Warman's ®
Flea Market
Price Guide

ELLEN T. SCHROY & DON JOHNSON

Published by

**krause
publications**

700 E. State Street • Iola, WI 54990-0001
Telephone: 715/445-2214

Please call or write for our free catalog.
Our toll-free number to place an order or obtain a free catalog is 800-258-0929
or please use our regular business telephone 715-445-2214
for editorial comment and further information.

ISBN: 0-87341-742-9

Printed in the United States of America

Table of Contents

Abbreviations

The following are standard abbreviations which are used throughout this edition of *Warman's Flea Market Price Guide.*

3D: three dimensional
4to: 8" x 10"
8vo: 5" x 7"
12mo: 3" x 5"
ADS: Autograph Document Signed
adv: advertising
ALS: Autograph Letter Signed
approx: approximately
AQS: Autograph Quotation Signed
attrib: attributed
b&w: black and white
C: century
c: circa
chlth: chromolithograph
cov: cover
CS: Card Signed
d: diameter or depth
dec: decorated
dj: dust jacket
DQ: Diamond Quilted
DS: Document Signed
ed: edition, editor
emb: embossed
ext.: exterior
Folio: 12" x 16"

ftd: footed
gal: gallon
ground: background
h: height
horiz: horizontal
hp: hand painted
illus: illustrated, illustration, illustrator
imp: impressed
int.: interior
irid: iridescent
IVT: inverted thumbprint
j: jewels
k: karat
l: length
lb: pound
litho: lithograph
ls: low standard
LS: Letter Signed
MBP: mint in bubble pack
mfg: manufactured
MIB: mint in box
MIP: mint in package
mkd: marked
MOC: mint on card
MOP: mother of pearl
n.d.: no date

No.: number
NRFB: never removed from box
opal: opalescent
orig: original
oz: ounce
pat: patent
pc: piece
pcs: pieces
pg: page
pgs: pages
pr: pair
PS: Photograph Signed
pt: pint
qt: quart
rect: rectangular
Soc: Society
sgd: signed
SP: silver plated
SS: sterling silver
sq: square
TLS: Typed Letter Signed
unp: unpaged
vol: volume
w: width
yg: yellow gold
#: numbered

❖ Introduction ❖

Maybe it was under the scorching summer sun of Pasadena. Perhaps it was on the rain-soaked grounds of Brimfield. Big flea markets. Big finds. Or was it during one of the countless small markets that spring up in community halls and edge-of-town parking lots? There was that special object you'd been searching for. The crowning glory of your collection or simply a piece of your childhood you'd been seeking. And of all places, you found it at a flea market.

But then, you really shouldn't have been surprised.

Flea markets have become a great American pastime. We love them because of the promise they hold, and we enjoy them because they allow us to be ourselves. We can dress as we like and look for whatever we want, and everyone else is doing the same. Big or small, indoors or outdoors, all flea markets have one thing in common—a promise that something great might be waiting just ahead.

The element of surprise that surrounds flea markets attracted us to this project. Forget the stereotype that irregular tube socks and Taiwanese wrench sets are all you'll find there. The antiques and collectibles market is alive and well at flea markets, where dealers make an honest living and where shoppers walk away smiling, their purchases carefully tucked under their arms.

Young at heart

One benefit of today's flea market is the emphasis placed on the family. While some dealers at higher-end markets twitch nervously at the sight of strollers and young children, most flea markets are promoted as events for everyone, young and old. Look around the next time you're at an outdoor flea market. Notice the number of parents pulling children in wagons. And, pay close attention to the smiles on those kids' faces.

Where else are kids encouraged to dig through a box of fast-food toys or spend a portion of their allowance on a 10-cent baseball card? And, an ice-cold drink or a soft pretzel is often all that's needed to give them a boost when they're wearing down.

No segment of the antiques and collectibles industry does a better job catering to the interests of children than do flea markets. These microcosms of the antiques trade offer youngsters appealing items at reasonable prices. For many adults, their love of collecting germinated in childhood and blossomed into adulthood. The legion of flea markets across the United States assures a bright future for the antiques and collectibles trade by creating tomorrow's collectors today.

And the fun isn't just for kids. If you haven't been to a flea market in a while, you're in for a treat. What are you waiting for?

In the beginning...

The thrill of the hunt continues to drive the antiques and collectibles market. People delight in the search for treasured items. Nowhere is that hope more alive than at a flea market. Whether you're looking for a Sesame Street record you remember from your childhood or a goblet to fill the void in your collection of American pattern glass, flea markets offer the realistic hope that the search will be successful. Better yet, chances are good the item can be purchased for a reasonable price.

Flea markets offer plenty of affordable treasures for children, like this 50-cent Garfield postcard.

Don't assume this book is another run-of-the-mill price guide. It's much more than that! *Warman's Flea Market Price Guide* contains valuable information about attending flea markets, and we've honed this edition specifically toward your needs as a flea market shopper or seller. We understand that flea markets are fun, family-oriented events. With that in mind, we've kept the tone lighthearted. A sufficient amount of information about each topic has been provided, complete with notes relating to periodicals, collectors' clubs and reference books. However, the listings are the backbone of the work, since that's what flea market enthusiasts really want.

In compiling the listings for *Warman's Flea Market Price Guide*, we put our fingers on the pulse of the marketplace, carefully checking to see what's being sold at flea markets. There's not much sense in listing prices for potholders if no one is collecting them. And, we've added categories you won't find in any other book. Pigeon Forge Pottery is one example of a collecting field that is gaining new interest. An increasing amount of the pottery is changing hands at flea markets, making it a prime candidate for inclusion here. Other new categories include 4-H, air guns, ballerinas, birdhouses, Boyd's Bears, Care Bears, Desert Storm, egg timers, Flygsfors glass, Garfield, Hawaiiana, jelly glasses, Michael Jordan, kaleidoscopes, Little Tikes, Longaberger baskets, My Little Pony, show jars, and taxidermy.

Photographs are a key component of this work. *Warman's Flea Market Price Guide* contains more photographs, and illustrates more categories than does any other flea market price guide. From the beginning of this project, photography has been a priority. While detailed listings are vital, clear photographs are invaluable for identifying an item.

In preparation for this book we asked you, flea market buyers and sellers, to tell us what you think. That input allowed us to fine-tune the end product to fit your needs. This isn't just another general-line price guide with the upper-end merchandise stripped away and the words "Flea Market" added to the title. From start to finish, we've focused on creating the best flea market book possible. Included is inside information about what's happening on the flea market scene, what's being offered for sale, and the value of that merchandise.

Our goal was to accurately reflect a typical flea market. We were literally thinking on our feet as we prepared this book. We walked hundreds of miles during a multitude of flea markets, talked to countless dealers, and listened to innumerable shoppers while observing the collectibles landscape.

You'll find an intriguing mix of merchandise represented here, from things that are readily available to scarce objects that, much to the delight of collectors, do occasionally surface at flea markets. Values in this price guide begin at 25 cents for labels and trading cards and range upward from there, highlighting the diversity of items that can be found even within specific categories.

Organization is the key

How do you combine roughly 700 photographs, nearly 800 categories, and countless listings into one cohesive unit? We started with "A." It's a pretty basic concept, but one that works just fine. Categories are listed alphabetically, from ABC plates to Zanseville pottery. Within each section, you may find the following:

Category: In an effort to make this book as enjoyable to read as it was to write, we intentionally omitted dry discourses on a category's history. If you wanted to do research, you'd be at a library, not at a flea market. Levity aside, that doesn't mean we shied away from useful information. Instead, we utilize a mix of key facts and fun tips. If you're not smiling as you read this book, we haven't done our jobs. For anyone wanting additional insight into a topic, we include information on periodicals, reference books, and collectors' clubs.

Periodicals: The advantage to periodicals is their ability to keep abreast of a changing marketplace. Newsletters are great sources of insider information. Weekly and monthly trade papers and magazines can also help you understand the market. We included those publications we consider helpful.

References: Due to the seemingly infinite number of books about the antiques and collectibles industry, we limited reference works to current titles we believe provide the most useful historical information as well as accurate prices. Most of the titles listed are readily available from booksellers, and many are offered for sale at flea markets.

Collectors' Clubs: It's hard to keep a good thing to yourself. Collectors love to share their enthusiasm with others, and collectors' clubs offer the perfect avenue for that. We've included many clubs, but there may be others we are not aware of, and new groups may become active. Use our suggestions as a starting point, but don't hesitate to ask fellow collectors and dealers about other clubs they may know of.

Reproduction Alert: Reproductions remain a problem throughout the antiques and collectibles trade. When we were aware of reproductions within a specific category, we used this alert to call your attention to their existence.

Listings: Looking for the heart of this book? You just found it. The individual listings are short but sweet, giving detailed descriptions that aid in identification. You'll find the listings presented alphabetically, each with a current value.

What's a flea market?

Attempting to define a flea market is like trying to describe all restaurants with a single statement. Sure, McDonald's and the White House kitchen both serve food, but there's a world of difference between the two.

Flea markets suffer from the same identity problem. They come in innumerable varieties, from multi-thousand-dealer events at Brimfield, Mass., to the local volunteer fire department's annual flea market and chili supper, featuring only a handful of merchants. The first may attract full-time dealers, while the latter may appeal to neighbors who have just cleaned out their garages. Yet, good sales and exciting buys can be made at both events.

Typically, flea markets are stereotyped as having low- to middle-market merchandise displayed in a haphazard manner. Imagine a herd of nude Barbies sprawled on the bare ground under a wobbly folding table holding a scattered array of chipped glassware and musty *TV Guides*. However, that's not always the case. In today's market, a shopper is just as likely to find a selection of 19th-century mechanical banks grouped in a professional setting, complete with risers and lights.

Additionally, a number of events considered flea markets are actually seasonal antique shows, such as the Sandwich Antiques Market in Sandwich, Ill. Ask someone in the Midwest to name his favorite flea market, and Sandwich is likely to be it. The Sandwich Antiques Market remains dedicated to providing both affordable and quality antiques and collectibles, while filtering out those dealers who carry bottom-of-the-line material. Is Sandwich a flea market? No, but it exhibits many of the qualities that attract flea market dealers and shoppers—a well-established event with indoor and outdoor spaces, good facilities, and the promise of finding a bargain.

The reputation of a particular market often dictates the quality of the merchandise presented. Better-known flea markets typically attract upper-end dealers who are just as comfortable at sophisticated antique shows, while lower-end markets tend to adopt a more laid-back approach. Booths may have a cluttered look, and there may be more merchants selling items from outside the antiques and collectibles field, everything from ferrets to football jerseys.

Flea markets also run the gamut from daily markets held in strip malls to monthly shows at 4-H fairgrounds. Outdoor summer markets tend to be a favorite with shoppers. During good weather, the flea market becomes a haven for families wanting to do something together. Children who normally whine at the suggestion of going to an antique mall or auction will often put on a happy face when told the destination is a flea market.

State of the flea market

Flea markets are alive and well. That's good news in an industry that is undergoing none-too-subtle changes, due in large part to the Internet. In a day when many antique malls are losing dealers who have decided they can more easily do business selling

Flea market merchandise ranges from lower-end affordable collectibles to more expensive antiques, such as this Ohio tool chest and barber's trade sign.

online, flea markets still appear to be strong. What's their secret? Actually, it's the Internet!

An increasing number of people have discovered fun and profit through selling antiques and collectibles on the World Wide Web. Although they might have gotten started cleaning out the attic, they're soon looking for additional sources of inventory. Flea markets have proven to be the perfect place to find inexpensive items for resale.

Nor have seasoned collectors abandoned flea markets. Shoppers still root through showcases and burrow under tables for prizes waiting to be found, sometimes at a fraction of their value. The thrill of the hunt continues to lure collectors and dealers to their favorite flea markets.

Those flea markets that serve as tag-team partners with more traditional antique shows are also doing well. Consider the Springfield Antiques Show & Flea Market, held monthly in Springfield, Ohio. While shoppers find a variety of upper-end antiques there, from American art pottery to country furniture, the show also attracts a number of dealers selling more affordable wares. Looking for Beanie Babies? They're there. Need vintage hardware for a kitchen cabinet? No doubt, someone's got it. Interested in Little Golden Books? Bring a large bag to carry them home.

Many promoters who combine traditional antique shows with flea markets are careful to limit the number of dealers selling new items, such as T-shirts and shrubbery. Because they are offered a range of items across a broad spectrum of prices, shoppers have the hope of finding exactly what they're looking for. Not even the Internet can dampen that enthusiasm.

The Flea Market Zone

If Rod Serling were still with us, he might sum things up this way: "There is a fifth dimension beyond that which is known to man. It is a dimension as vast as collectibles and as timeless as antiques. It is the middle ground between wanting and owning, between seeing and sacking, and it lies between the pit of man's coveting and the balance of his checkbook. This is the dimension of collecting. It is an area which we call The Flea Market Zone."

Is there a signpost up ahead? Collectors hope so, and they get excited when it reads "Flea Market" in large, bold letters. However, there are more efficient ways to find flea markets than by relying on chance. For starters, several guides have been published that cover American flea markets. These books are valuable for the detailed information they provide, listing flea markets, locations, dates, times, admission rates,

Collectors look for the signpost up ahead, especially when it reads, "FLEA MARKET."

Inexpensive smalls such as this Little Golden Book can interest every member of the family, from a 6-year-old to the adult collector.

dealer rates, and contact information. Check your favorite bookseller for titles and availability.

Trade publications are another excellent source of information. National and regional publications contain a fair number of advertisements for flea markets. In addition, don't overlook the free tabloids available at many flea markets, antique shows and antique malls. Ads for smaller flea markets and festival-related events can often be found in these publications.

Of course, nothing beats a good recommendation from other collectors and dealers. Ask around, especially when at a flea market you like. Talk to the dealers to find out which markets they prefer and which venues offer similar types of merchandise.

Check, please!

You've done your homework. You've found a great-sounding flea market. You managed to finagle a Saturday off from work. The rest of the family is dressed and ready to go. Have you forgotten anything?

How about a phone call?

Sure, the flea market guide states that Billy-Bob's Flea-Spectacular is open every Saturday and Sunday. However, circumstances do arise that cause flea markets to change their hours, move to a different location, or even go out of business. There's nothing more frustrating than driving 100 miles in the wee morning light, enduring two hours of your kids drubbing each other in the back seat, and drinking three cups of luke-warm coffee, only to find a "CLOSED" sign hanging crookedly on the chain-link fence surrounding what used to be Billy-Bob's. Such experiences can generally be avoided by confirming the details of the market ahead of time.

When contacting the promoter, double-check the date, hours of operation, and admission fees. If you aren't familiar with the area, ask for directions. And remember, if the drive involves much distance, find out if you will be changing time zones. Otherwise, a road trip from Illinois to Michigan could find you arriving 45 minutes after the gate opened instead of 15 minutes early, as you had planned. Time zones have crushed more than one collector's hopes of getting into a market with the opening surge of shoppers.

While you're at it, don't forget to check the weather forecast. It might be sunny when you leave your home in San Jose, but Pasadena could be in the midst of a thunderstorm. Rain and outdoor flea markets are natural enemies. A quick check of The Weather Channel would have shown you that a low-pressure system had stalled directly above the Rose Bowl Flea Market and Swap Meet. Sure, the event might be held "rain or shine," but that doesn't mean you feel like slogging through puddles on your day off.

Dress for success

Boy Scouts are pretty intelligent kids. They've got that neat hand sign, and they're good at expecting the unexpected. We should all be so smart.

Wise flea market dealers and shoppers know to prepare for stormy weather.

Veteran flea market shoppers also know to be prepared. To begin with, they dress for success. Nothing will kill a day at a flea market faster than being uncomfortable—whether you're too cold, too hot, or suffering from achy feet. Dressing appropriately for the season and accounting for changes in the weather are essential components of an enjoyable hunt for flea market treasures. Two key rules are: dress in layers, and take a change of clothes.

Many flea market shoppers are early birds, wanting to jump into the action as soon as possible. When arriving at a Wisconsin flea market in the chill of the morning, a wool sweater and a cup of steaming coffee will keep you warm. But once the coffee cup is empty, Mr. Sun peeks from behind the clouds, and the temperature climbs, it's likely your wardrobe will become a hindrance. Suddenly you're concentrating on the hot, itchy sweater instead of the under-priced Art Deco candlesticks you just walked past.

At the very least, expect the temperature to fluctuate during the day. Layers of light clothing will prepare you for any variations in the weather. It's better to wear a light jacket that can be removed and carried in your cloth bag or backpack, serving as packing material if needed, than to be stuck in a heavy hooded sweatshirt all day because it's the only thing you tossed on that morning.

Never wear clothes that haven't been worn and washed several times. Everything should fit and be comfortable. A new pair of jeans might be a little tighter than you had imagined, or an unwashed T-shirt could cause an unexpected rash. And don't even think about breaking in a new pair of shoes at a flea market. You're just asking for trouble (read: blisters) if you think your new Nikes are going to travel miles of hot pavement and acres of uneven terrain at an outdoor market without revolting against your toes or heels. Comfortable, well-worn walking shoes are your best bet.

Don't forget something to cover your noggin, also. On cold days, nothing keeps you warm like a stocking cap. In hot weather, a wide-brimmed hat will protect your head, face, and neck, lessening the possibility of sunburn and headaches. At the very least, a baseball-style cap affords shade for your face, and it can easily be stuffed in a back pocket when no longer needed.

In addition to those items you're wearing, pack a second set of clothes to keep in your vehicle. Give yourself the option of warmer or cooler clothes, depending on the weather. You may start the day wearing long pants, but by noon the shorts in your car might feel more comfortable. A quick trip to change will be time well spent. Don't forget to pack an extra pair of shoes and socks as well. More than one rainy day at the flea market has been salvaged when the cloudburst stopped and the shopper changed out of soaked sneakers and into a dry pair of shoes and socks. Better yet, pack a pair of boots. You'll be glad you did when the other shoppers are slogging through a rain-soaked field, mud oozing between their toes.

The right stuff

The right clothes are important, but wise flea market shoppers know that it takes more than a comfortable pair of khakis to ensure a good day shopping. Here are some other items you'll find useful.

Cash: Money talks. Cash speaks a universal language that everyone understands. Do more than just take along enough to get you through the day, keeping in mind that you'll probably eat and put gas in the car before returning home. Make sure you have a sufficient number of small bills, as well as some change in your pocket. Ones and fives come in handy when buying low-priced items, especially if a dealer has a handful of twenties or doesn't want to break your $100 bill for a postcard tagged $1.50. And, the quarters jingling in your pocket will speed the transaction at the concession stand when all you want is a glass of iced tea before heading down the next aisle.

Other funds: Although not all dealers accept checks, many do. Before leaving home, make sure you have a sufficient number of checks with you. Credit cards are honored by some dealers, primarily at the larger events; however, don't expect to use your VISA at many of the smaller flea markets. An ATM/debit card offers the best of both worlds. When you unexpectedly find a Pairpoint cornucopia just as you are running low on cash, the dealer will likely hold it for you while you dart off to the nearest automated teller machine. Many large flea markets now have ATMs available on the property.

Meals and snacks: Flea market food ranges from fantastic to repulsive, and to make matters worse, what some markets charge for a hot dog and a cold drink could finance a small Third World nation. Depending on the market, a better solution might be to pack your lunch and keep it in a cooler in the car. A quick trip to the parking lot will take less time than waiting in line for a greasy cheeseburger.

Pack high-energy food that's easily digested and, if desired, can be eaten while you walk. As a snack, fruit is always a good option, as are many sports-related energy bars. Don't forget to take along some drinks. A thermos of coffee, tea, or even soup is great for chilly mornings, while a cooler of iced soft drinks or juice will be worth its weight in gold by the end of the day. And don't forget the water. Not only will it quench you thirst, but it can also be used to clean and cool your face, neck, and hands on hot, sunny days.

After a long day of shopping, you may be too tired (or too poor) to stop at a restaurant. A cold drink and that box of crackers you stashed in your vehicle might be just what it takes to see you through the miles home.

The car kit: If you've spent much time at flea markets, you know how important it is to pack some things in the car "just in case." Among the items to consider are sunblock, Chap Stick, a travel-size medical kit, pain reliever, antacid, a small package of facial tissue, a container of anti-bacterial wipes or hand cleaner, bug spray, and even a hairbrush for those windy days at outdoor markets.

A box of your most frequently used reference books can serve as your traveling library. And don't forget to toss in some empty boxes, newspapers, wrapping supplies, and tape to pack your purchases safely for the trip home. A clipboard or several sturdy pieces of cardboard will protect items that are easily bent.

Some shoppers also include a black light, Bakelite and gold test kits, plastic bags for holding smalls, maps, a flashlight, a tow chain, gloves, hand warmers, an umbrella, and a small bag of tools with screwdrivers of various types and sizes.

Tools of the trade: Although your goal is to travel as lightly as possible, you will still want to carry a number of items with you. Begin with a cloth bag, fanny pack, or backpack for storing needed tools of the trade as well as your flea market finds. Some shoppers prefer to use collapsible carts.

A pen and a pocketsize notebook are useful for jotting down information on a dealer's location or for noting a specific item you want to quickly research using the reference books in your vehicle. A small tape measure can be used to determine whether the yellow ware bowl you're considering is the size needed for your nesting set, or whether the Victorian marble-top table will fit next to your sofa. A collapsible jeweler's loupe will prove invaluable in reading small marks or enhancing details in vintage photographs. Some shoppers prefer a magnifying glass with a battery-powered light.

A magnet can be used to determine if a painted frog doorstop is cast iron or brass, and a set of batteries will come in handy for testing toys or other battery-operated collectibles.

Handing out a want list or cards printed with your name, telephone number and what you collect can help secure items after the event. Most business supply stores and copy centers can create inexpensive versions. You might also want to carry an inventory to refer to so you don't purchase duplicate items.

Durable paper towels can be tucked in your pocket, serving a multitude of functions. They can be used to wrap your newly acquired Davenport Cigars match safe so it doesn't get scratched, wipe a runny nose, clean up blood from a cut finger, or serve as a backup when the Port-A-John is out of toilet paper.

Communication: Cellular phones and walkie-talkies have become standard equipment for many flea market shoppers. The cel phone allows you to inform your spouse when you're running a little late, to ask a friend if he's interested in the *Creature From the Black Lagoon* model kit you just found, or to call to have someone check a reference book you forgot to pack. Walkie-talkies and other two-way radios allow teams of shoppers to stay in contact with each other, checking to see if a Pepsi tray is a good buy or whether a team member still needs a specific Camp Snoopy drinking glass.

Let the games begin!

When it comes to flea markets, most veteran collectors attack the event with forethought. There's method to their madness. Here are some of the approaches used.

Run and gun: In the run and gun, the shopper hurries down the aisles, glancing in each booth for certain items, but not stopping unless he sees something he wants to buy. Sometimes he resorts to shouting, "Got any...?" as he's scurrying past. After going through the entire show, he'll begin a second loop, this time checking each booth more carefully.

Slow and steady: In this approach, the shopper figures he has a better chance of finding something if he methodically looks at all of the merchandise in each booth. This method allows him to scrutinize the items in each booth, but by the time he gets to the last aisle, several hours may have passed. He feels what he might miss in those latter booths (because it's already sold by the time he gets there) will be offset by the treasures he discovers later on.

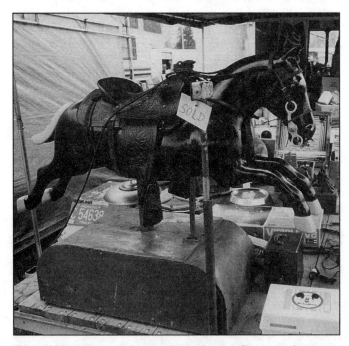

The right approach to shopping a flea market can mean the difference between taking home a prized piece and finding that special something already tagged "Sold."

FDS (Favored Dealer Status): Knowing certain dealers carry the type of merchandise he's looking for, the collector will immediately head to those booths. This is generally a good approach, and the dealers are easy to find since most flea markets allow them to reserve the same booth space for each show.

Walking advertisement: In this method, the customer wears a shirt or sign noting what he collects. Who could miss a neon-orange shirt with large black letters that read, "Old Cameras Wanted." Dealers with cameras for sale will eagerly flag down the shopper. No doubt, the resulting sale will be a Kodak moment.

Dickering 101

It's well understood that most flea market dealers are willing to lower their prices. Surely you've had this experience: You're shopping a flea market when, out of curiosity, you pick up an item. Immediately, you are hit with a rapid-fire, "Icandobe'eronthat!" Translated, it means, "I can do better on that." It doesn't matter if you're holding a $125 Blue Ridge teapot, a $10 PEZ dispenser, or the gum wrapper your daughter just dropped on the ground, the phrase speaks volumes about the fact that flea markets are places where prices can be negotiated.

Some dealers will automatically volunteer to provide a discount, while others may have signs announcing, "Ask for a better price" or "No reasonable offer refused." Yet, often it's up to you to make the first move. Here are some rules for the game of dickering.

Rule No. 1: Politeness is everything. This is a good rule to follow in all your dealings at a flea market, from negotiating with a seller to ordering a hot dog at the concession stand. Put a smile on your face and enjoy the day. When seeking a better price from a dealer, a cheery countenance can work wonders. Talk to him with the same tone and manner you would use when asking a friend for a favor. You can never go wrong when treating people with kindness and respect.

Common courtesy will also put you in good stead when seeking additional information about an item that's for sale. You might want to know who previously owned a particular cedar chest or whether an oil painting has had touch-up work. Do as your mother told you, and mind your manners. A non-threatening approach will help put the dealer at ease and could put you both on the path to a sale.

Rule No. 2: Play with a poker face. Conceal your enthusiasm until after you've purchased the item. If you spot a Chef egg timer you recall from your grandmother's kitchen, don't squeal, "OH MY GOSH!" and immediately rush into the booth to gleefully snatch the piece off the table. To a dealer, that's tantamount to announcing, "I hereby waive all my rights to bargain on the price of this item." The dealer knows you want the egg timer, and he sees a sale coming at full price. Instead, wait until you get the little Chef character back to the car before jumping for joy.

Rule No. 3: Be willing to pay a fair price. Don't let your pride keep you from owning something you want, especially if it's already affordable. If you find a Hummel lamp worth $475 that's only priced $200, it's okay to ask if the dealer will negotiate the price. However, don't be offended if he tells you the price is firm. Pay the $200 and be happy with your bargain. Remember, collecting should be fun. Don't let the absence of a discount ruin your day.

Rule No. 4: Know how to bargain. There are a number of methods that work for buyers. The one we prefer is a straightforward, non-threatening approach. Politely call the item to the dealer's attention and ask, "Is this your best price?" The dealer then has the option of quoting a lower figure or telling you the price is firm. If a discount is offered, we recommend you either accept it or thank the dealer and walk away.

Some people delight in dickering back and forth until a price is agreed upon. If that's your style, and the dealer doesn't mind, the best of luck to you both. But keep in mind that some dealers will be insulted if you respond to their offer by undercutting it with a counteroffer.

Rule No. 5: Bargain seriously. Don't ask for a discount unless you are truly interested in buying the item. Otherwise, you're wasting both your time and that of the dealer. We've all seen it happen. Someone picks up a Hubley airplane tagged $165 and asks the dealer, "Can you do any better on the price?" The dealer says he really wants to move merchandise, so he'll take $85 for it. The customer then mumbles something unintelligible, sets down the plane and walks out of the booth. Obviously, the individual never intended to buy the toy.

3 little words

They're just three little words, but they can have a big impact on your life. We're all familiar with the phrase "All sales final." The general rule at most flea markets is that the deal is finalized when money changes hands. If you experience buyer's remorse or find an identical item for less just two booths later, don't expect the seller to refund your purchase price or give you a rebate.

Even if the item is later determined to be a reproduction, your avenues of recourse may be limited. While reputable dealers will refund the purchase price if an honest mistake has been made, others will point out that you should not have bought the piece if you weren't sure of its authenticity.

The best thing you can do is to carefully examine all merchandise before you buy.

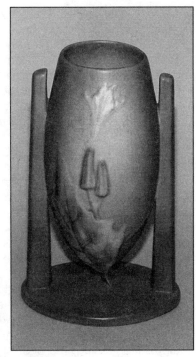

Check for damage. A hairline crack would greatly diminish the value of this Roseville Thorn Apple vase.

Check, please! The sequel

You've found a McCoy cookie jar, the sticker price seems fair, and the dealer appears willing to negotiate. But before you strike a deal, there are some other steps you'll want to take.

Examine the item: Carefully check prospective purchases. If the price seems low, the piece may be damaged. Examine glassware and pottery for chips and cracks. Check toys to see if all the parts are original and to determine whether the item has been repainted. Look for stains and holes in textiles. And, make sure you're dealing with an authentic item, not a reproduction.

Ask about it: Even if you are convinced the item is perfect, ask the dealer if he's aware of any damage. You might have missed a hairline crack or a carefully concealed repair. An honest dealer will tell you what he knows. And, most dealers are honest.

The bad and the ugly

This is the part of the book in which we get to use the Latin phrase every antiquer knows, *caveat emptor*—let the buyer beware. Although flea markets are enjoyable and hold the promise of turning up a prized collectible at a reasonable price, there are also some pitfalls that seem more troublesome than in any other segment of the market.

We want to stress that most flea market dealers are honest, reputable sellers who enjoy what they're doing and wouldn't think of jeopardizing their business by cheating a customer. However, it's important to discuss the proverbial "one bad apple" that can spoil the rest of the fruit in the barrel.

Reproductions: Reproductions, fakes, and fantasy items are often found at flea markets. One must understand that sales of reproductions are not dependent on the items being represented as old merchandise. Quite the contrary. At some flea markets, reproductions are stacked ten deep on the table and are offered at wholesale prices. That repro tin windup penguin may be bought as new here, passed off as authentic there. *There* may be one no farther than three aisles away, so *caveat emptor.*

Knowledge is your best defense. If the price seems too good to be true, even at a flea market, then maybe it is. When examining an item, use all your senses. Look at it. Are the details crisp, or does a cast-iron bottle opener have the worn molding of many recasts? Examine the hardware. Are the screws in a mechanical bank the right type for when the piece was made? Study the lithography. Is the printing of a die-cut sporting goods sign a little fuzzy, indicating a later printing method? Feel the piece. Does the wear on the base correspond to the age of the planter? Some old merchandise even has a slightly different texture than the reproductions. Using your nose can also provide some clues about the item. Does a small curly maple candle box have the smell of a 150-year-old piece, or is the scent that of freshly cut wood or new varnish?

Tall tales: Unscrupulous dealers always have a story to tell about their merchandise. Listen carefully, and *caveat emptor.* You might be told that a crystal goblet traveled across the Atlantic Ocean with a family of Pilgrims aboard the Mayflower. But, if that goblet is

Knowledge is the key when deciding how much to pay for fantasy items such as this Coca-Cola belt buckle.

pressed glass, you can rest assured it's not as old as the dealer suggests.

Some mistakes are made honestly, but they're mistakes nonetheless. How about the Lucy doll with a 1963 copyright date. The price tag read: "Lucy, 1963, all original, $45." But, Lucy's dress was fastened with Velcro tabs. Does anyone see a problem here? The Velcro shows the clothes to be of a more contemporary design.

Copyright dates are tricky things, and worth a brief mention. They indicate when a particular copyright was issued, not necessarily the date of manufacture for the object on which the copyright appears.

Look for clues that indicate an item's true age. For instance, a Royal Staffordshire platter marked "Dishwasher Safe" is definitely from the second half of the 20th century, not from the 19th century, no matter how old the transferware pattern looks. Knowledgeable collectors are always on the lookout for price tags with incorrect information. Among the common mistakes are pressed glass said to be cut glass, molded pottery marked as hand-thrown, machine-molded glassware claimed to be mouth-blown, plastic tagged as Bakelite or celluloid—need we go on?

Knowledge is your friend. The best purchases you will ever make are good reference books. Some of your most productive time will be spent with dealers and collectors who allow a hands-on examination of authentic antiques and collectibles. Armed with knowledge, you can shop any market safely.

The good

Don't let "The Bad and the Ugly" scare you away from flea markets. The nasties are far outweighed by "The Good" that can be found at these events. Topping the list of those positives is the family atmosphere at flea markets. Here's the perfect way to spend a day with loved ones. Because flea markets offer something for everyone, even children enjoy tagging along. The hunt for inexpensive collectibles will keep them interested for hours.

Although children seem to have a natural interest in the merchandise at flea markets, they don't always have the stamina to spend an entire day walking aisles and darting into booths. One popular solution is to take a wagon. Your youngsters will enjoy the ride, especially at outdoor markets. Toss in a coloring book or handheld video game, and you've made great strides toward boredom-proofing the day. Add a small cooler with juice and snacks, and you'll be a hero in their eyes.

Strollers can also be used, and they're particularly good for infants. But whether you're pushing little Susie in a stroller or pulling Johnny Jr. in a wagon, don't be surprised if you get the evil eye from at least a few shoppers. Some adults think children should be banned from all markets. Don't let such cavalier attitudes ruin your day. Remember, you're spending time with your family, and there are few things in the world more important than that. Behaving courteously when maneuvering through the show and using common sense when parking your children to examine an item will certainly be appreciated though.

Due to the inexpensive nature of some of the merchandise, flea markets are good places for children to learn the value of money. Permitting them to spend their allowance on a collection of their own teaches them to make decisions regarding how that money is used.

The other side

What's more fun than shopping at a flea market? How about selling at one? Most flea markets are a mix of full-time dealers running a business and one-time sellers looking for a way to get rid of the stuff that has piled up in the garage. As such, these markets are perfect for anyone looking to make a little cash from the extra things around the house.

Here are some tips to help you succeed if you're new to the role of flea market dealer.

Finding fleas: The first thing you need to do is decide which flea market you want to try. Check flea market directories and trade publications to see which events are held in your area. Before making a commitment to take a booth, attend several flea markets. Ask the dealers what they like about the event and what they would change. Question them about what's selling well and what price ranges attract buyers. Decide whether your merchandise will fit in at a particular market. Inquire about other flea markets the dealers use,

Finding merchandise to sell at a flea market can be as simple as cleaning out the attic. This dealer was selling her grown children's unwanted toys.

as well as the ones they like to shop. Don't forget to find out how and where the flea market is advertised. The greater the number of people who hear about the market, the more customers you will likely have.

Next, study the environment. Are there plenty of shoppers? Are the facilities well kept? Are there affordable concessions and clean restrooms? All of these are important considerations for keeping shoppers happy. As a dealer, you'll quickly learn that an unhappy customer is less likely to make a purchase.

Calculating costs: It's important to know how much you'll have to spend to get started in the flea market business, whether you're interested in selling only once or want to set up every weekend. Talk to the promoter about rates and the availability of booth space. Do the dealers also rent tables for displaying their goodies, or will you need to bring some from home? Of course, don't overlook the incidental expenses, such as gas for travel, meals while away from home, and the cost of a motel if you're traveling any distance. All those things can quickly cut into your profit.

Factoring time: If you are retired, you might have unlimited time to devote to your new hobby. But if you're still holding down a 9-to-5 job, can you get away from your desk in time to get on the road and set up at your favorite flea market? Before committing to a particular market, ask the promoter about the event's set-up policy. Because dealers often arrange their booths before the show begins, you may need to spend Friday traveling to your destination and setting up, in preparation for the crowd that will spill through the gates early Saturday morning.

One other factor to consider is how early you plan to arrive at your booth during the show. When we asked flea market dealers for tips, they repeatedly told us, "Arrive early." After only one flea market experience, you'll appreciate the need to be ready before the show opens, in order to maximize sales to early shoppers as well as other dealers.

Some dealers also mentioned that it's important to be willing to stay late at a show. Leaving too soon might get you home in time to catch that made-for-TV movie you wanted to see, but it can also mean you miss out on sales to last-minute bargain hunters.

Deciding what to take: In addition to your merchandise, you'll need the following.

Tables—Unless tables are provided by the promoter, you'll need something to display your items on. Card tables and larger folding tables are ideal.

Chair—Don't forget something to sit on during lulls in the action.

Cash box and change—A small locking cash box and adequate change, both bills and coins, will be essential.

Spending money—In addition to the money for your cash box, you'll want to take along some extra funds for any purchases you might make or to buy lunch.

Wrapping material—Newspapers, tissue, and bubble wrap will protect your customers' purchases on the trip home.

Tape—This can be used to secure the wrapping material around an item or for posting signs in your booth.

Bags and boxes—You will need paper or plastic bags to hold sold merchandise if the customer doesn't have their own carry-all. Cardboard boxes are good for packaging larger pieces or multiple items.

Receipt books—You'll want to record your sales, and your customer will appreciate a copy of the transaction.

Price tags—Pack some extra price tags for any items you purchase for resale while traveling to the flea market or while at the event. You might also discover you've forgotten to mark some merchandise, and extra tags will come in handy.

Business cards—Don't be bashful about handing out business cards to anyone who is interested in your merchandise. It may result in a sale long after you've packed and gone home. When a shopper has time to reconsider your *Wizard of Oz* book he walked away from at the show, knowing how to contact you could put that one in the sold column.

Price guides—Pack a few of your favorite price guides, including one general-line guide that covers the market as a whole. (Of course, we strongly recommend this book!) They'll come in handy for determining whether an Annie lunchbox is a good buy or for showing a customer where to find information on a club for jelly glass collectors.

Showcase—Consider keeping any valuable smalls in a showcase, which will discourage theft.

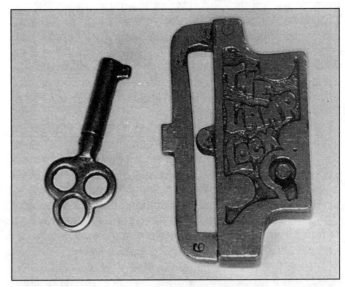

Small items such as this lock and key are best kept under ... well ... lock and key! Showcases help discourage theft of valuable smalls.

Sheets or tarps—You might also want to take some light, unfitted bed sheets to cover your merchandise when you're out of your booth, keeping ne'er-do-wells from being tempted by your miniature Blue Willow tea set. For outdoor shows, a light covering will also prevent dew from forming on your merchandise, while a water-resistant tarp will be more appropriate when the skies threaten rain.

Creating the display: There is no right or wrong way to display merchandise at a flea market. Some dealers achieve satisfactory results by simply placing their wares on a blanket on the ground. Others adopt a more professional approach, using tables with table covers, risers and lights. We believe the latter provides better exposure for your merchandise, and increased visibility can translate to increased sales.

One of the best things you can do to encourage sales is to price all of your merchandise. Some shoppers hesitate to ask for the price of an item that's untagged. Others may not ask out of principal, believing the dealer will quote a figure that's artificially inflated if the shopper is dressed nicely and appears to be financially fit. Don't run the risk of losing a sale because your merchandise isn't marked.

Providing customer service: The manner in which you treat your customers is the single most important factor in ensuring your success as a flea market dealer. Never underestimate the importance of greeting every individual who enters your booth. A genuine smile and polite conversation might be all it takes to win over a shopper who's debating whether to buy your hula girl nodder. Customers who are treated with courtesy will remember you, and a friend you make today might well be a customer you keep for life.

A word about cyberspace

The Internet has been the greatest single force in reshaping the antiques and collectibles industry since antique malls spread like wildfire in the 1980s. Promoters are using the Internet to advertise flea markets—a trend that is beneficial to both dealers and collectors looking for new events.

Although there are numerous websites serving as online antiques malls, countless smaller sites and individual web pages have given the Internet the feeling of a worldwide flea market. Even eBay, the largest of the online auctions, resembles your favorite marketplace, where just about anything can be found. The difference is that, instead of haggling with the dealer across the table to negotiate a price, you're engaged in a bidding war with other collectors.

In the coming years, look for more websites and online auctions to specialize in specific categories of antiques and collectibles. What you don't see at your local flea market can probably be found somewhere on the World Wide Web. And, don't be surprised when you discover it's being offered by a flea market dealer you know.

By now you've probably noticed a new feature for this edition of *Warman's Flea Market Price Guide*—boxes with two different icons. Both signal you have just found a category which is special.

The ✹ icon denotes a Hot Topic. We are defining a Hot Topic as a field that has generated a lot of collector interest and/or in which prices have risen dramatically in the last six months. As the current flea market season progresses, additional Hot Topics may surface, and some of the current ones may even cool a bit.

The ☆ icon denotes a New Warman's Listing. This is the first time they have appeared as a separate category, like Little Tikes. No other edition of Warman's has ever covered the pricing structure of this collectible before. Marx Toys are a good example of a New Warman's Listing. This edition of *Warman's Flea Market* is the first to include a brief history of and prices for Marx Toys under "M." Previous Warman's titles have carried some listings for these colorful toys, but under "T" for toy. Our intention is to make this edition as user-friendly as possible. To that end, we divided some large collecting categories into specific makers, etc.

Longaberger Baskets represents a topic that is Hot and also New to Warman's. These beautiful baskets can now be found on the secondary market and are often seen at flea markets, where dedicated Longaberger Basket collectors can find interesting examples to add to their collections. Because these baskets are so contemporary, they have never been listed in *Warman's Antiques & Collectibles*, so therefore, constitute a new listing.

❖ <u>Survey Results</u> ❖

The survey says...

Remember "Family Feud," the game show that pitted two families against each other to guess survey results? When it was time to reveal the answers, host Richard Dawson would smile and enthusiastically proclaim, "The survey says..."

Utilizing a questionnaire in *Warman's Today's Collector*, we asked shoppers and dealers to share their thoughts, ideas, and concerns about flea markets. Readers responded enthusiastically. They told us about their favorite flea markets as well as those they least like. They gave us insight into how much time and money they're willing to spend at an event, as well as the types of merchandise they look for. Respondents included tips for buying and selling at flea markets, as well as opinions on reproductions. Their choice of items to take to a flea market proved that many shoppers are veterans with years of experience. They recounted tales of great finds that will leave you eager to locate a nearby flea market, while their worst flea market experiences will have you shaking your head in disbelief.

Sound interesting? Some of the results follow. Keep in mind, this was by no means a scientific survey, but it does offer a glimpse into what's happening in today's marketplace.

By the numbers

For the record, the survey drew more than 100 responses.

The question concerning how much time people spend shopping at a flea market generated the widest range of answers. One respondent stays "5 minutes plus," while another spends 8 to 10 hours shopping a flea market. The most common answers put buyers at a flea market for 2 to 5 hours.

What are those shoppers looking for? Only 7% said they look solely for antiques, another 7% said they are specifically interested in collectibles, and 39% of those who answered search for both antiques and collectibles. Another 45% of the respondents search for both collectibles and non-antique items of various types. Only one individual was not interested in either antiques or collectibles, and she attends flea markets to find crafts and second-hand goods.

How much are flea market shoppers willing to spend? Here again, the diversity among answers was interesting. One shopper will spend as little as $1, while another sets a limit of $15,000. Most commonly, respondents set a limit of $200 or less. Two responses were especially creative. One individual said he would spend "As much as is in my pocket," while another said he limits the price he pays at a flea market to half of an item's value.

Because reproductions are often found at flea markets, we wanted to know how shoppers felt about them. Twelve percent felt reproductions are okay, while 45% admitted to being bothered by them. Not expressing an opinion one way or the other, 30% felt that you deserve what you get if you buy a reproduction, citing "let the buyer beware."

What are buyers searching for at flea markets? Everything is fair game, from Matchbox toys to bumper cars.

Everyone has a favorite. While the big-name events receive a lot of attention, many smaller flea markets enjoy a faithful following.

On the road again

When it comes to flea markets, everyone has a favorite. We've generated an alphabetical list of the best-loved flea markets, according to those who answered the survey. Many respondents offered more than one pick, and a few markets received multiple votes.

By no means is this a complete list of the best flea markets in the United States. It does, however, highlight some of the events shoppers and dealers return to again and again. What sets these markets apart? To some, a show is good if they can add to their collections. To others, merchandise isn't the key. Instead, it takes low prices for a market to earn high marks. For dealers, a market's worth is generally tallied in dollars and cents—whether sales were good.

Regardless of the different yardsticks people use to measure a flea market, here are some of the events respondents praised.

Alabama
Montgomery, Blue Ridge Treasure Hunt
Watumpike, Blue Ridge Treasure Hunt

Arizona
Glendale, Glendale 9 Swap Meet
Phoenix, American Park N Swap
Phoenix, Phoenix Fairgrounds Antique Market

Arkansas
Pine Bluff, 270 & 65 Flea Market

California
Fullerton, Troubleshooters Antiques and Collectibles Round-Up
Long Beach, Outdoor Antique and Collectible Market
Napa, Napa Flea Market
Niles, Niles Antique Faire
Oceanside, Oceanside Drive-In Swap Meet
Old Sacramento, Old Sacramento Street Fair
Pasadena, Rose Bowl Flea Market and Swap Meet
San Diego, Kobey's Swap Meet
Santa Cruz, Skyview Flea Market
Spring Valley, Spring Valley Swap Meet
Stockton, San Joaquin Delta College Flea Market

Delaware
Laurel, Bargain Bill

District of Columbia
Washington, Georgetown Flea Market

Florida
Mount Dora, Florida Twin Markets
Orlando, Colonial Flea Market
Port Richey, USA Fleamarket

Webster, Sumter County Farmer's Market
Webster, Webster Westside Flea Market

Georgia

Savannah, Keller's Flea Market

Illinois

Bloomington, Third Sunday Market
Grayslake, Lake County Antiques and Collectibles
    Show and Sale
Rosemont, Wolff's Flea Market
St. Charles, Kane County Flea Market

Indiana

Cedar Lake, Uncle John's Flea Market
Indianapolis, Indiana Flea Market
Lafayette, market unspecified
Shipshewana, Shipshewana Auction and
    Flea Market

Iowa

Fort Dodge, Hillbilly Sales
Walnut, American Legion town-wide market

Kansas

Kansas City, American Royal
Topeka, Boyle's Joyland Flea Market
Wichita, Mid-America Flea Markets

Massachusetts

Brimfield, multiple markets

Minnesota

Albany, Pioneer Days Flea Market

Missouri

Kansas City, Jeff William's Flea Market

New Hampshire

West Lebanon, Colonial Antiques & Flea Market

New Jersey

Columbus, Columbus Farmer's Market
Lambertville, Golden Nugget Antique Flea Market
Neshanic Station, Neshanic Flea Market
North Cape May, Victoria Commons Flea Market
Ocean Grove, market unspecified
Rancocas Woods, William Spencer's Antique Show

New Mexico

Sante Fe, market unspecified

New York

Clarence, Antique World and Marketplace
Manhattan, Antiques, Arts & Crafts Flea Market

New York City, The Annex Antiques Fair &
    Flea Market
Staten Island, market unspecified
Stormville, Stormville Airport Antique Show and
    Flea Market

North Carolina

Charlotte, Metrolina Expo

Ohio

Mansfield, market unspecified
Rogers, Rogers Community Auction and
    Open-Air Market
Springfield, Springfield Antique Show & Flea Market

Oklahoma

Tulsa, The Tulsa Flea Market

Pennsylvania

Adamstown, Renninger's #1 Antique Market
Adamstown, Shupp's Grove
Adamstown, Stoudt's Black Angus Antique Market
Barto, Jake's Flea Market
Evans City, Evans City Flea Market
Greensburg, Greengate Flea Market
Hannastown, market unspecified
Hazen, Warsaw Township Volunteer Fire Company
    Flea Market
Kutztown, Renninger's #2 Antique Market
Matamoras, Matamoras Drive-In
New Hope, New Hope Country Market
Philadelphia, market unspecified
Pittsburgh, market unspecified
Saylorsburg, Blue Ridge Flea Market
Sciota, market unspecified
Meadowlands, The Meadows
Watsontown, Route 180

Tennessee

Nashville, Tennessee State Fairgrounds Flea
    Market

Texas

Austin, market unspecified
Canton, First Monday Trade Days
Dallas, market unspecified
Houston, Traders Village

Virginia

Front Royal, Double Tollgate Flea Market

Wisconsin

Adams, Adams Flea Market
Elkhorn, Walworth County Flea Market
Princeton, market unspecified

All types of trading cards were among the items collected by the children of flea market shoppers.

Angels
Art Deco
BB guns
Beanie Babies
Beatles
Brass keys
Buttons
Candles
Coins
Davy Crockett
Depression glass
Dice
Dolls
Dolphins
Felix the Cat
Fishing lures
Harley Davidson
Hot Wheels
Hummels

Jewelry
Keychains
Knives
Lustre ware
McDonald's
Movie memorabilia
Painted masks
PEZ dispensers
Postcards
Roy Rogers
Salt and pepper shakers
Santas
Sports memorabilia
Star Wars
Teapots
Toy soldiers
Valentines
Wizard of Oz

It's the best

Are there still great things to discover at flea markets? You bet! Almost everyone who responded to the survey had a story about a fantastic find. Some purchases were remembered because they filled a void in a collection, while others were notable for the low price. Just what are shoppers unearthing from the packed aisles of their favorite events? Here are some of the highlights.

* 1950s boy Angel of the Month

* 1962 Dick and Jane book

* Whistler golf club

* Rare telegraph instrument

* Michael Jackson California raisin

* Sterling silverware set purchased for $25

* Early metal railroad calendar in near-mint condition purchaosed for $22.50 and sold two weeks later for $450

* Rolex watch

* 1st edition *Tarzan of the Apes* book

* 1890s school desk purchased for $7

* Little Friends metal lunch box

* *Boston Cooking School Cookbook* in excellent condition purchased for 25 cents

* 19th century 19" bulbous New England Peachblow vase purchased for $10

* Rare Judaica

* Autographed baseball of the 1931 Philadelphia A's

* Vintage Maxfield Parrish print purchased for $3

* Faberge clock

On the flip side

Just as one man's junk is another man's treasure, it can also be true that one man's treasure might be another man's junk. When we asked people to identify their least favorite flea markets, five of the events that made the cut as favorites were also chosen as the worst, with one market garnering three votes for the losers list. Some respondents defined their least-favorite flea markets in more generic terms. Among the events to earn thumbs-down ratings were roadside markets, indoor markets, small flea markets in Arizona, any flea market in Florida, and those events misadvertised or featuring mostly crafts.

The future of collecting

Want to know where the future of collecting lies? The next time you attend a flea market, the answer might be right in front of you. And, more likely than not, she'll be little more than knee high and digging through a box of Beanie Babies.

Our survey queried respondents about the collecting habits of their children. By a margin of more than 4 to 1, those shoppers who had children reported that their kids have collections of their own. What's really interesting is the broad range of items those youngsters actively seek. The list included the following (keeping in mind that some of the "children" are adults).

* L.C. Tiffany lion stickpin in 24k gold, found in the bottom of a tin of buttons
* Vintage DeLaval milking sign in its original paper wrapper
* 20 pieces of Stangl in a hard-to-find pattern
* Niloak vase purchased for 25 cents
* Red Holly bowl purchased for $50
* Tiffany Studios bronze inkwell with blown glass
* Pristine 1964 Ringo Starr bobbing-head doll purchased for $1.50
* 14k gold brooch signed Ronald Hayes, purchased in a $3 box of junk jewelry and sold for $700
* 1929 Erector set purchased for $10
* Occupied Japan silver candlesticks purchased for $1
* 4 gallons of early buttons
* Victor V phonograph
* Shoebox of Dresden Christmas ornaments for $45
* Near-mint, original insert poster from *Breakfast at Tiffany's* purchased for $70

This insert poster for Breakfast at Tiffany's was considered a best buy by one flea market shopper.

How bad can it get?

There's a scene during the movie *Stripes* in which the character played by Bill Murray has just lost his job and had his car repossessed. Upon returning to his apartment, his girlfriend walks out on him. He sums up the day with one simple statement, "Then, depression set in."

Love 'em though we do, flea markets can still have a down side. We asked collectors and dealers to share their worst flea market experiences, hoping it would help others avoid those troublesome situations. What we discovered is that many of the bad experiences are beyond a person's control, with the vagaries of weather most commonly cited. Dealers mentioned hot summer days that drew only a few buyers, winds that wrecked tents and merchandise, and four inches of rain that turned an outdoor market into a quagmire.

Other complaints included markets featuring only new merchandise and those allowing reproductions. Short tempers and rudeness (mentioned by both buyers and sellers) also made the black-list, as did finding hidden damage on an item said to have been in mint condition, and making long drives to markets no longer in business.

There were cases of bad luck as well. One shopper mentioned losing his wallet, while a dealer told of a $250 beer tray stolen while the thief's accomplice was buying an inexpensive item. One customer spent $350 for five items, but returned home to find only four of them in the bag the dealer had packed. The shopper returned to the market on two occasions, but could not locate the dealer.

In the "You Never Know What You'll Find at a Flea Market" department, one person told of examining a Johnson Bros. casserole, when it was regrettably discovered the piece contained a dirty diaper.

Drum roll, please...

Of the many nominations received, we chose five flea market experiences as being exceptionally bad. Here are the winners of our first-ever Fleabite Awards.

Award No. 1—The grand-prize for the worst flea market experience goes to the shopper who lost her 4-year-old daughter at one market. The story has a happy ending though, as the girl was later found at an ice cream stand.

Award No. 2—The runner-up for the Fleabite Award is presented to the dealer who endured above and beyond the call of duty. He described his worst experience as "Having to set up next to a player piano dealer who played that awful music all day long."

Award No. 3—You can't fight Mother Nature, as this winner found out at a New England show in 1989. The person recounted spending "the better part of the show in water over the top of my boots. A poorly anchored tent got about 50 feet of air and landed several rows over on a glass booth."

Award No. 4—When you gotta go... This recipient endured "horrible traffic and 2-hour lines to use smelly outhouses" at one New York market.

Award No. 5—It's a little different, but that's why we like this answer. "I bought a puppy and it was so cute," the person wrote. "It's now 5 years old and the bane of my existence."

Of course, the best answer to our question about worst flea market experiences would be to hear, "I've not had a bad one yet." Yes, it's easy to complain about things, but most flea markets are still great places to spend a day.

What have we learned from our survey? In summary, a call ahead to confirm hours and the type of merchandise offered can prevent a wasted trip. Courtesy is appropriate in any situation. Dress for the weather. Closely watch your merchandise. Knowledge is your best defense against buying reproductions and repaired items. Most importantly, smile and have fun. After all, isn't that what flea markets should be all about?

❖ Acknowledgments ❖

How do two people who live 600 miles apart work together to create a flea market price guide? We did it primarily through e-mail. In fact, we have yet to meet, but we've shared many laughs while completing this book. There was the night we played "Stump the Price Guide Editor," sending electronic images back and forth, trying to determine the makers and patterns of various pieces of glassware. (Contestant Ellen did brilliantly, it should be pointed out.) Telephone calls filled in when typed messages proved too slow, but we'll both cherish a friendship made possible by advancing technology.

From the beginning, we've envisioned *Warman's Flea Market Price Guide* as a book geared toward the family. It seems fitting, then, that our families played such important roles in making this book possible. Family members listened to our ideas, offered suggestions, tabulated survey results, read copy and assisted with photographs. They understood and tolerated the long hours required to complete this project. And, they correctly reminded us that this book wasn't all there was to life.

It is in this small bit of space that we publicly offer our gratitude for their time, effort, and understanding. There are no words to fully express how we feel, short of saying, "We love you." Thanks to Ellen's husband, Jeff, and to her patient parents, Naomi and Lawrence. Thanks to Don's wife, Liz, and to Carrie and Hope, two precious girls who saw their papa spending more time with his fingers on a keyboard and less time with his hands on a storybook. Yes, we can finally make that trip to the museum, and there will be more time for fairy tales on the couch.

Books such as this one are made possible by the many people behind the scenes who carry out their jobs with enthusiasm and proficiency, but often with little or no credit. At Krause Publications, those individuals include two top-notch editors, Tracy Schubert and Jon Brecka. They're more than just editors—we're glad to call them our friends. Thanks for a job well done!

When our survey was published in *Warman's Today's Collector*, flea market shoppers and dealers from across the country responded willingly to help make sense of the marketplace. Thanks a million to every one of you. The time you took is truly appreciated.

We also owe a debt of gratitude to those who provided items to be photographed. Our sincere thanks go to Barry and Barbara Carter, owners of the Knightstown Antique Mall, Knightstown, Ind., and their dealers; auctioneer Jim Dragoo; auctioneer Shane Hawkins; Don and Linda Hopkins, owners of the former Lindon's Antique Mall, Knightstown, Ind., and their dealers; auctioneers Dave and Bruce Kessler; auctioneers Rex Sigler and Jim Pickering; as well as family members Richard and Phyllis Johnson, Tom and Pete Johnson, Barry and Meg Schnieders, John and Char Schnieders, and Sally Schnieders.

Publishing books is not a business without risks, and generating a new title is fraught with even more peril. We owe a special thanks to Krause Publications for their willingness to take a chance on this project and for allowing us the time needed to create this new edition. It's been a fun journey since we talked on the phone during the summer of 1998 and said, "Sure, let's do the book together." The matter was complicated slightly by the state of Ohio, which physically and symbolically represented the vast distance between our offices in Indiana and Pennsylvania. We bridged that gap with e-mail and telephone calls, which speaks volumes about the trust implied in such a situation—both Krause's trust of us and our trust in each other. But doesn't that same trust also extend to those who deal and shop at flea markets? Without trust, we'd all be out of business.

Finally, and reverently, we give thanks to God, who is still in the business of helping ordinary people with everyday projects. We acknowledge His work in our lives and in this project.

Ellen Tischbein Schroy
Don Johnson
March 1999

☆ 4-H

Pledging head, heart, hands and health, 4-H club members have been awarded (and have made) a multitude of 4-H collectibles since the organization's inception around 1902. Expect renewed interest in this field as the centennial of the 4-H Youth Development Program is 2002. While pins, ribbons and trophies are the traditional finds, don't overlook 4-H projects themselves. Entomology collections—those small display boxes filled with bugs and butterflies—are especially attracting attention for their folk art nature.

Advertisement, National Dairy Products Corp. & 4-H, 1946, depicts boy with calf, 10-1/2" x 6-3/4" 15.50

Book, *Under the 4-H Flag* by John F. Case, 1927 ....35.00

Cookbook, *Prize Winning Recipes: 4-H and F.H.A. Favorite Food Shows*, Suburban Propane Gas, 1957, paperback, 62 pages, worn spine, 8-1/2" x 5-1/2" 2.00

Fruit jar rings, full box, mkd "4-H" 5.00

Magazine, *National Geographic*, November 1948, feature on 4-H clubs, worn spine 6.50

Pin
1st Year, 1950s.....................2.50
3rd Year, mkd "Presented by N.Y. State Bankers Assn," 3.00
4th Year, green, black and silver, clover logo, mkd "sterling," orig card....................................5.00
1987 Ohio State Fair Participant, shaped like state of Ohio ..3.50
Japanese, white background, green clover logo, Oriental characters, 3/4" d..............8.00
Junior Leadership, gold, enameled clover logo, 1960s 4.25
Swine, gold, enameled clover, pig's head in relief, mkd "County Honor Swine Moorman Mfg Co. in Coop. Ext. Ser. 1/20th 10K G.F.," 1" x 7/16"..........................3.00

Print, "The 4-H Fair," sgd "J.L. Munro 1998," fair scene, 8" x 10-1/4"..........................80.00

Songbook, *National 4-H Club Song Book*, 1946, 64 pgs, 8-3/4" x 6" 4.00

Tie tac, gold, green enamel clover logo..3.25

U.S. postage stamps, SC1005, 4-H club issue, 1952, full sheet of 50, unused................................ 14.50

❖ ABC Items

Generations of nannies and mothers have been teaching children their ABC's by using colorful china with letters of the alphabet, numbers, etc. Often these charming children's wares have nursery rhymes or sayings meant to inspire goodness in the user.

Collectors' Club: ABC Collectors Circle, 67 Stevens Ave, Old Bridge, NJ 08857.

For additional listings, see *Warman's Antiques and Collectibles Price Guide* and *Warman's English & Continental Pottery & Porcelain.*

Cup, small, pink luster 145.00

Mug
Bird perched on branch, printed alphabet on side, brown transfer with blue accents 245.00
DEF letters and children playing shuttlecock, pink transfer 165.00
Franklin's Maxim, "Slough Like Rust Consumes Faster Than Labor Wears," black transfer 165.00

Plate, bird design, handcolored transfer pattern, 6-1/2" d, $125.

Plate, china
Bible Pictures, The Destruction of Pharaoh, brown printed scene and alphabet, poly-chrome accents 195.00
Crusoe at Work, brown transfer, blue and yellow accents, brown printed alphabet border 225.00
F's for The Fowls And The Farm…, scene of animals inside barn, blue transfer, raised alphabet border 185.00
Franklin's Proverb, Make Hay While The Sun Shines, 6" d 175.00
Little Goose Box, Germany. 45.00
Timely Rescue, 8" d.......... 165.00
Two boys in cart pulled by dog, Staffordshire, 7" d......... 125.00

Plate, tin
Girl on swing, lithographed center, printed alphabet border 60.00
Who Killed Cock Robin..... 120.00

❖ Abingdon Pottery

The Abingdon Sanitary Manufacturing Company, Abingdon, Illinois, was founded in 1908 for the purpose of manufacturing plumbing fixtures. An art pottery line was started about 1933. In 1945, the company changed its name to Abingdon Potteries, Inc. Production of the art pottery line continued until 1950, when fire destroyed the art pottery kiln. After the fire, the company once again placed its emphasis on plumbing fixtures. Eventually, Abingdon Potteries became Briggs Manufacturing Company, a firm noted for its sanitary fixtures.

References: Susan and Al Bagdade, *Warman's American Pottery and Porcelain*, Wallace-Homestead, 1994; Joe Paradis, *Abingdon Art Pottery*, Schiffer Publishing, 1996.

Collectors' Club: Abingdon Pottery Collectors' Club, 210 Knox Hwy S, Abingdon, IL 61410.

For additional listings, see *Warman's Americana & Collectibles*.

Ashtray, #456............................36.00

Bookend
    Goose, single, #98 ....42.00
    Seagull, single, #305...........70.00

Candleholders, pr, double scroll, blue, gold trim, wear to gold 35.00

Console Bowl
    #377, yellow, handle continues into bowl, stamped "Abingdon, U.S.A.," 14" w, 3-3/4" h 50.00
    #532, Scroll/MD/14.5SL/1941, blue, some craze lines, 14-1/2" l, 3-3/4" h.........................25.00

Cookie Jar, Pineapple, lid repaired 75.00

Cornucopia, pink.......................20.00

Figure, goose, blue, #571........45.00

Planter, fan-shaped ribbon, mkd "Abingdon U.S.A.," also imp mark, 8" l, 4-1/2" h...............45.00

Salt and Pepper Shakers, pr, Little Bo Peep 45.00

Console bowl, floral design, gold trim, 3-3/4" h, 14-1/2" l, 6" w, $35.

Vase
    7" h, white, ship motif 58.00
    7" h, white, swirl.................. 46.00
    11" h, blue, swirl 75.00
    10" h, #117, handle, c1940. 45.00
    18" h, yellow 150.00
Window Box, #476.................. 20.00

❖ Action Figures

An action figure is a die-cast metal or plastic posable model with flexible joints that portrays a real or fictional character. In addition to the figures themselves, clothing, personal equipment, vehicles, and other types of accessories are also collectible.

The earliest action figures were the hard-plastic Hartland figures of popular television Western heroes of the 1950s. Louis Marx also included action figures in a number of playsets during the late 1950s. G.I. Joe, introduced by Hassenfield Bros. in 1964, triggered the modern action figure craze. In 1972, Mego introduced the first six super heroes in what would become a series of 34 different characters. Mego also established the link between action figures and the movies when the company issued series for "Planet of the Apes" and "Star Trek: The Motion Picture." Kenner jumped on the wagon with production of Star Wars figures in 1977.

References: John Bonavita, *Mego Action Figure Toys*, Schiffer Publishing, 1996; Paris & Susan Manos, *Collectible Action Figures*, 2nd ed., Collector Books, 1996; John Marshall, *Action Figures of the 1980s*, Schiffer Publishing, 1998.

Periodicals: *Action Figure News & Review*, 556 Monroe Tpk, Monroe, CT 06468; *Tomart's Action Figure Digest*, Tomart Publications, 3300 Encrete Ln, Dayton, OH 45439.

Collectors' Clubs: Captain Action Collectors Club, PO Box 2095, Halesite, NY 11743; Captain Action Society of Pittsburgh, 516 Cubbage St, Carnegie, PA 15106.

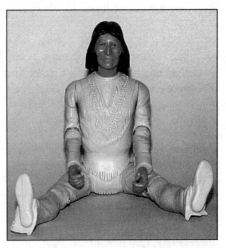

Geronimo, Marx, Best of the West series, 11-1/2" h, $40.

Boba Fett, Star Wars, 2 circles, MIP 25.00
Brett Hull, Starting Lineup, 1994....................................10.00
Death Star Commander, Star Wars............................10.00
Dream Team, Starting Lineup, 1996 Basketball, set 1 of 2 ....30.00
Hannibal, A-Team, Galoob, MOC 20.00
Human Torch, Fantastic Four....7.50
Jim Carey, Starting Lineup, 1996....................................15.00
Joker, Legends of Batman 15.00
Leia Organa, Star Wars 20.00
Luke Skywalker, Star Wars, 1st issue, 12" h, MIP...........38.00
Phantasm, Batman, animated, foreign card.........................24.00
Picard, Star Trek 10.00
Sabretooth #1, X-Men.............10.00
Spider-Man, super posable, 10" h 10.00
Troll, Spawn 15.00
Wild Wolf, Mask, Kenner, MOC 15.00
Willie Mays, Starting Lineup....20.00

❖ Adams

The name Adams denotes quality English pottery to collectors. Throughout their production from 1770 to the present, there have been Adams potteries in seven different locations, with

Coffeepot, Calyx Ware, Lowestoft, rose decor, 8" h, $125.

their wares marked from a simple "Adams" to more complex names, and sometimes it was not marked at all.

Reference: Susan and Al Bagdade, *Warman's English & Continental Pottery & Porcelain,* 3rd ed., Krause Publications, 1998.

Creamer, scene of three people in front of English buildings, dark blue transfer, wishbone handle, imp "Adams".......................165.00

Cup and Saucer, handleless, Adam's Rose pattern, red, green, and black dec, imp "Adams".............................225.00

Dish, rect, Cries of London-Ten Bunches A Penny Primrose..............................50.00

Mush Mug, The Farmers Arms 90.00

Pitcher, Adam's Rose pattern, green and red design, scalloped rim 110.00

Plate
 Adam's Rose pattern, late75.00
 English scene, dark blue transfer, imp "Adams"...................270.00
 Shakespeare Series, Sir John Falstaff, black transfer, blue and green accents, orange border.............................35.00

Teapot, Log Cabin, medallions with General Harrison on border, pink transfer..............................450.00

❖ Advertising

Manufacturers learned the valuable lesson of advertising their wares early. By using colorful, clever, and appealing packaging, consumers were attracted to certain items. Just as today's manufacturers lure us with pretty girls and adorable babies, vintage sellers also employed this type of ploy.

References: Warren Dotz, *Advertising Character Collectibles*, Collector Books, 1993, 1997 values updated; —, *What a Character! 20th Century American Advertising Icons*, Chronicle Books, 1996; Ted Hake, *Hake's Guide to Advertising Collectibles*, Wallace-Homestead, 1992; Bill and Pauline Hogan, *Charlton Standard Catalogue of Canadian Country Store Collectables*, Charlton Press, 1996; Bob and Sharon Huxford, *Huxford's Collectible Advertising*, 3rd ed., Collector Books, 1996; Ray Klug, *Antique Advertising Encyclopedia*, vol. 1 (1978, 1993 value update) and vol. 2 (1985), L-W Promotions; Mary Jane Lamphier, *Zany Characters of the Ad World*, Collector Books, 1995; Patricia McDaniel, *Drugstore Collectibles*, Wallace-Homestead, 1994; Don and Carol Raycraft, *Wallace-Homestead Price Guide to American Country Antiques*, 15th ed., Krause Publications, 1997; David and Micki Young, *Campbell's Soup Collectibles from A to Z*, Krause Publications, 1998.

Periodicals: *Creamers*, PO Box 11, Lake Villa, IL 60046; *Paper Collectors' Marketplace*, PO Box 128, Scandinavia, WI 54977; *Advertising Collectors Express*, PO Box 221, Mayview, MO 64071.

Collectors' Clubs: Antique Advertising Association of America, PO Box 1121, Morton Grove, IL 60053; Inner Seal Collectors Club, 4585 Saron Drive, Lexington, KY 40515; National Association of Paper and Advertising Collectibles, PO Box 500, Mount Joy, PA 17552; Porcelain Advertising Collectors Club, PO Box 381, Marshfield Hills, MA 02051; Ephemera Society of America, PO Box 95, Cazenovia,

Ben Hur Marjoram, litho tin, 2 oz, $25.

NY 13035; Tin Container Collectors Association, PO Box 440101, Aurora, CO 80044.

For additional listings, see *Warman's Antiques and Collectibles Price Guide* and *Warman's Americana & Collectibles*, as well as specific categories in this edition.

Advertisement, Lee Overalls, fabric sample, 1920s 20.00

Banner, Holsum Bread, illus by Howard Brown, 58" w 125.00

Billhook, Ceresota Flour..........50.00

Blotter
 Levi's, 2-3/4" x 6-1/4", stiff cardboard, full color art, black and white imprint for local dealer, unused, 1960s................20.00
 Pan-Am Gasoline, 3" h, 7-3/4" l, celluloid cover with country scene and adv, Dufe W. Fling Oil Co. 90.00

Book, *Chase & Sanborn Coffee & Tea Importers*, 1889............30.00

Box, Baker's Chocolate, 12 lb, wood 25.00

Box Opener, Wrigley's, 1940s.................................70.00

Bowl, Bird's Eye, General Goods 27.50

Cleanser, Pow Wow, multicolored graphic of Indian in headdress 55.00

Coat Hanger, San Francisco Cleaning & Drying Works, wood....................................10.00

Coffee Cup, White Castle........35.00

Coffee Measure, "Coffee Satisfaction is assured by A & P Coffee Service," aluminum, 3-3/4" l....................................8.00

Coffee Tin, H & K Coffee, 3 lb 55.00

Container, Early's Best Ribbon Cane Syrup....................................22.00

Counter Display, Gillette Blue Blades, cardboard, easel back, 1930s, 30" x 22" 85.00

Crate, Warners Kidney Liver & Remedy, wood, holds 2 doz bottles..............................165.00

Emery Board, Wead's Bread ...20.00

Folder, Marcelle Face Powder, samples................................18.00

Jar, Horlick's Malted Milk, orig lids, set of 4 ....125.00

Liquor Jug, Fleischmann's, dark blue pottery 90.00

Lunch Box, Slim Jims, no thermos, Aladdin 20.00

Mending Kit, Real Silk Hosiery ..5.00

Plate, Quick Service Laundry, tin, c1900 ....35.00

Record Buffer, Victor 40.00

Ruler, Clark Bars, wood.............8.00

Salesman's Brochure, Superior Matches, matchbook covers, "Glamour Girls Series" 45.00

Sample, Mavis Face Powder...14.00

Soap Box, Rub-No-More, shows elephants............................40.00

Tape Measure, Fab..................35.00

Theater Slide, advertising Kingnut Oleo margarine, pair in orig box 30.00

Mazola Karo corn popper, metal, 4-1/4" h, 8-3/4" d, $35.

Tip Tray, Clysmic Water, lady, deer, giant bottle 45.00

Tray, 3-3/8" w, 5" l, copper, Angelus Marshmallows, shows early Angelus Chocolate Marshmallows box, mkd "Rusckheim Bros & Eckstein, Chicago" 50.00

Tumbler, Small Grain Distilling, Louisville, etched, paneled sides, 4" h 55.00

Wallet, Rock Island Plow, cloth.................................... 24.00

Whetstone, Lavacide, For Fumigation, Innis, Speiden & Co., NY, celluloid 35.00

Whistle, Atwater Kent Radios 15.00

Wrapper, Huskey Ice Cream Bar, snow dog 15.00

Yardstick, Smith's Furniture Store................................. 10.00

❖ Advertising Characters

Just as advertisers used colorful labels to get attention, the use of characters became quite important. When consumers didn't know what brand to buy, they often decided to trust the character or personality promoting the project and could identify their favorite brands by the smiling images.

Today many of these characters have continued to have strong collector interest. From Mr. Peanut to the Campbell Kids, collectors seek items of various materials to add to their collections.

References: Warren Dotz, *Advertising Character Collectibles*, Collector Books, 1993; ——, *What a Character*, Chronicle Books, 1996; Mary Jane Lamphier, *Zany Characters of the Ad World*, Collector Books, 1995; David and Micki Young, *Campbell's Soup Collectibles from A to Z*, Krause Publications, 1998.

For additional listings, see *Warman's Antiques & Collectibles Price Guide* and *Warman's Americana and Collectibles*, as well as specific categories in this edition.

Aristocrat Tomato, Heinz, figure, 2-1/16" x 2-1/16" x 5-3/4" h, detailed smiling red tomato head wearing black monocle and top hat, name "Heinz" in relief on front of base and "57" logo in circle around three sides, c1950................................245.00

Bud Man, Budweiser Beer, 18" h flesh-colored foam rubber doll, red outfit, dark blue gloves, boots, black, white, and red bow tie, "Budweiser" and "Bud Man" on applied stickers on chest, late 1960s................................120.00

Charlie the Tuna
Alarm Clock, Lux Time Co., brass, wind-up..........................65.00

Doll, 7-1/2" h, vinyl..............30.00

Dutch Boy Paint, hand puppet, 11" h, vinyl head, fabric body, orig cellophane bag, 1960s...............45.00

Elsie the Cow, Borden's
Badge, white ground, blue lettering, 1-1/2" d 10.00

Ball, West Texas State Buffaloes, white, blue lettering, 4" d 15.00

Fountain Glass, 6-1/4" h, clear glass, frosted white image of Elsie and name, tiny Borden Co. copyright, c1940, pr...................35.00

Postcard, Elsie and Elmer, color, traveling scene....................25.00

Ring, dark gold luster plastic, center clear plastic dome over multicolored Elsie image, 1950 ....35.00

Plastic mug, Keebler elf, 3-1/4" h, $14.50.

Noid figurines, Dominos Pizza, rubber, 1987, 2-1/2" h, each $3.

Salt and Pepper Shakers, pr, Elsie and Elmer, china, c1940 ....125.00

Eveready Cat, bank 10.00

Florida Orange Bird, bank, 4-3/4" h orange vinyl, yellow accent, green leaf petal hair and wings, Hong Kong, c1960 ....35.00

Hamburger Helper Helping Hand, figure, 1-1/4" x 2" x 3" h, gold painted plaster, four-fingered glove, smiling face on palm, sealed in orig cellophane bag, generic box...........................18.00

Hamm's Bear, Hamm's Beer, cup, 5" h, blue and red artwork of trademark bear relaxing in back yard, beret and glasses on one side, running with tray of beer on other side, Dixie, c1970, set of four 16.00

Johnny, Philip Morris
Pinback Button, black, white, red, and fleshtone, 1930s.......35.00
Sign, emb tin, well worn, 12" x 14".........................95.00

Johnny Walker Red, mug 15.00

Kool Cigarettes
Dr. Kool, figure, 4-1/2" h, black and white, painted plaster, full figure walking along carrying satchel with name on side, wearing stethoscope, late 1930s, professional repair to base chip.......................136.00
Willie and Millie, salt and pepper shakers, figural, 3-1/2" h, black and white plastic, yellow accent beaks, red accent necklace and dark red hair bow on Millie, c1950 ....35.00

Mr. Clean, Procter and Gamble, figure, 8" h, painted vinyl, muscular, bald-headed figure, green earring in one ear, c1961 ....135.00

Nipper, RCA Victor
Coffee Mug, plastic..............8.00
Snowdome 40.00
Oscar Mayer, weinermobile, bank, plastic 30.00

Pillsbury Doughboy, Pillsbury Co.
Doll, 7-1/4" h, vinyl, smiling full figure boy, blue accent eyes, button on cap, copyright 1971 Pillsbury Co. Minneapolis18.00
Salt and Pepper Shakers, 4" h Poppin Fresh, 3-1/4" h Poppie, names on bases, blue accents, copyright 1974...............28.00

Reddy Kilowatt
Figure, 5" h plastic, 1/4" x 1-1/2" x 3" black plastic base, translucent pink body and white plastic head, hands and boots glow after being exposed to bright light, name on base, mid-1930s 300.00
Identification Badge, 3-3/4" sq, red and white paper envelope, 3" d still paper peel-off "E-Z Stick-On" badge with yellow upper and lower bands, red and white Reddy portrait, 1950s, unused...............20.00
Magic Gripper, 5-1/4" sq red and white paper envelope, 4-3/4" d thin textured dark yellow rubber disk, printed on one side with title and image of Reddy the Chef, c1950..............20.00
Magnepad, 5-3/4" sq white quilted fabric hot pad with magnet, red image of Reddy, red slogan, yellow fabric border trim, tray fabric reverse, unopened clear cellophane bag with red, white, and blue insert instruction sheet, c1950..................30.00
Pin, 1" h brass and red enamel figure, orig 2-1/4" x 2-3/4" diecut card with clear plastic window, c1950...............40.00
Plate, 9" d, white china, 2-1/2" h smiling full figured Reddy at left, dark red accent rim, early 1950s 60.00

Tony the Tiger
Radio 30.00
Spoon, SP, emb "Kellogg's" 10.00
Westinghouse Tuff Guy, figure, 5" h, gold painted plaster, chef with muscular crossed arms, image of woman at stove on shirt, "Westinghouse Tuff Guy 1952" in relief on front of base..................60.00

☆ Airguns

"You'll shoot your eye out!" That warning is still uttered from mothers everywhere, yet kids continue their love affairs with BB and pellet guns. Airguns trace their roots to Napoleon's day, but most collectors set their sights on examples manufactured since the late 19th century. Airguns made in the 1800s can still command premium prices, while models from the 20th century are kinder to the bank account. Collectors also search for go-withs, such as ammunition containers.

Periodicals: *The Airgun Letter*, 4614 Woodland Rd., Ellicott City, MD 21042; *Airgun Ads*, Barry Abel, P.O. Box 33, Hamilton, MT 59840.

Collectors' Club: Toy Gun Collectors of America, 3009 Oleander Ave., San Marcos, CA 92069.

Benjamin 30-30 BB carbine, rust-blistered barrel 42.00
Book, *The Complete Book of the Air Gun* by George C. Nonte, Stackpole Books, 1970 ....100.00
Daisy
Model 21 double-barrel BB gun 425.00
Model 25 commemorative BB gun, c1986, MIB 250.00

Daisy Model 188 air pistol, edge wear, $17.50.

Model 1894 ....65.00

Postcard, depicts American Youth's Bill of Rights poster, c1947, 5" x 7" 31.00

Red Ryder BB gun, c1983, sundial, large compass, orig box noting "A Christmas Story" 395.00

Red Ryder 60th anniversary BB gun, c1998, retail production model, MIB......................................40.00

Token, depicts Red Ryder and Beaver, brass, 2" d..............15.00

Upton, Model 40, 1,000-shot, nickel-plated, c1921...................350.00

❖ Airline Collectibles (Commercial)

Come fly with me! The friendly skies beckon collectors today. And, as airlines merge, change names, etc., more and more collectibles will emerge.

Periodical: *Airliners*, PO Box 52-1238, Miami, FL 33152.

Collectors' Clubs: Aeronautic & Air Label Collectors Club, PO Box 1239, Elgin, IL, 60121; C.A.L./N-X-211 Collectors Society, 226 Tioga Ave, Bensenville, IL 60106; Gay Airline Club, PO Box 69A04, West Hollywood, CA 90069; World Airline Historical Society, 3381 Apple Tree Lane, Erlanger, KY 41018.

For additional listings, see *Warman's Americana and Collectibles*.

Cigar Cutter, pocket, Pan Am, 1901 ....70.00

Cup and Saucer, Delta Airlines, for VIP International flights, Mayer China....................................25.00

Dinner Plate, Delta Airlines, for VIP International flights, Mayer China........................20.00

Continental pin, plastic, 2-5/8" l, $4.

Figure, Air-India, 4-1/2" h, painted plastic statuette, green flying carpet base, traditional red, white, and blue striped turban, green clasp, red jacket, white harem trousers, curled red shoes, orig label "Ameya Industries/Bombay, India," c1970........................ 35.00

Napkin Holder, American Airlines, 1" h, 1-1/2" d, open ended metal clasp, center with "AA" soaring eagle symbol, c1930 .... 15.00

Place Setting, United, china.... 42.00

Playing Cards, 3/4" x 2-1/4" x 3-1/2" box, c1960-80

American Airlines, US mail plane 10.00

Delta Airlines, white pyramid design............................... 8.00

Eastern/Ryder, text with logo design............................... 8.00

Ozark, snow covered Rockies design............................ 10.00

TWA Collectors Series, Douglas DC-9, 1966...................... 12.00

Postcard, unused

Aerolineas Argentinas, 1950s, Carrasco Airport, Montevideo Uruguay, black and white 10.00

Air Canada preparing for takeoff, oversized.......................... 6.00

Air Transat, Lockheed L1011, color, oversized 6.00

Alitalia, Caravelle III S.E. 210, radio print on back............ 8.00

KLM, Douglas DC-6, airline issued, slight crease......... 7.00

Lufthansa DC10, airline issued............................... 5.00

Pan American, Super 6 Clipper, color 8.00

Piedmont Airlines, Boeing 737-300 series, color, oversized......................... 6.00

Pluna, Uruguayan Airline, Boeing 737, radio club.................. 6.00

For exciting collecting trends and newly expanded areas look for the following symbols:

✪ Hot Topic

★ New Warman's Listing

(May have been in another Warman's edition.)

Trans-Canada Airlines, airline issued, Viscount at Windsor Airport, Windsor, Ontario, Canada............................8.00

Stewardess Wings, United Airlines, 2-1/2" x 3-1/4" orig black and white card, 2" w silver accent wings, red, white, and blue center logo, c1960, unused 20.00

Toy Car, TWA Airlines, airport service car, tin friction, 11" l ...120.00

Toy Plane

Corvair Inter-continental Jet, friction, 14" l, MIB 145.00

Pan Am Boeing 747, battery operated, automatic stop and go action, see thru cockpit, flashing jet engines, realistic sound, 13" l, MIB 225.00

Pan Am Boeing 747, friction, 7" l, MIB 225.00

Royal Dutch Airlines, KLM Corvair jet, friction, 14" l 95.00

Travel Bag, Pan Am World...... 10.00

❖ Akro Agate

The Akro Agate Co. was formed in 1911 to produce marbles. By the time they moved in 1914, they began production of other glass items, including floralware and children's dishes.

References: Gene Florence, *Collectors Encyclopedia of Akro Agate Glassware*, Revised Edition, Collectors Books, 1975, 1992 value update; Roger and Claudia Hardy, *Complete Line of Akro Agate*, published by author, 1992.

Collectors' Clubs: Akro Agate Art Association, PO Box 758, Salem, NH 03079; Akro Agate Collector's Club, 10 Bailey St., Clarksburg, WV 26301.

For additional listings, see *Warman's Americana & Collectibles*.

Reproduction Alert.

Ashtray, 2-7/8" sq, blue and red marble..................................8.50

Basket, 2 handles, orange and white 35.00

Children's Play Dishes, creamer

Interior Panel, topaz
transparent......................20.00

Stacked Disk, pink...............25.00

Stippled Band, green,
large 30.00

Children's Play Dishes, cup

Chiquita, transparent cobalt
blue 14.00

Interior Panel, green transparent,
large 15.00

Octagonal, closed handle, dark
green, large......................8.00

Children's Play Dishes,
cup and saucer

Chiquita, green opaque.........8.00

Stippled Band, green, large or
small...............................30.00

Children's Play Dishes, plate

Concentric Rib, green 8.00

Interior Panel, blue opaque,
medium 15.00

Interior Panel, topaz
transparent.....................10.00

Octagonal, green, large.........8.00

Stacked Disk, medium
blue 6.00Stippled Band, topaz,
large 10.00

Children's Play Dishes, saucer

Concentric Rib, white 3.00

Interior Panel, medium blue,
opaque, large 9.00

Stacked Disk and Panel, transparent green, small 12.00

Children's Play Dishes, set, Interior
Panel, topaz transparent, service
for 4, cups, saucers, plates,
creamer and sugar, teapot
with lid 215.00

**Miniature flower pots, green and
orange, 2-3/8" h, each $12.**

Children's Play Dishes,
sugar, cov

Chiquita, green opaque or transparent cobalt blue............. 8.00

Stacked Disk, pink.............. 50.00

Children's Play Dishes,
teapot, cov

Chiquita, green opaque 18.00

Interior Panel, green, white lid,
large 45.00

Stippled Band, green,
small.............................. 35.00

Children's Play Dishes, tumbler,
Stacked Disk and Panel, transparent green, 2" h............... 12.00

Children's Play Dishes, water set,
octagonal, open handle, blue
pitcher, 2 dark and 2 light green
tumblers............................. 70.00

Cornucopia, orange and white.. 8.00

Flowerpot, 2-1/2" h, Stacked Disk,
green and white................. 12.00

Lamp, 12" h, brown and blue marble,
4" d, black octagonal top, Globe
Spec Co............................. 75.00

Marbles, Chinese Checkers, set of
60, orig box...................... 130.00

Mexicalli Jar, cov, orange and
white 40.00

Powder Jar, Colonial Lady,
yellow 65.00

Vase

3-3/4" h, green, marble....... 15.00

4-5/8" h, 4-1/4" w, flared, green
and white marble, rust streaks,
raised flower on each side,
mkd "Made in USA" with
backwards S, crow over
letter A............................ 28.00

☆ Aladdin

Aladdin is the name used by many
collectors to describe the wares of the
Mantle Lamp Company of America.
Known for its lamps, this company was
founded in Chicago in 1908. It became
one of the leading producers of lunch
boxes in the 1950s through 1970s.

Vintage Aladdin lamps were made
of metal and glass. Among the glass
lamps are those made of Alacite, which

has a creamy yet translucent color.
Collectors insist that lamps possess all
the correct parts, including original
shades, which can be difficult to find.

References: J. W. Courter, *Aladdin
Collectors Manual & Price Guide
#16*, published by author (3935
Kelley Rd, Kevil, KY 42053), 1996;—,
*Aladdin, The Magic Name In Lamps,
Revised Edition*, published by author,
1997.

Collectors' Club: Aladdin Knights of
the Mystic Light, 3935 Kelley Rd,
Kevil, KY 42053.

Reproduction Alert.

Electric Lamp

Alacite table lamp, ivory,
embossed leaf design, cut-
through scalloped base,
wreath-shaped Alacite finial,
22-1/4" h.........................92.00

Alacite wall lamp, white,
U-shaped arm, 8-1/2" h ..93.50

G-217 table lamp, ivory Alacite,
gold metal base, vase design
with leaf spray in high relief,
c1940.............................75.00

Hopalong Cassidy bullet lamp,
Alacite, decal worn, no shade,
10" h 325.00

M-123, lady figural, metal, orig
fleur-de-lis finial 405.00

Kerosene Lamp

B-26 Simplicity "Decalmania"
lamp, pink Alacite,
c1948-53 ....325.00

Beehive, ruby, complete with B
burner, wick, chimney, insect
screen and shade,
c1937.............................795.00

Model 6 hanging lamp, no smoke
bell, small chip on orig shade,
older replaced chimney,
c1915.............................256.00

Model 8, 401 shade 380.00

Moonstone Quilt, green, B burner,
wick, chimney, c1937........335.00

Moonstone Quilt, white, B burner,
wick, chimney, c1937........350.00

Ruby flash Tall Lincoln drape, ruby
flashed, 1940s shade........861.00

Tall Lincoln Drape, cobalt... 1,100.00

Alacite lamps, electric, red and cream, 9-1/2" h, pr, $90.

Tall Lincoln Drape, c1941, old formula Alacite, complete with B burner, wick, chimney and shade 325.00

Venetian, rose, c1932, A burner, wick and chimney..............295.00

Vertique, yellow, B burner, wick, chimney and shade, c1938 ....735.00

Washington Drape, amber, plain stem, B burner, wick, chimney, shade, c1940.....................195.00

❖ Albums

Albums are a grouping of pages, bound together, used for a similar purpose. Albums can range in size from small ones used for autographs to larger, ornate types used to store photographs. They offer unique glimpses into a person's life. An autograph album might show one's friends and their sentiments at a particular time. Photograph albums are often found at flea markets filled with unidentified photographs of people and interesting places. Usually the individual values of these individual "instant relatives" are not great, but if there happens to be a famous person, or perhaps an interesting pose, the value may be enhanced.

Autograph
  Leather cover, 2" x 5", NY, 1877 ....100.00
  Velvet cover, word "Autograph" emb across front, faded red, filled with autographs, some including caricatures 75.00

Photo album, Victorian, embossed leather cover, brass hardware, 6-1/8" x 5-1/8", $110.

Daguerreotype, gutta percha, scrolling motif, dark brown 50.00

Photograph
  Celluloid cover, floral motif 85.00
  Leather cover, worn cover, some pages blank.................... 30.00
  Velvet cover, faded green, pages with diecut openings to accommodate studio sized portraits, some unidentified portraits 65.00
Scrapbook, made by Everett S. Pratt, Amherst College, class of 1897, details of campus activities glued in, pages fragile 750.00
Tintype, holds 24 tintypes, leather cover, 1-1/2" x 1-1/4" 225.00

❖ Aliens, Space-Related

From little green creatures to Martians, collectors are fascinated by science fiction and aliens. As you can see from this sampling, they come in all types of objects, from scary and spooky to just plain fun. Any alien collection is sure to be out of this world!

References: Dana Cain, *UFO & Alien Collectibles Price Guide,* Krause Publications, 1999; T. N. Tumbusch, *Space Adventure Collectibles*, Wallace-Homestead, 1990.

Periodicals: *Starlog Magazine*, 275 Park Ave, South, New York, New York, 10016; *Strange New Worlds*, PO Box 223, Tallevast, FL 34270.

Collectors' Clubs: Galaxy Patrol, 22 Colton St, Worcester, MA 01610; Lost in Space Fan Club, 550 Trinity, Westfield, NJ 07090; Society for the Advancement of Space Activities, PO Box 192, Kent Hills, ME 04349.

For additional listings, see *Warman's Americana & Collectibles* and related listings in this edition.

Action Figure, Space Marine Drake, Kenner, 1992, MIP 16.00
Book, *The Great Book of Movie Monsters*, Jan Stacy and Ryder Syverson, Contemporary Books, 1983, 351 pgs 15.00
Cap, from movie Alien, 1992, black, neon green writing, adjustable strap, officially licensed by Universal Industries, Inc............... 10.00
Christmas Ornament, Kringles Bumper Cars, Santa, reindeer, and space alien, Hallmark, 1991, MIB 50.00

Comic book, *UFO & Outer Space*, Gold Key, No. 16, Aug. 1978, 10-1/4" x 6-5/8", $5.

Keychain, Toy Story, Pizza Planet vending machine type, antenna lights, orig Basic Fun blister pack......................................4.75

Toy, Liddle Kiddles Kozmic Space Ship, red space ship, orange int, lime green wheels, clear dome, Mattel, 1969-70, 5-1/2" h.....80.00

Magazine

Cinemacabre, #2, George Stover, includes film characters, Alien, Superman, and Dawn of the Dead, late 1970s.......15.00

Famous Monsters of Filmland, #143, Close Encounters, Alien, and Star Wars 8.00

Famous Monsters of Filmland, #159, Time After Time and Alien 12.50

Famous Monsters of Filmland, #169, The Hearse, Contamination: Alien on Earth and Zombie 8.00

Puppet, Alf, red shirt and cap, Alien Productions, 1988, played with.......................................10.00

Stuffed Toy, green plush, 5" l, hanging ring 6.00

❖ Almanacs

While few of us today rely on almanacs for weather, it wasn't too long ago that many folks did. And, they got much more than weather, all kinds of useful information and health tips. Today these little almanacs are fun to collect and read. You never know what kind of wisdom you'll find.

Almanac Calculations for 1913, adv for Alonzo O. Bliss Co. Native Herbs, health tips and info, brittle covers...................................2.50

B. F. Goodrich Farmer's Handbook and Almanac, 1947, practical info, household hints, creased and torn cover 2.50

Farmers Almanac, 1974, Vol. 157, edited by Ray Geiger, copyright 1973 by Almanac Publishing Co., dusty.....................................1.00

Grier's Almanac, Johnson Drug Co., 1978, copyright 1978, Grier's Almanac Publishing Co., Atlanta, GA 2.00

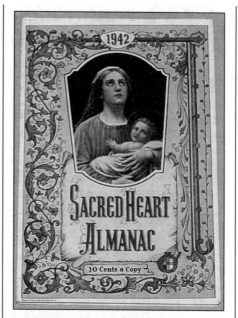

1942 Sacred Heart Almanac, 8-7/8" x 5-3/4", $5.

Healthway Products Almanac, Illinois Herb Co., 1968, 64 pgs 3.00

MacDonald's Farmer's Almanac, 1938, Atlas Printing Co., 6" x 9" 15.00

Maine Farmer's Almanac, 1916, wear and stains 15.00

Old Farmer's Almanac, 1857, wear and stains 12.00

Rexall Almanac & Moon Book, Yvonne DeCarlo on cov, 5" x 8" 15.00

Royster's 1944 Almanac, 59th C, published by F. S. Royster Guano Co., Norfolk, VA, staining on cov, 1" tear at spine 2.00

Telephone Almanac, 1940, printed for Bell System Telephone Subscribers, American Telephone & Telegraph Co. 5.00

Trail Blazer's Almanac and Pioneer Guide Book, 1965, wear to cover 3.00

Uncle Sam's Almanac, 1948, published by Haskin Service, soiled covers and pages 2.00

❖ Aluminum, Hand Wrought

The aluminum giftware market began in the 1920s, providing consumers with an interesting new medium, replacing fancy silver and silver-plate items. In order to be more competitive, numerous silver manufacturers added aluminum articles to their product lines during the Depression. Many well-known and highly esteemed metalsmiths contributed their skills to the production of hammered aluminum. With the advent of mass-production and the accompanying wider distribution of aluminum giftware, the demand began to decline, leaving only a few producers who have continued to turn out quality work using the age-old and time-tested methods of metal crafting.

References: Everett Grist, *Collectible Aluminum*, Collector Books, 1994; Frances Johnson, *Aluminum Giftware*, Schiffer Publishing, 1996; Dannie A. Woodard, *Hammered Aluminum Hand Wrought Collectibles*, Book Two, Aluminum Collectors' Books, 1993; ——, *Revised 1990 Price List for Hammered Aluminum*, Aluminum Collectors' Books, 1990; Dannie Woodard and Billie Wood, *Hammered Aluminum*, published by authors, 1983.

Periodical: *Aluminist*, PO Box 1346, Weatherford, TX 76086.

Collectors' Clubs: Aluminum Collectors, PO Box 1346, Weatherford, TX 76086; Wendell August Collectors Guild, PO Box 107, Grove City, PA 16127.

For additional listings, see *Warman's Americana & Collectibles*.

Ashtray, Stanhome, Stanley Home Product, center relief dec of house, 3-1/4" d 5.00

Everlast Metal casserole, 9-1/2" d, $12.

Basket, rose handle, 9" l, mkd "Continental Trade Mark Hand Wrought Silverlook 754" 25.00

Bowl, leaf design around base 10.00

Candy Tray, chrysanthemum dec, unmarked, 8" d 10.00

Casserole, cov, mkd "B. W. Buenilum," 10" d, 7-1/2" h 18.00

Coaster, flying ducks and cattails, set of six ..... 12.00Crumb Catcher Set, unmarked 10.00

Dish
Floral design, 5" d 3.00
Leaf shape, 4" l 3.00
Tulip design, raised sides, 7-1/2", Buenilum 24.00

Ice Bucket, cov, insulated, mkd "Krome Enduring Beautiful and Pat Pending," large knob on top, blister on bottom, use marks, plastic rim cracked, 10" h 20.00

Pitcher, Regal, some scratches and wear 15.00

Plate, flying ducks and cattails, 5" d 6.00

Scoop, 6-1/2" l, handle curled under 6.00

Serving Dish, marine motif, shells and shrimp dec, 16-1/2" x 16-1/2", mkd "B & B, St. Paul, Minn, USA" 65.00

Silent Butler
Flower design, unmarked 18.00
Moon and star design, 6-1/2" x 11" 24.00

Tidbit Tray, 3 tiers, dogwood pattern, mkd "Wilson Specialties Co., Inc., Brooklyn, NY," 10" h, 13" d ..30.00

Tray
Flower design, unmarked, 11-1/4" d..........................15.00
Four flying ducks, mkd "Hand Wrought by Federal S. Co.," wrapped handles, 18" d..............................30.00
Leaf design, mkd "Hand Forged Everlast Metal" with anchor and arm with hammer in hand, 14" x 9-1/4", wear...........15.00
Two handles, mkd "Hand wrought Rodney Kent" 28.00

❖ American Bisque

The American Bisque Company was founded in Williamstown, West Virginia, in 1919. Although the pottery's original product was china-head dolls, it quickly expanded its inventory to include serving dishes, cookie jars, ashtrays, and various other decorative ceramic pieces. B. E. Allen, founder of the Sterling China Company, invested heavily in the company and eventually purchased the remaining stock. In 1982, the plant was sold and operated briefly under the name American China Company. The plant closed in 1983.

Sequoia Ware and Berkeley are two trademarks used by American Bisque, the former used on items sold in gift shops, and the latter found on products sold through chain stores. Cookie jars produced by this company are marked "ABC" inside blocks.

Reference: Susan and Al Bagdade, *Warman's American Pottery and Porcelain,* Wallace-Homestead, 1994.

For additional listings, see *Warman's Americana & Collectibles.*

Bank, elephant, gray, standing on circus platform, 6" h 85.00

Clothes Sprinkler, figural, cat, marbles for eyes 165.00

Cookie Jar
Baby Elephant, bonnet 165.00
Bear with Cookie, mkd "USA" 80.00
Beehive, 11-3/4" h, mkd "USA" 165.00
Coffee Pot, 9-1/2" h, mkd "USA" 110.00
Cookie Truck, 11-1/2" h, mkd "USA 744"............. 195.00
Donald Duck, standing 385.00
Jack-in-the-Box, 12" h, imp "USA" on back............. 195.00
Kitten, 11-3/4" h, mkd "USA" 165.00
Milk Wagon, 9" h, mkd "USA 740" 165.00
Toy Soldier, Sentry, 11-1/4" h, mkd "USA 743"............. 225.00

Food Mold, fish, 10" l, white, red trim, ring for hanging, incised "ABC" 15.00

Pitcher, chick, gold trim 48.00

Planter
Flamingo, 7-1/4" x 10" l.......65.00
Lamb, 4-3/4" h, 6-1/2" l.........8.00
Teapot, Red Rose, 6-1/2" h, gold trim.........................55.00

Vase
6" h, white heart, blue bow . 28.00
7-1/4" h, green, fern frond handles...........................20.00

❖ Amusement Parks

Whhheeee, what a fun a trip to an amusement park can be. And doesn't everybody bring home some sort of souvenir. Today's collectors are starting to scout flea markets for these treasures, keeping the excitement of that trip alive a little longer.

Ashtray, metal, double hearts, cutout with cupid, scenes of Convention Hall and Steel Pier, Atlantic City, NJ, mkd "Made in Japan," 4" x 4-3/4" 22.00

Candy Box, James Bank, Atlantic City, Salt Water Taffy, 7" h 18.00

Charm Bracelet, Disneyland, six charms, copyright Walt Disney Productions, MIB 40.00

Desk Calendar, mechanical, Great Adventure Amusement Park, NJ, metal, shows Ferris wheel and other rides, paper label "Made in Japan," 3" h 24.00

Photograph, S. S. Morro Castle, Asbury Park, NJ, Sept., 1934, copyright 1934 Cole & Co., caption reads "As she appeared, still burning, the night her fire gutted hulk drifted out of the storm and the darkness through a driving rain to her final resting place; the doomed ship burning at daybreak six miles off the Jersey coast. There she lies...as millions of people have viewed this grim relic of one of the sea's major disasters," 11-1/2" x 19" 65.00

Pinback Button

Disneyland, "100 Million Smiles," Walt Disney Productions, Western Badge, Anaheim, 2-1/4" d..............................15.00

Plainfield, 885, attached ribbon reads "Asbury Park, June 22, 1933," attached key tag mkd "B.P.O.E.", some fraying to ribbon 28.00

Plaque, Disneyland, given to first visitors on July 17, 1951, emb brass, 10" h, 3-3/4" w 100.00

Plate, Hershey Park, Hershey, PA, lusterware, hand painted pastoral scene, black ink mark "Painted and Imported for Hershey Park," palette mark, "The Jonroth Studios Germany," 7" d.............45.00

Postcard

Disneyland, 1969 ....3.00
Heinz Ocean Pier, Atlantic City, unused 10.00

Coney Island frosted glass, 5" h, $10.

Snow White & Friends visit Disneyland, 1970 ....3.00
Tray, 12" d, tin litho, Young's Ocean City Pier, Atlantic City, NJ, scene includes huge fish tank, roller coaster, children's carnival, and scenic view of entire pier, C. W. Shonk Co. litho 175.00
Trinket Box, 2-1/2" d, 2" h, Minnie Mouse sewing little teddy bear, copyright "Walt Disney Productions," orig Disneyland price sticker, 1970s 70.00
Wallet, child's, Asbury Park, NJ, surfing and sailing scenes ..20.00

✪ Anchor Hocking

An American glassware producer, Anchor Hocking has been located in Lancaster, OH, since 1905 when the Hocking Glass Company opened its doors there. In 1937, they merged with the Anchor Cap & Closure Company, forming the highly successful Anchor Hocking Corporation.

Their principal areas of production are household glass articles and they grace many tables. Many of the kitchen and table wares are marked, helping collectors to identify these pieces. Several Depression-era glass patterns were made by this company. One production line is called "Fire-King," and a sampling of prices in that hot area of collecting can be found later in this edition.

References: Gene Florence, *Kitchen Glassware of the Depression Era, 6th Edition*, Collector Books, 1997; Garry Kilgo and Dale, Jerry, and Gail Wilkins, *Collectors Guide to Anchor Hocking's Fire-King Glassware*, K & W Collectibles Publisher, 1991.

Animal Covered Dish, fish, clear glass 20.00
Batter Bowl, set of nested bowls, 7", 8", 9", and 10" d, transparent green 95.00
Berry Bowl, Coronation pattern, 8" d, handle, ruby.......................15.00
Bowl, Desert Gold pattern, amber, orig sticker 8.00

Condiment Set, cruet and salt and pepper shakers, blue trim ...25.00
Food Chopper, red tin top, mkd "Anchor Hocking, Federal Tool Corp."................................18.00
Mixing Bowl, Vitrock, 8-1/2" d 18.00
Mug, Bo Peep 12.00
Salad Set, hand painted salad bowl, two cruets, salt and pepper shakers, all marked "AH" on bottom, c1950.................................25.00
Salt and Pepper Shakers, pr, green.................................45.00
Syrup Pitcher, 5-1/2" h, red top, mkd "Anchor Hocking, Federal Tool Corp.".................................15.00
Tom and Jerry Set, large bowl with 5 matching cups, white ground, red dec.....................................12.00
Tumbler, Manhattan pattern, 10 oz, pink, set of 6 ....150.00

✭ Angels

Perhaps they believe in guardian angels, but many flea market shoppers are looking for angels to add to their collections. And, they are finding them on all kinds of objects, from figurines to artwork.

Collectors' Clubs: Angel Collector Club, 14 Parkview Court, Crystal Lake, IL 60012-3540; Angels Collectors' Club of America, 12225 South Patomac, Phoenix, AZ 85044.

Advertising Mirror "Angelus Marshmallows," angel holding box of marshmallows.....................80.00

McDonald's mug, milk glass, 3-1/2" h, $5.

Book, *Angel Unaware*, Dale Evans
   Rogers, 1953, dj..................10.00
Candleholders, pr, Clay Art,
   4" x 3"................................12.00

Christmas Ornament
   Cardboard and wood, pink gown,
      flanked by two trees, 2-3/4" d,
      Japan..............................22.00
   Wax over composition, human
      hair wig, spun glass wings,
      cloth dress, Germany......55.00

Christmas Tree Topper
   Papier-mâché, blue dress, silver
      cardboard wings and crown,
      kneeling on silver sparkle cov-
      ered sphere, silver tube ..45.00
   Spun glass and cardboard,
      6" h................................24.00

Chromolithograph, diecut
   7" h, tinsel trim, German......18.00
   8" h, tinsel and lametta trim.10.00

Figure
   Artgift Corporation, Angel of
      Africa, pottery, copyright 1958
      ....55.00
   Fenton Glass, amber, opalescent,
      c1990, 7-1/4" h................40.00
   Josef Originals, gold trim and
      halo 20.00

**Lefton birthday angel, February,
orig box, 4-3/8" h, $32.**

Pair of hands with pink angel
   nestled in them, gold trim,
   applied roses, 5-1/4" h ... 35.00
Young boy playing ball with an
   angel 7.00
Fireplace screen, French, bronze
   dore, angel and torch motif,
   c1870........................... 2,850.00
Gargoyle, gypsum, winged cat, orig
   box, 12" h 72.00
Lamp, table, 26-1/2" h, cast metal,
   figural cherub on vase, bronze
   finish, French label, shade
   missing 165.00
Light Switch Cover, angel dec,
   Bernat................................. 5.00
Pin, goldtone, small rhinestone
   accents 5.00
Planter, angel on cloud, Lefton
   China 40.00
Plate, pink flowers border, center
   with woman in forest with angel
   lying asleep in her lap, c1880,
   Limoges, H & C with a line and
   Limoges under in green,
   9-1/2" d............................. 65.00
Postcard
   A Happy New Year, Victorian
      angel, postmarked Minneapo-
      lis, Dec 30, 1909 .... 4.00
   Easter Greetings, angel painting
      on egg, postmarked Jackson,
      Michigan, 1909, 1 cent stamp,
      printed in Germany........... 7.50
Salt and Pepper Shakers, pr, porce-
   lain, 3-3/4" h 25.00
Shoe, angel in green with fired gold
   wings, gold accents, mkd
   "Japan," 3-1/4" h................. 20.00
Tie Tac, angel head, brasstone, mkd
   "HNS" 12.00

❖ Animal Dishes, Covered

   These clever covered dishes were
first popular with the Victorians. They
used them to hold foods and sweets on
their elaborate sideboards. Some
examples were made by china manufacturers, but the vast majority are
glass and represent many major companies. They are found in milk glass
(opaque) in white and some colors,
clear glass, and many colors of translucent glass.

**Duck on nest, caramel slag, Impe-
rial, 4" h, 4-1/2" l, $50.**

Dolphin, chocolate glass, Green-
   town, chip on tail 195.00
Duck, milk glass, painted brown
   top, painted green base,
   Vallerystahl 95.00
Eagle, milk glass, eggs and nest on
   base, front emb "The American
   Hen," mkd "Porto Rica/Cuba/
   Philippines" 75.00
Fish, walking, white milk glass, red
   glass eyes......................... 195.00
Hen On Nest
   Marbleized, head turned to left,
      lacy base, white and deep
      blue, Atterbury 185.00
   Opaque aqua, Vallerystahl.. 75.00
   Transparent blue, Kemple Glass,
      mkd "K"........................... 35.00
Owl, green slag, Imperial Glass, mkd
   "IG".................................... 60.00
Rabbit
   Amber, Greentown............ 250.00
   Frosted, white, Vallerystahl. 65.00
Setter Dog, white milk glass, sgd
   "Flaccus," repair to lid 150.00
Swan, opaque blue,
   Vallerystahl 100.00

❖ Animation Cels

   A "cel" is an animation drawing on
celluloid. The technique is attributed to
Earl Hurd. Although the technique
reached perfection under animation
giants such as Walt Disney and Max
Fleischer, individuals such as Ub
Iwerks, Walter Lantz, and Paul Terry—
along with studios such as Columbia,

Charles Mints and Screen Gems, MGM, Paramount/Famous Studios, UPA, and Warner Brothers, did pioneering work.

A second of film requires over 20 animation cels. The approximate number of cels used to make that cartoon can be determined by multiplying the length of a cartoon in minutes times 60 times 24.

References: Jeff Lotman, *Animation Art: The Early Years*, Schiffer Publishing, 1995; ——, *Animation Art at Auction: Since 1994*, Schiffer Publishing, 1998; ——, *Animation Art: The Later Years*, Schiffer Publishing, 1996.

Periodicals: *Animation Film Art*, PO Box 25547, Los Angeles, CA 90025; *Animation Magazine*, 4676 Admiralty Way, Ste 210, Marina Del Ray, CA 90292; *Animato!*, PO Box 1240, Cambridge, MA 02238; *In Toon!*, PO Box 217, Gracie Station, New York, NY, 10028; *Storyboard/The Art of Laughter*, 80 Main St, Nashua, NH 03060.

Collectors' Club: Greater Washington Animation Collectors Club, 12423 Hedges Run Dr #184, Lake Ridge, VA 22192.

For additional listings, see *Warman's Americana and Collectibles.*

Fred and Wilma Flintstone, Barney and Betty Rubble, orig production cel, multi-cel setup, mounted on full celluloid, framed, glazed, 16" x 19" 425.00

Jungle Book, Walt Disney, 1967, Baloo, 6-1/2" x 4" gouache on celluloid, cel trimmed, unframed 925.00

Scooby Doo, sgd "246/11 #601 SC36," 14-3/4" x 11-3/4"....150.00

Smurf, #240 21 65 F-17, matted, 11" x 14" 95.00

Sylvester, orig production cel, gouache on full celluloid, accompanied by orig layout drawing, c1960, mounted, framed, glazed, 17" x 32" 450.00

Teenage Mutant Ninja Turtle, Certificate of Authenticity, copyright dates 1985 to 1991, matted, 11" x 14" 85.00

Winnie the Pooh with Rabbit and Piglet, 1960s orig film 350.00

☆ Anri

This Italian ceramics manufacturer has impacted the limited edition collectibles craze. Their wares can be found in various forms, with several different artists' works featured.

Periodical: *Collectors Mart Magazine*, 700 E. State St, Iola, WI 54990.

Collectors' Club: Club Anri, 55 Parcella Park Drive, Randolph, MA 02368.

Egg, J. Ferrandiz, baby coming out of egg, dated, 1980s, firing check 18.00

Figure
    Girl with three bunnies, 3" h...85.00
    Morning Chores, Sarah Kay, 1983 .... 465.00
    Season's Greetings, Sarah Kay, 1990 .... 225.00

Limited Edition Plate
    Disney Four Star Collection, Maestro Mickey, 1989, MIB................................. 75.00
    J. Ferrandiz, Heavenly Strings, 1989, MIB..................... 175.00

Music Box, Ave Marie De Lourdes by Ferrandiz 275.00

❖ Appliances

Appliances of all types fascinate collectors. Who made it, when, what does it do, does it work. All important questions to ask. And, please, please be careful when attempting to see if it works. Original instructions, parts, and boxes add greatly to the value of vintage appliances. Here's a sampling of what you can find at flea markets.

References: E. Townsend Artman, *Toasters*, Schiffer Publishing, 1996; Linda Campbell Franklin, *300 Years of Kitchen Collectibles*, 4th Edition, Krause Publications, 1998; Michael J. Goldberg, *Groovy Kitchen Designs for Collectors*, Schiffer Publishing, 1996; Helen Greguire, *Collector's*

Guide to Toasters & Accessories, Collector Books, 1997; Gary Miller and K. M. Scotty Mitchell, *Price Guide to Collectible Kitchen Appliances*, Wallace-Homestead, 1991; Diane Stoneback, *Kitchen Collectibles*, Wallace-Homestead, 1994; *Toasters and Small Kitchen Appliances*, L-W Book Sales, 1995.

Collectors' Club: Electric Breakfast Club, PO Box 306, White Mills, PA 18473.

For additional listings, see *Warman's Americana & Collectibles.*

Blender, Dorby Whipper, Model E, chrome motor, black bakelite handle, clear Vidrio glass measuring body 50.00

Chafing Dish, Manning Bowman, 1930s, bright chrome Art Deco design, two part top, hot plate base, black bakelite knob and handles 75.00

Coffee Set, Landers, Frary & Clark, c1915, coffee urn, large wood ear-shaped handles, nickel bodies, oval tray, 4 pc set 85.00

Drink Mixer, Made-Rite, Weining Made Rite Co., 1930s, lightweight metal, cream and green motor, single shaft..........................25.00

Egg Cooker, Hankscraft Co., 1930s, yellow china base, instructions on metal plate on bottom 35.00

Flour Sifter, Miracle Flour Sifter, 1934, electric, cream body, blue wood handle 35.00

Heater, Westinghouse Cozy-Glow, nickel-plated radiant heater, scallop shell shape, 17" h 150.00

Hot Plate, El Stovo, c1910, solid iron surface, clay filled int, pierced legs, pad feet 25.00

Juicer, Vita-Juicer, Kold King Distributing Corp., 10" h, cream-colored cast metal, base motor 35.00

For exciting collecting trends and newly expanded areas look for the following symbols:

✿ Hot Topic

☆ New Warman's Listing

(May have been in another Warman's edition.)

Percolator, Model No. 61, The Coleman Lamp and Stove Co., $65.

Mixer, Kenmore Hand Mixer, 1940s, cream-colored plastic case, single 4-1/2" beaker, orig box, booklet, warranty, and hanger plate 37.50

Popcorn Popper, Excel, 1920s, cylindrical nickel body, metal handles form legs, hand crank, black wood knob, top vent holes....................................25.00

Toaster

General Mills, early 1940s, 2 slice, chrome body, wheat dec on side, black bakelite base 35.00

Sunbeam, early 1920s, chrome body, round, reeded legs, hexagonal bakelite feet, double wire cages flip over horizontally, carrying handles ...125.00

Toastmaster, 1927, chrome Art Deco body, louvered sides, orig box 200.00

Waffle Iron, Coleman, 1930s, chrome Art Deco body, small black and white porcelain top, impala insert, black bakelite handles...............................65.00

❖ Art Deco

Named for the Paris Exhibition of 1927, "L'Exposition International des Arts Déecorative et Industriels Mondernes," it changed the style of the day to sleek. Art Deco style is angular, with simple lines and was reflected in everything of the period from artwork to skyscrapers.

References: Jean L. Druesedow (ed.), *Authentic Art Deco Interiors*

and Furniture in Full Color, Dover Publications, 1997; Mary Gaston, *Collector's Guide to Art Deco*, 2nd edition, Collector Books, 1997.

Periodical: *Echoes Report*, PO Box 2321, Maaspee, MA 02649.

Collectors' Clubs: Canadian Art Deco Society, #302 884 Bute St., Vancouver, British Columbia V6E 1YA Canada; International Coalition of Art Deco Societies, One Murdock Terrace, Brighton, MA 02135; Miami Design Preservation League, PO Bin L, Miami Beach, FL 33119; Twentieth Century Society, 70 Cowcross St, London Ec1M 6DR England.

For additional listings, see *Warman's Antiques and Collectibles Price Guide*.

Alarm Clock, plastic, mkd "Television," lighted, mahogany red, cream, and gold, minor wear to case, working 75.00

Bowl, 10" d, mottled beige ground, orange, tan, green, and copper flowers and leaves, sgd "Charlotte Rhead," mkd "Crown Ducal" 235.00

Brush, pink pearlized, matching comb, 1925, Fuller.............. 65.00

Cigarette Lighter, woman's head, heating oil in mouth 250.00

Dish, 7-1/4" l, free-form oval, clear glass, internally dec with alternating white and dark aubergine purple stripes, sgd "Walter" between two stripes (for Almeric Walter) 635.00

Wooden magazine rack, 15" h, 13-3/4" w, $52.50.

Percolator, Manning-Bowman & Co., chrome, wooden handle, 9-1/2" h, $35.

Lamp, table, chrome airplane, vertical glass airship, chrome base 525.00

Planter, pink poodle, ceramic, 8-1/2" w, 3-1/2" d............................ 45.00

Rug, 3'10 x 2', two diagonal rows of dark red, gold, aubergine, royal blue, tan, and green half circles, stippled field, Chinese, slight edge wear......................... 300.00

Tile, 8" sq, rust, tan, off-white, and purple design of lady, four short feet, mkd "Longwy, France, Primavera" with shield and crown 415.00

Vase, 6" d, ball shape, mottled blue, #601, mkd "Rumrill" 125.00

❖ Art Nouveau

This style is identified by flowing and sensuous female forms. The period started during the 1890s, and continued for the next 40 years, and was popular in Europe and America. Leading designers incorporated these sweeping lines into their works, as well as using florals, insects and other forms from nature.

References: Constance M. Greiff, *Art Nouveau*, Abbeville Press, 1995; Albert Christian Revi, *American Art Nouveau Glass*, reprint, Schiffer Publishing, 1981.

For additional listings, see *Warman's Antiques and Collectibles Price Guide*.

Belt Buckle, polychrome enamel, silver mount, minor enamel loss 245.00

Bird Cage, 33" h, beechwood, onion domed body, wirework sides, scrolled feet........................800.00

Brush, SP

Nude woman on back, 7-1/4" l.............................50.00

Scrolls, initials, dated 1916, 7-1/4" l.............................50.00

Woman's face, 5" l...............75.00

Bud Vase, metal circle of nudes supporting vaseline bud vase....................................190.00

Clock, green bisque, gold and pink highlights, gilt metal, imp Charenton marks, France, c1900, hand missing, nicks....................825.00

Desk Set, onyx, inlaid lapis lazuli band, two inkwells, blotter, note pad, card, and pen holders, imp hallmarks, London, c1921, 6 pc set.............................300.00

Mirror, 19-1/2" h, cast bronze, Rococo, kidney shape.......250.00

Picture Frame, 4-3/4" h x 6-1/2", rect, silver, English hallmarks 90.00

Umbrella Stand, 28-1/2" h, cast iron, emb floral dec, old green repaint 150.00

❖ Art Pottery

The Art Pottery "Movement" in America lasted from about 1880 until the first World War. During this time, over 200 companies, in most states, produced decorative ceramics ranging from borderline production ware to intricately decorated, labor intensive artware establishing America as a decorative art powerhouse.

Below is a sample listing of the work by various factories and studios, with pricing, from a number of these companies. However, remember that many more exist. Remember when buying art pottery that condition is critical to the price. Chips, cracks, or damage of any kind may drastically devalue the price of art pottery.

References: Susan and Al Bagdade, *Warman's Americana Pottery and Porcelain*, Wallace-Homestead, 1994; Paul Evans, *Art Pottery of the United States*, 2nd ed., Feingold & Lewis Publishing, 1987; Lucile Henzke, *Art Pottery of America*, revised ed., Schiffer Publishing, 1996; Ralph and Terry *Kovel*, Kovels' *American Art Pottery*, Crown Publishers, 1993; David Rago, *American Art Pottery*, Knickerbocker Press, 1997.

Collectors' Clubs: American Art Pottery Association, PO Box 1226, Westport, MA 02790; Pottery Lovers Reunion, 4969 Hudson Dr, Stow, OH 44224.

For additional listings, see *Warman's Antiques and Collectibles Price Guide,* as well as specific categories in this edition.

Bowl, 5" d, Pewabic Pottery, ext covered in shimmering burgundy glaze, int with richly lustered gold glaze, stamp mark 450.00

Candlestick, Walley Pottery, 10" h, bulbous top, flared base, striated brown-yellow high glaze, smooth green ground, looped handle, imp mark 290.00

Creamer, 3-1/2" h, Owens Pottery, Aqua Verdi, green matte, imp mark 75.00

Inkwell, 3-3/4" d, Owens Pottery, lime leaves, brown ground, sgd.....................................110.00

Mug, 4-1/2" h, Walrath Pottery, reddish-brown foliate design, brown ground, imp mark, pr 435.00

Pitcher, 6-3/4" h, 6-1/2" h, Merrimac Pottery, rich matte green glaze, restoration to chip at rim, stamped mark 300.00

Tile, 7-1/2" d, Walley Pottery, circular, large relief turtle dec, thick crackle matte green glaze, imp mark 460.00

Vase

4" h, 5" d, Pewabic Pottery, irid purple and turquoise high glaze, orig paper label.. 250.00

6" h, 4" d, Arequipa Pottery, hand modeled, stylized flowers, blue matte glaze, imp mark.... 850.00

Muncie lamp, blue-to-pink drip glaze, base 10" h, $135.

6" h, 4-3/4" d, Teco, bulbous, flaring rim, satin matte green glaze, two imp marks.... 410.00

12-3/4" h, Wheatley Pottery, ovoid, white and green flowers, mottled blue and light blue high glaze, inscribed mark ... 865.00

❖ Arts and Crafts

The Arts and Crafts Movement in America reflects a period when decorative arts took on a new look. This movement, from 1895 and 1920 saw leading proponents such as Elbert Hubbard and his Roycrofters, the brothers Stickley, Frank Lloyd Wright, Charles and Henry Greene, George

Niedecken, and Lucia and Arthur Mathews.

The national movement was marked by individualistic design and re-emphasis on handcraftsmanship and appearance. Most pieces favored a rectilinear approach, and most furniture was made of oak.

References: *Furniture of the Arts & Crafts Period With Prices*, L-W Book Sales, 1992, 1995 value update; Bruce Johnson, *Official Identification and Price Guide to Arts and Crafts*, 2nd ed., House of Collectibles, 1992; ——, *Pegged Joint*, Knock on Wood Publications, 1995; Thomas K. Maher, *The Jarvie Shop: The Candlesticks and Metalwork of Robert R. Jarvie,* Turn of the Century Editions, 1997; James Massey and Shirley Maxwell, *Arts & Crafts*, Abbeville Press, 1995; ——, *Arts & Crafts Design in America: A State-By-State Guide*, Chronicle Books, 1998; Kevin McConnell, *More Roycroft Art Metal*, Schiffer Publishing, 1995; Richard and Hilary Myers, *William Morris Tiles*, Richard Dennis (distributed by Antique Collectors' Club), 1996; David Rago, *American Art Pottery*, Knickerbocker Press, 1997; Paul Royka, *Mission Furniture, from the American Arts & Crafts Movement*, Schiffer Publishing, 1997.

Periodicals: *American Bungalow*, PO Box 756, Sierra Madre, CA 91204

Collectors' Clubs: Foundation for the Study of the Arts & Crafts Movement, Roycroft Campus, 31 S Grove St, East Aurora, NY 14052; Roy-crofters-At-Large Association, PO Box 417, East Aurora, NY 14052; William Morris Society of Canada, 1942 Delaney Dr, Mississauga, Ontario, L5J 3L1, Canada.

For additional listings, see *Warman's Antiques and Collectibles Price Guide.*

Box, jeweled lid, 5" x 7" 300.00

Creamer, 3-1/4" h, silver, oviform, rolled rim, mkd with Arthur Stone logo and initial "G" for Herman Glendenning, c1920 ....290.00

Desk, 36-3/4" h, 25" w, 20-1/2" d, walnut, old finish, elaborate geometric and foliage dec fretwork, replaced pigeon hole int, lid and gallery top are also replaced, some damage to fretwork. 220.00

Fish Tureen, 12" d, 12-1/2" h, hand hammered pewter, applied fish handles, orig ladles, imp Old Newbury marks................. 460.00

Furniture

Bookcase, 20-3/4" sq, 44" h, revolving, three int shelves, dark finish, mortise and tenons 575.00

Chair, dining, set with one arm chair, seven side chairs, refinished...................... 865.00

Morris Chair, four vertical slats, through tenons, adjustable pins, orig finish 1,495.00

Sewing Rocker, three vertical slats, orig finish 460.00

Table, library, two drawers, flat medial stretcher, worn orig dark brown finish, Stickley Brothers/Quaint label ... 750.00

Label, Stickley Bros., furniture type.................................... 30.00

Print, color woodblock on paper, William Rice, lone pine tree off Carmel, CA, coast 1,000.00

Tray, 12" l, silver, openwork handles, mkd with Arthur Stone logo, initial "C", minor scratches 865.00

Stickley Brothers table, maple, refinished, mkd "Stickley, Fayetteville, Syracuse," 25" h, top 15" x 24", $500.

Vase, 8" h, 3-1/2" d, bronze, applied silver tree design, imp logo, patent Aug 27, 1912, orig patina, Heinz Art Metal Shop, some denting.............................. 175.00

★ Ashtrays

Now that smoking is becoming unfashionable, ashtray collectors are finding more to choose from at their favorite flea markets. Many collectors have chosen to specialize in a particular kind of ashtray, whether it's advertising, souvenir, or figural ashtrays.

References: Art Anderson, *Casinos and Their Ashtrays*, 1994, printed by author; Nancy Wanvig, *Collector's Guide to Ashtrays*, Collector Books, 1997.

Arizona Grand Canyon, metal. 10.00
Black Cat, head........................35.00
Calico Ghost Town, California, pot metal 10.00
Canada Souvenir, Mountie, Indian 7.50
Capitol Metals Co., emb brass .. 10.00
Carnation Ice Cream, glass 5.00
Courtyard, New Orleans, porcelain 8.00
Esso, 4-1/4" x 4-1/4" x 1" h, clear heavy glass, blue and red dealer inscription, c1950................ 35.00
Hawaii, Aloha, pot metal, emb, 1939.................................... 20.00
Hotel Tropicana, Nevada, Follies Bergere, glass....................... 7.50

Burger Chef, glass with pyro label, 3-9/16" sq, $5.

Palm Springs, Calif,
porcelain.............................10.00
Pasadena Tournament of Roses,
ceramic..................................9.00
Penske Racing 1984 Indy 500 Win-
ner, auto racing driver helmet
shape 15.00
Reddy Kilowatt, K-Listo Kilovato,
4" d, 1" h, clear glass, bright red
and white reverse painted image
on bottom, c1950 ....38.00
Ryan's Wharf, glass...................8.00
White Horse Whiskey, glass 10.00
Winston Aged Tobacco, copper-
toned metal 8.00

❖ Aunt Jemima

Who's that great looking black gal
with the red kerchief and jovial smile?
Could be you've found Aunt Jemima,
one of those popular advertising characters who has her own following.

References: Patiki Gibbs, *Black
Collectibles Sold in America*, Col-
lector Books, 1987, 1996 value
update; Dawn Reno, *Encyclopedia
of Black Collectibles*, Wallace-
Homestead/Krause, 1996; J. P.
Thompson, *Collecting Black Memo-
rabilia*, L-W Book Sales, 1996; Jean
Williams Turner, *Collectible Aunt
Jemima*, Schiffer Publishing, 1994.

Collectors' Club: Black Memorabilia Collector's Association, 2482
Devoe Terrace, Bronx, NY 10468.

Bell, 5" h, red and white outfit ..75.00
Button, "Aunt Jemima Breakfast
Club," tin litho, 4" d, color image
of smiling Jemima, red back-
ground, black text "Eat a Better
Breakfast," Green Duck Co.,
Chicago, c1960 ....35.00
Cookbook, *Aunt Jemima's Album of
Secret Recipes*, 1935, 33 pgs,
soft cover, booklet form 32.00
Creamer and Sugar, Aunt Jemima
and Uncle Moses, plastic, F & F
Mold & Die Works, Dayton, Ohio
....150.00
Doll, stuffed vinyl, c1940, 12" h
....165.00
Hat, Aunt Jemima's Breakfast Club,
paper, fold-out style.............20.00

Magazine Tear Sheet
Aunt Jemima Pancakes, 1949,
13" x 5"........................... 15.00
Nelson Family with Aunt Jemima
Pancakes, 1956,
full page......................... 25.00
Paper Plate, c1950, 9-1/4" d... 30.00
Place Mat, paper, full color, unused
Aunt Jemima at Disneyland, "The
Story of Aunt Jemima" in
drawings based on N. C.
Wyeth paintings, "From first
Aunt Jemima Restaurant at
Frontierland in Disneyland,"
also shown, 1955, 13-3/4" x
9-3/4"............................... 55.00
Aunt Jemima's Kitchen 20.00
Story of Aunt Jemima, "Story of
Aunt Jemima and her Pan-
cake Days, ...has devoted her
time to working with service
clubs ...on her community
Pancake Day Festivals...,"
1950s, 10-1/2" x 13-1/2". 45.00
Restaurant Table Card, diecut face,
full color, "Folks...It's a treat to eat
out often...Bring the whole family...time for Aunt Jemima Pancakes," 1953, 4-3/4" x 3" 55.00

**Aunt Jemima Pancake Club fold-
over button, litho tin, 1-1/4" d, $14.**

Salt and Pepper Shakers, pr, Aunt
Jemima and Uncle Moses, plas-
tic, mkd "F & F Mold & Die Works,
Dayton, Ohio, Made in USA,"
3-1/4" h 45.00
Sheet Music, *Aunt Jemima's Picnic
Day*, 1914............................ 25.00
Thimble, porcelain, Aunt Jemima
and Uncle Moses, c1980,
1-1/8" h 12.50

❖ Autographs

Folks have been asking, "May I
have your autograph?" for decades.
Most celebrities will gladly oblige. But
because many items have been signed
in the past by auto pen and other
mechanical devices, it's tough to
always know if the signature is real.
And, at a flea market, you might find a
few celebrities around, but more than
likely you're going to have to trust your
instincts and the honesty of the dealer.

References: Mark Allen Baker, *All-
Sport Autographs*, Krause Publica-
tions, 1995; —, *Collector's Guide to
Celebrity Autographs*, Krause Publi-
cations, 1996; Susan and Steve
Raab, *Movie Star Autographs of the
Golden Era*, published by authors,
1994; Kenneth W. Rendell, *Forging
History: The Detection of Fake Let-
ters & Documents*, University of
Oklahoma Press, 1994; —, *History
Comes to Life*, University of Okla-
homa Press, 1996; George Sanders,
Helen Sanders and Ralph Roberts,
*Sanders Price Guide to Sports Auto-
graphs*, 1994 ed., Scott Publishing,
1993; —, *1994 Sanders Price
Guide to Autographs*, Number 3,
Alexander Books, 1994.

Periodicals: *Autograph Collector*,
510-A S Corona Mall, Corona, CA
91720; *Autograph Review*, 305 Carlton Rd, Syracuse, NY 13207; *Autograph Times*, 2303 N 44th St, No.
225, Phoenix, AZ 85008; *Autographs
& Memorabilia*, PO Box 224, Cof-
feyville, KS 67337; *The Collector*, PO
Box 255, Hunter, NY 12442.

Collectors' Clubs: Manuscript Society, 350 N Niagara Street, Burbank,

CA 95105; Universal Autograph Collectors Club, PO Box 6181, Washington, DC 20044.

For additional listings, see *Warman's Antiques and Collectibles Price Guide* and *Warman's Americana & Collectibles.*

Belson, Louie, real photo postcard, autographed 1948, several other signatures 65.00

Berra, Ford, and Rizzuto, sepia photograph, 11" x 14" 90.00

Bush, Barbara, First Lady, Blair House stationery, 3" x 2" 60.00

Campbell, Earl, autographed football 125.00

Dawson, Andre, autographed baseball 25.00

Day, Doris, letter sgd 45.00

Dors, Diana, letter, sgd, personal stationery, 1959 .... 95.00

Elkington, Steve, US Open golf cap 35.00

Fields, WC, promotional 10" x 13" photo, as Poppy, playing cigar box cello 90.00

Foreman, George, black and white glossy photograph, 8" x 10" 40.00

Gill, Vince, black and white glossy photograph, 8" x 10" 35.00

Griebling, Otto, hp watercolor cachet of clown, sgd on back 45.00

Houston, Whitney, black and white glossy photograph, 8" x 10" 60.00

Ives, Burl, letter, sgd 38.00

Jones, Spike, radio photo, sgd 75.00

Kemp, Jack, black and white glossy photograph, 16" x 20" 60.00

Leigh, Vivian, letter, sgd, personal stationery, 1959 .... 650.00

Rogers, Ginger, black and white photograph, 8" x 10" 70.00

Roland, Ruth, silent film queen, wedding photo, sgd, inscribed 45.00

Ryan, Nolan, *Legends Magazine* cover 150.00

Sellers, Peter, letter, sgd, personal stationery, 1959 .... 125.00

Sousa, John Philip, card mounted to album page 125.00

West, Mae, theater playbill, 6" x 9" program for stage production of Kenley Player's production of "Come On Up, Ring Twice," July 7, 1952, 12 pgs 75.00

Whitehouse, Eula, book, *Texas Flowers in Natural Colors*, first edition, 1936 .... 48.00

☉ Automobilia

Collectors have always loved their cars, and automobilia represents one of the biggest collecting areas found in today's market. Flea markets are excellent places to find all types of materials relating to automobiles, parts, accessories, etc. Specialized flea markets often held in conjunction with car shows are the best places to find automobilia, but a general flea market may usually lead to some choice items for collectors.

References: Mark Anderton, *Encyclopedia of Petroliana Identification and Price Guide*, Krause Publications, 1999; Mark Allen Baker, *Auto Racing Memorabilia and Price Guide*, Krause Publications, 1996; Leila Dunbar, *Automobilia*, Schiffer Publishing, 1998; Bob and Chuck Crisler, *License Plates of the United States*, Interstate Directory Publishing Co., 1997; Ron Kowalke and Ken Buttolph, *Car Memorabilia Price Guide*, 2nd ed., Krause Publications, 1997; Rick Pease, *A Tour With Texaco*, Schiffer Publishing, 1997; Jim and Nancy Schaut, *American Automobilia*, Wallace-Homestead, 1994.

Periodicals: *Hemmings Motor News*, PO Box 256, Bennington, VT 05201; *Mobilia*, PO Box 575, Middlebury, VT 05753; *Petroleum Collectibles Monthly*, 411 Forest St, LaGrange, OH 44050; *WOCCO*, 36100 Chardon Rd, Willoughby, OH 44094.

Collectors' Clubs: Classic Gauge & Oiler Hounds, Rte 1, Box 9, Farview, SD 57027; Hubcap Collectors Club, PO Box 54, Buckley, MI 49620; International Petroliana Collectors Association, PO Box 937, Powell, OH 43065; Spark Plug Collectors of America, 14018 NE 85th St, Elk River, MN 55330.

For additional listings, see *Warman's Antiques and Collectibles Price Guide.*

Annual Report, General Motors, 1948, 8" x 10-1/2", magazine format, color cover showing various GM vehicles, 44 black and white and color pages 15.00

Ashtray, Chrysler, 1933 .... 45.00

Book, *Edison Spark Plugs* 15.00

Cartoon Book, Volkswagen, 1960s 25.00

Catalog, showroom type
  Austin Healey Spirit MK III, 8-1/4" x 11", color art of car and engine, early 1960s 10.00
  Buick, 1963, 8-1/4" x 10-3/4", 20 pgs 8.00
  Mercedes-Benz 190SL, 8-1/4" x 12-1/4", 16 pgs, four models, interiors and other features, 1959 .... 40.00
  Volvo P1800, 8-1/4" x 11-3/4", color, 8 pgs, four gray insert pgs, 1961 .... 12.00

Demonstration Card, Chevrolet Knee-Action Wheels, 2-1/4" x 3-3/4", black, white, and orange card, clear filmstrip of optic design to create flicker movement when pulled back and forth, additional text, mid 1930s 35.00

Folder, advertising
  Buick, 7-3/4" x 10-3/4", 8 color pages, showing models, 1950 .... 25.00
  Mercedes-Benz Passenger Cars, 7-1/4" x 11-3/4", eight models, full color 25.00
  MGB 1100, 8-1/2" x 11", color, ink stamp of PA dealer, 1964 .... 15.00
  Oldsmobile, 10-1/2" x 10-1/2", color, six different models, 1963 .... 5.00
  Pontiac Strato-Streak V8, 1955, 5-3/4" x 8-1/4", full color . 15.00

Pinto nameplate, 5-1/8" x 1-3/4", $4.

Model Kit, Mazda Rotary Engine, 1972 ....25.00

Patch, DeSoto, 2-1/4" x 5-1/2", woven fabric, car name in red on white, gray wing tips, orange and blue logo, c1937, orig price tag on reverse 15.00

Picnic Set, 13" x 14" bright red fabric bag, plastic box, two Aladdin thermos bottles, one missing top, c1950 ....22.50

Pinback Button

Chevrolet, 2-1/8" d, "Harrisburg Zone Salesmen's Jamboree, Bloomsburg-1937," Chevrolet logo in center 20.00

Hudson, 1939......................35.00

Promo Car, Mustang, 1964, hardtop 55.00

☆ Autry, Gene

One of the famous singing cowboys that most Baby Boomers grew up with, Gene Autry left a wide range of items for collectors to enjoy. Since he delighted us on the movie screen, radio, and later television screens, many interesting collectibles can be found at today's flea markets. A visit to the Gene Autry Western Heritage Museum in Los Angeles is a must for all dedicated Gene Autry collectors.

Periodicals: *Cowboy Collector Newsletter*, PO Box 7496, Long Beach, CA 90807; *Gene Autry Star Telegram*, Gene Autry Museum, PO Box 67, Gene Autry, OK 73436; *Spur*, Gene Autry Western Heritage Museum, 4700 Western Heritage Way, Los Angeles, CA 90027-1462; *Westerner*, Box 5232-32, Vienna, WV 26105; *Westerns & Serials*, Route 1, Box 103, Vernon Center, MN 56090.

Collectors' Clubs: Gene Autry Fan Club, 4322 Heidelberg Ave, St Louis, MO 63123-6812; Gene Autry International Fan Club, 20 Cranleigh Gardens, Stoke Bishop, Bristol B59 1HD, UK.

Arcade Card 4.00
Banner, felt 35.00

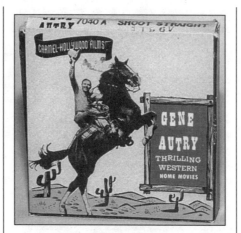

16mm film, "Shoot Straight," Carmel-Hollywood Films, $18.

Better Little Book, *Gene Autry and the Bandits of Silver Tip*, Whitman, 1940 .... 15.00

Book, *Gene Autry and the Thief River Outlaws*, Whitman, 1944, colorful dust jacket.............. 25.00

Bust, copyright 1995 "Autry Museum of Western Heritage, Gene Autry, the Singing Cowboy by McMee Productions" Gene Autry' s signature across back, 15" h..... 225.00

Cap Pistol, 8" l, silvered metal, simulated pearl handle, c1950 ... 35.00

Christmas Card, 1938, unused 20.00

Comic Book, Gene Autry, Dell

#5, 1947 .... 50.00

#99, 1955 .... 10.00

Counter Display, Personal Appearance, 11" x 14", cardboard, 1930s, full color 50.00

Guitar, Emenee, orig box 75.00

Handout, Sunbeam Bread, 8" x 10" color photo of Gene and Champ, 1950s.................................... 5.00

Little Golden Book, *Gene Autry and Champion*, 1956 .... 25.00

Lunch Box, 1954, steel, glass bottle.............................. 600.00

Pennant, large 55.00

Postcard

Gene Autry's Colorful Rodeo Parade, Stryker's Photogloss, 24" h, black and white, used 10.00

Standing pose, wear and pinholes.......................... 12.00

Record Album, Gene Autry's Western Classics, Columbia, 78 rpm, 1947, 4-record set............... 45.00

Sheet Music, *Red River Valley* 22.50

Sheet Music Book, *Gene Autry Song Hits*, Oahu Guitar Folio, c1950, 31 pgs 35.00

Souvenir Program, personal appearance giveaway, colorful cover, autographed....................... 55.00

Watch 110.00

Writing Pad, full color cover, 9" x 5-1/2" 32.00

❖ Autumn Leaf

This pretty dinnerware pattern was a premium for the Jewel Tea Co., being produced from 1933 until 1978. After it gained a wide popularity with America's housewives, other companies started to make accessories, like table cloths.

References: C. L. Miller, *Jewel Tea Company*, Schiffer Publishing, 1994; Jim and Lynn Salko, *Hall's Autumn Leaf China and Jewel Tea Collectibles*, published by authors, 1996.

Collectors' Clubs: Autumn Leaf Reissues Association, 19238 Dorchester Circle, Strongsville, OH 44136; National Autumn Leaf Collectors Club, 7346 Shamrock Drive, Indianapolis, IN 46217.

For additional listings, see *Warman's Americana &Collectibles*.

Berry Bowl, 5-1/2" d 5.00
Bread and Butter Plate..............8.00
Butter Dish, cov, 1 lb 190.00
Coasters, set of 8 ....48.00
Coffeepot, 11" h, metal infuser, lid missing, mkd "Hall's Superior...Mary Dunbar...," used condition....................40.00
Creamer and Sugar, cov, ruffled 35.00
Cream Soup Bowl 20.00
Cup and Saucer 16.00
Dinner Plate 16.00
Drippings Jar...........................40.00
Fruit Bowl, 5-1/2" d, stamp mark "Superior Hall Quality Dinnerware" on outside of circle, inside

Ball jug with ice lip, 7" h, $70.

of circle reads "Tested and approved by Mary Dunbar, Jewel Homemakers Institute." 14.00

Jug, ball, 7" h, gold circle mark "Hall's Superior, Tested and Approved by Mary Dunbar, Jewel Homemaking Institute, Superior Ware"....................................70.00

Mixing Bowl, 7-1/2" d, gold mark 20.00

Pitcher, 7" h, little wear to gold trim 40.00

Range Set 42.00

Salad Plate 12.00

Teapot, Aladdin, infuser, finial with 3 gold stripes, gold mark "Hall's Superior Quality Kitchenware" 120.00

Vegetable, cov 165.00

❖ Aviation Collectibles

Up, up, and away—aviation collectibles are soaring at flea markets around the country. Collectors can find material relating to early flight, more modern planes, hot air balloons, dirigibles and zeppelins, etc. From paper items to toys and figural models, the sky's the limit for this collecting category.

Periodical: *Airliners*, PO Box 52-1238, Miami, FL 33152.

Collectors' Club: World Airline Historical Society, 3381 Apple Tree Lane, Erlanger, KY 41048.

Matchcover, French, 1981 Paris Air Show, 1-7/8" x 2", 50 cents.

For additional listings, see *Warman's Americana & Collectibles.* Also see Airlines, and Lindbergh, and other related categories in this edition.

Ashtray, Naval Aviation Museum, Pensacola, Florida, figural airplane, souvenir decal, gold lettering, incised "Japan," 7" l 24.00

Book, *Official Guide of Commercial Aviation*, in Spanish, shows schedules of all companies operating in South America (Aerolineas Argentinas, Panair, Panagra, Pan American, Air France, etc.), Nov, 1957 .... 25.00

Cigarette Lighter, chrome plated, desk type, propeller, lighter compartment in wing, c1937 ..... 95.00

Comic Book, *Jim Ray's Aviation Sketchbook*, No. 2, 1946, ink stain on front cov, wear, yellowing, 64 pgs......................... 18.00

Game, Wings, The Air Mail Game, Parker Brothers, 4" x 5-1/2", flying Air Mail plane, set of 99 cards, orig instruction sheet, copyright 1928 .... 25.00

Gum Cards, Aviation Pioneers, Hugo Junkers, Otto Lilienthal, Orville Wright, biographies in German, set of three 15.00

Magazine Tear Sheet, Bendix Aviation Corp, 1947, *Saturday Evening Post* 2.00

Palm Puzzle, silvered rim, plastic cover, full color paper playing surface, Vosin box aircraft in flight,

inscription "1908 80 Kahen/Frankreich," German, c1970 ....35.00

Plate, Martin Aviation, Vernon Kilns, brown illus of 5 aircraft, titles, c1940, 10-1/2" d 55.00

Postcard, unused
    Friendship Airport, Baltimore, MD, textured paper, tinted art, C. T. Art-Colortone, mid-1950s, 3-1/2" x 5-1/2", unused, set of four 18.00
    Zeppelin flying over Montevideo, Uruguay, black and white 28.00

Teaspoon, Aviation Building, NY World's Fair, 1939...............15.00

Toy, Graf Zeppelin, 2-1/2" x 4-1/2", red, white, and blue diecut paper mounted to wood, rubber bands, toy whizzes when swung, Japanese, c1930 ....25.00

❖ Avon

Ding, dong...Avon calling! After years of producing fine cosmetics and interesting containers, Avon has branched out into all types of items that collectors are looking for, including jewelry and representative premiums. Expect to find Avon products well marked, and original contents and packaging will increase the values.

References: Bud Hastin, *Bud Hastin's Avon Products & California Perfume Co. Collector's Encyclopedia,* 13th ed., published by author, 1994; —, *Bud Hastin's Avon Collectible Price Guide,* published by author, 1991.

Periodical: *Avon Times,* PO Box 9868, Kansas City, MO 64134.

Collectors' Clubs: National Assoc. of Avon Collectors, Inc., PO Box 7006, Kansas City, MO 64113; Shawnee Avon Bottle Collectors Club, 1418 32nd NE, Canton, OH 44714; Sooner Avon Bottle Collectors Club, 6119 S Hudson, Tulsa, OK 74136; Western World Avon Collectors Club, PO Box 23785, Pleasant Hills, CA 94523.

For additional listings, see *Warman's Americana & Collectibles.* Also see Cape Cod in this edition for a listing of their glassware line.

Reproduction Alert.

Bell, frosted, orig box, 3-1/2" h ..9.00

Bottle, figural
  Boot, empty 5.00
  Ford Car, 1936 model, new, box in fair condition................20.00
  Liberty Bell, full, new 10.00
  Shoe, empty 5.00
  Steam Locomotive, The General, 4-4-0, full, end of box torn.................................40.00
  Toby Mug, empty...................5.00
Chamberstick, pewter, mkd "Avon American Heirlooms"...........10.00

Insect repellent, glass bottle, paper label, 2 oz, $6.50.

For exciting collecting trends and newly expanded areas look for the following symbols:

✪ Hot Topic

★ New Warman's Listing

(May have been in another Warman's edition.)

Cologne Bottle, Moodwind, dogwood flower design, paper label, 3" h 15.00
Decanter, totem pole................. 7.00
Jewelry
  Locket, 1-1/2" l, faux pearls around edge, blue and lavender violets in center, space for 2 photos 12.00
  Pin, leaf shape, held solid perfume, 2-1/4" x 1-1/2" 5.00
  Stick Pin, key, goldtone, 2" l 15.00
  Suite, bracelet, clip earrings, and ring, imitation amethyst........................ 15.00
Magazine Tear Sheet, Avon for Men, 1967 .... 5.00

Perfume Bottle
  Elusive, clear, silver top, 3" h 9.00
  Owl, frosted glass, 4-1/2" h, 2" d.................................. 9.00
Plate
  For Avon Representatives Only, 1977 .... 5.00
  Strawberry, 7-1/2" d, 1978 .... 12.00
  Wildflowers of the Eastern States, 8" d, Wedgwood............. 15.00
  Wildflowers of the Southern States, 8" d, Wedgwood 15.00
Potpourri, figural pig, orig sticker 5.00

Soaky
  Mickey Mouse, 7" h, 1969, orig bubble bath and box....... 25.00
  Pluto, 6" h, empty 20.00
Soap
  Aristocat Kitten Soap, orig box, 1970s........................... 65.00
  Christmas Children, girl holds doll, boy holds toy rocking horse, 1983 .... 9.00
Thimble, porcelain, blue and red flowers, mkd "Avon" 6.00

Figurine, Best Friends, bisque, 6-3/8" h, $12.50.

The ups and downs of toy values.

1. The original box in very good or better condition adds significantly to the price.
2. Original instruction sheet and/or packaging may add to the price.
3. Documentation from existing toy company catalog may add to the price.
4. Documentation from dated advertising may add to the price.
5. Missing pieces can detract from the price.

⭐ ⚙ Baby Related Collectibles

Grandmas and politicians love them, and today more and more collectors are seeking baby-related items. Perhaps it's nostalgia, perhaps it's the delightful colorful images, but whatever the reason, these appealing items are easily found at flea markets. Here's just a sampling of what kinds of items can be found.

Reference: Joan Stryker Grubaugh, *A Collectors Guide to the Gerber Baby,* published by author, 1998; Marcia Hersey, *Baby Rattles & Teethers Identification and Value Guide,* Krause Publications, 1998.

Baby Book, 1940, illus, unused 30.00
Bath Tub, oblong, tin 200.00
Blanket, 38" x 45", light blue and white, jointed teddy bears in various poses, 1940s 100.00

Flintstones figural baby bottles, Pebbles, Fred, Barney, Bamm-Bamm, Evenflo Products Co., 1977, plastic, 4-1/8" h to 5-3/4" h, set of 4, $32.

Calendar, 1941, Mennen, baby products illus 15.00
Crib Toy, lucite, Georg Jensen, MIB 48.00
Nanny's Pin, thread in holder, opal set...................................... 225.00
Nursery Set, Mrs. Tiggy Winkle, MIB 95.00
Rattle, sterling silver, 6-1/2" l .. 70.00
Talcum, Bauer & Black Baby Talc; oval, 4-1/2" x 3-1/2" 80.00
Tintype, 2-1/4" x 3", case 40.00

❖ Baccarat Glass

This French glassware manufacturer is still producing lovely wares. Their lovely paperweights are well known to collectors. Vintage Baccarat glass commands a higher value, but their contemporary pieces may also be found at flea markets.

Box, cov, 2-3/4" d, 2-1/4" h, white airplane design on sides, etched mark 125.00
Cologne Bottle, Rose Tiente, pinwheel swirled body, 5" h 90.00
Figure
    Baker, MIB 95.00
    Bull............................... 190.00
Finger Bowl, 4-3/4" d, 6-3/4" d underplate, ruby ground, gold medallions and flowers dec.................................... 350.00
Paperweight, Zodiac, sulphide, Pisces, c1955 .... 150.00
Toothpick Holder, Rose Tiente............................. 110.00

⚙ Badges

Name tags and identification badges are a hot collectible area. Some are found with photographs and other pertinent information about the original user. Each gives the collector a brief glimpse of history.

Bulldogging Champ, tin, back "Post's Raisin Bran," 1-1/2" d 20.00
Captain, Boy's State, American Legion logo 38.00
Chauffeur
    Chicago, 1920 .... 25.00

Child's detective badge, tin and copper, pinback, 2-5/8", $3.

    Illinois, 1950........................ 25.00
    Michigan, 1928 .... 35.00
Concordia Salus, sterling silver, white, red, and green enameled stars, fleur-de-lis, and crown, center "X" with thistle, beaver, shamrocks, and rose, and Latin words, c1902............................... 110.00

Employee
    National Cash Register Co., Dayton, OH, emb metal, 1-5/8" h, 2" l.................... 90.00
    Pepsi, celluloid, made by Phila Badge Co, 1" d, back rusting............................. 45.00
General, Suburban Aid System, 1-7/8" x 2-1/2" 28.00
Junior Police, Brattleboro, VT, 1950s 35.00
Lone Ranger, masked cowboy, sheriff, and gun, metal, orig package, 1960s, mkd "Made in Japan".................................. 8.00

Police
    Brattleboro, VT, Sergeant ... 55.00
    Commonwealth of North Marianas.......................... 55.00
    Special Officer, brasstone, 1-3/4" x 2-1/2" 30.00
Police Hat Type, Special Officer, Brattleboro, VT, 7-1/4" 55.00
Radio Premium, Eddie Cantor 30.00

Service Station Attendant
    Conoco, 1-5/8" h, 2-1/4" l, nickel over brass, cloisonné porcelain lettering.......................... 170.00

Standard Oil, 1-5/8" h, 2-1/4" l, nickel over brass, cloisonné porcelain lettering..........325.00

Texaco, 1-3/4" h, 2" l, bronze finish, cloisonné porcelain logo 275.00

Town Attorney, Town of Islip, Asst. T. A. #262, brasstone, 2" x 2-1/4" 58.00

❖ Bakelite

Bakelite is an early form of plastic and was first produced in 1907. The name "Bakelite" is a registered trade name based on the name of the inventor, Leo H. Baekeland. Items made of Bakelite are made in molds which are subjected to heat and pressure, then cooled. Bakelite is found in bright colors and many forms of household items.

For additional listings, see *Warman's Americana and Collectibles* and *Warman's Jewelry, 2nd ed.*

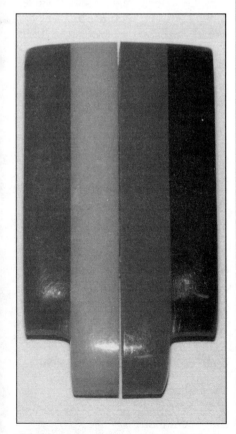

Clip, green, yellow, red and black, 1-13/16" x 1", $20.

Ashtray, 8" d, black and white. 45.00

Bracelet, bangle, octagon, chocolate marble with butterscotch swirls, 2-1/2", some wear 50.00

Bracelet, stretch, lemon slices, brown cylinder shapes...... 100.00

Buckle, 2-1/2" w, rect, carved flower on each end, dark blue 20.00

Button, translucent amber and brown swirl, 5 pc set on orig card 15.00

Cake Server, green handle 12.00

Corn Cob Holder, diamond shape, 2 prongs, red or green, pr... 15.00

Desk Set, Art Deco, butterscotch, ink tray, two note pad holders............................. 225.00

Napkin Ring, chick 30.00

Pie Crimper, marbleized butterscotch handle 4.50

Salt and Pepper Shakers, pr, gear shape, chrome lids, marbleized caramel, 2" h 85.00

Stationery Box, molded brown, Art Deco winged horse design, American Stationery Co., 1937 ... 75.00

Toothpick Holder, figural dachshund, green 95.00

⭐ Ballerinas

What little girl is there who hasn't dreamed of being a ballerina? Although it might not be as graceful as dancing, collecting ballerina items is certainly a lot easier on the toes. Swirling images of dancing ladies are found gracing many kinds of objects, all to the delight of ballerina collectors.

Bookends, Art Deco, brass ballerina, 4-1/4" x 6-1/2"..................... 85.00

Clock, United, rosewood-colored case with gilded trim, twirling ballerina, doubles as music box.................................. 235.00

Clothing, Fisher-Price ballerina outfit for My Friend dolls, MOC 16.00

Doll
　My Size Barbie, 1992, MIB.............................. 102.50
　Swan Lake Barbie, 1st in series, musical, 1991, NRFB ... 105.00

Terri Lee ballerina, MIB..... 985.00

Figurine
　Dresden, porcelain, 1977, 3-1/2" 90.00
　Josef Originals, porcelain, 4" 37.00
　Lefton, The Christopher Collection, 1982, 5-1/4" x 6-3/4" 20.00
　Lefton China, 5-3/4" h 36.00
　Occupied Japan, porcelain on bisque heart-shaped base, 7" 45.00
　Pen set, Ballerina Smurf, MIB 15.00

Music Box
　Bisque figure with glass eyes, cylinder base, French, 9" h 300.00
　Jewelry Box type, when opened ballerina twirls in front of mirror on lid int, divided jewelry box int, c1960 .... 10.00

❖ Banks

Saving pennies for a rainy day has been a popular idea for decades. Today's flea market shoppers can find interesting examples of banks to add to their collections. Found in every type of medium, they can range in price from very affordable to quite expensive.

Still banks, as listed below, are those with no moving parts. Mechanical banks, where action occurs, are thoroughly listed in *Warman's Antiques & Collectibles Price Guide.* Refer to one of the latest editions of that book to discover the high prices these banks now command, along with a comprehensive listing of which ones have been reproduced.

References: *Collector's Encyclopedia of Toys and Banks*, L-W Book Sales, 1986, 1993 value update; Don Duer, *Penny Banks Around the World*, Schiffer Publishing, 1997; Earnest Ida and Jane Pitman, *Dictionary of Still Banks*, Long's Americana, 1980; Andy and Susan Moore, *Penny*

Bank Book/Collecting Still Banks, Schiffer Publishing, 1984, 1997 value update; Tom and Loretta Stoddard, *Ceramic Coin Banks*, Collector Books, 1997.

Periodical: *Glass Bank Collector*, PO Box 155, Poland, NY 13431.

Collectors' Club: Still Bank Collectors Club of America, 4175 Millersville Rd, Indianapolis, IN 46205.

For additional listings, see *Warman's Antiques and Collectibles* and *Warman's Americana and Collectibles*.

Reproduction Alert.

Baseball Book of Knowledge, cast iron, mechanical, pitcher tosses coin to batter 225.00

Still bank, Big Boy, Marriott Corp., 1973, mkd "A Product of Big Boy Restaurants of America," rubber, 9" h, $12.50.

Mechanical bank, William Tell, cast-iron, $850.

Baseball Player, cast iron, A. C. Williams 400.00
Big Boy, 8" h, smiling vinyl full figure, black lettered name on chest, dark blue eye accents, base stamped "Niagara Plastics, Erie, PA," c1960 .... 75.00
Church, tin litho, U. S. Metal Co. 18.00
Cylinder, litho tin, 3" d, 3-1/2" h, black, white, red, yellow, and blue designs of young children, white top with smiling sun as coin slot, late 1930s 35.00
Elephant, seated, blue pants, Hubley 325.00
Girl Yarn Doll, American Bisque 35.00
Hubert the Lion, Lefton 40.00
Humpty Dumpty, American Bisque 455.00
Indian and Teepee, ceramic, young Indian gesturing towards teepee with TP Thompson logo, c1950, 5" x 6-1/4" x 6-3/4" h 140.00
London Tour Bus, Warner Brothers 35.00
Pabst Blue Ribbon Beer, miniature beer can, 1936-37 patent date, coin slot in top, 2-13/16" h .. 38.00
Pinocchio on the Whale, musical, Schmid 35.00
Popeye, American Bisque 250.00
Snappy Service, smiling figure, blue and white outfit, red and white company label on chest, name in relief in white letters on red base, c1970 .... 60.00

Squirrel, Goebel 35.00
The Jetsons, spaceship, licensed by Hanna-Barbera 375.00
Thermos Anti-Freeze, 2" d, 2-3/4" h, tin litho replica of can, red, white, and blue design of scurrying snowman holding thermometer and product can smiling in blizzard, car steaming in background, slogan "Fill Up-Or Freeze Up," 1940s 85.00
Uncle Sam, figural, glazed ceramic, 3" x 4-1/2" x 6-1/4", red, white, blue, and fleshtones............ 45.00

❖ Barber Bottles

Barber bottles are colorful glass bottles that were found on shelves and counters in barber shops and used to hold the liquids barbers used daily. Barber bottles are found in many types of glass—art glass with various decorations, pattern glass, and commercially prepared and labeled bottles.

References: *Barbershop Collectibles*, L-W Book Sales, 1996; Keith E. Estep, *Shaving Mug & Barber Bottle Book*, Schiffer Publishing, 1995; Richard Holiner, *Collecting Barber Bottles*, Collector Books, 1986.

For additional listings, see *Warman's Antiques and Collectibles*.

Reproduction Alert

Amber, Hobb's Hobnail, orig stopper.............................250.00
Baker's Best, emb, dug........... 12.00
F. W. Fitch, emb, dug 15.00
Lucky Tiger, red, green, yellow, black, and gilt label under glass, emb..................................... 85.00
Mary Gregory, white enameled girl chasing butterfly, sapphire blue, orig pewter stopper........... 175.00
Milk Glass, Witch Hazel, painted letters and flower dec, 9" h 115.00
Satin Glass, lime green, classical bird claw grasping ball, ground mouth, orig pewter stopper................................ 60.00
Stripe, cranberry opalescent 210.00
Swirl, blue opalescent 125.00

❖ Barber Shop and Beauty Shop Collectibles

Flea markets are a great place to find neat additions to collections relating to barber or beauty shops. There are some really great advertising items and barbering equipment to be found that add color and style to collections.

References: *Barbershop Collectibles,* L-W Book Sales, 1996.

For additional listings, see *Warman's Americana and Collectibles.*

Barber Brush
   Half doll porcelain handle 20.00
   Penguin handle, wood, paint chipped, 1940s.................35.00
Beer Mug, Barber Shop Whistle Stop, "For Good Cheer, Whistle for Your Beer," applied googly eyes, barber pole handle with whistle, mkd "G. C. Japan," 5-1/4" h................................ 50.00
Display Case, West Hair Nets, 15" h, 6" w, 5" d, tiered display case, tin litho picture of flapper lady in touring car inside lid 60.00
Facial Kit, Revlon, Moondrops at Home, orig packaging 45.00

Magazine Tear Sheet, adv
   All New Remington 60 Electric Shaver, 1962......................6.00
   Eversharp Schick Safety Razor, 1958..................................8.00
   Lady Schick, 1956.................6.00
   Norelco Speedshaver, 1957..6.00
   Remington Princess, 1959 ....5.00
   Remington Rollectric, 1958 ...6.00

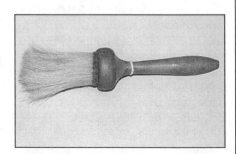

Shaker-style barber brush, wooden handle, 9" l, $12.

Sunbeam Blade Electric Shavemaster Razor, 1957.......... 6.00
Match Book Cover, Norman's Modern Barber Shop 6.00
Razor, Burham Razor, 1-1/2" w, 3-3/4" l, 3/4" h, tin litho safety razor tin, orig razor, 3 blades in orig envelope, complete, unused, red background, black lettering............................. 160.00
Razor Tin, Yankee Blades, 1-1/4" w, 2-1/4" l, tin litho, eagles and center image of man shaving, red background...................... 200.00
Record, Famous Barber Shop Ballads, Mills Brothers, 3 record set, 45 rpm, 1948 .... 45.00
Shaving Brush, Rubberset, #153 .... 5.00
Sign, Beauty Shoppe, two-sided, flanged porcelain, Art Deco lady with finger wave hairdo, 12" h, 24" l 275.00

Tin
   Bouquet Talcum Powder 25.00
   Magic Shaving Powder....... 25.00

❖ Barbie

Barbie, one of the first fashion dolls, was created by Mattel in 1958. Her friends, such as Ken and Skipper, came along in the following years. Accessories, clothes, and all types of merchandise soon followed. Barbie's life and success with collectors is well documented and she remains one of the most collectible dolls ever created.

References: J. Michael Augustyniak, *Collector's Encyclopedia of Barbie Doll Exclusives and More,* Collector Books, 1997; ——, *Thirty Years of Mattel Fashion Dolls, 1967 Through 1997: Identification and Value Guide,* Collector Books, 1998; Marcie Melillo, *Ultimate Barbie Doll Book,* Krause Publications, 1996; Patrick C. Olds and Myrazona R. Olds, *Barbie Doll Years, 2nd ed.,* Collector Books, 1997; Jane Sarasohn-Kahn, *Contemporary Barbie,* Antique Trader Books, 1996.

Periodicals: *Barbie Bazaar,* 5617 6th Ave, Kenosha, WI 53140; *Barbie Fashions,* 387 Park Ave So, New York, NY 10016; *Barbie Talks Some More,* 19 Jamestown Dr, Cincinnati, OH 45241; *Collector's Corner,* 519 Fitzooth Dr, Miamisburg, OH 45342; *Miller's Price Guide & Collectors' Almanac,* West One Summer #1, Spokane, WA 99204.

For additional listings, see *Warman's Americana and Collectibles.*

Activity Book, *Skipper and Scott Beauty Sticker Fun,* 1980 .....5.00
Book, *Portrait of Skipper,* 1964.....................................5.00
Camera, Super Star Cameramatic Flash Camera, 1978 ....20.00
Car, Hot Rod, #1460, 1963 ...195.00
Carrying Case, Barbie and Midge, pink, 1964 ....30.00

Doll
   Barbie, brunette bubble cut...................................125.00
   Barbie, ponytail, curly bangs, red head, 1958 ....200.00
   Fantasy Bride..................... 18.50
   Holiday, 1995 .... 60.00
   Ken 25.00

1992 Birthday Surprise Barbie, orig box, $35.

Ken, 1960, plaid pants,
turtleneck, blue coat......150.00
Midge, #1080, 1964 ....675.00
Ricky 25.00
Scott, #1019, 1979 ....70.00
Skipper, #950, 1963 ....120.00

Lunch Box
Barbie and Francie, vinyl, 6-1/4" x
9" x 4" deep, black, yellow,
blue, white, and pink graphics,
copyright 1965 Mattel, King-
Seeley Thermos Co. 55.00
The World of Barbie, vinyl, 6-3/4"
x 8-3/4" x 4" deep, blue, multicolored images of Barbie,
copyright 1971 Mattel, King-
Seeley, used 50.00
Pencil Case, Skipper and Skooter,
Standard Plastic, 1966 .... 15.00
Playset, Fashion Plaza,
1976 .... 80.00

Record, 12-1/2" x 12-1/2",
33-1/3 rpm, sealed
Birthday Album......................6.50
Sing-Along.............................6.00
Western Dress-Up Set, 5" x 14-1/2"
x 19", display box holding Barbie
theme western outfit for child,
vest, wrist cuffs, rope tie, belt,
spats, western hat, copyright
1981 Mattel, H-G Industries,
unused 35.00

❖ Barware

Back in the days when "rec rooms"
were popular in homes, bars were
often an important part of that scene.
Of course, a bar needed to be well
equipped. Many such novelty items
are now making their way to the flea
markets.

Reference: Stephen Visakay, *Vintage Bar Ware Identification & Value Guide,* Collector Books, 1997.

Ashtray, whiskey adv, glass...... 5.00
Bar Set, stemware and glasses, 11
pcs, sgd "Georges Briard" .. 70.00
Cocktail Mixing Spoon, sterling, mkd
"Black, Starr," 15" l 80.00
Cordial Set, six glass cordials
with cut floral dec, 1-1/2" x 3",
matching 12" x 3-1/2" aluminum
tray 95.00

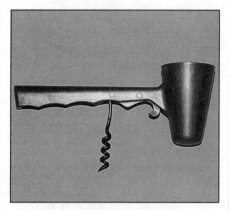

Bar Boy measure, opener, corkscrew, aluminum, 7" l, $4.

Lamp, drunk leaning on lamp post,
painted................................. 45.00
Pitcher, sterling overlay of golfer on
both sides 100.00
Sculpture, two men at bar, bartender
behind bar, #9, Brayton Laguna,
8" h 85.00

Sign
5-1/2" h, 13" l, Feigenspan Beer
P.O.N. (Pride of Newark), Ales,
beveled edge celluloid over
cardboard, gold, red, and
black, chain hung 90.00
27-1/2" d, Bartholomay's Beer,
Rochester, NY, reverse painting on glass, made inside oak
porthole, trademark winged
wheel............................ 225.00

Utensil Set
Barber Shop Quartet, 7-1/2" w
bar with four 4" h figures,
Corky Sr. and Corky Jr. (corks);
Screwy (corkscrew), Cappy
(bottle cap remover), souvenir
of Prince Albert, Canada,
orig box 85.00
Functional, carved wood
handles.......................... 50.00
Three Blind Mice, sitting on
wooden bench, each one different utensil, cork screw,
bottle opener, and cork,
7" l............................... 125.00

❖ Baseball Cards

Baseball cards were first printed in
the late 19th century. By 1900, the
most common cards were those
made by tobacco companies such as
American Tobacco Co. The majority
of the tobacco-related cards were
produced between 1909 and 1915.
During the 1920s, American Caramel, National Caramel, and York Caramel candy companies issued cards
identified in lists as "E" cards.

During the 1930s, Goudey Gum
Co. of Boston (from 1933 to 1941)
and Gum Inc. (in 1939) were prime
producers of baseball cards. Following World War II, Bowman Gum of
Philadelphia (B.G.H.L.I.), the succes-
sor to Gum, Inc., lead the way. Topps,
Inc., (T.C.G.) of Brooklyn, New York,
followed. Topps bought Bowman in
1956. Fleer of Philadelphia and Donruss of Memphis became competitive
in the early 1980s.

References: *All Sport Alphabetical Price Guide,* Krause Publications, 1995; *Baseball Card Price Guide, 12th ed.,* Krause Publications, 1998; Tol Broome, *From Ryan to Ruth,* Krause Publications, 1994; *Charlton Standard Catalogue of Canadian Baseball & Football Cards, 4th ed.,* The Charlton Press, 1996; Jeff Kurowski and Tony Prudom, *Sports Collectors Digest Pre-War Baseball Card Price Guide,* Krause Publications, 1993; Alan Rosen, *True Mint,* Krause Publications, 1994; *Standard Catalog of Baseball Cards, 6th ed.,* Krause Publications, 1996.

Periodicals: *Baseball Update,* 220 Sunrise Hwy, Ste 284, Rockville Centre, NY 11570; *Beckett Baseball Card Monthly,* 4887 Alpha Rd, Ste 200, Dallas, TX 75244; *Beckett Focus on Future Stars,* 4887 Alpha Rd, Ste 200, Dallas, TX 75244; *Card Trade,* 700 E State St, Iola, WI 54990; *Diamond Angle,* PO Box 409, Kaunaka-kai, HI 96748; *Old Judge,* PO Box 137, Centerbeach, NY 11720; *Sports Cards Magazine & Price Guide,* 700 E State St, Iola, WI 54990; *Sports Collectors Digest,* 700 E State St, Iola, WI 54990; *Your Season Ticket,* 106 Liberty Rd, Woodsburg, MD 21790.

Reproduction Alert.

The following listing is a mere sampling of the thousands of baseball cards available.

Bowman, common player
   1950, cards 1-72 ....30.00
   1952, cards 1-216 ....12.00
   1954, cards 1-112..................8.00
   1955, cards 225-320 ....16.00
Topps, common player
   1951, cards 1-52 ....30.00
   1953, cards 166-220 ....20.00
   1955, cards 1-150 ....11.00

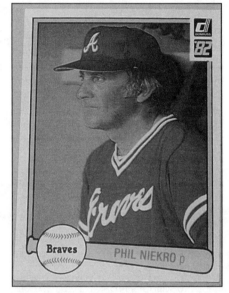

1982 Donruss, #475, Phil Niekro, 60 cents.

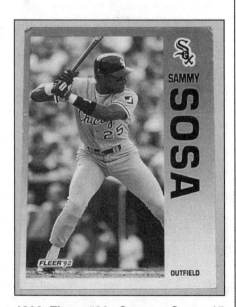

1992 Fleer, #98, Sammy Sosa, 15 cents.

☼ Baseball Memorabilia

Play ball! How those words excite fans and collectors. Because of America's fascination with this game, there are lots of baseball-related collectibles to be found at flea markets.

References: Mark Allen Baker, *All Sport Autograph Guide*, Krause Publications, 1994; ——, *Sports Collectors Digest Baseball Autograph Handbook*, 2nd ed., Krause Publications, 1991; ——, *Team Baseballs*, Krause Publications, 1992; David Bushing and Joe Phillips, *Vintage Baseball Bat 1994 Pocket Price Guide*, published by authors, 1994; ——, *Vintage Baseball Glove Pocket Price Guide, No. 4*, published by authors (217 Homewood, Libertyville, IL 60048), 1996; Mark Larson, *Complete Guide to Baseball Memorabilia*, 3rd ed., Krause Publications, 1996; Mark Larson, Rick Hines, and Dave Platta (eds.), *Mickey Mantle Memorabilia*, Krause Publications, 1993.

Periodicals: *Baseball Hobby News*, 4540 Kearney Villa Rd, San Diego, CA 92123; *John L. Raybin's Baseball Autograph News*, 527 Third Ave, #294-A, New York, NY 10016; *Sports Cards Magazine & Price Guide,* 700 E State St, Iola, WI 54990; *Sports Collectors Digest*, 700 E State St, Iola, WI 54990; *Tuff Stuff*, PO Box 1637, Glen Allen, VA 23060.

Collectors' Clubs: Glove Collector, 14057 Rolling Hills Lane, Dallas, TX 75210; Society for American Baseball Research, PO Box 93183, Cleveland, OH 44101

Reproduction Alert.

Baseball, autographed by Steve
   Carlton 50.00
Book, *Thrilling True Story of Baseball's Yankees,* 1951 .... 295.00
Charm, 1-1/2" x 8-1/2" l, green thin plastic wiener, "Pittsburgh Pirates Official Green Weenie" for "Buc Fever," copyright 1966 .... 10.00
Coaster Set, Ruppert Knickerbocker Beer, 3-1/2" d, tin litho, blue and

white cartoon image of 1880s base runner sliding into base, Colonial garbed umpire, Knickerbocker scoreboard, c1950, set of four......................................35.00
Coffee Cup, plastic, Detroit
   Tigers 25.00
Figure, Babe Ruth, striped cloth uniform, orig box, pictures of Yankee Stadium and history of Babe and stadium on box 75.00
Folder, Amazin' Willie Mays, speaker's bureau type, 4" x 9", lightly textured stiff orange paper, four pgs, published by Art Flynn Associates, public relations and advertising agency, c1950 ..24.00
Mug, figural, comic batter
   handle 70.00
Place Mat, Yankee Stadium Baseball's Proud Heritage, 9-1/2" x 14-1/2" white paper, scalloped edge, pink and blue accents, text, and photo showing aerial view of Yankee Stadium, history of baseball, early 1960s....................7.50
Puzzle, 8" x 10", Phillies Pro-Sports, color, orig clear vinyl bag, red, white, and blue header card, copyright April 1976 Stadium Photo, Philadelphia, Pa, smiling full figure image of Mike Schmidt, Allen, and Luzinksi................8.00
Record, Hank Aaron The Life Of A Legend, LP, unopened 12-1/2" x 12-1/2" album, single 33-1/3 rpm record on Fleetwood label, interviews and career highlights, mid 1970s 10.00

Salt and Pepper Shakers
   Batter and Umpire, bisque ..95.00
   Bugs Bunny and Taz with
     baseball 15.00
Spinner, Walter Johnson Baseball Game, 1-1/2" d, 2-1/2" l, lead type metal spinner, perimeter inscriptions for baseball plays, threaded, removes for storage of miniature

For exciting collecting trends and newly expanded areas look for the following symbols:

☼ Hot Topic

★ New Warman's Listing

(May have been in another Warman's edition.)

aluminum baseball coins, 11 picture Johnson, other with baseball batter, inscribed "National Ball Game," c1920 .... 125.00

Store Sign, Johnny Mize Red Man Chewing Tobacco, premium baseball cap offer, 11" x 15-1/2" color paper sign.................. 95.00

Toothbrush, bat shape, 6" l, beige plastic, Oracare, early 1970s

Cincinnati Reds, red team imprint 8.00

Minnesota Twins, blue team imprint 8.00

Wiffle Ball, Tim McCarver, 2-1/2" sq black and white box, red accents, 2-1/4" d white vinyl ball, smiling photo of McCarver on lid, c1960 .... 10.00

Window Card, 10" x 13-1/2", red on white thin cardboard, announcing "Savvy Skipper of the Red Sox" article to appear in *Saturday Evening Post,* July 21, 1956 .... 75.00

Yearbook, 1975 Phillies, 8-1/2" x 11", color cover, players with childhood photos inset next to them, 72 black-and-white and color pages 15.00

Cleveland Indians bank, 1984, can shape, tin, 4-1/2" h, 3" d, $7.

❖ Basketball Cards

This relatively new collecting area is growing. Like baseball card collecting, know your subject in order to spot values and interesting cards. This list is a mere sampling of the thousands of basketball cards available to collectors.

Periodicals: *Sports Cards Magazine & Price Guide,* 700 E State St, Iola, WI 54990; *Sports Collectors Digest*, 700 E State St, Iola, WI 54990.

Fleer

1985 Series, 90 cards, with stickers 30.00

1998, #1 .... 15.00

Johnson, Larry, Stadium Club .. 10.00

Olympics Dream Team, 1992, orig collector's album, includes Larry Bird, Charles Barkley, Michael Jordan, Scottie Pippen, Karl Malone, coaches, set of 25 cards................................... 15.00

SkyBox Series, 15 cards per pack, series of 36 factory sealed packs, 1990 .... 18.50

Topps

1995, complete #1 set 35.00

1997, factory set 25.00

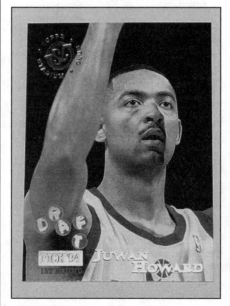

1994 Topps, Stadium Club, #210, Juwan Howard, $4.

Upper Deck, 10 cards per pack, series of 30 packs, 1995..... 15.00

❖ Basketball Memorabilia

Since its 1891 beginnings, the game of basketball has been enjoyed by players and spectators. With the recent difficulties in the NBA, expect to find higher prices for 1999 basketball collectibles because of the shortened season for team-related items.

References: Mark Allen Baker, *All Sport Autograph Guide*, Krause Publications, 1994; James Beckett, *Official Price Guide to Basketball Cards*, 6th ed., House of Collectibles, 1996; David Bushing, *Sports Equipment Price Guide*, Krause Publications, 1995; *Standard Catalog of Football, Basketball & Hockey Cards*, 2nd edition, Krause Publications, 1996.

Periodical: *Sports Collectors Digest*, 700 E State St, Iola, WI 54990.

Action Figure, MOC

Barkley, Charles, Headliners NBA 10.00

Drexler, Clyde, Rockets, Headliners NBA 5.00

Frazier, Will, Starting Lineup, 1997 .... 15.00

Hill, Grant, Detroit Pistons, Headliners NBA 7.50

Autograph, 8" x 10" photo

Bird, Larry 34.00

GAF View-Master reel No. H69, Harlem Globetrotters, 1977, $15.

Magic Johnson/Kentucky Fried Chicken plastic drinking cup, 1991, 6-3/4" h, $3.

Johnson, Magic 36.00
Mercer, Ron.........................15.00
Van Horn, K.........................25.00
Autographed Jersey
Bryant, Kobe 340.00
Jones, Eddie 185.00

Christmas Ornament,
Hallmark Treasury series
Hill, Grant, 1998, includes Fleer SkyBox trading card, 4-1/4" h 12.00
Johnson, Magic, 1997, includes Fleer SkyBox trading card, 5-1/2" h 14.00
New York Knicks, 1997, ceramic, orig box 8.00
Seattle Super Sonics, 1997, ceramic, orig box...............8.00
Doll, Dennis Rodman, extra outfit, wig, vinyl, 12" h 40.00
Dribbler, Knicks, black, 1959, Japan 35.00
Game, Cadaco, #165, 1973, unused, MIB 30.00
Photograph
Grove City, OH, early 1930s, 5" x 7"...............................30.00

Petrovic Drazen, wire service photo of young Yugoslav player, 1989...................... 3.50
Plaque, David Robinson, photo of him wearing Spurs jersey, copyrighted 1990 NBA, and cards, matted, display frame, 8" x 10" 35.00
Seals and Diecuts, Dennison, package of 4 pcs, unused, orig cellophane packaging 7.50
Tie tac with chain, male basketball player 12.00

❖ Baskets

Wonderful examples of all types of baskets can be found at flea markets. Check carefully for signs of age, wear, and damage and make sure they are priced accordingly.

Baby Basket, wicker, hood formed at one end, carrying handles, some damage and splits 75.00
Banana, large, two handles woven into side, loosely woven sides, damage 45.00
Market, woven splint single handle................................. 90.00
Melon shape, 15" d, woven splint, bentwood handle 85.00
Nantucket
5-7/8" d, 4-1/2" h, turned wooden bottom, splint and cane, bentwood swivel handle, traces of paper label, two small holes............................. 525.00

Picnic basket, caning stained green and red, 8-1/2" h, 12-1/2" sq, $38.

6" h, pocketbook type, whalebone plaque on lid, imperfections 175.00
Peach, 11-1/2" h, wide slats, wooden base 2.00
Picnic, woven splint, two folding lids attached to sides by leather loops, c1950 ....25.00
Sewing, cov, round, ring-type handles, slight wear 45.00

❖ Batman

Holy Cow Batman! This super hero and his cast of cohorts can be found at flea markets in various forms. Watch for examples from the recent movies as well as television-related and comic book-related collectibles.

References: Bill Bruegman, *Superhero Collectibles,* Toy Scouts, 1996; Joe Desris, *Golden Age of Batman,* Artabras, 1994.

Collectors' Club: Batman TV Series Fan Club, PO Box 107, Venice, CA 90291.

Action Figure, Batman Superfriends, Kenner license, Argentina...30.00
Bubble Bath, 1990s, 8-3/4" h, unused 25.00
Escape Gun, black or red, sealed in orig blister, 1966 ....45.00
Figure
Batman, Ertl, cast metal, 1990, sealed in orig blister pack with collector card, 2" h.......... 15.00
Penguin, Batman Returns, Applause tag, plastic, 1992, 9" h 25.00
Inflatable Figure, plastic, 1989, 13" h 40.00
Kite, Batman & Robin, plastic, 1982, sealed in orig package........20.00
Pen Set, Batman & Robin, DC Comics, 1978.....................30.00
PEZ, Batman, #5, 1985, used.35.00
Pin, plastic, pack of 12 assorted figures, 1989 ....12.00
Plastic Bag, 1989, 7-1/2" x 4-1/2", unused 1.00

Drinking glass, "Robin, The Boy Wonder," Pepsi Super Series, 1976, National Periodicals Publications Inc., 6-1/2" h, $15.

Puzzle, Batman & Robin, 130 pcs, 1981, 10-3/4" x 8-1/2", unused 12.00

Robot, wind-up tin, Biliken, Made in Japan, MIB 175.00

Scale Model, Bat Car, Valtoys, 3-3/4" l, MOC...................... 25.00

Toy
    Bat Cave, 1960s, orig box 85.00
    Pix-A-Go-Go, featuring the Penguin, National Periodical Publications, 1966, sealed in orig shrink wrap......................75.00

❖ Battery-Operated Toys

Perhaps it whizzes about, or clatters when it moves—battery-operated toys have amused children of all ages for decades. These inexpensive toys were made in large quantities, so fine examples exist today. The values of battery-operated toys are increased by great condition of the toy, all parts being present, interesting action, working condition, and the original box.

Reference: Richard O'Brien, *Collecting Toys,* Krause Publications, 1997.

BMW 3.5 CSL turbo car, Dunlop and Bosch Electric advertising, tin, MIB 120.00

Brainstorm Beany, blue felt beanie, yellow lettering and trim, orig 6" x 6" x 4" deep box, light bulb attached to top center of hat, back cord connects to cardboard and tin cylinder for battery, Electric Game Co., Inc., c1950 .... 45.00

Brave Eagle, beating drum, raising war hoop, MIB 145.00

Bubble Blowing Monkey, raises hand from pan on lap to mouth, MIB 195.00

Lamborghini Countach car, red, black trim, MIB.................. 120.00

Love-Love Volkswagen Beetle, blinking light in back window, tin, orange, Mobil, Champion, Goodyear sayings, VW on hubcaps, MIB 145.00

McGregor, Scotsman smoking cigar, raises up and down from pirate chest, MIB 195.00

My Fair Dancer, litho tin, dancer in naval outfit, sea horse graphics on base, 11" h, MIB 225.00

Rosko, bartender, shakes mixer, pours, and drinks, smoke rises from ears, MIB 75.00

School Bus, tin litho, switch to open front and back doors, headlights light up.............................. 175.00

Taxi Cab, Andy Gard, yellow, remote control wheel steering, dome signal light, 10" l, MIB............ 250.00

"Western" train, Japan, tin, missing its cowcatcher, 12" l, $20.

❖ Bauer Pottery

Brightly colored California-type pottery is usually what folks think about when they hear the name Bauer Pottery. Actually, it was started back in 1885 by John Bauer. The company moved around the United States, changed names and focus several times, and finally closed in 1962.

Coffee Cup, green-gray, 4" d 14.00

Console Bowl, cream colored 20.00

Cookie Jar, strawberries snack bar dec....................................225.00

Corsage Vase, Russel Wright, white 350.00

Dog Dish, large, cobalt..........150.00

Flowerpot, large, peach colored 65.00

Gravy Boat, bright yellow, imp "Bauer USA Los Angeles," 10" w, 4" h...........................30.00

Mixing Bowl, Ring pattern, #36, orange, 5-3/4" d 40.00

Muffineer, strawberries dec, "For Cinnamon Toast," some crazing 95.00

Salt Box, Grape & Cherries, wood lid..............................145.00

Salt Shaker, Strawberries, oval canister, no lid.....................35.00

Serving Dish, gray, 9" l............25.00

❖ Bavarian China

Flea markets are great places to find pieces of this colorful china. There were several manufacturers of china in the Bavarian, Germany, porcelain center.

For additional listings, see *Warman's Antiques and Collectibles Price Guide.*

Bowl, 9-1/2" l, large orange poppies, green leaves 85.00

Creamer and Sugar, purple and white pansy dec, mkd "Meschendorf, Bavaria" 65.00

Hair Receiver, apple blossom dec, mkd "T S. & Co." 60.00

Portrait Plate, elaborate portrait of lady, sgd "L. B. Chaffee, R. C. Bavaria," 16" l 100.00

Salt and Pepper Shakers, pr, pink apple blossom sprays, white ground, reticulated gold tops 35.00

Shaving Mug, pink carnations, mkd "Royal Bavaria" 65.00

Sugar Shaker, hp, pastel pansies 60.00

Teapot, yellow, colorful iris dec 60.00

☆ ⊙ Beanie Babies

Here's a partial listing of those popular Ty toys. Because this topic is so hot, be aware the prices may have changed before the ink dried on this edition.

References: Shawn Brecka, *The Beanie Family Album and Collectors Guide,* Antique Trader Books, 1998; Les and Sue Fox, *The Beanie Baby Handbook,* West Highland Publishing, 1997; Peggy Gallagher, *The Beanie Baby Phenomenon, Retired,* published by the author, 1997; Rosie Wells, *Rosie's Price Guide for Ty's Beanie Babies* Rosie Wells Enterprises, 1997.

Ally the Alligator 40.00
Blizzard the Snow Tiger 18.00
Bongo the Monkey (tan tail, sitting) 10.00
Chilly the Polar Bear 1,850.00
Cubbie the Bear (new tag) 20.00
Curly the Bear 15.00
Digger the Crab (new tag, red) 100.00

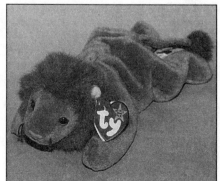

Roary Lion, retired, $12.

Flip the Cat 35.00
Gracie the Swan 12.00
Humphrey the Camel 1,850.00
Jolly the Walrus 15.00
Magic the Dragon (light pink stitching) 45.00
Peace the Tie-Dye Bear 20.00
Princess the Bear 15.00
Scorch the Dragon 20.00
Spooky the Ghost 35.00
Squealer the Pig 20.00
Tabasco the Bull 150.00
Twigs the Giraffe 12.00
Valentino the Bear 20.00
Wise the Owl 25.00
Zero the Empire Penguin 28.00

❖ Beatles

"She Loves Me, Yeah, Yeah, Yeah"—The Fab Four created quite a sensation with their music in the early 1960s. Through their records and movies, there are numerous examples of items to be collected.

Reference: Jeff Augsburger, Marty Eck and Rick Rann, *Beatles Memorabilia Price Guide,* 3rd edition, Antique Trader Books, 1997.

Periodicals: *Beatlefan,* PO Box 33515, Decatur, GA 30033; *Instant Karma,* PO Box 256, Sault Ste. Marie, MI 39783.

Collectors Clubs: Beatles Connection, PO Box 1066, Pinellas Park, FL 34665; Beatles Fan Club, 397 Edgewood Ave, New Haven, CT 06511; Beatles Fan Club of Great Britain, Superstore Productions, 123 Marina, St. Leonards on Sea, East Sussex, England TN38 OBN; Working Class Hero Club, 3311 Niagara St., Pittsburgh, PA 15213.

For additional listings, see *Warman's Americana & Collectibles.*

Reproduction Alert.

Bag, textured vinyl, red, portraits, black inscription and signatures, cord carrying strap, 1965 .... 170.00

Collector's plate, "The Beatles at Shea Stadium," 6th in The Beatles collection, 1992, 8-1/2" d, $60.

Beach Towel, terry cloth, four characters in bathing suits, c1960 .... 115.00
Billfold, red, 4 white signatures on 1 side, photo on other 90.00

Book
The Ballad of John & Yoko, 1982, 317 pgs 10.00
Yellow Submarine, Signet Book, 1968, paperback, 128 pgs 20.00
Coin Holder, red plastic, faces and names on front 12.00
Game, *Flip Your Wig,* Milton Bradley, 1964 .... 95.00

Magazine Article
Sixteen, Aug, 1966 .... 15.00
Time, Dec 22, 1980, John Lennon's death 12.00

45 rpm single, "What Goes On/Nowhere Man," Capitol Records, $30.

Postcard, 1964 .... 25.00

Sheet Music, *Day Tripper,*
    1964 .... 20.00

Sunglasses, black plastic, green
    lenses, Solarex................... 25.00

Sweatshirt, white, NEMS,
    1964 .... 150.00

✷ Beatrix Potter

Since the 100th anniversary of
Peter Rabbit in 1993, collectors have
been hot on the trail of this lovable
English hare. Flea markets are a
good place to spot him and the rest of
the Beatrix Potter family, especially
since many items are in current production.

Book

The Pie and the Patty-Pan,
    Warne & Co., 1905,
    1st ed 310.00

The Roly-Poly Pudding or
    The Tale of Samuel Whiskers,
    Hoen & Co.,
    1936 printing 22.00

Box, Jemima Puddle-Duck miniature
    trinket box, Border Fine Arts, mkd
    "Scotland, 1992," 3" h......... 38.00

Figurine

Mittens and Moppet, Royal Doul-
    ton, mkd "BP-6a"...........117.00

Peter Rabbit, Royal Doulton,
    1992, 6-1/2" h 50.00

Simpkin, mkd "BP-3b," 1975,
    4" h...............................375.00

**Hallmark Easter ornaments, Peter
Rabbit, 1996, 1st in series, MIB,
$50; Jemima Puddle-Duck, 1997,
2nd in series, MIB, $5.**

Lamp, Tom Kitten, shade pictures
    Mrs. Tabitha and kittens, mkd
    "Frederick Warne & Co 1994,
    Licensed by Copyrights,
    Designed by Charpente, Made in
    China," 14" h...................... 50.00

Mug, Peter Rabbit, John Beswick,
    1987, 2-3/4" h 65.00

Music box, Mrs. Tittlemouse, plays
    "It's a Small World," rotating base,
    6-1/2" h 31.00

Nightlight, bisque, mother rabbit
    rocking 2 babies, mkd "Schmid
    copyright 1990 F.W. & Co.," MIB,
    3-1/2" h 23.50

Ornament, Peter Rabbit holding
    1995 sign, Schmid,
    2-1/2" h 21.50

Pinback button, "Christmas with
    Beatrix Potter and Selfridges,"
    pictures Peter Rabbit, mkd "F.
    Warne & Co., Ltd. 1979, London
    Emblem Co. Ltd.
    01-390-4911" 22.50

Plaque, Jemima Puddle-Duck with
    Foxy Whiskered Gentleman, 1st
    ed, MIB 150.00

❖ Beer Cans

After Prohibition, the first beer
cans appeared. The first patent for a
lined can was issued to the American
Can Co. in 1934. Different types of
cans were developed, including a
cone top, and finally today's aluminum creations. If you're selling beer
cans at a flea market, make sure
you're not selling full cans to a minor!

Reference: Thomas Toepfer, *Beer
Cans,* L-W Book Sales, 1976, 1995
value update.

Collectors' Club: Beer Can Collectors of America, 747 Merus Court,
Fenton, MO 63026.

Ballantine, Newark, NJ, pull top,
    12 oz..................................... 6.00

Bantam, Goebel, Detroit, MI, flat top,
    8 oz..................................... 30.00

Budweiser, Anheuser-Busch, pull
    top, 10 oz.............................. 5.50

Colt 45 Malt Liquor, National, pull
    top, 8 oz............................... 2.00

**Hudepohl Salutes the 1975 World-
Champion Cincinnati Reds, 12 oz,
steel, $3.**

Falstaff Premium Quality Beer, Fal-
    staff Brewing Company, St. Louis,
    Mo., opened at bottom........ 35.00

Lucky Lager, San Francisco, CA, flat
    top, 7 oz.............................. 15.00

North Star, Associated, pull top,
    12 oz.................................... 4.50

Red Top, Drewrys, South Bend, IN,
    pull top, 11 oz...................... 10.00

Schlitz Light, Schlitz, pull top,
    12 oz.................................... 1.50

Topper, Eastern, Hammton, NJ, pull
    top, 12 oz.............................. 5.00

❖ Belleek

There's an old Irish saying that
newlyweds who receive a wedding
gift of Belleek will have their marriage
blessed with lasting happiness. It's a
great saying, and Belleek certainly
does make a nice wedding gift. Belleek is a pretty, very thin, ivory-col-
ored porcelain with an almost

iridescent look. It dates back to 1857 in Fermanagh, Ireland.

Several American firms also produced a Belleek-type porcelain, including Willets and Lenox.

Collectors' Club: The Belleek Collectors' Society, 144 W. Britannia St., Tauton, MA 02780.

For additional listings, see *Warman's Antiques and Collectibles Price Guide* and *Warman's English & Continental Pottery & Porcelain.*

Biscuit Barrel, cov, Basket
   weave pattern, 6th mark,
   1965-80 .... 100.00
Cake Plate, cream and gold,
   6th green mark, 1965-80,
   10-1/2" d........................... 90.00
Creamer
   Cleary pattern, 3rd green
     mark..............................60.00
   Pastel yellow ribbon and bow
     accents, green mark 60.00
Creamer and Sugar
   Clover pattern, 6th green mark,
     1965-80.........................100.00
   Shamrock pattern, married pair,
     green marks, 1945-55...120.00
Cream Jug, Lily of the Valley
   pattern, 2nd black mark, 1891-
   1926 .... 195.00
Cup and Saucer, Shell pattern, 2nd
   black mark, 1891-1926..... 195.00

Pitcher, Ott & Brewer, 5" h, $125.

Demitasse Cup and Saucer, green
   mark on cup, gold mark on
   saucer, c1956 .... 50.00
Dish, Shamrock pattern, 3rd green
   mark 60.00
Dresser Vase, detailed rose
   and leaves, green mark,
   3-3/4" h........................... 185.00
Figure, pig, 2" h, 3" l 90.00
Honey Pot, barrel type, clover
   leaves dec, 7th gold-brown mark,
   c1980-93 .... 80.00
Nut Bowl Set, Shell pattern, white
   ext, yellow int, black mark,
   9 pcs............................... 700.00
Potpourri Vase, Basket weave pat-
   tern, 6th green mark, 1965-80,
   4-1/2" h........................... 100.00
Salt, open, star, 3rd black
   mark 60.00
Sugar Bowl, open, yellow ribbon and
   box accents, green mark 45.00
Tea Set, Basket weave pattern, 6th
   green mark, 1965-80, repair to
   teapot spout..................... 275.00

✧ Bells

From the slight ringing of a silver bell to the clanging sound of a ship's bell, bells have enchanted collectors for decades. Check for signs of use and to make sure the clapper is original.

Collectors' Clubs: American Bell Association, Alter Rd, Box 386, Natrona Heights, PA 15065; American Bell Association International, Inc, 7210 Bellbrook Dr, San Antonio, TX 78227.

Ceramic
   Hawaiian Hula Girl, mkd "Made in
     Japan," 4-1/2" h.............. 36.00
   Mermaid, 4-1/2" h 24.00

Church, cast brass, wrought iron
   ringer, suspended from chain,
   Reading, PA, late 18th C,
   20" h 990.00

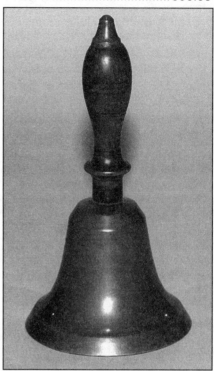

School bell, brass, turned wooden handle, 7" h, 3-3/4" d, $65.

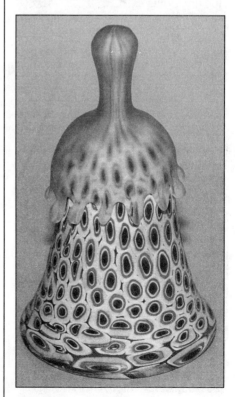

Millefiori, 5" h, $75.

Desk, bronze, iron base, ornate mechanism, Victorian, 3" w, 5" h 135.00

Glass

Fenton, Statue of Liberty, hand painted dec 35.00

Murano, gold wash, orig sticker, 4" h 65.00

Princess House, cut design, 6-3/4" h 10.00

Porcelain, Danbury Mint, Mother's Day, pink flowers 18.00

✯ Belt Buckles

Belt buckle collecting is an interesting way to amass a neat collection of items that are small, easy to store (and carry at flea markets), and represent many different types of materials. Some of the more ornate ones are set with precious and semi-precious stones, or are elaborately cast.

Reproduction Alert.

ARA Bull Riding Champion, 1981, dec copper, 4-1/2" w, 3-1/4" h 50.00

Elephant, brass 10.00

Hockey, brass 10.00

Initials "WJR," sterling silver ... 22.00

Koalas, brass 10.00

Masonic emblem, 2" x 2-7/8" .. 12.00

Military

31st 28.00

34th 28.00

39th 28.00

141 Inf 28.00

Rectangular, plastic, green 8.00

Shriner emblem, silvertone 20.00

Brass buckle, "American Bowling Congress League Award, Season 1957-58, Most Improved Average," $8.

Squirrel, brass 10.00

Steam shovel, brass 12.00

Tiffany, mono, 14K 275.00

Western, Wil-Aren Originals, 2-1/2" h, 3-3/4" w 20.00

❖ Bennington

Bennington Pottery is another classic American success story. Started in 1845 in Bennington, Vermont, the Fenton brothers first developed useful stoneware. In 1849, Fenton patented his famous flint glaze, called "Rockingham." This technique could add streaks of blue, green, yellow, or orange color to the traditional brown glaze. After this development, more forms were added to the production at Bennington Pottery, including candlesticks, flasks, creamers, and other items.

Other potteries began to copy their designs. Some Bennington Pottery pieces are marked, but not all. Genuine pieces of Bennington Pottery are getting expensive when the condition is good.

For additional listings, see *Warman's Antiques and Collectibles Price Guide* and *Warman's American Pottery and Porcelain.*

Bowl, shallow, brown and yellow Rockingham glaze, Fenton's 1849 mark, 7-1/8" d 775.00

Canning jar, half-gallon, $55.

Candlestick, flint enamel glaze, 8-1/4" h 875.00

Curtain Tiebacks, pr, Rockingham glaze, 1849-58, one chipped 185.00

Flask, book shape, titled *Bennington Battle*, thick brown and tan mottled glaze, some age lines, 5-5/8" h 210.00

Nameplate, 8" l, Rockingham glaze 135.00

Picture Frame, oval, chips and repairs, 9-1/2" h 245.00

Pie Plate, brown and yellow Rockingham glaze, Fenton 1848-58 mark, wear, 9" d 925.00

Pitcher, hunting scene, Rockingham glaze, 8" h, chips 175.00

✯ Beswick

Beswick characters are well known to collectors and include figures from children's literature as well as animals and other subjects. The firm was created by James Wright Beswick and his son, John Beswick, in the 1890s. By 1969, the company was sold to Royal Doulton Tableware, Ltd., who has continued the fine tradition.

References: Diana Callow et al., *The Charlton Standard Catalogue of Beswick Animals, 2nd ed.,* Charlton Press, 1996; Diana and John Callow, *The Charlton Standard Catalogue of Beswick Pottery,* Charlton Press, 1997; Harvey May, *The Beswick Price Guide, 3rd ed.,* Francis Joseph Publications, 1995, distributed by Krause Publications.

Child's Feeding Dish, Mickey and Donald on bicycle 140.00

Figure

Barnaby Rudge 60.00

Chippy Hackee, Beatrix Potter, copyright 1979 .... 55.00

Hereford Bull, 6" h 225.00

Horse, 4" h 40.00

Mr. Alderman Ptolemy, BP38 .... 150.00

Palomino Horse, #1261, 6-3/4" h 165.00

Samuel Whiskers, BP2 ..... 250.00

Scottie, white, ladybug on nose,
HN804, 1940-69............225.00
Siamese Cat Standing, #1896,
1963-80, oval mark, 6-1/2" h
......................................100.00
Swish Tail Horse, #1182, orig
Beswick sticker, 8-1/2" h
......................................225.00
Timmy Willie, from Johnny
Townmouse, BP2..........200.00
Tom Kitten and Butterfly, BP3C
......................................275.00
Tony Weller............................85.00
Modelle Jug, shape #694, leaves,
stems, flowers, rabbit, stamped
"Made in England, 694, Beswick
Ware," 1939-62, 9-1/4" h,
6" w 135.00

Mug, small
Falstaff, inscribed "Pistol with Wit
or Steel, Merry Wives of Wind-
sor," #1127, 1948-73,4" h
....85.00
Hamlet, inscribed "To Be or Not
To Be," #1147, 4-1/4" h ...85.00
Plate, 7" d, Disney characters 95.00
Tulip Vase, shape #843, semi-gloss
white, 1940-43, 4" h 50.00

❖ Bibles

Bibles are one area of the antiques
and collectibles marketplace that is
only occasionally found at flea markets. Why? Because most families
prefer to keep Bibles of their loved
ones, or donate them to a local
church. We think this is a great idea.

Some large old family Bibles do
surface at flea markets and book
sales from time to time. Their prices
range from a few dollars to several
hundred, depending on the illustrations, date, type of Bible, condition,
etc. Often potential buyers will be
more interested in the genealogical
information that might be contained
there. Before selling a family Bible,
consider sharing any historical or
genealogical information with family
members. Many small historical societies, libraries, etc. are also grateful
for such genealogical information.

Sometimes military issued Bibles
come into the marketplace. Often the

Gideons New Testament, Psalms and Proverbs, 1968, 50 cents.

history of the owner or where the
Bible has traveled to is of more value
than the monetary one attached to it.

⭐ Bicentennial

Remember all that hoopla of
1976? How many of you have
stashed some bit of Bicentennial
trivia away? This type of memorabilia
is starting to show up more and more
at flea markets and a whole new generation is collecting it. Perhaps their
bits and pieces will turn into treasures.

Calendar Plate, 200th Anniversary,
mkd "1975 Spencer Gifts"... 15.00
Doll Clothing, Skipper, #9165 . 50.00
Drinking Glasses, Elsie Family,
Spirit of '76, red, white, and blue
patriotic dec, family in colonial
garb, Elsie playing drum in
center, Elmer plays fife, Beaure-
gard plays smaller drum,
5-1/2" h, pr......................... 28.00
Lunch Box, Disney's America on
Parade, Mickey, Goofy, and
Donald as Spirit of '76, no thermos, raised tin, Aladdin, some
wear.................................... 70.00

Medal, 1-1/2" d, $10.

Medal, gold plate, 1-1/2" d, orig dis-
play case and pamphlet......50.00
Mug, brown and white decal,
Federal Glass, "F" in shield
mark......................................8.00
Pinback Button, 3-1/2" d
1776-1976 Bicentennial, eagle
and shield 20.00
Spirit of '76, America's Bicenten-
nial, 1776-1976...............20.00
Plate
Fenton Glass, red, 13 stars,
eagle, 1776-1976, quote from
Daniel Webster on back . 30.00
Frankoma, Patriots Leaders,
white sand, 8-1/2" d........45.00
Scottsbluff-Alliance, Nebraska,
gold trim, back mkd "Nile Valley
Federal Savings & Loan Asso-
ciation, Scottsbluff-Alliance,"
10" d 10.00
St. Clair, Joe, carnival glass, blue,
5-1/2" d 40.00
Walt Disney's, 1776-1976,
Schmid, Japan, MIB 65.00
Postcard, St. Louis 1764-1964
Bicentennial, unused 8.00

❖ Bicycle

"Look, Ma—no hands!" Gee,
haven't we all shouted that once or
twice. And how many of us wish we
still had those neat old bikes, banana
seats and all.

References: Fermo Galbiati and Nino Ciravegna, *Bicycle,* Chronicle Books, 1994; Jim Hurd, *Bicycle Blue Book,* Memory Lane Classics, 1997; Jay Pridmore and Jim Hurd, *The American Bicycle,* Motorbooks International, 1996; Neil S. Wood, *Evolution of the Bicycle,* Vol. 1 (1991, 1994 value update), Vol. 2 (1994), L-W Book Sales.

Periodicals: *Antique/Classic Bicycle News,* PO Box 1049, Ann Arbor, MI 48106; *Bicycle Trader,* PO Box 3324, Ashland, OR 97520; *Classic & Antique Bicycle Exchange,* 325 W. Hornbeam Drive, Longwood, FL 32779; *Classic Bike News,* 5046 E. Wilson Rd., Clio, MI, 48420; *National Antique & Classic Bicycle,* PO Box 5600, Pittsburgh, PA 15207.

Collectors' Clubs: Cascade Classic Cycle Club, 7935 SE Market St, Portland, OR 97215; Classic Bicycle and Whizzer Club, 35769 Simon, Clinton Twp, MI 48035; International Veteran Cycle Assoc., 248 Highland Dr, Findlay, OH 45840; National Pedal Vehicle Assoc., 1720 Rupert, NE, Grand Rapids, MI 49505; The Wheelmen, 55 Bucknell Ave, Trenton, NJ 08619.

For additional listings, see *Warman's Americana & Collectibles.*

Bicycle

Ace Clyde and Motor Works, metal label, as found condition 150.00
Columbia, Fire Arrow 300.00
Columbia, Twinbar 3,200.00
Huffy, Radiobike 2,000.00
Monark, Silver King, hexagonal tube 900.00
Roadmaster, Luxury Liner, restored 620.00
Schwinn, Corvette 300.00
Schwinn, Hornet 425.00
Sears, Elgin, Skylark, very good orig condition..............2,250.00
Bicycle Ornament, Bambi, celluloid, 1940s, 4" h 125.00
Book, *Bicycle Stamps: Bikes and Cycling on the World's Postage Stamps,* Bicycle Books, hardcover 15.00

Schwinn Tornado Sting-Ray owner's manual, 7-1/2" x 3-3/4", $5.

Handle Bar Grips, wooden, unused, for high wheeler.................. 65.00
Limited Editions, building, Bicycle Shop, Village Series, Princeton Galleries, porcelain, 1-1/4" h 15.00

Magazine Tear Sheet
Murray Bicycles, Strato-Flite, LeMans, and Wildcat, *Boys' Life,* 1966 .... 3.00
Raleigh, Chopper, *Boys' Life,* 1970 .... 3.00
Roadmaster, half sheet, *Saturday Evening Post,* 1951 ... 2.00
Schwinn Bicycles, from back cover, reverse slightly scuffed.............................. 2.00
Schwinn Christmas, Krates, Orange Krate, Lemon Peeler, Apple Krate, and Pea Picker 3.00
Sears, The Screamer Bicycle............................. 3.00

Pin, shaped like bicycle
Goldtone, front wheel turns, faux pearls, 2-1/4" x 2-5/8" 8.50
Silvertone, clear stones in center, 2" x 1-1/4" 15.00
Pinback Button, Schwinn, 7/8" d 28.00
Print, Donald Duck riding a bicycle, glow-in-the-dark, orig frame, Walt Disney Productions, 9" x 11"...............................38.00
Stickpin, United States Tire Co., 1-1/4" x 3" card, blue ink imprint of company, holds brass stickpin of happy bug wearing hat and peddling bicycle, c1920 ......25.00

❖ Big Little Books

The Whitman Publishing Company trademarked this type of book in the 1930s. The first series were based on typical children's stories. Soon Big Little Books became popular with advertisers as premiums. This was followed by titles about movies and later television characters.

References: Bill Borden, *The Big Book of Big Little Books,* Chronicle Books, 1997; Larry Jacobs, *Big Little Books: A Collector's Reference & Value Guide,* Collector Books, 1996; Lawrence Lowery, *Lowery's Collector's Guide to Big Little Books and*

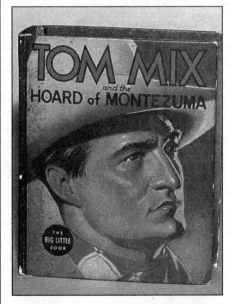

***Tom Mix and the Hoard of Montezuma* by Wilton West, 1937, $45.**

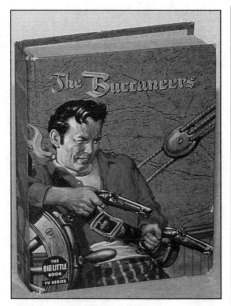

The Buccaneers, 1958, $15.

Similar Books, privately printed, 1981; *Price Guide to Big Little Books & Better Little, Jumbo, Tiny Tales, A Fast-Action Story, etc.,* L-W Book Sales, 1995.

Collectors' Club: Big Little Book Collector Club of America, PO Box 1242, Danville, CA 94526.

Buck Jones, Roaring West 48.00
Don Winslow, USN, #1107,
    1935 .... 60.00
Little Women........................... 20.00
Mickey Mouse and Bobo the
    Elephant, #1160, 1935 .... 85.00
Mickey Mouse Runs His Own News-
    paper, #1409, 1937 .... 40.00
Skeezix at the Military Academy,
    #1408, 1938 .... 35.00
Treasure Island, #1141, Jackie Coo-
    per, Wallace Berry............. 110.00

✴ Billiards

"Rack 'em up boys" was the cry heard in many pool halls. Today collectors enjoy poking around flea markets looking for vintage equipment and decorating accessories with a billliard theme.

Ashtray, Joe Camel shooting pool, 6-
    1/4" x 4-1/2" 20.00

Match safe, sterling silver, English, billiards scene, 1-5/8" d, $250.

Balls, complete set, Catalin,
    colorful 50.00
Bridge, brass mounted standard
    cue 70.00
Magazine Tear Sheet, The Irish Skir-
    mishers Blind Pool, from *Puck*,
    Sept, 1882 .... 25.00
Mirror, 1-3/4" x 2-3/4", celluloid,
    advertising "The Wonders Pool
    Parlors," Scranton, PA, multicol-
    ored graphics of topless women
    surrounded by cherubs, American
    Art Works, some light surface
    scratching 575.00
Pool Cue, Budweiser, Pabst ... 30.00
Wall mounted cue case, ornate Vic-
    torian type, painted and ebonized
    wood frame....................... 200.00

❖ Bing and Grondahl

This Danish company has produced fine quality Christmas plates for decades. However, many collectors also include some of their other products, like bells and figurines in their collections.

Reference: Pat Owen, *Bing & Grondahl Christmas Plates,* Landfall Press, 1995.

Periodical: *Collectors Mart Magazine,* 700 E. State St., Iola, WI 54990.

Bell
    1976, Old North Church, Boston,
        MA, 5" h.......................... 25.00
    1991, Independence Hall, 4" h,
        MIB 30.00

Figurine
    Boy with Accordian, #1991, boy
        seated on barrel, 9" h ... 225.00
    Fish woman, #2233, old woman
        sitting on bench, box of eels on
        one side, basket of flounder
        and other fish in front, old pail
        with scales, Axel Locher, 8" l,
        7" w.............................. 500.00
    Girl with Doll, #1721, 8" h . 110.00
    Girl with Flowers, #2298,
        6" h 140.00
    Girl with Puppy, #2316,
        5-1/4" h......................... 125.00
    Penguin, #1821, black and white,
        3-1/8" h......................... 150.00
    Skier, 8-1/2" h 130.00
    Youthful Boldness, #2162,
        7-1/2" h......................... 175.00

Limited Edition Collector Plate
    Aotearoa, 150 Years of New
        Zealand Nationhood,
        #12285/619, 7" d 40.00
    Christmas at Home, 1971,
        #8000/9071, green
        backstamp 27.00
    Christmas in Greenland, 1972,
        green backstamp........... 22.00
    Christmas in the Village, 1974,
        #8000/9074, green
        backstamp 26.00
    Christmas Peace, 1981 ...... 35.00
    Christmas Tree, 1982 .... 35.00
    Country Christmas, 1973 .... 20.00
    Fox and Cubs, 1979, Mother's
        Day, 6" d 35.00
    Hare and Young, 1971, Mother's
        Day, 6" d 40.00
    Lion and Cubs, 1982, Mother's
        Day, 6" d 55.00
    Raccoon and Young, 1983,
        Mother's Day, 6" d 55.00
    Stork and Nestling, 1984,
        Mother's Day, 6" d 50.00
    Woodpecker and Young, 1980,
        Mother's Day, 6" d 35.00
Planter, Dutch Shoe 275.00

Thimble, soaring seagull,
     mkd "B & G 4831, Made in
     Denmark" 20.00

⋆ Birdcages

Birds of a feather flock together—
they don't have a choice when kept
behind bars. Birdcages have long
been used for practical purposes.
Now many are being purchased for
their decorative touch.

Brass, rectangular with slightly
     domed top, dated 1876, 13" h,
     11" l, 8-1/2" w 30.00

Wire and metal

Art Deco design, 2 stories, orig
     paint, 25" h, 20" l,
     12" w 245.00

Bamboo, spring-loaded door, old
     yellow paint, 16" h, 11" l,
     8" w 300.00

Genykage, English pavilion style,
     brass plate, glass panel in
     back, some rust, 15" h, 12" l,
     10" w 175.00

Grain-painted, 2 doors, 33" h,
     14" l, 9" w 182.50

Hendryx, round with domed top,
     attached pedestal, 19" h,
     11" d...............................39.00

Hendryx, round with domed top,
     painted red and black, 17" h,
     13" d.............................150.00

Round with domed top, metal
     floor stand with round
     base 122.50

**Hendryx, brass with tin tray, 11" h,
$60.**

Round with domed top, slight
     mushroom look, gold paint
     over orig white enamel,
     18" h, 14" d..................... 47.00

Wood, German, "Provol's Golden
     Bird," paper label, 6-1/2" h, 6-1/2" l,
     4-1/2" w.......................... 133.50

⋆ Birdhouses

Due to their folk art nature, many
vintage birdhouses can be found in
collectors' living rooms, instead of
their usual places in pine trees and
on fence posts. Vintage birdhouses in
good original condition are in
demand, but don't overlook some of
the high-quality contemporary examples on today's market.

Metal, contemporary, made from 5
     Colorado license plates, 9" h,
     5" l, 5" w............................ 18.00

Metal, vintage, made from 2-qt tin
     can, orig gray paint, some
     rust 22.50

Pottery, contemporary, house
     design, brown sponging, painted
     chimney, doors and windows,
     5" h, 4" l, 3" w 33.00

Pottery, Michael Crocker,
     contemporary, gourd design,
     tan-green glaze, 8" h 30.00

**House-shape, orig paint, metal roof,
repaired side, 13" h, 13" l, 8" w,
$220.**

Wood, vintage, traditional form,
     metal roof, orig red paint, 7" h,
     6" l, 4-1/2" w.......................65.00

Wood, Wayne Sims, contemporary,
     church design, rough cedar sid-
     ing, 10" h, 4-5/8" l, 4" w.......20.50

Wood, Wayne Sims, contemporary,
     house design, American flag motif
     on roof and front, rough cedar sid-
     ing, 6" h, 4-5/8" l, 4" w.........16.50

❖ Bisque

Bisque is a rather generic term
given to china wares that have been
fired, but not glazed. It usually has a
slightly rough texture and is highly
susceptible to chips.

Boot, 3-1/8" h, 2" l, applied roses
     and leaves 7.50

Box, cov, round, hp violets and
     leaves, small gold bow........45.00

Figure

Bird, 3-1/2" h, gray, crown on
     head 12.00

Jester, 8-1/2" h.................... 15.00

Kate Greenaway Girl, 3-1/2" h,
     German 50.00

Pocahontas at Jamestown, dated
     1607-1907, 6" h 30.00

**Figures, mkd "Made in Japan," 4" h
woman, 3-1/2" h boy, each $18.**

Snow White and 7 Dwarfs.600.00
Match Holder, figural, Dutch girl,
    copper and gold trim 48.00
Piano Baby, crawling, crying, mkd
    "Made in Japan" 20.00

❖ Black Memorabilia

Black Memorabilia is a term used to describe a very broad range of the collecting field. It deals with Black history and ethnic issues, good and bad, and those cultural items that have affected many through the years. America's flea markets are a great place to find interesting Black Memorabilia as more and more dealers are offering related items.

References: Patiki Gibbs, *Black Collectibles Sold in America*, Collector Books, 1987, 1996 value update; Kyle Husfloen (ed.), *Black Americana Price Guide*, Antique Trader Books, 1997; J. L. Mashburn, *Black Americana: A Century of History Preserved on Postcards*, Colonial House, 1996; Myla Perkins, *Black Dolls 1820–1991* (1993, 1995 value update), *Book II* (1995), Collector Books; Dawn Reno, *Encyclopedia of Black Collectibles*, Wallace-Homestead/Krause, 1996; J. P. Thompson, *Collecting Black Memorabilia*, L-W Book Sales, 1996.

Periodical: *Lookin back at Black,* 6087 Glen Harbor Dr., San Jose, CA 95123.

Collectors' Club: Black Memorabilia Collector's Association, 2482 Devoe Ter, Bronx, NY 10468.

For additional listings, see *Warman's Antiques & Collectibles Price Guide* and *Warman's Americana & Collectibles.*

Bank, 4-1/2" h, Mammy,
    cast iron 95.00
Carry Out Box, Coon Chicken
    Inn 200.00
Clock, luncheon type, black women
    dec, 1950s.......................... 45.00
Cookbook, *Dixie Southern
    Cookbook* 50.00

Mammy grocery list, wooden, with wooden pegs, 8-1/4" x 6", $30.

Dart Board, 23" h, 14" w, tin over
    cardboard, Sambo, name on
    straw hat, Wyandotte Toy Mfg.,
    some denting and scratching
    .... 80.00
Doll, Crissy, 24" h 100.00
Humidor, 10-1/2" h, majolica, boy
    sitting on large melon, pipe in
    hand, small chip on foot and
    top 875.00
Magazine, *Life,* Dec 8, 1972, featuring Diana Ross on cover 18.00
Menu, 12-1/2" h, Coon Chicken Inn,
    1949, price insert.............. 300.00

Nodder
    Girl, hp, porcelain, mkd
        "Japan"........................ 300.00
    Mammy........................... 125.00

Photograph,
unidentified subject
    Little boy, in front of train 75.00
    Man, formal dress, graduation,
        1910 .... 45.00

Poster
    19-1/2" h, 15-1/2" w, paper, black
        man going off to war, saying
        good-bye to wife, all colored
        regiment marching by, © 1918,
        framed 75.00

22" h, 14" w, Ragtime Jubilee,
    Big Time Minstrel Review,
    cardboard, black with big
    red lip............................... 25.00
Recipe Holder, Mammy,
    wood 45.00
Reserve Card, Coon Chicken
    Inn 100.00
Salt and Pepper Shakers, pr
    Jemima & Uncle Moses, F & F,
        damaged 35.00
    Mammy & Chef, 5" h........... 55.00
    Mammy & Chef, ceramic, 8" h,
        Japan, 1940s................ 115.00

Sign, diecut cardboard
    Gold Dust Washing Powder, Gold
        Dust Twins shown on package,
        large letter "L" on top, formerly
        part of larger hanging sign,
        13-1/2" h, 9-1/2" w 60.00
    Hambone Sweets, 7" d, color
        graphics on both sides, black
        caricature aviator smiling and
        puffing on cigar while seated in
        aircraft, titled "Going Over,"
        orig string loop handle, late
        1920s............................. 38.00
    Oxydol, Mammy, 1939, small
        tear 100.00
Tea Towel, boy and girl eating watermelon, pr........................... 25.00
Tea Towel Transfers, Pickaninnies,
    orig envelope 30.00

Toy
    Dancing Dan, in front of lamp post
        on stage, microphone remote
        attached to stage, 13" h,
        MIB 375.00
    Strutting Sam, tap dancer on
        pedestal, tin, battery operated,
        11" h, MIB 475.00

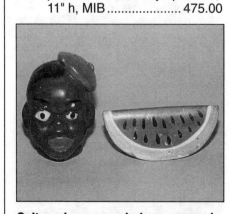

Salt and pepper shakers, ceramic, Japan, boy's head 2-3/4" h, $45.

Wall Plaque, head, chalk,
pr 125.00

❖ Blenko

Blenko Handcrafted Glass was made in Milton, West Virginia. It is known for its strong colors and crackle glass wares. Original labels read "Blenko Handcraft" and are shaped like a hand.

Beaker, 7" h, crystal body, applied green leaves, c1940-50...... 90.00

Candlesticks, pr, clear
crystal 30.00

Decanter
10" h, 5-1/2" w, bright green, ground stopper, orig label35.00
13" h, clear crystal, teardrop stopper............................85.00

Paperweight
Apple, crackle glass, emerald green, applied crystal stem and leaf, 6" h.........................55.00
Mushroom, orig label, c1960 ....48.00

Vase
4" h, 4" w, double neck, turquoise 50.00
6-1/4" h, amberina, hand blown, c1950 ....25.00
7-1/2" x 7", crackle, clear body, applied blue rosettes.......85.00
8" h, 8" d, ruby red, crimped, ftd, 1950s 150.00
9-1/4" h, 6-1/2"h, emerald green, fluted, pontil scar.............95.00
9-1/2" h, 8" w, crystal, four applied blue rosettes, orig label 135.00
9-3/4" x 6-1/4", crackle, clear body, applied blue-green leaves............................135.00

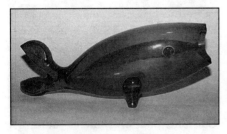
Amberina fish, 7" h, 17" l, $35.

10-1/2" h, 8-1/2" w, crackle, reddish-orange body, crimped top 135.00
11" h, 6" d, crackle, Rose Crystal 125.00
16" h, amberina, ftd 40.00

❖ Blue & White Pottery/Stoneware

This utilitarian stoneware delighted early housewives and can be found in many forms and patterns. It was durable and many examples have survived.

Reproduction Alert.

Bowl, large, molded arches, blue and white sponge dec 125.00
Creamer, Eagle pattern, 3" h .. 85.00

Pitcher
Grape and Trellis pattern, molded star mark, 9" h 395.00
Rose on Trellis pattern, 7-7/8" h......................... 225.00
Tavern scenes, 9-1/4" h.... 140.00
Wildflower, 7-1/2" h, two hairline cracks........................... 135.00

Butter crock, blue over white, 6-1/2" h, 9-1/4" d, $85.

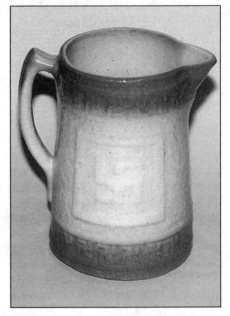
Pitcher, Good Luck sign, 8-3/8" h, $250.

Salt Box
Blackberry pattern, orig lid............................ 225.00
Butterfly pattern, maple replacement lid......................... 185.00

❖ Blue Ridge Pottery

Blue Ridge Pottery was made in Ervin, TN. The company started in the 1920s and continued until 1957. They developed a technique for hand painting china when most other manufacturers were relying on stamps and decals.

References: Betty and Bill Newbound, *Collector's Encyclopedia of Blue Ridge Dinnerware,* Collector Books, 1994; —, *Southern Potteries, Inc.,* 3rd ed., Collector Books, 1989, 1995 value update; Frances and John Ruffin, *Blue Ridge China Today,* Schiffer Publishing, 1997.

Periodicals: *Blue Ridge Beacon Magazine,* PO Box 629, Mountain City, GA 30562; *National Blue Ridge Newsletter,* 144 Highland Drive, Blountville, TN 37617.

Collectors' Club: Blue Ridge Collectors Club, 208 Harris St., Erwin, TN 37650.

For additional listings, see *Warman's Americana & Collectibles* and *Warman's American Pottery and Porcelain.*

Bon Bon, Dorothy pattern 55.00
Bowl, Bluebell Bouquet pattern, 9" d, some crazing 20.00
Cake Plate, Maple Leaf, #2 .... 85.00
Cake Tray, Verna pattern, maple leaf shape 70.00
Candy Dish, Chintz 90.00
Celery Tray, leaf shape
    Easter Parade 75.00
    Tuffie Muffie, edge repaired.40.00
Cereal Bowl, Daffodil pattern, 6" d 12.00
Creamer, Daffodil pattern 12.00
Creamer and Sugar, Carnival pattern 30.00
Cup and Saucer, Daffodil pattern 12.50
Demitasse Cup and Saucer, French Peasant pattern 75.00
Eggcup, Becky pattern 30.00
Pie Plate, Mardi Gras pattern, used, age spots 20.00
Pitcher
    Annette's Wild Rose pattern, antique shape, 5" h 75.00
    Big Blossom pattern, Grace shape, 5-3/4" h...............95.00
    Faimede Fruit pattern, Alice shape, 6-1/4" h...............90.00
Plate
    Daffodil pattern, 10-1/2" d, dinner..............................15.00
    French Peasant pattern, 9" d...............................100.00
    Queen's Lace, 10-1/2" d, used 10.00
    Sweet Clover, dinner 8.00
Platter, Cocky Locky pattern 140.00
Relish, hand painted, handle, 10-1/4" l 80.00
Soup, two handles, French Peasant pattern 135.00
Teapot, Calico pattern, colonial shape 170.00

Vase, Hampton pattern, hibiscus shape, 5-1/2" h 80.00

❖ Blue Willow

This intricate pattern is based on a weeping willow by the bank of a Japanese village. Over 200 different manufacturers have made variations of this pattern, mostly in blue with a white background. The first pattern was developed by Josiah Spode in 1810. This pattern is still being made today.

References: Leslie Bockol, *Willow Ware: Ceramics in the Chinese Tradition,* Schiffer Publishing, 1995; Mary Frank Gaston, *Blue Willow,* 2nd ed., Collector Books, 1990, 1996 value update.

Periodicals: *American Willow Report,* PO Box 900, Oakridge, OR 97463; *The Willow Transfer Quarterly, Willow Word,* PO Box 13382, Arlington, TX 76094.

Collectors' Clubs: International Willow Collectors, PO Box 13382, Arlington, TX 76094-0382; Willow Society, 39 Medhurst Rd, Toronto Ontario M4B 1B2 Canada.

Berry Bowl, small, Homer Laughlin 6.50
Bouillon and Underplate, Ridgway............................. 85.00
Cake Plate, tab handles, Royal China Co. 24.00
Cereal Bowl, unmarked 8.00
Creamer and Sugar, Allerton 125.00
Cup, mkd "USA"........................ 3.00
Cup and Saucer
    Buffalo Pottery 25.00
    Shenango 15.00
Dessert Plate, unmarked 5.00
Funnel 85.00
Gravy Boat, mkd "Willow, Woods Ware, Woods & Sons, England," 8-1/4" l 100.00
Grill Plate, mkd "Moriyama," 10-1/2" d 45.00
Kerosene Lamp, c1950, 8-1/2" h 85.00
Pie Plate, 10" d 50.00

Miniature tureen, mkd "Made in Japan," 5-1/2" x 3-1/4", $80.

Plate, dinner
    Booth's................................. 65.00
    Buffalo Pottery 20.00
    Dudson, Wilcox & Till Ltd., Hanley, England, 10" d, set of 10........................ 325.00
    Unmarked 8.00
Platter, 17-3/4" l, mkd "J. J. & Co.," hairlines 60.00
Saucer, unmarked 3.00
Soup Bowl, unmarked 10.00
Teapot, cov, emb "Sadler, England" 165.00
Tray, metal, wear.................... 15.00
Vegetable Dish, Johnson Bros., England, 10" d 48.00

❖ Boehm Porcelain

Starting from a studio in Trenton, NJ, Edward Marshall Boehm has created exquisite porcelain sculptures. A second production site, called Boehm Studios, was started in Malvern, England in the early 1970s and continues today.

Collectors' Club: Boehm Porcelain Society, PO Box 5051, Trenton, NJ 08638.

Limited Edition Plate
    American Redstart, 1975, based on designs of Edward Marshall Boehm, made by Lenox China, 24 kt gold edge, orig box, certificate 70.00
    Lion, Great Animals of the World, World Wildlife Fund, 1978, 10-1/2" d, orig round walnut frame 48.00

Poodle, white, contemporary, 5" l, $22.50.

Mountain Bluebirds, 1972, based on designs of Edward Marshall Boehm, made by Lenox China, 24 K gold edge, orig box, certificate...............100.00

Sculpture
American Eagle..............1,000.00
Blue Jay, #436, 4-1/2" h 150.00
Cardinal, female, #425, 15" h..............................700.00
Crocus, 5" h.......................210.00
Daisies, #3002 ....800.00
Madonna La Pieta, 4-1/2" h, c1958 ....110.00
Pelican, #4016 ....1,000.00
Saw Whet Owl, #20078, Made in England, 5-1/2" h 250.00
Screech Owl, #20079, Made in England, 5-1/4" h 250.00

❖ Bookends

What comes in pairs and only stands around all day—bookends! These useful objects can be found in every medium and range from purely functional to whimsical.

Arts & Crafts, hammered copper, Craftsman Studios, LA 135.00
Baby, seated on pillow, bronzed spelter, 4" x 5-1/2" 150.00
Boy, writing in diary, brightly polished bronzed spelter, 6-1/2" h 95.00
Bull and Bear, Merrill Lynch logo, solid marble base, 7-3/4" h................................ 85.00

The Arab, mkd "Hubley 314," 5-1/2" x 5", pr, $110.

Cocker Spaniels, chalkware, 5-1/2" h................................ 30.00
Grazing Horses, mkd "Bronzmet, Pat 22, '24," darkened patina.................................. 95.00

Hand Crafted
Copper and sheet metal, 5" h................................ 22.00
Wood, figural black boy, ebony finish, "Simeon" scratch carved on base 195.00
Indian Chief Bust, full leather headdress.......................... 130.00
Laurel and Hardy 340.00
Law and Order, Woodspirit, policemen with acorn badge, four-leaf clover in cap, 3" h 25.00
Liberty Bell, bronze, 5" h......... 35.00
Pirate Girls, bronze colored, patinated cast lead, 8-1/2" h... 195.00
Pirates, cold painted cast iron170.00
Puppies, three puppies resting, cast metal................................... 70.00

Scotties
Seated 160.00
Standing, tail mended....... 145.00
Wagon Train, painted cast iron, American Hardware Co., 1931 .... 110.00

❖ Bookmarks

Ranging from delicate clips to intricate embroidered pieces, bookmarks have been assisting readers for decades. Interesting examples can be found at flea markets if one looks carefully.

Periodical: *Bookmark Collector,* 1002 W. 25th St., Erie, PA 16502.

Collectors' Club: Antique Bookmark Collector's Association, 2224 Cherokee St., St. Louis, MO 63118.

Beadwork, 8-1/4" l, 1-3/4" w, rect, navy blue ground, rose flowers, 3 beaded tassels, leather top and thong, some loss to beading 125.00
Cloisonné, figural butterfly, brass marker................................. 15.00
Cross Stitch on punched paper, "Love," 6-1/4" l, beige, salmon, and green dec....................... 9.00

Diecut Paper
Climax Catarrh Cure, woman with fur coat, multicolored 10.00
James Fitzgerald, Bookseller & Stationer, MA, rural scene................................ 8.00

"Compliments of the Globe-Wernicke Co., Cincinnati, Sectional Bookcases," paper, 6-15/16" x 2-1/16", $17.50.

Mr. Peanut, 3" x 7-7/8" h, stiff paper, diecut, black and white, orange accents, full figure of Mr. Peanut in classic pose, text at bottom "Greetings From Mr. Peanut," additional text for "The Peanut Store," c1940 .... 15.00

Sterling Silver, etched lace design, multicolored silk string and thread, mkd "Sterling, R & G Co." 15.00

❖ Books

All types of books can be found at flea markets, from vintage titles to new. A book's value can be increased by a great binding, an early copyright, a first printing, interesting illustrations, an original dust jacket, or a famous writer.

Many book collectors are turning to their computers and using the Internet to find books. There are several sites devoted to antique books and also several ways to search out titles.

Prices at flea markets for books can range from a dime to thousands of dollars. To remove a musty smell from a book, sprinkle baking soda onto several pages, close, and let it rest for a few days. When you remove the baking soda, the smell should disappear. Avoid books with mold or you might be bringing home a big problem.

References: *American Book Prices Current,* Bancroft Parkman, published annually; *Huxford's Old Book Value Guide,* 10th ed., Collector Books, 1998.

Periodicals: *AB Bookman's Weekly,* PO Box AB, Clifton, NJ 07015; *Biblio Magazine,* 845 Wilamette St., PO Box 10603, Eugene, OR 97401; *Book Source Monthly,* 2007 Syosett Dr, PO Box 567, Cazenovia, NY 13035; *Rare Book Bulletin,* PO Box 201, Peoria, IL 61650; *The Book Collector's Magazine,* PO Box 65166, Tucson, AZ 85728.

Collectors' Club: *Antiquarian Booksellers Association of America,* 20 West 44th St., 4th Floor, New York, NY 10036.

The following listing is a sampling of books that may be found at flea markets.

An Old Sweetheart of Mine, James W. Riley, Bobbs Merrill, illus by H. Christy, 102 pgs, decorated front cover 18.00

Fifteen Flags, Ric Hardman, Little Brown, 1968, 1st ed., history of 27th Inf. Reg. 50.00

Great Women, Beacon Lights of History, John Lord, Ford-Howard, NY, 1886, 522 pgs, worn 8.00

Homespun Tales, Kate Douglas Wiggin, Grosset Dunlap, NY, 1920, 344 pgs 18.00

Hoosier Zion, Presbyterians in Early Indiana, L. C. Rudolph, Yale Univ. Press, 1963, 218 pgs 10.00

Journey Through A Century, Biography of Alice Young Lindley, 1853-1951, Ethlyn Walkington, 1966, 119 pgs 10.00

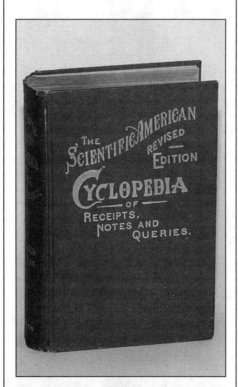

The Scientific American Cyclopedia of Receipts, Notes and Queries, 25th Edition edited by Albert A. Hopkins, New York, Munn & Co., 1906, 9-1/4" x 6-1/4", $30.

My Garden of Hearts, A New Book of Stories and Human Life, Love & Experience, Margaret E. Sangster, Christian Herald, 1913, 439 pgs 13.00

Navy Yearbook, Andrews & Engel, 1944, 1st ed., 376 pgs, illus 105.00

Pennsylvania, Guide to Keystone State, WPA Writers Program, Univ. of PA, 1940, 660 pgs, ex-library copy 16.00

The Adventures of Snooki and Snak, Lillian Elizabeth Roy, c1928, hardcover, some pgs colored 35.00

The Art of Egypt Through The Ages, Sir E. Densin Ross, Edwin Rudge, 1931, 6 color plates, 410 black and white illus, cloth binding 75.00

The Honeymoon Is Over, Shirley and Pat Boone, autographed, 1977, 185 pgs 22.50

The Mammoth Hunters, Jean Auel, Crown, 1985, 1st ed., 645 pgs, maps, dj 12.00

The Treasures of Louis Comfort Tiffany, Doubleday, 1980, 304 pgs, color and black and white illus, orig dj 75.00

The Wise Garden Encyclopedia, A Complete & Convenient Guide To Every Detail of Gardening, Wise & Co., 1951, 1,380 pgs, color and black and white illus 14.50

The Writings of Abraham Lincoln, 8 volume set, Centennial edition, 1905, illus 55.00

❖ Books, Children's

Like adult books, flea markets offer many types of books. Condition is just as critical to price, and more emphasis is placed on good illustrations.

References: E. Lee Baumgarten, *Price Guide for Children's & Illustrated Books for the Years 1880–1960 Sorted by Artist* and *Sorted by Author,* published by author, 1996; David & Virginia Brown, *Whitman Juvenile Books,* Collector Books, 1997; E. Christian Mattson and Thomas B. Davis, *A Collector's Guide to Hardcover Boys' Series Books,* published by authors, 1996; Diane McClure Jones and Rosemary Jones, *Collector's Guide to Children's Books, 1850 to 1950*, Collector Books, 1997.

Periodicals: *Book Source Monthly,* 2007 Syossett Dr, PO Box 567, Cazenovia, NY 13035; *Martha's KidLit Newsletter,* PO Box 1488, Ames, IA 50010; *Mystery & Adventure Series Review,* PO Box 3488, Tucson, AZ 85722; *The Authorized Edition Newsletter,* RR1, Box 73, Machias, ME 04654; *Yellowback Library,* PO Box 36172, Des Moines, IA 50315.

Collectors' Clubs: Many specialized collector clubs exist.

A Child's Garden of Verses, Marla Kirt, 1919, 4th imprint 17.50

Baby Animals, Marg. Wise Brown, Random House, 1941, 46 pgs 8.00

Children's Praise & Worship for Sunday School, A. L. Byers, Anderson College, IN, 1928 .... 6.50

Elsie's Girlhood, Martha Finley, Dodd, Mead & Co., 1872, emb pansies on covers 20.00

Guess Who, Dick & Jane, Scott Foresman, c1951 .... 45.00

How the Grinch Stole Christmas, Dr. Seuss, 1957, red and green cover 25.00

Jo's Boys, Louisa May Alcott, 1918, 10 plates, gold top pages ... 10.00

Raggedy Ann in the Snow White Castle, Johnny Gruelle, Bobbs-Merrill, 1960, 95 pgs 21.50

The Password To Larkspur Lane, Nancy Drew, 1933, blue and orange cover, dj 25.00

Treasure Island, Robert Louis Stevenson, illus by Paul Frame, Whitman, 1955 .... 5.00

Uncle Arthur's Bedtime Stories, 5 volumes, 1976, Arthur S. Maxwell, set 25.00

Wooden Willie, Johnny Gruelle, M. A. Donohue & Co., 1927, Colland Co., cover illus by Gruelle .. 70.00

❖ Bootjacks

Bootjacks are clever devices to aid in removing one's boots. Flea market shoppers should be aware that many bootjack reproductions exist. *Reproduction Alert.*

Beetle, brass, 10" l 95.00

Mermaid
    Cast iron, antique 95.00
    Cast iron, reproduction,
        10" l 10.00

Naughty Nellie
    Cast iron, antique 65.00
    Cast iron, reproduction,
        9" l 10.00
    Copper finished reproduction,
        9" l 10.00

Traditional, wood
    Maple, tiger striped, 10" l 30.00

Beetle shape, cast iron, good paint, 10-1/2" l, $30.

Pine, oval ends, sq nails,
    25" l 30.00
Walnut, carved heart and openwork, 22" l 45.00

❖ Bottle Openers

Back in the dark ages, before pull tops and twist-off tops, folks actually used these wonderful bottle openers. Today collectors seek them out at flea markets. Some collectors prefer the figural types and try to find interesting examples with good paint. Other collectors concentrate on finding interesting advertising bottle openers.

Collectors' Clubs: Figural Bottle Opener Collectors Club, 3 Ave A, Latrobe, PA 15650; Just for Openers, 3712 Sunningdale Way, Durham, NC 22707.

For additional listings, refer to *Warman's Americana and Collectibles.*

Reproduction Alert.

Bartender, Syroco 48.00
Blatz Milwaukee Beer, adv, some rust 8.00
Canadian Act Brand Beer & Ale, church key type, some rust ... 6.50
Coca-Cola, mkd "Starr Brown Co., Newport News, VA, Made in USA" 25.00
Donkey, cast iron, 3-5/8" h 50.00
Drunk, cast iron 35.00
Elephant, sitting, trunk raised, brown, pink eyes and tongue, 3-1/2" h 44.00
Genesee Beer, adv, some rust ... 8.00
Goldberg's, Philadelphia, some rust 6.00
Guitar Man 18.00
Holsten Beer, adv, mkd "Made in Germany," some rust 8.00

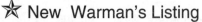

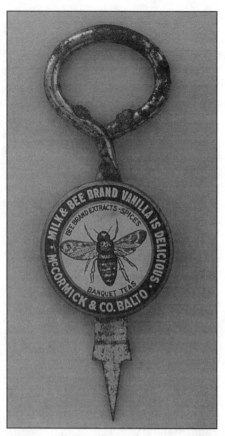

Metal milk cap lifter and bottle opener, litho disc, "Milk & Bee Brand Vanilla Is Delicious, McCormick & Co. Balto., Bee Brand Extracts—Spices, Banquet Teas," 4-3/4" l, 1-5/8" d, $55.

Horlocher Pilsner, church key type,
    some rust 6.00
Hotel Commodore, Vaughn, USA,
    some rust 8.00
Jeweled, tempered steel blade 20.00
Mr. Dry, wall mounted, man with
    black top hat, Wilton Co. 75.00
Parrot, cast iron, John Wright,
    5-1/4" h 95.00
Pepsi-Cola, adv, some rust..... 10.00
Pittsburgh Paint, PPG Industries,
    adv, some rust 8.00
Scottie................................... 18.00
Souvenir, piece of tree, bark on one
    side, Delaware Turnpike
    decal 10.00
Sunshine Premium Beer, church key
    type, some rust..................... 6.00
Wagner Lockheed International, adv,
    plastic handle 8.00
Winking Man 65.00

❖ Bottles

Many types of bottles are found at flea markets. Prices range according to rarity, condition, and color. There are several excellent reference books available to assist collectors.

References: Ralph & Terry Kovel, *Kovels' Bottles Price List*, 10th ed., Crown Publishers, 1996; Michael Polak, *Bottles*, 2nd ed., Avon Books, 1997; Carlo and Dorothy Sellari, *The Standard Old Bottle Price Guide,* 1989, 1997 value update, Collector Books.

Periodicals: *Antique Bottle and Glass Collector*, PO Box 187, East Greenville, PA 18041; *Canadian Bottle and Stoneware Collector*, 179D Woodridge Crescent, Nepean, Ontario K2B 7T2 Canada.

Collectors' Clubs: American Collectors of Infant Feeders, 5161 W 59th St, Indianapolis, IN 46254; Federation of Historical Bottle Collectors, Inc.; 1485 Buck Hill Drive, Southampton, PA 18966; Midwest Antique Fruit Jar & Bottle Club, PO Box 38, Flat Rock, IN 47234; New England Antique Bottle Club, 120 Commonwealth Rd, Lynn, MA 01904.

For additional listings, see *Warman's Antiques and Collectibles Price Guide* and *Warman's Glass.* The following listing is a small sampling of the types of bottles that may be found at flea markets.

Acme Nursing Bottle, clear, lay-
    down type, emb 70.00
Bull Dog Brand Liquid Glue, aqua,
    ring collar 6.50
Cole & Southey, Washington, DC,
    soda water, aquamarine ... 110.00
Empire Nursing Bottle,
    bent neck 50.00
Everett & Barron Co. Shoe Polish,
    oval, clear 5.00
Kranks Cold Cream, milk glass. 6.50
Lysol, cylindrical, amber, emb "Not
    to be Taken"........................ 12.00
Neamand's Drug Store,
    clear 30.00

Hutchison-type, embossed "Monroe Cider & Vinegar Co., Eureka, Cal.," aqua, 6-7/8" h, $45.

Owl Drug Co., cobalt blue, owl sitting
    on mortar 70.00
Pre Cream Rye, bartender's
    type 35.00
Sloan's Liniment, Castor Oil.... 20.00
USA Hospital Dept, Acetate
    Potassa, cylindrical, aqua ... 70.00

❖ Boxes

Collectors love boxes of all kinds. Interior decorators also scout flea markets for useful boxes too. The colorful labels of these vintage packages are delightful to display. Locked boxes offer the mystery of a treasure inside, but don't be lured into paying too much!

Andy Gump Sunshine Biscuits, cardboard, 5" x 3" x 2" 425.00
Apple, pine, old red paint, conical
    feet, 9-3/4" x 10" x 4" h 310.00

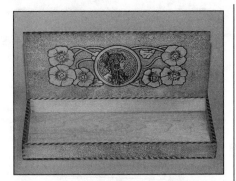

Pyrography glove box, 5-1/8" h, 12" l, 1-3/8" d, $20.

Baker's Chocolate, 12 lb size, wood 25.00

Book shape, green onyx, brass and wood trim, wear and chips, 5" l 165.00

Candle, hanging, pine and hardwood, old worn gray paint, 10-1/4" w 330.00

Candy, Whitman's Pleasure Island Chocolates, cardboard, pirate scenes on 5 sides, map on bottom, 1924 .... 28.00

Cigarette, Crystolite pattern, Heisey Glass 85.00

Dresser, rect, white ground, small pink flowers and green leaves, mkd "Nippon" 35.00

Fairies Bath Perfume, unopened, 1920s 12.00

Heart shape, silver plated, small gold bow trim, velvet lining . 35.00

King Brand Rolled Oats 45.00

Ladies Favorite Polish, paper label, 4" 10.00

National Lead Co., paint chip samples 25.00

Pine, worn orig brown graining, yellow ground, machine dovetail, 16-1/4" l 200.00

Swift's cream cheese box, wooden, dovetailed, 3 lb, 3" h, 10-7/8" w, 3-1/2" d, $15.

Regal Underwear, cardboard .. 20.00

Snuff, shoe shaped, curved toe, worn black lacquer, inlaid pewter trim, 3" l 225.00

Ward Baking Co., wood 100.00

❖ Boy Scouts

"On my honor, as…" is a pledge that has been recited by millions of boys through the years. Collectibles relating to scouting troops, jamborees, etc. are eagerly sought and readily found at flea markets.

Reference: George Cuhaj, *Standard Price Guide to U.S. Scouting Collectibles,* Krause Publications, 1998.

Periodicals: *Fleur-de-Lis*, 5 Dawes Court, Novato, CA, 94947; *Scout Memorabilia,* PO Box 1121, Manchester, NH 03105.

Collectors' Clubs: American Scouting Traders Association, PO Box 210013, San Francisco, CA 94121; National Scouting Collectors Society, 803 E. Scott St., Tuscola, IL 61953; World Scout Sealers, 509-1 Margaret Ave., Kitchener, Ontario N2H 6M4 Canada.

For additional listings, see *Warman's Americana & Collectibles.*

Appreciation Plaque, Onward to God & Country, 1959, laminated .. 6.00

Book, *The Boy Scout Aviators,* George Durston, 1921, dj ... 15.00

Bookmark, 3/4" x 3-1/2" l, Cub Scouts BSA, gold accent metal, relief image of wolf against dark blue ground, c1960 .... 3.00

Button, 3/8" d yellow cello button with blue accent lettering, "I Care About Cub Scouting" 4.50

Canteen, BSA, 1 qt, canvas cov, New York City logo 10.00

Handbook, *Patrol Leaders Handbook,* 1962 .... 5.00

Jacket Patch, 1957 National Jamboree 45.00

Medal, Beaver, orig box 98.00

Patch

First Class, cut edge, brown border 2.50

Certificate of registration, National Council, 1957, 3-13/16" x 2-1/2", $5.

Scout Lifeguard, diamond shaped 5.00

Scoutmaster, gold letters 10.00

Ring, sterling silver 35.00

Signaler, BSA, 2-key set, orig box 40.00

❖ Boyd Crystal Art Glass

The Boyd Family of Cambridge, OH, has made some interesting colored glassware through the years. Many of their molds were purchased from leading glass companies, such as Imperial.

Reference: Boyd's Crystal Art Glass, *Boyd Crystal Art Glass: The Tradition Continues,* published by author.

Periodical: *Boyd's Crystal Art Glass Newsletter,* 1203 Morton Ave., PO Box 127, Cambridge, OH 43725.

Collectors' Club: Boyd Art Glass Collectors Guild, PO Box 52, Hatboro, PA 19040.

Doll, Louise, yellow slag 25.00

Duckling, 1-1/2" h, periwinkle .. 10.00

Elephant, Zack, Mardi Gras, red and gold slag, 3-1/2" 35.00

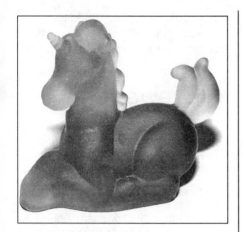

Unicorn figurine, 2-1/8" h, $10.

Hand, rubina, 4" l.................... 20.00
Horse, Joey, 4" h
    Amethyst, 1st logo 30.00
    Delphinium...................... 21.00
    Mardi Gras, orange slag . 20.00
Horse, Rocky, Black Beauty,
    4" l 20.00
Paperweight, Golden Delight,
    2-1/2".................................. 11.00
Pig, Candyland purple,
    2" h 15.00
Salt
    Bird, orange and gold slag,
        3" l 26.00
    Chick, Spring Surprise, red and
        gold slag, 2" 10.00
Shoe, Daisy and Button, bow on
    front, ribbed bottom, 5-1/2", mkd
        Cobalt Slag 20.00
Vaseline 20.00
Tomahawk, cobalt blue, 7" l.... 26.00
Wine Glass, chocolate slag, lst logo,
    4" h.................................... 20.00

✷ ⊛ Boyd's Bears & Friends

What's better than a teddy bear? How about collectible figurines that feature teddy bears? That combination has made Boyd's Bears highly popular with collectors, who now search for a variety of lines. Here are just a few examples.

Aunt Becky, MIB, 12" 27.50
Aunt Yvonne 20.50

Auntie Harestein Rabbit, Archive
    Collection, sgd "Justin
    Lowenthal," #75 of 350,
    15" h 128.50
Betty Lou, Bubba Bear, 1996, orig
    tag, 17" h 350.00
Celeste, Angel Bunny, #2230,
    1st ed................................ 200.00
Clarissa, 16" h........................ 34.00
Corinna, 16" h......................... 46.00
Lisa, 16" h 42.50
Ogden, 10" h........................... 23.00
Winnie II, 14" h........................ 29.50

❖ Brass

Brass has long been a favored metal to use for decorative and functional objects. Its durable nature leads to many brass examples being found at flea markets.

Avoid pieces with unusual wear, that might be broken, or are poorly polished.

Reproduction Alert.

Andirons, pr, ball top, unmarked,
    14" h 250.00
Ashtray, figural, bull's head,
    protruding curved horns 50.00

Blow torch, Clayton & Lambert Mfg. Co., Dearborn, Mich., red wooden handle, 10-3/4" h, $18.

Bell, 3-1/8" h, $4.

Bed Warmer, pierced brass pan,
    long wooden handle.......... 135.00
Boot Scraper, lyre shape, cast iron
    pan base 300.00
Bucket, tapered, rolled rim, iron bail
    handle, 19th C, 22-1/2" d.. 350.00
Candlesticks, pr, push-ups,
    8" h 100.00
Cigar Cutter, pocket type 40.00
Frame, ornate, emb animals,
    elephants, early photo of young
    girl.................................... 250.00
Kettle, spun, iron bail handle, mkd
    "Hayden Patent," dents....... 45.00
Mortar and Pestle, 4-1/2" h 65.00
Pedestal, 8" h, Putti dec on 4 legs,
    19th C 175.00
Sundial, round...................... 250.00

❖ Brastoff, Sascha

This internationally known designer and artist began to produce ceramic artware in 1953. He did produce items in other mediums, but is most well known for the brightly colored ceramics. If a piece has his full name, it was made by him. Pieces marked "Sascha B" only indicate that he supervised the production, but didn't necessarily make the item himself.

Bowl, 3 feet, black and gold, 2-5/8" h, 5-3/4" d, $25.

Ashtray
   Eskimo, 7" d 60.00
   Horse with flowing mane and tail, off-white, olive, brown, and pink, matching 2-3/4" h cigarette holder, both pcs mkd, 7" d..................................80.00
   Rooster head, ink stamp on back, 4-1/4" x 3" 32.00
Candleholders, pr, walrus, 8" h 80.00
Charger, 17" d 150.00
Compote, striped white design, 12" h.................................... 85.00
Fruit Bowl, Surf Ballet, gold dec, emerald green ground, ftd.. 42.00
Lighter, rooster and signature on bottom, 4" h, needs flint...... 40.00
Mug, Eskimo and walrus 75.00
Plaque, enameled clusters of grapes, olive, green, brown, and black, #414T, sgd, 13-3/4" d95.00
Plate, pagoda design, curled lip, 12" d 85.00
Vase, Alaskan series, 12" h.. 250.00

❖ Brayton Laguna Ceramics

Founded by Durline E. Brayton, a potter who made his wares in his home in South Laguna Beach, CA. Upon Brayton's death in 1951, employees operated the company until it closed in 1963.

Covered box, pottery, green glaze, yellow and red molded fruit and leaves, 2-1/2" h, 5-1/2" l, 3-1/2" d, $15.

Cookie Jar, teal background, golden brown partridges, black branches, #V-11, incised mark 260.00
Creamer and Sugar, Calico Cat and Gingham Dog 90.00
Figure
   Bull and cow, purple, minor glaze rub on top of bull's horn 475.00
   Figaro, crouching, 1940s, 3-1/2" l, repaired chip to ear 45.00
   Horses, pr, sgd "Betsy 1942, 5", black ink stamp "B.R.," one with damage to ears....... 40.00
   Sally.................................... 35.00
   Snow White's Deer, 6-1/2" h......................... 125.00
Flower Ring............................. 35.00
Oak Bucket, glazed dec.......... 45.00
Planter, black and white, mkd "M18 Brayton Laguna Calif"......... 55.00
Salt and Pepper Shakers, pr, Mammy and Chef, c1940 . 150.00

❖ Bread Boxes

Bread boxes used to be a staple of a well-equipped kitchen. Today, these boxes are finding their way to flea markets. Make sure the interior is clean and free of rust if you're going to use this flea market treasure.

Chrome, rect, black Bakelite handle................................. 15.00
Graniteware, sq, gray, raised red handles and letters "Bread" 35.00
Metal, painted white, 1950s type decal on pull-down front...... 15.00
Plastic, Tupperware, orig top .. 10.00

❖ Breweriana

Collectors have enjoyed finding new examples of Breweriana at their favorite flea markets for years. Some specialize in one brewery, while others might collect only one type of item, like beer trays. Whatever they enjoy, their collections are bound to be colorful and constantly growing.

References: Herb and Helen Haydock, *World of Beer Memorabilia*, Collector Books, 1997; Herb and Helen Haydock, *World of Beer Memorabilia*, Collector Books, 1996.

Periodicals: *All About Beer*, 1627 Marion Ave, Durham, NC 27705; *Barley Corn News*, PO Box 2328, Falls Church, VA 22042; *Suds 'n' Stuff*, 4765 Galacia Way, Oceanside, CA 92056.

Collectors' Clubs: American Breweriana Assoc., Inc., PO Box 11157, Pueblo, CO 81001; East Coast Breweriana Assoc., PO Box 64, Chapel Hill, NC 27514; National Assoc. of

Schlitz mug, pottery, McCoy, 6" h, $7.50.

Breweriana Advertising, 2343 Met-To-Wee Lane, Wauwatosa, WI 53226.

Reproduction Alert.

Bank, Miller Beer, miniature beer can 8.00

Beer Ladle, hand crafted gourd, brown patina, front hp "Craven Co. NC, 1862, Gesundheit"...................... 245.00

Bottle, Coors Brewery, George Killian's Dome, Lite............. 55.00

Figure

Blatz Beer, colorful plastic, smiling bartender holding mug of beer in left hand, blue bow tie and pants, tin litho beer can as torso, Tilmac Handcraft, MI, late 1960s, 10-1/2" h.......48.00

Old Crow Whiskey, hard plastic, 9-1/2" h 35.00

Menu, Budweiser, card stock, multicolored, beer bottle next to schooner of ale on silver platter, simulated frame and wood paneling motif, Anheuser-Busch, Inc., St. Louis, c1950, blank, 11-1/4" x 14-1/4"................................. 8.00

Poster, Budweiser, Arlington Milton................................ 100.00

Sign

7-1/4" h, 10" l, Max Sellinger's Nutwood Kentucky Whiskey, reverse painting on glass, wrap around chain edging along borders...........................150.00

16-3/4" h, 15-1/2" w, Acme Beer, octagonal, self-framed tin over cardboard, titled "good tobacco, great beer, and a successful hunt which makes for a very good day," artist sgd "Blaenzer," © 1938 ....60.00

17-1/2" d, Moerlbach Brewing Co., tin litho, adv on reverse, pretty girl on front 60.00

Tip Tray

4-1/4" d, Tivoli Brewing Co., bottle of Altes Lager Beer, H. D. Beach Co. litho, overall crazing 60.00

5" d, Ruhstaller's Beer, titled "Purity," lady with dove in lap, Kaufmann & Strauss Co. litho, some minor spotting........60.00

Container, Big Ben's Birch Beer, conical waxed paper, 1 qt, 9-3/4" h, $3.50.

6-1/8" x 4-3/8", Stagmier Beer; oval, some crazing 195.00

Tray, Wright & Taylor Old Charter Whiskey, factory scene, chipping and rubbing to rim 175.00

Whiskey Bottle, 11-1/2" h, bulbous, inverted flare, faceted neck, acid-cut script adv for McGinnis Pure Rye 350.00

☆ Breyer

Founded in 1943, the Breyer Molding Company of Chicago has created some interesting radio and television cases. But they are best known for the animals they started as a sideline. By 1958, this sideline had turned into a real barnyard of animals. The facility continued to develop new techniques, creating interesting new animals, primarily horses. The production operation was moved to New Jersey after the firm was acquired by Reeves International.

References: Felicia Browell, *Breyer Animal Collector's Guide,* Collector Books, 1998; Nancy Atkinson Young, *Breyer Molds and Models,* Schiffer Publishing, 1997.

Periodicals: *The Hobby Horse News,* 2053 Dryehaven Drive, Tallahassee, FL 32311; *The Model Horse Trader,* 143 Mercer Way, Upland, CA 91720; *TRR Pony Express,* 71 Aloha Circle, North Little Rock, AR 72120.

Collectors' Clubs: Breyer Collectors Club, 14 Industrial Road, Pequannock, NJ 07440; North American Model Horse Show Association, PO Box 50508, Denton, TX 76206.

Andalusian Mare, dapple gray, Club 99 ....15.00

Clydesdale in harness.............42.00

Fighting Stallion

Leopard Appy 72.00

Sorrel 30.00

Goliath, the American Cream, #7498, 1995.......................30.00

Midnight Sun TWH #60...........30.00

Miniature, 2-1/2" h

Brown, 1975.......................12.00

Medium brown, 1976 ....10.00

Buck, 8-1/2" h, 8" l, $20.

Medium brown, white feet,
1975 ....12.00
Spotted, 1975 ....11.00
Yellow, 1975 ....11.50
Palomino Azteca.................. 250.00
Rearing Mustang, sorrel 50.00
Serenity Set, JC Penney,
1995 .... 40.00
Saddlebred Filly, Weanling, Dancing
Queen 100.00
SR Belgian, alabaster............ 60.00

❖ Bride's Basket

The term "Bride's Basket" usually refers to a decorative glass bowl in a fancy silver or silver plate holder. This traditional gift to brides was meant as a show piece for the young couple's sideboard. Over the years, sometimes the bowl becomes damaged, so it is not uncommon to find a bowl that is mismatched to the base. This type of "married" piece would have a lesser value than a bowl and base that started life together.

Blue, ruffled, leaves, blossom, gold
dec, no frame 150.00
Cranberry, applied glass trim, SP
holder, 6" d 195.00
Cranberry Opalescent,
no frame 140.00
Fenton, maize, amber and crystal
crest, hp roses on int., white ext.,
SP holder, 10-1/2" d 275.00

Fenton, white hobnail, paper label, 7-1/2" h, $18.

Overshot, ruby crimped edging, polished pontil, 10" d 350.00
Silverplated, mkd "Middletown
Plate Co., Quadruple Plate 1857,"
9-1/2" d, 5-1/2" h plus
handle.............................. 140.00
Tiffany, Favrile, #516, art glass insert
with opalescent swirl, amethyst
tint, bronze base,
sgd................................. 1,450.00

❖ British Royals

Generations of collectors have been fascinated with the British Royal family and have saved bits and pieces relating to them. A great quantity of items survive from past Royals as well as those generated by present day royal weddings, births, and state visits.

Periodical: British Royalty Commemorative Collectors Newsletter, PO Box 294, Lititz, PA 17543.

Collectors' Club: Commemorative Collector's Society, Lumless House, Gainsborough Rd, Winthrope, New Newark, Nottingham NG24 1NR UK.

For additional listings, see *Warman's Antiques and Collectibles Price Guide,* as well as "Princess Diana Collectibles" in this edition.

Bell, Queen Elizabeth Coronation,
1953 .... 30.00
Box, cov, Elizabeth the Queen
Mother, 1980, 80th Birthday, color
portrait, Crown Staffordshire,
4" d 75.00
Cup and Saucer, Elizabeth II,
portrait flanked by flags, corona-
tion, pairs of flags inside cup and
saucer................................ 45.00
Goblet, Royal Wedding Commemo-
rative, 6" h, MIB 70.00
Loving Cup, Elizabeth II and Philip,
1972 Silver Wedding Anniversary,
Paragon, 3" h.................... 175.00
Magic Lantern Slide, Victoria and
Albert 25.00
Mug, Queen Elizabeth Coronation,
1953 .... 24.00
Plate, Queen Victoria, Jubilee Year,
Royal Worcester,
10-1/2" d 275.00

Coronation plate, "H.M. Queen Elizabeth II, June 2nd Coronation 1953," mkd "Tuscan fine English bone china," 4-1/4" d, $25.

Stamp Set, Coronation Souvenir, 4"
x 6" envelope with 9-1/2" x 12"
stamp block sheet, 60 perforated
commemorative stamps for King
George IV and Queen Elizabeth I
coronation, c1937, portraits of
family members, envelope neatly
opened at one end.............20.00

❖ Bronze

Bronze is sturdy metal that has been used for functional and decorative objects for centuries. Collectors should be aware that some objects merely have a bronze coating and are not truly solid bronze. The value of these pieces is considerably less than a solid bronze object.

Ashtray, 7-1/2" d, circular leaf form,
applied salamander,
c1910...............................120.00
Cricket Cage, 5-3/4" h.............85.00
Dish, cov, bird finial,
Sorensen 110.00
Elevator Buttons, from PA Ave,
Washington, hotel, bronze body,
MOP button, 10" h 750.00
Figure, reproduction
Lady with wolfhound, black and
gilt trim, black marble base,
16-1/2" h 250.00
Three girls, dancing hand in hand,
base scratch engraved "Villanis,
German," 9-1/4" h.......... 165.00

Vase, Neoclassical style, after Clodion, baluster form, continuous bacchanalian scene of infant satyrs, putti, and goats, light brown patina, 15" h 350.00

Wall Plaque, Indian head, oval, greenish patina, 10-3/4" w, 13-1/4" h........................... 175.00

❖ Brush-McCoy Pottery

The Brush-McCoy Pottery was a result of a merger between the Brush Pottery Company and the J. M. McCoy Pottery in 1911. This new company produced all kinds of utilitarian wares, including such wares as cookie jars, garden items, and kitchen wares.

References: Sharon and Bob Huxford, *Collector's Encyclopedia of Brush-McCoy Pottery*, Collector Books, 1996; —, *Collector's Encyclopedia of McCoy Pottery*, Collector Books, 1980, 1997 value update; Martha and Steve Sanford, *Sanfords' Guide to Brush-McCoy Pottery*, Book 2, Adelmore Press (230 Harrison Ave., Campbell, CA 95008), 1996; —-, *Sanfords' Guide to McCoy Pottery*, Adelmore Press, 1997.

For additional listings, see *Warman's Antiques and Collectibles Price Guide, Warman's Americana & Collectibles, Warman's American Pottery and Porcelain,* and "McCoy Pottery" in this edition.

Bowl, glazed beaded berries on front, mkd "Brush USA 6," sgd "M. T.", some glaze missing...... 12.00

Cookie Jar
    Cookie House, mkd "W31," c1962 ....195.00
    Happy Bunny, gray, mkd "W25 Brush USA," c1960 ....395.00
    Humpty Dumpty 375.00

Flower Bowl, Onyx
    4" d.....................................30.00
    6" d.....................................35.00

Flower Frog, figural bluebird, 3-1/2" h.............................. 85.00

Pitcher, Fish & Waterlily........ 100.00

Frog garden ornament, 6" l, $25.

Planter
    Frog, reclining, 10" l.......... 120.00
    House 45.00
    Squirrel, chipped 15.00

Vase
    Cantaloupe, swirl with speckles, 7" h................................. 45.00
    Onyx, 6" h........................... 70.00
    Onyx, 8" h, brown and green.............................. 95.00

❖ Bubblegum Trading Cards

Bubblegum trading cards were big business in the late 1930s, especially for the Goudey Gum and National Chicle Companies. They produced several series that had collectors clamoring for more. Bowman, Donruss, Topps, and Fleer eventually got into the market too, creating many cards for folks to collect.

The following list is a mere sampling of the many bubblegum cards available. The prices listed are for complete sets in excellent condition.

Periodicals: *Non-Sport Update*, 4019 Green St, PO Box 5858, Harrisburg, PA 17110; *Non-Sports Illustrated*, PO Box 126, Lincoln, MA 01773; *Wrapper*, PO Box 227, Geneva, IL 60134.

Collectors' Club: United States Cartophilic Society, PO Box 4020, St Augustine, FL 32085.

The Osmonds, #12 (taxi zone) and #32 (group) from set of 66, 1973, Osbro Production, 25 cents each.

Batman, Topps, 1966, Riddle back series, 38 cards to a set....250.00

Battlestar Galactica, Topps, 132 cards and 22 stickers to set..40.00

Combat, Series 2, Donruss, 1964, 66 cards to a set 250.00

Fabian, Topps, 1959, 115 cards to a set......................................120.00

Good Guys & Bad Guys, Leaf, 1966, 72 cards to a set 275.00

Mars Attacks!, Topps, 1962, 55 cards to a set 1,650.00

Movie Stars, Bowman, 1948, 36 cards to a set 360.00

Rock Stars, Donruss, 1979, 66 cards to a set 48.00

Tarzan, 1966, Philadelphia Chewing Gum Co., 66 cards to a set......................................185.00

Wild Man, Bowman, 1950, 72 cards to a set........................... 1,250.00

✴ Bunnykins

These charming bunny characters have delighted children for many years. But did you know that they were created by a nun? Barbara Vernon Bailey submitted her designs from the convent. Many of her designs were inspired by stories she remembered her father telling her. The concept of Bunnykins began in 1934. A new series was modeled by Albert Hallam in the 1970s.

Baby Plate, Letter Box, Barbara Vernon Bailey.....................75.00

Bowl, 6-1/2" d..........................40.00

Plate, "Happy Birthday from Bunnykins," 8-1/8" d, orig box, $30.

Child's Cup, two handles, mkd
  "English Fine Bone China, Bunnykins, Royal Doulton Tableware
  Ltd, 1936" 55.00
Child's Plate, mkd "English Fine
  Bone China, Bunnykins, Royal
  Doulton Tableware Ltd,
  1936" 50.00
Christmas Plate, 8" d 18.00
Coupe, 3-1/2" d, slight use
  scratches 30.00
Figure
  Bridesmaid, DB173, 3-3/4"..40.00
  Buntie Bunnykins helping Mother,
    DB2 .... 85.00
  Doctor Bunnykins, 4-1/2" h..40.00
  Easter Greetings 55.00
  Fisherman Bunny, DB170,
    4" h 50.00
  Mother and Baby Bunnykins,
    DB167, 1997 .... 45.00
  Nurse 45.00
  Policeman, DB64 .... 45.00
  Reginald Up To No Good, cold
    cast, discontinued 20.00
  Sailor Bunny, 1997,
    discontinued 55.00
  Seaside, 1998 .... 55.00
  Uncle Sam, 4-1/2" h, brown back-
    stamp, c1985 .... 45.00

❖ Business & Office Machines

Folks who collect things have always been attracted to objects that are no longer in style. And, it's good someone saves these wonderful gadgets for the next generations to marvel over. Business and office machines fall into that kind of category.

Collectors' Club: Early Typewriters Collectors Association, 2591 Military Ave., Los Angeles, CA 90064-1993.

Adding Machine, working condition
  Burroughs 17.50
  Star 15.00
  Victor 10.00
Advertising Mirror, Monarch Type
  Writer Co., black and white celluloid, shows Monarch Visible typewriter with letterhead of sponsor,
  early 1900s 50.00
Bookkeeping Machine, Remington
  Model 23, working condition,
  extra parts 300.00
Business Seal, cast iron and bronze,
  table-top model, interesting
  impression 45.00
Checkwriter, SafeGuard 25.00

Seal stamp, cast iron, 8-1/4" h, 4-7/8" l, $17.50.

Dictaphone, Model 10,
  Type A 50.00
Erasure Shield, Remington Typewriter Co., diecut black and white
  celluloid, red and black lettering,
  early 1900s 45.00
Notary Seal, bronze, orig carrying
  case, commission expired .. 10.00
Pinback Button, Remington Electric
  Typewriter, black and white,
  orange image of shipping crate,
  "In-Box Delivery," 1960s 25.00

✶ Buster Brown

This sandy-haired boy and his dog, Tige, were pretty busy early in the 20th century. As a creation of R. F. Outcault, they delighted children and adults with their adventures. But, their biggest contribution to the collector's world are the numerous products that carry advertisements with Buster Brown.

Booklet, *Buster Brown's Latest,*
  Buster Brown Hosiery Mills, Chattanooga, TN, 1909, R. F. Outcault
  signature on cover art, 3 different
  stories 100.00
Box, Buster Brown Shoes,
  empty 15.00
Camera 65.00
Cup and Saucer 50.00

Fork, coin silver, 6" l, $12.

Still bank, Buster Brown & Tige, cast-iron, orig paint, 5-1/4" h, $350.

Lapel Stud, white metal, silver finish, c1900, 1-1/4" d 45.00

Pinback Button, "Vote for Buster Brown," red outfit, tugging black stocking held by Tige, c1970 .... 25.00

Whistle, figural, bisque 75.00

❖ Busts

Busts were a way of immortalizing a hero or someone special. Made of materials such as marble, bronze, or alabaster, they have endured. It was a sign of wealth to display a popular bust as part of your home decor.

Value is added when a plaque identifying the subject, foundry or maker, and date are present.

Child, 6-3/4" h, bronze, gilt, green onyx base, mkd "S. Klaber & Co. Foundry NY" 85.00

For exciting collecting trends and newly expanded areas look for the following symbols:

✪ Hot Topic

★ New Warman's Listing

(May have been in another Warman's edition.)

Abraham Lincoln, milk glass, $95.

Franklin, Benjamin, 15" h, carved oak, old brown alligatored finish, black carved base, sgd "Harris" 800.00

Locke, 7-3/4" h, black basalt, rised base, imp title and mark, Wedgwood, c1865 .... 525.00

Virgin Mary, 18-1/2" h, bronze, two-tone finish, black granite base, sgd "F. de Luca" 120.00

Washington, George, 35" h, cast plaster, orig bronze finish ... 125.00

Young Woman, 7-1/2" h, marble, head piece, cowl neck 250.00

❖ Buttonhooks

Used originally for hooking tiny buttons on gloves, dresses, and shoes, these long narrow hooks are sometimes found hiding in vintage sewing baskets.

Celluloid handle
6-1/8" l, mkd "Parisian Ivory," Loonen France trademark 25.00
7-1/8" l, black etched floral design 12.50

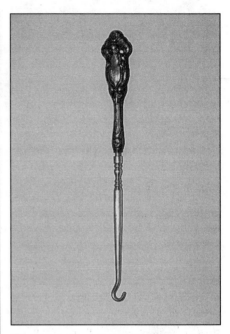

Sterling silver, 6-3/4" l, $20.

Sterling
6" l, floral and leaf design, mkd "Tiffany & Co. Pat'd '98" 800.00
6-1/8" l, feather paisley type design 35.00
6-1/4" l, swirling design, mkd "Tiffany & Co." 100.00
7-1/4" l, Art Nouveau design 45.00

❖ Buttons

Buttons are collected according to age, material, and subject matter. The National Button Society, founded in 1939, has designated 1918 as the dividing line between old and modern buttons. Shanks and backmarks are important keys to determine the age of buttons. It is the older buttons which attract the most attention of collectors.

References: There are many excellent button books available to collectors. Some of the standard reference books are Fink & Ditzler, *Buttons, The Collector's Guide To Selecting, Restoring and Enjoying New & Vintage Buttons, 1993;* Elizabeth Hughes and Marion Lester, *The Big Book of Buttons,* 1981 (reprint by

New Leaf Publishers); Florence Zacharie Nicholls, *Button Handbook, with three supplements, 1943-1949,* (reprints by New Leaf Publishers).

Periodical: *Button Bytes,* http://www.tias.com/articles/buttons. An internet magazine devoted to buttons.

Collectors' Clubs: National Button Society, 2733 Juno Place, Apt. 4, Akron, OH 44313-4137; Pioneer Button Club, 102 Frederick St., Oshawa, Ontario L1G 2B3 Canada; The Button Club, PO Box 2274, Seal Beach, CA 90740.

Bakelite
Log, carved, red 2.50
Tortoiseshell, large disc,
2-1/8" d 5.00

Black Glass
Gold luster, fabric-look, self shank, mkd "Le Mode," 1950s, 7/8" l 4.00
Silver luster, petal look, self shank with threaded groove, mkd "Le Chic," 1950s, 13/16" 4.00

Carnival Glass, purple
Buckle & Scrolls, 5/8" d 10.00
Lazy Wheel, 5/8" d 12.00
Windmill, 5/8" d 14.00

Czechoslovakian Glass, diminutive
Cobalt blue, inlaid ribbons of light green glass, multicolored foil, 4-way metal box shank, 3/8" d 5.00
Floral bouquet, set of 12....... 2.00

Figural, plastic
Apple, realistic coloring, metal shank................................ 1.25
Flower basket, pastels, metal shank................................ 1.50
Mouse, small, blue, shelf shank................................ 3.00

Moonglow (glass)
Black with red, colorless glass molded with plants and flowers, back mark is straight line with angled line at both ends, self shank, 1/2" d.............. 5.00
Green flower, gold trim, 1/2" d................................ 2.00

White, gold trim, four lobed, self shank, 1/2" d.................... 2.00
Paperweight, complicated millefiori by John Gooderham, white base, 8 flower canes, center small red, white, and blue cane, brass wire shank, sgd with "J" cane on back, 5/8" d, 1/2" h 20.00

Stenciled China
Black and white zebra stripes............................. 1.00
Blue and white flower........... 2.00

Newer buttons, minimal value but good collectibles for children.

Fellow collectors:

Name: _____
Address:_____
_____
Phone:_____
E-mail:_____

Name: _____
Address:_____
_____
Phone:_____
E-mail:_____

Name: _____
Address:_____
_____
Phone:_____
E-mail:_____

Name: _____
Address:_____
_____
Phone:_____
E-mail:_____

Name: _____
Address:_____
_____
Phone:_____
E-mail:_____

Name: _____
Address:_____
_____
Phone:_____
E-mail:_____

C

✫ Cake Collectibles

Here's a sweet collectible for you. However, in our recent trips to flea markets, we're finding more and more of these kinds of items appearing. Doesn't anyone bake anymore? It certainly seems like there are a lot of cake pans for sale!

Cookie Board, wood, metal top, 12 impressions 35.00
Cupcake Pick, baker with hat, Yeakel's Bakery 5.00
Pan
    Bird shape, old 30.00
    Child's building block shape 10.00
    Garfield shape.....................15.00
    Weight Lifter shape 10.00

Tin cake carrier, 6" h, 12" d, $12.

Topper
    Bells, pink satin 25.00
    Bride and Groom, tulle on base, orig flowers, c1946 .... 65.00
    Bugs Bunny, six matching birthday candle holders, Wilton, 1978 .... 24.00
    Comic Character................. 24.00
    Disney 24.00
    Mickey & Minnie Mouse...... 24.00
    Snoopy 24.00
    Snow White 24.00

❖ Calculators

What would we do without pocket calculators? Some of the first models are beginning to command steep prices. However, like many other collectibles, condition is very important. Add that to the collector's desire for the original box and instruction sheet.

References: Bruce Flamm and Guy Ball, *Collector's Guide to Pocket Calculators,* Wilson/Barnett Publishing, 1997; Thomas F. Haddock, *Collector's Guide to Personal Computers and Pocket Calculators,* Books Americana, 1993.

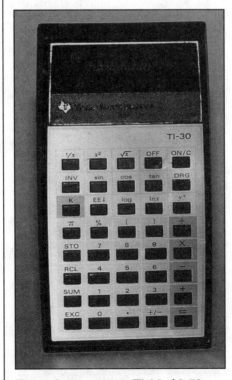

Texas Instruments TI-30, $8.50.

Collectors' Club: International Association of Calculator Collectors, PO Box 70513, Riverside CA, 92513.

Addiator Duplex, brass............25.00
Bohn Instant............................30.00
Bowmar 901B 70.00
Casio HL-809, 2-3/4" x 4-1/2", MIB 25.00
Commodore, MM1 ....75.00
Crag, 4502 ....55.00
Crown CL 130 ....150.00
Keystone, 390 ....55.00
Lloyds 303.............................20.00
National 25.00
Radio Shack EC 425...............50.00
Royal Digital 3 ....110.00

❖ Calendar Plates

Many of these interesting plates were made as give-aways for local merchants. Sometimes these were made by popular manufacturers of the day, like Homer Laughlin or Royal China. Many have fanciful gold borders and trim and interesting scenes along with the advertising.

Expect to pay more for a local calendar plate when sold in the area where it originated. This is a collectible category where location is as important as condition.

Periodical: *The Calendar*, 710 N. Lake Shore Drive, Barrington, IL 60010.

1909, Compliments of Stadt Hardware Co., Grand Rapids, MI, Hudson, Homer Laughlin, 8" d 45.00
1910, Compliments of Crviest Bros., Hudson, Homer Laughlin, 9-1/4" d 50.00
1910, Compliments of E. E. Kelly, Lincolnville, PA, scene of children playing at swimming hole, James Whitcomb Riley verse, back stamped E.E.C.CO. Porcelain, some small cracks, 9-1/4" d 25.00
1912, Martha Washington 42.00

"God Bless Our House Throughout 1972," Edwin Meakin, 9" d, $10.

1916, man in canoe, Iowa,
　7-1/2" d 35.00
1917, scene of cat in center ... 35.00
1920, The Great War, MO 35.00
1929, Compliments of Oliver Reese
　General Merchandise, Serena, IL,
　6-1/2" x 7" 30.00
1967, sports theme, gold trim,
　10" d 7.00
1976, Bicentennial theme 12.00
1981, children, animals, and
　flowers, Deborah Bell Jarratt
　design 30.00
1984, Hail Columbia, Spencer
　Gifts, Inc., Series IX, Japan,
　9" d 15.00

❖ Calendars

With a brand new century, what's a better collectible than calendars? They often have great artwork from the best illustrators of the day, perhaps advertising, and often household hints, etc. besides the necessary numbers and days of the week.

1893, Hood's Sarsaparilla, titled
　"The Young Discoverers," little
　boy and girl looking at globe,
　8-1/2" h, 6" w, some paper
　loss 75.00
1894, Hoyt's, lady's perfume .. 15.00
1901, Colgate, miniature,
　flower 20.00
1909, Bank of Waupun, emb
　lady 35.00
1914, Youth's Companion, marching scene, easel back 12.00

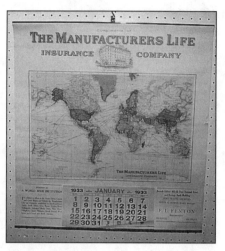

"Compliments of The Manufacturers Life Insurance Company," paper, tear-off calendar sheets, 24" x 23", $35.

1922, Warren National Bank,
　Norman Rockwell illus 300.00
1928, Hartney Machine & Motor
　Works, titled "Discovered," two
　dogs pointing at prey in forest
　scene, 16-1/2" h, 10-1/2" w,
　full pad 55.00
1929, Socony Products, 2-1/4" x 3-
　3/4", red, white, and blue celluloid
　pocket calendar, Standard Oil Co.
　of NY, Socony Motor Oils symbols
　and monthly calendar on one
　side, "Socony Special Gasoline"
　inscription and 1930 monthly
　calendar on other side 20.00
1942, Tydol-Veedol, 8" x 8-1/2", wall
　type, opens to 8-1/2" x 13-1/2",
　color art of US military aircraft for
　each three months of year, closed
　cover has orange, sepia, and
　black and white design of
　Independence Hall 40.00
1954, Shell Marine Lubricants,
　2-1/4" x 3-1/2" thin plastic, yellow,
　Shell logo in center of saver
　ring, reverse side with red
　calendar 25.00

❖ ☆ California Raisins

Savvy collectors were stashing California Raisins collectibles as soon as they appeared. So far, their investments haven't risen much, but hopefully they are enjoying their collections.

Bank, Sunmaid Raisins, Claymation,
　Made in China, 1987, 6-1/2" h,
　some wear 10.00
Cereal Box, figural, promotion on
　back for Raisin People key chain,
　some damage to back,
　13" h 45.00
Figure
1987, 2-1/2" h
　Blue sneakers, one hand points
　　up, other points down 4.00
　Holding gold saxophone, eyes
　　closed 4.00
　Microphone in hand 5.00
　Orange sunglasses, one hand
　　points up, other points
　　down 4.00
1988, Applause
　Boom Box Male, one hand points
　　up, yellow shoes, sunglasses,
　　2" h 12.00
　Christmas, green sunglasses,
　　holding candy cane, red sneakers, 2-1/2" h 10.00
　Microphone Female, holding
　　microphone in one hand, other
　　hand pointed up, yellow shoes,
　　bracelet, 2-1/4" h 8.00
　Microphone Male, one hand
　　extended with open palm,
　　2-1/4" h 8.00
　Saxophone, black beret, blue
　　eyelids, 2-1/4" h 14.00
　Tambourine, green shoes and
　　bracelet, 2-3/4" h 12.00
Pillow, figural, 1987, all orig tags,
　26-3/4" l, 13-1/4" w 22.00

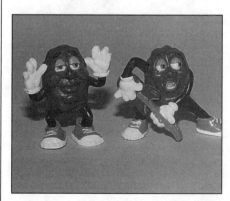

Hardee's, 1988, 2-1/8" h, each $4.

Print, Claymation, designed by Will Vinton Productions, gold metallic frame, 10" x 8" 12.00

Wind-Up, Applause, 1988, 4" h
Hands both point up, blue sneakers 10.00
Hands both point up, orange sunglasses and sneakers 12.00
Microphone in one hand, other hand as fist......................12.00

Wrapping Paper, light green, shows Raisin Band, licensing trademark, 44" x 35-1/2" sheet, unused 20.00

❖ Camark Pottery

Founded in Camden, Arkansas, this pottery was started in 1926 by Samuel Jack Carnes. The factory produced earthenware, art pottery, and decorative accessories. Several of the head potters had migrated to Camark from Weller Pottery. The company remained in business until 1966.

Reference: David Edwin Gifford, *Collector's Guide to Camark Pottery: Identification and Values,* Collector Books, 1997.

Cambridge Plainware sherbet, pink, 4-3/8", $15.

Collectors' Club: Arkansas Pottery Collectors Society, PO Box 7617, Little Rock, AR 72217.

Bowl, large, green 85.00
Casserole, cov, chicken-shaped lid 48.00
Pitcher, figural cat handle 50.00
Planter
Elephant, 11" x 8" 65.00
Rooster 30.00
Tulip-shape, pink, orig label: "Camark, Deluxe Artware, or shape #051, finish #90," 4-1/2" h, 5" w, pr 50.00
Vase
Crescent, blue, small 17.50
Double handles, chartreuse, 1930s 55.00
Double handles, mirror black............................... 64.00

❖ Cambridge Glass

Cambridge Glass Company, Cambridge, Ohio, was incorporated in 1901. Initially, the company made clear tableware, later expanding into colored, etched, and engraved glass. Over forty different hues were produced in blown and pressed glass. They used five different marks, but not every piece was marked. The plant closed in 1954. Some of the molds were later sold to the Imperial Glass Company, Bellaire, Ohio.

References: Gene Florence, *Elegant Glassware of the Depression Era,* Revised 6th ed., Collector Books, 1995; National Cambridge Collectors, Inc., *Cambridge Glass Co., Cambridge, Ohio* (reprint of 1930 catalog and supplements through 1934), Collector Books, 1976, 1996 value update; ——, *Cambridge Glass Co., Cambridge, Ohio, 1949 thru 1953* (catalog reprint), Collector Books, 1976, 1996 value update; ——, *Colors in Cambridge Glass,* Collector Books, 1984, 1993 value update; Bill and Phyllis Smith, *Cambridge Glass 1927–1929* (1986) and *Identification Guide to Cambridge Glass 1927–1929* (updated prices 1996).

Collectors' Club: National Cambridge Collectors, Inc., PO Box 416, Cambridge, OH 43725.

For additional listings, see *Warman's Antiques and Collectibles Price Guide* and *Warman's Glass.*

Bell, Blossom Time, crystal 95.00
Bowl and Underplate, Wildflower, crystal, gold trim................ 385.00
Butter Dish, cov, Gadroon, crystal 45.00
Champagne, Wildflower, crystal 24.00
Cocktail, Diane, crystal 15.00
Cordial, Caprice, blue 124.00
Creamer and Sugar, Cascade, emerald green..................... 35.00
Cup and Saucer, Martha Washington......................... 45.00
Flower Frog, Draped Lady, amber................................ 200.00
Goblet, Diane, crystal.............. 25.00
Iced Tea Tumbler, Lexington ... 18.00
Plate, Crown Tuscan, 7" d....... 45.00
Relish, Mt. Vernon, 5 part, crystal 35.00
Server, center handle, Decagon, blue 20.00
Swan, crystal, sgd, 7".............. 35.00
Tumbler, Caprice, blue, 12 oz, ftd....................................... 40.00
Vase, Songbird and Butterfly, #402, blue, 12" h................ 395.00
Wine, Caprice, crystal 25.00

❖ Cameo Glass

Here's a collecting area that shows up sporadically at flea markets. However, when you find a great example, you'll feel like you've hit the jackpot.

Antique cameo glass is actually several layers of glass that are cut in a cameo technique. Look for examples that are aesthetically pleasing, free of damage, and possibly having a signature or paper label. The following listings are a quick overview of what kind of prices cameo glass brings.

For additional listings, see *Warman's Antiques and Collectibles Price Guide* and *Warman's Glass.*

Reproduction Alert.

Miniature Vase, 3" h, oval body, frosted pink with opal amber, layered in olive green, cameo etched nasturtium blossoms, bud, and leafy vines, sgd "Galle" at side.............................. 500.00

Vase

5-1/4" h, quatraform body, pink and colorless, overlaid in maroon, etched berry and leaf dec, sgd "Legras" at side, rim nick.............................200.00

6" h, shaped body, frosted pink, fiery amber and colorless, overlaid in butterscotch yellow, blossoming nasturtiums and leafy vines, sgd "Galle" at side 575.00

6-3/4" h, transparent topaz, footed urn shape, faceted scalloped rim, deeply recessed etched panels of six repeating vertical units, base inscribed "Schneider LeVerre Francais".......................250.00

8" h, swelled pink oval body, overlaid in red, burgundy-black, cameo etched riverside scene, church and mountains on far shore, cameo sgd "Richard" at edge..............................600.00

9-3/4" h, flared oval body, pink, white, and colorless, overlaid in white, green and yellow, cameo etched decumbent seed clusters hanging from leafy branches, Asian-style "Galle" mark on side......950.00

12" h, colorless oval body, overlaid in bright cobalt blue, faceted and etched, wide medial band, classical chariot scene, European 750.00

❖ Cameos

Most jewelry collectors include a few cameos in their treasures. These carved beauties enchant buyers. When purchasing a shell-carved cameo, check closely for the style, be sure the setting is secure and original to the cameo, and hold it up to the light. If you can see light passing through the carved layers you're in luck, for if you cannot see the image when held this way it's probably a modern copy.

Bracelet, carved lava, various colored cameos, Victorian 14K yg mounting........................ 1,500.00

Brooch

Scenic, house in center of oval plaque, white gold setting........................... 900.00

Woman, flapper style hair-do, off-shoulder dress, white gold setting........................... 600.00

Woman, head and shoulders, flowers in her hair, Victorian carved agate, gold beadwork frame, 18K yg setting ... 850.00

Compact, onyx cameo, marcasite ring, yellow guillouche enamel.............................. 425.00

Pendant, diamond-shaped frame, cameo with dancing figure, flowing dress and scarf, 14K yg setting.............................. 850.00

Ring, small woman's profile, diamond necklace ornament, white gold basket setting 1,250.00

Stickpin, carved shell with woman's profile, 14K yg mounting and pin.................................... 400.00

Costume jewelry cameo on chain, unmarked, 2" x 1-1/2", $20.

❖ Cameras and Accessories

"Say cheese" is the usual cry of a photographer. The fun of photography has been around for years and many cameras and their accessories and ephemera find their way to flea markets. Check carefully for completeness and condition. The value may be affected by the type of lens or special features offered by a particular model.

For additional listings, see *Warman's Antiques and Collectibles* and *Warman's Americana & Collectibles.*

Reference: James and Joan McKeown, *McKeown's Price Guide to Antique & Classic Cameras, 1997-1998*, 10th ed., Centennial Photo Service, 1997.

Periodicals: *Camera Shopper*, PO Box 1086, New Cannan, CT 06840; *Classic Camera,* PO Box 1270, New York, NY 10157-2078; *Shutterbug*, 5211 S. Washington Ave., Titusville, FL 32780.

Collectors' Clubs: American Photographic Historical Society, Inc, 1150 Avenue of the Americas, New York, NY 10036; American Society of Camera Collectors, 4918 Alcove Ave, North Hollywood, CA 91607; International Kodak Historical Society, PO Box 21, Flourtown, PA 19301; Leica Historical Society of America, 7611 Dornoch Lane, Dallas, TX 75248; Nikon Historical Society, PO Box 3213, Munster, IN 46321; Zeiss Historical Society, 300 Waxwing Drive, Cranbury, NJ 08512.

Book, *A Century of Cameras from the Collection of the International Museum of Photography at George Eastman House,* Eaton S. Lothrop Jr., Morgan & Morgan, 1973, 150 pgs 38.00

Box, Eastman Kodak Brownie Developing, sgd..................65.00

Camera

Agfa, Paramat, 35mm half frame, Color-Apotar f2.8/30mm lens, automatic metering, c1963..............................30.00

Argus, Ciro-Flex Model D, twin-lens reflex camera, 1940s 30.00

Eastman Kodak, Anniversary Box, No. 2, Hawk-Eye Model C, tan, foil seal, given away at 50th anniversary in 1930 ....35.00

Konishiro Kogaku, Pearlette, trellis-strut folding camera, 127 rollfilm, Rokuosha Optar f6.3/75mm lens, Echo shutter, c1946, mkd "Made in Japan" 40.00

Zeiss Ikon, Contessa, folding 35mm rangefinder, Tessar f2.8/45mm lens, Synchro Compur shutter, c1950 ....100.00

Target Brownie Six-20 box camera, $5.

Argus C-44 35mm, Argus Cintagon f 2.8 50mm lens, $35.

Exposure Meter, Zeiss Ikon Ikophot, orig instruction booklet, clear plastic case 20.00

Sign
  Ansco Film, 10" h, 24" l, two sided, diecut, box shape, Ansco Plenachrome Film, one side fair, other good........ 70.00
  Premo Camera, 34" h, 17" w, diecut cardboard, lady holding up hand, titled "It's easy to make good pictures with a Premo" 50.00

⭐ Campbell's Soup

"Mmmm, good!" is the advertising cry of the two cute Campbell's Soup Kids. Their image has graced many products and advertising since they were created in 1905 by Grace Drayton.

Reference: David and Micki Young, *Campbell's Soup Collectibles from A to Z,* Krause Publications, 1998.

Collectors' Clubs: Campbell Kids Collectors, 649 Bayview Dr, Akron, OH 44319; Campbell's Soup Collector Club, 414 Country Ln Ct, Wauconda, IL 60084.

Bank, can shape, "Tomato Soup," paper label with torches on sides, red and white, 4" h, 1995...... 5.00

Bell, Fishing Buddies, custard glass, mail-in premium, Fenton Glass, 1988 .... 35.00

Calculator, credit-card size, Conrad Electronics 15.00

Clock, wall, schoolhouse type, boy and girl holding soup can on face, 1983 .... 120.00

Comic Book, Captain America and the Campbell's Kids, Marvel Comics, 1980 .... 23.00

Cookbook, *Easy Ways to Delicious Meals,"* 1967 .... 12.00

Doll, boy chef, chef's hat, composition, Horsman, 1947 .... 265.00

Kitchen Timer, Tomato Soup can shape, MIB 15.00

Mint Tray, Campbell's Kids 15.00

Soup Bowl, Campbell's Soup ... 5.00

Thermometer, 12" h, diecut porcelain, tomato soup can shape, round thermometer in center 3,650.00

❖ Candlesticks

Designed to hold a burning candle upright, candlesticks can be found in all shapes and sizes at flea markets.

5-7/8" h, brass, sq base, spool stem, one base slightly battered, pr 445.00

Child's plate, Campbell's Kids, Buffalo China, 1-3/8" h, 7-5/8" d, $95.

Bank, 125th anniversary, tomato soup tin can, 4" h, $5.

Cherokee Pottery, blue, 6-1/2" h, pr, $45.

6" h, copper, sq base, handle stamped "6," battered, replaced push-up 95.00

6-1/4" h, wrought iron and tin, side push-up 225.00

6-1/2" h, brass, push-ups, minor battering and repair, Victorian, pr 90.00

6-3/4" h, hogscraper, push-up, lip handle, brass ring, dents .. 375.00

7-1/2" h, pewter, Jack-O-diamonds style, English, 19th C, pr ...115.00

8-1/8" h, brass, Queen Anne style, petal base, poorly resoldered stem and base.................. 275.00

8-1/2" h, glass, amethyst, baluster style................................... 50.00

❖ Candlewick

Imperial Pattern No. 400, known as Candlewick, was introduced in 1936 and became a real hit with American consumers. It was continuously made until 1982. After Imperial declared bankruptcy, several of the molds were sold and other companies then started to produce this pattern, often in different colors.

References: Gene Florence, *Elegant Glassware of the Depression Era, Sixth Edition,* Collector Books, 1994; *National Imperial Glass Collector's Soc., Imperial Glass Encyclopedia, Vol. I: A–Cane,* The Glass Press, 1995; —, *Imperial Glass Catalog Reprint,* Antique Publications, 1991; Virginia R. Scott, *Collector's Guide to Imperial Candlewick, 4th ed.,* available from author; Mary M. Wetzel-Tomalka, *Candlewick: The Jewel of Imperial, Book I,* available from author; —, *Candlewick: The Jewel of Imperial, Book II,* available from author, 1995; —, *Candlewick, The Jewel of Imperial, Personal Inventory & Record Book,* available from author, 1998; —, *Candlewick, The Jewel of Imperial, Price Guide '99 and More,* available from author, 1998.

Periodicals: *Glasszette,* National Imperial Glass Collector's Soc., PO Box 534, Bellaire, OH 43528; *The Candlewick Collector Newsletter,* National Candlewick Collector's Club, 275 Milledge Terrace, Athens, GA 30606.

Collectors' Clubs: National Candlewick Collector's Club, 275 Milledge Terrace, Athens, GA 30606; National Imperial Glass Collector's Society, PO Box 534, Bellaire, OH 43528. Check with these organizations for clubs located in your area.

For additional listings, see *Warman's Americana & Collectibles* and *Warman's Glass.*

Reproduction Alert.

Ashtray, eagle 70.00
Bon Bon, #51H, heart shape, 6", handle 35.00
Bowl, 12" d, #106B, belled 70.00

Wine glasses, 3400 line, clear, 7-1/2" h, each $35.

Bud Vase, 87F, 8-1/2" h, fan, floral cutting 90.00
Cake Plate, sterling silver pedestal 65.00
Canape Plate, #36 .... 12.00
Celery, #105, 13".................... 40.00
Cigarette Holder, eagle 95.00
Cup and Saucer, #37, coffee... 14.00
Jelly Server, 1 bead stem, 2 bead cover 50.00
Pastry Tray, #68D, 11-1/2" l, floral cutting 80.00

Plate, beaded edge
 6" d 6.50
 8-1/2" d 12.00
 10-1/4" d 32.00
Relish, #55, 4 part.................. 30.00
Salt and Pepper Shakers, pr, #247...................................... 45.00
Sherbet, #19, 5 oz, low 18.00

Vase
 #87C, 8" h, crimped, plain top 50.00
 #143C, 8" h, crimped, flip, cut leaves 200.00

❖ Candy Containers

Figural glass candy containers have been part of childhood since 1876, when they were first introduced at the Centennial Exposition in Philadelphia. Historical changes from that date can be seen in the interesting glass containers. Candy containers were also made of papier-mâché, cardboard, tin, etc. These are also highly collectible and eagerly sought at flea markets.

References: *Candy Containers,* L-W Book Sales, 1996; Douglas M. Dezso, J. Lion Poirier & Rose D. Poirier, *Collector's Guide to Candy Containers,* Collector Books, 1997; George Eikelberner and Serge Agadjanian, *Complete American Glass Candy Containers Handbook,* revised and published by Adele L. Bowden, 1986; Jennie Long, *Album of Candy Containers,* published by author, Vol. I (1978), Vol. II (1983).

Collectors' Club: Candy Container Collectors of America, PO Box 352, Chelmsford, MA 01824-0352.

For additional listings, see *Warman's Antiques and Collectibles* and *Warman's Americana & Collectibles.*

Reproduction Alert:

Battleship, glass, orig cardboard closure, printed "Victory Glass Inc." 48.00

Black Cat, with pumpkin, papier-mâché, Germany................ 75.00

Boot, papier-mâché, red and white...................................... 24.00

Bulldog, glass, orig paint 90.00

Dog, glass, blue..................... 15.00

Duck, cardboard, nodding head 18.50

Football, tin, Germany 18.00

Hen on Nest, glass, 2 pc, Millstein 15.00

Lantern, large, glass and metal 35.00

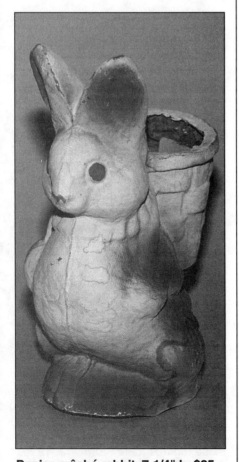

Papier-mâché rabbit, 7-1/4" h, $25.

Model T, glass......................... 24.00

Owl, glass, stylized feathers, painted, screw-on cap 90.00

Pistol, glass............................. 30.00

Pumpkin Man, bisque 45.00

Rabbit, papier-mâché, pulling basket, pasteboard wheels 55.00

Rooster, glass, screw-on cap................................... 125.00

Telephone, glass, candlestick type.................................... 50.00

Turkey, chalk, metal feet, Germany........................... 35.00

Witch, bisque 40.00

❖ Cap Guns

"Bang, bang!" was the cry of many a youngster playing "cowboys and Indians." Whether you were the good guy or the bad guy, you needed a reliable six shooter. Actually, the first toy cap gun was produced in the 1870s and was made of cast iron. That was the material of choice until around World War II, when paper, rubber, glass, steel, tin, wood and even zinc were used. By the 1950s, diecast metal and plastic were being used.

References: Rudy D'Angelo, *Cowboy Hero Cap Pistols,* Antique Trader Books, 1997; James L. Dundas, *Cap Guns with Values,* Schiffer Publishing, 1996; Jerrell Little, *Price Guide to Cowboy Cap Guns and Guitars,* L-W Book Sales, 1996; Jim Schlever, *Backyard Buckaroos: Collecting Western Toy Guns,* Books Americana/Krause Publications, 1996.

Periodical: *Toy Gun Collectors of America Newsletter,* 312 Sterling Way, Anaheim, CA 92807.

Collectors' Club: Toy Gun Collectors of America, 3009 Oleander Ave., San Marcos, CA 92069.

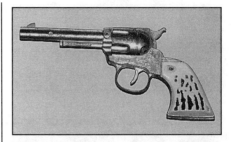

Daisy, plastic grips, 9-1/4" l, $32.50.

Cheyenne Shooter, Hamilton .. 70.00

Dragnet, Badge 714, Joe Friday, 1955................................. 120.00

Grisley, 1950s, box only 95.00

Hubley, western style 55.00

Ideal, Yo Gun, red and yellow, plastic, 1950s..................... 35.00

Kelmar Corp, Pow's Pop, automatic, Bakelite, maroon................ 45.00

Kilgore, Buck, No. 407, red, navy, and white, black grips, orig box 125.00

Mattel, Shoot N Shell 42.00

Nichols Derringer, orig card, diecast gun, caps, and bullets, 1950s................................. 65.00

Stevens, J & E, Buffalo Bill, repeating, 1920s, orig box 320.00

Western Pioneer, 1950s, box only 40.00

☆ Cape Cod by Avon

This pretty ruby red pattern was an instant hit with Avon lovers. Today more and more pieces are showing up at flea markets. Remember that this is a mass-produced pattern and very good examples are available.

Candlesticks, pr
2-1/4" h, grooved pattern 20.00
8-3/4" h, one with Bird of Paradise, other with Patchwork Cologne 25.00

Creamer and Sugar 22.00

Cruet, 5-3/4" h....................... 12.50

Luncheon Plate 10.00

Salad Plate............................... 7.00

Salt and Pepper Shakers, pr, 4-1/2" h 15.00

Candleholders, 4-5/8" h, pr, $18.

Vase, 8" h, ftd 22.00
Wine Goblet............................. 5.00
Wine Set, 10" decanter, four match-
    ing wine tumblers 35.00

☆ Care Bears

Some people wear their hearts on their sleeves. Care Bears wear them (and other symbols representing personality traits) on their tummies. Kids of all ages have welcomed these lovable creatures into their homes—and collections—since they were introduced by American Greetings Corp. in 1982.

Air mattress, 1983 .... 15.00
Bedspread, twin size 61.00
Curtains, 34" x 28".................. 21.00
Doll
    Baby Hugs, 1984,
        orig box 38.00
    Bedtime Bear, plush, 13" h....8.00
    Cozy Heart Penguin, plush, orig
        box, 11" h 66.00
    Grams, with shawl...............40.00
    Secret Bear, talks, peach, 1985,
        worn box 70.00
Drinking glass, Grumpy,
    Pizza Hut............................. 5.50
Ice skates, MIB........................ 17.00
Lunch Box, metal, orig thermos,
    copyright MCMLXXXIII
    American Greetings, Aladdin
    Industries............................ 18.00
Mug, stoneware, Care Bear
    Cousins, 1985 .... 10.00
Music box, ceramic, plays "Close to
    You" as bear twirls.............. 37.00

Good Luck Bear glass, Pizza Hut, 6-1/8" h, $15.

Sleeping bag, 1983, tags
    attached.............................. 52.50
Sneakers, girls size 3, blue,
    MIB 20.00

❖ Carlton Ware

This brightly colored pottery was first manufactured by Wiltshow and Robinson at the Charlton Works, Stoke-on-Trent factory, about 1890. The company's name was changed to Carlton Ware, Ltd. in 1957. Some of the items have great sayings on them, which collectors seem to enjoy.

Collectors' Club: Carlton Ware International, PO Box 161, Sevenoaks, Kent Tn15 6GA UK.

Bowl, Bleu Royale, #17359, 9-1/4" d,
    slight scratches 85.00
Dish
    Bleu Royale, hp, imp "#1226/1,"
        painted mark "Carlton Ware,
        Made in England" 155.00
    Lettuce leaf shape, mkd "Made in
        England, Trade Mark Regis-
        tered, Australian Design, Reg-
        istration Applied For,"
        10-1/2" l 50.00
    Rouge Royale, Mandarin scene,
        hp, gold edge, #1608/2,
        10-1-4" l 115.00
    Vert Royale, imp "1698/2," orig
        sticker, gold trim, 10" l, slight
        scratch............................ 60.00
Honey Pot, cov, underplate,
    registered Australian design,
    imp "2120," light crazing under
    glaze 60.00
Jug, hp, cream ground resembles
    wood grain, registered Australian
    design, imp "#2211,"
    6-3/4" h 255.00
Mug
    Dreamer, "I dreamed that I died &
        to heaven did go, I rang the
        bell gaily and bowed very low, I
        said I'm from Canada, My how
        they did stare, Come right in
        said Peter, You're the first one
        from there," 3-3/4" h 45.00
    "Tobacco-Tobacco is a hateful
        weed-I like it. It makes you thin,
        it makes you lean, it takes the
        hair right off your bean, it's the
        worst darn stuff I've ever seen,
        but I like it," 3-3/4" h........ 50.00
Pitcher, hp, blue mark, repair to
    handle, 3" h........................ 30.00
Salad Set, figural, 9-1/2" d, bowl,
    8-1/2" l fork and spoon, sgd,
    c1930 .... 180.00

❖ Carnival Chalkware

Brightly painted plaster-of-Paris figures that were given away as prizes at carnivals continue to capture the eye of collectors as they wander through flea markets. Most of these figures date from the 1920s through the 1960s.

Cat bank, 11-1/2" h, $45.

Basset Hound, paint flecked,
  11" h 25.00
Bugs Bunny 65.00
Cat, bank, c1940 .... 45.00
Dog
  8-3/4" h, with ashtray...........25.00
  9-1/2" h...............................35.00
Horse, unpainted flat back, 5-1/2" h,
  few chips 15.00
Lone Ranger.......................... 75.00
Miss America, 15" h, c1940.... 35.00
Singing Cowboy, 1950s 65.00
Wimpy, 18" h, 1940s.............. 48.00

❖ Carnival Glass

Carnival glass can be found in many different colors, including marigold, purples, greens, blues, reds, and pastels, all with a metallic-looking sheen or iridescence. Many different manufacturers were responsible for creating hundreds of patterns.

The following listings are a mere sampling of the thousands of carnival glass pieces available to collectors.

References: Carl O. Burns, *Collector's Guide to Northwood Carnival Glass,* L-W Book Sales, 1994; —, *Dugan/Diamond Glass,* Collector Books, 1998; —, *Imperial Carnival Glass 1909-1930 Identification and Values, Collector Books,* 1996; Dave Doty, *A Field Guide To Carnival Glass,* Pageworks, 1998; Bill Edwards, *Standard Encyclopedia of Carnival Glass, 6th ed.,* Collector Books, 1998; Tom and Sharon Mordini, *Carnival Glass Auction Price Reports,* published by authors; The Australian Carnival Enthusiasts Associated, Inc., *Carnival Glass of Australia,* Australian Carnival Enthusiasts Associated, Inc.; Glen and Steve Thistlewood, *Carnival Glass-The Magic and the Mystery,* Schiffer, 1998.

Periodical: *Network,* Pageworks, PO Box 2385, Mt. Pleasant, SC 29465.

Collectors' Clubs: American Carnival Glass Assoc., 9621 Springwater Ln, Miamisburg, OH 45342; Canadian Carnival Glass Assoc., 107 Montcalm Dr., Kitchner, Ontario N2B 2R4 Canada; Carnival Glass Collectors Assoc. of Australia, Inc., 24 Kerstin St., Quakers Hill, NSW 2763; Collectible Carnival Glass Assoc., 2360 N. Old S. R. 9, Columbus, IN 47203-9430; Heart of America Carnival Glass Assoc., 43-5 W. 78th St., Prairie Village, KS 66208; International Carnival Glass Assoc., P. O. Box 306, Mentone, IN 46539; The Carnival Glass Society (UK), 162 Green Lane, Edgeware, Middsix HA8 8EJ, England; WWW.CGA at http://www.woodsland.com. Many of these have regional chapters, contact the national organization for information about a club in your area.

For additional listings, see *Warman's Antiques and Collectibles Price Guide* and *Warman's Glass.*

Reproduction Alert.

Bon Bon, 7" d, Grape & Cable,
  blue..................................... 90.00
Bowl
  Fruits & Flowers, amethyst,
    7-1/4" d.......................... 70.00
  Grape & Cable, ftd, pastel,
    7-1/2" d........................... 70.00
  Holly & Berry, peach
    opalescent 110.00
  Peacock & Grape, marigold,
    9" d 50.00
  Raindrops, peach opalescent,
    8-3/4" d........................... 85.00
  Strawberry, amethyst,
    8-3/4" d........................... 85.00
  Vintage Leaf, green,
    7-1/2" d........................... 72.00
Bushel Basket
  Ice Green 200.00
  White, Northwood 120.00
Candy Dish, Drapery,
  white 125.00
Compote, Petals, amethyst,
  7-1/2" x 3-3/4" 45.00
Hat, Luster Flute, amethyst..... 32.00
Mug, 3-1/2" h
  Orange Tree, aqua 60.00
  Singing Birds, amethyst.... 215.00
Pitcher, 9" h, Butterfly & Berry,
  marigold........................... 265.00
Plate, Vintage, green,
  7-1/2" d 140.00
Rose Bowl
  Double Stem, domed foot, peach
    opalescent................... 160.00
  Grape Delight, white 95.00
Tankard Pitcher, 12-1/2" h, Paneled
  Dandelion, marigold.......... 400.00
Tumble-Up, Smooth Rays,
  marigold 60.00
Tumbler
  Butterfly & Berry, marigold .. 30.00
  Paneled Dandelion,
    marigold.......................... 48.00

Grape pattern bowl, 3 feet, purple, unmarked, 6-1/2" d, $65.

Raspberries, amethyst 75.00
Vase, Ripple
    Amethyst, 11" h 110.00
    Green, freeform top,
        8-7/8" h 110.00

❖ Cartoon Characters

They've entertained generations for decades and now collectors seek them out at flea markets. Their charm and humor light up collections all across the country.

References: Ted Hake, *Hake's Price Guide To Character Toys,* Gemstone Publishing, 1998; Jim Harmon, *Radio & TV Premiums,* Krause Publications, 1997.

Periodical: *Frostbite Falls Far-Flung Flier* (Rocky & Bullwinkle), PO Box 39, Macedonia, OH 44056.

Collectors' Clubs: Betty Boop Fan Club, 6025 Fullerton Ave, Apt 2, Buena Park, CA 90621; Peanuts Collector Club, 539 Sudden Valley, Bellingham, WA 98226; Pogo Fan Club, 6908 Wentworth Ave S, Richfield, MN 55423; Popeye Fan Club, Ste 151, 5995 Stage Rd, Barlette, TN 38184; R. F. Oucault Soc, 103 Doubloon Dr, Slidell, LA 70461.

Birthday Card, Ziggy, unused ... 1.00
Bubble Gum Wrapper, Popeye,
    1981, 5-1/2" x 5-1/2" 45.00
Comic Book, Popeye, large size
    format, 1972, 14" x 11" 15.00
Cookie Jar
    Bugs Bunny.........................40.00
    Felix the Cat 50.00
Doll, Felix the Cat 8.00
Figure
    Archie, Sirocco, painted brown
        military uniform and hat,
        1944 ....24.00
    Popeye, jointed wood, 4-1/2" h,
        copyright K.F.S..............145.00
Game, Barney Google an' Snuffy
    Smith, Milton Bradley, 1963,
    orig box 42.00
Harmonica, Underdog 35.00

Ziggy candle tin, American Greetings Corp., 2-5/8" h, 2-1/2" sq, $1.

Music Box, Betty Boop as
    cowgirl 45.00
Napkin Holder, Popeye,
    ceramic............................... 15.00
Pencil Holder, plastic, figural,
    Garfield 2.00
Perfume Set, Little Lulu 85.00
Pinback Button, New Funnies, Andy
    Panda, black, white, red, bright
    yellow 25.00
Ring, Little Lulu 40.00
Salt and Pepper Shakers, pr
    Betty Boop 15.00
    Bugs Bunny and Taz 15.00
    Felix the Cat 20.00
Talking Doll, Bugs Bunny, Mattel,
    seven phrases, 1971 .... 95.00
Teapot, Betty Boop 35.00
Thermos, Casper The Friendly
    Ghost................................. 75.00
Vase, Betty Boop 30.00
Wall Plaque, figural, Andy Panda,
    ceramic, mkd "Napco Ceramics,"
    1958 .... 65.00

❖ Cash Registers

One of the necessities of any store is a good cash register. However, with today's electronic gadgets, the large ones of yesterday have been cast aside. Today, collectors gather these units up, often restore them, and then enjoy their purchases.

Magazine, The NCR, Vol. XVII, No. 4, Sept. 1904, information on 1904 World's Fair, 8-5/8" x 6-1/8", $12.50.

National, candy store size
    Ornate cast detail, milk glass
        shelf on front, 21-1/4" x
        10-1/4" x 16".................. 675.00
    Polished brass, cast detail,
        milk glass shelf, oak base has
        1" chip on corner, minor edge
        chips on glass, top banner
        missing,
        17" x 10-1/4" x 16"........ 715.00
National Model 5 ....2,200.00
Model 5 2-1/4", medium, emb brass,
    ornate ledge on three sides, side
    casing to hold tape, 17" h, missing "Amount Purchased" marquee, restored................... 750.00
Model 313, small, emb brass,
    marble ledge, 17" h, missing
    "Amount Purchased" marquee,
    restored............................. 750.00
Model 317, small, emb brass,
    marble ledge, 17" h, missing
    "Amount Purchased" marquee,
    restored............................. 500.00
Wooden, loose money in
    back 125.00

❖ Cassidy, Hopalong

Another one of the cowboy heroes who went from movies to radio and television. Hoppy was also a master at self promotion and did a lot of advertising, like many of the other early cowboy heroes.

Collectors' Club: Friends of Hopalong Cassidy Fan Club, 4613 Araby Church Rd, Frederick, MD 21701-7791; Westerns & Serials Fan Club, Route 1, Box 103, Vernon Center, MN 56090-9744.

Bread Label, Bond Bread 100.00
Child's Sweater, button down
   type 275.00
Collector's Plate, Hoppy and Topper,
   orig box and certificate 35.00
Poster
   Riders of the Deadline.......185.00
Spunny Spread, 16" x 20", black and white, Hoppy seated on Topper, c1950 .... 35.00
Soap, Topper, orig box.......... 125.00
Store Display, diecut, Hoppy leaning on rock 75.00

Neckerchief, Hopalong Cassidy and Topper, black, 37" l, $75.

Target Game, tin, orig back holders, 27" h 180.00
Writing Pad, hardcover, multicolored graphics, 8" x 10" 70.00

❖ Cast Iron

Cast iron has long been a favorite metal for creating durable goods, such as cooking utensils, farm implements, and tools.

Periodicals: *Cast Iron Cookware News,* 28 Angela Ave, San Anselmo, CA 94960; *Kettles n' Cookware,* Drawer B, Perrysburg, NY 14129.

Collectors' Club: Griswold & Cast Iron Cookware Assoc., 54 Macon Ave., Asheville, NC 28801.

Baker's Lamp, attached pan, hinged lid, mkd "No. 2. B. L.," pitted................................. 250.00
Boot Scraper, scroll ends, green granite base..................... 110.00
Hat Rack, painted, flower basket form, late 19th C.............. 825.00
Mortar and Pestle, urn shape, pitted................................. 50.00
Skillet, Griswold No. 7............. 35.00
Toy, motorcycle cop, mkd "Champion"......................... 65.00
Trivet, round, mkd "Griswold Mfg Co., Erie, PA/USA/8/Trivet/206," 7-3/4" d 35.00
Windmill Weight, bobtail horse, Dempster Mill Manufacturing, old black repaint 110.00

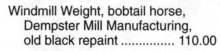

Cigar Cutter, "The Champion Knife Improved, Enterprise Mf'g Co., Philadelphia, U.S.A.," 19" l, $75.

❖ Catalina Pottery

Catalina Pottery is another California pottery that has been gaining in collector interest in the past years. It was founded in 1927 on Santa Catalina Island. Dinnerware production was added in 1931. In 1937, Gladding, McBean & Co. bought the firm and closed the island plant.

Ashtray
   Fish, small, blue.................. 60.00
   Sleeping Mexican, matte green, cold paint 285.00
Cigarette Box, cov, horse's head, ivory 475.00
Cup and Saucer, green........... 60.00
Head Vase, terra cotta and turquoise........................... 185.00
Jug, red, handle 80.00
Tray, Catalina Blue, 13-1/2" d 150.00
Vase
   4" x 10", white ext., white int., fluted, blue ink mark 225.00
   8" x 12", white ext., blue int., incised mark 260.00

❖ Catalogs

Old trade and merchandise catalogs are sought by collectors. They are sometimes the best source of information about what a particular company was producing for that particular time period.

Reference: Ron Barlow and Ray Reynolds, *Insider's Guide To Old Books, Magazines, Newspapers and Trade Catalogs,* Windmill Publishing, 1996.

For additional listings, see *Warman's Antiques and Collectibles* and *Warman's Americana & Collectibles.*

Hartz Mountain Products, c1933, 32 pgs 18.00
John Deere Co., Chicago, IL, 1970, 24 pgs 14.00
Jordan, Marsh & Co., Boston, MA, 1895, 254 pgs.................... 33.00
Kaywoode Pipes, 1937 .... 25.00

Theo. A. Kochs Company Barbers' Supplies, No. 29, 12-1/4" x 9-1/8", $225.

Lincoln Mercury, Detroit, MI, 1947,
    48 pgs 16.00
Montgomery Ward & Co., 1956,
    1,144 pgs, Fall & Winter..... 32.00
Murray Iron Works, Co., Burlington,
    IA, 1919, 95 pgs 44.00
Oriental Treasures, auction
    catalog, 1915, illus, penciled in
    prices.................................. 38.00
Paine Furniture Co., Boston,
    MA, 1902, 24 pgs, binding
    cut off 37.00
Risom, Contemporary Furniture,
    hard bound, 1940s 45.00
Sears, 1930s,
    Modern Homes................... 30.00
Sherwin-Williams Co., Columbus,
    OH, c1930, 14 pgs, paint
    samples............................. 22.00
Standard Mail Order Catalog,
    377 pgs, 1915 .... 35.00
Starlette Precision Tools,
    1938 .... 25.00
Winnisimmet Yarns, Chelsea, MA,
    1960, 6 pgs 19.00

For exciting collecting trends and newly expanded areas look for the following symbols:

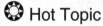 Hot Topic

⭐ New Warman's Listing

(May have been in another Warman's edition.)

❖ Cat Collectibles

It's usually purrfectly obvious to cat collectors, they love their cats, no matter if live and furry, or some interesting collectible. More often than not, they are purchasing objects which resemble their favorite furry friends.

Collectors' Club: Cat Collectors, 33161 Wendy Drive, Sterling Heights, MI 48310.

Reproduction Alert.

For additional listings, see *Warman's Americana & Collectibles.*

Avon Bottle, Kitten's Hideaway,
    white kitten in brown basket,
    1974 .... 8.00
Bookends, ceramic, black cats, gold
    trim, mkd "Japan," c1950.... 30.00
Bookmark, figural cat face, celluloid,
    reverse mkd "don't kiss me," 22" l
    green cord, c1920, 1-3/4" w x
    1-3/4" h 65.00
Comic Book, *Felix the Cat,* All
    Pictures Comics, 1945........ 50.00

Pull toy, wooden, black cat, mustard base, 9-5/8" h, 9-1/4" l, 3-7/8" w, $25.

Plate, "Souvenir of Effingham, Ill.," Dresden China, 7-1/2" d, $30.

Figure
    Cat Band, ceramic, 6 white cats in
        blue jackets, gold instruments,
        Japan............................. 60.00
    Country Christmas, cats among
        presents, Lowell Davis,
        1984 .... 525.00
Pitcher, figural, tail forms handle,
    clear glass, incised "WMF Germany," 8-1/4" h.................. 25.00
Planter, brown and white cat, blue
    bow, standing upright, one paw
    raised 12.00
Print, French artist, H. Gobin, titled
    "Le Tigre," 1840 .... 80.00
Salt and Pepper Shakers, pr, black
    and white figures, blue bows,
    porcelain, mkd
    "Czechoslovakia" 18.50
Teapot, figural, Norcrest.......... 40.00
Tea Towel, linen 10.00
Thermometer, hammered aluminum,
    white metal cat on base...... 45.00
Toy, tin, yellow and red cat, red ball
    and wheels, mkd "MAR Toys
    Made in USA," 6" l 115.00
Wall Plaque, Kitty Kat Family, Miller
    Studios, chalkware, orig box,
    unused 30.00

❖ Celluloid

Being the first commercially successful form of plastic, celluloid has been a part of life since the 1870s. Modern plastics have proved safer and easier to manufacture, so items made from celluloid are becoming quite collectible.

Calendar holder, brown landscape decor, 4-1/8" h, 3-7/8" w, $20.

For additional information, see *Warman's Antiques and Collectibles,* and *Warman's Americana & Collectibles.*

Animal, horse, 7" l, cream, brown highlights, hp eyes, marked with VCO intertwined mark 48.00

Bar Pin, ivory-grained, orange and brown layered pearlescence, hp rose motif 15.00

Bookmark, cream colored, diecut, poinsettia motif, Psalm 22 printed on front 15.00

Brush and Comb Set, child's, orig box 20.00

Doll, 6-1/2" l, crepe paper cone-shaped body...................... 100.00

Doll, blue glass eyes, moveable arms and legs, dressed in fabric skirt, crochet top, bandanna around head, earrings, 9" h.................................... 90.00

Dresser Tray, imitation tortoiseshell rim, glass and lace center .. 35.00

Necklace, red chain, berries ... 50.00

Picture Frame, oval, ivory grained, easel back, 8" x 10"............ 20.00

Pocket Mirror, oval, souvenir of Niagara Falls, printed colored drawing of falls, 2-1/2" h.............. 20.00

Rattle, blue and white, egg shape, white handle 18.50

Roly Poly, chicken, weighted base, 2-1/2" d............................. 38.00

❖ Central Glass

Central Glass Works, Wheeling, West Virginia, was established as a cooperative in 1863 by workmen from J. H. Hobbs, Brockunier and Company. It failed shortly thereafter, and was reorganized as a stock company in 1867. Production continued until 1939, and consisted of tablewares and barware for commercial and domestic use.

Bowl, 11" d, Frances, green, crimped,............................. 40.00

Butter Dish, cov, Chippendale pattern, colorless 20.00

Candlestick, 9" h, ribbed deep blue, silver trim 42.00

Cocktail, Balda, lavender 30.00

Creamer, Balda, lavender 30.00

Decanter Set, decanter, 6 cordial glasses, Balda, lavender .. 660.00

Fruit Bowl, Frances, 10" d, 3 toes, green 35.00

Goblet, water
    Acorn, colorless 15.00
    Balda, lavender 30.00
    Veninga, colorless 15.00

Hair Receiver, cov, Chippendale, colorless 15.00

Jug, Yodel, lotus etch, pink and crystal, 64 oz 300.00

Mayonnaise, Morgan, ftd, 2 handles, matching ladle, rose 165.00

Pitcher, water
    Acorn, colorless 35.00

Tumbler, Yodel, lotus etch, pink and crystal
    2-3/4 oz, ftd 40.00
    7 oz, ftd............................. 30.00
    12 oz, ftd............................ 35.00

Water Set, Greek, pitcher and six 7 oz tumblers, pink and crystal 500.00

❖ Ceramic Arts Studio

Created as a pottery which made wheel-thrown ceramics, this studio was located in Madison, Wisconsin and founded by Lawrence Rabbett and Ruben Sand in 1941. They continued making interesting ceramics until 1955.

Collectors' Club: Ceramic Art Studio Collectors Assoc., PO Box 46, Madison, WI 53701.

Bank, Tony the Barber 125.00

Figure
    Angel Blessing 90.00
    Colonial Woman 65.00
    Dance Modern Man 90.00
    Farmer Boy and Girl, orig bench, fishing pole and fish...... 225.00
    Fighting Leopards 250.00
    Lillabell, orig ribbon and bell................................ 150.00
    Little Bo Peep, lamb, pr 55.00
    Mexican Couple, 7" h.......... 90.00
    Parakeets, Budgie & Pudgie, slight roughness on beak............................. 125.00
    Running Boy 100.00
    Winter Willy....................... 50.00

Head Vase, Becky................. 250.00

Madonna & Child, blue.......... 150.00

Salt and Pepper Shakers, pr
    Elephant and Sabu 225.00
    Fish up on tails................... 60.00

Shelf Sitter, Maurice and Michelle, pr 225.00

Wall Plaque
    Cockatoos, A and B 185.00
    Comedy and Tragedy 200.00
    Harlequin and Columbine . 325.00

❖ Cereal Boxes

Cereal boxes have contained clever advertising, premiums, and activities for years. Early boxes were designed to appeal to the cook of the household, but as children began to request their favorite brands and wanted to save enough box tops to get a specific premium, the whole industry refocused on that group. By the 1970s, special promotional boxes were created, giving collectors even more opportunities to expand their collections.

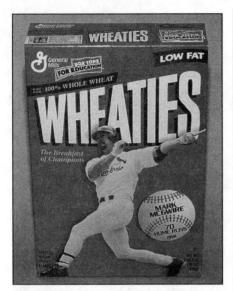

Wheaties, Mark McGwire 70 Home Runs 1998, 18 oz, unopened, $5.

Collectors' Club: Sugar-Charged Cereal Collectors, 5400 Cheshire Meadows Way, Fairfax, VA 22032.

Batman, Ralston, hologram t-shirt
   offer, 1989 .... 9.00
Cap'n Crunch, Treasure Hunt game
   board on back 75.00
Cheerios, aircraft carrier premium,
   1960s 120.00
Corn Kix, Rocket Space O-Gauge,
   1950s 90.00
Donkey Kong Junior, Ralston, base-
   ball card pack, 1984 .... 32.00
Froot Loops, Kellogg's, Mattel Fun
   on Wheels contest, 1970.... 30.00
Highland Oats........................ 32.00
Kellogg's Corn Flakes, sample size,
   c1920 .... 17.50
Kix, General Mills, Rocket
   Trooper............................. 150.00
Quaker Puffed Rice, 5 oz,
   1919 .... 22.00
Rice Chex, red check design,
   1950s 65.00
Sugar Jets 80.00
Wheaties, 1988 Redskin NFL
   Champions 25.00

❖ Cereal Premiums

This category is for all those fun things we saved from eating all that cereal. Sometimes these goodies were tucked into the box. Other premiums were things that you earned, through saving box tops, coupons, etc. Whatever the method, the treasure was the premium, and, at today's prices, collectors are having the most fun now.

Batman Bank, Ralston Cereal,
   plastic, sealed in orig package,
   1989 .... 25.00
Canteen, Rin Tin Tin, Nabisco, plas-
   tic, raised inscription "Official Rin
   Tin Tin 101st Cavalry," copyright
   1955, Screen Gems Inc.,
   orig box............................... 75.00
Cereal Bowl, Tom Mix, Hot Ralston
   Cereal for Straight Shooters,
   white china, illus, copyright 1982,
   Ralston Purina.................... 35.00
Coloring Kit, Post Corn Crackos,
   color-by-number pictures, box of
   colored pencils, instruction sheet,
   1967, unused.................... 125.00
Comics, The Adventures of Little
   Orphan Annie, 1941, Quaker
   Puffed Wheat & Rice
   Sparkles 65.00

Wheaties coin collection, 15 coins, complete, $15.

Manual, Tom Mix, *Life of Tom Mix,*
   Ralston, 1933,
   orig envelope 75.00
Pin, Pep Cereal, Squadron back,
   1930s 25.00
Quisp Smoke Gun, plastic,
   1950s 120.00

❖ Character and Promotional Drinking Glasses

Everybody's got one or two of these in the cupboard. However, there are also dedicated collectors who find flea markets to be great hunting grounds for new additions. Thanks to modern advertisers, like Coca-Cola and McDonald's, there are many examples to find.

Periodical: *Collector Glass News,* PO Box 308, Slippery Rock, PA 16057.

Collectors' Club: Promotional Glass Collectors Association, 3001 Bethel Road, New Wilmington, PA 16142.

Annie and Sandy, Swenson's,
   1982...................................... 8.00
Bugs Bunny, Pepsi, 1973, copyright
   Warner Bros. Inc. 9.00
Bullwinkle, Crossing the Delaware,
   Arby's, 1976....................... 12.00
Charlie Chaplin, Movie Star series,
   Arby's.................................... 9.00
Charlie Tuna, 3-3/4" h, 3" d, clear
   glass, single image of Charlie in
   white, no inscription, heavily
   fluted base, c1970, pr 25.00
Daffy Duck, Pepsi, Warner Bros.,
   1976.................................... 18.00
Empire Strikes Back, Luke Sky-
   walker, Burger King, 1980... 17.50
Endangered Species, Bengal Tiger,
   Burger Chef, 1978 .... 7.50
Little Bamm-Bamm, Flintstones,
   Hardee's, 1991 .... 6.00
Mayor McCheese taking Pictures,
   McDonald's 5.00
Noid, beach chair, Domino's Pizza,
   1988...................................... 2.50
Santa and Elves, Coca-Cola..... 9.00
Superman, Pepsi, 1975 .... 18.00

Goofy, Pepsi Collector Series, 1978, 6-3/8" h, $5.

Superman In Action, National
Periodical Publications, 1966,
4-1/4" h............................... 35.00
Underdog, Brockway Glass Co.,
Pepsi, 16 oz, small logo 25.00
Wendy, Brockway Glass Co.,
16 oz 15.00

❖ Character Banks

Banks that represent various cartoon, fictional, and even real characters are popular with collectors. Because so many of them are figural, they create a colorful scene when displayed.

Batman, glazed ceramic, 1966,
7" h..................................... 24.00

Donald Duck, nodding head, composition, Walt Disney Enterprises, 6" h, $175.

Betty Boop 20.00
Bugs Bunny, pot metal............ 60.00
Buster Brown and Tige, cast iron,
c1910............................... 165.00
Captain Marvel, dime register type,
litho tin, Fawcett Publications,
1948 .... 85.00
Fred Flintstone, vinyl,
12-1/2" h 20.00
Laurel and Hardy, plastic,
14" h 45.00
Old Dutch Cleanser, litho tin ... 25.00
Woodsey Owl, pottery............. 45.00

❖ Character Clocks and Watches

Telling time is more fun when your favorite character gives you a hand. Condition of the item is important when collecting clocks and watches. Examples with original bands, boxes, stands, and works will bring a higher price.

Autry, Gene, wristwatch 135.00

Betty Boop
Clock 45.00

Ronald McDonald alarm clock, metal, red, made in China, orig box, 6-3/4" h, $55.

Watch................................... 35.00
Charlie the Tuna, wristwatch, full
color image of Charlie on silver
background, copyright 1971 Star-
Kist Foods, grained purple leather
band.................................... 75.00
Flintstones, wall clock, battery
operated............................. 15.00
Jetsons, watch, lunch-box type,
Fossil, MIB......................... 80.00
Lone Ranger, wristwatch, metal
case, Lone Ranger on galloping
Silver, orig tan strap,
c1940............................... 165.00
Rogers, Roy, alarm clock, color dial,
c1970................................. 30.00
Smitty, wristwatch, gray aged dial,
white, red, and green figure, New
Haven Clock Co., 1935,
orig case 250.00
Snoopy, alarm clock 30.00
Star Wars, alarm clock,
talking 35.00

❖ Character Collectibles

Character collectibles range from items relating to fictional and real characters. Some of these characters got their start to fame from early radio programs, others were popular advertising spokesmen, while still others were found in newspapers, etc. As collectors become younger and younger, so do the ages of the characters they search for. Foxy Grandpa is giving way to Gumby and now even Rugrats.

For additional listings, see *Warman's Antiques and Collectibles* and *Warman's Americana & Collectibles,* as well as numerous specific categories in this edition.

References: Bill Bruegman, *Cartoon Friends of the Baby Boom Era,* Cap'n Penny Productions, 1993; ——, *Superhero Collectibles,* Toy Scouts, 1996; ——*Cartoon & Character Toys of the 50s, 60s, & 70s,* L-W Book Sales, 1995; Ted Hake, *Hake's Guide to Cowboy Character Collectibles,* Wallace-Homestead, 1994; ——, *Hake's Price Guide to Character Toys,* Gemstone Publishing, 1998; Jim Harmon, *Radio & TV Premiums,* Krause Publications, 1997; Jack Koch, *Howdy Doody,* Collector Books, 1996; Cynthia Boris Liljeblad, *TV Toys and the Shows That Inspired Them,* Krause Publications, 1996; David Longest, *Character Toys and Collectibles* (1984, 1992 value update), 2nd series (1987, 1990 value update), Collector Books; Rex Miller, *The Investor's Guide To Vintage Collectibles*, Krause Publications, 1998; Richard O'Brien, *Collecting Toys,* 8th ed., Krause Publications, 1997; and Micki Young, *Campbell's Soup Collectibles from A to Z,* Krause Publications, 1998.

Collectors' Clubs: Charlie Tuna Collectors Club, 7812 NW Hampton Rd, Kansas City, MO 64152; Dick Tracy Fan Club, PO Box 632, Manitou Springs, CO 80829; Howdy Doody Memorabilia Collectors Club, 8 Hunt Ct, Flemington, NJ 08822; Official Popeye Fan Club, 1001 State St, Chester, IL 62233.

Bullwinkle, coloring book, *Bullwinkle & Dudley Do Right*, Saalfield, copyright 1971, unused 30.00
Charlie Tuna, doll, vinyl 30.00

Stuffed doll, George Jetson, Nanco, 1989, 16-1/2" h, $10.

Dennis the Menace
 Book, *Dennis The Menace,* Hank Ketchum, Holt & Co., 1952, 1st ed., hardcover 35.00
 Lamp, figural 50.00
Dick Tracy
 Candy Bar Wrapper, premium offer, 1950s 10.00
 Toy, two way radio set, 1950, MIB............................... 40.00
Garfield, telephone, figural...... 48.00
Jetsons
 Colorforms Set, copyright Colorforms and Hanna-Barbera, 1963 .... 40.00
 Record, *The Jetsons, First Family on the Moon,* 33 RPM, 1977 .... 60.00
Kayo and Moon Mullins Pinback Button, black and white, *Los Angeles Evening Express* contest, 1-1/4" d 45.00
Popeye, flashlight, figural, King Features 30.00
Tom and Jerry, pinback button, Tom and Jerry Go For Stroehmann's Bread, black, red, and white litho, 1950s................................. 25.00

❖ Chase Chrome and Brass

This American company produced many interesting chrome and brass forms. They are well marked and quite stylish.

Bell, 3" h, Art Deco style, chrome, black ball handle 65.00
Bud Vase, four tubes, polished chrome, logo on base, 9" h 115.00
Candle Snuffer, Puritan, MIB 85.00
Candlestick, 2-1/2" h, polished chrome, cobalt blue glass bubble, 2-1/2" sq base....................48.00
Coaster, Art Deco, for Bovano, set of 4 ....200.00
Folding Tray, chrome satin finish, ribbed handle with two raised stars, emb fruit, fish, and fowl designs, 3 tiers, few minor scratches 70.00
Serving Dish, polished chrome, two compartments, glass liner, stationary handle, some wear to handle 45.00

✫ Chein Toys

An American toy company, Chein produced quality toys from the 1930s through the 1950s. Many Chein toys were lithographed on tin and are clearly marked.

Cabin Cruiser Motor Boat, litho tin, 15" l, 4" w, sgd "Princess Pat," 1940s, MIB......................275.00
Carousel, litho tin, wind-up......60.00
Disneyland Roller Coaster, one car.............................640.00
Donald Duck, litho tin wind-up ... 65.00
Motor Boat, litho tin, sgd "Peggy Jane," 14" l, 3" w, 1930s, MIB 225.00
Penguin, wind-up, played with condition 75.00
Roller Coaster, 2 cars, MIB ...590.00
Sand Pail, litho tin, fish dec.....35.00
Sand Shovel, litho tin 25.00
Waddling Duck, litho tin, windup, c1935 ....75.00

Ancient Rome chess set, 1st in series, Classic Games Co., 1963, king 4-1/8" h, complete set with board and box, $75.

✵ Chess Set

This game of kings has been played for centuries. Be certain to make sure all the playing pieces are present and the age of the board fits the age of the playing pieces.

Carved ivory, natural and "antique" color, 18" l, fitted case with inlaid playing surface, mkd "Hong Kong"................................. 275.00

Carved marble pieces, fitted case, no playing board................. 40.00

Pewter, exquisitely detailed playing pieces, fitted case, no playing board 200.00

Plastic, molded, black and white, cardboard board................. 15.00

Wood, hand carved, c1920..... 80.00

❖ Children's Collectibles

This category is a bit of a catch-all. It covers things that children played with and also items that were used in their rooms.

Bib Clips, sterling silver, clothespin type 75.00

Blocks, wood, bright colors, c1950, some wear.......................... 20.00

Cloth Book, handmade, things to teach children hand skills, buttons, zipper, etc. 10.00

Diaper Holder, fabric, clown face, head, striped body.............. 10.00

Kitchen Cupboard, some old paint, some restoration............... 400.00

Lamp, clown in rocking chair, music box base, orig shade 40.00

Night Light, plug-in type, figural teddy bear, plastic 5.00

Piano, "Concert," baby grand 110.00

Scooter, steel frame and wheels, wooden platform and handle, worn orig red paint, black, and yellow striping, partial label "...Arrow Deluxe".............. 150.00

The Bobbsey Twins And The Goldfish Mystery and **The Bobbsey Twins, The Red, White and Blue Mystery**, Grossett & Dunlap, ex lib, each $4.

Cloth book, *Animal Friends*, **Saalfield, $7.**

Wagon, Roller Bearing Coaster, wood, metal fittings, black stenciled label, old red and brown paint, some touch-up to paint.................................385.00

Wall Plaques, plaster-of-paris, Jack and Jill on one, Humpty Dumpty on other, self-framed, pr......20.00

Wastebasket, tin, yellow ground, hp teddy bear on side, wear and dents...................................15.00

❖ Children's Dishes

We've all made mud pies and other goodies. And what better way to serve them to our dolls and teddies than pretty dishes. Collectors today eagerly seek out these colorful dishes.

Collectors' Club: Toy Dish Collectors, PO Box 159, Bethlehem, CT 06751.

Baking Set, tin, cookie tin, canister, bowl, pie pan, cake pans, angel food pan, cup cake pan, etc. 25.00

Chocolate Pot, china, decal with Model T and passengers 90.00

Cup and Saucer
   Blue Willow pattern............. 15.00
   Cherry Blossom pattern, depression glass 45.00
   Moss Rose pattern................ 7.50

Dinnerware Set
   Depression Glass, Diana, crystal, gold trim, rack, 12 pc set...................... 125.00

Little Orphan Annie miniature tea set, 4-1/4" h teapot, 2-1/4" creamer and sugar, German, $150.

Plastic, Tinkerbelle, Walt Disney,
9 pcs 25.00
Plate, Laurel pattern, depression
glass 15.00
Silverware Set, aluminum,
4 spoons, forks, knife, and
pie server 15.00

Teapot
Aluminum, black wood knob,
swing handle 25.00
China, Occupied Japan.......85.00

Tea Set
Akro Agate, orig box mkd
"The Little American Maid,
No. 3000" 300.00
Geisha Girl pattern, china, service
for 4...............................125.00

❖ Chintz Ware

Chintz Ware is the general term for
brightly colored multiflower china patterns made primarily in England.
These popular patterns resemble
chintz fabrics and were made by
many manufacturers. After declining
for years after World War II, chintz
has enjoyed a lively comeback with
collectors for the past several years.

References: Eileen Busby, *Royal
Winton Porcelain*, The Glass Press
Inc.,1998; Linda Eberle and Susan
Scott, *Charlton Standard Catalogue
of Chintz,* Charlton Press, *2nd Edi-
tion*, 1997, *3rd Edition*, 1999;
Heller/Feljoy, *Chintz by Design*,
Chintz International, 1997; Muriel
Miller, *Collecting Royal Winton
Chintz,* Francis Joseph Publications,
1996; Jo Anne Welch, *Chintz Ceram-
ics*, 2nd Edition, Schiffer Publishing,
1998.

Collectors' Clubs: Royal Winton
International Collectors' Club,
Dancer's End, Northall, Bedfordshire,
England LU6 2EU; Royal Winton Col-
lectors' Club, 2 Kareela Road,
Baulkham Hills, Australia 2153.

For additional listings, see *Warman's Antiques and Collectibles* and
*Warman's English & Continental Pot-
tery and Porcelain.*

Reproduction Alert.

**Plate, Rose Chintz, Johnson
Brothers, 10" d, $12.50.**

Biscuit Barrel, Erphila,
Czech 225.00
Bread Tray, Old Cottage, Royal
Winton 200.00
Breakfast Set, Rosebud Iridescent,
green 250.00
Cake Tray, 2 tiers, Cotswald, Royal
Winton 145.00
Creamer and Sugar, Nantwich,
Royal Winton 235.00
Cup, #12586, Shelley 50.00

Cup and Saucer
Marguerite, Shelley, cup
damaged 50.00
Rosina 20.00
Dish, Dubarry, Kent.............. 125.00
Mustard, cov, Summertime,
Royal Winton 175.00

Plate
Dubarry, Kent, 8-1/2" d 165.00
Old Cottage, Royal Winton,
8" d................................ 50.00
Sweet Pea, Royal Winton,
5" sq 100.00
Soup Bowl, two handles, underplate,
Old Cottage, Royal
Winton 145.00

**For exciting collecting trends
and newly expanded areas look
for the following symbols:**

 Hot Topic

☆ **New Warman's Listing**

(May have been in another Warman's edition.)

Teapot, cov, Marina, Lord
Nelson.............................325.00
Tray
Old Cottage, Royal
Winton 150.00
Summertime 95.00

☆ Chocolate Related

Many collectors suffer from a
sweet tooth. Happily there are won-
derful examples of items relating to
chocolate to satisfy this urge.
Candy Box, tin, Whitman 5.00
Chocolate Set, 9-1/2" h chocolate
pot, 4 cups and saucers, dark
mauve and pink lily, white phlox,
green leaves, overall shading,
unmarked.........................250.00
Comic Book, *Major Inapak Space
Ace, #1,* 1951, Magazine Enter-
prises, NY, giveaway for "Inapak-
The Best Chocolate Drink in the
World" 10.00
Cup and Saucer, Johnston's
Hot Chocolate, mkd
"Salem China"....................35.00
Fudge Sauce Heating Pot,
Johnston Hot Fudge, Helmco,
Chicago.............................80.00

Mold
Dog 45.00
Dutch Boy 55.00

**Hershey's Christmas ornament,
wooden train, 1986 premium, 3" h,
4-1/4" l, $10.**

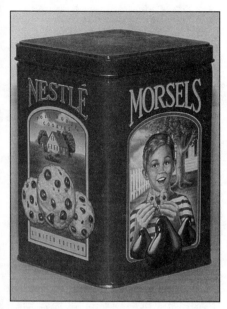

Collectors' tin, Nestle Morsels, Toll House Cookies, 6-3/8" h, 4-1/2" sq, $4.50.

Rabbit 45.00
Sample, Cocomalt Drink, orig powdered drink contents 50.00
Tin, milk can shape, "Huyler's Milk Chocolate," 4" h 45.00
Tin, Monarch Cocoa 50.00
Toy Truck, Hershey's Milk Chocolate, plastic truck, Buddy L, mkd "Made in Japan," two removable Hershey Kisses, 1982 .... 15.00

☆ Christmas and Easter Seals

The National Tuberculosis Association issued seals, pinback buttons, etc., in order to educate and raise funds for their work. The American Lung Association also issued seals.

Full Sheet
American Lung Association, 1977 .... 2.50
Christmas, sheet of 100, 10-1/2" x 8-1/4", 1950 .... 1.50
Christmas, sheet of 100, 10-1/2" x 8-1/4", 1951 .... 1.50
Pinback Button, Santa Claus image, small red cross Easter Seal Society, LJ Amber Co., Chicago 20.00

1951 Christmas Seals stamps, full sheet of 100, 10-1/2" x 8-1/8", $1.50.

1922 TB Assn. Christmas Seal, red, white, blue and yellow 45.00
1923 TB Assn. Christmas Seal, red and green 40.00
Sign, Santa, Buy Christmas Seals, easel type, diecut cardboard, Santa carrying sign on shoulder, 1923, 7-1/2" x 10-1/2" 60.00

❖ Christmas Collectibles

One of the most celebrated holidays of the year has given us many collectibles. Some collectors specialize in only one type of object or one character, like Santa. Others just love Christmas and collect a wide variety of objects.

References: Beth Dees, *Santa's Guide to Contemporary Christmas Collectibles,* Krause Publications, 1997; George Johnson, *Christmas Ornaments, Lights & Decorations* (1987, 1998 value update), Vol. II (1996), Vol. III (1996), Collector Books; Clara Johnson Scroggins, *Silver Christmas Ornaments,* Krause Publications, 1997; Lissa and Dick Smith, *Holiday Collectibles*, Krause Publications, 1998.

Collectors' Club: Golden Glow of Christmas Past, 6401 Winsdale St, Golden Valley, MN 55427.

For additional listings, see *Warman's Antiques and Collectibles* and *Warman's Americana & Collectibles.*

Blotter Pad, Christmas and New Year's Greetings, celluloid, 3" x 7-1/4", color graphics, scene with

Star of Bethlehem, Eckerson Co., Jersey City, c1920 .... 12.00
Bubble Light, Santa, 1950s, working condition, good paint 45.00
Figure, Santa, 2" h, bisque, full figure, holding green sack over left shoulder 35.00
Light Bulb, figural
Santa, 4-1/4" l, white glass, yellow sack over shoulder, right hand in pocket, dark blue trimmed red outfit 25.00
Santa, 9" l 110.00
Sparkle Plenty 75.00
Lights, figural, 23 different large figures, Japanese, orig box, 1926 .... 425.00
Ornament
Aladdin, orig package, 1993 .... 18.00
Clown bust, glass 35.00
Rudolph, plastic 4.00
Santa, glass, 3" h 35.00
Postcard, A Hearty Christmas Greeting, Victorian scene of children sledding 3.50
Store Display, Swift's, Santa, inflatable, sand in bottom, holds two Swift's hams in hands, red and white, 32" h 30.00
Tile, Royal Delft, 1974 .... 20.00
Toy, battery-operated Santa, rings bell, eyes light up, head turns, orig box, mkd "Made in Japan," c1950, 13" h 125.00

Bank, "Save Your Pennies and Your Dollars Will Take Care of Themselves," oval, litho tin, $250.

Chalkware Santa Claus bank, 9-1/2" h, $65.

Tree Topper, angel, cardboard and spun glass 24.00
Twinkle Tree, 1950s, changes color, orig box 40.00

❖ Cigar Collectibles

The late 1990s certainly have revived the fine art of cigar smoking. And, with this revival, collectors are finding numerous examples to add to their collections.

Periodicals: *The Cigar Label Gazette,* PO Box 3, Lake Forest, CA 92630; *Tobacco Antiques and Collectibles Market*, Box 11652, Houston, TX 77293.

Collectors' Clubs: Cigar Label Collectors International, PO Box 66, Sharon Center, OH 44274; International Lighter Collectors, PO Box 536, Quitman, TX 75783; International Seal, Label and Cigar Band Society,

8915 E. Bellevue St., Tucson, AZ 85715; Pocket Lighter Preservation Guild, PO Box 1054, Addison, IL 60101.

Box, advertising, Yellow Cab, rect, illus on front of Yellow Cab, lettering above, litho on lid, 7" l, 5-1/2" w 130.00
Box, cov, glass, covered with cigar bands 45.00
Bowl, small, glass, covered with cigar bands 35.00
Jar, La Flor De, General Arthur, orig lid, paper label 185.00
Sign
    American Havana Cigars, oval tin, titled "As Good As The Name," trademark label crest with lady on each sign, 9-1/2" h, 13-1/2" w................................... 325.00
    Chas. Mattheas, beveled tin over cardboard, titled "Mildred," fair hair lady, American Art Works, 1884, 13-1/4" h, 9-1/4" w 175.00
    Henrietta Cigars, tin over cardboard, titled "It Surely is a MASTERPIECE," gentleman admiring his cigar while sitting next to candlestick telephone, full box of cigars, 13-1/4" h, 9-1/4" l 200.00
    Merry Prince Cigar 5 Cents, reverse painted on glass, scalloped edge, 6" h, 16" l 250.00
    Portia Cigars, self framed tin, oval, portrait of young lady, Haeusermann litho, c1910, 17" h, 14" w, in painting and some restoration ... 250.00
Tin, Between The Acts, little cigars, full, 1920s 20.00

Larks cigar box, wooden, $10.

❖ ✿ Cigarette Collectibles

The cigarette industry is taking a beating for its product and advertising methods during the 1990s. However, the collecting interest in the topic is hot! Whether this politically incorrect habit will be snuffed out is anyone's guess.

Periodicals: *Tobacco Antiques and Collectibles Market*, Box 11652, Houston, TX 77293.

Collectors' Clubs: Ashtray Collectors Club, PO Box 11652, Houston, TX 77293; Camel Joe & Friends, 2205 Hess Drive, Cresthill, IL 60435; Cigarette Pack Collectors Association, 61 Searle St, Georgetown, MA 01833; International Lighter Collectors, PO Box 536, Quitman, TX 75783; International Seal, Label & Cigar Band Society, 8915 E. Bellevue St., Tuscon, AZ 85715; Pocket Lighter Preservation Guide, PO Box 1054, Addison, IL 60101.

Bridge Booklet, Chesterfield adv, 1937..................................... 25.00
Carton Sleeve, Camel, Christmas, c1940.................................. 20.00

Chesterfield tin sign, some rust, 23-1/4" x 17-1/2", $65.

Cigarette Card

Album with complete Player's King George series 48.00

Album with complete Player's military uniforms series........48.00

Series, airplanes, Wings, set of 81 ....125.00

Display, Royaliter Lighters, 6 boxed lighters, 1940s.................... 90.00

Game, Camel, MIB, 1992 .... 10.00

Poster, Camel Cigarettes, 10" x 21", multicolored, copyright 1935 by R. J. Reynolds Tobacco Co., image of cigarette pack and close-up portrait of unidentified model, slogan "I'd Walk A Mile For A Camel" in white and yellow letters 55.00

Silk, Wm. Randolph Hearst for Governor 10.00

Store Display, Chesterfield, Christmas, 1940s 10.00

Thermometer, Marlboro Man.. 42.00

Tin, Pall Mall, 1929, Christmas, colorful, large..................... 85.00

❖ Circus Collectibles

Whether it's the allure of the big tent or the dazzling acts, circuses have delighted kids of all ages since the 18th century. Of course this has helped to generate lots of collectibles, advertising, schedules, etc.

Periodical: *Circus Report,* 525 Oak St. El Cerrito, CA 94530.

Collectors' Clubs: Circus Fans Association of America, PO Box 59710, Potomac, MD 20859; Circus Historical Society, 3477 Vienna Court, Westerville, OH 43081; Circus Model Builders International, 347 Lonsdale Ave., Dayton, OH 45419.

Advertising Booklet, Ringling Bros and Barnum & Bailey Combined Circus, 1937, 10 pgs, 11" x 8-1/2" 60.00

Book, *Life of P. T. Barnum,* hard cover 20.00

Circus Pass

Circus Hall of Fame, Sarasota, FL 3.50

Ringling Bros. and Barnum & Bailey Circus Printing Set, box damaged, $90.

Covina, California Jr. Chamber of Commerce....................... 3.50

United Nations Circus, Bridgeport......................... 3.50

Wallace & Clark Trained Animal Circus 3.50

Clock, chrome and beige painted metal, seal with ball on top, other circus animals, 5" x 6" 75.00

Clown, celluloid figure riding fuzzy horse, mkd "M. M.," orig box............................... 75.00

Figure, ring master, lead, most of orig paint, Barclay, 2-1/4" h 40.00

Flyer, Herald 10.00

Little Golden Book, *Howdy Doody's Circus*, 1st edition, 1950 ..... 16.00

Pop-Up Book, *Circus,* 1979 .... 15.00

Postcard, giant........................ 15.00

Poster

Al G. Kelly & Miller Bros. giraffe, 28" h, 21" w 60.00

Camel Cigarettes, Capt. Terrell Jacobs/World-Famous Lion Trainer, "Healthy Nerves," 10" x 21", full color, copyright 1935 by R. J. Reynolds Tobacco Co., image of cigarette pack and lion tamer in action......................... 65.00

Ringling-Barnum-Bailey, 28" x 41", full color, charging lion and tiger, 1940s............................... 175.00

Ring, giant.............................. 20.00

❖ Civil War

This sad time in American history has led to an interesting range of collectibles.

Periodicals: *Military Collector Magazine,* PO Box 245, Lyon Station, PA 19536; *Military Collector News,* PO Box 702073, Tulsa, OK 74170; *North South Trader's Civil War,* PO Drawer 631, Orange, VA 22960.

Collectors' Clubs: American Society of Military Insignia Collectors, 526 Lafayette Ave., Palmerton, PA 18071; Association of Military Uniform Collectors, PO Box 1876, Elyria, OH 44036; Company of Military Historians, North Main Street, Westbrook, CT 06498; Military Collectors Society, 137 S. Almar Drive, Fort Lauderdale, FL 33334; Orders and Medals Society of America, PO Box 484, Glassboro, NJ 08028.

Reproduction Alert.

Badge, Daughters of the Union, Veterans Encampment, 1-1/4" x 4", red, white, and blue, striped fabric ribbon, bronze luster oval brass hanger bar with detailed covered wagon drawn by team of six horses, cello pendant of Gen. John F. Reynolds, ribbon inscribed "19th Annual Encampment, Lancaster, PA, 1931" 25.00

Tintype, ninth plate, tinted, cavalry soldier with Burnside carbine, holstered revolver, saber, $1,075.

Belt, enlisted man's black leather, brass retaining clips, oval brass "US" buckle 175.00

Button, brass, U.S. eagle imprint 10.00

Cabinet Card, Mathew Brady, No. 395, Shipping of 1st Conn. Siege Train at Yorktown, Union soldiers............................ 350.00

Inkwell..................................... 20.00

Photograph, ambro-type, soldier with weapons 475.00

Print, Battles of the Rebellion, 1863, Charles Magnus, lithographer, hand coloring, framed 400.00

Tintype, unidentified Union soldier................................. 30.00

❖ Clarice Cliff

To some collectors, hearing the name Clarice Cliff means Art Deco. To others, it's the bright ceramics created by this talented English woman. Clarice's work is becoming very popular and very expensive.

Collectors' Club: Clarice Cliff Collector's Club, Fantasque House, Tennis Drive, The Park, Nottingham, NG7, 1AE, England.

For additional information and listings, see *Warman's Antique and Collectibles* and *Warman's English & Continental Pottery & Porcelain*.

Reproduction Alert.

Lotus Jug, 11-1/2" h, Bizarre, Crocus, printed factory marks 900.00

Miniature Vase, 2-3/4" h, Original Bizarre, printed factory marks 360.00

Plate, 9-3/4" d, Bizarre, Blue Chintz, printed factory marks........ 625.00

Sandwich Plate, 10-1/2" d, Bizarre, Gayday............................ 400.00

Sugar Sifter, 5" h, Bizarre, Lynton shape, printed factory marks 425.00

Vase, 10" h, Fantasque Bizarre, Pastel Trees and House, blue and orange bands, printed factory marks 1,450.00

❖ Cleminson Pottery

This California pottery is known for its hand-decorated pieces. Started by Betty Cleminson in her El Monte, CA, home, the business soon grew and expanded in 1943.

Reproduction Alert.

Child's Cup, modeled as clown's head, comical hat cover, large ears, colorful 80.00

Cookie Jar, Candy House 100.00

Creamer and Sugar, figural, King and Queen, bright colors 85.00

Egg Separator......................... 20.00

Lazy Susan, Distlefink 90.00

Pie Bird, figural bird, yellow, blue, and lavender, mkd, 4-1/4" h............................... 95.00

Pie Bird Reproduction, rooster, 4-1/2" h, c1980 .... 20.00

Plate, hillbilly dec 25.00

Figural shaker, mkd "The California Cleminsons," 6-1/2" h, $20.

Razor Bank, white and green, old-time-looking man on front ...45.00

Ring Holder, bull dog, white and peach, rings go on tail.........27.50

Salt and Pepper Shakers, pr, male sailor "Old Salt," and female sailor "Hot Stuff," 5-1/4" h 75.00

String Holder, "You'll always have a 'pull' with me!," 5" h...........100.00

Wall Pocket, clock 24.00

❖ Clickers

These little giveaways were popular with early advertisers and children too.

Flavor-Kist Saltines, 1-3/4" l....40.00

Gun, figural
Red, 1950s 35.00
Tommy Gun, plastic, yellow and green, 1950s 8.00

Cartoon face, T. Cohn Inc., 2-1/2" x 1-1/4", $10.

Halloween, cat, plastic, 2-1/4" l20.00
Oshkosh 65.00
Poll Parrot Shoes.................... 27.50
Quaker State, 1-7/8" 65.00
Reach for Old Style Beer........ 25.00
Red Goose Shoes, tin, 2" l 40.00
Smile... 50.00
Twinkle Shoes, 1-7/8" l 80.00
Weatherbird Shoes, 1-3/4" l.... 27.50
Weston's 38.00

❖ Clocks

Tick-tock. Collectors have been enjoying clock collecting for decades. Some have specialized and seek particular manufacturers or types of clocks. Buyers should carefully examine a clock to determine if it's in working order. Missing parts may add considerable expense to the purchase price.

Reference: Robert and Harriet Swedberg, *Price Guide to Antique Clocks,* Krause Publications, 1998.

Periodicals: *Clocks,* 4314 W 238th St, Torrance, CA 90505.

Collectors' Club: National Association of Watch and Clock Collectors, Inc, 514 Poplar St, Columbia, PA 17512.

For additional listings, see *Warman's Antiques and Collectibles Price Guide* and *Warman's Americana & Collectibles.*

Advertising
  Purina Poultry Chows, electric, 3
    dials, red, white and blue
    checkered bag style,
    alarm 45.00
  Rexall, wooden Seth Thomas
    clock, 1954 Rexall Award of
    Merit, small mortar and pestle
    at top, 23" h......................50.00

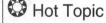

For exciting collecting trends and newly expanded areas look for the following symbols:

✪ Hot Topic

✯ New Warman's Listing

(May have been in another Warman's edition.)

Animated
  Ballerina, music box,
    United........................... 150.00
  Fireplace, Mastercrafter's. 125.00
  Grandmother, rocking chair,
    Haddon......................... 190.00
  Spinning Wheel, Lux 85.00
Ansonia, carriage,
  metamorphic...................... 28.00
Electric, Cincinnati Reds, logo,
  wood frame, 1940s............. 65.00
Marshall Fields, mantel........... 65.00
Seth Thomas, beehive, 5" h, 4 jewel,
  mahogany case 55.00
Weatherstation, LL Bean, clock,
  thermometer, hygrometer, moon-
  phase, oak jointed round case,
  11-3/4" d, bezel................... 75.00

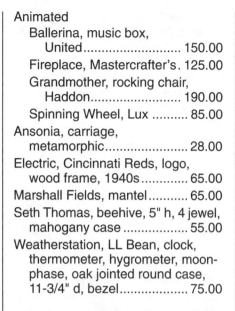

Panasonic model RC-1091 clock radio, yellow plastic case, 5-1/2" h, $12.50.

Figural fireplace clock, electric, wooden hearth, United Clock Corp., 8-1/2" h, 10-1/4" w, 3" d, $80.

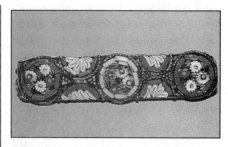

Bar pin, 1-15/16" l, $30.

❖ Cloisonné

Cloisonné is an interesting technique where small wires are adhered to a metal surface and then the design filled in with enamel, creating a very colorful design. The more intricate the design, the enameling, or the older the piece, the higher the price can be.

Collectors' Club: Cloisonné Collectors Club, PO Box 96, Rockport, MA 01966.

For additional listings, see *Warman's Antiques and Collectibles Price Guide.*

Reproduction Alert.

Box, 2" x 3"...........................100.00
Button, red ground, multicolored
  design, 1-1/4" d..................25.00
Charger, roosters and floral dec,
  black ground, Chinese, late 19th
  C, surface scratches,
  14" d 190.00
Cigarette Case, green, 3 dragons,
  Chinese...........................175.00
Cross Pendant, blue ground, rose
  and white dec, Russian
  hallmarks 150.00
Vase, dark colors, wide rust band,
  small flowers, bird in flight,
  Japanese, 8-1/2" h...........235.00

✯ ✪ Clothes Sprinklers

Here's a part of the flea market world that has taken off. Who would have ever thought that Grandma's way of preparing ironing would ever be so popular with collectors? Because many of these handy sprinklers are figural, they make a great display.

Chinese Man, ceramic
  Blue and white.....................45.00
  Green and yellow 35.00
Dutch Boy, ceramic,
  8-1/4" h............................ 295.00
Elephant, ceramic
  Pink and gray 135.00
  White 110.00
Glass, clear recycled bottle, black rubber and tin stopper top 5.00
Mammy, ceramic, white dress,
  7" h.................................. 495.00
Merry Maid, plastic, mkd "Made in USA"..................... 15.00
Nude Baby Boy, "Guess What I Am," bisque, back incised "G501F Germany," c1930,
  8-1/2" h............................. 395.00
Sprinkle Plenty....................... 45.00

❖ Clothing

As fashions change from year to year, collecting vintage clothing never seems to go out of style. Many clothing collectors look for prestigious labels as well as garments that are in good condition.

Collectors' Clubs: The Costume Society of America, PO Box 73, Earleville, MD 21919; Vintage Fashion and Costume Jewelry Club, PO Box 265, Glen Oaks, NY 11004.

For additional listings, see *Warman's Antiques and Collectibles Price Guide* and *Warman's Americana & Collectibles*.

Bathing Suit, girl's, cotton print, ruffles, 1950s......................... 15.00
Bed Jacket, satin, pink, ecru lace trim, labeled "B. Altman & Co. NY," 1930s......................... 35.00
Blouse
  Beaded taffeta, black, black glass beads at yoke, hand sewn...............................90.00
  Cotton, white, Victorian cutwork...........................25.00

Bridesmaid's Gown, pink chiffon, satin ribbon trim, size 10..... 50.00
Cape, mohair, black, ankle length, c1930............................. 90.00
Christening Gown, cotton, white, lace trim, matching bonnet,
  47" l 115.00
Coat
  Boy's, linen, hand stitched, dec cuffs........................ 35.00
  Lady's, Persian Lamp, black, matching hat and muff.... 95.00
Dress
  Girl's, georgette and chiffon, pink, c1920 .... 75.00
  Lady's, black satin, 1920s .. 90.00
Pajamas, lady's, silk, red,
  1920s................................. 75.00
Pants Suit, top and palazzo pants, Andrea Gayle, bright green, orange, yellow, pink, gray, and purple satiny material,
  2 pc.................................... 65.00
Skirt, lady's, black wool, Victorian............................. 45.00
Suit
  Boy's, navy wool blazer, short pants, orig Tom Sawyer brand 45.00

Child's bib overalls, blue and white, unused, original "Size 2" paper tag, $8.

Lady's, linen, straight skirt, jacket with shoulder pads and fitted waist, English 70.00
Man's, black garbardine, jacket, vest, trousers, size 42, c1940............................. 50.00
Wedding Gown, satin, ivory, padded shoulders, sweetheart neckline, waist swag, self train, c1940 .... 140.00

❖ Clothing Accessories

Clothing accents and accessories are perhaps more collectible than vintage clothing. Perhaps this is because many of these accessories are just as fun to use today as when they were originally created. And, like with vintage clothing, with proper care and handling, it's perfectly acceptable to use these collectibles.

References: Roselyn Gerson, *Vintage & Contemporary Purse Accessories*, Collector Books, 1997; ——, *Vintage Ladies Compacts,* Collector Books, 1996; ——,*Vintage Vanity Bags and Purses*, Collector Books, 1994, 1997 value update; Michael Jay Goldberg, *The Ties That Bind, Neckties,* Schiffer Publishing, 1997; Susan Langley, *Vintage Hats & Bonnets, 1770-1970,* Collector Books, 1997; J. J. Murphy, *Children's Handkerchiefs,* Schiffer Publishing, 1998.

Periodicals: *Glass Slipper,* 653 S Orange Ave, Sarasota, FL 34236; *Lady's Gallery,* PO Box 1761, Independence, MO 64055; *Lill's Vintage Clothing Newsletter,* 19 Jamestown Dr, Cincinnati, OH 45241; *The Vintage Connection,* 904 N. 65th St., Springfield, OR 97478; *Vintage Clothing Newsletter,* PO Box 88892, Seattle, WA 98138; *Vintage Gazette,* 194 Amity St, Amherst, MA 01002.

Collectors' Clubs: The Costume Society of America, PO Box 73, Earleville, MD 21919; Vintage Fashion and Costume Jewelry Club, PO Box 265, Glen Oaks, NY 11004.

Beatles necktie, $30.

For additional listings, see *Warman's Antiques and Collectibles Price Guide,* and *Warman's Americana & Collectibles.*

Apron, child's, pink, lace and silk ribbons, 24" x 14" 70.00

Baby Bonnet, white cotton, pink ribbon ties, c1960 .... 10.00

Collar, beaded and fur, white, early 1950s 10.00

Gloves, lady's, satin, long, white 20.00

Handkerchief
 Child's, Little Miss Muffet, sq 20.00
 Lady's, lace edge 10.00
 Man's, monogrammed, silk 5.00

Muff
 Child's, white rabbit fur 25.00
 Lady's, dark brown sable fur, hand crocheted liner 35.00

Shawl, paisley, dark background, long fringe, small holes 70.00

Stole, marabou, white 50.00

Sweater, child's, hand knit, train on back 30.00

Teddy, yellow, pink emb trim on bodice, 1920s 25.00

Tie, hp scene of New York harbor, 1940s 12.00

Yoke, crocheted, ribbon trim... 15.00

✩ Cobalt Blue Glassware Items

Blue has always been a favorite color for interior decorating. Today there is a bit of a resurgence in the popularity of cobalt blue glassware items. A quick tip to tell the age of cobalt glass is the "greasy fingers test"—try rubbing your fingertips over the surface of a piece. If you get a slightly greasy feeling or leave behind streaks on the glass, it's a modern creation.

Animal Dish, cov, hen on nest, Kemple Glass 15.00

Bell, figural handle of man, 6" h 18.00

Bottle, violin shape.................. 12.00

Cocktail Shaker Set, dumbbell-shaped shaker, chrome lid, four cone-shaped tumblers, West Virginia Specialty Co............. 200.00

Paperweight, apple shape, cobalt blue crackle glass body, hand blown, hand applied crystal stem and leaf, Blenko Glass Co., 6" h, 3-1/2" w 65.00

Plate, 3 bunnies at top, Westmoreland Glass Co. 15.00

Rose Bowl, white stripes and white edging............................. 20.00

Water pitcher, Hazel Atlas, ribbed ball shape, 6-1/2" h, $45.

Tumbler, 5" h, white frosted design, "Atlantic City," with skyline, ocean, and hotels 45.00

❖ Coca-Cola

Coca-Cola was invented by John Pemberton, an Atlanta, GA, pharmacist in 1886. First introduced as a patent medicine, it became a popular soft drink in the 1890s. Many advertising items were issued with "Coca-Cola," but the first to use the nickname "Coke" didn't appear until 1941.

References: Bob and Debra Henrich, *Coca-Cola Commemorative Bottles,* Collector Books, 1998; Allan Petretti, *Petretti's Coca-Cola Collectibles Price Guide*, 10th ed., Antique Trader Books, 1997; Allan Petretti and Christ Beyer, *Classic Coca-Cola Serving Trays,* Antique Trader Books, 1998; B. J. Summers, *B. J. Summers' Guide to Coca-Cola*, Collector Books, 1996; Al and Helen Wilson, *Wilson's Coca-Cola Guide*, Schiffer Publishing, 1997.

Collectors' Club: Cavanagh's Coca-Cola Christmas Collector's Society, 1000 Holcomb Woods Parkway, Suite 440B, Roswell, GA 30076; Coca-Cola Collectors Club, 400 Monemar Ave., Baltimore, MD 21228-5213; Coca-Cola Collectors Club International, PO Box 49166, Atlanta, GA 30359-1166.

For additional listings, see *Warman's Antiques and Collectibles Price Guide* and *Warman's Americana & Collectibles.*

Reproduction Alert.

Advertisement, picture of Eddie Fisher.................................. 8.00

Blotter, 3-1/2" x 7-1/2" stiff paper, colorful graphics of smiling Coca-Cola Sprite elf digging bottle of Coke out of snow bank, copyright 1953 Coca-Cola Co. 10.00

Book, *Portrait of a Business,* 1961, autographed by W. G. Kurtz 75.00

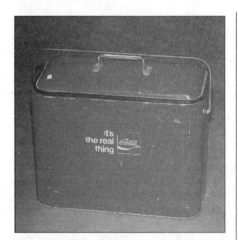

Picnic cooler, "it's the real thing," 16" h, 18" w, 8-1/2" d, some wear, $75.

Book Cover, 10" x 14", dark green stiff paper, advertising "Safety A.B.C.'s" motif in brown and red, copyright 1940, unfolded 5.00

Bottle, Dodgers/Jackie Robinson, 50th Anniversary, full 20.00

Bottle Carrier, 12 bottles, aluminum, red graphics front and back, 16" l, c1950 .... 125.00

Broadside, 30" h, 22" w, shows four different variations of Coca-Cola carriers, 1922, 1929, 1935, and 1939 models, black on white, fold marks 35.00

Calendar Panel, 22" h, 13" w, 1947 January/February, pretty girl with skis 25.00

Cooler, 12" h, 18" l, 8-1/2" d, metal, wire carrying handle, orig red paint scratched 100.00

Playing cards, 1994, double deck in collector's tin, 4-3/8" x 5-3/4", $5.

Blotter, 1953, 3-1/2" x 7-9/16", $12.

Coupon, 5-1/2" x 6-1/2", postcard type, stiff paper sheet, perforated for tearing apart, red, white, and dark green illus of carton of Coke, fleshtone hand, top half with full color "Take Home A Carton" with young lady, sponsored by Coca-Cola Bottling Works, Ft. Wayne, IN, c1930 .... 15.00

Dominoes............................... 15.00

Door Push, 31-1/2" h, 3" w, porcelain, Canadian 100.00

Figure, polar bear, ceramic 15.00

Serving Tray, 10-1/2" x 13-1/2" x 1", tin litho, pretty girl in restaurant booth holding bottle of Coke, color cartoon art of outdoor activities on rim, mid-1950s 85.00

Sign
    Candy Express, 1960s, plastic, clown illus....................... 45.00
    Friendly Pause, three teens, c1948, cardboard, 27" h, 16" w, poor condition................. 70.00

Tip Tray, 4-1/2" d, tin litho, smiling pretty girl, wearing embroidered hat, rose accents, pink dress, pink shawl, dark green background, red letters "Coca-Cola," green and gold accent rim, Passaic Metalware Co., NJ, 1914 .... 220.00

Toy, Junior Coca-Cola Truck, Corgi 35.00

Tray, 1930, summer scene ... 300.00

❖ Cocktail Shakers

"Make mine a dry martini," was the plea of many well-heeled party guests we gazed at in the movies. To make that perfect drink, a clever device called the cocktail shaker was used. Today these shakers are finding their way to flea markets and collectors.

Reference: Stephen Visakay, *Vintage Bar Ware,* Collector Books, 1997.

Pitcher type, chrome top, catalin finial, green glass body, self feet 120.00

Set, chrome, chrome cocktail shaker, matching tray, etched designs, center medallion, black composite handle, 4 cocktails with flared bowls 120.00

Set, glass
    Black, Call of the Wild sterling silver overlay, 4 ftd cups, Lotus Glass, c1934 .... 450.00
    Golfer motif, silver overlay, six cups, Czechoslovakia 1,000.00
    Ribbed, clear, chrome top, six matching glasses............ 60.00

Glass, 3 frosted panels, aluminum lid, 8" h, $30.

Spiral design, 22 oz shaker, built-in strainer, chrome lid, four glasses, chrome tray with wooden handles, silk-screened "Professional Cocktails" and "Cheers/Here's How" in six different languages........................... 45.00

Shaker

  Chrome, Farberware, incised bands, 13-1/2" h..............50.00

  Chrome, penguin shape....400.00

  Glass, silk-screened American and Foreign gold coins, brass lid, 12-1/4" h....................40.00

  Glass, silk-screened French waiter, policeman, poodle, ballerina, 12 drink recipes, 9-1/2" h 45.00

❖ Coffee Mills

The secret to a really great cup of coffee has always been freshly ground coffee beans. Today's collectors are discovering this is still the case, and with the current popularity of coffee, perhaps we'll see an increase in coffee mills.

Collectors' Club: Association of Coffee Mill Enthusiasts, 657 Old Mountain Road, Marietta, GA 30064.

Arcade #4, crystal................. 250.00
Arcade, telephone style........ 800.00

Maple dovetailed case, cast-iron works with Victorian decor, wooden handle, 9" h, $95.

Enterprise #0 .... 100.00
Enterprise #1 .... 500.00
Enterprise #12 .... 1,000.00
Fairbanks Morse #7 .... 800.00
National Specialty, single wheel..................... 850.00
Right, double wheel 275.00
Swift Lane Bros, #12............ 750.00
Wright, double wheel 275.00

❖ ⊚ Coffee Tins

Here's one of the advertising categories that has gotten hot over the last few years. Collected for their colorful labels, these tins are found in many sizes and shapes.

Anchor Coffee, 1 lb 25.00
Bowers Bros. Coffee, Richmond, VA, round, large, emb top 50.00

Chase & Sanborn Coffee, tin, 1 lb, $10.

Blue Flame Coffee, paper label, 1 lb, $65.

Breakfast Call Coffee, round slip top, 3 lb.................... 125.00
Del Monte Coffee, key lid........45.00
Folger's Coffee, 5 lb, keywind.50.00
Gold Bond Coffee, 1 lb, screw top....................................35.00
Hersh's Best...........................70.00
King Cole 70.00
Luzianne Coffee, small size, Mammy illus........................95.00
Mammy Coffee, 4 lb size, Mammy illus...................................500.00
National's Best Blend, 1 lb, screw top....................................60.00
Red Rose, 1 lb, keywind 45.00
Sears Coffee Pail 200.00
Society Brand, tin litho, 2" h ..325.00
White House Coffee, 1 lb, tin vacuum pack, keywind......400.00

❖ Coin Ops & Trade Stimulators

Folks have been enchanted by getting something from a machine since the time a penny bought a piece of candy. Some machines told fortunes, others were games, while others were to help stimulate trade at a place of business. Because many of these machines have seen a lot of use, expect to find signs of wear and some repairs.

References: Richard M. Bueschel, *Collector's Guide to Vintage Coin Machines,* Schiffer Publishing, 1995; ——, *Guide to Vintage Trade Stimulators & Counter Games,* Schiffer Publishing, 1997; ——, *Lemons, Cherries and Bell-Fruit-Gum,* Royal Bell Books, 1995; ——, *Pinball 1,* Hoflin Publishing, 1988; ——, *Slots 1,* Hoflin Publishing, 1989.

Periodicals: *Always Jukin',* 221 Yesler Way, Seattle, WA 98104; *Antique Amusements Slot Machines & Jukebox Gazette,* 909 26th St NW, Washington, DC 20037; *Around the Vending Wheel,* 5417 Castana Ave, Lakewood, CA 90712; *Coin Drop International,* 5815 W 52nd Ave,

Denver, CO 80212; *Coin Machine Trader*, 569 Kansas SE, PO Box 602, Huron, SD 57350; *Coin-Op Classics*, 17844 Toiyabe St, Fountain Valley, CA 92708; *Coin Slot*, 4401 Zephyr St, Wheat Ridge, CO 80033; *Gameroom Magazine*, 1014 Mt Tabor Rd, New Albany, IN 47150; *Jukebox Collector*, 2545 SE 60th Street, Des Moines, IA 50317; *Loose Change*, 1515 S Commerce St, Las Vegas, NV 89102; *Pin Game Journal*, 31937 Olde Franklin Dr, Farmington, MI, 48334; *Scopitone Newsletter*, 810 Courtland Dr, Ballwin, MO 63021.

Collectors' Club: Bubble-Gum Charm Collectors, 24 Seafoam St, Staten Island, NY 10306.

Duck Hunter, 1¢, arcade, shoots
    penny at target for gum ball, ABT
    Silver King, c1949 .... 250.00
Fortune Telling, Waitling, scale,
    #400, 1948 .... 400.00
Marklin Phillies, cigars,
    1930s 150.00
Skill Game, Kicker/Catcher, 5¢, 3
    balls, Baker Mfg.,
    c1940 .... 400.00
Stamp Machine, Shipman,
    1960 .... 35.00
Tally-Ho, 5¢, wood rail pinball
    machine............................ 250.00
Zeno Gum, 1¢, wooden case dispensed sticks of gum,
    c1910 .... 600.00

❖ Coins, American and Foreign

Coin collecting has been a favorite pastime for generations. Coin collectors are very particular about the grading of their coins and have established very specific guidelines. Coin collectors do find treasures for the collections at flea markets, partially because they are so dedicated, but also because they usually are very educated collectors.

For more information about this fascinating hobby, check the following references and periodicals.

References: Krause Publications is the country's premier publisher of books on coins. The following are all excellent references by this publisher. Colin Bruce and George Cuhaj, *Standard Catalog of World Coins, 1601-1700*; Richard Doty, *America's Money-America's Story;* Dave Harper, *1999 North American Coins & Prices,* 8th ed.; Chester Krause and Clifford Mishler, ed. by Colin Bruce, *Standard Catalog of World Coins, 1801-1900*; Richard Lobel, Mark Davidson, Alan Hallistone and Eleni Caligas, *Coincraft's 1998 Standard Catalog of English & UK Coins, 1066 to Date;* N. Douglas Nicol, ed. by Colin Bruce, *Standard Catalog of German Coins, 1601-Present,* 2nd ed.; Jules Reiver, *The United States Early Silver Dol-*

Foreign, Republique Francaise, 2 francs, 1946, 50 cents.

American, 1923 Peace silver dollar, $8.50.

lars, 1794 to 1804; Wayne G. Sayles, *Ancient Coin Collecting V*; Bob Wilhite, *1998 Auction Prices Realized,* 17th ed.

Periodicals: *Coin Prices*, Krause Publications, 700 E. State St., Iola, WI 54990; *Numismatic News,* Krause Publications, 700 E. State St., Iola, WI 54990.

❖ College Collectibles

Flea markets are a great place to find new additions for those who collect college-related items. Most concentrate on memorabilia from their alma mater.

Ashtray, Old South Ball, Memphis
    State College, 1955 .... 20.00
Coloring Book, University of Florida
    Gators, 1982, unused 15.00
Etching, interior of Chapel at Univ of
    Chicago, by Leon R. Pescheret,
    framed................................ 60.00
Lunch Box, oval, graphics of colorful
    college pennants................. 16.00
Mascot, Baylor University, bear, hard
    rubber, 1950s...................... 20.00
Pennant
    Indiana University, red and white,
        30" l 12.00
    Iowa State, maroon and gold felt,
        23" l 12.00

University of Evansville printer's block, 2-3/16" sq, $12.50.

Plate

Alma College, Alma, MI, Vernon Kilns 30.00

Robinson Hall, Albion College, Albion, MI, Wedgwood, 10-1/4" d 45.00

Susanna Wesley Hall, Albion College, Albion, MI, Wedgwood, 10-1/4" d 45.00

Postcard

A and M College, campus scene, unused 1.00

Bruce Hall, Central College, Conway, AR, unused 3.00

Campus, University of Chicago, IL, 1926, unused 2.50

Main Hall, Rutgers University, NJ, 1946, unused 2.00

Meridian Senior High School-Junior College, Meridian, MS, unused 4.00

The Student Center, Douglass College, New Brunswick, NJ, used 2.00

Program, Rice University vs University of Houston, Sept 11, 1971 .... 100.00

Range Shakers, porcelain, Boston University logo, 3" h, pr 35.00

Ribbon, University Day, April 11, 1894, "California Midwinter International Exposition-University of California," tan, gold lettering, California seal in center...... 70.00

Textbook, *Food for the Family,* Wilmot and Batter, hardcover, c1938, some writing inside............. 30.00

Yearbook, Columbia, MO, 1944 .... 15.00

❖ ⊙ Coloring & Activity Books

Here's another collecting area that is currently pretty hot. Coloring and paint books started in the early 1900s but didn't really catch on until the 1930s, when manufacturers started to introduce coloring books based on child stars such as Shirley Temple. Most collectors seek uncolored books, but some will buy books with neatly executed work.

Alf, 30 pages, Spanish text, 1989, unused..................... 12.00

Christmas Cut-Out and Coloring Book, illus by Florence Sarah Winship, Santa wearing flocked hat on cover, 1954, 15" x 11", unused................................ 35.00

Dumbo Press-Out Book............ 6.00

Esso/Humble, *The Tiger in the Tank*, 7-1/2" x 8-1/2", giveaway booklet, 16 pgs, tiger-related cartoon form coloring pages, full color art on cover, early 1970s, unused................................ 35.00

GI Joe, 16 pgs, Spanish text, 1990, unused................................ 12.00

Henry, 1956, one page colored 30.00

Lady and the Tramp Sticker Activity Book, unused 6.00

Mr. Peanuts, 12 months.......... 12.00

Pinocchio 20.00

Planet of the Apes, Artcraft, authorized edition, Apjac Productions, Twentieth Century Fox Film Corp., some pages colored............................... 20.00

Oh Susanna, Children's Musical Pack O'Fun, coloring book, punch-out toys, story book, unbreakable record, caricatures of black family, 1950s 95.00

Sambo's Restaurant *Family Funbook Activity Book*, 1978, unused............................... 42.00

Trace and Color, Merrill Company Publishers, 1962, 10-7/8" x 8-1/8", $3.

Spider-Man, 16 pgs................. 12.00

The Love Bug, Hunt's Food promotional, 1969, full page promo on back cover, unused.............20.00

ThunderCats, red cover, printed in Mexico, 1989, unused.........15.00

Winnie Winkle, copyright 1953....................................75.00

☆ Comedian Collectibles

Those who can make us laugh seem to find a way to our hearts. Some collectors are now choosing to concentrate on these folks and are having a great time doing it.

Also check Autographs, Character Collectibles, Movie Collectibles, etc. in this edition.

Autograph, pin mounted with photo, autographed card, nicely matted, Phyllis Diller, from "Traveling Saleslady" 40.00

Book

Don't Shoot, It's Only Me: Bob Hope's Comedy History of the United States, Bob Hope, Putnam, 1990, 315 pgs, used................................ 7.50

The Odd Couple, Neil Simon, 1966, 116 pgs................ 12.50

Colorforms Set, Three Stooges, 1959, MIB 270.00

Coloring Book, Bob Hope, Saalfield, unused 18.00

Coloring Kit, Laurel and Hardy, Transogram, Larry Harmon Pictures Corp copyright, 1962, unused 28.00

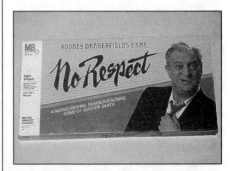

No Respect board game, Rodney Dangerfield, Milton Bradley, $7.50.

For exciting collecting trends and newly expanded areas look for the following symbols:

⊙ Hot Topic

☆ New Warman's Listing

(May have been in another Warman's edition.)

Comic Book, Jackie Gleason & The Honeymooners, #2 .... 35.00
Cookie Jar, I Love Lucy 100.00
Doll, Three Stooges, set of 3, 1980s 150.00
Game, Laurel and Hardy, Transogram, 1962 copyright...... 42.50
Notebook Binder, Laugh-In, 1969 .... 20.00
Pinback Button, Maryland Theater Komedy Klub, 1" d, blue letters, white ground, showing Mary Ann Jackson from Our Gang 45.00
Puppet, Jerry Lewis, 9" h, fabric, soft vinyl head, c1950 .... 55.00
Record Album, George Gobel, Decca, In Person at the Sands, LP 75.00
Salt and Pepper Shakers, pr, Three Stooges 20.00
Teapot, Lucille Ball.................. 45.00
Toy, Jackie Gleason, Away We Go, Reggie Van Gleason III, mint on card, 1950s 115.00
Waste Basket, Laugh-In, litho with show characters 45.00

❖ Comic Books

Comic Books date back to the 1890s when newspapers started to print their popular funnies strips in book form. By the late 1930s, comic book manufacturers were producing all kinds of tales to delight young readers. Through the years, the artwork found in comic books has gotten more and more sophisticated and many collectors now specialize in a particular artist or maker.

This is one of those topics where collectors have learned to rely on good reference books. We've listed a few of the current publications here, but more exist. Pay particular attention to the condition of a comic book, any damage will severely decrease value.

References: *Comics Buyer's Guide Annual*, Krause Publications, issued annually; Dick Lupoff and Don Thompson (eds.), *All in Color for a Dime*, Krause Publications, 1997; Alex G. Malloy, *Comics Values Annual 1998*, Antique Trader Books, 1997; Robert M. Overstreet, *Overstreet Comic Book Price Guide*, 27th ed., Avon Books, 1997; Maggie Thompson and Brent Frankenhoff, *Comic Book Checklist & Price Guide*, 4th ed., Krause Publications, 1997.

Periodical: *Comics Buyer's Guide*, 700 E State St, Iola, WI 54990.

Collectors' Clubs: American Comics Exchange, 351-T Baldwin Rd, Hempstead, NY 11550; Fawcett Collectors of America & Magazine Enterprise, too!, 301 E Buena Vista Ave, North Augusta, SC 29841.

Reproduction Alert.

Battlestar Galactica, 1978, 10" x 13-1/2" 15.00
Bewitched, #8 .... 3.75
Blondie, 1972, 14" x 11".......... 15.00
Crime Reporter, #2 .... 68.00
Daredevil, Oct, #114 .... 10.00
Fightin' Marines, #15 .... 5.00
Frankenstein, Classics Illustrated, #6 .... 4.50
Get Smart, #5 .... 5.00
Henry, 1971, 14" x 11" 15.00
Jim Ray's Aviation Sketchbook, Vol. 1, No. 2, 1946, ink stain, yellowed pgs, 10" x 7" 15.00
Jungle Adventures, #3 .... 2.00
Katy Keene, #45 .... 12.50
Mister Miracle, June, #2............ 9.00
Oliver Twist, Classics Illustrated, #17 .... 2.00
Red Ryder, Frame-Up, Dell, #133, August, 1954, slight wear ... 18.00
Sherlock Holmes, Classics Illustrated, #2 .... 40.00
Sleeping Beauty, Walt Disney, #1 .... 20.00
Spider-Man, 1974, 14" x 11" ... 15.00
Star Wars Galaxy, Dark Horse Special, Fall, 1984, premier issue, factory sealed, cards and comic book.................................... 12.50

The New Adventures of Superboy, DC Comics, Vol. 1 No. 8, Aug. 1980, worn, 50 cents.

Super Heroes, #4 .... 2.50
The Ghost in the Lady's Boudoir, Consolidated Book Publishers, 1945................................... 38.00
Woody Woodpecker, #194, copyright 1981, some wear 4.00
Zebra Jungle Empress, #1 ......22.00

❖ Commemorative Glasses

Decorative drinking glasses have always been a popular way to commemorate a special event or place.

Airplane, single propeller, green images of early planes, 1940s................................... 16.00
Florida, hard plastic, hand painted, c1950
   2-1/2" h, flamingo dec......... 10.00
   3-1/2" h, flamingo dec, mkd "ACM Rogers Plastic Warren, Mass".............................. 15.00
Lord's Prayer, etched on clear glass 20.00

Glass, emb "Walt Disney World, Remember the Magic," paper tag "McDonald's Celebrates the Magic of Walt Disney World," 25th anniversary, 5" h, $3.

Midwinter Fair, 1894, ruby stained
   Etched "B.F.V.B.," hp
      flowers 95.00
   Etched "Edward Doyle" 110.00
Niagara Falls, Prospect Point, gold
   rim 20.00
The Alamo, San Antonio, TX, three
   portraits 18.00
Whittier's Birthplace, etched,
   waisted tumbler 60.00

❖ Commemorative Medals

Commemorative medals are collected by type, subject matter, and maker. Collectors look for unusual examples and prefer those in very good condition.

Information on medal collecting is often found in coin references. Medals are often handled by coin dealers.

American Legion
   Circular, bronze and enamel,
      1-1/4" d 8.00

"Liliuokalani Queen of Hawaii 1891-1893 / Last Royal Ruler, 75th Anniversary, Hawaii State Numismatic Association," 1-1/2" d, $7.

With attached pinback button,
   "12th Grand Promenade,
   Camden, NJ, 1932" 12.00
Junior Baseball District Champs,
   American Legion,
   1-1/4" d 35.00
Knights of Pythias, medal with bar
   pin, "Conn Lodge 37," name on
   back 38.00
Kodak Movie Awards, bronze, by
   Medallic Art Co., NY, reads
   "Sponsored in Cooperation with
   UFF/UFPA and CINE,"
   3" d 19.00
Military
   Armed Forces Reserve, ribbon
      bar and pin, 1-1/4" d medal,
      MOC 28.00
   Cross with eagle, "1917-1918
      United States Forces," back
      reads "Presented by the peo-
      ple of Williamsburg, Mass to
      (blank for name) in grateful
      recognition of patriotic service
      in the World War 1917-1918,"
      1-1/4" x 1-1/4" 35.00
   Drill Corps 1944 on bar pin,
      medal reads "York Comy, New
      York, S. J. Ecker,"
      sterling 28.00
   Efficiency, Honor, Fidelity, back
      reads "For Good Conduct,"
      name inscribed 16.00
   For Merit, Army Air Forces, bar
      pin with medal, sterling... 35.00

   For Merit, 500 Hours, Army Air
      Forces, bar pin with medal,
      sterling 38.00
   For Merit, 1000 Hours, Army Air
      Forces, bar pin with medal,
      sterling 38.00
   Heroic or Meritorious Achieve-
      ment, no name, ribbon ... 12.00

❖ Compacts & Purse Accessories

Ladies have been powdering their noses for years and using interesting compacts to perform this task. Today's collectors have many interesting shapes, materials, and makers to search for at flea markets.

References: Roselyn Gerson, *Ladies Compacts,* Wallace-Homestead, 1996; —, *Vintage and Contemporary Purse Accessories, Solid Perfumes, Lipsticks, & Mirrors,* Collector Books, 1997; —, *Vintage Ladies Compacts,* Collector Books, 1996; ——, *Vintage Vanity Bags and Purses: An Identification and Value Guide,* 1994, 1997 value update, Collector Books.

Collectors' Club: Compact Collectors Club, PO Box 40, Lynbrook, NY 11563.

For additional listings, see *Warman's Antiques and Collectibles Price Guide* and *Warman's Americana & Collectibles.*

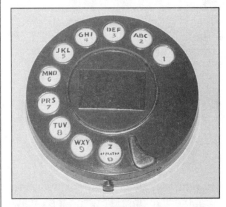

Phone Dial compact, burgundy enamel, 3-1/2" d, $140.

Coty, #405, envelope box 65.00
Djer Kiss, with fairy 95.00
Dorset, 3-1/8" sq, white, all over gold
    birds, flowers, and leaves, mkd
    "Dorset, Fifth Avenue," slight dis-
    coloration around edges..... 15.00
Dunhill, Mary, rouge............... 28.00
Elp Talcum, blue plastic box,
    unused 24.00
Flamingo Motif 90.00
German, 2-7/8" d, double mirror,
    couple in colonial dress, mkd
    "Made in West Germany," slight
    discoloration 10.00
Halston, SP, name on puff,
    used 150.00
Mondane Beauty Box, goldtone,
    rhinestone basket,
    3 reservoirs 125.00
Norida, emb lady, silver tone .. 75.00
Petit Point, 2-1/4" x 2-3/4", gold
    metal edge, red and yellow roses,
    blue flowers, green leaves, plain
    black petit point on back..... 15.00
Princess Pat, rouge and large puff,
    orig package...................... 20.00
Souvenir, Atlantic City, NJ, rouge
    compartment and puff 48.00
Timepact, enamel, black, elongated
    horseshoe shape, case and
    watch 190.00
V8, clear rhinestone perimeter, black
    enameled metal hinged lid, raised
    V8 symbol accented with rhine-
    stones, some orig powder, puff,
    little wear to case 95.00
Volupte, 2-7/8" sq, gold metal, top
    black, beaded bold edge, gold
    center medallion with shell-like
    raised edge, inlaid on gold leaves
    and rhinestone flowers, flannel
    case, orig Franklin Simon
    box 75.00
Whiting & Davis, vanity bag, silvered
    mesh, etched and engraved lid,
    braided carrying chain,
    1920s 425.00

❖ Computers & Computer Games

With the Y2K problem, many more computers might be finding their way to flea markets. Make sure you've got all the parts and as many original

Toshiba T1000 laptop, works, $55.

documents as possible when buying a computer on the secondary market.

Atari XL 800, additional
    modem 125.00
Miniature Game, Tetris,
    electronic...................... 18.50
Zenith, pc, 5-1/4" floppy drive,
    28K hard drive, working
    condition........................ 25.00

❖ Condiment Sets

Condiment or castor sets are useful tableware containers. Usually they contain salt and pepper shakers as well as mustard pots, perhaps bottles for vinegar, oil, etc. Early castor sets are found with pressed or cut glass bottles held in a silver frame and had matching tops and stoppers. China condiment sets became a little more whimsical.

Bellflower pattern, 5 clear pattern
    glass bottles, orig stoppers,
    pewter frame 325.00
Blue Willow, 6 china bottles,
    matching frame................. 150.00
Creased Bail, opaque rose milk
    glass, Dithridge, 4 pc........ 200.00
Cut Glass, 4 green cut to clear
    square bottles, SP frame.. 350.00
Hobnail, salt and pepper shakers,
    creamer, sugar, mustard, white
    milk glass, matching round tray
    with chrome loop handle 95.00

Castor set, 5 clear glass bottles, swirl design, 15-1/2" h, $165.

Pixieware, Holt Howard
    Mayonnaise 60.00
    Relish...................................55.00
Ruby Thumbprint pattern, 4 ruby
    stained bottles,
    glass frame 315.00

❖ Consolidated Glass Co.

Formed in 1893, Consolidated Glass produced interesting glassware and lamps until 1964 when a fire destroyed the plant. Some of the Consolidated patterns, such as Ruba Rombic and Dancing Nymph are highly sought by collectors. However, don't overlook some of the other interesting color combinations and shapes produced by this firm.

Collectors' Club: Phoenix and Consolidated Glass Collectors, PO Box 81974, Chicago, IL 60681.

For additional listings, see *Warman's Antiques and Collectibles Price Guide* and *Warman's Glass.*

Berry Bowl, master, Cone, pink, glossy, SP rim 115.00

Bowl, Catalonian, yellow, 9-1/2" d 48.00

Butter Dish, cov, Cosmos pattern, pink bands 200.00

Candlestick, Five Fruits, Martele, green 32.00

Celery Dish, two part, Ruba Rombic, smoky topaz 450.00

Cigarette Box, Catalonian, ruby flashed lid, crystal base 65.00

Cup and Saucer, Catalonian, green 265.00

Lamp, Dogwood, brown and white 140.00

Night Light, blown-out floral shade, silvered base, 10" h 660.00

Nut Dish, Ruba Rombic, smoky topaz 350.00

Pitcher, Cosmos pattern, 9" h 265.00

Puff Box, cov, Lovebirds, blue 115.00

Tumbler, Ruba Rombic, jade 325.00

Vase
    Hummingbird, #2588, turquoise on custard, 5-1/2" h 100.00
    Katydid, fan shape, white frosted body 172.00

❖ Construction Toys

Building toys have delighted children for many years. Today's collectors look for sets in original boxes with all the tools, vehicles, instructions, etc.

A. C. Gilbert
    Chemistry Experiment Lab, 3 pc metal box 35.00
    Erector Set, No. 4, complete, orig instructions 285.00

Mysto Erector set, No. 1, 1913, cardboard box, $500.

Erector Set No. 10181, Action Helicopter 80.00
American National Building Box, The White House, wood pieces, landscaping, orig wood box 120.00
Auburn Rubber, Building Bricks, 1940s 25.00
Embossing Company, No. 408, Jonnyville Blocks, deluxe edition, blocks, trees, hook and ladder, village plan 65.00
Halsman, American Plastic Bricks, #717 .... 45.00
Lego, Main Street Set, orig box and pcs, unused 120.00
Lincoln Logs, #25 .... 75.00
Tinkertoy, box with odd parts and pieces 10.00

❖ Cookbooks and Recipe Leaflets

Whether you're whipping up a cake or a gourmet meal, you might need a cookbook. Collectors have long treasured these books and leaflets promoting different household products. Today new collectors are eager to find those with advertising or displays that show depression glass, etc.

Periodicals: *Cook Book,* PO Box 88, Steuben, ME 04680; *Cookbook Collector Exchange,* PO Box 32369, San Jose, CA 95152-2369; *Cook Book Gossip,* PO Box 56, St. James, MO 65559; *Old Cookbook News & Views,* 4756 Terrace Drive, San Diego, CA 92116-2514.

***Good Things to Eat**, Arm & Hammer Baking Soda, 79th ed, 1924, 5-11/16" x 3-1/2", $7.50.*

Collectors' Club: Cook Book Collectors Club of America, PO Box 56, St. James, MO 65559.

Any One Can Bake, Royal Baking Powder, 1929, 100 pgs 10.00
Betty Crocker's Cooky Carnival, Gold Medal Flour adv, 1957, used 15.00
Betty Crocker's Picture Cook Book, McGraw-Hill, 1950, 1st ed., 9th printing, 463 pgs 18.50
Cutco Cutlery, 1961, 128 pgs, hardback, 8-1/2" x 5-1/2" 3.00
Dainty Junkets, 32 pgs, 1915 .... 18.00
Everyday French Cooking for the American Home, Henry Paul Pellaprat, 1968, 562 pgs, dj 22.00
Great Italian Cooking, Luigi Carnacina, Abradale Press, 851 pgs, dj 30.00
Hershey's Index Recipe Book, 1934 .... 12.00
Luchow's German Cookbook-Famous Restaurant in NY, Jan Mitchell, 1960, 224 pgs, book club edition 9.50
Pillsbury Family Cookbook, 1863 .... 12.00

Rawleigh's Good Health Guide Almanac Cookbook, 1951, 31 pages 18.00

Shumway's Canning Recipes, booklet form 5.00

The Cooking of China, Food of the World, Emily Hawn, 1968, Time-Life Books 9.50

The Poultry Cookbook, Southern Living Cookbook Library, 1977, 192 pgs 9.50

The Soup and Sandwich Handbook, Campbell Soups, thermal mug on cover, 1971......................... 12.00

The White House Chef Cookbook, Rene Verdon, 1968 .... 7.50

❖ Cookie Cutters

Cookie cutters may be found in several different kinds of metal and plastic. Look for cutters in good condition, free of rust and crumbs. The prices listed below are for tin or aluminum figural cookie cutters.

Periodicals: *Around Ohio,* 508 N. Clinton, Defiance, OH 43512; *Cookie Crumbs,* 1167 Teal Road, S. W., Dellroy, OH 44620; *Cookies,* 9610 Greenview Lane, Manassas, VA 20109-3320.

Collectors' Club: Cookie Cutters Club, 1167 Teal Road, S. W., Dellroy, OH 44620.

Biscuit, red wood handle, 2-3/4" d............................... 10.50

Bunny, 2-5/8" l, 1920s............. 22.50

Chicken, 2" w x 2" h, 1920s.... 22.50

Club, green wood handle, 2-3/4" d................................ 7.50

Cowboy, gingerbread type, 6" h, stamped design, aluminum........................... 15.00

Elephant, orig box mkd "Campaign Cookie Cutter-Vote Republican" 50.00

Flower, red wood handle, 2-1/2" d.............................. 10.00

Lion, green wood handle, 4-1/2" l............................... 22.50

Rabbit, green wood handle, 4" l....................................... 12.50

Reindeer, tin, 3" l 12.00

Rabbit, aluminum with green metal handle, 4-1/8" l, $2.

Santa, green wood knob......... 15.00

Squirrel, soldered handle, used.................................. 10.00

Star, tin, 2" l............................. 6.50

Turkey, tin, 2" l 8.50

❖ Cookie Jars

Cookie jars have been a highly-desirable collectible for years. Today more and more cookie jars are appearing at flea markets, some new, some vintage. If you're looking for new jars, check for a signature by the artist or the company's mark and (the original box will add to the value). If vintage jars are more your interest, check for signs of use and damage.

Periodicals: *Cookie Jar Collectors Express,* PO Box 221, Mayview, MO 64071-0221; *Cookie Jarrin',* RR2, Box 504, Walterboro, SC 29488-9278; *Crazed Over Cookie Jars,* PO Box 254, Savanna, IL 61074.

Collectors' Club: Cookie Jar Club, PO Box 451005, Miami, FL 33245-1005.

For additional listings, see *Warman's Americana & Collectibles.*

Animanics 80.00

Basket, brown, lemons 20.00

Bear with night cap, blue striped shirt.................................... 20.00

Blue Bonnet Sue..................... 40.00

Bugs Bunny 40.00

Buzz Lightyear, Treasure Craft.................................. 225.00

McCoy covered wagon, 10-1/2" l, $100.

Cactus, wearing bandana and cowboy hat, Treasure Craft 50.00

Cathy, Papel............................ 75.00

Chef, American Bisque 90.00

Chef, RRP 10.00

Curious George....................... 50.00

Elvis, in car............................. 100.00

Felix 50.00

Flintstones.............................. 50.00

Foghorn Leghorn 50.00

Handy Harry, Pfaltzgraff 185.00

I Love Lucy............................. 100.00

James Dean............................ 50.00

Magilla Gorilla, Twin Winton.. 275.00

Marilyn Monroe 50.00

Marvin Martian 50.00

Maxine 60.00

Michael Jordan Space Jam.... 175.00

Mrs. Potts............................... 35.00

Olympics, Warner Bros, 1996.... 75.00

101 Dalmatians 40.00

Pillsbury Funfetti 45.00

Pink Panther, Treasure Craft ... 125.00

Quaker Oats, 120th Anniversary........................ 70.00

Ranger Bear with Badge, Twin Winton, mkd "Code #84" 60.00

Sailor Boy, Shawnee Commemorative, limited to 100 jars, designed by S. A. Corl, produced by Mark Supnick, 1992, black hair... 495.00

Smokey Bear, 50th Anniversary...................... 275.00

Smiley Pig, unmarked Shawnee, 11-1/4" h, $325.

Socks, White House Cat......... 40.00
Superman 85.00
Sylvester and Tweety,
    Applause 55.00
Three Stooges........................ 50.00
Troll, Norlin 55.00
Uncle Sam, American Cookie
    Jar Co.............................. 150.00
Yosemite Sam 40.00
Wile Coyote 40.00

❖ Cooper, Susie

This English designer founded her own pottery in 1932. Her designs were bright and innovative.

Collectors' Club: Susie Cooper Collectors Group, PO Box 7436, London N12 7GF UK.

For additional listings, see *Warman's English & Continental Pottery & Porcelain.*

Coffeepot, Dresden Spray 150.00
Cup and Saucer
    Dresden Spray 90.00
    Orchid..................................85.00

Fruit Bowl, hp florals 185.00
Jug, gray-green, incised leaping
    rams 90.00
Place Setting, plate, cup and saucer,
    polka dot............................. 35.00
Plate
    Apple 42.00
    Tigerlily 32.00
Soup Bowl, Dresden Spray..... 18.00

❖ Coors Pottery

Founded in Golden, Colorado, Coors Pottery produced industrial, chemical, and scientific porcelain wares at first. They then developed a household cooking ware and, later, six dinnerware lines. The company went out of business in the early 1940s, lasting for only 30 years.

Periodical: *Coors Pottery Newsletter,* 3808 Carr Place, N. Seattle, WA 98103.

Batter Jug
    Corrado, large 95.00
Rosebud, small 110.00
Bowl, cov, Rosebud 60.00
Cake Knife, Rosebud, maroon,
    yellow rosebud, green
    leaves 37.50
Cup and Saucer, Rosebud
    Blue 35.00
    Turquoise........................... 35.00
    White 50.00
    Yellow 35.00
Dish, cov, Rosebud, square.... 82.00
Gravy Boat, attached underplate,
    Mello-Tone, azure blue 30.00
Honey Pot, orig spoon,
    Rosebud 350.00
Percolator 125.00
Pitcher, Mello-Tone, 2 qt,
    coral pink 30.00
Platter, Mello-Tone, oval, canary
    yellow 24.00
Teapot, large, Rosebud,
    rose 70.00

❖ Copper

Copper has long been a favored metal with craftsmen as it is relatively easy to work with and durable. Copper culinary items are lined with a thin protective coating of tin to prevent poisoning. It is not uncommon to find these items relined. Care should be taken to make sure the protective lining is intact before using any copper pots, etc. for domestic use.

Baking Pan, 11" d, turk's head,
    swirled design, worn
    tin lining.............................70.00
Bed Warmer, 38-1/2" l, engraved lid,
    wood handle, wrought iron ferule,
    European 75.00
Bowl, hand hammered, scrolled rim,
    brown patina, stamped "Harry
    Dixon San Francisco,"
    c1920.............................350.00
Colander, punched star design,
    10-3/4" d 80.00
Fish Poacher, cov, oval, rolled rim,
    iron swing bail handle, C-form
    handle on lid, 19th C.........350.00
Measure, haystack type, dovetailed
    construction, conical body, flared
    rim, tubular scroll handle, mkd
    "Anderson Brothers Makers Glasgow, 4 gallons,"
    19th C 170.00
Plate, 8" d, Yankee Doodle,
    1978...................................30.00
Tea Kettle, sturdy construction,
    swivel handle, stamped "1840,"
    8-1/4" h 65.00
Tray, rect, hammered, Dirk Van Erp,
    imp mark, orig patina with wear,
    14-1/2" x 9-3/4" 425.00

Pot, brass handle, 2-1/2" h, 4-7/8" d, $6.

✯ Costumes

Playing dress-up has always been fun for children. Collectors today enjoy finding vintage Halloween and other type of costumes. It's possible to find some very interesting costumes and accessories at flea markets.

Collectors' Club: The Costume Society of America, PO Box 73, Earleville, MD 21919.

Bat Masterson, orig box........ 140.00

Batman, display bag, vinyl cape, mask, cuffs, and badge, copyright 1966 National Periodical Publications...................... 120.00

Captain Action, cloth outfit, mask, knife, 2 pistols, skull, brass knuckles, holster and belt, rifle, boots, orig box, copyright 1966 Ideal Toy Corp. 225.00

Cowboy, child size
 Boots, Acme........................85.00
 Chaps..................................90.00
 Outfit, 4 pcs, 1960s 200.00
 Vest and Chaps, hide rosettes 150.00

Fred Flintstone, vinyl plastic mask and outfit, Ben Cooper, copyright 1973 Hanna-Barbera, orig box 40.00

Yoda mask/costume, Star Wars, The Empire Strikes Back, Ben Cooper, $17.50.

Matador, adult size, heavily embroidered, sequins and gold metallic thread, minor wear 120.00

Red Riding Hood, red cotton cape and skirt, yellow yarn braids sewn on hood, home made, c1950................................... 35.00

Star Wars, R2-D2, plastic mask, vinyl costume, Ben Cooper, copyright 1977, orig box............. 40.00

✯ Cottage Ware

Cottage Ware is the name given to charming English tea ware that is shaped like a cottage. You can find all the necessary pieces to serve a proper tea in this pattern. It is beginning to become quite popular with those who explore flea markets for that charming accent piece.

Biscuit Jar, wicker handle, Price Bros., 7-1/2" h..................... 95.00

Butter Dish, cov, Fox and Hounds pattern, Kensington Cottage Ware 165.00

Creamer and Sugar, brown, yellow, green, and pink, Ye Old Cottage, Made in England, ink stamp in wreath "Price Bros. Made in England, Cottage Ware, Reg. No. 845007" 120.00

Teapot, mkd "Keele St. Pottery Co. Ltd. England, handpainted," 6-1/4" h, 9" l, 4" w, $55.

Cup and Saucer, Price Bros....35.00

Jam Jar, cov, mkd "Kensington, England" 35.00

Milk Pitcher, mkd "Price Brothers, England," 7-1/4" h..............75.00

Teapot, brown, yellow, green, and pink, Ye Old Cottage, Made in England, ink stamp in wreath "Price Bros. Made in England, Cottage Ware, Reg. No. 845007"
 8" w, 5-1/2" h................. 100.00
 8-1/2" w, 6" h, slight crazing to glaze 90.00

✯ Counter Culture

"Cool, man." Whether you lived through the 1960s or just fantasize about that era of hippies and beatniks, collectors are starting to seek out those love beads and psychedelic things.

Lamp, smiley face, plastic, base 4-1/2" sq, $12.

Bolo Tie Medallion, star design, pink star, circles and checks shading from gray to light tan in background, Peter Max.............. 15.00

Book, *Psychedelic Pscounds,* Alan Vorde, interviews with psychedelic bands 30.00

Bumper Sticker, Save the Whales 1.00

Cigarette Holder, Beatnik, figural man or woman, orig cardboard and plastic pkg, Hong Kong, 1950s 40.00

Medallion, peace sign, bronzed metal 10.00

Mood Ring, adjustable band... 12.00

Pet Rock, MIB........................ 35.00

Pinback Button
    Feed Twiggy, black and white center photo, mkd "1967 Design Unlimited 1896 Pacific, S.F."................................20.00
    Go Mod, white lettering, deep pink background, 1970s, 2-1/4" d 10.00
    Jerry Garcia for President, 1980, 2-1/8" sq, black and white photo, yellow lettering 15.00

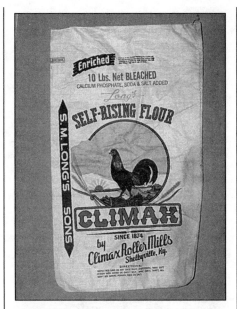

Climax flour sack, Climax Roller Mills, Shelbyville, Ky, cloth, stains, 17-1/4" x 10-1/4", $7.50.

Display
    Beechnut Gum, tin, 27-1/2" x 15-1/2", c1950, 3 tiers .. 130.00
    Chiclets Gum, 8" w, 10" l, box, glass top, mfg by Frank H. Fleer & Co., orig scalloped spoon 125.00
Lance Crackers, 3 metal wire shelves 55.00
Wrigley's Gum, wooden, counter type.................................. 250.00
Yeast Foam, tin, wall mounted, "Eat Yeast Foam" 27-1/2" h, 2-1/2" d 60.00

Mannequin
    Child 110.00
    Female 90.00
    Male.................................. 100.00
Scoop, 5", tin, wood handle 28.00
Sign, 11" x 23-1/4" l, emb metal litho over cardboard, red background, one side reads "5 Cent Window," other reads "10 Cent Counter," 1920s............................... 750.00
Spice Bin, 32" l, 10-3/4" d, twelve compartments, rolled front, names of different spices on front, beveled mirror at top 800.00
Store Tin, 12" h, front glass view window with stenciled adv on three sides, Hoarhound Lumps............................... 125.00

☆ Country Store Collectibles

Today we tend to think of old time store items as "Country Store" when, in reality, much of the memorabilia we collect was from small stores located in cities as well as country locales. These stores offered people a place to meet, stock up on supplies, and catch up on the latest gossip. They were filled with advertising, cases, cabinets, and all kinds of consumer goods.

Reference: Richard A. Penn, *Mom and Pop Stores,* R. S. Pennyfield's, 1998.

Bill Peg, 6-1/2" h..................... 15.00
Bin, Butter Cup Popcorn, round, paper label, snap top, nursery rhyme scenes, 10" h, 8" d .. 30.00
Cracker Bin, glass cover inside, solid outside lid, blue paint 50.00

☆ Country Western

Even if you've never been to Nashville, you've probably tapped your foot to a few country western tunes. Country Western collectors know their favorite stars and eagerly seek out memorabilia, autographs, as well as records, etc., relating to them. As the music industry continues to lure us, expect to find more and more country western collectibles at local flea markets.

Periodical: *Goldmine,* 700 E State St., Iola, WI 54990.

Album, LP
    Browns, RCA, Sweet Sounds 50.00
    Cash, Johnny, Sun, Hot & Blues Guitar............................ 100.00
    Harris, EmmyLou, Emus, Gliding Bird 50.00
    Lewis, Jerry Lee, Sun, Jerry Lee's Greatest..........................50.00
    Tubbs, Ernest, Decca, Golden Favorites........................60.00

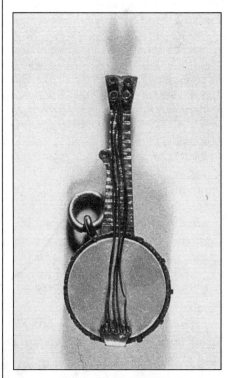

Watch fob, banjo, mother of pearl face, 1-5/8" l, $35.

Autograph, black and white glossy
photo, 8" x 10"
- Gill, Vince 35.00
- Judd, Wynona 40.00
- lang, k. d.............................42.00
- Parton, Dolly........................35.00

Book, *The Judds: A Biography,* Bob
Millard, Doubleday, 1988,
206 pgs 6.50

Compact Disc
- Chestnut, Mark, Summer Country
Concert, 8/98 Nashville 15.00
- Gill, Vince, The Key, album
premiere concert.............20.00
- McGraw, Tim, Summer Country
Concert, 8/97 ....15.00

T-Shirt, Garth Brooks, "The Hits,"
promo, face image and "Garth"
on front 35.00

❖ Cowan Pottery

Cowan Pottery encompasses both
utilitarian wares and artistic wares. R.
Guy Cowan started making pottery in
Ohio around 1915 and continued until
1931. Most pieces are marked with
an incised name. Later a black stamp
mark and initials were used.

For additional listings, see *Warman's Antiques and Collectibles Price Guide, Warman's Americana & Collectibles,* and *Warman's American Pottery and Porcelain Price Guide.*

Bookends, pr, Sunbonnet Girl, yellow glaze 245.00

Candlesticks, pr, sea horses,
green 75.00

Cigarette Holder, sea horse,
aqua 42.00

Compote, 2" h, diamond shape, tan
ext., green int. 38.00

Cup and Saucer, melon dec, tan
glaze.................................. 40.00

Plaque, plain, turquoise glaze,
11-1/2" d 220.00

Trivet, scalloped rim, bust of young
girl framed by flowers,
6-1/2" d............................. 325.00

Vase, fan shape, apple green, gold
specks, 5" h........................ 90.00

❖ Cowboy Heroes

Thought of mostly as matinee
heroes, some cowboy heroes got
their start in radio, and others tran-
scended to television. Many of
today's collectors specialize in one
character or show, but some are fascinated with all kinds of cowboy hero
memorabilia.

Reference: Jim and Nancy Schaut,
Collecting the Old West, Krause Publications, 1999.

Periodicals: *Collecting Hollywood,*
American Collectors Exchange, 2401
Broad St., Chattanooga, TN 37408;
Cowboy Collector Newsletter, PO
Box 7486, Long Beach, CA 90807;
Westerner, Box 5232-32, Vienna, WV
26105; *Westerns & Serials,* Route 1,
Box 103, Vernon Center, MN 56090.

For additional listings see *Warman's Americana & Collectibles* and
additional categories for specific cow-
boys in this edition.

Autograph, Ken Maynard, 8" x 10"
black and white glossy pic.,
1941 .... 135.00

Big Little Book, *Bobby Benson on
the H-Bar-O Ranch,* Whitman,
1934 .... 42.00

Hobby Kit, diecut leather parts,
makes gun belt and double
holster, grained western motifs,
plastic stitching cords, orig packaging and box, 1954 copyright,
Street & Smith Publications,
unused.............................. 60.00

Red Ryder child's gloves, 2-tone brown cloth with red-and-black vinyl, worn, $25.

Lobby Card, Rustlers of Red Dog,
Universal Pictures, Johnny Mack
Brown, 11" x 14" 10.00

Photograph Collection, group of
100+ color pictures, various sizes,
all 1940s cowboys 150.00

Platter, western scene with "Star
Hotel, Dale Robertson" on top,
Wellsville China Co., signature on
bottom, 12-1/2" l 80.00

Target Game, Straight Arrow, litho
tin board, 3 magnetic feather
tipped arrows, National Biscuit
Co., c1950 .... 75.00

Writing Tablet, Picture Land Stars
series, William S. Hart,
c1920................................. 40.00

❖ Cow Collectibles

Cows have been a part of the folk
art and country decorating schemes
for years. But cow collectors will be
the first to tell you that cows are also
popular on many types of advertising
and even on children's items.

Periodical: *Moosletter,* 240 Wahl
Ave., Evans City, PA 16033.

Bank, cast iron, orig gold
paint.................................245.00

Blotter, Cow Brand Baking Soda,
c1920, 4" x 9-1/4" 15.00

Butter Print, wood, cow with tree and
flowers, scrubbed, 1 pc turned
handle 190.00

Old McDonald butter dish, Regal China, $200.

Cookie Jar, Purple Cow,
Metlox.............................. 575.00

Pinback Button
Farm Maid Milk, Junior Member,
red, white, and blue.........24.00
Guernsey's Rich Inheritance,
yellow, brown, and white,
c1935 ....20.00
Whitings Milk, red, white, and
blue, gold circle accents
around logo, 1930s 24.00

Poster, Evaporated Milk-Pure Cow's
Milk, black and white illus, green
ground, c1940 .... 35.00

Toy, ramp walker, brown and white,
plastic, orig sealed cellophane
pkg, mkd "Made in Hong Kong,"
1950s 18.00

❖ Cracker Jack

Collectors have been searching
for the prize in every box ever since
1912. Prizes can range from paper to
plastic and tin. To date, over 10,000
examples of prizes have been issued
by the Borden Company.

Collectors' Club: Cracker Jack Collectors Association, 108 Central St.,
Rowley, MA 01969.

Book, *Cracker Jack Painting &
Drawing Book,* Saalfield, 1917,
24 pgs 45.00
Booklet, *Cracker Jack Riddles,* red,
white, and blue cover, 42 pgs,
1920s 60.00
Bookmark, spaniel, brown and
white, diecut litho tin 38.00
Doll, vinyl, Vogue Dolls, 1980 copyright, 12" h, MOC................ 37.50
Pencil, 3-1/2" l, red name 15.00
Prize
Battleship, red enameled white
metal 18.50
Gun, Smith & Wesson, .38
replica, black finished white
metal 24.00
Magnet, silver-wire horseshoe
shape, orig red and white
paper wrapper, mkd "Made in
Japan"............................17.50
Owl, red, blue, and yellow, stiff
paper..............................42.00

**Collector's tin, 2nd in series,
8-1/8" h, 5-7/8" d, $5.**

Rocking Horse, dark blue
wash.............................. 24.00
Spinner Top, red, white and blue
litho............................... 35.00
Toy Truck, tin, "Marshmallows" on
side, 1" x 1"....................... 125.00
Watch, litho, 1940s 85.00

★ ✪ Crackle Glass

Crackle Glass can be identified by
the light cracks found throughout the
surface of the glass. These cracks
are an intentional part of the design,
but are random, causing no two
pieces to be identical. By the late
1930s to the early 1970s, crackle was
quite popular in the West Virginia
glass houses, including Pilgrim,
Blenko, Kanawha, and Viking, and
many others.

References: Judy Alford, *Collecting
Crackle Glass with Values,* Schiffer,
1997; Stan and Arlene Weiman,
*Crackle Glass Identification and
Value Guide,* Book I (1996), Book II
(1998), Collector Books.

Collectors' Club: Collectors of
Crackle Glass Club, PO Box 1186,
Massapequa, NY 11758.

For additional listings, see *Warman's
Glass.*

Beaker, 7" h, 5" w, hand blown crystal, hand applied mint green
leaves, Blenko Glass 75.00
Bowl, 8-1/4" h, 5-1/4" d, crystal bowl,
amethyst foot, Blenko Glass85.00
Bud Vase, amberina, Kanawha, orig
label, 7-1/4" h......................60.00
Candy Dish, cov, amberina,
Kanawha, 3" h 45.00
Creamer, emerald green body, clear
handle, Pilgrim....................35.00
Ladle, amethyst handle, crystal
bowl, Blenko, 15" l 160.00
Nappy, 5" x 5-1/4" x 2" h, heart
shaped, amberina, hand blown,
pontil scar, Blenko Glass 65.00
Paperweight, 6" h, apple, amethyst,
applied crystal stem and leaf,
Blenko Glass.......................55.00
Punch Cup, emerald green body,
clear handle, Pilgrim 20.00
Rose Bowl, blue, 6" h, 9" w, Blenko
Glass, c1950......................75.00

**Ewer, amber with clear handle,
Pilgrim paper label, 4-1/2" h, $12.**

Vase
    4" h, 4" w, double neck, Blenko
        Glass..............................35.00
    5-1/2" h, smoke gray 65.00

❖ Cranberry Glass

When a glass maker puts a small amount of powdered gold into a warm blob of molten glass, it changes color to a rich cranberry color, hence the name. Because different glass makers used slightly different formulas, there are slight differences in cranberry glass shades.

For additional listings, see *Warman's Antiques and Collectibles Price Guide* and *Warman's Glass*.

Reproduction Alert.

Basket, Hobnail, clear twisted thorn
    handle, Fenton 20.00
Bottle, Inverted Thumbprint pattern,
    white enameled dot flowers and
    bands, gold trim, clear faceted
    ball stopper, 8-1/2" h 150.00
Box, 4", crystal rigaree 140.00
Candlestick, applied yellow eel dec,
    10-1/2" h........................... 125.00
Creamer, Optic pattern, fluted top,
    applied clear handle 90.00
Pitcher, Ripple and Thumbprint
    pattern, bulbous, round mouth,
    applied clear handle,
    6-1/2" h............................. 125.00
Sauce Dish, Hobb's Hobnail
    pattern................................ 45.00

Fenton hobnail bowl, 4-1/2" h, $70.

Toothpick Holder, crystal
    prunts 48.00
Tumble-Up, Inverted Thumbprint
    pattern 75.00
Vase, 8-7/8" h, bulbous, white enam-
    eled lilies of the valley dec, cylin-
    drical neck 125.00

❖ Credit Cards and Tokens

Some people use these to shop and others shop for interesting credit cards to add to their collections. Plastic charge cards became big business in the 1950s. Before that, folks had charge plates, coins, and tokens. Some stores issued paper cards before plastic became so popular with card vendors.

Periodical: *Credit Cards and Phone Cards News,* PO Box 8481, St Petersburg, FL 33738.

Collectors' Clubs: Active Token Collectors Organization, PO Box 1573, Sioux Falls, SD 57101; American Credit Card Collectors Society, PO Box 2465, Midland, MI 48640; American Numismatic Association, 818 N. Cascade Ave., Colorado Springs, CO 80903; American Vecturist Association, PO Box 1204, Boston, MA 02104; Token & Medal Society, Inc., 9230 SW 59th St., Miami, FL 33173.

Cards
    American Express, 1971, green,
        large centurion profile..... 24.00
    Arco, Lifetime Credit Card,
        gold top 24.00
    Bloomingdale's, white,
        tan border......................... 7.50
    Carte Blanche, 1968, First
        National City Bank.......... 27.50
    Diner's Club, 1966, colored
        blocks, blue top 50.00
    Leh's Department Store, yellow,
        black lettering.................. 3.50
    Lit Brothers, metal charge plate,
        leather carrying case...... 24.00
    Mobil, 2" x 3-1/2", white plastic,
        full color illus of typical Mobil-
        gas service station, mkd "2nd
        Series".............................. 12.00

5-cent token, mkd "Indiana Cigar Store," brass, 13/16" d, $13.50.

    Montgomery Ward, punched data
        charge-all card................ 12.00
    Saks Fifth Avenue,
        paperboard 24.00
    TWA, Getaway Card, couple in
        swim suits, 1974............. 15.00
    Visa, hologram...................... 4.00
Tokens
    Bamberger & Co.,
        celluloid 225.00
    Gimbel Bros., rect., lion and
        shield 15.00
    Plotkin Bros., Boston, white
        metal, lion's head over shield,
        PB logo, rect................... 18.00
    Strawbridge & Clothier, arrow-
        head shape..................... 22.00

❖ Crockett, Davy

"King of the Wild Frontier" was used to described Walt Disney's version of this popular American character.

Bank, dime register type, litho metal,
    full color, 2-1/2" x 2-1/2"......80.00
Belt, figural metal buckle, leather
    belt......................................35.00
Bow Tie 15.00
Game, Davy Crockett's Alamo
    Game, Lowell Toy Corp., mid
    1950s 55.00
Hat, rabbit fur tail and sides, plastic
    top with imprinted image of Davy,
    1950s 60.00
Pocket Knife 65.00

Drinking glass, pyro design, 5-1/8" h, $15.

Ruler, paper, adv for Atlas Soap,
    6" l 7.50
Scarf, silk, 1950s 30.00
School Bag, fabric, brown and tan,
    vinyl fringe, scene on side, brown
    shoulder strap, brass buckle,
    1950s, unused.................... 80.00

❖ Crooksville Pottery

Semi-porcelain dinnerware and housewares were made by the Crooksville Pottery, in Crooksville, OH, from 1902 until 1959. Some pieces were marked.

Batter Jug, cov, Silhouette...... 48.00
Casserole, cov, Silhouette 32.00
Creamer and Sugar,
    Silhouette 20.00

Bowl, floral pattern, 2-5/8" h, 8-3/4" d, $6.50.

Cup and Saucer, Petit Point
    House 7.50
Gravy Boat, Quadro................ 12.50
Pie Baker, Petit Point House... 18.50
Plate, Petit Point House, 9" d.... 9.00
Soup Bowl, Ivora.................... 10.00
Syrup Jug, Dartmouth............. 24.00
Teapot, Petit Point House 35.00
Tumbler, Silhouette 17.50
Utility Jar, cov, Petit Point
    House 48.00

❖ Crown Devon

Crown Devon is a type of English pottery dating from 1870 to 1982. The factory was located at Stoke-on-Trent and produced a wide range of pottery, from majolica, luster wares, figurines, souvenir wares, etc.

Reference: Susan and Al Bagdade, *Warman's English & Continental Pottery & Porcelain,* Krause Publications, 1998.

Ashtray, Hot Scent 25.00
Bowl, oval, pedestal base, painted
    green, orange, and black geometric banding, gilt accents, paper
    label, 11" l 90.00
Cheese Dish, Spring pattern, red
    and blue flowers and urn, scattered ivy, tan shaded ground,
    slant top 5.00
Cigarette Box, Tally Ho 75.00
Jug, musical
    Auld Lang Syne, dec of men in
        tavern, 4-1/2" h............... 85.00
    Here's A Health Unto Her Majesty, raised tinted portraits of
        Queen Elizabeth II, color
        bands, gold trim............ 145.00
Vase, multicolored flowers and crest
    on front, flowers on reverse,
    shaded tan ground, raised gold
    leaf design, matte gold handles
    and rim, 11-1/4" h 75.00

❖ Cuff Links

Some styles of fashion dictate long sleeves that need to be fastened with a decorative cuff link. These little jewelry treasures have been making a colorful statement for many years.

Watch for different styles of backs and closures.

References: Most jewelry books will contain some information about cuff links, including Christie Romero's *Warman's Jewelry,* 2nd edition, Krause Publications.

Collectors' Club: National Cuff Link Society, PO Box 346, Prospect Heights, IL 60070.

Cuff Links, pr
    Gold filled, yellow and white gold,
        dumbbell style, swivel back,
        marquise shape, engine turning design on top, plain back,
        sgd "S & W" (Sturtevant and
        Whiting Co.).................... 30.00
    Gold filled, yellow and white gold,
        dumbbell style, swivel back,
        octagon shape, machine and
        hand engraved design on top,
        plain back, sgd "S & S"... 45.00
    Gold, 10K yellow, hexagon
        shape, engine turned engraved
        design on front, sgd "NJSC" in
        four leaf clover,
        c1920........................... 125.00
    Gold, 14K rose, cushion shape
        top, inlaid turquoise, crescent
        shape back, late 19th C, wear
        and some cracking to
        turquoise...................... 175.00
    Gold, 14K yellow, round, engine
        turned design on front and
        back, sgd "c" in arrowhead,
        c1920........................... 225.00
    Gold, 14K yellow, two rubies set
        in each, c1960 .... 395.00
    Gold, 18K yellow, Art Deco style,
        little diamonds in center of
        MOP plaques, set in platinum
        bezels 350.00

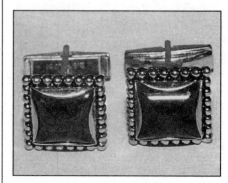

Green stone, gold finish, $1.

Silver-plated, mkd
"Correct Links" 4.00
Silvertone, clear glass stone,
5/8" d..............................5.00

Cuff Links and Tie Clip Set
LaMode Originals, black stone
and goldtone, orig box 25.00
Mask shape, unmarked.......12.00
Square, gold plated, inset MOP
disk..................................18.00
Swank, gold and silver plated,
orig box 25.00

⭐ Cupids

Cute little cupids have been charming our hearts since the Victorian times. Their form is found on many types of objects—just watch out for those arrows they might be pointing at you.

Bookends, pr, cast iron, 8" h, some damage 75.00
Box, cov, bisque, olive green, gold and bronze accents, white glazed emb cameo of woman and cupid on lid, Schafer and Vater, 5" x 3", small chip 225.00
Bud Vase, amber shading to clear, white enameled cupid , in the style of Mary Gregory, 8-5/8" h, some wear, slight gold loss at top rim 175.00
Dresser Box, ceramic, heart-shaped, cupids on top, bow pattern on base 35.00
Dresser Set, beveled mirror with red cupids, brass handles with filigree............................... 250.00
Figure, bisque, 4-1/2" h 20.00
Jar, cov, porcelain, orange and gold, center scene of Victorian woman and cupid, 4-1/2" d 35.00

Bisque figurine, Japan, 2-1/2" h, 4" w, $22.

Pin, shooting arrow
Brass, Coro, lavender and white rhinestones, c1940, 2" x 2" 42.00
Sterling Silver, intent expression, stamped "Sterling" on back, c1940, 2" l, 2-1/2" w 110.00
Pitcher, ceramic, beige ground, cupid on each side, black wreath and "Japan" on bottom, 7-3/4" h 45.00
Postcard, cupid sharpening arrow, holding bow, unused............. 5.00

Print, orig frame
Cupid Asleep 115.00
Cupid Awake 115.00

Valentine, postcard type
Cupid with heart in wheelbarrow, "It's all for You," leather postcard, postmarked Indianapolis 6.00
Man and woman in floral heart wreath with cupid, "A Token of My True Love," used 7.50
Vase, figural, mkd "Japan," 3" h 5.00

❖ Cups and Saucers

Cup and saucer collecting is a hobby that many different generations have enjoyed. Some porcelain makers have created special cups and saucers for collectors. Other collectors prefer collecting cups and saucers that were made as dinnerware or even depression glass patterns.

Adam's Rose, green and red design, black stripe on rims........... 140.00
Bavaria, blue luster ext., MOP int., black handle and rim, mkd "Bavaria"............................ 10.00
Belleek, Limpet pattern, 3rd black mark 100.00
Beswick, Benjamin Bunny, Royal Albert mark 17.50
Bone China, purple thistles, green leaves and pods, brown stems, gold trim............................. 17.50
Coronation, George and Elizabeth, sepia portraits, multicolored royal crest on saucer, gold trim, Aynsley 95.00

Cupids motif, unmarked, $35.

Deldare Ware, street scene, Buffalo Pottery 225.00
Flow Blue, Hamilton pattern....45.00
Forget Me Not, white shaded to cobalt blue ground, gold int., gold striped handle and rim, mkd "Made in Germany"............. 12.00
Moss Rose, gold trim, mkd "H & Co. Limoges" 30.00
Remember Me, brown and pink flowers, scalloped saucer, mustache guard in cup 35.00

❖ Cuspidors

Called cuspidors or spittoons, these functional items can be found in metal or ceramic. They were originally found in bars, on trains, and even homes.

Brass, Redskin Cut Plug Chewing Tobacco 125.00
Cast iron and tin, turtle shape, damaged copper insert, mkd "Den Jacobs, Chicago".............. 250.00
China, lady's hand shape, violets, turquoise beading, Nippon, green M in wreath mark 145.00

Bennington, 1-pc, molded shell design, slight chip, 4" h, 9" d, $95.

Pewter, Gleason, Roswell, Dorchester, MA, c1850, 8" d 225.00

Redware, tooled bands, brown and green glaze, brown dashes, 8" d 245.00

Red Wing Stoneware, company logo stamped on side 285.00

Rockingham Glaze, columnar side design, minor chips 55.00

Yellow Ware, green, blue, and tan sponged glaze, 7-1/2" d 80.00

❖ Custard Glass

Custard glass is a yellowish opaque glass that derives its color from the uranium salts that are added to the hot molten glass. Because different manufacturers used slightly different amounts, you can see some variations in color from maker to maker.

For additional listings, see *Warman's Antiques and Collectibles Price Guide* and *Warman's Glass.*

Berry Bowl, master
    Jackson 90.00
    Louis XV, good gold 110.00

Butter Dish, cov, Georgia Gem, enamel dec....................... 300.00

Celery, Ring Band................. 300.00

Compote, Argonaut Shell 80.00

Creamer, Jackson................... 70.00

Goblet, Grape and Gothic Arches, nutmeg stain....................... 75.00

Napkin Ring, Diamond with Peg.................................... 150.00

Plate, Grape and Cable 55.00

Pitcher, "Souvenir Washington C.H. Ohio, 1904," 2-3/4" h, $37.

Punch Cup, Northwood Grape 50.00

Sauce, ftd, Intaglio 90.00

Spooner, Intaglio 95.00

Table Set, cov butter, creamer, cov sugar, spooner, Argonaut Shell 425.00

Tumbler, Cherry Scale 50.00

❖ Cut Glass

One of the prettiest glass' ever made, cut glass should be sparkly and sharp to the touch. It has been made by American and European companies for many years. Most companies didn't sign their work, but collectors can identify different makers by their intricate patterns.

Collectors' Club: American Cut Glass Association, PO Box 482, Ramona, CA 9205.

For additional listings, see *Warman's Antiques and Collectibles Price Guide* and *Warman's Glass.*

Basket, diamond miters, diamond points, small stars, 6" x 4-1/4" x 6" h, pinhead nick 55.00

Bowl
    Brilliant cut pinwheels, hobstars, and miters, 8" x 3-3/4" .. 145.00
    Heavy blank, serrated rim, two rows of vertical rays, star bottom, 8-1/4" d.................. 45.00

Carafe, 2-1/2" floral leaf band, star, file, fan, and criss-cross cutting, molded neck, 8" h............... 70.00

Creamer and Sugar, hobstar, American Brilliant Period, 3" h 50.00

Decanter, stopper, large hobstars, deep miters, fan, file, hallmarked silver neck and rim, 11" h, 3" square 130.00

Dish, heart shaped, handle, American Brilliant Period, 5" d 45.00

Goblet, strawberry diamond, pinwheel, and fan, notched stem, 7 pc set............................. 350.00

Nappy, hobstar center, intaglio floral, strawberry diamond button border, 6" d 45.00

Pickle Tray, checkerboard, hobstar, 7" x 3" 45.00

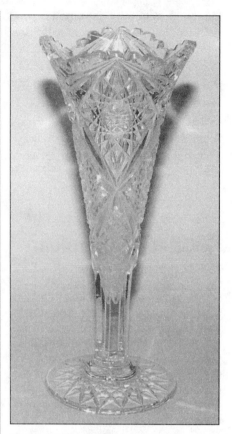

Vase, 12" h, $120.

Tumbler, cut panels, fans, sheaves, roundels, strawberry diamonds, 3-1/8" h 40.00

Vase, trumpet form, Florentine pattern, large graduated circles and fans, notched miters, hobstars, 15-3/4" h, Higgins & Seiter 250.00

☆ Cybis

Opened as an artists' studio by Polish immigrants, Boleslaw Cybis and his wife Marja. They created porcelain sculpture of exquisite detail.

Bear, 1968............................400.00

Bluebirds, nesting, 1978 ....250.00

Buffalo, 1968........................200.00

Dandy Dancing Dog, 1977 ....300.00

Easter Egg Hunt, 1972..........220.00

Independence Celebration, 1972.................................210.00

Kitten Chantilly, 1984 ....215.00

Lullaby Pink, 1986................195.00

Madonna, with bird, damage to
bird's tail 100.00
Merry Christmas, 1982 .... 315.00
Pinto, 1972 .... 225.00
Raccoon, with berries, 8-3/4" 170.00
Recital, 1985........................ 300.00
Sebastian Seal, 1976 .... 250.00
Snail, 1968, 4" l, 2-3/4" h...... 125.00
Summer, 1982 .... 210.00
Windy Day, 1972 .... 215.00

❖ Czechoslovakian Collectibles

Finding an object marked "Made in Czechoslovakia" assures you that it was made after 1918, when the country proclaimed its independence. Marks that include other countries, like "Bohemia" or "Austria," indicate that the piece is before the 1918 date. Expect to find good quality workmanship and bright colors.

Periodical: *New Glass Review*, Bardounova 2140 149 00 Praha 4, Prague, Czech Republic.

Collectors' Club: Czechoslovakian Collectors Guild International, PO Box 901395, Kansas City, MO 64190.

For additional listings, see *Warman's Antiques and Collectibles Price Guide* and *Warman's Glass.*

Belt Buckle, metal, 4 amber rhinestones, mkd "Czechoslovakia 81-Ges Gesch" 18.00
Bowl, brightly colored dec, incised mark, 9" d 60.00
Box, cov, blue glass, sterling rosary 120.00
Lemonade Set, 13" h blown pitcher, 4 matching glasses, bright orange, black silhouettes of children at play, trees, birds, animals, applied handle 225.00
Necklace
    Fringed, multicolored, 2 baroque pearls, 4" w, 20" l...........110.00
    Glass, red center pendant, brass setting, red glass and brass filigree beads, 13" l, mkd on "O" ring 95.00
    Marbleized green stone, set in brass, small green spacer beads, clear rhinestones set at top 80.00

For exciting collecting trends and newly expanded areas look for the following symbols:
❂ Hot Topic
★ New Warman's Listing
(May have been in another Warman's edition.)

Perfume Bottle, small, heavily cut Amethyst 125.00
    Crystal, large faceted stopper 60.00
    Pink................................... 125.00
    Smoky Topaz, enameled dec, large stopper 90.00
Pitcher, cream, blue stripes, stamp mark, 4-1/4" h 45.00
Place Card Holders, glass, set of 6, orig box 80.00
Vase
    9-1/4" h, 4" w, pottery, 6 sides, 3 legs, glaze flake........... 225.00
    10" h, pottery, brightly painted, incised numbers 118.00
    11-1/4" h, glass, luster finish, orange, green, and cream 125.00

Tea set, 3 pcs, white lustre with orange trim, teapot 3-3/4" h, $38.

Want List:

1. _____
2. _____
3. _____
4. _____
5. _____
6. _____
7. _____
8. _____
8. _____
10. _____

D

❖ Dairy Collectibles

Collecting items that pertain to dairies is a popular part of the antiques and collectibles marketplace. Some collectors specialize in items from local dairies, while others concentrate on things like milk bottles or milk bottle caps.

Reference: C. H. Wendel, *Encyclopedia of American Farm Implements & Antiques,* Krause Publications, 1997.

Periodicals: *Creamers,* PO Box 11, Lake Villa, IL 60046; *Cream Separator and Dairy Collectors Newsletter,* Route 3, PO Box 488, Arcadia, WI 54612; *Fiz Biz,* PO Box 115, Omaha, NE, 68101; *The Milk Route,* 4 Ox Bow Rd, Westport, CT 06880.

Collectors' Clubs: Cream Separator and Dairy Collectors, Rt 3, PO Box 488, Arcadia, WI, 54612; National Association of Milk Bottle Collectors, 4 Ox Bow Rd, Westport, CT 06880; National Association of Soda Jerks, PO Box 115, Omaha, NE, 68101.

Booklet, *Walt Disney's Snow White Dairy Recipes-Fun For The Whole Family,* American Dairy Association, 1958, 16 pgs, 6" x 7" 35.00

Change Tray, tin, "Compliments of the Chas. Skidd Mfg Co., Manufacturers of Chilly-King Coolers for Milk or Cream," by Chas. W. Shonk Co., Chicago, 4-1/2" 35.00

Container, painted white, galvanized, raised lettering "Property of Homestead Dairy," insulated, 10" x 13-1/2" 25.00

Cookbook
Delicious Dairy Dishes, Borden's Farm Products Company of Michigan, 1935 .... 12.00
Healthful Dairy Dishes, Ruth Berlozheimer's Culinary Arts Institute, 1950, softcover 5.00
Modern Approach to Everyday Cooking, American Dairy Association, 1966, hardcover, spiral bound 15.00

Map, No. 95, Arbuckle Map of the World series, dairy products from the Netherlands, copyright 1889 .... 10.00

Milk Bottle, clear, "Rogers Riverside Dairy since 1919 Fulton NY Producers Processors Distributors" in orange letters, picture of calf, 8-5/8" h 15.00

Milk Box, metal, Cumberland Case Co., Chattanooga, TN, 12" x 10" 20.00

Salt and Pepper Shakers, pr, St. Lawrence Dairy Cream, metal tops, 3-1/4" h 50.00

Serving Tray, Howerton Sanitary Dairy, Northampton, PA, 13-1/4", chips to rim 150.00

Spinner, Dellwood Milk and Dairy Products, plastic, paper inlay 30.00

Tin, Tarzin Rub, dairy veterinary use, 1-1/4" h 38.00

Trade Card, Borden milk wagon pulled by horse, diecut 25.00

☆ Dakin

What's something fun and cuddly to collect? Dakin collectibles fit easily into this category. Look for original tags to help identify genuine Dakin.

Coca-Cola Polar Bear, white, red scarf, 1993, no tag, 14" h ... 20.00

Doll, cloth, three faces 55.00

Donald Duck, articulated, orig string tag, c1972, 9" h 37.50

Garfield Snowman, United Feature Syndicate, Inc., Dakin, Inc. San Francisco, CA tags, 1981, 10-1/4" h 18.00

Teddy bear, 1984, 15" h, $5.

Mouse, tagged "Dream Pets R. Dakin Company Japan" 10.00

Polar Bear, Jelly Roll Oldetyme Bear, white plush, 12" h 15.00

Rooster, bright yellow plumage, red jersey, Denver, CO radio station promotional piece, 1980, tush tag 7.50

Smokey Bear, orig tags, c1970, 8" h 40.00

☆ Decorative Accessories

Call it "kitsch" or "bric-a-brac," but decorative accessories are the things that help make a statement about who we are as we decorate our living spaces. Decorators have been using objects d'art for years. Now that many of these objects are coming into the flea market scene, collectors get a second chance to add some of these decorative objects to their domain.

Bird House, snow covered, DeForest 110.00

Bust, Sheherazade, chalkware painted to resemble bronze 250.00

Cigar Store Indian, chief, 70-1/4" h, pine, carved and painted, red, white, and blue feathered headdress, gold and red gown, holding dagger in right hand, tobacco and cigars in other hand, black painted base, 19th C 2,750.00

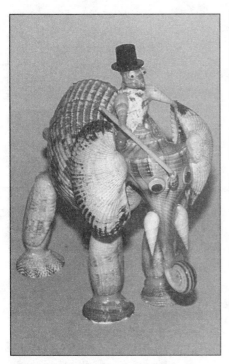

Shell art, elephant with rider, 6-1/4" h, 6" l, $7.

Compote, 12" d x 4-1/2" h, alabaster, sixteen pieces of polychrome dec fruit, minor wear and damage 1,150.00

Cornucopia Vase, pierced rim, painted floral motif, four feet with fish scales, stamped and imp mark, 1913, orig paper label reads "Fisher, Budapest".. 300.00

Crocus Pot, ceramic, white ground, purple floral design, unmarked 2.00

Figure
    Gooney Bird, 6-5/8" h, chip carved wings, black and orange paint, blue and yellow details, long legs, rect base, PA, early 20th C 525.00
    Rooster, 5-1/4" h, pine, cross-hatched wing detail, orange, red, yellow, pink, and green, standing on grassy mound,Carl Snavely, Lititz, PA, 20th C 400.00

Garden Set, ceramic, blue and white, 18-1/2" h, Chinese 600.00

Inkwell, figural, rose, brass, color wash, pink and red petals, green stem 250.00

Lamp, traffic meter base, cloth shade.................................. 50.00

Mantel Ornaments, 12-1/2" h, fruit and foliage design, chalkware, American, made in 19th C, some paint wear, pr 475.00

Paperweight, multicolored concentric millefiore base, dated 1848 cane, Whitefriars 190.00

Rug, hooked, "Home Is Where The Heart Is," log cabin center, pine trees and fence.............. 1,000.00

Theorem, watercolor on velvet, basket of fruit, unidentified maker, framed 200.00

Urn, Capo-di-Monte, ovoid, central molded frieze with figures and cupids, molded floral garlands, multicolored dec, pedestal base 450.00

Wall Plaque
    Basket shape, chalkware, paint dec 45.00
    Masks, Comedy and Tragedy, white ceramic, unmarked 70.00

Wall Sconce, 15" h, bronze, doré finish, crystal drop pendants, cast foliage dec, French, pr...... 600.00

✯ Decoys

Carved wooden birds of all types are referred to as decoys. Some collectors prefer decoys that were designed to be used by hunters. Many decoys exhibit fine carving and intricate details. Of course, this may help push the price higher, as will a signed decoy and the locale of the carver.

Periodicals: *Decoy Magazine*, PO Box 787, Lewes, DE, 19558; *North America Decoys*, PO Box 246, Spanish Fork, UT 84660; *Sporting Collector's Monthly*, RW Publishing, PO Box 305, Camden, DE 19934; *Wildfowl Art*, Ward Foundation, 909 South Schumaker Dr, Salisbury, MD 21801; *Wildfowl Carving & Collecting*, 500 Vaughn St, Harrisburg, PA 17110.

Collectors' Clubs: Midwest Collectors Association, 1100 Bayview Dr, Fox River Grove, IL 60021; Minnesota Decoy Collectors Association,

PO Box 130084, St Paul, MN 55113; Ohio Decoy Collectors & Carvers Association, PO Box 499, Richfield, OH 44286.

For additional listings, see *Warman's Antiques and Collectibles Price Guide*.

Reproduction Alert.

Bluebill Drake, carved by Jim Kelson, Mt. Clemens, MI, carved wing detail, feather stamping, glass eyes, orig paint, orig keel and weight, c1930...............25.00

Canada Goose, carved by Bill Eminght, Toledo, OH, cork body, wood head and keel, orig paint, shot scars, sgd and dated 1968................................. 650.00

Canvasback Drake, carved by Miles Smith, Maine City, MI, high head, balsam body, glass eyes, orig paint, c1933 .... 200.00

Mallard Drake
    Carved by Bert Graves, hollow body, orig weighted bottom, branded "E. I. Rogers" and "Cleary"......................... 900.00
    Manuf by Mason Factory, standard grade, carved wood, glass eyes, orig paint.... 225.00

Merganser Drake, Mason Factory challenge grade, orig paint 700.00

Merganser Hen, carved by Hurley Conklin, hollow body, carved wing tips, branded "H. Conklin" on bottom.................................... 375.00

Sickle Bill Curlew, carved by unknown maker, carved wood, glass eyes, pitchfork line beak, orig paint, 30" l 150.00

Mallard drake decoy, composition, painted, glass eyes, 14" l, $38.

❖ Dedham Pottery

Dedham Pottery is usually thought of as the pottery with the crackle glaze and rabbit border. Actually, this American pottery has produced interesting art pottery type wares, as well as over 50 different patterns with the popular crackle glaze. Dedham pottery is marked with several distinct marks that represent different time periods.

Collectors' Club: Dedham Pottery Collectors Society, 248 Highland St., Dedham, MA 02026.

For additional listings, see *Warman's Antiques and Collectibles Price Guide.*

Reproduction Alert.

Bowl, rabbit pattern, registered
  stamp mark, 8-1/2" sq 600.00
Candlesticks, pr, rabbit pattern, registered blue stamp............ 425.00
Creamer and Sugar, duck pattern, blue stamp, type #1,
  3-1/4" h............................ 650.00
Pitcher, turkey pattern, blue
  stamp 600.00
Plate
  Dolphin pattern, blue registered
    stamp mark, 6" d,
    chip 225.00
  Duck pattern, blue stamp mark,
    Maude Davenport's "O" rebus
    mark, 8-1/2" d 390.00
  Elephant pattern, blue registered
    stamp, 10" d, rim
    nicks..............................450.00
  Magnolia pattern, blue stamp,
    8-1/2" d 165.00
  Rabbit pattern, blue stamp mark,
    8-1/2" d 175.00
Tea Cup and Saucer
  Azalea pattern, registered stamp
    ....135.00
  Duck pattern, registered stamp
    ....155.00
  Iris pattern, registered stamp
    ....155.00
  Rabbit pattern, registered stamp
    ....165.00

❖ Deeds and Documents

Collectors seek out interesting vintage deeds and other documents to glean historical information. When purchasing a deed, check for authentic signatures, revenue stamps, seals, etc. Prices for deeds vary according to age, size, and location. Expect to pay $10 and upward for a common deed, more if some famous person's name appears, etc. Documents also range in price greatly and their values too are determined by content, date, signature, etc.

Arrest Warrant, Marion Co., KY,
  1887-1891, 9 pgs, 8" x 12-1/4",
  group of 5 warrants ranging from
  stealing chickens, breach of
  peace, construction problems,
  handwritten, sgd, dated 24.00

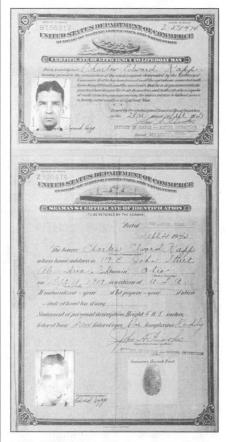

U.S. Merchant Marine documents, "Certificate of Efficiency to Lifeboat Man" and "Seaman's Certificate of Identification," 1943, pr, $40.

Help Wanted Poster, W. R. Parsons,
  Chicago, IL, c1900, "Agents
  Wanted by Manufacturers of the
  Daisy Stair Corner" 18.00
Invoice, New Jersey Auto Top Mfg.,
  Newark, NJ, 1916, company letterhead, illus of 1909 auto with
  man in it, attached business card
  on heavy stock, light green
  ....25.00
Letterhead
  Clipless Paper Fastener, Newton, IA, 1913, 2 pgs, illus of
    fasteners......................... 10.00
  H. E. Hessler Co. Syracuse, NY,
    Rural Mail Box 8.50
Parry Mfg. Co., Indianapolis, IN,
  1906, picture of factory 15.00
Price List, George W. Rogers, Chesterfield, MA, 1895, illus of Newman Best & Cheapest Wire Truss
  Fence.................................. 15.00
Program, Leap Year Party by Young
  Ladies, 1888, dance program
  inside 10.00

❖ Degenhart Glass

Operating from 1947 until 1978, John and Elizabeth Degenhart created glass novelties under the name of Crystal Art Glass. They created some unusual colors. When Crystal Art Glass went out of business, many of the molds were purchased by Boyd Crystal Art Glass, also located in Cambridge, OH.

Collectors' Club: Friends of Degenhart, Degenhart Paperweight and Glass Museum, Inc., 65323 Highland Hills Rd, PO Box 186, Cambridge, OH 43725.

Reproduction Alert.

Animal Covered Dish
  Hen, mint green, 3" 22.00
  Turkey, custard 60.00
Bell, Bicentennial, amethyst...... 7.50
Candy Dish, cov, Wildflower, twilight
  blue 32.00
Cup Plate, heart and lyre,
  mulberry............................. 15.00
Hand, tomato red 30.00

Priscilla figurine, orange, 5-1/4" h, $55.

Hat, daisy and button, milk blue
.... 10.00

Owl
    Bluebell 32.00
    Midnight Sun 30.00
Salt, bird, amber 12.00
Toothpick Holder, basket, milk white
.... 20.00

Vase, Forget-Me-Not,
    crystal 20.00

❖ Delftware

Delftware is a popular ware with a white dense body over a red clay body which features a tin enamel glaze. Early examples had a white background with blue decoration and polychrome enameling followed.

Muffineer, Colonial Williamsburg reproduction, made in Holland, 6-3/4" h, $22.

For additional listings, see *Warman's Antiques and Collectibles Price Guide* and *Warman's English & Continental Pottery & Porcelain.*

Reproduction Alert.

Bowl, blue and white, landscape
    with figure, 12" d, edge
    chips 500.00
Charger
    Blue and white, foliate dec, Dutch,
    19th C, 13-1/8" d, chips, glaze
    wear 410.00
    Polychrome floral design, blue,
    red, yellow, green, and black,
    13-1/4" d, edge chips ... 880.00
Mug, blue and white, armorial
    surrounded by exotic landscape,
    palm trees, mkd on base, Dutch,
    19th C, minor chips, glaze wear
    .... 590.00

Plate, blue and white floral dec,
    Dutch inscription on front, edge
    chips 200.00
Tea Caddy, blue and white floral dec,
    scalloped bottom edge, mkd
    "MVS 1750," cork closure, wear,
    edge flakes, old chips 550.00

✺ Depression Glass

Depression glass was made from 1920 to 1940. It was an inexpensive machine-made glass and was produced by several companies in various patterns and colors. The number of forms made in different patterns also varied.

References: There are many excellent reference books on Depression Glass. Gene Florence, Carl Luckey, Kent G. Washburn and others have all authored books on Depression Glass. Hazel Marie Weatherman wrote the first and most referred to editions, titled *Colored Glassware of the Depression Era*, Books 1 and 2, plus several supplements.

Periodicals: *The Daze*, PO Box 57, Otisville, MI 48463; *Depression Glass Shopper On-Line Magazine*, www.dgshopper.com.

Collectors' Clubs: Canadian Depression Glass Club, 1026 Forestwood Drive, Mississauga, Ontario L5C 1G8, Canada; National Depression Glass Association, Inc., PO Box 8264, Wichita, KS 67209; 20-30-40 Society, Inc, PO Box 856, LaGrange, IL 60525.

Divided relish, Miss America pattern, pink, 8-3/4" d, $25.

For additional listings, see *Warman's Depression Glass.* The listings below are a mere sampling of the current Depression Glass market.

Reproduction Alert.

Ashtray

Adam, Jeannette Glass Co., 4-1/2" d, green 25.00

Diana, Federal Glass Co., pink 4.00

Early American Prescut, Anchor Hocking, crystal, 4" d 3.00

Forest Green, Anchor Hocking Glass Co., 4-5/8" sq, green...................................5.50

Manhattan (Horizontal Ribbed), Anchor Hocking Glass Co., crystal.............................11.00

Moroccan Amethyst, Hazel Ware, amethyst, 3-1/2" d.............5.75

Windsor (Windsor Diamond), Jeannette Glass Co., 5-3/4" d, pink 35.00

Berry Bowl, individual

Anniversary, Jeannette Glass Co., 4-7/8" d, irid...............4.50

Bowknot, green 16.00

Colonial Fluted (Rope), Federal Glass Co., green.............11.00

Normandie (Bouquet and Lattice), Federal Glass Co., 5" d, irid 5.00

Old Café, Hocking Glass Co., ruby...................................6.00

Patrician (Spoke), Federal Glass Co., amber 12.00

Sharon (Cabbage Rose), Federal Glass Co., pink...............10.00

Berry Bowl, master

Aunt Polly, US Glass Co., blue 45.00

Cameo (Ballerina, Dancing Girl), Hocking Glass Co., pink 150.00

Heritage, Federal Glass Co., pink 42.00

Indiana Custard, (Flower and Leaf Band), Indiana Glass Co., French Ivory 32.00

Raindrops (Optic Design), Federal Glass Co., green......45.00

Strawberry, US Glass Co., green or pink 20.00

Bowl

American Pioneer, Liberty Works, crystal, 9" d 24.00

Bamboo Optic, Liberty, 4-1/4" d, green 6.00

Carolyn, Lancaster, 1" d, topaz 36.00

Early American Prescut, Anchor Hocking, crystal, 8-3/4" d, ruffled 9.00

Iris (Iris and Herringbone) Jeannette Glass Co., 9-1/2" d, irid 10.00

Jody, Lancaster, 12" l, oval, topaz 35.00

Jubilee, Lancaster Glass Co., 8" d, pink 265.00

Moonstone, Anchor Hocking Glass Co., cloverleaf, opal 13.00

Oyster and Pearls, Anchor Hocking Glass Co., 5-1/4" w, heart shape, ruby 15.00

Roxana, Hazel Atlas, golden topaz 12.00

Butter Dish, cov

Anniversary, Jeannette Glass Co., pink........................ 60.00

Block Optic (Block), Hocking Glass Co., green 50.00

Doric, Jeannette Glass Co. green 90.00

Floral, (Poinsettia), Jeannette Glass Co., green 90.00

Moderntone, Hazel Atlas, cobalt blue, metal cov 100.00

Royal Lace, Hazel Atlas, pink............................... 150.00

U.S. Swirl, US Glass Co., green or pink 115.00

Windsor (Windsor Diamond), Jeannette Glass Co., pink............................... 60.00

Cake Plate

Adam, Jeannette Glass Co., green 32.00

Anniversary, Jeannette Glass Co., crystal, round 7.50

Block Optic (Block), Hocking Glass Co., crystal 18.00

Cameo (Ballerina, Dancing Girl), Hocking Glass Co., 10" d, green 22.00

Holiday (Buttons and Bows), Jeannette Glass Co., 10-1/2" d, pink 100.00

Miss America, (Diamond Pattern), Hocking Glass Co...........25.00

Primo (Paneled Aster), US Glass Co., green or yellow 23.50

Thistle, Macbeth-Evans, green 150.00

Candy Dish, cov

Cloverleaf, Hazel Atlas, green 45.00

Floragold, Jeannette Glass Co., irid................................. 15.00

Moroccan Amethyst, Hazel Ware, amethyst, tall 32.00

Ribbon, Hazel Atlas, black 38.00

Cereal Bowl

Aurora, Hazel Atlas, pink 14.00

Cherry Blossom, Jeannette Glass Co., green...................... 35.00

Daisy (No. 620), Indiana Glass Co., fired-on red 25.00

Horseshoe (No. 612), Indiana Glass Co., green or yellow 25.00

Old Café, Hocking Glass Co., crystal or pink 8.00

Coaster

Adam, Jeannette Glass Co., pink................................32.00

Cherry Blossom, Jeannette Glass Co., green or pink.......... 15.00

Miss America, (Diamond Pattern), Hocking Glass Co., crystal 20.00

Comport

Anniversary, Jeannette Glass Co., crystal, ruffled 6.50

Floragold, Jeannette Glass Co., irid, 5-1/4" d, ruffled 695.00

Manhattan (Horizontal Ribbed), Anchor Hocking Glass Co., crystal, 5-3/4" h............... 32.00

Windsor (Windsor Diamond), Jeannette Glass Co., crystal 6.00

Console Set, Block Optic (Block), Hocking Glass Co.,11-3/4" d bowl, pr 1-3/4" h candlesticks, amber............................... 160.00

Cookie Jar, cov

Manhattan (Horizontal Ribbed), Anchor Hocking Glass Co., crystal.............................35.00

Mayfair (Open Rose), Hocking Glass Co., green 575.00

Princess, Hocking Glass Co., blue 875.00

Creamer

Adam, Jeannette Glass Co., green...............................22.00

Bamboo Optic, Liberty, ftd, green...............................10.00

Christmas Candy (No. 624), Indiana Glass Co., crystal.............................12.00

Cube (Cubist), Jeannette Glass Co., green 10.00

Holiday (Buttons and Bows), Jeannette Glass Co., pink 12.50

Newport (Hairpin), Hazel Atlas, cobalt blue.......................20.00

Ovide, Hazel Atlas, black 7.00

Raindrops (Optic Design), Federal Glass Co. 8.00

Sunflower, Jeannette Glass Co., green or pink 20.00

Cream Soup

American Sweetheart, Macbeth-Evans, monax 120.00

Mayfair, Federal Glass Co., amber...............................18.00

Moderntone, Hazel Atlas, 5" d, ruffled, amethyst 30.00

Patrician (Spoke), Federal Glass Co., amber 16.00

Cup and Saucer

Cameo (Ballerina, Dancing Girl), Hocking Glass Co., crystal..............................14.00

Dogwood, Macbeth-Evans, green..............................40.00

Doric & Pansy, Jeannette Glass Co., ultramarine 21.00

Lorain, Indiana Glass Co., crystal or green...........................15.00

Madrid, Federal Glass Co., amber 9.00

Parrot (Sylvan), Federal Glass Co., green 55.00

Fruit Bowl

Bubble (Bullseye Provincial), Hocking Glass Co., crystal, 4-1/2" d 5.00

Floragold, Jeannette Glass Co., irid 8.50

Heritage, Federal Glass Co., crystal.................... 15.00

Iris (Iris and Herringbone) Jeannette Glass Co., 11-1/2" d, ruffled 15.00

Oyster and Pearls, Anchor Hocking Glass Co., pink 10.00

Raindrops (Optic Design), Federal Glass Co., green 11.00

Goblet

Block Optic (Block), Hocking Glass Co., green 24.00

Bubble (Bullseye Provincial), Hocking Glass Co., forest green 15.00

Colonial Block, Hazel Atlas, crystal.................... 9.00

Diamond Point, ruby stained, 7-1/2" h 35.00

Moroccan Amethyst, Hazel Ware, amethyst.................... 10.00

Old English (Threading), Indiana Glass Co., amber, green, or pink.................... 30.00

Ring, (Banded Rings), Hocking Glass Co., crystal 7.00

Iced Tea Tumbler, ftd, 12 oz

Circle, Hocking Glass Co., green or pink 17.50

Dewdrop, Jeannette Glass Co., crystal.................... 17.50

Diamond Quilted, (Flat Diamond), Imperial Glass Co., green or pink 10.00

Hobnail, Hocking Glass Co., crystal.................... 8.50

Homespun (Fine Rib), Jeannette Glass Co., crystal or pink 32.00

Ships (Sailboat, Sportsman Series), Hazel Atlas, cobalt blue 18.00

Juice Tumbler, ftd

Fortune, Hocking Glass Co., crystal.................... 8.00

Old Café, Hocking Glass Co., crystal or pink 10.00

Peanut Butter, unknown maker, crystal.................... 9.00

Royal Ruby, Anchor Hocking, ruby 5.00

Mayonnaise Set, Underplate, Orig Ladle

Christmas Candy (No. 624), Indiana Glass Co., crystal 24.00

Diamond Quilted, (Flat Diamond), Imperial Glass Co., blue..................65.00

Patrick, Lancaster Glass Co., yellow 80.00

Mug

Block Optic (Block), Hocking Glass Co., green 35.00

Moderntone, Hazel Atlas, white................................8.50

Pitcher

Adam, Jeannette Glass Co., 32 oz, pink 125.00

Crystal Leaf, Macbeth-Evans, pink...............................45.00

Floragold, Jeannette Glass Co., irid...............................40.00

Forest Green, Anchor Hocking Glass Co., 22 oz, green 22.50

Fruits, Hazel Atlas, green ...85.00

New Century, Hazel Atlas, ice lip, 80 oz, cobalt blue 45.00

Ring, (Banded Rings), Hocking Glass Co., 60 oz, decorated or green 25.00

Plate

American Pioneer, Liberty Works, 6" d, crystal....................12.50

American Sweetheart, Macbeth-Evans , 9" d, monax 10.00

Aurora, Hazel Atlas, 6-1/2" d, cobalt blue 12.00

Bowknot, 7" d, green 12.50

Bubble (Bullseye Provincial), Hocking Glass Co., 6-3/4" d, crystal 3.50

Cameo (Ballerina, Dancing Girl), Hocking Glass Co., 8" d, green 12.00

Cherry Blossom, Jeannette Glass Co., 9" d, grill, green or pink................................22.00

Circle, Hocking Glass Co., 8-1/4" d, green or pink 11.00

Colonial Fluted (Rope), Federal Glass Co., 8" d, green 10.00

Columbia, Federal Glass Co., 9-1/2" d, pink 32.00

Doric, 6" d, green or pink 6.50

Doric & Pansy, Jeannette Glass Co., ultramarine, dinner 35.00

Early American Prescut, Anchor Hocking, crystal, 10" d....10.00

Egg Harbor, Liberty, luncheon, green or pink.....................9.00

Floragold, Jeannette Glass Co., 8-1/2" d, dinner, irid.........35.00

Floral, (Poinsettia), Jeannette Glass Co., 8" d, salad, pink 15.00

Floral and Diamond Band, (Poinsettia), Jeannette Glass Co., 8" d, luncheon, green or pink 40.00

Florentine No. 1 (Old Florentine, Poppy No. 1), Hazel Atlas, 10" d, dinner, green 16.00

Florentine No. 2 (Poppy No. 2), Hazel Atlas, 10" d, yellow, dinner 15.00

Fortune, Hocking Glass Co., 8" d, luncheon, crystal or pink 17.50

Georgian (Lovebirds), Federal Glass Co., green, 8" d, luncheon 10.00

Hobnail, Hocking Glass Co., 8-1/2" d, luncheon, crystal..............................5.50

Holiday (Buttons and Bows), Jeannette Glass Co., pink, 6" d, sherbet.....................6.00

Homespun (Fine Rib), Jeannette Glass Co., 9-1/2" d, dinner, crystal or pink..................17.00

Horseshoe (No. 612), Indiana Glass Co., 8-3/8" d, salad, green or yellow...............10.00

Iris (Iris and Herringbone) Jeannette Glass Co., 9" d, dinner, irid 45.00

Jubilee, Lancaster Glass Co., 9-3/4" d, luncheon 16.50

Laced Edge (Katy Blue), Imperial Glass Co., 10" d, blue 90.00

Madrid, Federal Glass Co., 8-7/8" d, amber 8.00

Manhattan (Horizontal Ribbed), Anchor Hocking Glass Co., 7" d, crystal............................6.00

Mayfair (Open Rose), Hocking Glass Co., 8-1/2" d, pink 25.00

Miss America, (Diamond Pattern), Hocking Glass Co., dinner, crystal............................15.00

Moderntone, Hazel Atlas, 7-3/4" d, cobalt blue 12.50

Moroccan Amethyst, Hazel Ware, amethyst, 9-3/4" d, dinner 7.00

Newport (Hairpin), Hazel Atlas, 8-1/2" d, dinner, fired on color 15.00

Normandie (Bouquet and Lattice), Federal Glass Co., 6" d, irid 3.00

Old Café, Hocking Glass Co., crystal or pink, 6" d, sherbet 4.00

Old Colony (Lace Edge, Open Lace), Hocking Glass Co., crystal, dinner................. 33.00

Parrot (Sylvan), Federal Glass Co., 9" d, dinner, green 38.00

Patrician (Spoke), Federal Glass Co., 7-1/2" d, amber 15.00

Patrick, Lancaster Glass Co., 8" d, luncheon, pink........ 45.00

Peanut Butter, unknown maker, crystal, 8" d, luncheon 5.00

Petalware, Macbeth-Evans, 9" d, dinner, monax................. 10.00

Pineapple & Floral (No. 618), Indiana Glass Co., 6" d, sherbet, amber 6.00

Pretzel (No. 622), Indiana Glass Co., 9-3/4" d, dinner, crystal 10.00

Primo (Paneled Aster), US Glass Co., 10" d, dinner, green 22.50

Princess, Hocking Glass Co., 9-1/2" d, grill, green or pink.................................. 15.00

Queen Mary (Prismatic Line, Vertical Ribbed), Hocking Glass Co., 6" d, crystal..... 4.00

Romansque, 8" d, octagonal, gold 8.00

Rose Cameo, Belmont Tumbler Co., 7" d, salad, green ... 16.00

Rosemary (Dutch Rose), Federal Glass Co., 9-1/2" d, dinner, green 15.00

Roulette (Many Windows), Hocking Glass Co., 8-1/2" d, luncheon, crystal 7.00

Round Robin, 6" d, sherbet, irid or green 7.00

Roxana, Hazel Atlas, 6" d, sherbet, crystal................ 4.00

Royal Lace, Hazel Atlas, 8-1/2" d, luncheon, cobalt 30.00

Royal Ruby, Anchor Hocking, ruby, 7" d, salad............... 3.00

Sandwich, Anchor Hocking, 9" d, crystal 20.00

Ships (Sailboat, Sportsman Series), Hazel Atlas, 9" d, dinner, cobalt blue 32.00

Sierra Pinwheel, Jeannette Glass Co., 9" d, dinner, green 18.00

Starlight, Hazel Atlas, 9-1/2" d, dinner, crystal 7.00

Tea Room, Indiana Glass Co., 8-1/4" d, luncheon, green 37.50

Thistle, Macbeth-Evans, 8" d, luncheon, green.............. 22.00

Vernon (No. 616), Indiana Glass Co., 8" d, luncheon, green or yellow 10.00

Waterford (Waffle), Hocking Glass Co., dinner, crystal.......... 10.00

Windsor (Windsor Diamond), Jeannette Glass Co., 9" d, dinner, green or pink....... 25.00

Platter

Cherry Blossom, Jeannette Glass Co., green.....................48.00

Georgian (Lovebirds), Federal Glass Co., green 70.00

Indiana Custard, (Flower and Leaf Band), Indiana Glass Co., French Ivory 30.00

Laced Edge (Katy Blue), Imperial Glass Co., 13" l, blue.... 165.00

Royal Lace, Hazel Atlas, pink.................................. 40.00

Windsor (Windsor Diamond), Jeannette Glass Co., 11-1/2" l, oval, green.....................25.00

Punch Bowl Set, Royal Ruby, Anchor Hocking, bowl, 12 cups, ruby.................................. 110.00

Relish

Doric, Jeannette Glass Co. green 32.00

For exciting collecting trends and newly expanded areas look for the following symbols:

✪ Hot Topic

✪ New Warman's Listing

(May have been in another Warman's edition.)

Early American Prescut, Anchor Hocking, crystal, 4-part, 11" d 10.00

Lorain, Indiana Glass Co., 4-part, 8" d, crystal or green.......17.50

Miss America, (Diamond Pattern), Hocking Glass Co., 4-part, crystal.............................11.00

Pretzel (No. 622), Indiana Glass Co., 3-part, crystal.............9.00

Princess, Hocking Glass Co., 4-part, apricot................100.00

Tea Room, Indiana Glass Co., divided, green 30.00

Salt and Pepper Shakers, pr

Adam, Jeannette Glass Co., green........................100.00

American Sweetheart, Macbeth-Evans, monax 325.00

Florentine No. 2 (Poppy No. 2), Hazel Atlas, green...........40.00

Hex Optic (Honeycomb), Jeannette Glass Co., green or pink 30.00

Manhattan (Horizontal Ribbed), Anchor Hocking Glass Co., crystal...........................50.00

Ribbon, Hazel Atlas, green .25.00

Waterford (Waffle), Hocking Glass Co., crystal, tall 7.00

Sandwich Server, center handle

Daisy (No. 620), Indiana Glass Co., amber 14.50

Landrum, Lancaster, topaz..55.00

Old English (Threading), Indiana Glass Co., amber............60.00

Ring, (Banded Rings), Hocking Glass Co., decorated or green...........................15.00

Spiral, Hocking Glass Co., green.........................30.00

Twisted Optic, Imperial, canary 35.00

Sherbet

Adam, Jeannette Glass Co., green........................40.00

April, Macbeth-Evans, 4" h, ftd, pink 15.00

Bowknot, unknown maker, green........................24.00

Cherry Blossom, Jeannette Glass Co., pink........................17.00

Florentine No. 1 (Old Florentine, Poppy No. 1), Hazel Atlas, yellow............................16.00

Florentine No. 2 (Poppy No. 2), Hazel Atlas, yellow 8.00

Forest Green, Anchor Hocking Glass Co., Boopie, green 7.00

Fruits, Hazel Atlas, pink........ 7.50

Hex Optic (Honeycomb), Jeannette Glass Co., green or pink.................................. 5.00

Iris (Iris and Herringbone), Jeannette Glass Co., 2-1/2" h, irid 15.50

Old English (Threading), Indiana Glass Co., green 20.00

Parrot (Sylvan), Federal Glass Co., cone shape, green.. 24.00

Peanut Butter, unknown maker, crystal............................. 4.00

Raindrops (Optic Design), Federal Glass Co., crystal............................. 4.50

Sunflower, Jeannette Glass Co., green 13.50

Thumbprint, Federal Glass Co., green 7.00

Windsor (Windsor Diamond), Jeannette Glass Co., pink 13.00

Sugar, cov

Bamboo Optic, Liberty, ftd, green 10.00

Cameo (Ballerina, Dancing Girl), Hocking Glass Co., 3-1/4" h, pink............................. 100.00

Cube (Cubist), Jeannette Glass Co., 3" h, green or pink .. 25.00

Holiday (Buttons and Bows), Jeannette Glass Co., pink............................. 25.00

Madrid, Federal Glass Co., amber............................. 7.00

Ring, (Banded Rings), Hocking Glass Co., decorated 10.00

Sierra Pinwheel, Jeannette Glass Co., pink 20.00

Tulip, Dell Glass Co., blue 20.00

Vernon (No. 616), Indiana Glass Co., crystal 12.00

Tumbler

Bamboo Optic, Liberty, 5-1/2" h, 8 oz, ftd, pink.................... 15.00

Bubble (Bullseye Provincial), Hocking Glass Co., crystal............................. 5.00

Cherryberry, US Glass Co., 3-5/8" h, irid..............................20.00

Columbia, Federal Glass Co., 4 oz, crystal 30.00

Forest Green, Anchor Hocking Glass Co., 9 oz, green......7.00

Hex Optic (Honeycomb), Jeannette Glass Co., 7 oz, 4-3/4" h, green or pink......8.00

Horseshoe (No. 612), Indiana Glass Co., 9 oz, ftd, green 22.00

Madrid, Federal Glass Co., 5-1/2" h, amber 18.00

Mayfair (Open Rose), Hocking Glass Co., 6-1/2" h, ftd, pink.................................40.00

Moderntone, Hazel Atlas, cone, white 4.00

Peanut Butter, unknown maker, crystal, milk glass 7.00

Princess, Hocking Glass Co., 9 oz, green 28.00

Pyramid (No. 610), Indiana Glass Co., 8 oz, ftd, crystal or pink.................................50.00

Rose Cameo, Belmont Tumbler Co., green......................22.50

Ships (Sailboat, Sportsman Series), Hazel Atlas, 9 oz, cobalt blue 14.00

Vernon (No. 616), Indiana Glass Co., yellow.....................35.00

Vegetable, open

Cameo (Ballerina, Dancing Girl), Hocking Glass Co., green 30.00

Daisy (No. 620), Indiana Glass Co., dark green..............10.00

Doric, Jeannette Glass Co., pink.................................30.00

Florentine No. 2 (Poppy No. 2), Hazel Atlas, yellow, cov.................................55.00

Horseshoe (No. 612), Indiana Glass Co., 8-1/2" d, green or yellow 30.00

Pineapple & Floral (No. 618), Indiana Glass Co., amber or crystal 30.00

Rosemary (Dutch Rose), Federal Glass Co., green 37.00

Sharon (Cabbage Rose), Federal Glass Co., amber, oval...............................20.00

Star, Federal Glass Co.,
    amber..............................10.00
Tea Room, Indiana Glass Co.,
    green...............................75.00
Whiskey
    Diamond Quilted, (Flat Dia-
      mond), Imperial Glass Co.,
      pink 12.00
    Hex Optic (Honeycomb),
      Jeannette Glass Co., green or
      pink 8.50
    Hobnail, Hocking Glass Co., crys-
      tal 5.00
    Raindrops (Optic Design),
      Federal Glass Co.,
      green.................................9.00

✴ Desert Storm

Collectibles from this sad bit of history are starting to make it to flea markets. Because of their relative newness, expect to find them in very good condition.

Magazine 2.00
Newspaper, headline edition 1.00
Welcome Banner 10.00
Yellow Ribbon.......................... 1.00

Desert Storm, Pro Set, 253 cards, $10.

For exciting collecting trends and newly expanded areas look for the following symbols:

❂ Hot Topic

✴ New Warman's Listing
(May have been in another Warman's edition.)

✴ Dexterity Puzzles

Small enough to hold in your palm, these little puzzles have brought hours of enjoyment to collectors. Considering most were made as premiums or giveaways, they certainly have increased in value over the years.

Black Woman, tin rim, glass over full color paper with caricature portrait of young woman wearing jewelry and fur cape 72.00
Camel Driver, tin rim, glass over lightly emb full color surface, merchant and camel, two pyramids in background......................... 65.00
Chimney Cleaner, tin rim, glass over paper playing surface, sooty black chimney sweep emerging from top of chimney 60.00
Cracker Jack Man, plastic over cardboard backing, cartoon figure wearing polka dot bow tie, 1920s.............................. 70.00
Dancing Couple, silvered tin rim, glass over color paper playing surface, Bavarian couple, scenic outdoor scene.................... 90.00
Jack-In-The-Box, silvered tin rim, glass over full color paper surface, bearded character wearing fez 45.00
New York-Paris Aero Race 65.00
Old Lady, tin rim, glass over full color emb playing surface, elderly lady with jiggle eyeballs, ad insert for Worcester, MA, clothier 100.00
Quints, 1930s......................... 90.00
Touring Car, tin rim, glass over full color paper playing surface, touring car with male driver, female passenger.......................... 50.00

❖ Dick Tracy

Here's a comic strip character who made it to the movies! And, along the way, he and his pals generated some great collectibles.

Badge, Detective Club 78.00
Big Little Book, *Dick Tracy Encounters Facey,* #2001, 1967 ..... 10.00

Trading cards, Topps, 16 glossy movie cards and 1 sticker, 25 cents.

Candy Bar Wrapper, premium offer, 1950s 10.00
Card Game, 1934 .... 55.00
Crimestoppers Club Kit, MIB 110.00
Doll, Breathless, Madonna...... 15.00
Game, Dick Tracy Master Detective Board Game, 1961 ....25.00
Lunch Box 135.00
Salt and Pepper Shakers, pr, Dick Tracy and Junior, painted plaster, c1940 .... 32.00
Toy, two-way radio set, 1950, MIB 40.00

❖ Dionne Quints

Born in Ontario, Canada, on May 28, 1934, this set of little girls excited the world. They lead an interesting, but sheltered life and attracted visitors and interest from around the world. Of course, all this created collectibles and souvenirs for their fans.

Collectors' Club: Dionne Quint Collectors, PO Box 2527, Woburn, MA 01888.

Blotter, celluloid cov, quints on toy designed for five, c1935......24.00
Book, *The Dionne Quintuplets Growing Up,* 1935...............42.00

1937 advertising calendar, 7-3/8" x 10-1/2", $30.

Calendar, 1936, Watch Us Grow 20.00

Fan, 8-1/4" x 8-3/4" diecut stiff paper, image of five Quints wearing bonnets playing with sand pails at beach, reverse text for Allentown, PA, Dodge-Plymouth dealer, copyright 1936 NEA Services, Inc., B & B St. Paul, Minn, wooden handle, slight damage 15.00

Magazine Cover, *Woman's World,* Feb, 1937 .... 12.00

Paper Dolls, "Let's Play House with the Dionne Quints," unused 55.00

Picture, "The Darling Dionnes," holding dolls, framed 50.00

Postcard, Dr. Dafoe and babies 18.00

Spoon, set of five 135.00

❖ Disneyana

Walt Disney created a wonderful cast of characters that still delights children of all ages. Through the many Disney movies and television shows, many collectibles are available.

Check for the official "Walt Disney Enterprises" logo.

Reference: Ted Hake, *Hake's Guide to Character Toys*, Gemstone Publishing (1966 Greenspring, Ste. 405, Timonium, MD 21093), 1998.

Periodicals: *Mouse Rap Monthly*, PO Box 1064, Ojai, CA 93024; *Tomart's Disneyana Digest*, 3300 Encrete Ln, Dayton, OH 45439; *Tomart's Disneyana Update*, 3300 Encrete Ln, Dayton, OH 45439.

Collectors' Clubs: Imagination Guild, PO Box 907, Boulder Creek, CA 95006; Mouse Club East, PO Box 3195, Wakefield, MA 01880; National Fantasy Fan Club for Disneyana Collectors and Enthusiasts, PO Box 19212, Irvine, CA 92713.

Bank, Cinderella 35.00

Book, *Mickey Never Fails,* DC Heath, 1939, hardcover, school reader 32.00

Bookends, pr, Donald Duck carrying school books, chalkware 25.00

Bubble Gum Card, Mickey Mouse, #23 .... 8.00

Canasta Card, Elmer the Elephant, factory sealed, 1930s 50.00

Christmas Light Set, 1930s 135.00

Snow White and the Seven Dwarfs ironing board, Wolverine Toy, metal, $55.

Doll, Pollyanna, 30" h 100.00

Drinking Glass, Donald Duck, "Full, Going, Going, Gone!," 1940s, 4-3/4" h 40.00

Figure
    Dumbo 35.00
    Son of the South, bear 45.00

Film, Donald the Skater, c1935, black and white, 16mm, orig box 24.00

Hair Brush, Mickey Mouse, Walt Disney Enterprises, c1930, orig box 45.00

Bambi Cartoon Kit, Colorforms, box 12-1/2" x 8", $18.50.

4-record set, "Walt Disney's So Dear To My Heart," Capitol Records, 1949, 78 rpm, 10-1/2" x 12-1/8", $28.

Movie Projector, orig films, Milk Mouse 375.00

Music Box, Happy, figural 30.00

Scuffy Shoe Polish Bottle, Mickey Mouse, c1950, hard black contents 20.00

Stamp, Mickey Mouse, Walt Disney Enterprises 40.00

Teapot, cov, large, Mickey Mouse 95.00

Thermos, Disney's Wonderful World, Aladdin, 6-1/2" h 10.00

Toy, Mickey Mouse Train, battery operated 100.00

Valentine, Jiminy Cricket, diecut, movable arms, 1939 .... 27.50

Wall Plaque

    Mickey Mouse as band leader, mkd "Ceramica De Cuernavaca," 1970s 95.00

    Minnie Mouse, figural, mkd "Ceramica De Cuernavaca," 1970s 95.00

❖ Disneyland and Disney World

From celebrities to kids of all ages, lots of folks enjoy Disneyland and Disney World. Collectibles from the wonderful amusement parks created by Walt Disney are eagerly sought.

Reference: Ted Hake, *Hake's Guide to Character Toys*, Gemstone Publishing (1966 Greenspring, Ste. 405, Timonium, MD 21093), 1998.

Periodicals: *Mouse Rap Monthly*, PO Box 1064, Ojai, CA 93024; *Tomart's Disneyana Digest*, 3300 Encrete Ln, Dayton, OH 45439; *Tomart's Disneyana Update*, 3300 Encrete Ln, Dayton, OH 45439.

Collectors' Clubs: Imagination Guild, PO Box 907, Boulder Creek, CA 95006; Mouse Club East, PO Box 3195, Wakefield, MA 01880; National Fantasy Fan Club for Disneyana Collectors and Enthusiasts, PO Box 19212, Irvine, CA 92713.

Lunchbox, tin, Aladdin Industries, $22.50.

Book, *Disneyland,* hardcover, 1969 edition, 9-1/2" x 1" 40.00

Coke Cans, Toon Town, 6 pack, Mickey, Roger Rabbit, Donald, Goofy 20.00

Guide Book, 20 pgs, c1955 .. 125.00

Little Golden Book, *Donald Duck in Disneyland,* 1955 .... 15.00

Locket, brass, heart shape, raised castle on front, pink and blue accents, late 1950s 28.00

Pinback Button, Main Street Commemorative, blue text, 3000th Performance, Sept 4, 1991, color photo 37.50

Plate, Disneyland, lace edge, multicolored center design, 7-1/4" d 6.00

Tray, metal, white designs around rim, 1960s........................... 15.00

Wrist Watch, 35 Years of Magic-Disneyland, Mickey's face, band with relief of Fantasy Land Castle, the Matterhorn, and Ferris wheel, Japan, MIB 25.00

❖ Dog Collectibles

Woof Woof! Collecting dog related items is a fun sport for many collectors. Some specialize in collectibles showing a certain breed, or perhaps a dog that looks like a favorite pet. Others seek out famous dog characters, like Tige and Rin Tin Tin or Lassie.

Salt and pepper shakers, ceramic, Japan, 3" h, pr, $9.

Collectors' Clubs: Canine Collectors Club, 736 N. Western Ave., Ste. 314, Lake Forest, IL 60045; Wee Scots, PO Box 1597, Winchester, VA 22604.

Bank, St. Bernard, cast iron, black and gold paint 135.00

Book, *Lassie Come Home,* Eric Knight, John Winston Co., 1944, illus by Marguerite Kirmse 6.00

Bookends, pr, Cocker Spaniels, chalkware, 5-1/2" h, few paint chips 28.00

Brush

    Bulldog, ceramic face, leather collar, full brush, 9" l 70.00

    Dalmatian, Norcrest, Japan, 1960s, 6-1/4" l 14.00

    Figural, ceramic, Marutomoware, Made in Japan, c1950, 6-3/4" l 22.00

Doorstop, Spaniel, Staffordshire style 225.00

Dresser Tray, four French Poodles doing can-can, sgd "Clement" 125.00

Figure

    Basset Hound, Napco......... 45.00

    Bulldog, glass, amber stain, Tiffin............................... 35.00

    Dalmatian, Sparky, Hagen-Renaker......................... 75.00

    Irish Setter, Mortens Studios, #856 .... 95.00

    Spaniel, Ceramic Arts Studios, standing......................... 58.00

Jewelry, pin, Cocker Spaniel, sterling silver, emb detail, mkd "Cini" 90.00

Magazine, *Dog*, 1941 .... 24.00
Nodder, German Shepherd 75.00
Painting, French Poodle and boy, oil
    on canvas, 1950s 200.00
Stuffed Toy, Cocker, Steiff type,
    mohair, 5" h 45.00
Tape Measure, Bulldog, brass, glass
    eyes.................................... 85.00

❖ Doll House Furniture

Doll house furnishings are the tiny articles used to furnish and accessorize a doll house. Materials and methods of production range from fine handmade wooden pieces to molded plastic items. Several toy manufacturers, such as Tootsietoy, Petite Princess, and Renwal, made doll house furnishings.

Reference: Dian Zillner, *Antique Dollhouses and Their Furnishings*, Schiffer Publishing, 1998.

Periodicals: *Doll Castle News*, PO Box 247, Washington, NJ 07882; *Miniature Collector*, 30595 Eight Mile, Livonia, MI 48152; *Nutshell News*, PO Box 1612, Waukesha, WI 53187.

Collectors' Clubs: Dollhouse & Miniature Collectors, PO Box 16, Bellaire, MI 49615; National Assoc. of Miniature Enthusiasts, PO Box 69, Carmel, IN 46032.

Arm Chair, Petite Princess, matching
    ottoman 27.50
Bathroom Set, Tootsietoy, 10 pcs,
    orig box 85.00
Bear Rug, white, purple velvet lining,
    glass eyes 35.00

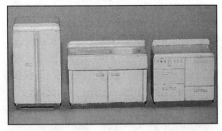

Wooden appliances, white with red bases, 3 pcs, 2-1/2" to 3-1/2" h, $45.

Bed, Renwal, twin size.............. 9.00
Bedroom Suite, Tootsietoy, 6 pcs,
    orig box............................... 65.00
Chest of Drawers, walnut, hand
    made 65.00
Desk, maple, hinged front, royal blue
    and black int. 115.00
Fireplace, Renwal, brown
    plastic 37.50
Kitchen Suite, Ideal, plastic, c1940,
    7 pcs, orig box 40.00
Living Room Suite
    Arcade, cast iron, sofa and
        chair 185.00
    Tootsietoy, sofa, two chairs,
        library table, 2 lamps, phonograph stand, 7 pcs.......... 90.00
Piano, Ideal, plastic, litho,
    mirror 30.00
Wing Chair, Petite Princess,
    MIB 15.00

❖ Doll Houses

Flea markets are often only temporary addresses for doll houses. From large, custom castles to ordinary houses, collectors enjoy collecting doll houses.

Reference: Dian Zillner, *Antique Dollhouses and Their Furnishings*, Schiffer Publishing, 1998.

Periodicals: *Doll Castle News*, PO Box 247, Washington, NJ 07882; *Miniature Collector*, 30595 Eight Mile, Livonia, MI 48152; *Nutshell News*, PO Box 1612, Waukesha, WI 53187.

Collectors' Clubs: Dollhouse & Miniature Collectors, PO Box 16, Bellaire, MI 49615; National Assoc. of Miniature Enthusiasts, PO Box 69, Carmel, IN 46032.

Bing, Germany, garage, litho tin,
    double doors, complete with 2
    orig cars............................ 600.00
Bliss, Victorian, litho on wood,
    2 rooms, 2 story, high steeple
    roof, dormer windows, spindled
    porch railing, second floor
    balcony 1,400.00
Converse, cottage, red and green
    litho on redwood, printed bay windows, roof dormer 550.00

Fisher-Price #952, $6.

Ideal, colonial style, 3 rooms up, 3
    rooms down, balcony,
    back open 300.00
McLoughlin, folding, 2 rooms, dec
    int, orig box 925.00
Schoenhut, mansion, 2 story, 8
    rooms, attic, large dormer, 20
    glass windows, orig decal,
    1923.............................. 1,850.00
Tootsietoy, printed Masonite, half
    timbered style, 4 rooms, removable roof 200.00

✯ ✪ Doll Toys

Collectors are finding out what all little girls know - you can't play dolls without beds, cribs, bassinets, and all the equipment found in a real nursery. Barbie has her own furniture, accessories, plus an extensive wardrobe, but she wasn't the first to be so fortunate. Collectors are able to find all kinds of miniature treasures.

Reference: Jean Mahan, *Doll Furniture, 1950s-1980s, Identification and Price Guide,* Hobby House Press, 1997.

Bassinet, fold-up type 65.00
Bed, four poster, 1920............. 95.00
Blanket Chest, pine, old worn
    repaint, six board type 450.00
Bunk Beds, wood, orig bedding,
    c1960................................. 80.00
Chest of Drawers, Empire style,
    mahogany and mahogany
    veneer, 3 dovetailed drawers,
    scrolled feet, some veneer
    damage............................500.00

Bed, oak, 9" h, 9-1/4" l, 8" w, $18.50.

Kitchen Set, metal, sink, stove, refrigerator, colorful litho dec 175.00

Outfit, Crissy, orange and white polka dot blouse, matching bell bottom pants 10.00

Stroller, red plaid seat, white metal frame, c1960, played with condition............................. 20.00

Trunk, dome back, lined with wallpaper, orig handles 75.00

Wash Tub, aluminum, 5" d...... 15.00

❖ Dolls

Doll collectors are a very dedicated group. Some specialize in a particular doll style or company, while others love them all. There are many examples of dolls for collectors to consider. Condition, age, markings, orig clothing all help determine a doll's value.

References: J. Michael Augustyniak, *Thirty Years of Mattel Fashion Dolls, 1967 Through 1997: Identification and Value Guide,* Collector Books, 1998; Kim Avery, *The World of Raggedy Ann Collectibles,* Collector Books, 1997; Linda Crowsey, *Madame Alexander Collector's Dolls Price Guide,* Collector Books, 1998; Maryanne Dolan, *The World of Dolls, A Collector's Identification and Value Guide,* Krause Publications, 1998; Jan Foulke, *32nd Blue Book of Dolls and*

Values, Hobby House Press, 1997; R. Lane Herron, *Warman's Dolls,* Krause Publications, 1998; Michele Karl, *Composition & Wood Dolls and Toys: A Collector's Reference Guide,* Antique Trader Books, 1998; plus many others.

Periodicals: *Antique Doll World,* 225 Main St, Suite 300, Northport, NY 11768; *Cloth Doll Magazine,* PO Box 2167 Lake Oswego, OR 97035; *Costume Quarterly for Doll Collectors,* 118-01 Sutter Ave, Jamaica, NY 11420; *Doll Castle News,* PO Box 247, Washington, NJ 07882; *Doll Collector's Price Guide,* 306 East Parr Rd, Berne, IN 46711; *Doll Life,* 243 Newton-Sparta Rd, Newton, NJ 07860; *Doll Reader,* 6405 Flank Dr, Harrisburg, PA 17112; *Doll Times,* 218 W Woodin Blvd, Dallas, TX 75224; *Doll World,* 306 East Parr Rd, Berne, IN 46711; *Dollmasters,* PO Box 151, Annapolis, MD 21404; *Dolls—The Collector's Magazine,* 170 Fifth Ave, 12th Floor, New York, NY 10010; *National Doll & Teddy Bear Collector,* PO Box 4032, Portland, OR 97208.

Collectors' Clubs: Doll Collector International, PO Box 2761, Oshkosh, WI 54903; Madame Alexander Doll Fan Club, PO Box 330, Mundeline, IL 60060; United Federation of Doll Clubs, PO Box 14146, Parkville, MO 64152.

Artist Type

Yollanda Bell, Picture Perfect, Baby Sarah, pink nightgown, teddy bear, bunny slippers, 14" h............................. 125.00

Dianna Effner, Sweetness, 1988, Christening dress 125.00

Annie Wahl for Richard Simmons, Sister Mary Margaret, hallmarked, cloth tag, developed with L. L. Knickerbocker Co.,.............................. 80.00

Bed Doll, silk face, painted bangs, gray wig, sewn shoes, undressed 100.00

Boudoir Type

French, cloth face............. 160.00

Spanish, silk face, bisque feet, mini.............................. 175.00

Cloth, Raggedy Ann, Christmas box......................................35.00

Composition

Anne Shirley, 18" h, orig clothes, Effanbee 195.00

Deanna Durbin, 15" h, orig box 245.00

Dream Baby, 20" h, Arranbee, redressed......................... 115.00

Judy Garland, 18" h, Ideal, Wizard of Oz costume.......................675.00

Nancy, 2" h, Arranbee, orig outfit 410.00

Plastic

Bonnie Walker, 17" h, Ideal, redressed 90.00

Ginger, 8" h, hard plastic, sleep eyes, several outfits, including cowgirl outfit, roller skater outfit, tagged Terri Lee Brown dress, hat and shoes, dresses, coats, accessories, hats, some outfits commercially made, some hand made.......... 185.00

Mary Ellen, 3" h, Madame Alexander, orig clothes 225.00

Penny Brite, orig clothes..... 45.00

Tammy, Ideal, orig clothes..... 45.00

Tiny Terri Lee, 10" h, Terri Lee Dolls, trunk with six orig outfits 450.00

Buffy and Mrs. Beasley, vinyl, talks, Mattel, 11" h, $150.

Vinyl
  Butterball, Effanbee, all orig
    ....65.00
  Mary Poppins, Horsman, extra
    clothes.............................70.00
  Truly Scrumptious, 11-1/2" h,
    Mattel 95.00
Vinyl and hard plastic
  Andy, 12" h, Eegee..............25.00
  Brenda Starr, 12" h, Madame
    Alexander, played with
    ....450.00
  Chatty Cathy, Mattel, talking,
    MIB.................................85.00
  Littlest Angel, 1" h, Arranbee
    ....45.00

❖ Doorknobs

If a man's home is his castle, it's no wonder that collectors have latched onto the idea of collecting the ornamental doorknobs and other types of hardware. A doorknob often gives a house personality and a bit of pizzazz.

Reference: H. Weber Wilson, *Antique Hardware Price Guide*, Krause Publications, 1999.

Periodical: *American Bungalow*, PO Box 756, Sierra Madre, CA 91204.

Collectors' Club: Antique Doorknob Collectors of America, Inc., PO Box 126, Eola, IL 60519.

Door Bell, mechanical, brass 125.00
Door Bell Plate, Toulon pattern, Neoclassic design, Reading,
  6" l, 2-1/4" w 60.00
Door Knob
  Arts and Crafts, stamped metal, rose motif, one nickel plated, other copper plated, 2" d knobs, matching 9" h x 1-1/2" w plates, pr..........................50.00
  Eastlake style, brass 40.00
  Mineral, multicolored, brass shank, 2-1/4" d...............30.00
  Passage, sunburst vase and foliage, Branford, c1880 ......35.00
  Porcelain, hand painted, fixed brass rosette, mkd "H & S Pitts Patent," 19th C,
    2-1/2" d 275.00

Victorian, scales and key motif, brass, pr, $75.

Rustic, hammered bronze, thumb action, tapered pickets with serrated ends form 12-1/2" h x 3-3/4" w back plate....... 250.00
Door Knocker, dog, heavy cast iron, old tan paint 235.00
Mail Slot Cover, brass, emb "Letters," Victorian 48.00

❖ Doorstops

Functional figural doorstops became popular in the late 19th C. Today's collectors can find many colorful examples which have been made by several different manufacturers. The condition of the doorstop is critical to its price and collectors prefer doorstops with as much original paint as possible. The sampling of prices below are for examples with at least 80% of their original paint.

Collectors' Club: Doorstop Collectors of America, 1881-G Spring Rd, Vineland, NJ 08630.

Reproduction Alert.

Basket of Flowers, Hubley
  #152 .... 125.00
Fireside Cat 150.00
Mammy, Hubley
  Blue dress, small 240.00
  Red dress, large 385.00
Parrot 65.00
Percheron, dapple gray,
  Hubley 225.00

Fruit basket, cast iron, Hubley, mkd "#456," 7" h, $95.

Petunias & Daisies Basket,
  Hubley............................... 115.00
Poppies & Daisies 125.00
Show Horse, Chestnut, Hubley,
  slight retouch to nose........ 150.00
Twin Cats, iron 250.00

❖ Dr. Seuss

Remember reading *Green Eggs and Ham* or *The Cat In The Hat*? Both those titles are dear to Dr. Seuss collectors. Here's a topic where collectors are still establishing the fair market values, mainly because so many of the Dr. Seuss-related items have just recently been entering the secondary market. The other interesting part about collecting Dr. Seuss is that collectors are learning to look for the many pseudonyms used by this favorite writer.

Barrettes, set of 2 on orig card, figural heads, from *5,000 Fingers of Dr. T.* 37.50
Book, *Cat In The Hat,* later printing, well read 20.00
Grow Chart, The Cat in the Hat Grow Chart, paper, orig packaging 17.50
Lunch Box, metal, several characters on sides 85.00
Pin, pewter, figural, Cat in the Hat...................................12.00
Slippers, Cat in the Hat, figural stuffed head, new 12.00

Grinch doll, Coleco, orig box, $130.

❖ Drinking Glasses

Here's a collecting category that's liable to make you thirsty! Collecting drinking glasses and tumblers of all sizes is an interesting way to study different types of materials, manufacturers, colors, etc. Many drinking glasses start life in sets, but, due to breakage and other tragedies, they sometimes get orphaned and end up at flea markets, just waiting for a new home.

Bohemian Glass, ruby flashed, cut design, gold dec, 4 pc set
.... 150.00

Carnival Glass, Grape pattern,
pastel.................................. 30.00

Depression Era
Flowers, yellow and green ..12.00
Stars, white 10.00

Sunbonnet Girl, red, white, and blue 15.00

Early American Glass, blown
Cobalt blue, paneled, pinpoint flakes on foot,
3-1/8" h.......................... 125.00
Olive green, old paper label, broken blisters, Midwestern, 4" h............................... 700.00

Fenton Glass, Diamond Optic, Aqua 6.00

Fiesta Ware, cobalt blue 75.00

Heisey, Rose Etch, 12 oz, ftd.. 50.00

Libbey Glass, green, slight swirl pattern, mkd, set of 6.............. 72.00

Northwood, blue, opalescent white band at top, mkd................. 10.00

Pattern Glass, clear
Colorado pattern................. 15.00
Kokomo pattern 25.00
Yale pattern 25.00

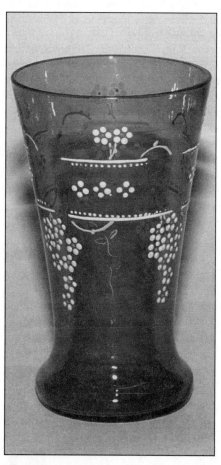

Victorian, green with enameled floral decor, set of 6, $90.

❖ Drug Store Collectibles

Aacchhoo! Here is another collecting field where the collectors are beginning to really specialize. Whether they collect paper ephemera relating to drug stores, things related to a favorite local drug store, bottles, or old packaging, this is a fun category. However, please don't try any of the remedies you might find. Those old compounds might not be stable anymore.

Periodical: *The Drug Store Collector,* 3851 Gable Lane Drive, #513, Indianapolis, IN 46208.

For additional listings, see *Warman's Americana & Collectibles.*

Badge, 7/8" d, celluloid, attached ribbons and names, Mrs. D. B. Crawford, and Dean B. Crawford, "72nd Annual Meeting, New Jersey Pharmaceutical Association, Atlantic City, N.J., June 23-24-25-26," 1942, pr 12.00

Blotter, "Crawford Apothecary, Pacific Ave., Cor. Florida, Atlantic City, N.J." 6.00

Sloan's Liniment bottle, Standard Laboratories, emb glass with paper label, 6 oz, $4.

Bottle, Sodium Phosphate, 4 ounces, by United Drug Company, corked, aluminum screw-on top 30.00

Burma-Bey After-Shave Lotion, red and black glass bottle, background map, 2 oz, full 12.00

Burn-A-Lay, medical cream for burns, Kendall Co. Health Care Division, 1 oz type, orig contents 8.00

Display, 16" h, Phalon's Flor De Mayo, figural wooden countertop type, reverse painted on glass advertising on back, some paint loss, silver loss to mirror, other damage 75.00

Dr. Scholl's Ball-O-Foot, orig cellophane wrapper 4.00

Jar

6-3/4" h, cylindrical, recessed reverse painted label, "Lavender Salt," raised bottom with same pattern as ribbed top, ground stopper 100.00

7" h, rect, recessed reverse painted label, Hayden's Jockey Club Sachet Powder, ground stopper with ribbed top, chip on lip 225.00

11-1/2" h, cobalt blue, paper label mkd "Sundries," domed lid 275.00

License, "Registered Pharmacist" from "The Board of Pharmacy of the State of New Jersey," 1936, 1938, 1942, 1943, 1944 ..... 30.00

Medical Dosage Glass, "The Druggist," J. W. Anderson, Rockville, MO 45.00

Order Form for Opium, etc. To Crawford's Drug Store, Atlantic City, N.J., 1920s, 8-1/2" x 10-1/2" 20.00

Permit, No. 4, State of NJ, The Board of Pharmacy, 1934-1935 to D.B. Crawford, Inc., Atlantic City, NJ, raised seal, 8-1/2" x 10-1/2" 12.00

Prescription Blank—National Prohibition Act, Pleasantville, NJ, 1920s, set of four 10.00

Sign, Choice Perfumes, reverse painted on glass, mother-of-pearl and glitter trim, 15-3/4" h, 53-1/2" l, framed 400.00

❖ Duncan and Miller Glassware

The glass company known as Duncan & Sons and later Duncan and Miller, was founded in 1865 and continued through 1956. Their slogan was "The Loveliest Glassware in America", and many collectors agree with that.

Collectors' Club: National Duncan Glass Society, PO Box 965, Washington, PA 15301.

For additional listings, see *Warman's Antiques and Collectibles Price Guide* and *Warman's Glass*.

Animal

Goose, fat 280.00

Heron 100.00

Swan, red bowl, 7-1/2" h 45.00

Bowl, Caribbean, blue, 8-1/2" d 72.00

Candelabra, pr, First Love, crystal, 2–light 75.00

Candy Jar, cov, Sandwich, chartreuse, 8-1/2" h 95.00

Champagne, Terrace, red 95.00

Cocktail Glass, Caribbean, blue, 3-3/4 oz 48.00

Creamer and Sugar, Passion Flower, crystal 42.00

Cup and Saucer, Radiance, light blue 24.00

Goblet

Caribbean, blue 40.00

Festival of Flowers, crystal 30.00

Oyster Cocktail, First Love, crystal 24.00

Plate

Radiance, light blue, 8-1/2" d 12.00

Sandwich, green, 8" d 24.00

Relish Dish, divided, Caribbean, blue 30.00

Sherbet, Sandwich, green 12.00

Tumbler, Terrace, red 40.00

Wine Glass, Festival of Flowers, crystal 27.50

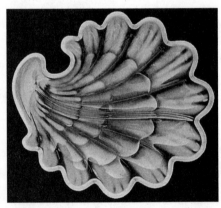

Relish, Sanibell, pink, 8-3/4" l, $35.

E

☆ Earp, Wyatt

Another cowboy hero, this one was also the best looking one of the bunch.

Big Little Book, *Hugh O'Brian: TV's Wyatt Earp,* Whitman #1744, 1958 .... 20.00

Cap Gun, holster, and badge, orig card 145.00

Color and Stencil Set, Hugh O'Brian, MIB 145.00

Gun, holster, belt 120.00

Puzzle, frame tray, full color portrait, Whitman, 1958 .... 25.00

Statue, Hartland.................... 125.00

❖ Easter Collectibles

Here's a holiday that's always hopping to be collected. From chicks to bunnies, this one is fun and whimsical, as well as having serious religious overtones.

Decoration, tissue paper, "Easter Greetings," rabbit with potted lily, 11" x 14" 15.00

Easter Egg, papier-mâché, 2 baby chicks on front, easter basket filled with lily of the valley flowers, int with flowered paper, 3" w, 4-1/2" l................................ 75.00

Pin, Easter Lilies, cast silver, mkd "Taxco 980," c1940............. 65.00

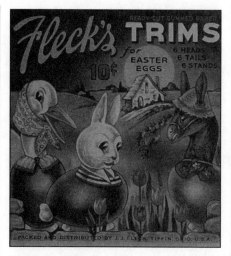

Fleck's Trims egg decorations, paper, 5-5/8" x 5-1/2", $6.50.

Postcard, Gibson Lines, Gibson Art Co., Cincinnati, $2.00.

Plate, "Easter, Jesus is Risen, He is not here," Frankoma, sand glaze, date stamp 1972, mkd "Oral Roberts Association, Tulsa, Frankoma, O.J. F. 1972," 7-1/2" d 24.00

Postcard

Best Easter Wishes, 2 roosters, April 1908 postmark 6.00

Easter Wishes, Victorian girl with rabbits, Raphael Tuck & Sons, printed in Germany, unused 10.00

Happy Easter, children playing in open egg, unused 6.00

Pair of Cupids with Easter egg, unused 5.00

Snowbunnies Figures, Dept 56

Counting the Days Til Easter 1997, MIB....................... 24.00

I'll Color the Easter Egg, MIB................................. 18.00

Wishing You a Happy Easter, MIB................................. 32.50

☆ ⊙ Eggbeaters

Before modern kitchens were outfitted with powerful appliances, egg beaters were run by hand. Naturally, there were all types, sizes, styles of handles, and manufacturers. These clever gadgets make a great wall display and are enjoyed by many collectors.

Reference: Linda Campbell Franklin, *300 Years of Kitchen Collectibles,* 4th ed, Krause Publications, 1997.

A & J, fits glass bowl, mkd "Pat Oct 9, 1923 A & J, Made in U.S.A.," painted white wooden handles, 5" from lid to end of beaters 20.00

A & J Lite, wood handle, 12" l.15.00

Androck, red handle, red wooden knob, mkd "Another Androck Product, Made In The United States of America" 15.00

Ekco Best, 2 arrowheads mark, turquoise plastic handle and knob, 12" h, 3-1/4" w 8.00

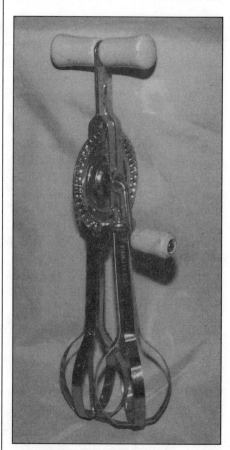

Androck, yellow wooden handles, 10-1/2" h, $6.

Fries, wood handle,
    10" h, 7" w 145.00
Ladd
    Blue handle, 11" l 18.00
    Green handle, 10-3/4" l 18.00
Turbine Egg Beater, wood crank
    knob, mfg by "Cassady-Fairback
    Mfg Co., Chicago, U.S.A. Pat.
    Aug 20, 1912," 10-1/2" l 32.50
Ullman, wood handle, 11" l 18.00
Unknown maker, aluminum,
    10-1/2" l 22.50

❖ Egg Cups

Delicate egg cups make a wonderful collection and are useful and pretty to look at. Egg cups are found in many kinds of dinner services. Other egg cups were made in various materials by many manufacturers as novelties.

Collectors' Club: Eggcup Collectors' Corner, 67 Stevens Ave., Old Bridge, NJ 08857.

Ceramic or Porcelain
    Child's, Indian motif, gold trim,
        blue Japan stamp,
        2-1/4" h 18.00

Across The Continent pattern, red transferware design, 4-1/2" h, $45.

Figural, chick, green, flake on
    base 18.00
Hand painted, mkd
    "Japan,"1950s, 4" h 12.00
Hen on nest, mkd "Worcester
    Royal Porcelain Co., Ltd.,
    Worcester, England,"
    4-5/8" h 30.00
Light blue 6.00
Organdie, Vernon Kilns 15.00
Rabbit leaning against eggshell
    house, incised "Germany
    6458" on back, red stamped
    "69" on bottom, 3-1/4" h,
    2-1/2" w 50.00
Rabbit with cane, incised "Germany 6450" on back, red
    stamped "76" on base, 3-1/4"
    h, 2-1/2" w 50.00
Turquoise blue ground, tree limb,
    leaves and acorns dec 8.00
Jasper, blue, white dec, Wedgwood,
    Portland vase mark,
    c1910 .... 85.00
Silver plate, chicken foot, 2" h,
    2" d 48.00
Wood, hand painted leaves and
    flowers, mkd "Wien," 2-1/2" h,
    1-1/4" d 5.00

✦ ✿ Egg Timers

Figural egg timers are really catching on with collectors. They are colorful, cute, and useful, too.

Bellhop, kneeling, earthenware, 3" h,
    worn.................................... 85.00
Building, emb details, plastic, glass
    timer, emb "Casdon,"
    4" h 40.00
Chef, porcelain, red "Germany"
    mark, incised numbers on back,
    3-3/4" h 110.00
Chef, standing, porcelain, Japan,
    3-3/4" h 60.00
Chick, wooden diecut, paper label
    "Lorri Design," 3-3/4" h 50.00
Dutch Girl, porcelain, black
    "Germany" mark,
    3-1/4" h 110.00
Elf with Mushroom, plastic, back
    emb "A. Casdon Product, Made in
    England," 3" h, 5" w 60.00
Housemaid with Towel, earthenware, Japan, 4" h................ 70.00

Humpty Dumpty, hard plastic, mkd
    "A. Casdon Product, Made in
    England," 4" h 95.00
Isle of Man, hard plastic,
    unused 32.00
Jenny Jones, hard plastic, apron
    emb "Jenny Jones," back emb "A.
    Casdon Product, Made in
    England," 4-1/4" h 75.00
Kitchen Pixie, Enesco, recipe clip on
    back, 5-1/2" h 45.00
Milk bottle shape, People Dairy Co.,
    5-1/8" x 2-1/4", orig box 85.00
Pine Bark, pinecone decal dec,
    3-1/4" h 30.00
Sailor Boy, white suit, blue details,
    stamped "Germany,"
    3-1/4" h 110.00
Windmill with Bird, earthenware,
    mkd "Germany" and incised
    "Germany 825," 3-3/4" h 95.00
Woman with Shawl, porcelain,
    incised lettering on front "Cymru
    am byth," stamped "Foreign" in
    red ink on bottom, incised "Germany" and numbers on back,
    4-1/4" h 110.00

❖ Elephant Collectibles

Collecting elephants was considered to be lucky by many folks. Particularly lucky are those elephants with their trunks raised. Perhaps it is because elephants are exotic or so large, folks just seem to enjoy them.

Periodical: *Jumbo Jargon,* 1002 W. 25th St., Erie, PA 16502.

Frankoma pottery, emb "1968 / GOP," white glaze, 4" h, 5" l, $35.

Bank, metal, red elephant, green base, mkd "Vasio," c1936, 5" h 65.00

Bottle opener, figural, cast iron, sitting, trunk raised

Brown, pink eyes and tongue, 3-1/2" h 55.00

Pink, "GOP" on base, 3-1/4" h 55.00

Figure

Glass, trunk raised, 3" h, 2-1/2" l 12.00

Porcelain, acrobat, pastel blue, white, beige, triangular gold "Royal Dux" sticker, oval "Made in Czech Republic" sticker, 4-1/4" h 55.00

Teak, carved adult and baby, 20th C, one tusk missing, 23-1/2" h 140.00

Lamp, elephant with girl, hand painted, Japan, 14" h 45.00

Napkin Ring, Bakelite, navy blue, c1940 .... 65.00

Pin, gold tone, figural.............. 25.00

Planter, figural, pottery, unmarked
5" h, glossy finish............ 18.00
8" x 5-1/2" 20.00

Postcard, Elephant Hotel, Margate City, NJ, 1953...................... 7.50

Salt and Pepper Shakers, pr, figural, mkd "Japan" 24.00

Toy, Elmer Elephant, gray, bow tie and hat, rubber, Sieberling, 5" h 165.00

✴ Enesco

This company has made quality limited editions for years. Some are marked with a stamp; others have foil labels or paper tags. They are also well known for the Precious Moments collection. A listing for Precious Moments is found later in this edition.

Bank, Garfield, arms folded, 6" h...................................... 60.00

Dealer Sign, "The Rose O'Neill Kewpie Collection by Enesco," 3-3/4" h, 1991..................... 45.00

Figure

Betsy Ross and Friend, 4-1/2" h 18.00

Blot, Dalmatian, 1960s, 3-3/4" h........................ 125.00

Irish Mouse, hard plastic, 2-1/2" h............................. 5.00

Penny Whistler Lane, Mummy & Weeney, 1-1/4" h.............. 4.00

Pluto, 1960s, © Walt Disney Productions, 6-1/4" h 60.00

Shaggy Dog, © Walt Disney Productions, orig paper tag, foil sticker, 5" h..................... 65.00

Snow White and Seven Dwarfs, Walt Disney Productions Japan, 1960s................ 275.00

Mug, Mouseketeers, emb Mickey Mouse face, foil label, c1960.................................. 50.00

Music Box, Love Story, Mickey and Minnie Mouse, plays "Love Makes The World Go Round," 6" h, orig paper label 75.00

Salt and Pepper Shakers, pr
Blue jays, orig paper labels, 3-3/4" h.......................... 15.00

Pixies, orig foil labels, 4" h.. 24.00

Snow Dome, Nag's Head, NC, mouse on skis, oval 15.00

"Jesus" figurine, Little Bible Friends, 1980, sgd "Lucas," 5" h, $10.

❖ Ertl

Ertl is well known as a farm toy manufacturer. However, they have also made many other kinds of toys and figures. Ertl also specializes in promotional or commemorative trucks and banks. The sale of these toys and banks probably have assisted quite a few volunteer fire companies and other civic groups.

Collectors' Club: Ertl Collectors Club, PO Box 500, Dyersville, IA 52040.

Airplane

Alaska Airlines, DC-3.......... 40.00
Allegheny Airlines, DC-3..... 60.00
American Airlines............... 40.00
Continental Airlines, DC-3 .. 45.00
McDonald's Air Express...... 30.00
Shell Oil, trimotor 50.00
TWA, DC-3 .... 45.00
United Airlines, trimotor 50.00
US Navy Air Express 30.00

Bank

American Telephone & Telegraph, replica 1918 Model T Ford, MIB 35.00

Fina, replica 1917 Model T Ford van, MIB 100.00

Kodak, replica Ford's first delivery car, MIB 75.00

Smokey The Bear Ford Truck, 8" l 125.00

Car

Atlanta Braves Headbopper, 3" l 8.00

Deere lawn tractor, orange and white, metal, rubber tires, orig box, $300.

For exciting collecting trends and newly expanded areas look for the following symbols:

✪ Hot Topic

✴ New Warman's Listing

(May have been in another Warman's edition.)

Boss Hogg's, Dukes of Hazzard,
1981 ....35.00
Figure, diecast
Captain Marvel, 2" h, collector
card, 1990, MOC.............15.00
Daffy Duck, driving a fire engine,
Looney Tunes, 1980s,
MOC...............................40.00
Duck, cast, 2-1/2" h 20.00
Road Runner, Looney Tunes,
1980s, MOC....................40.00
Sylvester, Looney Tunes, 1980s,
MOC...............................40.00
Wondergirl, 2" h, 1990,
MOC...............................15.00
Tractor
John Deere, utility tractor, 1993,
1/16th scale....................36.00

McCormick-Deering, Farmall,
1/16th scale.................... 85.00

☆ Eyeglasses

Some collectors look for vintage
eyeglasses. Eyeglasses tend to
make a neat decorator accent.
Other flea market buyers look for
period eyeglasses to use for theatrical purposes.

Gold rim, broken nose piece... 18.00

Horn rimmed, c1920 .... 20.00

Monocle, gold frame 25.00

Prince Nez, orig case, gold ear
hook 30.00
Silvertone frames, lady's,
c1950 .... 10.00

**Cosmeian cat-eye sunglasses,
taupe, 1960s, $35.**

Favorite dealers:

Name: _____

Shop name:_____

Address:_____

_____

Phone:_____

Hours:_____

Comments:_____

Name: _____

Shop name:_____

Address:_____

_____

Phone:_____

Hours:_____

Comments:_____

Name: _____

Shop name:_____

Address:_____

_____

Phone:_____

Hours:_____

Comments:_____

Name: _____

Shop name:_____

Address:_____

_____

Phone:_____

Hours:_____

Comments:_____

Name: _____

Shop name:_____

Address:_____

_____

Phone:_____

Hours:_____

Comments:_____

Name: _____

Shop name:_____

Address:_____

_____

Phone:_____

Hours:_____

Comments:_____

F

❖ Farber Brothers/ Krome Kraft

Farber Brothers was located in New York City from 1919 to 1965. Their principal business was the sale of fine table accessories. Some of these had ceramic inserts by such quality manufacturers, like Lenox, or glass inserts by Cambridge. The bases were chrome, silver plate, or mosaic gold. Most of their items were marked Farber Brothers, and they did use some paper labels with the Krome Kraft name.

Candy Dish, cov, Cambridge, black, etched dec 75.00
Compote, Cambridge, nude stem, amethyst 70.00
Decanter, Cambridge, Dutchess, filigree, amber, 12" h 75.00
Goblet, amber glass bowl, chrome stem, 5-7/8" h, set of four . 125.00
Mustard, cov, cobalt blue Cambridge bowl, chrome lid 50.00
Salt and Pepper Shakers, pr, Cambridge, amber, 2-1/2" h 30.00
Tray, crystal and chrome, 9-1/2" l 42.00
Tumbler, 12 oz, varied colors, Cambridge #5633, set of six 150.00
Wine, Cambridge, amethyst, 6-1/2" h, set of six 150.00

Cocktail shaker, plastic handle, 10-3/4" h, $20.

❖ Fans, Electric

Summer heat often melts other collectors, but not those who specialize in electric fans. Almost every manufacturer has made electric fans and there are many varieties to collect. Look for clever designs, well made fans, and prominent names. Check the wiring and other mechanicals before plugging in any electrical appliance. Then sit back and cool off!

Emerson Sea Gull, cast-iron base, 12-3/4" h, $68.

References: John M. Witt, *Collector's Guide to Electric Fans*, Collector Books, 1997; ——, *Witt's Field Guide to Electric Desk Fans*, published by author, 1993.

Collectors' Club: American Fan Collector Association, PO Box 804, South Bend, IN 46624.

Ceiling
Emerson CF28, 2 blade, restored 3,000.00
Emerson CF30, 5 blade, good orig condition 4,000.00
Desk, oscillating, brass cage and blades, orig tags 125.00
Table Top
Emerson, #444A, black, gold painted blades, 2 speed, 1926, 8" 35.00
General Electric, #2364327, Whiz, polished brass blades, glossy hunter green finish, c1924, 9" 40.00
Knapp-Monarch, brown finish, 1940, 9" 18.00
Western Electric, #6100, cast iron and metal, 10" d 70.00

❖ Fans

Today we tend to think of fans as a decorative accessory, but to our ancestors, they were a primary way of cooling themselves. Collectors can find a wide range of advertising fans, practical fans, and highly decorative fans. Care needs to be taken in handling some of the more delicate ones, as they may be made of real feathers, ivory, mother of pearl, or even very fine kid.

Paper fan, portrait of woman, advertises "Frankie's Forest Park, Dayton's Family Playground," stains, 10-1/8" x 9-7/8", $9.50.

Collectors' Club: FANA, Fan Association of North America, Suite 128, 1409 N. Cedar Crest Blvd., Allentown, PA 18104.

For additional listings, see *Warman's Antiques and Collectibles Price Guide.*

Advertising

Alva Hotel and Restaurant, 8" x 9-1/2", diecut cardboard, 5-1/2" l wooden handle, full color art of nude toddler holding thermometer in process of shattering from heat while talking on candlestick phone, sweating puppy looks on, minor wear 60.00

Compliments of E. W. Hoyt & Co., Proprietors of Hoyt's Germany Cologne and Rubifoam for the Teeth, chromolithograph of young girl in peach dress and lace bonnet, surrounded by calendar sheets from Ladies' Calendar 1890, bottle of tooth powder and cologne and adv text on back, split wood stick, c1890 ....150.00

Southern Belles on front in Cypress gardens scene, 3 panels, funeral home adv on back 15.00

Tums for the Tummy, hand screen type, young boy beckons to girl leaving drug store, express wagon pulled by terrier, self handle with adv text 35.00

Bridge Tally, yellow, used.......... 5.00

Dance Card, ivory, gilt metal, folding type, room to pencil in names, European, c1870.............. 175.00

Egret Feathers, hand made, 12" l, 9" d, starting to shed 35.00

Silk, mother-of-pearl, shaped feather panels printed with lithographed hand colored scenes, including Christening of Prince Imperial, brisé, French, c1865 .... 225.00

❖ Farm Collectibles

Farm collectors are saving an important part of our American heritage. By collecting and protecting the bits and pieces of items relating to or used on a farm, future generations will be able to have some idea of what hard work farming really is.

References: C. H. Wendel, *Encyclopedia of American Farm Implements & Antiques,* Krause Publications, 1997; ——, *Unusual Vintage Tractors,* Krause Publications, 1996.

Periodicals: *Antique Power,* PO Box 1000, Westerville, OH 43081; *Belt Pulley,* PO Box 83, Nokomis, IL 62075; *Country Wagon Journal,* PO Box 331, W Milford, NJ 07480; *Farm & Horticultural Equipment Collector,* Kelsey House, 77 High St, Beckenham Kent BR3 1AN England; *Farm Antiques News,* 812 N Third St, Tarkio, MO 64491; *Farm Collector,* 1503 SW 42nd St, Topeka, KS 66609; *Iron-Men Album,* PO Box 328, Lancaster, PA 17603; *Rusty Iron Monthly,* PO Box 342, Sandwich, IL 60548; *Spec-Tuclar News,* PO Box 324, Dyersville, IA 52040; *Toy Farmer,* H C 2, Box 5, LaMoure, ND 58458; *Toy Tractor Times,* PO Box 156, Osage, IA 50461; *Tractor Classics,* PO Box 191, Listowel, Ontario N4H 3HE Canada; *Turtle River Toy News & Oliver Collector's News,* RR1, Box 44, Manvel, ND 58256.

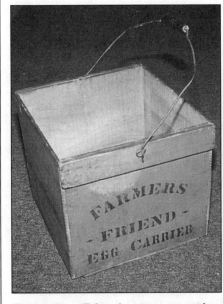

Farmer's Friend egg carrier, wooden, mustard paint, $65.

Collectors' Clubs: Antique Engine, Tractor & Toy Club, 5731 Paradise Rd, Slatington, PA 18080; Cast Iron Seat Collectors Assoc., PO Box 14, Ionia, MO 65335; CTM Farm Toy & Collectors Club, PO Box 489, Rocanville, Saskatchewan S0A 3L0 Canada; Early American Steam Engine & Old Equipment Soc., PO Box 652, Red Lion, PA 17356; Ertl Replicas Collectors' Club, Hwys 136 and 20, Dyersville, IA 52040; Farm Toy Collectors Club, PO Box 38, Boxholm, IA 50040; International Harvester Collectors, RR2, Box 286, Winamac, IN 46996.

Barn Hinge, wrought iron, strap type, 27" l......................................75.00

Booklet

Allis-Chalmers Gleaner Combine, 34 pgs, 1950s 5.00

International Harvester, Make Soil Productive, 64 pgs, 1931 ....8.50

Charm

Cow's Relief, diecut brass profile of milk cow, inscribed "Cow's Relief Saves Your Cows," reverse "Our Husband's Mfg. Co/Lyndon, Vt./Makers," early 1900s.............................25.00

Newton Farm Wagon, diecut brass, "Newton Wagon Co/Batavia, Ill" on back 35.00

Chick Feeder, tin 24.00

Egg Carton, cardboard separators.........85.00

Egg Crate, wooden

Large, for 2 dozen eggs, mkd "Star Egg Crate & Tray Mfg. Co., Rochester, NY," orig inside cardboard, 12-1/2" l, 8-1/4" w, 3" h 155.00

Small, wooden bail handle.. 45.00

Flax Comb, wrought iron, ram's horn finials, 17-1/2" l 135.00

Goat Yoke, single, wood, bentwood bow 60.00

Grain Shovel, wood, carved dec 300.00

Horse Feeding Box, wood, 13" x 17" x 8"............30.00

Memo Book, Agrico Fertilizer, 1947 calendar 3.50

Needle Book, Globe Fertilizer ...6.50

Pinback Button, celluloid

Lamb Wire Fence Co., red and white, black accents, early 1900s 15.00

Lindsey Incubator Co., red image, blue letters, white background, early 1900s 30.00

O. I. C. Swine, black and white, silver rim, multicolored patriotic bunting, plump pig, early 1990s 35.00

Purina Chicken Chowder, red and white checkered feed sack, blue background, white slogan "If Chicken Chowder Won't Make Your Hens Lay They Must Be Roosters," 1920s 10.00

Rain Gauge, John Deere, c1940 .... 35.00

Ruler, International Harvester Co, folding, celluloid, printed monthly calendars for 1909 and 1910, lists of farm products, black inscriptions on 1 side, red on reverse, 1/2" x 4-1/2" 27.50

Seed Dryer, chestnut frame, pine spindles, 21" x 43" 85.00

Sickle, 21" l, wood frame, iron blade 25.00

Sign, Threshermen & Farmers Insurance, 8" x 15" 45.00

Stickpin

Deering, circular brass, reverse with slogan "A Good Machine To Stick To" 20.00

J. I. Case Co., figural brass logo, eagle on world globe, inscribed "J. I. Case Threshing Machine Co./Racine, Wis., U.S.A.," early 1900s 25.00

❖ Farm Toys

Toy and farm machinery manufacturers have provided young fans with wonderfully detailed farm toys. Today's collectors are eager to find good examples and can find additions to their collections ranging from toys from the 1920s to the present.

Periodicals: *Toy Tractor Times*, PO Box 156, Osage, IA 50461; *Turtle River Toy News & Oliver Collector's News*, RR1, Box 44, Manvel, ND 58256.

Tractor, John Deere 4020, 1/16 scale, Ertl, Precision #3, metal, rubber tires, MIB, $95.

Collectors' Clubs: Antique Engine, Tractor & Toy Club, 5731 Paradise Rd, Slatington, PA 18080; CTM Farm Toy & Collectors Club, PO Box 489, Rocanville, Saskatchewan S0A 3L0 Canada; Ertl Replicas Collectors' Club, Hwys 136 and 20, Dyersville, IA 52040; Farm Toy Collectors Club, PO Box 38, Boxholm, IA 50040.

Baler, Oliver 45.00
Bulldozer, Case, diecast, Matchbox, 2-1/2" 10.00
Caterpillar, yellow, Matchbox, 1965, 2" 20.00

Combine

International Harvester, 1950s 55.00

New Holland, zinc alloy, diecast, Ertl.................................. 40.00

Corn Picker, John Deere, steel, Ertl 55.00
Disc, Case, four gang, Ertl...... 20.00
Goat Cart, large ears, 7" l 85.00
Harrow, tandem disc, Corgi, 1967 .... 15.00
Hay Rack, Arcade, 7" l 85.00
Horse Cart, stake sides, cast iron, 7" l 35.00
Log Skidder, John Deere, front blade 24.00
Manure Spreader, McCormick-Deering, team of horses, Arcade 65.00
Ox Cart, Kenton, 7" l 45.00

Pickup Truck

Ford, Buddy L, 1950 .... 20.00
Model A, Hubley 35.00

Plow

Case, Ertl............................ 10.00

John Deere, trailer, steel, Ertl Eska 60.00

Tractor

Allis-Chalmers, lawn and garden type, Ertl, 1972 .... 24.00

Avery, Hubley, cast iron, 1920 .... 150.00

Farmall M, cast iron, wood wheels.................. 95.00

International Harvester, Cub Cadet, lawn and garden type, front end blade, trailer, 1976 .... 35.00

Oliver 70 Row Crop, driver, rubber, Arcor.................. 15.00

Wagon

International Harvester, four-wheels, steel, Tru-Scale 30.00

McCormick-Deering, two horses, cast iron, 12-1/2" l.......... 45.00

⚙ Fast Food Collectibles

The hamburger has long been a popular American food, and our favorite fast food restaurants learned how to make them even better. By adding toys and premiums, they tried to lure us in even more often. These special extras have become an interesting part of the collectibles market.

Reference: Gail Pope and Keith Hammond, *Fast Food Toys,* 2nd ed., Schiffer Publishing, 1998.

Periodicals: *Collecting Fast Food & Advertising Premiums,* 9 Ellacombe Rd, Longwell Green, Bristol, BS15 6BQ UK; *The Fast Food Collectors Express,* PO Box 221, Mayview, MO 64071-0221.

For additional listings, see *Warman's Americana & Collectibles,* and "McDonald's" in this edition.

Ashtray, Big Boy, glass, red and white logo.............................4.00

Bank

Big Boy, 9-1/4" h, figural, vinyl, smiling full-figure boy, blue letters, red and white checkered overalls, incised trademark on bottom, c1960................. 85.00

Kentucky Fried Chicken, Col. Sanders, 12-1/2" h, white hard vinyl smiling full-figured figure, name incised on front, Canadian premium, c1970 ......75.00

Calendar, Burger King, Olympic games theme, 1980 .... 4.00

Doll, Burger King, orig box...... 20.00

Drinking Glass, Howard Johnson's Restaurant, multicolored logo, 4-1/4" h.............................. 32.00

Flying Ring, Wendy's, Fun Flyer, plastic, 3-1/2" d................... 3.50

Glider, King Glider, Burger King, Styrofoam, 1978.................. 2.50

Nodder, Big Boy, papier-mâché head, 5" h.......................... 10.00

Paper Napkin, Pizza Hut, logo .... .50

Pinback Button, Vote for Col. Sanders, KFC, blue and white, c1972, 1-1/2" d.............................. 24.00

Puppet, hand
Denny's, Deputy Dan, 1976................................3.00
Pizza Hut, Pizza Pete............2.00

Menu, Howard Johnson's, ice cream cover 2.00

Burger Chef paper cup, 5" h, $9.75.

Salt and Pepper Shakers, pr, KFC Col. Harland Sanders, figural, 4-1/4" h, smiling full figures, one on white base, one on black base, incised name, Starting Plastics Ltd., London, Canadian premium, c1970...................... 34.00

Dairy Queen, salt shaker, choclate dip ice cream cone, 4-1/4" h.......................... 22.00

Store Display, Taco Bell, Godzilla, 18" h, 18" w, holds 6 premiums, 1 missing 75.00

Sundae Dish, 3-1/2" x 8-1/4" x 1-1/4" deep, green molded plastic, designed like boat, curlicue of simulated ice cream scoop for handle, diecut Dairy Queen name, Lynn-Sign Molded Plastic Co., Boston, early 1960s 12.00

Tee Shirt, Big Boy, white ground, red, white, and black trademark 10.00

Yo-Yo, Burger King Yum Yum, Duncan Yo-Yo, 1979............. 5.00

❖ Fenton Glass

Founded by Frank L. Fenton in 1905, the Martin's Ferry, Ohio, firm first decorated glass for other makers. By 1907, the company was making their own glass and had relocated to Williamstown, West Virginia. Today they are still making quality glass, and collectors are encouraged to visit the factory site and museum in Williamstown.

References: There are several very good older reference books about Fenton Glass.

Periodicals: *Butterfly Net,* 302 Pheasant Run, Kaukauna, WI 54130; *Glass Messenger,* 700 Elizabeth St., Williamstown, WV 26187.

Collectors' Clubs: Fenton Art Glass Collectors of America, Inc., PO Box 384, Williamstown, WV 26187; National Fenton Glass Society, PO Box 4008, Marietta, OH 45750.

For additional listings and a complete listing of reference books, see *Warman's Antiques and Collectibles* and *Warman's Glass.*

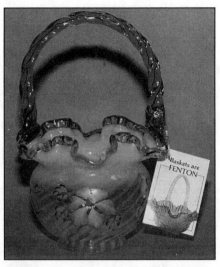

Bride's basket, clear with white swirled stripes, aqua rim and handle, hp flowers, sgd "handpainted by S. Shepherd," orig box, 8" h, $65.

Ashtray, Lincoln In, ruby..........27.50

Basket, Beatty Waffle, green opalescent, #6137 .... 48.00

Bell, Velva Rose, Whitton, #906.............................25.00

Bowl
Peach Crest, shell shape, 10" d 75.00
Rosalene, basketweave...... 32.00

Cake Dish, Silver Crest, white, 13" d 65.00

Candlesticks, pr, Ming, cornucopia, 5" h 50.00

Candy Dish, cov
Lamb's Tongue, turquoise..... 35.00
Teardrop, white 55.00

Compote, Waterlily, Rosalene............................30.00

Condiment Set, Teardrop, white 55.00

Cruet, #418 Coin Dot, cranberry opalescent 120.00

Fairy Light, Persian Medallion, blue satin, 3 pc................... 35.00

Float Bowl, Silver Crest, 13" d 45.00

Flower Frog, Nymph, blue opalescent, 6-3/4" h, 2-3/4"w.............................. 48.00

Goblet, Lincoln Inn, red...........24.00

Hat, Swirl Optic, French opalescent, #1922............................... 115.00

Lamp, Erwin Hall, Mariette College, sgd "Gloria Finn," #9 of 150 .... 300.00

Pitcher, 4" h
   #421 Coin Dot, cranberry opalescent.....................65.00
   #422 Dot Optic, cranberry opalescent......................65.00

Plate
   Fenton Rose, dolphin handles, #1621, 6" d...............27.50
   Ming Rose, #107, 8" d.........32.00

Salt and Pepper shakers, pr, Hobnail, cranberry opalescent, flat, #3806 .... 50.00

Sherbet, Lincoln Inn, pink 15.00

Tumbler, Lincoln Inn, red, 5 oz, ftd 25.00

Vase
   5-3/4" h, fan shape, Hobnail, ruffled rim, white milk glass.................................18.00
   7" h, Burmese, roses, sgd "Sue Foster".................120.00
   10" h, Apple Tree, milk glass 95.00
   11" h, cranberry Snow Crest, swirl...............................60.00

Wine Goblet, Lincoln Inn, red 25.00

❖ Fiesta

Frederick Rhead designed this popular Homer Laughlin pattern. It was first introduced in 1936 and became a real hit after a vigorous marketing campaign in the early 1940s. Original colors were red, dark blue, light green, brilliant yellow, and ivory. Turquoise was added in 1937. Red was removed in 1943, but brought back in 1959. Light green, dark blue, and ivory were retired in 1951 and replaced by forest green, rose, chartreuse, and gray. Medium green was added in the late 1950s. By 1969, the popular pattern was redesigned and finally discontinued in 1972. However, by 1986, Homer Laughlin reintroduced the pattern, but in a new formula and new colors, including a darker blue, black, white, apricot, rose, and even pastels some years later.

Bugs Bunny cup and saucer, mkd "What's Cookin', Doc? / made exclusively for The Warner Bros. Studio Stores," blue-gray, $32.50.

Nappy, medium green, 8-1/2" d, $150.

Collectors' Clubs: Fiesta Club of America, PO Box 15383, Loves Park, IL 61115; Fiesta Collectors Club, 19238 Dorchester Circle, Strongsville, OH 44136.

For additional listings, see *Warman's Antiques and Collectibles Price Guide, Warman's Americana & Collectibles,* and *Warman's American Pottery and Porcelain.*

Reproduction Alert.

Ashtray, red............................ 55.00

Bowl, medium green, 5-1/2" d 65.00

Calendar Plate, ivory, 1954, 10" d 55.00

Candleholders, pr, bulb, ivory.................................. 115.00

Carafe, cov, light green......... 185.00

Casserole, cov
   Cobalt Blue...................... 200.00
   Gray.................................. 375.00

Chop Plate, gray 80.00

Coffee Pot
   Cobalt Blue...................... 300.00

Green.............................225.00
Rose 850.00
Compote, red 110.00

Creamer
   Cobalt Blue, stick handle 50.00
   Medium Green................... 80.00
Cream Soup, rose 95.00

Cup and Saucer
   Chartreuse 28.00
   Gray.................................. 26.00
   Ivory 24.00
   Light Green 20.00
   Medium Green................... 60.00
   Red 30.00
   Turquoise 24.00
   Yellow 24.00
Deep Plate, gray 50.00

Egg Cup
   Gray 175.00
   Light Green 65.00
   Yellow 45.00

Fruit Bowl, 11-3/4" d
   Cobalt Blue 350.00
   Red 420.00
Gravy, turquoise 40.00
Juice Pitcher, cobalt blue 70.00
Juice Tumbler, rose................. 60.00
Marmalade, red.................... 400.00
Mixing Bowl, #4, light green 85.00

Mug
   Gray 95.00
   Rose 75.00
Mustard, cobalt blue.............. 245.00
Nappy, ivory, 9-1/2" d 50.00
Onion Soup, cov, ivory 375.00

Plate, 6" d
   Forest Green....................... 5.00
   Ivory 7.50
   Turquoise 5.00

Plate, 9" d
   Light green......................... 10.00
   Turquoise 10.00
   Yellow 10.00

Salad Bowl, individual size
   Medium Green.................. 135.00
   Red 110.00
Salt and Pepper Shakers, pr, yellow................................. 40.00
Soup Bowl, turquoise 35.00

Sugar, cov

    Chartreuse 70.00

    Gray 80.00

Teacup, chartreuse................ 28.00

Teapot, cov, red 175.00

Utility Tray, red....................... 60.00

Vase, 8" h, light green........... 580.00

Water Pitcher, turquoise,

    disk....................................... 90.00

❖ Figurines

Here's a topic where collectors can usually find great examples to add while browsing at their favorite flea market. Some specialize in certain types of figurines, while others might concentrate on specific makers. Here's a general sampling of what they might find.

Aloha, Treasure Craft,

    1959 .... 45.00

Angel Fish, green "Japan" mark,

    2" h.. 7.00

Blue Jar, mkd "Homco"........... 25.00

Boy Graduate 30.00

Friar, holding sausages, pewter and

    ceramic, 3-1/4" h 50.00

Girl with Watering Can, Japan 35.00

Lion and child, porcelain, mkd

    "Japan" on bottom, 5" w,

    4" h...................................... 38.00

Homco child with lamb, 4-1/2" h, $13.

Man, glass, blue head, hands, and

    shoes, applied bushy hair,

    4" h 12.00

Oriental Girl, 6" h 15.00

Parrot, chip on tail.................. 15.00

Polar Pal, paddling kayak, with Mal-

    amute puppy, icy blue pool base,

    Westland Resin, retired 35.00

Ram, 6-1/4" h, small chip on

    base.................................... 10.00

Snowbunny, "I'll Love You Forever,"

    Dept 56, 4-3/4" h 15.00

Woman, wearing evening gown,

    holding feather fan.............. 12.00

❖ Finch, Kay

Kay Finch is another California potter who started in her home studio about 1935. Her son George and husband Braden, both artists and sculptors, joined her and continued making interesting figures and tablewares until 1963.

Angel, white and blue,

    4-1/2" h 95.00

Bank, Sassy Pig.................... 140.00

Bowl, egg shape, daisies at top, pink

    ext, Kay Finch pink int, mkd,

    5-1/2" l, 3-3/4" h.................. 95.00

Candleholder, white flower,

    14" h 35.00

Dish, shell, chartreuse, mkd,

    12" x 10", slight crazing 40.00

Figure

    Cherub............................. 160.00

    Doves, #1502 .... 295.00

    Peep the Duck.................... 45.00

    Toot the Owl 115.00

    Vicki, as is......................... 350.00

Mug, Santa, #4950 .... 145.00

Planter, baby block and bear

    .... 100.00

Soup Tureen, Turkey 500.00

Wall Pocket, Santa................. 90.00

❖ Firearms Accessories

Collectors of firearm accessories and related memorabilia find flea markets are a great source to add to

their collections. Collectors of firearms are well advised to ask to see any required licenses of vendors who they are dealing with as some states are getting strict about this collecting area. For that reason, we've decided not to include firearm prices in this edition, as fewer quality dealers are choosing to use flea markets to sell guns.

But, memorabilia, advertising, and related items are still being sold by general flea market dealers around the country.

References: John Ogle, *Colt Memorabilia Price Guide,* Krause Publications, 1998; Ned Schwing, *Standard Catalog of Firearms,* 8th ed., Krause Publications, 1998; John Walter, *Rifles of the World,* Krause Publications, 1998.

Periodicals: *Gun List,* 700 E. State St., Iola, WI 54990; *Military Trader,* PO box 1050, Dubuque, IA 52004; *The Gun Report,* PO Box 38, Aledo, IL 61231.

Collectors' Club: The Winchester Arms Collectors Association, PO Box 6754, Great Falls, MT 59406.

Advertisement, Daisy M-25, framed,

    engraved BB gun..............285.00

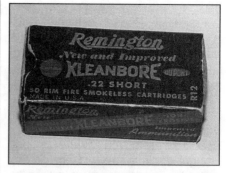

Remington Kleanbore .22-cal. shell box, no shells, $3.

Book, *Bullets by the Billion,* Chrysler Corp., © 1946, hardcover 20.00

Bullet Mold, Winchester, 45-75 caliber 125.00

Folder, 2" x 6-1/4", Winchester New Rival Shells, shotgun shape diecut, dark blue, yellow, and red stiff paper, 1930s 85.00

Pinback Button

Peters Ammunition, red, white, and blue, gold letters, c1910 .... 50.00

Shoot Peters Shells, multicolored, brass and red shell on white background, black letters, Pulver Co., early 1900s ... 40.00

Shoot UMC .22 Smokeless Cartridges, red and white, c1910 .... 35.00

Winchester Products, red and white "W" on blue and silver design, early 1900s 40.00

Razor Blade, Marlin Gun Makers since 1870/Guaranteed by the makers of Marlin Guns/New Haven, Connecticut, blue and white, unopened paper over single edge razor, c1940 .... 15.00

Watch Fob, Dead Shot, brass rim, multicolored celluloid insert, c1920 .... 150.00

❖ Firefighters

Hats off to fire fighters, those brave folks who help others in a time of need. Many of them are also collectors of fire memorabilia.

Periodical: *Fire Apparatus Journal,* PO Box 121205, Staten Island, NY 10314.

Collectors' Clubs: Antique Fire Apparatus Club of America, 5420 S Kedvale Ave, Chicago, IL 60632; Fire Collectors Club, PO Box 992, Milwaukee, WI 53201; Fire Mark Circle of the Americas, 2859 Marlin Dr, Chamblee, GA 30341; Great Lakes International Antique Fire Apparatus Association, 4457 285th St, Toledo, OH 43611; International Fire Buff Associates, Inc, 7509 Chesapeake Ave, Baltimore, MD 21219; International Fire Photographers Assoc, PO Box 8337, Rolling Meadows, IL 60008; Society for the Preservation & Appreciation of Motor Fire Apparatus in America, PO Box 2005, Syracuse, NY 13320.

Alarm Box, cast iron, pedestal, emb "City of Chicago," restored 285.00

Badge

1-3/4" x 1-3/4", relief image of fire hydrant on one side, hook and ladder on other, Mineola Fire Dept, c1950 .... 10.00

2" x 2", relief image of fire hydrant on one side, hook and ladder on other, Mineola Fire Dept, c1950 .... 10.00

Bell, brass, 12" 85.00

Belt, black leather, white lettering 75.00

Bucket, galvanized tin, red lettering, "Fire Only" 35.00

Daguerreotype, fireman, hat, horn, and uniform, tinted 500.00

Fire Engine Name Plate

Ahrens-Fox 15.00

LaFrance 17.50

Mack Trucks, bulldog.......... 25.00

Hose Nozzle, brass................. 50.00

Negative, glass, Chicago Fire Dept #6 pumper 45.00

Pinback Button, convention Pennsylvania State Firemen's Convention

Dark blue cello button, colorful image of Irishman smoking pipe, shaking hands with fireman, light blue ribbon, 1-1/4" green and white "guest" cello button, Harrisburg, PA, Oct, 1914 .... 20.00

Fire department buttons, mkd "Scovill Mfg. Co, Waterbury," 3/4" d and 1/2" d, each $2.

White button, colorful image of firehouse and hat, black text around border "Lebanon Co. Fireman's Convention, Myerstown, PA, June 15, 1929," red, white, and blue ribbon 15.00

Ring, Jr Fire Marshall, Hartford Insurance, 1950s 20.00

Toy

Chief Car, litho tin, friction powered, 1960s, 16" l 75.00

Mickey Mouse Fire Truck, Sun Rubber 80.00

Watch Fob, 1-1/4" d, aluminum, accented by small red fire helmet, New Kensington, PA, firehouse, inscription "1928 West Penna. Volunteer Fireman's Assn," back reads "33rd Annual Convention/The Aluminum City/Aug 1926," black leather strap................................... 15.00

⊗ Fire-King

Made by Anchor Hocking Glass Co., Fire-King is currently one of the hottest collectibles in the glass segment of the collectibles market.

Production began on oven-proof Fire-King glass in 1942 and continued until 1972. Dinnerware was made in several patterns, some more extensive than others. Fire-King wares were made in several colors, including azurite, forest green, gray, ivory, jade-ite, peach luster, pink, plain white, ruby red, sapphire blue, opaque turquoise, and white. Some pieces were also decaled. Jade-ite, a light green opaque color, is currently the most popular and is commanding high prices. Fire-King also made useful utilitarian kitchenware items that are also popular with collectors.

References: Gene Florence, *Anchor Hocking's Fire-King & More,* Collector Books, 1998; ——, *Collectible Glassware from the 40s, 50s, 60s,* 4th ed., Collector Books, 1998; Gary Kilgo et. al., *A Collectors Guide to Anchor Hocking's Fire-King Glassware,* 2nd ed., published by authors, 1997.

Periodical: *The Fire-King News,* PO Box 473, Addison, AL 35540.

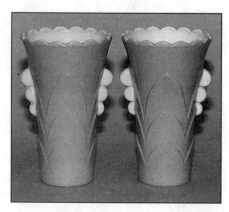

Deco vases, blue, 5-1/4" h, each $6.

Collectors' Club: The Fire-King Collectors Club, 1406 E. 14th St., Des Moines, IA 50316.

For additional listings, see *Warman's Americana & Collectibles* and *Warman's Glass.*

Dinnerware

Alice, jade-ite
Cup and Saucer	12.00
Dinner Plate	70.00
Salad Plate	14.00

Jane Ray
Berry Bowl, ivory	55.00
Cup and Saucer	15.00
Demitasse Cup and Saucer, jade-ite	85.00
Dinner Plate, 9" d, ivory	55.00
Soup Bowl, 7-5/8" d	30.00

Laurel Gray
Bowl, 4-1/2" d	6.00
Creamer and Sugar	7.00
Cup and Saucer	5.00
Dinner Plate	8.00
Serving Plate, 11" l	40.00

Restaurant Ware, Jade-ite, heavy
Bowl, 4-3/4" d	15.00
Cereal Bowl, 5" d	35.00
Chili Bowl	15.00
Creamer and Sugar, cov	35.00
Cup and Saucer	18.00
Dinner Plate, 9" d	32.00
Grill Plate	35.00
Luncheon Plate	85.00
Mug	15.00
Platter, 9-1/4" l	60.00
Platter, 11-1/2" l	65.00
Salad Plate	15.00

Swirl, Azurite
Cup and Saucer	8.00
Dinner Plate	8.50
Platter, oval	20.00
Salad Plate	7.00

Swirl, Ivory
Cup and Saucer	7.00
Dinner Plate, orig label	11.00
Pie Pan, orig label	15.00
Range Shaker, orig tulip top	24.00
Soup, flat, orig label	12.00
Starter Set, orig pictorial box, 4 dinner plates, 4 cups and saucers, set	60.00

Turquoise
Bowl, Splashproof, 3 qt	25.00
Child's Plate, divided, 7-1/2" d	40.00
Starter Set, orig box	75.00

Kitchenware

Red Dots
Grease Jar, white	35.00
Mixing Bowl Set, 7", 8", 9", white	70.00
Salt and Pepper Shakers, pr, white	45.00

Stripes
Grease Jar	35.00
Salt and Pepper Shakers, pr	37.50

Tulip
Bowl, 9-1/2" d	35.00
Grease Jar, ivory	35.00
Grease Jar, white	35.00

Ovenware
Baker, Sapphire Blue, individual serving size	4.50
Casserole, cov, Peach Luster, copper tint, tab lids, orig label	7.50
Custard Cup, crystal, orig label	3.00
Loaf Pan, Sapphire Blue	17.50
Pie Plate, crystal, 10 oz	4.00
Utility Bowl, Sapphire Blue, 7" d	14.00

❖ Fireplace Collectibles

Besides a place to hang your stocking at Christmas, fireplaces are an important decorative and sometimes functional element. And as such, they need to be accessorized. Flea markets offer a wonderful place to find interesting objects to accomplish this goal.

Andirons, pr, American
Brass, acorn finials, baluster turned shaft, spurred arched legs, ball feet, replaced log rests, c1800, 18-1/2" h	395.00
Brass, belted ball top, matching tongs and shovel, 15" h	550.00
Brass and wrought iron, minor imperfections, late 18th C, 20-1/2" h	350.00
Cast Iron, George Washington commemorative, painted, 20-1/2" h	375.00
Bellows, turtle back, orig green paint, red trim, yellow stenciled fruit and foliage, brass nozzle, old leather in tatters, chip on handle, 17" l	165.00
Coal Hod, hammered brass, emb tavern scenes, 25" h	90.00

Fire screen, tinsel art, oak frame, scene with pond, birds, butterfly and flowers, English, $125.

Fire Fender, brass and wire, English, 37-1/2" w, 9" d, 9-1/2" h, early 19th C 600.00

Fire Lighter, gun shape, Dunhill 90.00

Shovel, brass, steeple top, minor dents, 34" l 125.00

Tongs, brass, urn top, 32" l 120.00

✯ Fishbowl Ornaments

Perhaps you want to give Goldie a little company or a place to play hide-and-seek with her friends by adding an ornament. Imaginative collectors find interesting things to brighten up their aquariums. Check to be sure that the paint is non-toxic and the item is waterproof.

Ancient ruins, earthtones 4.00

Aquarium background panel, blues, greens 2.00

Castle, several openings, pastels 3.00

Ferns, flowers, vines, plastic, each .... .50

Figure

    Deep Sea Diver 2.00

    Mermaid, seated 3.00

Rocks, shells, large decorative-stones .... .25

Castle, pottery, 3-1/2" h, 3-3/4" l, $7.50.

✯ Fisher, Harrison

Harrison Fisher was a well known illustrator and portraitist of the 19th C. Many collectors seek out illustrations with his famous signature.

Magazine Cover

    Cosmopolitan, May 1919, Saltion Army Girl 30.00

    Ladies Home Journal, Oct, 1909, American Girls Abroad series, footer reads "The American Girl in the Netherlands, 9-1/2" x 14-3/4" 25.00

Postcard, typical view of American Girl series 15.00

Print Series, printed on heavy clay coated paper, vivid colors, published by Bobbs-Merrill Co.,1909, 9" x 12", set of 10 .... 100.00

✯ Fisher-Price

Unless you grew up in a closet, you probably played with Fisher-Price toys as a child. Founded in East Aurora, N.Y., in 1930, the company eventually became, and today remains, a leader in the market for children's toys. Collectors still search for, and sometimes play with, all types of Fisher-Price items. Flea markets are prime hunting ground for both old and new examples.

Reference: John J. Murray and Bruce Fox, *Fisher-Price, 1931-1963: A Historical, Rarity, Value Guide*, 2nd Edition, Books Americana/Krause Publications, 1991.

Collectors' Club: Fisher-Price Collector's Club, 1442 N. Ogden, Mesa, AZ 85205.

Buzzy Bee, #325 .... 30.00

Car and camper, #992 .... 30.00

Family Play Village, #997 .... 30.00

Floating Marina, with box 31.00

Hospital, #931, with 19 people 52.50

Houseboat, complete 45.00

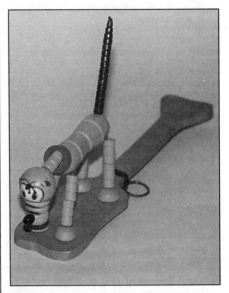

Mickey Mouse Pals Pluto Pop-Up Kritter, Walt Disney Enterprises, ears missing, 11-1/2" l, $85.

Huffy Puffy Train, #999 .... 50.00

Jumbo Jitterbug Pop-up, #422, restrung, ears replaced 195.00

Katy Kackler, #140 .... 63.00

Musical Sweeper, #225 .... 46.00

Play Family School, #923, 15 pcs plus letters 43.00

Quacky Family, #799, orig box 177.50

Snoopy Sniffer, #181, orig box 72.00

Super-Jet, #415 .... 300.00

Tailspin Tabby Pop-up, #400 .... 225.00

❖ ⊙ Fishing

Perhaps the only thing better than meandering through a flea market on a lazy summer afternoon is going fishing. This is one topic where a few auction houses have surprised us by selling some lures, ephemera, and other fishing items for record setting prices.

Periodicals: *American Fly Fisher*, PO Box 42, Manchester, VT 05254; *Antique Angler Newsletter*, PO Box K, Stockton, NJ 08559; *Fishing Collectibles Magazine*, 2005, Tree House Lane, Plano, TX 75023; *The*

Fisherman's Trader, PO Box 203, Gillette, NJ 07933.

Collectors' Club: American Fish Decoy Association, 624 Merritt St., Fife Lake, MI 49633; National Fishing Lure Collectors Club, 22325 B. Drive South, Marshall, MI 49068; Old Reel Collectors Association, 849 NE 70th Ave., Portland, OR 97213.

Bobber

    Panfish float, hp, black, red, and white stripes,5" l..............12.00

    Pike float, hp, yellow, green, and red stripes, 12" l..............27.50

Creel, wicker, center lid hole, early 1900, used 65.00

Decoy, Ice King, perch, wood, painted, Bear Creek Co., 7" l....................................... 70.00

Flies, Jorgenson, salmon...... 450.00

Lure

    Carters Bestever, 3" l, white and red, pressed eyes 9.00

    Creek Chub Co., Baby Beetle, yellow and green wings...40.00

    Hastings, frog, hollow rubber, hp, thick line tie wire, weed guard, c1895 ....200.00

    Heddon, King Bassor, red, gold spot, glass eyes 35.00

    Paw Paw, underwater minnow, green, and black, tack eyes, 3 hooks 18.00

    Pfleuger, polished nickel minnow, glass eyes, 5 hooks, 3-5/8" l...........................250.00

    Shakespeare, mouse, white and red, thin body, glass eyes, 3-5/8" l...........................30.00

Frog lure, rubber, 3-1/2" l, $7.50.

    South Bend, Panatella, green crackleback finish, glass eyes, orig box 50.00

    Strike-It, green, yellow, and red spots, glass eyes............ 40.00

Reel

    Chubb, Henshall-Van Antwerp, black bass 4,200.00

    Hardy, Perfect Fly Reel, English, 3-3/8" x 1-1/4" 150.00

    Hendryx Safety Reel, trout 1,200.00

    Pfleuger Summit 1993L, lightweight model, jeweled caps, on/off clicker, spool tension adjustment, c1936.......... 65.00

    Union Hardware Co., raised pillar type, nickel and brass 30.00

Rod

    Hardy, split bamboo fly, English, 2 pc, 1 tip, 7 feet.......... 250.00

    Heddon Co., casting, nickel silver fittings, split-bamboo fly, fish decal brown wraps, bag and tube, 5-1/2 feet 50.00

    Shakespeare Co., premier model, 3 pcs, 2 tips, split bamboo fly, dark brown wraps, 7-1/2 feet........................ 35.00

Tackle Box, leather 470.00

☆ Fitz & Floyd

Fitz & Floyd is an American success story. The company started as distributors in the late 1950s. After Pat Fitzpatrick died, Bob Floyd went on to establish a colorful niche in the dinnerware and table accessories business by introducing a mix–and–match philosophy. Most of Fitz & Floyd is sold through their own stores. Some items are marked "Fitz & Floyd" while others bear the mark of "OCI" for Omnibus, one of their subsidiaries.

Caddy, Sockhoppers............. 275.00

Candy Jar and Candle Holder, Old World Santa, incised "Copyright F, 1993," 9-1/2" h.................... 95.00

Cookie Jar

    Daisy the Cow, sgd OCI 125.00

    German Santa, incised "copyright OCI, 1989," 11-1/2" h 155.00

    Hampshire Pig, incised "Copyright F & F 1992" 195.00

    Mama Bear, 1991, 11" h 165.00

    Pig Waiter, incised "Copyright FF 1987" 165.00

    Prunella Pig, orig paper label............................... 150.00

    Queen of Hearts, incised "Copyright F & F 1992," 10-1/2" h 245.00

    Rio Rita, designed by Vicki Balcou, 10-3/4" h 195.00

    Russian Santa, incised "Copyright OCI, 1991," 10-1/4" h 145.00

    The Cookie Factory, © 1987, removable sign for Cookies and No Cookies Today............................ 125.00

Dish, cov, figural, pumpkin, few flakes on leaves,5" h.......... 18.00

Figure

    Cinderella/Godmother......... 75.00

    Giraffe 45.00

    Night Before Christmas..... 175.00

    Rio Rita 85.00

Rabbit Series Figure

    Ballooning Bunnies............. 85.00

    Bustles & Beaus 85.00

    Busy Bunnies..................... 85.00

    Floral Rabbit 60.00

    Hat Box 85.00

    Mayfair 85.00

    Mother............................... 65.00

Salt and Pepper Shakers, pr

    Cat and Ball of Twine, 3-3/4" h 25.00

    Ham & Eggs, c1987, 4" h ...30.00

    Kittens, 3-1/2" h 27.50

    Mama Bunny and Baby Bunny, 4" h 22.50

    Policeman and Patrol Car, 4-5/8" h 22.50

❖ Flags

Just driving to a flea market, you're bound to see a couple of flags flying—perhaps at the post office or a few colorful ones flying at homes or businesses. Collectors have been seeking flags and related memorabilia for decades.

Collectors' Club: North American Vexillological Association, Suite 225, 1977 N. Olden Ave., Trenton, NJ 08618.

Badge, Foresters of America, red, white, and blue ribbon 18.00

Booklet, *Our Flag, Display and Respect*, Marine Corps, 1942, 28 pgs 8.00

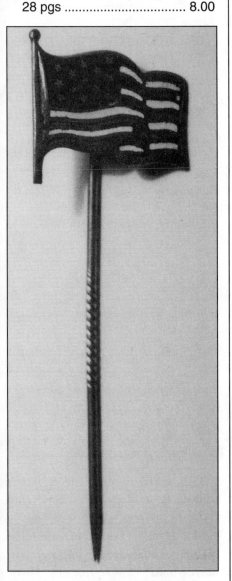

Stick pin, metal, 13 stars, $5.

Clock, mantel, Howard Miller Mfg., "God Bless America," World War II vintage, small American flag waves back and forth as second hand moves 175.00

Flag

    36 stars, parade type, printed muslin, 25" x 22" 115.00

    38 stars, coarse muslin, mounted on stick, 12-1/2" x 22" 50.00

    36 stars, 1908-12, stars sewn on, 4" x 5" 70.00

    49 stars, child's parade type, silk, wood stick, 1959-60, 4" x 5-1/4" 24.00

    Welcome Home, Support Our Troops, nylon, white background, center yellow ribbon design............................ 10.00

Lapel Stud, enameled brass, red, white, and blue enamel flag, white ground, Harrison/Morton campaign, 1888.......................... 40.00

Postcard, printed semblance of Stars and Stripes covering address side, picture of Wm H. Taft for President, July 4, 1908, 46 stars, unused 20.00

Trivet, America's Stars & Stripes, Flag of Freedom, 1776-1976, sand glaze, commemorative Frankoma backstamp, 6-1/2" d 20.00

Tobacco Silk, Egyptienne Straights Cigarettes

    Flag of Algiers 6.00

    Flag of Bolivia, first in series 7.50

    Flag of Edinburgh 6.00

    Flag of Holland 6.00

    Flag of Japan, Man of War Flag, last in series 6.50

    Flag of Madrid 6.00

    Flag of Wales....................... 6.00

Vanity Bag, enameled, flag, U.S. Army sentry and tents on lid 120.00

⭐ Flamingos

Long legged and often portrayed as bright pink, these feathered friends bring smiles to collectors. The famous pink plastic flamingo created as a yard ornament has now passed its golden anniversary, attesting to the lasting appeal of these birds.

Candy Dish, cov, incised "972 Sarsaparilla Deco Designs, WNY, NJ, Copyright 1983," 4" h, 6" l, 6-1/4" w.............................. 37.50

Condiment Set, 3-1/2" h creamer, 4-1/2" h sugar, pr salt and pepper shakers, Sarsaparilla Deco Design, 1982...................... 48.00

Figure

    5-1/4" h, attributed to Maddux, chip on back 35.00

    5-3/4" h, Deco, slight crazing to base........................... 30.00

    7" h, Deco 45.00

    11" h, bisque, wood base, sgd "Andrea"................. 175.00

    35-1/2" h, solid brass, c1940........................... 195.00

Flamingo Pond

    2-1/4" h, 13-1/2" w, mkd "Maddux of California Los Angeles, #1024" 40.00

    12" l, 7-1/2" w, Will George, sgd on bottom 45.00

Lawn Ornament, plastic, orig legs

    Pink, c1950......................... 50.00

    White............................... 35.00

Napkin Ring, 3" h, c1980, set of four.......................... 20.00

Cement yard ornament, flaking orig paint, 12" h, 14-1/2" w, $42.

Paperweight, bronze, brass petunia, incised "Lakeeny Malleagle Co., Cleveland, Ohio," c1930, 5-3/4" h................................ 65.00

Pin, pink flamingo, mkd "Lea Stein, Paris" on clasp, 2-1/2" l, 1-3/4" w 95.00

Planter

7-1/4" h, x 10" l, attributed to American Bisque.............65.00

10" h, unmarked..................75.00

12" h, base mkd "#402".....125.00

Salt and Pepper Shakers, pr, orig sticker "Kenmar, Japan," 4" h....................................... 37.50

Spoon Rest, "Florida, Let Me Hold The Spoon," 7" h 25.00

Toothpick Holder, orig foil sticker "GF, Made in Japan," 3" h....................................... 42.00

Vase, 8-3/4" h, Sunglow, pink flamingo, Hull 75.00

❖ Flashlights

Shall we shed a little light on an interesting collectible topic? Flashlights actually evolved from early bicycle lights. The first tubular hand-held flashlight was invented by Conrad Hubert in 1899. After that, several manufacturers developed flashlights and today collectors have a wide range to choose from.

Collectors' Club: Flashlight Collectors of America, PO Box 4095, Tustin, CA 92681.

Candle, Eveready, #1643, cast metal base, cream-colored painted candle, 1932.......... 40.00

Lantern

Delta Lantern, Buddy model, 1919................................15.00

Eveready, #4707, nickel-plated case, large bull's eye lens, 1912................................25.00

Novelty

Frankenstein, c1960, 9-1/2" l.............................48.00

Hulk Hogan, WWF Wrestling, 1991 ....12.00

Peter Pan, McDonald's premium, MIB...................................4.00

Bottle shape, plastic, Schlitz and Chief Oshkosh Beer, 10" h, each $12.

Rugrats, Nickelodeon, MGA Entertainment, combination keychain and flashlight, soft vinyl, orig blister pack, Chuckie or Tommy 7.25

Ultimate Warrior, WWF Wrestling, 1991...................... 10.00

Railroad, Jenks, brass, patent July 25, 1911 .... 90.00

Tubular

Aurora, all nickel case 20.00

Ray-O-Vac, Space Patrol ... 40.00

Yale, #3302, double ended, flood lens and spot lens 30.00

Vest Pocket

Eveready, Masterlight, #6662, nickel plated, ruby push button switch, 1904 .... 30.00

Franco, glass button switch 25.00

❖ Flatware

Whether you're setting an elegant table or searching for a more informal pattern, you need great looking flatware. There are many, many patterns to choose from, and they range in price to reflect the age, maker, and whether it's sterling silver or silver plate.

Besides some excellent reference books, there are many matching services that can help you complete a flatware set. But, many of us find it more fun to look at flea markets to find additional pieces or unique serving pieces to complete our sets.

References: Frances M. Bones and Lee Roy Fisher, *Standard Encyclopedia of American Silverplate,* Collector Books, 1998; Tere Hagan, *Silverplated Flatware,* revised 4th ed., Collector Books, 1990, 1998 value update.

Bacon Server, Old Maryland, Kirk-Steiff................................90.00

Bonbon, Princess Patricia, Gorham..............................18.50

Butter Knife

Bridal Rose, Alvin 30.00

Fleetwood, Manchester 15.00

Silver Wheat, Reed & Barton............................ 15.00

Carving Set, Cactus, Jensen 325.00

Cheese Knife, Allure, Rogers, 1939....................................8.00

Cocktail Fork

Contour, Towle 24.00

Spoon, silverplated, Vintage pattern, mkd "1847 Rogers Bros. A1," 6", $14.

Empress, International 10.00

Cold Meat Fork, Moselle, American
  Silver Co............................ 60.00

Cream Soup Spoon
  Bridal Rose, Alvin...............65.00
  Fleetwood, Manchester.......30.00

Dessert Spoon, Bridal Rose,
  Alvin 60.00

Dinner Fork
  Bridal Rose, Alvin...............55.00
  Concord, Whiting.................25.00
  Fleetwood, Manchester.......30.00
  Trianon, Dominick & Haff,
    pierced, sterling silver,
    set of 6 ....150.00

Dinner Knife
  King George, Gorham.........40.00
  Lily of the Valley, Gorham....27.50

Fish Knife, Acorn, Jensen....... 38.00

Grapefruit Spoon, Fleetwood,
  Manchester 20.00

Gravy Ladle, Horizon,
  Easterling 40.00

Iced Tea Spoon
  Lily of the Valley, Gorham....30.00
  Romansque, Alvin 20.00

Lemon Fork, Princess Patricia,
  Gorham 17.50

Luncheon Fork
  Chapel Bells, Alvin 24.00
  Della Robbia, Alvin..............20.00
  King Albert, Whiting.............20.00
  Silver Wheat, Reed &
    Barton 24.00

Luncheon Knife, King George,
  Gorham 35.00

Meat Fork, DuBarry,
  International 90.00

Olive Fork, Chippendale,
  Alvin 25.00

Pie Server, Acorn,
  Jensen............................ 135.00

Place Setting
  Contour, Towle 95.00
  Prelude, International 60.00

Salad Fork
  Chapel Bells, Alvin 20.00
  Horizon, Easterling..............20.00

Sardine Fork, Cambridge,
  Gorham 50.00

Steak Knife, King George,
  Gorham 40.00

Sugar Spoon
  Copenhagen,
    Manchester 24.00
  Fairfax, Dugan 28.00

Sugar Tongs, Bridal Rose, Alvin,
  large 90.00

Tablespoon
  King Albert, Whiting............ 30.00
  Rambler Rose, Towle 30.00

Teaspoon
  Bridal Rose, Alvin 24.00
  Fairfax, Dugan................... 18.00
  Princess Patricia,
    Gorham 15.00
  Rambler Rose, Towle 15.00

❖ Florence Ceramics

Florence Ward began creating ceramics in her Pasadena, CA, workshop, in 1939. By 1946, her business had grown into a full-sized plant when her husband and son joined the business and moved it to another Pasadena location. Their main production was semi-porcelain figurines and other decorative accessories. Operations ceased in 1977.

Collectors' Club: Florence Collector's Club, PO Box 122, Richland, WA 99352.

Bust, white, 9-1/2" h
  Choir Boy........................... 75.00
  Pamela and David 300.00

Cigarette Box, cov
  Lady's head, green,
    cameo 125.00
  Winter 245.00

Dealer Sign 350.00

Figure
  Abigail.............................. 160.00
  Blue Boy 295.00
  Camille 245.00
  Choir Boy.......................... 45.00
  Rebecca, gray and
    maroon 250.00
  Rhett................................ 300.00

Sarah 115.00
Scarlett.............................. 175.00

❖ Flow Blue

The name of this pretty china is derived from the blue design that seems to flow or blur on its white background, creating a distinctive appearance. Flow blue china was first produced in 1830 in the Staffordshire district of England. Many potters made flow blue, including some American firms.

References: There are several good older reference books that help identify patterns and their makers.

Collectors' Club: Flow Blue International Collectors' Club, Inc., PO Box 1526, Dickenson, TX 77539.

Reproduction Alert.

For additional listings, see *Warman's Antiques and Collectibles Price Guide, Warman's Americana & Collectibles,* and *Warman's English & Continental Pottery & Porcelain.*

Bacon Platter, Touraine,
  10" l................................245.00

Bone Dish, Albany 50.00

Butter Dish, cov, insert, Chapoo,
  Wedgwood.......................525.00

Butter Pat, Argyle, Grindley,
  3" d 50.00

Cake Plate, Richmond,
  10" d 250.00

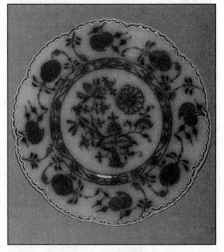

Plate, Holland pattern, Johnson Bros., England, 8-1/8" d, $95.

Coffee Cup and Saucer, Arcadia,
    large 85.00
Creamer, Fairy Villas,
    5" h.................................... 275.00
Cup, handleless, Amoy......... 250.00
Dessert Bowl, Manhattan,
    5-1/4" d............................... 42.00
Gravy Boat, Chapoo,
    Wedgwood 275.00

Plate
    Dundee, Ridgways,
        10" d..............................125.00
    Eclipse, Johnson Bros.,
        7" d.................................65.00
    Fairy Villas,
        10-1/2" d 135.00
    Idris, 10" d 75.00
    Touraine, Stanley Pottery,
        8-3/4" d 60.00
Platter, Gothic, c1850 .... 700.00
Sauce Tureen, underplate,
    Wedgwood 400.00
Serving Bowl, Conway,
    9" d 135.00

Soup Plate
    Alaska, Grindley 75.00
    Touraine, Stanley Pottery,
        7-1/2" d 75.00

Tea Cup and Saucer
    Astoria 120.00
    Touraine 90.00
Teapot, cov, Strawberry 200.00
Toothbrush Holder, Alaska,
    Grindley 145.00

✭ Flower Frogs

Flower frogs are those neat holders that were sometimes designed to compliment a bowl or vase. Others were made to be purely functional and had holes to insert flower stems, making flower arranging a little easier.

Turtle figurine, Brown County Hills Pottery, 6" l, $35.

Art Deco Lady
    6" h, white porcelain, dancing
        nude 90.00
    7-1/2" h, mkd "3941 Germany,"
        c1930 .... 195.00
Bird, figural, bright colors, mkd
    "Made in Japan," 5-1/2" h,
    chipped 50.00
California Pottery, candle holder
    type, made to hold fresh flowers
    around candle, mkd "Calif USA
    V17," 3-1/2" h,4" w.............. 20.00

Cambridge Glass
    Draped Lady, amber,
        8-1/2" h......................... 200.00
    Rose Lady, green 250.00
    Two Kids, crystal 155.00
German, nude, lavender scarf, porcelain, 9-1/2" h................... 135.00
Rookwood, figural nude, porcelain
    glaze, c1930 .... 325.00
Ruby Glass, 3" d.................... 12.00
Silver Deposit Glass, clear glass frog
    with candleholder, 4" d 45.00
Weller, Brighton Woodpecker, 6" h,
    3-1/2" w, 3" l...................... 520.00

☆ Flygsfors Glass

This might be a new name to glass collectors. This Swedish glass was created in the 1950s and can be very unique and almost flowing in appearance. It's usually a bright color cased in colorless crystal. Most pieces are signed on the base by creator Paul Kedelv. The glassworks was taken over by Orrefors in the 1970s and closed in 1980.

Dish, oval, organic shape, clear to
    orange to deep peach center, sgd
    "Flygsfors 53 Kedelv," 14" l,
        8-1/2" w, 4" h................ 250.00
Vase
    6" h, clear, orange dec, floral top,
        etched signature on base
        "Flygsfors, Coquille, 1959"
        .... 350.00
    12" h, 6-1/4" at top, sculptural
        type, clear to peach, sgd
        "Flygsfors Coquille," narrow
        base 400.00

❖ Folk Art

Folk art pieces are treasures that were created by craftsmen who wanted to delight and entertain. Perhaps it's the use of color or the whimsical attitude of some pieces of folk art that adds to their charm. The folk art creator was frequently an unknown and often untrained artisan. Today many craftsmen are continuing the folk art tradition.

Periodicals: *Folk Art Finder,* One River, Essex, CT 06426; *Folk Art Illustrated,* PO Box 906, Marietta, OH 45750.

Collectors' Club: Folk Art Society of America, PO Box 17041, Richmond, VA 23326.

Box, covered with nuts, inscribed "E.
    B. N. Bailey 1860," 5" h, 8-1/4" w,
    5" d, minor loss 275.00
Dish, layers of cigar bands, back
    painted gold 65.00
Figure, carved and painted wood
    Eagle, wings spread, clutching
        branches in claws.........350.00
    Gooney bird, stylized, chip-carved
        wings, black and orange paint,
        blue and yellow details, long
        legs, rect base, PA, early
        20th C 525.00
Outhouse, 13" h 85.00
Scherenschnitte, paper cutting, peacock in a tree, initialed and dated
    "MW 1806," circular gilt gesso
    frame,6-1/4" sq 475.00

Prison art wallet, made of folded cigarette packs, initials "LMO" in design on back side, 3-3/4" x 10", $38.50.

Theorem, watercolor of fruit on velvet, framed, toning, minor staining, 6-3/8" h,
8-3/8" w 925.00

❖ Food Molds

Flea markets are great places to find food molds. Originally designed to make interesting shapes, today many use them as decorative accents.

Basket, pewter ice cream mold, replaced hinge pins 30.00

Boy on Bicycle, 2–part chocolate mold, 8-1/4" h 410.00

Chick and Egg, 2–part chocolate mold, mkd "Allemange," Germany 75.00

Elephant, tin chocolate mold with 3 cavities 100.00

Flag, pewter ice cream mold 115.00

Pineapple, tin and copper pudding mold, oval......................... 100.00

Rabbit, cake mold, Griswold. 270.00

Steamboat, pewter ice cream mold 120.00

Witch, chocolate mold with 4 cavities 85.00

Fish, Wear-Ever No. 2930, aluminum, 11-3/4" x 8-3/4", $8.

❖ Football Cards

Trading cards for this sport are easily found at flea markets. Like baseball cards and other sports trading cards, it's easy for the collector to check on the values and scarcity of these cards. Here's a sampling of some current prices.

Periodicals: *Sports Cards Maga-*

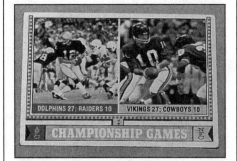

1973 Playoff Championship, #462, $2.50.

zine & Price Guide, 700 E State St, Iola, WI 54990; *Sports Collectors Digest,* 700 E State St, Iola, WI 54990.

Bowman's Best, 1997, set 55.00

Topps
    1989, factory set 15.00
    1989, hand set 12.00
    1998, factory set 55.00

Upper Deck
    1995, complete set, Premium 30.00
    1996, complete set 35.00
    1997, complete set 45.00

USFL
    1984 .... 339.00
    1985 .... 125.00

❖ Football Memorabilia

Every collector has their favorite team or player. Most can tell you more details about their collections and the game of football than you'll ever need to know. However, this dedicated clan usually really enjoys the sport and the collectibles it generates every year.

Reference: John Carpentier, *Price Guide to Packers Memorabilia,* Krause Publications, 1998.

Periodical: *Sports Collectors Digest,* 700 E State St., Iola, WI 54990.

Autograph, signed photograph
    Hampton, Rodney 25.00
    Montana, Joe...................... 50.00

    Payton, Walter 45.00

Book, *NFL, The First 50 Years,* NFL Ridge Press, 1970, 25 pgs, black and white photos................. 12.00

Can Proof Sheet, "Super Super Super Steelers 1979," Iron City Beer, Pittsburgh Brewing Co., Pittsburgh, PA, 5" x 8-1/4" litho tin, smiling team members, beer company and football helmet logo at top, white background................................. 10.00

Display Card, "All American Razor Blades," 8" x 13-1/2" manila envelope with imprint, 7" x 12" red, white, and blue card with orig attached 20 blue and white boxes of razor blades, five blades to a box, graphic of football player kicking off........................... 40.00

Folder, "Drink Coca-Cola" 1937 German Football Championship, 3" x 5-1/8", color artwork, showing players bumping into each other, ball in air, Coca-Cola logo, four pages include info about teams, league 15.00

Football, autographed by members of the Cleveland Browns, white Wilson ball, 25 signatures 250.00

Mug, Super Bowl IV, thermos type, Dallas vs Miami, Lombardi trophy illus, 1972........................... 35.00

Pennant, Chicago Bears, black felt, orange "Bears," orange, green, and red football art, orange felt trim strip, late 1940s 25.00

Program, Penn State-Navy Homecoming Game, Oct 14, 1955, Beaver Field, Penn State Centennial celebration, 64 pgs 35.00

Chip bowl, Super Bowl XXV, plastic, 8-1/4" x 11-1/2", $5.

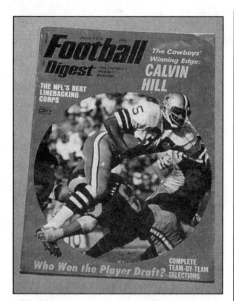

***Football Digest*, June 1974, Calvin Hill feature, 7-1/2" x 5-3/8", $1.**

Sign, Ballantine Beer, 12-1/2" x 30", diecut high gloss cardboard, easel back, full color action scene with NY Giants ball carrier hurdling thru tacklers in green helmets, TV and radio broadcast schedule border, copyright 1960 T. Ballantine & Sons 75.00

Yearbook, Green Bay Packers, 1974, autographed by coaches and players 40.00

❖ Fostoria Glass

The Fostoria Glass Company was first located in Fostoria, Ohio, but moved to Moundsville, WV, in 1891 and continued production of fine glass tablewares. They made pressed patterns, such as the popular American pattern, and also delicate engraved patterns. Like other American glass manufacturers of that era, some of their products were made in colors.

References: There are several very good older reference books about Fostoria Glass.

Collectors' Clubs: Fostoria Glass Collectibles, Inc., PO Box 1625 Orange, CA 92668; Fostoria Glass Society of America, PO Box 826, Moundsville, WV 26041.

Reproduction Alert.

For additional listings and a complete listing of reference books, see *Warman's Antiques and Collectibles* and *Warman's Glass.*

Ashtray, Coin, 7-1/2" d, red..... 30.00

Bookends, pr, Lyre 145.00

Bowl, Coin, amber, oval 30.00

Butter, cov, America, round... 125.00

Candy Dish, cov, Coin, amber, round 35.00

Celery Vase, Double Greek Key 140.00

Champagne Flute, Kimberly #2990 .... 15.00

Cigarette Holder with Ashtray, Two Tone, #5092, amethyst and crystal 75.00

Claret, June, blue.................... 95.00

Creamer and Sugar
　Alexis, hotel size, cut dec... 115.00
　Fairfax, green, ftd 35.00

Cream Soup, American 47.50

Cruet, Coin, olive green 50.00

Demitasse Cup and Saucer, June, topaz......................... 60.00

Goblet, water
　American, 7" h 17.50
　Baroque, blue 25.00
　Chintz 25.00
　Colonial Dame, 11 oz 15.00

Ice Tub, American, 6-1/2" d 60.00

Juice Tumbler, Navarre........... 24.00

Mayonnaise, underplate, Colony 25.00

Old Fashioned Tumbler, Coin, crystal 30.00

Pitcher
　Beverly, amber.................. 125.00
　Jamestown, green 115.00
　Meadow Rose 195.00

Plate
　Baroque, blue, salad 14.00
　Colony, dinner.................... 35.00
　Fairfax, green, salad............. 6.50
　Lafayette, wisteria, luncheon......................... 24.00

Platter, American, 12" l 60.00

Relish
　Chintz, 2–part 30.00
　Silver Spruce, 3–part 35.00

Salad Bowl, Fairfax, green......27.50

Sherbet
　Colonial Dame, 6-1/2 oz 10.00
　Fairfax, yellow..................... 12.00
　Jamestown, medium blue... 15.00
　Versailles, topaz.................. 18.00

Sugar, cov, Coin, olive green ..30.00

Syrup, glass lid, American 135.00

Top Hat, American, 4" h 50.00

Tumbler
　Chintz, ftd............................ 24.00
　Vernon, etched.................... 17.50

Vase
　American, flared, 9-1/2" h........................200.00
　Two Tone, #2470, red and crystal, 10" h 150.00

Water Pitcher, Coin, olive green 55.00

Vase, American pattern, bud vase with cupped top, 8-1/2" h, $30.

Wedding Bowl, Coin, red 65.00
Whiskey, American 17.50
Wine
    American 15.00
    Chintz 38.00
    Willowmere...........................17.50

❖ Franciscan Ware

This popular dinnerware was produced by Gladding, McBean and Co., Los Angeles, California, about 1934. Their use of primary colors and simple shapes was met with enthusiasm. More patterns, shapes, and colors were developed, including pastels. Production stopped in 1986.

Collectors' Club: Franciscan Collectors Club, 8412 5th Ave NE, Seattle, WA 98115.

For additional listings, see *Warman's Americana & Collectibles* and *Warman's American Pottery and Porcelain.*

Tumbler, Apple pattern, 5-1/4" h, $27.50.

Ashtray, Apple 25.00
Bowl
    Apple, ftd 22.00
    Coronado, turquoise,
        7-1/2" d 17.50
Bread and Butter Plate,
    Apple 14.00
Butter Dish, cov, Coronado,
    turquoise........................... 32.00
Cereal Bowl, Ivy 22.00
Chop Plate, Starburst 62.00
Creamer and Sugar
    Apple 60.00
    Magnolia 75.00
Cup and Saucer
    Apple 16.00
    Poppy 32.00
Demitasse Cup and Saucer,
    Rosemore 45.00
Dinner Plate
    Apple 20.00
    Poppy 37.50
Fruit Bowl, Poppy.................... 30.00
Grill Plate, Apple 140.00
Gravy and Underplate
    Apple 42.00
    Ivy 80.00
Jam Jar, Apple 135.00
Mixing Bowl, Apple, 9" d 90.00
Relish, Ivy, 11" l 58.00
Salad Plate, Apple 18.00
Salt and Pepper Shakers,
    pr, Apple, small................... 36.00
Side Salad Plate, Starburst,
    crescent shape 27.50
Snack Plate, Meadow Rose.. 170.00
Soup Bowl, Desert Rose......... 18.00
Teapot, cov
    Apple 65.00
    Meadow Rose 200.00
Turkey Platter, Apple............. 320.00
Tumbler, Ivy 30.00
Vegetable Bowl
    Apple, 7-1/2" l.................... 62.00
    Coronado, yellow................ 35.00

Creamer and sugar, Desert Rose pattern, $35.

> **For exciting collecting trends and newly expanded areas look for the following symbols:**
>
> ✪ Hot Topic
>
> ★ New Warman's Listing
>
> (May have been in another Warman's edition.)

❖ Frankart

Frankart is the name used by artist Arthur Von Frankenberg, who achieved his goal of mass producing "art objects" in the mid 1920s. Most of his works were stylized forms and consisted of ashtrays, bookends, lamps, vases, etc. The pieces were cast in white metal and finished in several popular finishes. Some of the better recognized finishes are bronzoid (bronze colored) and cream, but there were also an iridized copper, silver, or gold finish, plus a gunmetal iridescent gray, a very dark brown, a light verde green, and a pearl green which has a pale iridescence. Prices listed below are for bronzoid finish.

Ashtray
    Duck, outstretched wings support
        green glass ash
        receiver......................... 145.00
    Nude, kneeling on cushions, holding 3" d removable pottery
        ashtray.......................... 250.00

Bookends, pr
    Horse heads, flowing manes,
        5" h 65.00

Nude, seated, one arm arched
over head 265.00
Cigarette Box, back to back nudes
supporting green glass box
475.00
Lamp, standing nude holding 6"
round crackled glass globe
shade 450.00

❖ Frankoma Pottery

This pottery was founded in Oklahoma by John N. Frank in 1933. Production of dinnerware and accessory pieces was interrupted by several disastrous fires. The last one destroyed all molds that were used prior to 1983. Frankoma used a honey-tan colored clay from Ada, Oklahoma, prior to 1954. A clay from Sapulpa is brick-red. Since the early 1970s, a lighter pink clay has been used.

Collectors' Club: Frankoma Family Collectors Association, PO Box 32571, Oklahoma City, OK 73123.

For additional listings, see *Warman's Antiques and Collectibles Price Guide* and *Warman's American Pottery and Porcelain.*

Ashtray, fish, 7" l 17.50
Bird Feeder...........................28.00

Cowboy boot, tan, 4-1/2" h, $18.

Ashtray, "Consulting Engineers Council, 10th Anniversary Convention, May 3-5, 1966, Tulsa, Okla.," 9-1/4" d, $12.

Bowl, Prairie Green glaze,
red clay, #35, 6" l, 4" w,
3-1/2" h 40.00
Bud Vase, Desert Gold glaze,
red clay, mark #38 ....50.00
Casserole, cov, Wagon Wheel, tan
glaze 24.00
Christmas Plate, sand glaze, sgd-
John Frank, orig certificate
1977, The Birth of Eternal
Life 32.00
1978, All Nature
Rejoiced 30.00
Cornucopia, dark pink clay,
9-1/2" l, 4" w, 4-3/4" h 40.00
Deviled Egg Tray, green glaze,
mkd "Frankoma #819," 12" d
....35.00
Figure, dove, newer version ...30.00
Leaf Bowl, tan and reddish brown,
red clay, #226, 12" l, 6-1/2" w
....35.00
Mug, donkey, red, 1976 ....37.50
Pitcher, Wagon Wheel, Prairie
Green, #94D, 6-1/2" h 64.00
Pitcher and Tumblers, 7-3/4" h
pitcher mkd "Frankoma, 5D," six
4-1/4" tumblers 120.00
Planter, elephant...................17.50
Plate
Battles for Independence, white
sand, 1974, 8-1/2" d 45.00
Prairie Chicken, Wildlife Series,
1974 ....40.00
Salt and Pepper Shakers, pr,
Puma 128.00

Teapot, Wagon Wheels, Prairie
Green glaze, pink clay, 6 cup,
#94T....................................70.00
Toby Mug, Uncle Sam, blue glaze,
1976, small nick 45.00
Trivet, Cattle Brands,
6-1/4" d 18.00
Vase, Desert Gold glaze, red clay,
mark #37.............................40.00
Wall Pocket, boot, brown satin
glaze, red clay, "Mom, 1970" written on bottom, 5" h 60.00

❖ Fraternal and Service Collectibles

Folks have often saved family items relating to benevolent societies and service clubs. Today, many of these items are entering the flea market scene. This type of memorabilia tells an interesting story of how past generations spent some of their leisure time.

Apron, Masonic 40.00
Bookends, pr, bronzed, high relief of
BPOE elk 80.00
Compact, Rotary International...30.00
Cuff Links and Money Clip, Masonic
emblem, gold plate, MOP
accents, mkd "Anson," orig
box 65.00
Fez, Knights of Columbus 20.00
Goblet
IOOF, etched......................48.00
Shriners, ruby stained, St. Paul,
1907 ....70.00
Ice Cream Mold, circle, mkd "Kiwanis Club" and "E & Co. NY"
....30.00
Medal, Masonic, 1882.............40.00
Medallion with Pinback Button,
Plainfield Inter-City Track & Field
Meet, 1925, Rotary
International 16.00
Mug, Shriners, Syria Temple, Pittsburgh, 1895......................125.00
Pendant, Eastern Star, silvertone
setting, rhinestones and
rubies 48.00
Plate, Masonic, Shenango
China 85.00

Postcard, Pequod Tribe, No. 47, Improved Order of Red Man, Instituted April 17, 1874, Atlantic City, New Jersey, The Sunshine Tribe, red Indian and bow, reverse side with notification of election to membership, 3-1/2" x 5-1/2" 5.00

Ribbon Badge

Degree of Pocahontas, Notmia, 2" x 8-1/2", purple ribbon, silver lettering, Frederick, MD, Council No. 38, silver braids at bottom, brass accent hanger at top in three parts 15.00

Fraternal Order of Eagles, 2" braided copper rim, white cello button, colorful image of eagle flying American flag, sunburst background, red lettering "Pottsville Aerie No. 134, F.O.E.," red, white, and blue ribbon 10.00

Improved Order of Red Men, 2-1/2" x 8-3/4", green, blue, and red ribbon, gold braids at bottom, attached three part brass accent hanger badge with 1" d black and white cello of male Indian, yellow and red accents, silver text on ribbon "Menton Tribe, No. 511, Imp'd O-R-M Spring Glen, PA," early 1920s 15.00

Rotary Club, white, light blue and yellow lettering, US flag, Rotary flag in center, ship wheel, Cincinnati Rotary Club, Convention I. A. of R. C., San Francisco, 1915, bottom reads "Cincinnati Wants You In 1916".............................40.00

Murat fez, $35.

Shaving Mug, BPOE, pink and white, gold elk's head and name, crossed American flags and floral dec......................................95.00

Watch Fob, IOOF, 94th Anniversary, April 12, 1913 ....32.00

❖ Frog Collectibles

Ribbit, ribbit. From Kermit to Froggie, frog characters have been popular in advertising and other segments of our culture.

Collectors' Club: The Frog Pond, PO Box 193, Beech Grove, IN 46107.

Advertising Trade Card, Pond's Extract 7.50

Bank, pottery, seated frog, green glaze.................................32.00

Beanie Baby

Legs the Frog, retired Oct 97, MWBT and protector 55.00

Smoochy the Frog, MWBT and protector 16.00

Candy Mold, tin 48.00

Clicker, Life of Party Products, Kirchhof, Newark, NJ.................18.00

Condiment Set, figural salt and pepper shakers on tray, stamped "Hand Decorated, Shafford, Japan" 48.00

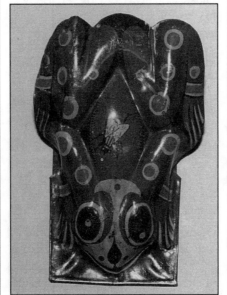

Tin clicker, 3" x 2-1/4", $10.

Cookie Jar, green frog with yellow bow tie 55.00

Figure

Bisque, German, 1" h 15.00

Budweiser, Boy Meets Girl, 5-3/4" w, 3-3/8" h 30.00

Pin, figural

Enamel, black, green eyes, Ciner, 1-1/2" x 2" 200.00

Gold plate, 8 pearls on back, emerald green rhinestone legs, red rhinestone eyes, sgd "Trifari Pat Pending," 1-1/2" h 110.00

Goldtone, clear rhinestones, emerald green cabochon eyes, 2" h 45.00

Sterling silver, green agate frog, sterling silver lily pad, prong set, mkd "Hand Wrought Sterling NHE," 2-1/2" h........225.00

Sterling silver, amethyst colored glass eyes, Taxco, 1-1/2" h 45.00

Planter, ceramic, black and white, 3-1/2" x 4" Flip the Frog and his Pup 125.00

Flip the Frog Lemonade Stand 125.00

Sculpture, The Frog Prince, Franklin Mint, 1986 ....40.00

Stein, Budweiser, frog posing with bottle, another on handle, mkd "Handcrafted by Ceramate," 6" h 28.00

Toothbrush Holder, frog playing mandolin, mkd "Goldcastle, Made in Japan," 6" h...................145.00

❖ Fruit Jars

Some parts of the country refer to these utilitarian glass jars as "canning jars" while others refer to them as "fruit jars" or "preserving jars." But, did you know that the first machine made jar was promoted by Thomas W. Dyott in 1829. The screw-type lid jar was patented in November of 1858. Other improvements followed which allowed housewives to preserve the fruits of their gardens.

References: There are several older reference books which aid in identification.

Periodical: *Fruit Jar Newsletter,* 364 Gregory Ave., West Orange, NJ 07052.

Collectors' Clubs: Ball Collectors Club, 22203 Doncaster, Riverview, MI 48192; Federation of Historical Bottle Collectors, Inc., 88 Sweetbriar Branch, Longwood, FL 32750; Midwest Antique Fruit Jar & Bottle Club, PO Box 38, Flat Rock, IN 47234.

Jar, machine made

Amazon Swift Seal, clear, qt, glass lid, wire bail 6.00

Atlas, qt, #109, cornflower blue 38.00

Boyds Mason, aqua, half gallon, 2-3/4" h domed glass and zinc lid 45.00

Dexter, aqua, qt, glass lid, screw band 30.00

Globe, #1123, qt, amber......25.00

Jewell Jar, clear, half gallon, glass lid, screw band 10.00

Mason, #1664-1, qt, aqua ...25.00

Mason, aqua, qt, emb backwards "s," zinc lid.........................4.50

Ball Ideal canning jar, 1 pt, aqua, $8.

Presto Wide Mouth, clear, half pint, glass lid, wire bail 3.50

Standard, aqua, qt, wax seal................................. 22.00

Tropical Canners, clear, pt, zinc lid 5.00

Jar Rings, price for full box

All Pack 7.50

American 5.00

Ball 4.50

Bulldog 5.00

Presto 5.00

ShurFine............................. 5.00

Tite Rite 6.00

Topseal 5.00

❖ Fry Glass

The H. C. Fry Glass Co. of Rochester, PA, is a great example of how a company changed to stay alive. This glass company started making brilliant cut glass. By the Depression, they switched to a patented heat resistant ovenware, known as Pearl Oven Glass. They also provided an art glass line, known as Foval, in 1926 and 1927.

Reference: The H. C. Fry Glass Society, *The Collector's Encyclopedia of Fry Glassware,* Collector Books, 1990, 1998 value update.

Collectors' Club: The H. C. Fry Glass Society, PO Box 41, Beaver, PA 15009.

Reproduction Alert.

For additional listings, see *Warman's Antiques and Collectibles Price*

Ovenglass casserole, 7-3/8" d, $20.

Guide and *Warman's Glass.*

Butter Dish, cov, Pearl Oven Ware 80.00

Canapé Plate, Foval, cobalt blue center handle 175.00

Cup and Saucer, Foval, cobalt blue handles 68.00

Nappy, brilliant period cut glass, pinwheel and fan with hobstar center, sgd 65.00

Platter, Pearl Oven Ware, 17" l................................65.00

Trivet, Pearl Oven Ware, 8" d 24.00

❖ Fulper

Fulper Pottery, located in Flemington, NJ, made stoneware pottery and utilitarian wares from the early 1800s until 1935. The pieces are usually well marked. Examples from the Arts and Crafts period are currently the strongest in value.

Collectors' Club: Stangl/Fulper Collectors Club, PO Box 583, Flemington, NJ 08822.

For additional listings, see *Warman's Antiques and Collectibles Price Guide* and *Warman's American Pottery and Porcelain.*

Vase, bulbous shape, mottled red and green apple-skin motif, stamped mark, 3-1/2" h, $85.

Basket, off-white, horizontal spiral ribs, twisted rope handle, applied rose, 15" x 7-1/4" vertical stamp 360.00

Bowl, curled edge, leopard skin type dec, crystalline glaze, early mark, 13" d 300.00

Carafe, blue drop, silver overlay of sailing ships...................... 175.00

Flagon, Norman Flower, four horizontal bands, braided handle, pear shape, ivory, mahogany, and cucumber flambé with mottled gunmetal black around base, vertical stamp, 10-3/8"x6" 400.00

Mushroom, 4-1/2" h, #92 .... 55.00

Vase, 9" h, green crystalline glaze, 4 buttresses...................... 500.00

❖ Funeral

Here are a few listings that might help price items for sale at a flea market that relate to funerals.

Advertising Pencil, Harvey Funeral Service, bullet shape, red, orig eraser, 4-1/4" l 5.00

Comic Book, *Superman Funeral for Friend*, epilogue #34, 1993 .... 90.00

Mourning photo, woman in casket, image 7-1/4" x 9-1/4", $22.

For exciting collecting trends and newly expanded areas look for the following symbols:

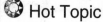 Hot Topic

✱ New Warman's Listing

(May have been in another Warman's edition.)

Fan

Cardboard, 3 folding sections, back mkd "McGinnis Funeral Home, A Father and Three Sons, All Licensed Morticians"...................... 20.00

Rattan, Winberg's Funeral Home.............................. 7.50

Funeral Home Basket, large, wicker, white 45.00

Magazine, *Life*

December 6, 1963, John F. Kennedy's funeral 25.00

February 5, 1965, Sir Winston Churchill's funeral.......... 28.00

Match Holder, wall type, tin, orig black paint, faded gold lettering "You can save Big Money by trading with the Smith-Clark Co., Home Outfitters and Funeral Directors, Goshen, Geo. W. Herr, Mgr. Undertaking Dept," lower lift lid with "Matches"................ 80.00

Memorial Card, typical

Black, gold lettering 5.00

Modern, folding type, poem or scripture 1.00

Railroad Sign, "Funeral Coach," emb, early 20th C 125.00

Wrapping Paper, pictures of hardware, stamped "Comstock Mercantile Co.-Hardware-Furniture-Funeral Directors," 24" w roll............................. 35.00

❖ Furniture

Flea markets are a great place to find furniture. And, you can expect to find furniture from almost every time period and in all kinds of condition. If shopping a flea market for furniture, make sure you take a measuring tape, measurements of rooms or sizes of desired pieces, and can figure out a way to get your treasures home. The listings below are a sampling of what you might expect to find at a flea market.

References: There are many excellent reference books. Some deal with specific time periods or types of furniture.

For additional price listings and a full listing of reference books, see

---

Warman's Antiques and Collectibles Price Guide.

Bed, rope, spool dec on headboard and footboard, stripped..... 100.00

Blanket Chest, 47-1/2" w, 21-1/2" d, 26" h, country, pine, dovetailed case, turned feet, base and edge moldings, walnut till and lid, wear and some edge damage ... 475.00

Bookcase, barrister type, stacking, glass front, 3 section, removable top and base 115.00

Bureau, molded crest over rect mirror, candle holders at side, 2 lidded boxes, 3 drawers, orig dark brown paint, gold striping, floral dec 500.00

Chair

Dining room type, newly caned seat................................ 75.00

Oak, pressed back........... 100.00

Windsor, high comb back, 1920s............................ 95.00

Chest of Drawers, country style, solid cherry, 4 large drawers, scrolled front piece, scrolled feet, refinished, old glass knobs 750.00

Church Bench

23" w, oak 135.00

61" l, primitive, solid ends . 165.00

Clothes Tree, oak, square center posts, all orig hooks 150.00

Stand, oak and cherry, 1 drawer, 1-board top, turned legs, $375.

Highboy, golden oak, serpentine front, refinished, 47-3/4" h, 30" w, $395.

Desk, 36" x 72-1/2" x 29-1/2" h, oak, light natural finish, traces of white, carved horseshoe detail, plate glass top, matching desk chair with cowhide back, Brandt Company 500.00

Filing Cabinet, oak, 4 drawers, worn finish 400.00

Jelly Cupboard, two doors, stripped 350.00

Kitchen Cabinet, painted surface, agateware sliding work surface, some wear 350.00

Morris Chair, as found condition, very worn orig cushions...........................200.00

Night Stand, sq top, slightly splayed legs, small drawer, refinished 200.00

Plant Stand, cast iron, worn orig gilding with red and green dec, onyx inset top, bottom shelf, 14" x 14" x 30" h..............................165.00

Rocking Chair
  Boston style, maple seat, worn 250.00
  Cane seat and back, newly caned................300.00

Table
  Coffee table, blue glass top, curving sides, lower shelf 120.00
  Dining, rect, extra leaves, mahogany colored, c1940 ....115.00
  Drop Leaf, cherry, refinished, burn mark on one leaf 400.00
  Kitchen, oak, drop leaf, some wear, c1890 ....200.00
  Side, wrought iron, demilune, gray stone top, 28-1/4" w, 15-1/4" d, 31-3/4" h.......525.00

Wash Stand, painted, new brasses, no back..............................125.00

Favorite periodicals:

1. *Maine Antique Digest*
2. *Antique Week*
3. *Warman's Today's Collector*
4. *Sports Collectors Digest*
5. *The Depression Glass Daze*

6. *Antique Trader Weekly*
7. _____
8. _____
9. _____
10. _____

G

❖ Gambling

Most of us are willing to take a chance on "winning it big" and may buy lottery tickets, chances, etc. Some collectors eagerly seek out memorabilia related to gambling, lotteries, and other games of chance.

Collectors' Club: Casino Chips & Gaming Tokens Collectors Club, PO Box 63, Brick, NJ 08723.

Book, *Scarne's Complete Guide to Gambling,* John Scarne, 1961, 10th printing, 714 pgs, dj.... 10.00

Card Counter, plated, imitation ivory face, black lettering 24.00

Cigarette Lighter, gun shape, enameled card suit signs on grips60.00

Dice, pr, celluloid 12.00

Ohio lottery tickets, 1975, each 25 cents.

Plastic roulette wheel, with layout and rules book, Lowe, 1941, 8" d, $45.

Faro Cards, sq corners, Samuel Hart & Co., NY 135.00

Faro Chip Rack, blue-green cloth lining, 18" l, 10" w................... 90.00

Poker Chips, wood holder
    Crown 60.00
    Dogs playing cards 65.00

Roulette Wheel, wood and metal, single and double zero decals, 4 prong spinner 45.00

❖ Games

Kids of all ages have enjoyed games for decades. Some played hard, but it's those who carefully saved the pieces, instructions, and took very good care that collectors love. Flea markets are a great source for vintage games as well as those featuring popular television and movie characters.

Periodicals: *The Games Annual,* 5575 Arapahoe Rd, Suite D, Boulder, CO 80303; *Toy Shop,* 700 E. State St, Iola, WI 54990; *Toy Trader,* PO Box Box 1050, Dubuque, IA 52004.

Collectors' Clubs: American Game Collectors Association, PO Box 44, Dresher, PA, 19025; Gamers Alliance, PO Box 197, East Meadow, NY 11554.

Alfred Hitchcock Presents Why, Milton Bradley, 1958 .... 27.50

Donald Duck Wagon Trail Game, Whitman, box 8-5/8" x 16-5/8", $10.

Autographs, Leister Game Co., 1945.................................30.00

Barney Miller, Parker Brothers, 1977...................................20.00

Bozo the Clown Circus Game, Transogram 12.00

Candy Land, Milton Bradley, first edition, 1949 ....45.00

Cribbage, Champion, orig box 50.00

Dr. Kildare, Ideal, 1962 ....40.00

Fox Hunt, E. S. Lowe Co., 1940s.................................20.00

Gong Show, American Publishing, 1977...................................15.00

Have Gun Will Travel, Parker Brothers, 1975 ....18.00

Lie Detector Game, Mattel, c1960, MIB 90.00

Magnatel, Mattel, 10 games in one, 1961, unused...................100.00

Parcheesi, Selchow & Righter ..8.00

Rook, Parker Brothers 5.00

Scoop! The Game, Parker Brothers, 14" x 19-1/2" , black, white, orange, and green box, copyright 1956...................................45.00

Scrabble, Selchow & Righter 7.50

Springrings, Spears Games, © Great Britain, c1930, 6" x 6" x 1" 25.00

Tic Tac Dough, Transogram, 1957, first edition 25.00

Woody Woodpecker, some missing parts....................................15.00

✯ Gardening

There's something therapeutic about gardening, and when the

Flowerpot, brown brushed terra cotta, 13-1/2" h, 12-3/4" d, $125.

weather is bad, why not collect gardening items to soothe your spirit? Many landscapers use antique elements to enhance a garden, so dig around flea markets for interesting gates, garden benches, etc.

Bird Bath, concrete, 2 pc 35.00
Flower Pot, clay, typical 1.00
Garden Bench, precast
　　concrete 45.00
Gardening Gloves, well worn.... 2.00
Hoe, heart-shaped blade, worn
　　wood handle 20.00
Seed Box, litho label, wood box
　　with lid 30.00
Seedling Bell, glass dome, knob top
　　.. 35.00

Seed Packet
　　Shaker 7.50
　　Typical 3.00
Shears, wood handle 25.00
Shovel, worn wood handle 15.00
Sprinkling Can, tin, wide brass
　　head 25.00
Sun Dial, brass, mounted on marble
　　base 125.00
Wheel Barrow, wood wheel and
　　body, removable sides,
　　weathered 125.00

☆ Garfield

Who's the coolest cat around the cartoon pages these days—Garfield! Flea markets are a great place to find him and his buddies.

Glass mug, "Use Your Friends Wisely," McDonald's, 3-1/2" h, $6.

Bank
　　Ceramic, arms folded, mkd
　　　　"Enesco," 6" h 60.00
　　Ceramic, wearing graduation
　　　　gown and cap, 5-1/2" h, mkd
　　　　"Enesco" 60.00
　　Plastic, gum ball type, "Can I Bor-
　　　　row A Penny," orig plastic key,
　　　　6-1/2" h........................... 20.00
Clock, alarm, talking, MIB 50.00
Keychain, Garfield playing tennis,
　　twistable chain, blister pack,
　　MOC 2.25
PEZ 6.50
Stuffed Toy, standing, 1981, United
　　Features Syndicate, Inc., Dakin
　　Inc., San Francisco, CA,
　　10-1/4" h 16.00
Window Sticker, stuffed figure, four
　　suction cups, faded body,
　　6-1/2" h 4.00

❖ Gas Station Collectibles

Whether you refer to it as Gas Station Collectibles, Service Station Memorabilia, or Petroliana, there are plenty of advertising items, premiums, and other items to collect that all relate to those places that sell us gas so we can drive to flea markets!

Reference: Mark Anderton, *Encyclopedia of Petroliana,* Krause Publications, 1999.

McGill High Speed Changer, metal, worn, 5-1/2" x 4", $15.

Periodical: *Petroleum Collectibles Monthly,* 411 Forest St., La Grange, OH 43065.

Collectors' Club: International Petroliana Collectors Association, PO Box 937, Powell, OH 43065.

Banner
　　8" l, Texaco Havoline,
　　　　plastic 65.00
　　36-1/2" x 60", Sunoco Winter Oil
　　　　and Grease, heavy cloth,
　　　　Mickey Mouse illus, © Walt
　　　　Disney 1939 .... 650.00
Car Attachment, Shell Oil, 3-3/4" x
　　5-1/2" metal domed image of
　　Shell symbol, three colorful
　　International Code Flags,
　　late 1930s 190.00
Charm Bracelet, Tidewater Oil Co.,
　　gold-plated metal, detailed Flying
　　A logos, Veedol Oil can
　　charms 150.00
Coloring Book, Esso Happy Motor-
　　ing, unused 25.00
Decal Sheet, Esso, 3-1/2" x 3-1/2",
　　white, red letters, beige back-
　　ground, Palm Brothers, Decalo-
　　mania Co., NY, c1950 .... 3.00
Employee Badge, Texaco,
　　enameled 350.00
Fan, 10-1/2" l, 7-5/8" w, Sinclair
　　Opaline Motor Oil, adv on
　　back 75.00
Kit, Amoco Word Building Contest,
　　4-1/4" x 8-3/4", black and white
　　envelope, instruction and blank

folder, perforated card spelling "American Oil Company," contest dated Jan 31, 1934, unused 20.00

License Plate Attachment, Sunoco, 1940 .... 100.00

Pin, Mobil Oil, 1932 .... 35.00

Radio, Texaco 65.00

Shirt, Texaco 45.00

Sign

Esso Elephant Kerosene, porcelain 875.00

Good Gulf Gasoline, porcelain, flange 550.00

Sinclair Gas, porcelain 100.00

Socony Motor Oil, 15" d, curved heavy porcelain, Standard Oil Co., NY, some damage 325.00

Thermometer

Shell Anti-Freeze.................85.00

Sunoco, 6-3/4" h, 3-3/4" w, tin, raised finish, diecut, emb airplane in flight, adv below, blue and white, black lettering 275.00

❖ Geisha Girl

Geisha Girl porcelain features over 150 different patterns. It was made primarily for export to western markets during the last quarter of the 19th Century and the 1940s. All the wares contain at least one elaborately dressed Geisha, and many have bright colors and hand painting. Because over 100 different manufacturers made Geisha Girl wares, many marks may be found.

Bowl, Bamboo Trellis, 7-1/2" d 37.50

Celery Set, Porch, Torii Nippon mark, 5 pcs 40.00

Hatpin Holder, Long Stemmed Peony, hourglass shape 40.00

Mug, Bamboo Trellis 20.00

Nut Bowl, Porch, Torii Nippon mark 30.00

Plate, Ikebana in Rickshaw, 7-1/4" d 20.00

Tea Cup and Saucer

Bamboo Tree, Torii, mkd "Made in Japan" 9.00

Bird Cage 15.00

Toothpick Holder, Parasol Modern, 2" h 12.00

Chocolate pot, repaired spout, 7-1/2" h, $14.

❖ GI JOE

Billed as "A Real American Hero," Hasbro's GI Joe has been a favorite for years. Today collectors seek out GI Joe action figures, accessories, vehicles, etc. Over the years, GI Joe has undergone changes in size and even attitude, creating many items for collectors. Most collectors prefer their treasures to be NRFB (never removed from box) or NRFP (never removed from package).

References: Vincent Santelmo, *GI Joe Identification & Price Guide, 1964-1998;* Krause Publications, 1999; ——, *The Complete Encyclopedia of GI Joe,* 2nd ed., Krause Publications, 1997.

Periodicals: *GI Joe Patrol,* PO Box 2362, Hot Springs, AR 71914.

Collectors' Clubs: GI Joe Collectors Club, 12513 Birchfalls Drive, Raleigh, NC 27614; GI Joe: Street Brigade Club, 8362 Lornay Ave., Westminster, CA 92683.

For additional listings, see *Warman's Americana & Collectibles.*

Accessory

Ammo belt......................... 18.00

Bullet proof vest, secret agent 8.00

Goggles, orange 14.00

Life ring 1.00

Navy flag......................... 28.00

Sand bag 5.00

Snowshoes 15.00

Sleeping bag..................... 24.00

Tent, poles missing 20.00

Action Figure

Action Pilot, #7800, 1964, NRFB............................ 370.00

Astronaut, Talking, #7915, 1969 .... 950.00

Canadian Mountie, with dog, complete 375.00

Marine Medic, painted hair, complete 390.00

Sailor, Target Exclusive, white, MIB............................ 125.00

Soldier, Wal-Mart Exclusive, black, MIB..................... 125.00

Super Joe, #7503, 1977, NRFB............................. 90.00

Clothing

Beret, green 85.00

Boots, short, black 4.00

Boots, tall, brown 8.00

Hat, Army......................... 28.00

Helmet, dark blue............... 18.00

Jacket, dress, Marine.......... 30.00

Jacket, Russian 12.00

Pants, dress, Marine............. 6.00

Pants, ski patrol 22.00

Shirt, Navy, 1 pocket............. 4.00

Shirt, soldier, no pockets....... 8.00

Coloring Book, 48 pgs, Spanish text, 1989................................. 15.00

Desert Patrol jeep, orig box, 20-1/2" l, $225.

Playset, Atomic Man Secret
  Outpost, good box.............. 85.00
Weapon
  Bayonet...............................15.00
  Flare pistol............................2.00
  M-16....................................30.00
  Night stick...........................20.00

❖ Girl Scouts

It's easy to identify Girl Scouts with their cookie campaigns, but they are as dedicated to community service and education as their male counterparts. Flea market finds may include clothing, badges, camping equipment, etc.

Reference: George Cuhaj, *U. S. Scouting Collectibles,* Krause Publications, 1998.

Periodicals: *Asta Report,* 9025 Alcosta Blvd, #230, San Ramon, CA 94583-4047; *Fleur-de-Lis,* 5 Dawes Court, Novato, CA 94947; *Scout Memorabilia,* PO Box 1121, Manchester, NH 03105; *Scouting Collectors Quarterly,* 806 E. Scott St., Tuscola, IL 61953.

Collectors' Clubs: American Scouting Traders Association, PO Box 92, Kentfield, CA 94914; International Badgers Club, 7760 NW 50th St., Lauder Hill, FL 33351; National Scouting Collectors Society, 806 E. Scott St., Tuscola, IL 61953; Scouts on Stamps Society International, 7406 Park Drive, Tampa, FL 33610.

Award, Gray Squirrel Award, black
  and gray, white background,
  1980s 12.00
Bear, Ginny Scout, complete with
  stand, bear outfit, tag "Bearly
  There, Inc., Westminister CA
  92683, Collector's Corner Exclu-
  sive Ginny Scout, #15 of 50, All
  New Materials, Made in U.S.A."
  Girl Scout pin on uniform.... 75.00
Booklet, *Cooking with a Purpose,*
  Campbell Soup, 10 pgs,
  1974 ....11.00
Canteen, aluminum, cloth jacket,
  Girl Scout insignia,
  7-1/4" d.............................. 25.00

First aid kit, Johnson & Johnson, cardboard, 5-1/2" x 4", $10.

Charter, tan textured paper, dated
  Jan 1921, dark brown inscription
  and design, inked
  signatures........................... 30.00
Hat, Brownie, wool, orig tag.... 18.00
Invitation, "Sister Scout," white and
  green, cartoon fishes,
  c1980.................................... 5.00
Magazine, *The American Girl,*
  June, 1934.......................... 10.00
Mug, white background,
  red insignia 7.00
Pin, Fiftieth Anniversary.......... 12.00
Pinback Button
  Boone Brownie Olympics, brown
    and orange, early
    1980s 12.00
  Brownie Day, brown and orange,
    cartoon clown image,
    1981 .... 10.00
  Girl Scouts Audubon Project,
    green and white, blue
    lettering, 1980s.............. 10.00
  Girl Scouts Meet the Challenge,
    green and yellow,
    1980s 8.00
Ring, Brownie, sterling silver, adjust-
  able, center image of dancing
  Brownie, 1930s................... 35.00
Sewing Kit, Brownies, red case,
  1940s................................. 15.00

❖ Glass Knives

Most glass knives date to the depression-era glass and the manufacturers who dominated the market at that period. They range in color and design. Like other collectibles, a premium is paid for one in the original box.

Block pattern, pink 45.00
Flower handle, pink, inscribed "Net-
  tie," mkd "Made in USA" 40.00
Plain, green, 9-1/8" l............... 42.00
Three Leaf pattern, crystal 18.00
Three Star pattern
  Blue.................................... 42.00
  Crystal, orig box.................. 40.00
  Pink.................................... 38.00

☆ Goebel

Many dealers and collectors associate the name "Goebel" with Hummels. They have created many other similar figures, animals and accessories. Look for the Hummel-type markings and well made porcelain.

Collectors' Clubs: Friar Tuck Collectors Club, PO Box 262, Oswego, NY 13827; Goebel Networkers, PO Box 396, Lemoyne, PA 17043.

Animal Figure
  Blue Bird, CV73, mkd
    "Germany" 20.00
  Ducks, pair..........................28.00
  Fish, incised mark, 3" 45.00
  Rabbit, purple, #803, stylized bee
    in V mark, mkd "Goebel W.
    Germany" 60.00
  Thumper, Walt Disney Produc-
    tions paper label, blue full bee
    mark, 2-1/2" h.................65.00
Decanter, Friar Tuck, large....130.00
Figure
  Bellhop, Sheraton, orig
    suitcases 425.00

Bird, blue glaze, mkd "CV74," 2-1/2" h, 3-3/4" l, $20.

Betsey Clark......................100.00

Dutch Boy on Tulip, It's A Small World, Walt Disney Productions, orig tags and box, 5-1/2" h 90.00

Eleanor, mkd "Made in West Germany," incised numbers, 8-3/4" h 75.00

Elisabeth, 1601, gold trim, mkd "Made in West Germany," incised numbers, 8-3/4" h 75.00

Isabella, 1503, gold trim, mkd "Made in West Germany," incised numbers, 8-5/8" h 75.00

Katharina, 1772, gold trim, mkd "Made in West Germany," incised numbers, 8-3/4" h 75.00

Seven Dwarfs......................70.00

Flower Pot, Oriental Man attached to side, crown mark 90.00

Perfume Lamp, Bambi, stylized bee mark, foil paper label, 6-1/2" h............................ 275.00

Salt and Pepper Shakers, pr

Flower the Skunk, orig foil label, full bee mark, black "Germany" mark, c1940, 2-3/4" h 225.00

Friar Tuck, full bee mark, "Made in West Germany," 4" h.145.00

Frog and toadstool 35.00

Peppers, one red, other green, full bee mark, black "Germany" stamp, 2" w ...30.00

Thumper, full bee mark, 2-1/2" h 225.00

Vase, Figaro Cat.....................90.00

❖ Goldschneider Porcelain

Vienna, Austria, was the site of the first Goldschneider productions in 1885, when Friedrich Goldschneider established a porcelain and faience factory. Production continued there until the early 1940s, when the family fled to the United States. The Goldschneider Everlast Corporation was located in Trenton, New Jersey, from 1943 until 1950, producing traditional figures and accessories.

Ashtray, German Shepherd 55.00

Figure

Lady with parasol, 8-1/2" h . 85.00

Madonna and Child, orig label, 4-1/2" h........................... 60.00

Southern Belle, 10-1/2" h ... 90.00

Music Box, Colonial Girl........ 120.00

Plate, mermaid pattern 175.00

Wall Mask, Art Deco, curly brown haired girl, aqua sash 220.00

❖ Golf Collectibles

"Fore!" When you consider the game of golf has been played since the 15th century, you can begin to imagine how many golf collectibles are available to collectors. Flea markets are a great source for finding interesting clubs, paper ephemera, as well as golf clubs and other items.

Reference: Chuck Furjanic, Antique Golf Collectibles: A Price and Reference Guide, Krause Publications, 1997.

Periodicals: Golfiana Magazine, 222 Levette Lane, #4, Edwardsville, IL 62025; US Golf Classics & Heritage Hickories, 5207 Pennock Point Rd, Jupiter, FL 33458.

Collectors' Clubs: Golf Collectors Society, PO Box 20546, Dayton, OH 45420; Logo Golf Ball Collector's Association, 2552 Barclay Fairway, Lake Worth, FL 33467; The Golf Club Collectors Association, 640 E. Liberty St., Girard, OH 44420.

Ball

Haskell, bramble, patent 1899 .... 50.00

Lynx, rubber core................ 18.00

Mitchell, Manchester, gutty . 60.00

Spring Vale Hawk, bramble 35.00

Book

Golf-A New Approach, Lloyd Mangrum, Whittlesey House, 1949, 127 pgs, illus of golf swings 10.00

Golf In The Sun All Year Round, Robert H. K. Browning, 1931 .... 38.00

Understanding Golf, John Gordon, 1926 .... 40.00

Club

Burke, juvenile, mashie, wood shaft.............................. 30.00

C. S. Butchart, square-head driver, stamped shaft 48.00

Hagen, iron-man sand wedge, wood shaft 170.00

McGregor, Tourney 693W driver, c1953, steel shaft 150.00

Spaulding, Cash-in Putter, steel shaft 65.00

Wilson, wedge, staff model, c1959, steel shaft 60.00

Golf Bag, Osmond Patent Caddy, ashwood, leather handles, straps,

Ashtray/planter, man with bag and clubs, ceramic, 8-1/2" h, $10.

canvas club tube, ball
pocket............................... 270.00
Mug, hickory shaft, pewter...... 45.00
Paperweight, US Open,
1980 .... 32.00
Pin Tray, figural, lady golfer, Schafer
& Vater............................. 235.00
Program, Bob Hope Desert Classic,
1967 .... 20.00

❖ Gonder Pottery

Established in 1941 by Lawton
Gonder, this pottery was located in
Zanesville, OH, until it closed in 1957.
Gonder pieces are clearly marked,
and many have interesting glazes.

Collectors' Club: Gonder Collectors
Club, 917 Hurl Drive, Pittsburgh, PA
15236.

Bowl, white, crackle glaze,
8" d...................................... 15.00
Candlesticks, pr, turquoise ext.,
coral-pink int., marked "E-14
Gonder"............................. 25.00
Ewer, Shell and Star pattern, green,
13" h.................................. 60.00
Figure, Coolie, kneeling, blended
turquoise and brown glaze,
#457 .... 45.00
Teapot, cov, brown and yellow glaze,
mkd "Gonder USA P-31,"
7" x 11" 85.00
Tea Set, 3 pc, purple drip over
cream glaze.......................115.00

**Creamer, mkd "996," green glaze,
$5.**

Vase
7" h, E-line, orig label 50.00
8" h, two swans at base...... 45.00
12" h, peacock tail motif, minor
glaze flaws 80.00

❖ Goofus Glass

Whether collectors identify it as
Goofus Glass, Mexican Ware, or
Hooligan Glass, it's got a unique
beauty. Goofus Glass is actually clear
pressed glass that has been painted,
usually on the back, with a metallic
gold ground and other colors to highlight the design. Because the colorful
decoration is not fired, it's very susceptible to flaking. Most Goofus
Glass was created from 1890 to
about 1920.

Periodical: *Goofus Glass Gazette,* 9
Lindenwood Court, Sterling, VA
20165.

Bowl, Carnations, 8" d 32.00
Cake Plate, Dahlia and Fan, red
flowers, gold ground 45.00
Coaster, Grapes, red grapes, gold
ground 4.00

Vase, red and gold, 7-1/8" h, $45.

Dish, Chrysanthemum Sprays, red
flowers, gold ground, scalloped
rim, 11" d............................85.00
Plate
Apples, red fruit, gold ground,
7-1/2" d...........................28.00
Roses, red flowers, green leaves,
gold ground, 11" d 50.00
Vase, red bird, brown ground,
7-1/2" h 35.00

❖ Graniteware

Graniteware is the name given to
metal kitchen and dinnerwares that
have an interesting speckled or swirled
paint decoration. The first graniteware
was made in Germany in the 1830s. By
World War I, American manufacturers
were taking over the market. Common
colors are gray and white, but savvy
collectors will tell you that graniteware
comes in a variety of colors. Graniteware is still being made.

Collectors' Club: National Graniteware Society, PO Box 10013, Cedar
Rapids, IA 52410.

Berry Pail, cov, Stransky Steelware,
gray and blue 225.00
Bowl
6-1/8" d, blue and white, medium
swirl, black trim, c1960 ... 35.00
8" x 10-1/2" l, gray, oval 35.00
Funnel, 6-1/2" x 6" gray,
handle 28.00
Grill Plate, 11-1/4" d, green and
white, large swirl, black trim,
c1960 ....42.50
Mold, ftd, melon, speckled
blue 185.00
Onion Bin 125.00
Pan, 11" x 6" , mottled gray,
handle 40.00
Plate
9" d, gray and white 20.00
10-1/4" d, orange and white, large
swirl, black trim, c1960 ... 35.00
Platter, 14" l, medium blue and white
swirl..................................195.00
Roaster, cov
Cobalt blue, emb "Savory,"
11-1/2" w, 17-1/2" l, 8" h,
used..................................60.00

Oval pan, blue and white, 3-3/4" h, 11-1/4" l, 9" w, $120.

Gray coffee kettle, wooden bail handle, 13-1/2" h, base 11-1/2" d, $80.

White lid, black base, 12" w, 18-1/2" l, 5" h, used.........75.00
Sieve, triangle shape, cream, blue trim 30.00
Syrup Holder
  Gray, some wear 125.00
  White, some wear 65.00
Tea Kettle, dark blue, white specks, stationary handle................ 70.00
Utensil Holder, wall, large, small dippers, skimmer, side dipper, 14-1/2" x 19", deep blue/green 250.00
Wall Pan, 10" w, white, blue trim, spout, mkd "Made in Germany" 35.00

❖ Greentown Glass

The term "Greentown Glass" generally refers to items made by the Indiana Tumbler and Goblet Co.,

which was located in Greentown, IN. This company made pressed pattern glass and bar wares beginning in 1894. By 1900, the factory had expanded several times, and Jacob Rosenthal developed an opaque brown glass, called "chocolate" glass. This color innovation saved the struggling company. Rosenthal went on to develop other opaque colors, including Golden Agate and Rose Agate. The factory closed in 1903 after a fire destroyed the operation.

Collectors' Clubs: Collectors of Findlay Glass, PO Box 256, Findlay, OH 45839; National Greentown Glass Association, 19596 Glendale Ave., South Bend, IN 46637.

Reproduction Alert.

For additional listings, see *Warman's Antiques and Collectibles Price Guide* and *Warman's Glass.*

Celery Vase, Beaded Panel, clear.................................. 100.00
Creamer
  Indian Head, opaque white450.00
  Shuttle, chocolate, tankard style............................... 95.00
Goblet, Overall Lattice, clear .. 45.00
Mug, 5" h, Nile Green 35.00
Mustard, cov, Daisy, opaque white 90.00
Nappy, Masonic, chocolate..... 90.00
Salt and Pepper Shakers, pr, Cactus, chocolate 275.00
Tumbler, 4" h, Cactus, chocolate 30.00
Water Pitcher, Squirrel, clear................................. 145.00
Wine, Cord Drapery, amber 280.00

☆ Greeting Cards

From Merry Christmas to Happy Birthday, we've grown up receiving and sending greeting cards. Some folks save all these remembrances and many find their ways to flea markets. Some collectors tend to look for ones with colorful images, or witty

Snow White and the Seven Dwarfs, Buzza, Gibson Greetings Inc., 7-3/4" x 5-3/8", $2.

sayings, while others are trying to find an interesting autograph. It's one of those collecting areas where secondary prices are still being established.

Birthday
  Amos & Andy, brown portraits, message includes song title "Check and Double Check," Rust Craft, inked birthday note 28.00
  Barbie, To My Sister On Your Birthday, ©1995 .... 1.00
  Blondie, Dagwood illus, full color, Hallmark, © 1939........... 20.00
  Space Patrol Man, diecut, full color, transparent green helmet, orig envelope 25.00
Christmas
  Christmas Greetings, emb holly, silver background, The Art Lithographic Co. 9.00
  Hearty Greetings, cut-out emb border, holly on front........ 6.50
Get Well, Amos n' Andy, black and white photo, Hall Bros., © 1951 .... 30.00

❖ Gregory, Mary

Here's a name that may be a myth. It seems there is some documentation that a lady named Mary Gregory did some decorating on glassware made in the Sandwich, MA, area, back when the American glass industry was young. However, it's highly doubtful that Mary painted all the wares attributed to her, if she painted any human figures at all. However, brilliantly colored glassware with white enameled painting continues to be called "Mary Gregory Glass", so the legend lives on.

Reproduction Alert.

For additional listings, see *Warman's Antiques and Collectibles Price Guide* and *Warman's Glass.*

Barber Bottle, deep sapphire blue ground, white enameled child playing tennis, long neck, pontil scar 150.00

Box, cov, deep amethyst ground, white enameled boy with bunch of flowers in hand, metal fittings, 3-3/4" l 375.00

Goblet, electric blue ground, white enameled children, pr 275.00

Plate, cobalt blue ground, white enameled girl with butterfly net, 6-1/4" d 135.00

Salt Shaker, sapphire blue ground, white enameled girl in garden, brass top 195.00

Tumbler, cranberry ground, white enameled boy on one, girl on other, facing pr 120.00

Vase, cranberry ground, white enameled boy with wagon, 4" h 100.00

Water Pitcher, colorless body, white enameled girl, colored hands and hair 225.00

☆ Griswold

Here's a name to evoke thoughts of cast iron skillets and kitchen implements. Griswold items are frequently found at flea markets. The company started in Erie, PA, to manufacture hardware. By 1914, the company started to make the cast iron cookware that is associated with the name by many folks. In 1946 the company was sold to a group of New York investors. The trade name Griswold

No. 6 skillet, cast iron, $35.

was sold to its major competitor, the Wagner Manufacturing Co. in the late 1950s. Wagner continued operations, but dropped the words "Erie, Pa" from the trademark.

Periodical: *Kettles 'n' Cookware,* Drawer B, Perrysville, NY 14129.

Collectors' Club: Griswold & Cast-Iron Cookware Association, Drawer B, Perrysville, NY 14129.

Damper Cover, 4", mkd "Griswold, New American," reversible . 20.00
Griddle, #10 .... 72.00
Muffin Pan, #10 948 .... 45.00
Patty Mold, orig box 70.00
Popover Pan, #10 .... 50.00
Skillet
    #3 .... 22.00
    #5 .... 45.00
    #8 .... 48.00
    #14 .... 175.00
Swedish Pancake Pan, #34, 9-1/2" 35.00
Trivet, #7, round 50.00

☆ Guardian Ware

Before aluminum came into its own as a great material for soft drink cans, it was put to use in making pots and pans. Light and versatile, aluminum became the cookware of choice for many years. Among the leading lines was Guardian Ware, with its distinctive symbol of a knight.

Cleaner, Guardian Service Cleaner, paper can, unopened, 8 oz 22.50

Coffee percolator and server, with basket and glass lid, black plastic handles 77.00

Coffeepot, glass lid 30.00

Cookbook, *Guardian Service Tested Recipes*, softcover, 72 pgs, shelf wear 24.00

Griddle, octagonal, 13" w 51.00

Omelet pan, plastic handles, 16" x 6" 35.00

Pan, triangular, domed metal lid 56.00

Pans, triangular shape, domed glass lids, made to fit together in a circle, set of 3 .... 93.00

Platter, 10" x 13" 21.00

Roaster, domed metal lid, 15" x 10" 105.00

Salt and pepper shakers, teapot form, glass bases, aluminum tops, 3" h, pr 71.00

Skillet, glass lid, 2 handle covers, clip-on handle 91.00

Tray, round, 15-1/2" d 40.00

Water pitcher, tilted ball shape, plastic handle 430.00

Ice bucket, basketweave motif, glass lid, 9-1/4" h, $55.

❖ Guitars

Guitars do show up at flea markets. And, if you're the strumming type, ask to try it out before agreeing on a purchase price. Interest in vintage guitars has increased over the past years, spirited on by record-setting prices at auction. It's a market a buyer must specialize in to find really good bargains at flea markets.

Periodicals: *Twentieth Century Guitar,* 135 Oser Ave., Hauppauge, NY 11788; *Vintage Guitar Classics,* PO Box 7301, Bismarck, ND 58507.

Gibson, J45, 1980 .... 1,300.00
Singing Cowboy, wooden, 1941, red and yellow stenciled campfire scene 155.00
Stanford, imitation rosewood finish 95.00

University, rosewood back and sides, vine and leaf pattern, spruce top, ebony guard plate, mahogany neck, MOP trim, 1905-10 .... 250.00

❖ Gunderson

In the late 1930s, Robert Gunderson took over the old Pairpoint Glass operations. Using the name Gunderson Glass Works, they manufactured table wares until 1952. One of the most distinctive glass colors made by Gunderson is peachblow. Their interpretation of this antique glass shades from an opaque faint pink to white to a deep rose.

Cornucopia, white shading to light pink to dark pink base, ruffled, etched mark, 6-1/4" h 395.00

Cup and Saucer, peachblow 275.00
Goblet, glossy finish, deep peachblow color, applied Burmese glass base 295.00
Luncheon Plate, deep raspberry to pale pink, matte finish 375.00
Punch Cup, soft peachblow colors 275.00
Vase, ruffled, soft peachblow colors, 5" h 245.00

For exciting collecting trends and newly expanded areas look for the following symbols:

 Hot Topic

⭐ New Warman's Listing

(May have been in another Warman's edition.)

Wise shoppers remember to:

1. Look under tables
2. Check display cases
3. Ask for assistance
4. Ask for items that may not be displayed
5. Ask for provenance

Receipts should contain:

1. Dealer's name
2. Dealer's address
3. Dealer's telephone number
4. Detailed description of item purchased
5. Purchase price
6. Date of purchase
7. Guarantee if any
8. Note of condition

Checklist for shopping with children.

1. Well packed wagon or stroller
2. Boxed drinks
3. Adequate snacks
4. Favorite blanket or stuffed toy
5. Sunglasses, hat, and sun screen.

Encourage children to search for a favorite animal or character.
Including youngsters in the treasure hunt enhances their enjoyment too.

✫ Haeger Potteries

Haeger Pottery has an interesting history. Starting as a brickyard in Dundee, IL, in 1871, the company began to produce an art pottery line in 1914. Because of their high quality luster glazes and soft pastels, the line was a success. A line named "Royal Haeger" was introduced in 1938. Today members of the Haeger family are still involved in the pottery.

Collectors' Club: Haeger Pottery Collectors of America, 5021 Toyon Way, Antioch, CA 94509.

Ashtray, #2043, slight bottom
chip 10.00
Candy Dish, cov, textured white, sgd
"Royal Haeger" 12.00
Candleholders, agate, pink mauve,
light blue swirled feathers,
4-1/2" h 45.00
Cigarette Holder and Ashtray, tex-
tured white, sgd "Royal Haeger,"
10" x 6-1/4" 10.00
Figure
Bull, gold weave glaze 200.00
Rooster, 20" h 175.00
Seal 35.00
Squirrel 35.00
Flower Frog, nude bather, #77, mkd
"Royal Haeger," c1927, 5" d,
7" h 165.00
Flower Pot, 4-1/4" h,
5-1/2" d 20.00

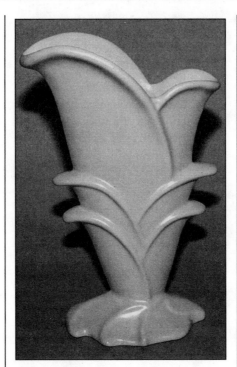

Vase, mkd "3454," white glaze, 11" h, $60.

Hanging Basket, owl, matte white,
mkd "Royal Haeger Owl,
#5015" 55.00
Pitcher, orig paper label, stamp
mark, 10" h 85.00
Planter, blue, antiqued gold trim,
5" h, 5" w, water marks, pr.. 30.00
Serving Dish, Gold Tweed,
16" 32.00
Swan, raised wings, light gray and
brown, 9" l, mkd "Royal Haeger"
.... 45.00
Tea Set, acorn finials 100.00
Vase
Agate, pink mauve, light blue
swirled feathers, 10" h.... 95.00
Creamy green, blue stamp
"Haeger, U.S.A.," and worn
silver stamp, 11-3/4" h,
7" w 25.00
Delft style, cylindrical,
11" h 36.00

✫ Hagen Renaker

Here's a name collectors recognize for quality miniature figurines
and other accessories.

Figure
Appaloosa and Colt, 3" h 18.00
Buckskin Mare, 2-1/2" h...... 12.50
Chihuahua, 1-1/2" h 4.50
Dragons, blue, wings, pair,
1-1/2" h, © 1995 .... 15.00
Ducks, male standing, 6-3/4" h,
female lying down, Studio Line,
pr 175.00
Hippo, 2" h Mama, 1" h Baby,
© 1995 .... 8.50
Hummingbird with flowers,
2-1/4" h, 2" l 7.50
Jock, Walt Disney's Lady and the
Tramp, 1-1/4" h, glued to orig
1-3/4" x 2-1/4" card 90.00
Pegasus, 2" h standing figure,
1" h lying figure, © 1995 ... 15.00
Saddlebred Horse, 2-1/2" h 12.50
St. Bernard, 2" h 6.00
Tramp, Walt Disney's Lady and
the Tramp, 2-1/4" h 195.00
Trusty, Walt Disney's Lady and
the Tramp, 1-7/8" h 75.00

Wall Plaque, irregular shape,
caveman style, high glaze
7" x 12", fish 250.00
10-1/2" x 5", fawn.............. 175.00
10-1/2" x 15", reindeer 250.00
14" x 9", butterfly 250.00
19" x 8", fish 350.00

❖ Hair Related

Today we've got a commodity the Victorians couldn't get enough of. And to think we pay barbers and beauticians to cut it off —hair! Victori-ans saved every loose strand in dresser jars called hair receivers and then used the hairs to make jewelry and ornate flower wreaths, etc. Of course, all the voluminous hair had to be brushed and tucked in place with hair combs, barrettes, etc.

Reference: Mary Bachman, *Collec-tor's Guide to Hair Combs, Identifica-tion and Values,* Collector Books, 1998; Christie Romero, *Warman's Jewelry,* 2nd ed., Krause Publica-tions, 1998.

Collectors' Club: Antique Comb Collectors Club International, 8712

Pleasant View Road, Bangor, PA 18013; Antique Fancy Comb Collectors Club, 3291 N River Rd, Libertyville, IL 60048; National Antique Comb Collectors Club, 3748 Sunray Dr, Holiday, FL 34691.

Hair Brush, sterling silver, Art Nouveau style, wear to bristles 125.00

Hair Comb

Celluloid, engraved grapes, tortoise shell motif 12.00

Celluloid, rhinestone trim..... 45.00

Gutta Percha, French jet, Victorian 95.00

Mexican Silver, mkd "Made in Mexico, 925" 15.00

Sterling silver, 3 turquoise stones, wave shape...................... 45.00

Hair Pin, silver twisted work, two-pronged comb, Victorian, c1890, 5" l 75.00

Hair Receiver, top with center hole, porcelain, roses dec 85.00

Jewelry

Brooch, central oval glazed compartment with braided light brown hair, stamped scrolled relief navette-shaped frame, convex back, 10K yg, c1840 .... 195.00

Locket, oval beveled edge glass front and back, braided knot of gray hair, plain gold-filled frame, c1850 .... 200.00

Wreath, ornate flowers made from hair, paper leaves, other period decorations, 19" x 23" shadow box 145.00

❖ Hall China

Hall China Company was located in East Liverpool, OH, and started making semi-porcelain dinnerware. By 1911, Robert T. Hall had perfected a non-crazing vitrified china, allowing the body and glaze to be fired at one time. Hall's basic product was hotel and restaurant wares. This line was extended to creating premium and retail wares, such as Autumn Leaf or Jewel Tea. An extensive retail line of teapots was created about 1920.

Kitchenware was introduced in 1931. The company is still in business today.

Collectors' Club: Hall China Collector's Club, PO Box 360488, Cleveland, OH 44136.

For additional listings, see *Warman's Antiques and Collectibles Price Guide, Warman's Americana & Collectibles,* and *Warman's American Pottery and Porcelain,* plus "Autumn Leaf" in this edition.

Bean Pot, Red Dot 95.00

Bowl, Orange Poppy, silver rim, 9" d 35.00

Casserole, cov, Rose White.... 30.00

Cereal Bowl, Pastel Morning Glory 17.50

Coffeepot, Dripolator, 6-1/2" h, 9" l, 5-1/4" w, floral design, base reads "The Enterprise Aluminum Co., Massillon, Ohio, Superior Quality Kitchen Ware Drip-O-Later, Trademark REG. U.S. PAT. OFF. PATENT NOS. 1370782-174-3925" 70.00

Coffee Set, coffee pot and mug, Sanka, white with orange trim, sticker "98% Caffeine Free Coffee," base mkd "Made Expressly for Sanka Brand Decaffeinated Coffee Furnished by Minners and Co., Inc., Hall China," 4-1/2" h x 5-1/4" l pot, 3-1/4" h x 3-3/4" l mug 60.00

Cookie Jar, Tootsie, inside chips 128.00

Creamer and Sugar, Chinese Red 95.00

Cup and Saucer, Taverne 20.00

Custard Cup, Orange Poppy 6.50

Drip Jar, Red Poppy................ 30.00

French Baker, Jewel Tea....... 158.00

Jug

Radiance............................. 48.00

Rose White, 7-3/4" 48.00

Leftover, gray and yellow bowl, mkd "Refrigerators, Hall Ovenware China., Made for General Electric," 3-1/4" h, 5-3/4" w 15.00

Mixing Bowl, Crocus, 7-1/2" d 55.00

Onion Soup, cov, Red Dot....... 48.00

Oyster Plate, mkd "Hall China Co., East Liverpool, Ohio, USA," 10-5/8" d 95.00

Pie Plate, Pastel Morning Glory 32.00

Pitcher, teal blue, glaze skip on lip, 6" h 20.00

Pretzel Jar, cov, Taverne 195.00

Sugar Bowl, cov, Century Fern, green, orange, blue, and gray dec, blue lid, mkd "Eva Zeisel H. Century, Hallcraft, Made in USA of Hall China Co.," 4-1/4" h, 5" w 27.50

Sugar Shaker, handle, Crocus 150.00

Stack Set, Red Poppy............. 75.00

Teapot

Aladdin, cobalt blue, gold trim......................... 50.00

Baltimore, yellow................ 50.00

Doughnut, cobalt blue....... 165.00

Globe, emerald green, gold trim...................... 115.00

Individual size, dark green, 4" h, chip on lid 10.00

Plume, pink......................... 22.00

Flare-Ware casserole, $20.

Teapot, light blue, 5-3/4" h, 9" l, $25.

Red Poppy, New York
shape 80.00

Tomorrow's Classic Spring,
"Hallcraft Classic Shape by
Eva Zeisel, H (inside square),
made in USA by Hall China
Co.," 5-3/4" h, 9" l..........155.00

Tea Tile, Wild Poppy 85.00

Tom and Jerry Set, bowl, 12 mugs,
black, gold lettering 65.00

Vegetable Bowl

Century Fern, mkd "Eva Zeisel H.
Century, Hallcraft, Made in
USA of Hall China Co.," 11-1/4"
l, 8-1/4" w 42.00

Wildfire, white, pink roses, green
leaves, blue ribbon, mkd "Hall's
Superior Quality Kitchenware,"
9" l....................................27.50

⭐ Hallmark

Hallmark is another American success story. Started by two brothers,
Joyce and Rollie Hall, in 1913, they
first sold Christmas cards. Through
purchases of printing and engraving
plants, they developed into a nation-
wide company. After World War II,
they expanded and attracted famous
artists to the company. Other innovations followed, including the popular
Keepsake Ornament series that was
started in 1973.

Reference: Rosie Wells, ed., *The
Ornament Collector's Official Price
Guide for Past Years' Hallmark Ornaments and Kiddie Car Classics,* 12th
ed., Rosie Wells Enterprises, 1998.

Periodicals: *Hallmarkers,* PO Box
97172, Pittsburgh, PA 15229; *The
Ornament Collector,* 22341 E. Wells
Rd., Canton, IL 61520.

Collectors' Club: Hallmark Keepsake Ornament Collectors Club, PO
Box 412734, Kansas City, MO 64141.

Christmas Card Holder, figural train,
orig instruction sheet, orig
envelope...........................18.00

Doll, Bride and Groom, Madame
Alexander, MIB...................35.00

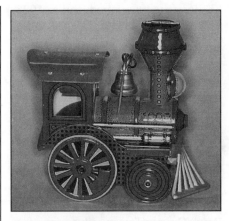

**Ornament, tin locomotive, 1982,
orig box, $225.**

Greeting Card, Birthday Card, black
characters, © Hall Brothers, Inc.,
c1940s, 4" x 5"....................25.00

Locket, First Christmas Together,
heart-shaped, brass, double picture type, 2-1/4", orig wrapping
and box..............................27.50

Lunch Box, Precious Moments,
Betsy Clark, 1975, orig
thermos 42.00

Magazine Advertisement,
Thanksgiving cards adv,
1959 ....5.00

Ornament

Baby's 1st Christmas, acrylic
baby cup filled with toys, 1985,
3-3/4" h..........................20.00

Enterprise, 1991, MIB....... 225.00

Forest Frolics, 1990, MIB ... 50.00

For The One I Love, porcelain,
1992, MIB......................20.00

Hark, the Herald, elf playing tuba,
1992, MIB......................20.00

Heavenly Angel, 1992, 3" h,
................................MIB32.00

Heart of Christmas, opens, 1992,
2" h.............................30.00

Holiday Wildlife, 1982, MIB
................................275.00

Jolly Trolley, 1982, MIB....... 60.00

Kringles Bumper Cars, 1991,
MIB.............................50.00

Mickey Mouse, Tree-Trimmer
Collection, satin, 1980, MIB
................................35.00

Mother, satin, roses on white
ground, 1981, 3-1/4" h, slight
damage to orig box 18.50

Mustang, Classic Car series,
1992, MIB 48.00

Our First Christmas Together,
bears in tunnel-of-love boats,
1991, orig instruction sheet,
some damage to box, orig
wrapping.........................55.00

Paz Sobre La Tierra, (Peace on
Earth), little girl holding globe,
boy with guitar, 1992, 3" h, MIB
27.50

Sailing Santa, 1981, MIB .. 120.00

Santa Deliveries, 1984, MIB40.00

Stocking, pressed tin, 1992, 4-
3/4" h, MIB 8.00

Star Trek Shuttlecraft, talking,
1992, MIB 48.00

Twelve Days of Christmas, 8
Maids A Milking 25.00

World-Class Teacher, 1992, 3-
1/4" h, MIB......................9.00

Pop-Up Book, *Walt Disney World,* ©
1972, 6-3/4" x 9-1/2" 65.00

Thimble, partridge, 1986, orig
wrapping and box 27.50

❖ Halloween

Trick or Treat! Collectors love to
find treats at flea markets. From costumes to postcards, there are plenty
of Halloween-related items.

Reference: Lissa Bryan Smith and
Richard Smith, *Holiday Collectibles,*
Krause Publications, 1998.

Periodicals: *Boo News,* PO Box
143, Brookfield, IL 60513; *Trick or
Treat Trader,* PO Box 499, Winchester, NH 03470.

Candy Container

Black Cat head, pressed cardboard, cut-out eyes and mouth,
wire handle, Germany 60.00

Clown's head on top, orange
crepe paper, celluloid
head 100.00

Clicker, litho tin, orange and black,
mkd "T. Cohn, USA"..............7.50

Costume, child's

Flipper, cloth, black velvet trim
................................50.00

Howard the Duck, Collegeville,
1986, orig box................60.00

Party hat, paper with cellophane covering, Japan, 7" h, $8.

The Fonz, Happy Days, Ben
  Cooper, 1976, orig box....35.00
Halloween Mask
  Deputy Dawg, 1960s...........32.00
  Esso Tiger, 1960s...............16.00
  Rabbit, 1960s.....................10.00
  Zorro, large brim, 1960s......35.00
Hat, cardboard and crepe paper,
  black and orange, Germany,
  4" h...................................... 17.50
Lantern, pumpkin, papier-mâché,
  paper eyes and mouth, wire
  handle, candleholder in base,
  Germany, 4" h 65.00
Postcard, witch riding broom through
  sky...................................... 12.00
Rattle, frying pan shape, goblins,
  pumpkins, mkd
  "T. Cohen" 50.00

✯ Hanna-Barbera

The partnership of William Denby Hanna and Joseph Roland Barbera came about slowly. They both worked for MGM, and, when a new cartoon division was started in 1937, they were teamed together. For twenty years they worked under this arrangement, creating such classics as Tom and Jerry. After striking out on their own, they started producing cartoons for television and created such great characters as Huckleberry Hound and the Flintstones. In 1966, Taft Communications purchased the

Plastic mug, mkd "Flintstones Multiple brand Vitamins," 3-1/4" h, $5.

company, leaving Hanna and Barbera to head the company.

Bank, Yogi Bear,
  Knickerbocker..................... 40.00
Colorform Set, Jetsons, © 1963,
  complete, orig box 42.00
Comic Book, *The Flintstones at the
  New York World's Fair,* official fair
  souvenir.............................. 25.00
Figure, Scooby Doo, metal, orig foil
  label: © 1977 Hanna-Barbera
  Productions, incised © Vanity Fair
  Ind., Inc., Made in Hong Kong,
  2-3/4" h 60.00
Halloween Costume, Fred Flint-
  stone, Ben Cooper,
  orig box.............................. 60.00
Pinback Button, Tom and Jerry Go
  For Stoehmann's Bread, black,
  red, and white litho, 1950s,
  1-1/8" d.............................. 27.50
Ramp Walker, Astro and George
  Jetson, Marx, plastic, © Hanna-
  Barbera, early 1960s 120.00
Record, Huckleberry Hound and
  Yogi Bear, Little Golden Record,
  1959, 45 RPM 25.00

❖ Hardware

Decorative and ornate hardware has graced our homes for decades. Vintage hardware is purchased by those restoring antique homes, those wanting to add a touch of class to newer homes, or collectors who appreciate the beauty of the object.

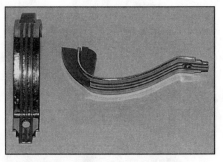

Cabinet handles, chrome and blue plastic, 1950s, pr, $10.

Reference: H. Weber Wilson, *Antique Hardware Price Guide,* Krause Publications, 1999.

Also see "Doorknobs," in this edition.

Coat Hook, cast iron, painted black,
  wall mounted, double
  hooks 15.00
Door Bell, mechanical,
  brass..................................125.00
Door Bell Plate, Marshall Field &
  Co., brass 25.00
Door Knocker, cast iron, figural fox
  head....................................85.00
Door Push Plate, Windsor pattern,
  Sargent, bronze, c1885,
  16" h 150.00
Hinges, pr, wrought iron
  Blanket chest, penny terminals,
  15-1/2" l 50.00
  Gate, weathered 45.00
Hook, cast iron, long 12.00
Mail Slot Cover, brass, "Letters,"
  Victorian.............................45.00
Shelf Bracket, wrought iron, ornate
  scrolling pattern, pr 20.00
Switch Plate Cover, Channel 7,
  brass, 5-3/4" 35.00

❖ Harker Pottery

The Harker Co. was another East Liverpool, OH, firm. Started by Benjamin Harker about 1840, it first produced yellow ware products from natural clay deposits. White ware was first made about 1879, and they then continued to create dinnerware and table accessories. The plant was destroyed by fire in 1975 and not rebuilt.

Plate, Cameoware, 10-3/8" d, $8.

For additional listings, see *Warman's Americana & Collectibles* and *Warman's American Pottery and Porcelain.*

Batter Bowl, Petit Point
   Rose 65.00
Cake Server, Petit Point
   Rose 20.00
Casserole, cov, Red Apple 35.00
Cheese Plate, Red Apple 24.00
Creamer, Kriebel's Dairy, Hereford,
   PA 50.00
Cup and Saucer, Cameo, Shell
   Ware, blue 17.50
Dinner Plate, Petit Point Rose 15.00
Pie Plate, Cameo, Dainty Flower,
   blue 75.00
Rolling Pin, Cameo, blue 75.00
Salad Bowl, Red Apple 27.50
Vegetable Bowl, Red Apple 32.00

❖ Harlequin China

This bright and cheery pattern was made by Homer Laughlin and originally sold by F. W. Woolworth Co. It was introduced in the 1930s in bright yellow, spruce green, maroon, and mauve blue. Eventually, it was produced in all the Fiesta colors except ivory and cobalt blue. The line was discontinued in 1964, but reissued in 1979. The reissue was made in turquoise, yellow, medium green, and coral. Look for the Homer Laughlin backstamp on most pieces.

Dinnerware
After Dinner Cup,
   chartreuse 95.00
After Dinner Cup and Saucer
   Maroon 100.00
   Red 130.00
   Spruce 195.00
Ashtray, saucer, red 90.00
Casserole, cov
   Chartreuse 240.00
   Maroon 200.00
   Spruce 195.00
   Yellow 165.00
Creamer, individual, green 125.00
Deep Plate, medium green ... 125.00
Eggcup, double
   Gray 40.00
   Mauve blue 30.00
   Red 40.00
   Rose 38.00
   Spruce 42.00
   Turquoise 25.00
Marmalade, maroon 325.00

Egg cup, mauve blue, 3-7/8" h, $25.

Nappy, medium green 195.00
Nut Dish, rose 95.00
Pitcher, ball, Spruce 95.00
Plate
   7" d, medium green 45.00
   10" d, medium green 135.00
   10" d, red 25.00
Spoon Rest, yellow 295.00
Sugar, cov, gray or maroon 45.00
Teapot, cov
   Gray 185.00
   Red 95.00
   Rose 100.00
Tumbler, red or yellow 65.00

Figure
Cat
   Mauve blue 175.00
   Spruce 275.00
   Yellow 175.00
   White and gold 160.00
Donkey
   Gold trim 80.00
   Mauve blue 225.00
   Spruce 325.00
   Yellow and gold 250.00
Duck
   Maroon 275.00
   Spruce 175.00
   Yellow 245.00
Fish
   Gold trim 80.00
   Maroon 350.00
   Yellow 250.00
Lamb
   Gold 125.00
   Mauve blue 325.00
   White and gold 125.00
Penguin
   Maroon 285.00
   Yellow 250.00
   White and gold 125.00

⭐ Harmonica and Related

Harmonicas used to be the musical choice of those who couldn't afford fancy instruments. Today their rich sounds are still enjoyed. Flea markets are a great place to find vin-

Swing Band harmonica, Japan, 1974, 4-5/8" l, $10.

tage harmonicas, often in their original boxes.

Harmonica
   American Ace Harmonica, Hohner-Panarmonic, Made in Rep. Of Ireland, orig box, orig instruction sheet..............28.00
   Bell Bird, orig box 18.00
   Marine Band Harmonica, M. Hohner, Germany, No. 1896, orig box 22.00
   Roy Rogers Harmonica, good luck emblem, Roy's picture framed by horseshoe, 4-1/4" l, 4-1/4" w..........................55.00
   Sousa's Band, orig box 24.00
Keychain, Harmonica for the Musically Hopeless, small plastic harmonica, orig blister pack 3.50
Photograph, snapshot, children's harmonica band, c1927........ 5.00
Set, Herb Shriner's TV Jamboree, 1955, boxed set with harmonica, instruction book, 2 records, membership pin, and holster, unused 25.00
Tape, Bonfiglio, Home for the Holidays 10.00

✶ Hartland Plastics

   This famous plastics maker produced figures of characters and animals. Look for examples with little or no damage.

Babe Ruth, 1960s 275.00
Bay Foal, mahogany.............. 12.00
Bullet...................................... 25.00
Cheyenne and horse 200.00
Dale Evans 75.00
Don Drysdale, 25th anniversary, MIB 72.00
Kilroy Was Here 7.50
Mustang, rearing, woodgrain 30.00
Nelson (Nettie) Fox, 25th anniversary, MIB 55.00
Pony Express, rider and horse 138.00
Rocky Colavito, 25th anniversary, MIB 55.00
Ted Williams, 1960s.............. 350.00
Wells Lamont Thunderchief .. 155.00
Wyatt Earp and horse 80.00
Yogi Berra, 1960s, mask missing 250.00

❖ Hatpin Holders and Hatpins

   Hatpins are coming back into vogue with collectors. Perhaps it's the renaissance of large hats or the romance that hatpins evoke. Whatever the reason, more and more hatpins are coming onto the flea market scene and the prices are rising. Of course, if you're going to collect hatpins, you've got to have a few hatpin holders to display your treasures.

Collectors' Clubs: American Hatpin Society, 20 Monticello Drive, Palos Veres Peninsula, CA 90274; International Club for Collectors of Hatpins and Hatpin Holders, 15237 Chanera Ave., Gardena, CA 90249.

   For additional listings, see *Warman's Antiques and Collectibles Price Guide* and *Warman's Jewelry.*

Doll, porcelain half doll, arms folded, satin dress as cushion for hatpins, 9" h 125.00

Hatpin
   Art Deco dec....................... 85.00
   Beaded and sequined head, black, 2-3/8" x 1-1/4" d, 6-1/4" l............................ 75.00

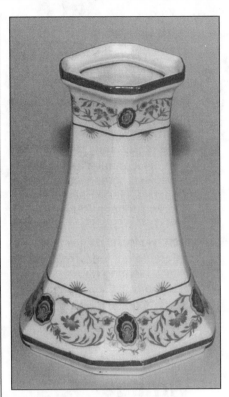

MZ Austria, 6-1/4" h, $39.

Faceted glass, black, 2-1/4" x 1-1/4" d, 5-5/8" l............... 150.00
Filigree, blank place for monogram, 1" d, 4-5/8" l, tip broken off 75.00
Filigree, eight point floral design, 9 clear prong set rhinestones, 1" d, 11-1/4" l 75.00
Filigree, teardrop, 3/4" l head, 7-5/8" l 65.00
Gold lustered metal, screw-type, c1920, 6-1/2" l 20.00
Iridized metal head, faceted dome, 1-3/4" d, 11-1/4" l............. 125.00
Military insignia, 2" d, 9-1/2" l 125.00
Rhinestones, round ball head, 12 prong set clear rhinestones, 3/8" d, 8-1/4" l................. 45.00
Shell, metal holder, 1-3/8" l x 1" d head, 8-3/4" l 75.00

Wood, black ebonized head, metal separator, 11-1/2" l 100.00

Hatpin Holder, porcelain

Bavarian, hexagonal, pastel florals, mkd "Z. S. & Co.," 4-3/4" h 45.00

Germany, yellow roses, 6-1/2" h 90.00

Nippon, pink, mauve and lavender flowers, green leaves, gold trim, mkd "Hand Painted Nippon The Jonroth Studios," c1900, 4" h....................200.00

Nippon, white, hp, 4" h 40.00

Royal Bayreuth, tapestry, portrait of lady wearing hat, blue mark 575.00

Souvenir, Capitol Building, Washington, DC, 4-1/2" h 125.00

❖ Hats, Lady's Vintage

A well-groomed lady used her hat to complete her ensemble. Some vintage hats are large and colorful, while others are a little more demure. There has been a resurgence in hat collecting, perhaps due to popular movies featuring stars in large bonnets. Whatever the reason, our hats are off to those who enjoy this collecting area.

Reference: Susan Langley, *Vintage Hats and Bonnets, 1770-1970,* Collector Books, 1997.

Felt

Black, trimmed in black ostrich feathers, small bowl crown, short back brim, wide in front, black ribbon with bow in back, orig label "Yowell Drew Ivey Co., Daytona Beach".....125.00

Brown, wide brim, beige feathers, green netting, 1930s 125.00

Rose, net and chiffon layers, flowers, and pearls, wire frame on each side for secure fit, label "Mary Louis Shaker-Shaker Heights"...........................45.00

Sapphire Blue, Art Deco style, small matching bow and netting 40.00

Straw with black bow, "Shelley Simpson for Stetson" label, $12.

Straw

Black, large brim, crown fabric, label "Schiparallei Jr. Paris".............................. 70.00

Black, pink, rose, and white flowers, green leaves, label "Neiman Marcus"............ 40.00

Navy, feathers and veil, small turned up brim, label "Gage Brothers & Co., Chicago, New York, Since 1856".......... 70.00

Velvet, black, red poppies, fully lined, wire in brim, 2" w front brim, back brim narrow... 60.00

❖ Haviland China

Haviland China has an interesting history in that it was founded in America by importer David Haviland who then moved to Limoges, France, to begin manufacturing. He was quite successful. His sons, Charles and Theodore, split the company in 1892. Theodore opened an American division in 1936 and continued to make fine dinnerware. The Haviland family sold the firm in 1981.

There are thousands of Haviland dinnerware patterns. There are some great reference books to help identify patterns and dates. Here's a sampling of what you might find at a flea market.

Collectors' Club: Haviland Collectors International Foundation, PO Box 802462, Santa Clarita, CA 91380.

For additional listings, see *Warman's Antiques & Collectibles Price Guide* and *Warman's American Pottery & Porcelain.*

Bone Dish, turtle dec..............65.00

Bowl, hp yellow roses, 8" d 37.50

Butter Dish, cov, Gold Band, mkd "Theo Haviland" 48.00

Cake Plate, Baltimore Rose, #1151, #1 blank, gold trim 145.00

Chop Plate, Chrysanthemum, #88, 11" d................................80.00

Coffee Cup, Marseille.............25.00

Compote, ftd, reticulated, gold trim...........................175.00

Creamer and Sugar, small pink flowers, scalloped, gold trim......65.00

Cup and Saucer, Montmery 30.00

Dinner Service, Gold Band, service for 12............................1,000.00

Plate

Blue flowers, green leaves, 7-1/2" d...........................15.00

Princess, 9-1/2" d 24.00

Rajah, mkd "Theo Haviland," 6" d 8.00

Platter, Baltimore Rose, large, #1151, smooth blank, gold trim...........................170.00

Relish Dish, Marseilles, #48, 8-1/2" d 30.00

Tea Cup and Saucer, small blue flowers, green leaves..........28.00

Gravy boat, attached base, rose decor, 3" h, 8-3/4" l, 6-1/4" w, $45.

Teapot, Baltimore Rose, #1151,
  #1 blank, lid missing 165.00
Vegetable Dish, Marseille,
  #9 .... 45.00

☆ Hawaiiana

Aloha. Some collectors are just naturally drawn to colorful Hawaiian objects. Perhaps it's the smiles of the hula girls or their alluring dance. It's a collecting category where prices aren't too high. Objects made in Hawaii do tend to be a little higher than those things imported from Japan, etc.

Ashtray, black glass, applied natural
  shells, "Hawaii" across center, 4-
  1/2" d 17.50
Bell, Hula Girl, ceramic, "Hawaii"
  written across skirt, "Made in
  Japan" sticker, 4-1/2" h 36.00
Coca-Cola Bottle, "Ronald
  McDonald House, Hawaii, 1996
  Maile Lei," 2nd ed 42.00
Doll, Hula Girl, felt, grass skirt,
  9" h 21.50
Figure
  Hula Girl, grass skirt, porcelain,
    10" h 150.00
  Hula Girl, Treasure Craft of
    Hawaii, foil label, 1968,
    11" h 65.00
  Nui-Nui Aloha, carved lava, orig
    label "CoCo Joe,
    Hawaii" 20.00

Ceramic figurines, Ucagco China, Japan, 6" h, pr, $125.

Sterility Goddess, carved lava,
  orig booklet and label "a Hip
  Original made in Hawaii,"
  6-1/4" h 30.00
Map, Kingdom of Hawaii, 1880,
  10-1/2" x 6-1/4" 87.00
Matches, safety, Hawaii the Home of
  the Hawaiian Lei on back ... 12.50
Napkin, Hula Girl fabric, "Aloha
  Hawaii," 12" sq 18.00
Nodder, Hula Girl, plaster, mkd
  "EFCCO Imports San Francisco
  Made in Japan," bottom magnet
  missing, 6-1/4" h 45.00
Pillow Cover, Honolulu, tropical
  themes and poem to mother,
  17-1/4" sq plus fringe 50.00
Plate
  Aloha from Hawaii, Hula maids
    and other colorful scenes, gold
    trim, 8" d 25.00
  Honolulu, Vernon Kilns, made
    exclusively for The Liberty
    House, 10-1/4" d, slight factory
    imperfection to back 75.00
  Iolani Palace, Vernon Kilns,
    10-1/2" d 118.00
Photograph, La Hula Rhumba,
  sepia, 1940s, orig folder 20.00
Postcard, Mauna Kea, real photo,
  unused 12.00
Program and Menu, "Christmas in
  Hawaii," 1947, Medical Dept,
  147th General Hospital,
  autographs from 147th,
  8-1/2" x 11" 50.00
Record, Blue Hawaii, Bing Crosby
  and Shirley Ross 18.00
Salt and Pepper Shakers, pr, figural
  suitcases 24.00
Shirt
  Duke Kahanamoku, rayon, minor
    stains, pocket restitched
    .... 105.00
  HRH His Royal Highness Hawaii,
    size 44, pink and gray,
    cotton 25.00
  Iolani Hawaii Executive, 2 front
    pockets, size M, light blue
    .... 22.50
  JCPenny's, Japanese print of
    pheasants, bonsai trees
    .... 75.00
  Malihini, made in Hawaii, cotton,
    light green with 2 surfboards,
    embroidered hats on
    pockets 42.00

Spoon, sterling silver, design of
  Kamehameha, Hawaiian king,
  bowl of spoon with enameled
  crest 211.00
Tin, Hawaiian Coconut Snow, Lihue
  Kauai, Hawaii, 10 oz,
  colorful 35.00
Tourist Pamphlet, shows 1930
  Hawaii calendar of events, 15
  pgs, 9" x 6" 36.00
Travel Brochure, Hawaii Tourist
  Bureau, Honolulu, 1942, wear,
  11" x 8-1/2" 15.50
Ukulele, Le Domino, JSR Company,
  decals worn, bridge
  repaired 160.00
View Book, "Aloha, Cordial Greet-
  ings from Hawaii," © 1944, C. Q.
  Pang Division, Royal Hawaiian
  Distributing Co., 18 full color
  views, unused 25.00
View-Master Reels, State Tour
  Series, orig 16 pg color booklet by
  Lowell Thomas, set of 3 ...... 16.00

❖ Hazel Atlas

When Hazel Glass Company merged with the Atlas Glass & Metal Company in 1902 in Washington, PA, Hazel Atlas was created. This merger led to a company that aggressively developed ways to automate the glassware industry. They concentrated on table wares, kitchen items, and tumblers.

References: Gene Florence, *Collectible Glassware from the 40s, 50s, 60s,* 4th ed., Collector Books, 1998; —, *Kitchen Glassware of the Depression Years,* 5th ed., Collector Books, 1995, 1997 value update.

Bowl, cobalt blue, metal
  holder 60.00
Cereal Bowl, Cowboy, white opaque
  glass, black cowboy
  scenes 25.00
Custard Cup, green 5.00
Berry Bowl, mkd "Hazel Atlas,"
  4-1/4" d 4.50
Child's Mug, animal characters, mkd
  "H/A" on bottom, 3" h, some wear
  to dec 22.00
Creamer, Aurora, blue,
  4-1/4" h 25.00

Child's cup, milk glass, space motif, 3-1/8" h, $6.

Dinner Plate, Moderntone, pink, 1940s, 9" d 7.50

Drinking Glass, Florida souvenir, frosted, yellow state image, sailfish, alligator, palm tree, and flamingo, 5" h 12.00

Lemon Reamer, green............ 20.00

Old-Fashioned Tumbler, Moroccan Amethyst, 3-1/2" h.............. 12.50

Salad Plate, Moderntone, mint green, 1940s, 6-3/4" d.......... 5.50

Salt and Pepper Shakers, pr, grapes, Hazel Atlas symbol on bottom, some wear to tops. 10.00

Sherbet, Moderntone, pink, early 1950s 5.00

Snack Set, cup and oblong plate with indentation for cup
    Capri Seashell, light blue 18.00
    Seashell, crystal 22.50

Sugar Bowl, cov, Ovide, black, two handles................................. 5.00

Syrup Pitcher, red plastic slide-top lid, mkd, 5-1/2" h 9.00

Tom and Jerry Set, 2 qt punchbowl, six 6 oz mugs 75.00

❖ Heisey Glass

Heisey Glass is one manufacturer that's easily recognized by many dealers. That H in a diamond logo is easy to spot. But, did you know that Heisey didn't mark any glass until 1901, and they used paper labels for years before starting to use the diamond mark. The Heisey Glass Company was known for its brilliant colors and excellent quality crystal.

References: Neila Bredehoft, *Collector's Encyclopedia of Heisey Glass, 1925–1938*, Collector Books, 1986, 1997 value update; Gene Florence, *Elegant Glassware of the Depression Era*, 7th edition, Collector Books, 1997.

Periodicals: *Heisey Herald*, PO Box 23, Clinton, MD 20735; *The Heisey News*, 169 W Church St, Newark, OH, 43055; *The Newscaster*, PO Box 102, Plymouth, OH 44865.

Collectors' Clubs: Bay State Heisey Collectors Club, 354 Washington St, East Walpole, MA 02032; Heisey Collectors of America, 169 W Church St, Newark, OH, 43055; National Capital Heisey Collectors, PO Box 23, Clinton, MD 20735; Southern Illinois Diamond H Seekers, 1203 N. Yale, O'Fallon, IL 62269.

Reproduction Alert.

For additional listings, see *Warman's Antiques and Collectibles Price Guide* and *Warman's Glass*.

Animal
    Goose, wings half up 90.00
    Plug Horse, Oscar 115.00
    Sparrow 140.00
Ashtray, Old Sandwich, #1404, moongleam, individual size 70.00
Basket, #480 .... 225.00
Bowl, Rose, 13" d, shallow 40.00
Cake Plate, Rose, pedestal .. 325.00
Candelabra, Ridgleigh, 7" h, bobeches and prisms, pr 140.00
Candlesticks, pr
    #18, 9" h 100.00
    Lariat, 2-lite........................ 60.00
Candy Dish, cov, recessed panels, crystal and black enamel, gold dec.................................... 45.00
Champagne
    Minuet.............................. 35.00

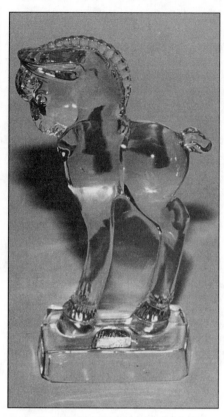

Colt figurine, clear, 5" h, $45.

    Tudor 20.00
Cheese Comport, Crystolite, ftd...25.00
Cheese Plate, Crystolite, 8" d, 2 handles 45.00
Cocktail
    Lariat, moonglo cutting 15.00
    Rosalie................................ 12.00
Creamer and Sugar, Twist, Sahara 170.00
Cruet
    Old Sandwich..................... 60.00
    Pleat and Panel, flamingo... 65.00
Coaster, Colonial, 4-1/2" d 5.00
Cocktail
    Colonial.............................. 14.00
    Steeplechase, Sahara 90.00
Cup and Saucer, Empress, yellow, round...................................42.00
Goblet
    Narrow Flute 30.00
    Provincial 19.50
    Tudor 17.50
Iced Tea Tumbler, Plantation, ftd... 75.00

Jug, Queen Anne #1509, dolphin ftd,
    silver overlay 125.00
Nappy, Colonial, 6-1/4" 4.00
Plate
    Colonial, 4-3/4" d 6.50
    Empress, yellow, 8" d 24.00
    Orchid Etch, 7-1/4" d 24.00
Punch Cup, Crystolite 10.00
Sandwich Plate, center handle,
    Rose 225.00
Sherbet, Orchid Etch 24.00
Spring Salad Bowl,
    Crystolite 90.00
Tankard, Greek Key 265.00
Toothpick Holder, Waldorf
    Astoria 115.00
Tumbler, Rose Etch, ftd 50.00
Vase, Prison Stripe, cupped,
    5" h 65.00
Wine, Orchid Etch 75.00

☆ Higgins Glass

Creating in a Chicago Studio,
Frances Stewart Higgins and Michael
Higgins designed some exciting
glassware in the early 1950s. Dearborn Glass provided space for them
between 1958 and 1964 when their
works were mass produced. Their
unique double layered glass wares
were usually signed with a gold-
screened signature. By 1966, they
returned to their own studio and
changed their focus a bit. Pieces
made after the 1970s have an
engraved signature on the back. The
company is still in business today.

Ashtray, blue and yellow ray, signa-
    ture inside casing, 10" 85.00
Bowl, white, green pulled feathers,
    gold signature, 13-1/2" d ...115.00
Charger, summer season dec,
    etched signature, 15" d 550.00
Dish, daisies dec, ftd,
    8-1/2" d 100.00
Plate
    6-1/2" d, amber and gold pulled
        scroll, etched signature ...60.00
    7-1/2" d, pink, blue, and yellow
        stripes, etched signature with
        stick man logo 100.00

8-1/2" d, chartreuse and white
    stripes, gold seaweed dec,
    gold signature 60.00
Platter, purple ground, green and
    light purple stripes, gold signa-
    ture, orig paper label,
    12-1/2" l 115.00
Tray, gold spiral dec, chartreuse and
    yellow rays, 14" 65.00

☆ Hobby Horses

Many children have played with
hobby horses. From primitive
wooden creations to more polished
professionally made examples, all
were loved and ridden for hours.

Cisco Kid, played-with
    condition 30.00
Colt 45, vinyl head, wood stick,
    played-with condition 5.00
Mobo, c1920 .... 475.00
Rich Toys, played-with
    condition 15.00
Snoopy, vinyl head, 36" l wood stick,
    played-with condition 5.00

❖ Hockey Cards

Like baseball, basketball, and football trading cards, hockey cards are
plentiful. Good price guides help the
collector understand the market.
Here's a sampling of some hockey
card prices.

Periodicals: *Sports Cards Magazine & Price Guide,* 700 E State St,
Iola, WI 54990; *Sports Collectors
Digest*, 700 E State St, Iola, WI
54990.

Donruss
    1996, complete set, Elite 25.00
    1997, complete set 20.00
    1997, complete set, Canadian
        Ice 25.00
Score, 1990, Canadian
    factory 20.00
Topps
    1987, complete set 115.00
    1989, complete set 29.00
Upper Deck
    1994, complete set 50.00
    1995, complete set 55.00

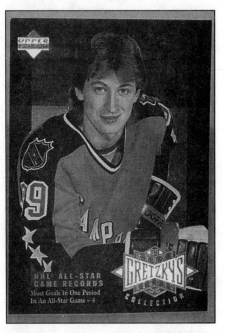

**1995-96 Upper Deck Gretzky's
Record Collection, G17, Wayne
Gretzky, Most Goals in One Period
in an All-Star Game, $4.**

❖ Hockey Memorabilia

Here's another type of sport that
generates lots of collectibles. Whether
you're into field hockey or ice hockey,
flea markets are a great place to score
a goal with this collectible.

Autograph, signed photograph
    Ballard, Harold 90.00
    Dionne, M. 17.00
    Gretzky, Wayne 38.00
    Hextall 15.00
    Lemieux, Claude 35.00
    Lenders, Eric 48.00
    Lindros, Eric 25.00
    Patrick, Roy 27.00
    Richard, Henry 20.00
    Richter 24.00
    Stevens, S. 20.00
Jersey, game type, used, Rangers,
    autographed by Wayne
    Gretzky 425.00
Mask
    PCI, autographed by Patrick
    Roy 70.00

Riddell, autographed by Eric
    Lindros 55.00
Puck, autographed
    Fedorov, Sergei 26.00
    Lemieux, Mario..................60.00
    Lindros, Eric 28.00
    Patrick, Roy......................30.00

❖ Holiday Collectibles

Aren't the holidays great? And, so many collectibles are available at flea markets for all types of holidays. We've made separate listings for Christmas, Easter, and Halloween and now we'll tackle some of the others for you.

Reference: Lissa Bryan Smith and Richard Smith, *Holiday Collectibles,* Krause Publications, 1998.

Periodicals: *Pyrofax Magazine,* PO Box 2010, Saratoga, CA 95070; *St. Patrick Notes,* 10802, Greenscreek Drive, Suite 703, Houston, TX 77070.

Bunting, red, white and blue muslin,
    Fourth of July type.............. 10.00
Candy Box, shamrock shape, cardboard, green, lithograph shamrocks on top, 8-1/2" h 17.50
Candy Container
    Hat, cardboard, green and gold, label on base, "Loft Candy Co.," 3" h.........................27.50
    Potato, pressed cardboard, brown, velvet green and gold shamrock, Germany........50.00
    Shield shape, red, white, and blue, 2-1/4" x 2-1/2" 15.00
    Turkey, composition, metal legs, removable head, 5" h......65.00
Figure
    Gobbler, hard plastic, 2-1/3" h 12.00
    Leprechaun, holding pig, celluloid, weighted, Japan, 7" h.................................37.50
    Man, composition, green felt coat, spring legs, beer stein, 6" h...............................65.00

Candy box, litho paper, Christmas and New Years, 3" h, 4-1/4" l, 1-3/4 w, $17.50.

Greeting Card, Mayflower, with Joyful Thanksgiving Wishes, unused.................................. 8.50
Nodder, Irish boy, bisque, Germany, 3" h 48.00
Nut Cup, green and white crepe paper, foil Irish symbols, twisted paper handle, Kupper Favor Co., Peru, IN, set of four, unused................................ 24.00
Pinback Button, Labor Day Justice for All, patent date 1911, 1-1/2" d 7.50
Placemat Set, four 16" x 11" hand embroidered mats, one center 11" x 30-1/2" mat, white linen, each mat with a different embroidered scene, one with Victorian ladies leaving a steepled church at Easter, Victorian ladies seated at Thanksgiving table, Victorian men seated at Hannukah table, Victorian family Christmas scene with tree, c1940 .... 35.00
Postcard
    A Joyous Thanksgiving, boy carving pumpkin, 1913............ 5.00
    Fourth of July spelled out in red firecrackers, Germany...... 5.00
    Love's greetings, boy and girl, Ellen Clapsaddle, artist, 1922 .... 15.00
    On March 17 May You Be Seen A'Wearing of the Green, Irish man standing on "17", Quality Cards, A. M. Davis Co., Boston, 1912 .... 4.00

On Memorial Day, Hail Columbia, musical score, angel flying with flag, 1908......................... 7.50

☆ Holly Hobbie

This cute country gal appeared on the scene in the late 1970s and continued to spread her brand of sunshine for several years. Holly Hobbie and her friends often had inspirational messages.

Bell, annual, bisque................40.00
Brunch Bag, vinyl, zipper closure, Aladdin Industries, 1978, orig thermos...............................65.00
Children's Play Dishes, plastic, large plate, 7 smaller plates, 2 mugs, mkd "Aluminum Specialty, Chilton toys, Manitowoc, WI," 10 pcs 25.00
Coffeepot, 8" h, 1973 ....35.00
Doll
    Amy, 15" h...........................30.00
    Fancy, MIB 25.00
Figure
    A Basketful of Wishes, girl wearing large hat, standing, black cat, #300, HHF-18, 1974 ....30.00
    Girl with pigtails carrying books and gift box, strolling by fence, #300, HHF-5....................35.00
Halloween Costume, Ben Cooper, American Greetings, small child size, worn............................ 15.00

Plate, "Love at Christmas is all around us! 1981," 8-1/4" d, $10.

Limited Edition Plate, Christmas, 1974, 10-1/2" d.................. 15.00

Lunch Box, metal, several different scenes, 1972..................... 20.00

Teapot, white porcelain, green trim, green and brown Holly, "Tea for two is twice as nice," base mkd "Country Living, WWA, Inc. MCM-LXXX, Cleveland, USA 46144, Made in Korea," 5-3/4" h 32.00

Tidbit Tray, 3 tiers, white porcelain, yellow, gold, orange and black Holly with cat and flowers, "Happiness is having someone to care for," gold trim, gold metal handle, base mkd "Holly Hobbie Porcelain, World Wide Arts, Inc., Cleveland, OH, MCMLXXII, Made in Japan," 13" h...................... 45.00

Toy Sewing Machine, plastic, mkd "Durham Industries," 1975 .... 20.00

✿ Holt-Howard

The partnership of brothers John and Robert J. Howard with A. Grant Holt created an import company in 1948 in Stamford, CT. Robert designed some novelty ceramic containers that proved to be very successful.

Reference: Walter Dworkin, *Price Guide to Holt-Howard Collectibles and Related Ceramic Wares of the '50s and '60s,* Krause Publications, 1998.

Rooster salt and pepper shakers, 1960, 4-5/8" h, pr, $35.

Baby Feeding Dish, warmer, horse, orig tail stopper, paper label and black stamp mark, 1958, 8-3/4" l, 5" h 195.00

Bud vase, green glaze, 1958, 7-1/2" h 160.00

Candle Climbers, pr
   Angels, Noel 60.00
   Mice..................................... 25.00
   Santa, orig box 35.00

Candleholders, pr
   Angel 28.00
   Santa 28.00
   Christmas angels............... 40.00
   Cocktail Cherries 90.00
   Cocktail Olives................... 90.00

Christmas Ornament, Santa, paper, boxed set of 6..................... 24.00

Drinking Glass, Santa, mkd "1959 Holt Howard," 3" h, 2" d, some paint missing, set of 4......... 25.00

Grease jar, Cozy Kitten......... 285.00

Ketchup, Pixieware 70.00

Jam n' Jelly Condiment Jar, Rooster, mkd, c1962, 4-1/2" d, small chips to paint.............................. 45.00

Lady's Head Vase, orig Christmas ball dangle earrings, holly, necklace, paper label, 1959, 4" h, 4" w, small nick on hair............... 80.00

Salt and Pepper Shakers, pr, Pixie................................. 400.00

Salt and pepper shakers, Raggedy Ann & Andy, 1966, 7-1/4" h 165.00

Salt and pepper shakers, stacking cat heads......................... 330.00

Sewing Box, Kitty, tongue tape measure 200.00

Snack Plate, pie crust edge, indent for cup, matte finish, stamped "1962 Holt Howard," foil Japan sticker, 8-1/2" d.................... 7.50

String Holder, cat head 80.00

String Holder, cat, orig sticker, 4-3/4" h 110.00

For exciting collecting trends and newly expanded areas look for the following symbols:

✿ **Hot Topic**

★ **New Warman's Listing**

(May have been in another Warman's edition.)

❖ Home Front Collectibles

While the "boys" were off to World War II, there was a real effort to create images to help those left behind contribute to the war effort. Today, these items are becoming choice collectibles. Some have powerful messages and bright graphics.

Blotter, "Getting a Kick Out of Our Job," 3-7/8" x 9" tan blotter, red text, Aug 1943 calendar, red and white striped pants and shoe kicking Hitler, Mussolini, and Hirohito, off the face of the planet, Essingers, Philadelphia, PA, beer imprint, unused 35.00

Bookmark, 2-1/2" x 7", "Prevent Forest Fires," orange stiff paper, red and black art, Hitler and Hirohito at top with blazing forest fire in background, US Dept of Agriculture, black and white reverse with text 45.00

Match Book, V for Victory, War Bond promotion, 1-1/2" x 3-3/4", red, white, and blue, V symbol on one side, image of Minuteman on reverse, Diamond Match Co., NYC, unused 12.00

Match Pack, Strike At The Seat Of Trouble, 1-1/2" x 4", cartoon of Hitler holding globe looking nervous while arrow points to seat of his pants, striker surface for matches, Anchor Packing Co. ad, some matches used............ 45.00

Pinback button, Remember Pearl Harbor, 1-5/16" d, $15.

Membership Card, Slap-A-Jap, 2-1/2" x 4", black and white cartoon card, Charter Member, Uncle Sam slapping Japanese soldier to ground, unused 50.00

Patch, Paper Trooper, 3-1/2" d, yellow fabric, blue and white "PT" letters 25.00

Score Card, 5-1/2" x 8-1/2", black inked bright yellow kitchen hanger card, reads "I Helped To Save His Life Today," young American soldier with Axis caricature portraits for 29 days of month to be scratched when saving tablespoon of fat, cooking instruction on other side 35.00

Sticker, "Salvage Will Win The War," 1-1/2" x 2" yellow, blue, white, and red, cartoon image of Japanese soldier choking on "v" portion of word "salvage".................... 25.00

Sweetheart Pin, pink lucite with two aluminum hearts, pair of palm trees, inscribed "N. G. 44," 1-1/2" d.............................. 38.00

Window Banner, 8-1/2" x 12", fabric panel, printed in red, white, blue, and bright gold, loop for hanging 35.00

❖ Homer Laughlin

The Homer Laughlin Company is another dinnerware manufacturer that helped make East Liverpool, OH, such a busy place. By the late 1880s, this company was producing white ware. When the firm was sold to a group of investors from Pittsburgh, expansion soon followed. New plants were built in Ohio and West Virginia and the dinnerware lines increased. Besides giving us such interesting patterns as Fiesta and Harlequin, the firm also designed Kitchen Kraft and Riviera, plus thousands of other designs.

Periodical: *The Laughlin Eagle,* 1270 63rd Terrace S, St. Petersburg, FL 33705.

For additional listings, see *Warman's Americana & Collectibles* and *Warman's American Pottery and Porcelain.*

Dogwood teapot, 8-1/2" h, $45.

Baker, Mexicana, oval............ 25.00
Bowl, Cavalier, egg shell, numbered, set of four 20.00
Butter, cov, Virginia Rose, jade..................................... 80.00
Casserole, cov, individual, Conchita 225.00
Casserole, cov, large
   Conchita 125.00
   Mexicana 145.00
Cereal Bowl, Rhythm, chartreuse, 5-1/2" d, ftd 5.00
Cup, Rhythm, forest green or gray 7.00
Deep Plate, Mexicana............. 45.00
Dessert Bowl, Rhythm, yellow, 5-1/4" d................................ 3.00
Fruit Bowl, Mexicana 15.00
Nappy, Rhythm, yellow, 8-3/4" d.............................. 18.00
Pie Baker, Mexicana 37.50
Plate, Virginia Rose, 9" d.......... 7.50
Platter, Rhythm, yellow, 11-1/2" l 12.00
Soup Bowl, Rhythm, yellow 9.00
Tray, Virginia Rose................. 30.00

❖ Horse Collectibles

Giddyap is known as the universal "go command" for horses. Perhaps it's also appropriate for horse memorabilia collectors. Some specialize in things that are related to horses, such as bridles and bits, while others prefer items that display images of horses. Whatever their preference, horse collectibles of all forms are to be found at flea markets.

Bells, worn leather strap with over 40 nickel bells, tug hook ...225.00
Bit, eagle, mkd "G. S. Garcia"..............................775.00
Book, *Quarter Horses, Story of Two Centuries,* Robert M. Denhardt, Univ. of Oklahoma Press, 1967, 192 pgs 12.00
Clock, brass horse standing next to western saddle, wood base, United 170.00
Contest Flyer, Dan Patch, illus..................................28.00
Cookie Cutter, prancing horse, bobtail, flat back..................80.00
Curry Comb, tin back, leather handle, early 1900s 45.00
Game, Pony Express, cast-metal horses, 1940s 85.00
Lasso, horsehair 135.00
Magazine, *Western Horseman,* Vol. 1., #1, 1935..................30.00
Men's Brush, horse head figural handle 10.00
Mug, Clydesdales, Budweiser, Christmas, Ceramarte, 1985..................................50.00
Postcard, bucking bronco, cowboy flying off, Prescott, AZ, rodeo, 1920s..................................15.00
Rosette, brass, Civil War.........25.00

Costume jewelry pin, Pegasus, blue and pink plastic, rhinestones, 2-1/4" h, 2" l, $2.

Saddle, McClelland type, large fenders for leg protection, early 1900s 900.00

Saddle Blanket, Navajo, early 1900s 950.00

Spurs, Crockett, arrow shank 700.00

Tray, Genessee Twelve Horse Ale, horse team illus, 12" d 115.00

❖ Horse Racing

Here's another horse-related category. This one's devoted to horse racing. See "Kentucky Derby Glasses" for specifics in that area.

Collectors' Club: Sport of Kings Society, 1406 Annen Lane, Madison, WI 53711.

Book, *American Trotting and Pacing Horses,* Henry T. Coates, 1902 .... 25.00

Doorstop, figural racehorse, stamped "Virginia Metalcrafters," 1949 .... 200.00

Game, Jeu De Course, France, 1895 .... 550.00

Pinback Button

Geo. Taylor, Jockey, M. McLoughlin Colors, blue and gold, High Admiral Cigarettes back paper, early 1900s 35.00

Jim Beam decanter, 95th Kentucky Derby, 10-7/8" h, $14.

Loates Celebrated English Jockey, red, white, and pale blue racing clothes, American Pepsin Gum back paper, early 1900s 25.00

Silky Sullivan Winner, multicolored, white ground, blue letters, c1950 .... 20.00

Topeka Derby Day, Sept 13, 1904, sepia..................... 20.00

Print, Currier & Ives, The Grand Racer Kington, by Spendthrift, 1891, unmatted, unframed 475.00

Sheet Music, *Dan Patch March* 40.00

Trophy, silver, typical.............. 50.00

✭ ⚙ Hot Wheels

Hot Wheels introduced their first diecast cars in 1968 after Harry Bradley, an automotive designer, Howard Newman, a Mattel designer, Elliot Handler, Mattel chairman, and Jack Ryan, also of Mattel, collaborated. Mattel designed Hot Wheels to be raced, and worked hard at creating continually changing styles and models.

Reference: Michael Thomas Strauss, *Tomart's Price Guide to Hot Wheels,* 3rd ed., Tomart Publications, 1998.

Periodicals: *Hot Wheels Newsletter,* 26 Madera Ave, San Carlos, CA 94070; *Toy Cars & Vehicles,* 700 E. State St., Iola, WI 54990; *Toy Shop,* 700 E. State St., Iola, WI 54990.

Accessories

Case, Sizzlers Race 75.00

Full Curve Accessory Pak .. 12.00

Gas Pumper, Mattel............ 12.00

Snake Mountain Challenge 20.00

Cars and Trucks

Beach Bomb, green............ 75.00

Bulldozer, #34 .... 28.00

Camaro Z28, red, chrome base, #33 .... 46.00

Chaparral, white, played with 35.00

Chevy, '57, Ultra Hots, #47 .... 110.00

McDonald's race car, 1993, 3-5/8" l, $1.

Coronet Car, NRFP............. 14.00

Corvette, billionth............... 10.00

Custom Firebird, blue 40.00

Delivery Truck, #52............. 32.00

Dump Truck, steel bed, #38 .... 7.00

Earthmover, #16 .... 85.00

Ferrari, #312, red enamel ... 50.00

Fire Truck, 1980.................... 2.00

Fleetside, purple 35.00

Ford Bronco, turquoise, #56 .... 18.00

GM Ultralite, #594, 1995, NRFP.............................. 3.00

GT Racer, #598, 1995, NRFP.............................. 3.00

Masarati Mistral, brown....... 55.00

McDonald's, Key Force Car, 1993, NRFP..................... 3.00

McDonald's, Tattoo Machine, 1993, NRFP..................... 3.00

Mercedes 500 SL, 1997, NRFP............................. 26.00

Pontiac Banshee, #457, 1995, NRFP.............................. 3.00

Pontiac Salsa, #596, 1995, NRFP.............................. 3.00

Set, 25th anniversary, 1993, NRFP, five cars............... 38.00

Tail Gunner, #29................. 75.00

Tractor Trailer, 1979............. 1.00

Van de Kamps, mail in premium, NRFP, Deora, 1997 .... 20.00

Van de Kamps, mail in premium, NRFP, Hiway Hauler Truck, 1996 .... 24.00

✭ Howdy Doody

"What time is it kids?-Howdy Doody Time!" Every Howdy Doody Show started with Buffalo Bob Smith asking the Peanut Gallery that question. It was a great kids' show, and today collectors are happy to find interesting items to add to their treasures as they find memorabilia about Howdy, Mr. Bluster, Clarabelle or some of the other characters.

Collectors' Club: Doodyville Historical Society, 8 Hunt Court, Flemington, NJ 08822.

Bank, plastic, NBC Broadcasting Co., c1970 .... 35.00

Book, *Howdy Doody's Lucky Trip,* 1953, edge wear 45.00

Box, for Howdy Doody rubber squeeze toy, bright graphics 42.00

Camera, Doody Sun Ray, 4 rolls of film, 6 developing papers, © Kagran, instructions printed on back, MOC 150.00

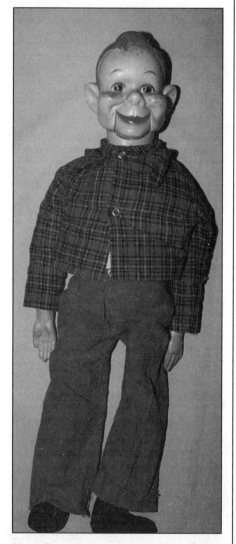

Ventriloquist's puppet, 1972, $40.

Cookie Jar, Vandor, orig paper label, 10" h 425.00

Cup, plastic, decal "Howdy Doody, Be-Keen, Be-Keen, Drink Chocolate Flavored Ovaltine," plastic, 1950s, mint 75.00

Ice Cream Spoon, silver plate, 7" l 38.00

Keychain, 3 dimensional, NRFP...................................... 4.50

Learn How to Tell Time Teacher, orig package 95.00

Little Golden Book
Howdy Doody & Clarabelle, 1951, some edge damage 45.00
Howdy Doody in Funland, 1953 .... 45.00
Howdy Doody's Circus, 1960 .... 17.50

Lunch Box, plastic................... 45.00

Program, Bill Graham's Fillmore East Theatre, Howdy Doody Revival, featuring Buffalo Bob Smith, April 4, 1971 .... 30.00

Puppet, Clarabelle, Peter Puppet, MIB 350.00

Ventriloquist Doll, 18" h........... 65.00

✫ Hubley Toys

Hubley Manufacturing was located in Lancaster, PA, starting in 1894. Their first toys were cast iron. By 1940, cast iron was phased out and replaced with other metals and plastic.

Periodicals: *Toy Cars & Vehicles,* 700 E. State St., Iola, WI 54990; *Toy Shop,* 700 E. State St., Iola, WI 54990.

Airplane, American Eagle, all metal, 11" wingspan, MIB............ 165.00

Baby Speedboat, cast iron, emb "Baby" on side, 4-1/2" l 90.00

Crash Car 65.00

Indian Motorcycle, 9" l, green repaint, repair 375.00

MG, diecast, red, nickel-plated windshield and grille, black rubber tires, Hubley Kiddie, c1950, 2" x 6" x 2" 15.00

Pickup, die cast, 11" l.............. 50.00

Pumper, cast iron, red, gold trim, nickel-plated driver, 11-1/4" l 500.00

Racer, die cast 170.00

Hubley Farm Set No. 50, box only, tears, 4-1/8" h, 14-1/2" l, 7" w, $20.

❖ Hull Pottery

In 1905, Addis E. Hull purchased the Acme Pottery Company, Crooksville, Ohio. In 1917, the A. E. Hull Pottery Company began making art pottery, novelties, stoneware, and kitchenware, later including the famous Little Red Riding Hood line. Most items had a matte finish with shades of pink and blue or brown predominating.

After a disastrous flood and fire in 1950, J. Brandon Hull reopened the factory in 1952 as the Hull Pottery Company. New, more-modern-style pieces, mostly with a glossy finish, were produced. The company currently produces wares for florists, e.g. the Regal and Floraline lines.

Hull pottery molds and patterns are easily identified. Pre-1950 vases are marked "Hull USA" or "Hull Art USA" on the bottom. Many also retain their paper labels. Post-1950 pieces are marked "Hull" in large script or "HULL" in block letters.

Each pattern has a distinctive letter or number, e.g., Wildflower has a "W" and a number; Waterlily, "L" and number; Poppy, numbers in the 600s; Orchid, in the 300s. Early stoneware pieces are marked with an "H".

References: Susan and Al Bagdade, *Warman's American Pottery and Porcelain,* Wallace-Homestead, 1994; Barbara Loveless Gick-Burke, *Collector's Guide to Hull Pottery,* Collector Books, 1993; Joan Hull, *Hull, The*

Heavenly Pottery, 6th ed., published by author (1376 Nevada, Huron, SD 57350), 1999; ——, *Hull, The Heavenly Pottery Shirt Pocket Price List,* published by author, 1998; Brenda Roberts, *The Ultimate Encyclopedia of Hull Pottery,* Collector Books, 1995; Mark and Ellen Supnick, *Collecting Hull Pottery's Little Red Riding Hood, Revised Edition,* L-W Books, 1998.

Periodicals: *Hull Pottery Association,* 11023 Tunnel Hill NE, New Lexington, OH 43764; *Hull Pottery Newsletter,* 7768 Meadow Dr, Hillsboro, MO 60350.

See *Warman's Americana & Collectibles* for more examples.

Bank, Corky Pig, rose and green dec 80.00

Basket
    Parchment & Pine, brown and green, 15" 140.00
    Water Lily, tan and brown, 10-1/2" 350.00

Candleholders, pr, Water Lily, pink and turquoise, L-22, 4" 150.00

Clock, Bluebird 175.00

Coaster/Ashtray, Gingerbread Man 20.00

Console Bowl

Lamb planter, 8-1/2" h, 7-1/2" l, $49.

Blossom Flite, T10 ....110.00
Water Lily, pink and turquoise, flaw nick 150.00
Cornucopia, double
    Bow Knot, pink and blue, B-13, 13-1/2" l 300.00
    Water Lily, pink and turquoise, L-27, 12" 225.00
Ewer, Tokay, 12" h 160.00
Jardiniere, Bow Knot, pink and blue, B-18 .... 200.00

Pitcher
    Water Lily, pink and turquoise, L-3, 5-1/2" h 95.00
    Wildflowers, pink and blue, W-11, 8-1/2" 165.00
Planter, Bandana Duck, #75 ... 60.00
Tea Set, Woodland, glossy ... 165.00
Tray, Gingerbread Man, large, brown 65.00
Urn, Wildflowers, yellow and brown, W-20, 15", 1" factory hairline 450.00

Vase
    Iris, Rose/Peach, #407-7 .. 125.00
    Magnolia, handle, #12, 6-1/2" 75.00
    Tulip, 103-33, suspended type 195.00

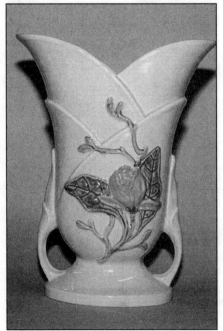
Magnolia high-gloss vase, 11-1/8" h, $100.

Water Lily, pink and turquoise, L-12 10-1/2" 200.00
Wildflower, W-15, fan 140.00

❖ Hummels

Created from original drawings by Berta Hummel, these charming children have delighted collectors for generations. Production of her figurines started in 1935. The story behind these figurines is quite interesting and well covered in the many reference books available.

References: Carl F. Luckey, *Luckey's Hummel Figurines and Plates: A Collector's Identification and Value Guide,* 11th ed., Krause Publications, 1997; Robert L. Miller, *No. 1 Price Guide to M. I. Hummel: Figurines, Plates, More...,* 6th ed., – ——, *Hummels 1978-1998: 20 Years of "Miller on Hummel" Columns,* Collector News, 1998.

Collectors' Clubs: Hummel Collector's Club, Inc, 1261 University Dr, Yardley, PA 19067; M. I. Hummel Club, Goebel Plaza, Rte 31, PO Box 11, Pennington, NJ 08534.

Annual Plate, Singing Lesson, 1979 ....50.00
Annual Bell, third edition, bas relief, 1980, MIB 70.00
Lamp, table, Culprits, #44, crown mark, c1930, orig wiring, 9-1/2" h 475.00
Figure
    Apple Tree Boy, #142/I, 6" 290.00
    Apple Tree Girl, #141/I, 6" 290.00
    Book Worm, #3/I 490.00
    Brother, #95 .... 230.00
    Chicken Licken 240.00
    Coquettes, #179 .... 280.00
    Crossroads, #331, 6 3/4" 360.00
    Doll Mother, stylized bee mark 135.00
    Farewell 325.00
    Feather Friends, #344 ..... 365.00
    Friend or Foe, #434 .... 285.00
    Goose Girl 250.00

Happy Birthday, #176/0,
6" 245.00
Home From Market 175.00
Happy Pastime, #69 ....190.00
Just Resting, #112 3/0 ......175.00

First Edition Annual Bell, 1978, orig box, $45.

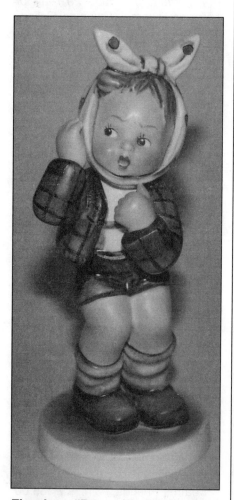

**Figurine, "Boy with Toothache,"
5-5/8" h, $110.**

Letter To Santa Claus,
#340 .... 350.00
Mischief Maker 290.00
Out Of Danger, #56B 290.00
Playmates, #580/0 .... 200.00
Sensitive Hunter 240.00
She Loves Me, She Loves Me
Not 225.00
Stormy Weather, #71/I 370.00

❖ Hummel Look-Alikes

Some folks love Hummels so much they are enchanted with figures that are designed to look like Hummels. A number of companies have made these figures, some better than others. If in doubt, check for the familiar Hummel mark and don't be surprised to find another maker's identification mark or label.

Schmid Christmas ornament, 2nd ed, 1984, $22.

Boy, standing
Hands behind back 15.00
Next to fence....................... 20.00
Girl, standing
Holding basket 17.50
Reading book..................... 15.00
With cat, 1973, Avon........... 10.00

❖ Hunting

Flea markets make great hunting, whether you're looking for big game or small treasures. Substitute a camera for the usual rifle or trap, and bring along a bag to tote your catch in.

Periodicals: *Sporting Collector's Monthly,* PO Box 305, Camden Wyoming, DE 19934; *Deer and Deer Hunting; The Trapper & Predator Caller; Turkey and Turkey Hunting; Wisconsin Outdoor Journal,* 700 E. State St., Iola, WI 54990.

Collectors' Clubs: Call & Whistle Collectors Association, 2839 E. 26th Place, Tulsa, OK 74114; Callmakers & Collectors Association of America, 137 Kingswood Drive, Clarksville, TN 37043.

Book
How To Hunt Deer, Edward A.
Freeman, 1960, dj 10.00
*The Art of Hunting Big Game in
North America,* O'Connor, Outdoor Life, 1967, dj........... 24.00
Calendar Top, 20" h, 14" w, Winchester, man atop rock ledge, hunting rams, artist sgd "Philip R. Goodwin," metal rim at top, some creasing 235.00
Call
Crow, Charles Perdew, Henry, IL, fair condition 190.00
Duck, Herter's orig box 40.00
Turkey, orig box 35.00
Counter Felt, "Shoot Where You Aim," Winchester 195.00
License
Deer, New York State, 1936, buff, black, and white, resident use, pinback style................... 35.00
Fishing, Connecticut, 1936, green and white, Resident Angling License, pinback style 20.00

Fishing, Delaware, 1936, black and white, resident use, pinback style, 1-3/4" d 60.00

Game, New York State, 1918, red and white, serial number in blue, brass lapel stud fastener, 1-1/2" d 75.00

Pinback Button

Infallible Shotgun Smokeless, multicolored, blue and white striped banner, gold wreath, red dots, green ribbons, turquoise background, back paper "Compliments of McCurdy & Norwell Co/Originators," early 1900s 80.00

Shoot Peters Shells, multicolored, Pulver Co., brass and red shell on white, early 1900s......45.00

Use Peters Shells, multicolored hunter and dog pursuing rabbit, c1907-20 ....90.00

Poster, 14" h, 20" w, limited edition titled "It All Started Here," young boy using his first Red Ryder BB gun, artist sgd "Les C. Kouba," matted and framed 100.00

Sign, split log, Hatchet Mountain Hunting Camps, Guide Service, Supplies, crude................. 150.00

Watch Fob, Dead Shot, bright luster brass rim, multicolored celluloid insert, reverse inscribed "Dead Shot Smokeless Powder Manufactured by American Powder Mills/Boston, Mass," 1920s............................... 175.00

For exciting collecting trends and newly expanded areas look for the following symbols:

✪ Hot Topic

✭ New Warman's Listing

(May have been in another Warman's edition.)

Match safe, sterling silver, high relief of fox hunt, 2-1/4" x 1-3/4", $70.

Fellow collectors:

Name: _____

Address:_____

_____

Phone:_____

E-mail:_____

Name: _____

Address:_____

_____

Phone:_____

E-mail:_____

Name: _____

Address:_____

_____

Phone:_____

E-mail:_____

Name: _____

Address:_____

_____

Phone:_____

E-mail:_____

Name: _____

Address:_____

_____

Phone:_____

E-mail:_____

Name: _____

Address:_____

_____

Phone:_____

E-mail:_____

❖ Ice Cream Collectibles

Cold and creamy, ice cream can be the perfect accompaniment to a few hours at a flea market. But, if your tastes run to ice cream collectibles, some great examples may be waiting for you, too.

Collectors' Clubs: National Association of Soda Jerks, PO Box 115, Omaha, NE 68101; The Ice Screamers, PO Box 465, Warrington, PA 18976.

Advertisement, Icy PI 5 Cents, Automatic Cone Co., blue and red letters, white ground, 18-3/4" h, 11-3/4" w, water stained on lower corner 10.00
Cone Dispenser, glass, copper insert 365.00
Doll, Eskimo Pie 15.00
Lid, Florida Ice Cream, Florida Dairy, Tampa, Florida, one vanilla, other chocolate, pr........................ 4.00
Mold
   Cherub 85.00
   Ram......................................75.00
Pinback Button, Arctic Rainbow Ice Cream Cones, multicolored, celluloid, c1912 .... 30.00
Plate, 7" d, Davis Ice Cream Co., Cambridge, green image of lady in large hat in center, white ground 200.00

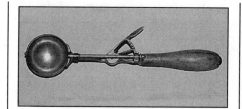

Gilchrest #16, wooden handle, 11" l, $24.

Scoop
   Gilchrest #31 .... 120.00
   Gilchrest #33 .... 145.00
   No-Pak, #31 .... 90.00
Sign
   Jack & Jill Ice Cream Cake Roll, full color, paper, painted image of smiling housewife holding slice of ice cream cake, yellow, red, and blue background, copyright "Newly Weds Baking Co.," c1940, 8-1/2" x 19-1/2"............................ 24.00
   Jack Frost Fontaine, Jack Frost blowing visions of children making candy, adults making ice cream, elderly couple making icing and cakes, cardboard, 14-1/4" h, 11-1/4" w, some paper loss at edges........ 25.00
Table, 24" sq display top, 32-1/2" h, filigree cast iron legs, four attached swivel seats 1,800.00
Tray
   Folmers Ice Cream............. 90.00
   Pure Milk Co., ice cream and milk, 1900..................... 120.00
Truck Driver's Manual, Jack & Jill Ice Cream, 4-1/2" x 6", black and white, 20 pg manual, red accent cover, late 1930s 18.00
Whistle, Puritan Dairy Ice Cream, yellow tin litho, black letters, c1930................................. 40.00

✫ Ice Picks

An ice pick was once a very useful household necessity. Today collectors search for interesting shapes and advertising slogans. Most have wooden handles with metal picks. Expect to find examples with wear and minor rusting.

"Peoples Ice Delivery Co., Save With Ice, Buy an Ice Refrigerator," 8" l, $9.

Bob's Ice Delivery 5.00
City Ice Works, Salem, Oregon, very worn 8.00
City Products Co. 4.00
Clarkson Peoples Coal & Ice .. 12.50
Coolerator, Seaboard Ice Company, combination adv ice pick and bottle opener...................... 18.00
Dr. Pepper.............................. 5.00
Hygenic Artificial Ice Co. 12.50
PRR, small, very worn 2.25
Union Ice Company 10.00
United Ice and Coal, very worn . 2.50
Wilson Ice and Coal.................. 5.50

✫ Ice Skating

Folk art skate, possibly a trade sign, wood with iron blade, 10-1/2" h, 18-3/4" l, $95.

Today we happily watch figure skating on television as skaters glide around. Ice skating is actually an old pastime, going back to a time when skates where hand made and much cruder than today's finely-shaped skates. Collecting ephemera related to ice skating is also quite popular with today's generation.

Ice Skates

Child's, aluminum, leather straps, beginner's type, double runners, c1950 ....20.00

Figure, white leather uppers, metal blades, worn, c196 ....10.00

Hockey, brown leather uppers, wide blades, c1960 ....25.00

Wooden, metal runners, leather straps 55.00

Film, 16mm, Donald the Skater, Walt Disney Character Film, Hollywood Enterprises, c1935, orig box 25.00

Pinback Button, Frosty Treat, female ice skater, red, white, and blue, c1930, 1-1/4" d 27.50

Program

Ice Capades, autographed by Peter Foss, pin-up on front cover by artist Lew, 1958 ....25.00

Ice Follies, Philadelphia, 1960 ....5.00

Ticket Stub, Holiday on Ice, 1975 .... 2.00

❖ Illustrators

Many flea market adventurers are starting to specialize in one particular illustrator. You'll find them scouring through magazines for illustrations and advertisements by their favorites. Others devote their search to prints, calendars, books, or other types of ephemera.

Periodicals: *Calendar Art Collectors' Newsletter,* 45 Brown's Lane, Old Lyme, CT 06371; *The Illustrator Collector's News,* PO Box 1958, Sequim, WA 98232; *The Philip Boileau Collectors' Society Newsletter,* 1025 Redwood Blvd, Redding, CA 96003.

Book, *The Story of Siegfried,* Peter Hurd 45.00

Magazine Cover

Flagg, James Montgomery, color 10.00

Mucha, Alphonse, *Literary Digest* 48.00

Howard Christy, "The World Before Them," Dresden China plate, 6-5/8" d, $25.

Parrish, Maxfield, *Ladies Home Journal,* Nov, 1912 .... 55.00

Smith, Jessie Wilcox, *Good Housekeeping* 27.50

Twelvetrees, Charles, *Pictorial Review,* small format, pre-1930 .... 15.00

Postcard

Atwell, Mabel Lucie 9.00

Christy, F. Earl 30.00

Clapsaddle, Ellen Hattie 25.00

Mucha, Alphonse.............. 200.00

Outcault, R. 17.50

Thiele, Arthur..................... 35.00

Sign, Maxfield Parrish, Edison Mazda Lamps, titled "Contentment," © 1927, matted and framed, 35" h, 23" w 600.00

❖ Imari

Imari is a Japanese porcelain that dates back to the late 1770s. Early Imari is a simple decoration, unlike the later renditions also known as Imari. As the Chinese and later the English copied and interpreted this pattern, it's developed into a rich brocade design.

Bowl, 15" d, blue and white, scalloped rim, early 20th C 225.00

Charger, 19th C 550.00

Dish, shaped rim, all–over flowering vine dec, gilt highlights, 9-1/2" d 150.00

Jardiniere, hexagonal, bulbous, short flared foot, alternating bijin figures and immortal symbols, stylized ground, 10" h 265.00

Sauce Tureen, Boston retailer's mark, imp "Ashworth Real Ironstone," 6-1/8" h, 5-1/4" w, 9-1/4" l 325.00

Teabowl and Saucer, floriform, floral spray dec 215.00

❖ Imperial Glass

Bellaire, OH, was the location of Imperial Glass, beginning in 1901. Through the years they have produced pressed glass in patterns imitating cut glass, interesting art glass, and animals, as well as tablewares in the style of elegant depression glass patterns.

Collectors' Club: National Imperial Glass Collectors Society, PO Box 534, Bellaire, OH 43906.

Animal, pony stallion, caramel, c1970 ....65.00

Baked Apple, Cape Cod 5.00

Berry Bowl, Katy Blue, opalescent, flat, rim 30.00

Bowl, Diamond Quilted, black, 7" d, crimped 20.00

Cake Stand, ftd, Cape Cod pattern, 10" d, 4" h 55.00

Candlesticks, pr, Katy Blue, opalescent, duo 125.00

Candy Box, cov, Grape, milk glass, ftd, satin finish....................40.00

Cereal Bowl, Katy Blue, opalescent 65.00

Cocktail, Cape Cod 12.00

Cracker Jar, cov, Americana, milk glass 60.00

Creamer and Sugar, Cape Cod 15.00

Cup and Saucer, Cape Cod 7.50

Jug, Doeskin, 8" h, 36 oz, milk glass 50.00

Juice, Cape Cod, ftd 8.00

Parfait, Cape Cod 11.00

Plate

Cape Cod, Verdi, 8" d 15.00

Vase, caramel slag, 5-1/4" h, 4-1/4" d, $40.

Diamond Quilted, black,
8" d...................................15.00

Punch Bowl Set
Crocheted, crystal, bowl,
12 cups 300.00
Mount Vernon, 15 pcs 90.00
Salt and Pepper Shakers, pr, Cape
Cod, Verdi 45.00
Soup Bowl, Katy Blue,
opalescent........................... 85.00
Sugar, cov, Diamond Quilted,
black.................................... 10.00
Tumbler, Katy Blue, opalescent,
10 oz 65.00
Vase, Katy Blue, cobalt blue... 65.00

❖ Indiana Glass

The good news is that Indiana Glass Company has a colorful history, dating back to 1907, when it was founded in Dunkirk, Ind. The bad news is that some of the company's popular patterns, as well as those originated by other firms, have been reproduced over the years. Color and detail are two clues used to help flea market shoppers distinguish vintage Indiana glass from newer production.

King's Crown compote, purple carnival glass, 5-1/4" h, 4-3/4" d, $15.

Reproduction Alert.

American Eagle, plate, #1960,
Bicentennial, carnival glass, gold,
7-1/2" d 12.50
Daisy Amber, plates, set of 6,
8-1/2" d 36.00
Grape and Cable, candy dish,
amethyst, 6" x 6"................. 32.00
Grape and Cable, cracker jar,
amethyst, 8-1/2" h 90.00
Grape and Cable, cream and sugar
on tray, amethyst, tray
8" x 3-1/4" 20.00
Near Cut, bowl, red, 4-3/4" h,
8-1/2" d 26.00
Pretzel, plates, fruit center,
8-1/8" d 25.00
Pretzel, soup bowls, set of 4,
7-1/2" d 20.00
Sandwich, luncheon plates, set of 6,
8-3/4" d 32.00
Sandwich, teacup, teal,
2-3/4" h 16.50
Tea Room, cream and sugar,
4" 31.50
Tea Room, vase, ruffled edge, pink,
11" 177.50

❖ Ink Bottles

Before the invention of the ballpoint pen, it was common for ink to be sold in bottles. Because most of

Aqua glass, emb "Carter's" on base, 3" h, $7.50.

them date back to the 1800s, they are pricey when found in excellent or better condition.

Periodical: *Antique Bottle and Glass Collector,* PO Box 187, East Greenville, PA 18041.

Carter's, hexagonal, cathedral panels, clear with yellow cast, machined mouth, smooth base, c1900, 9-7/8" h 700.00
Empire Ink, octagonal umbrella, label "Williams Black Empire Ink, New York," lime green, tooled mouth, smooth base, some damage to label 200.00
Harrison's Columbia Ink, cylindrical, cobalt blue, applied flared mouth, pontil scar, 5-5/8" h 225.00
Harrison's Columbia Ink, octagonal, light green 75.00
Laughlin's and Bushfield, Wheeling, WV, octagonal, aquamarine, inward rolled mouth, pontil scar 300.00
Senate Ink Co., house shape, full label "Bank of Writing Fluid, Manuf by Senate Ink Co., Philadelphia," aquamarine, tooled sq collared mouth, some fading to label, 2-5/8" h....................325.00

❖ Inkwells

Like ink bottles, ink wells were commonly used to hold ink. Because early ink bottles had a tendency to tip or spill, inventors soon came up with decorative and more stable ways of having ink available when they needed it.

Collectors' Clubs: St. Louis Inkwell Collectors Society, PO Box 29396, St. Louis, MO, 63126; The Society of Inkwell Collectors, 5136 Thomas Ave. S., Minneapolis, MN 55410.

Brass, figural rose, color wash, pink and red petals, green stem250.00
Double Desk Type, gilt metal and cast brass, Moorish pattern, hinged top, hooks to hold pen, imp "Tiffany & Co.," foot restored, pan missing 350.00
Snail, clear glass, ground mouth, America, 1830-70, flat chip.................................. 150.00
Teakettle Shape
    Ceramic, hexagonal, mottled ruby red and white glaze, French, 1830-60, 2-1/8" h 90.00
    Glass, brick red and burgundy slag, ground mouth, brass cap, America, 1830-60, two small chips..............................115.00

❖ Insulators

Insulators date back to 1837 when the telegraph was developed. Styles have been modified a bit over the years, and collectors are treated to a wide variety of shapes and colors.

Periodicals: *Bottles & Extras,* 88 Sweetbriar Branch, Longwood, FL 32750-2783; *Canadian Insulator Magazine,* Mayne Island, British Columbia, V0N 2J0 Canada; *Crown Jewels of the Wire,* PO Box 1003, St Charles, IL 60174; *Drip Point,* 1315 Old Mill Path, Broadview Heights, OH 44147; *Rainbow Riders' Trading Post,* PO Box 1423, Port Heuneme, CA 93044.

Collectors' Clubs: Capital District Insulator Club, 41 Crestwood Dr, Schenectady, NY 12306; Central Florida Insulator Collectors Club, 707 NE 113th St, North Miami, FL 33161; Central/Southern Counties Insulator Club, 234 N. 5th St., Port Hueneme, CA 93401; Chesapeake Bay Insulator Club, 10 Ridge Rd, Catonsville, MD 21228; Dixie Jewels Insulator Club, 6220 Carriage Court, Cumming, GA 30130-9111; Enchantment Insulator Club, 1024 Camino de Lucia, Corrales, NM 87048-8314; Federation of Historical Bottle Collectors, Inc., 88 Sweetbriar Branch, Longwood, FL 32750-2783; Greater Chicago Insulator Club, 34273 Homestead Road, Gurnee, IL 60031-4206; Lone Star Insulator Club, PO Box 1317, Buna, TX 77612; Missouri Valley Insulator Club, 52 Lakewood Lane, Council Bluffs, IA 51502; National Insulator Association, 1315 Old Mill Path, Broadview Heights, OH 44147; National Trails Insulator Club, 408 Arlington Rd, Brookville, OH 45309; North-Cal Insulator Club, 2551 Verna Way, Sacramento, CA 95821; OK Insulator Club, Route 2, Box 27, Carnegie, OK 73015; Triple Ridge Insulator Club, 2120 S. Vaughn Way, Aurora, CO 80014-1375; Yankee Polecat Insulator Club, 79 New Bolton Rd, Manchester, CT 06040.

Hemingray-42, green glass, 4-1/4" h, $3.

Boston Bottle Works, CD 728, light aqua, smooth base 90.00
General Electric, CD 134, light aqua....................................8.00
Hemingray
    CD 125, blue......................30.00
    CD 152, two tone aqua.......20.00
    CD 154, blue......................25.00
    CD 165, clear.......................7.50
Locke, CD 287, light aqua.......25.00
Lynchburg, CD 164, yellow-green 35.00
New England Telephone & Telegraph, CD 104, aqua......6.50
W. Brookfield, CD 133, light aqua 25.00

❖ Irons

Folks have been trying to keep their clothes pressed neatly since the 1100s. Of course, those irons are vastly different than the streamlined appliances we use today.

References: Dave Irons, *Irons by Irons,* published by author, 1994; —, *More Irons by Irons,* published by author, 1996; —, *Pressing Iron Patents,* published by author, 1994.

Periodical: *Iron Talk,* PO Box 68, Waelder, TX 78959.

Collectors' Clubs: Club of the Friends of Ancient Smoothing Irons, PO Box 215, Carlsbad, CA 92008; Midwest Sad Iron Collectors Club, 24 Nob Hill Dr, St Louis, MO 63138.

Acme, liquid fuel, tank in front....................................125.00

Fiery Feather travel iron, Gorgie Mfg. Co., red wooden handle, 7-3/4" l, 4" w, $6.50.

Best on Earth, flat iron, lift off cold handle 75.00

Dixie, laundry stove type, holds 8 irons 315.00

Geneva, hand fluted, dated 1886 .... 75.00

Kenrick, slug, hinged flip top, double patent 150.00

Magic #1, slug, top lifts off 15.00

Ne Plus Ultra, double chimney charcoal............................ 200.00

Pacific Electric Heating Co., 1906 .... 90.00

Sundry Mfg. Co., Buffalo, NY, fluted, 3 pcs............................... 325.00

❖ Ironstone

Ironstone has been a popular dinnerware material for decades. From the pristine white ironstone with its molded designs to wares which have painted or decaled decorations, it has served many housewives.

Bowl, Tamerlane pattern, Oriental design, J & M P Bell, 9-3/4" d........................... 165.00

Coffee Set, 11-1/4" h coffee pot, 3-1/4" h creamer, 3-1/4" h sugar, white ironstone, yellow and orange daffodils, mkd "Nikko Ironstone Dishwasher—Oven Safe, Made in Japan" 40.00

Decanter, hand painted guardsman, mkd "Mason's, No. 2574," 9-1/4" h.............................. 45.00

Dessert Set, white background, 8 decals representing different countries, 12" d cake plate, eight 7-3/4" plates, mkd "Kaysons Fine Ironstone China, Japan, 1966" 30.00

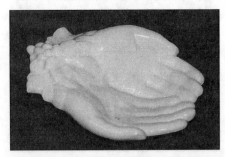

White ironstone hands dish, mkd "Warranteed Ironstone China, W.H.&Co.," 7-1/4" x 5-1/2", $30.

Dinner Plate, Stratford Stage, mkd "Royal Staffordshire Ironstone" 6.00

Jug, white, Strathmore, #30, mkd "Mason's," wear, 5-1/4" h 100.00

Ladle, white
Gray transfer print, flower and fern dec, worn gold edging, 6" l 45.00

Lavender daisies, gold trim, c1895............................. 50.00

Plain, 10-1/2" l, 3-1/2" d bowl, crazed............................... 48.00

Place Setting, Royal Mail, brown and white, mkd "Fine Staffordshire Ironstone...Made in England," 4 pcs 25.00

Platter, plain white
13-3/4" x 18-3/4", illegible incised mark 48.00
14" x 10", mkd "Royal Ironstone China, Alfred Meakin, England"......................... 65.00

Salad Plate, Stratford Stage, mkd "Royal Staffordshire Ironstone" 4.00

Tea Set, child's, painted pansies, faded gold trim, worn paint, 15 pcs............................... 75.00

Thimble, rose in an urn dec, mkd "Mason's Patent Ironstone, Made in England," 1" h 9.50

Vegetable Bowl, American Hurrah, mkd "J. & G. Meakin," 8-1/2" l 45.00

⭐ Italian Glass

Italian glassblowers have been crafting whimsical glass items along with functional items for generations. There is a keen interest in modern Italian glass. Look for bright colors and flowing forms.

Basket, bright red free flowing body, controlled bubbles, mica flecks, clear casing, attached self handle, 14" h, 9" w................... 70.00

Centerbowl, broad shallow clear irid bowl, bright blue rim wrap, molded dished pattern at center, Venetian Revival style, 18" d 300.00

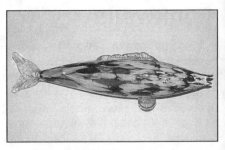

Fish, multicolor, 21" l, $37.50.

Circus Elephant, balanced on ball, Murano, 15" h 115.00

Decanter, spiral forest green and yellow twisted canes, unpolished pontil, matching stopper.... 115.00

Vase
3-3/4" h, oyster white, deep pink and green threading, one side of ruffled rim turned up 100.00
5-1/2" h, irid, green waves 125.00
7-1/2" h, round, shades of dark and medium green interspersed with blue spiral swirls, narrow top opening......... 50.00

❖ Ivory

Ivory is derived from the teeth or tusks of animals. It can be carved, and the resulting yellow-white object is quite durable. Some ivory objects have been highlighted with ink, metal, or stones.

Periodical: *Netsuke & Ivory Carving Newsletter,* 3203 Adams Way, Amber, PA 19002.

Collectors' Club: International Ivory Society, 11109 Nicholas Drive, Wheaton, MD 20902.

Earrings, pr, pierced, hand carved
Drops suspended from gold filled leaves, c1910, 1-1/4" l 180.00

Crochet hook, hand finial, 6-1/4" l, $40.

Two elephants on a ball, c1910, 1" l, new gold filled wires 75.00

Figure

Eagle attacking monkey, Japanese, 3" h 475.00

Medicine Woman, Chinese, 5-1/4" l..........................400.00

Measure, whalebone, ivory, and exotic wood, American shield inlay, inscribed "WH," 19th C, 14-7/8" l, minor imperfections................... 200.00

Necklace, hand carved beads, 15" l, 1-1/2" x 1-1/4" pendant, c1910................................ 165.00

Rolling Pin, exotic wood, baleen spacers, 19th C, 13-5/8" l, cracks 245.00

Seal, intaglio, handle, 19th C, 3-7/8" l, cracks................. 400.00

Snuff Bottle, elephant ivory, carved bird on one side, carved rose on other, orig wand, gold-tone neck chain, sgd "LRS".............. 125.00

Top, carved, sealing wax inlaid scribed lines, 19th C, 2-7/8" l, minor cracks and chips 365.00

For exciting collecting trends and newly expanded areas look for the following symbols:

✪ Hot Topic

★ New Warman's Listing

(May have been in another Warman's edition.)

Favorite dealers:

Name: _____

Shop name:_____

Address:_____

_____

Phone:_____

Hours:_____

Comments:_____

Name: _____

Shop name:_____

Address:_____

_____

Phone:_____

Hours:_____

Comments:_____

Name: _____

Shop name:_____

Address:_____

_____

Phone:_____

Hours:_____

Comments:_____

Name: _____

Shop name:_____

Address:_____

_____

Phone:_____

Hours:_____

Comments:_____

Name: _____

Shop name:_____

Address:_____

_____

Phone:_____

Hours:_____

Comments:_____

Name: _____

Shop name:_____

Address:_____

_____

Phone:_____

Hours:_____

Comments:_____

❖ Jade-ite Glassware

Jade-ite is one of the hottest colors of glassware of the late 1990s. It gets its name from the jade-like hue of the glass and, since it's opaque, it may vary slightly with the several manufacturers who created this color. The best known maker of jade-ite was Anchor Hocking in their Fire King line. Jade-ite has been around since the 1920s and is still being made today.

Bowl, 4-1/2" d 20.00
Bud Vase, Jeannette 20.00
Butter Dish, cov, 1 lb size 140.00
Canister, dark, Jeannette........ 90.00
Measuring Cup, 2 oz,
    Jeannette 50.00
Pitcher, sunflower in base....... 60.00
Range Shaker, sq, mkd "Flour,"
    Jeannette 45.00
Reamer................................... 60.00

Batter bowl, $40.

Refrigerator Dish Base,
    Philbe 32.00
Skillet, 2 spouts...................... 35.00
Tea Canister, 48 oz sq, light
    jade-ite.............................. 165.00
Water Dispenser, metal
    spigot................................ 160.00

❖ Japanese Ceramics

Japanese ceramics covers the many porcelain and ceramic makers found in Japan through the centuries. Each one brought a different style or perhaps glaze to their work. As the western world became interested in Oriental things, more Japanese ceramics were imported and remain today as treasured objects.

Charger, two large iron oxide carp, underglaze blue ground, peonies, stylized waves, flowering branches, Meiji period,
    13-1/4" d............................ 350.00

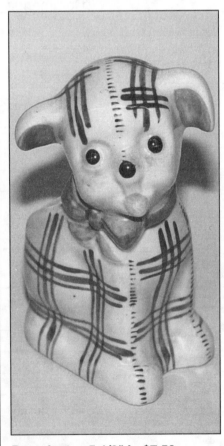

Dog planter, 5-1/2" h, $7.50.

Ewer, red and gilt motif, riverscape and figure dec, loop handle, dragon finial, Kaga, late
    19th C 570.00
Plate, Nabeschima style, relief and underglaze blue hibiscus dec, c1900, 8-1/2" d 225.00
Tea Bowl, Raku, hand modeled, irregular straight sides, small recessed ring foot, central well of flower heads, peach glaze, double crackle pattern 190.00
Teapot, Seven Gods of Wisdom, glazed and unglazed clay, polychrome dec, Banko,
    5" h 450.00
Vase, flowing blue dec, fan shape, 20th C 20.00

✭ Jeannette Glass

This glassmaker was located in Jeannette, PA, and produced mainly depression era glasswares. Their colors were as bright as the competitors of that era, and the patterns reflected the tastes too. Some of the wares they produced from 1900 to 1983 have a mark which is a "J" inside a square.

References: Gene Florence, *Collectible Glassware From the 40s, 50s, 60s,* 4th ed., Collector Books, 1998; ——, *Collector's Encyclopedia of Depression Glass,* 13th ed., Collector Books, 1998.

For additional listings, see *Warman's Depression Glass.*

Ashtray
    Butterfly, clear 7.00
    Cowboy Hat, Delphite 22.75
Banana Split Dish, oval, clear ... 5.00
Bowl, 6" d, Jennyware, clear..... 8.00
Canister, cov
    3" h, jade-ite, labeled, Allspice, Ginger, Nutmeg, or Pepper, each............................... 72.00
    5-1/2" h, sq, Delphite,
        coffee............................. 85.00
Creamer and Sugar, green 15.00
Drippings Jar, cov, jade-ite 35.00

Tumbler, Tree Bark Variant, marigold, 5" h, $20.

Mixing Bowl, 6" d, clear	16.00
Reamer, Delphite	90.00
Refrigerator Dish, cov	
4-1/2" h, jade-ite, sq	20.00
8-1/2" x 4-1/2", clear	20.00
Salt and Pepper Shakers, pr, ribbed, jade-ite	30.00
Tray, sq, handle, pink	18.00
Tumbler, Cosmos pattern, irid	4.50

✫ Jelly Glasses

Collecting jelly glasses is a win-win proposition, at least when it comes to the newer lines on today's market. Not only does your local grocery store offer an interesting collectible at a reasonable price, but you get to eat the contents as well. Flea markets are a great source for jelly glasses that have already moved from store shelf to consumer and beyond.

Collectors' Clubs: Jelly Jammers, 110 White Oak Dr., Butler, PA 16001.

Archie, "Jughead Wins the Pie Eating Contest," 1973, design faded	5.00

Welch's Pooh's Grand Adventure: The Search for Christopher Robin, 10 oz, orig lid, 4" h, $3.

Archie, "Reggie Makes the Scene," Welch's, 1971	5.75
BAMA Racing, Tim Fedewa	3.75
Flintstones, "Fred and His Pal at Work," 1962, 4-1/4" h	10.00
Flintstones, "Fred's Newest Invention," 1962, 4-1/4" h	10.00
Flintstones, "Pebbles' Baby Sitters," 1963, 4-1/4" h	16.50
George Jetson, Kraft, 1990, Hamilton Projects, 5-1/2" h	28.00
Howdy Doody, "Dilly Dally is Circus Big Shot," Welch's, 4-1/4" h	18.00
Speedy Gonzales, "Speedy Snaps Up the Cheese," 1974	3.00
The Wubbulous World of Dr. Seuss, "The Grinch and Friends," Welch's, 1997	4.00

❖ Jewel Tea Company

Most flea market browsers think about the Autumn Leaf pattern when they hear the name Jewel Tea. But, actually it's much more. The Jewel Tea Company, headquartered in Barrington, IL, has been supplying household necessities for years, in addition to the popular Autumn Leaf pattern.

Baker, Poppy pattern, gold band, mkd "Hall's Superior Kitchen Ware, Made in USA," 9" d	10.00
Beverage Coaster Set, Autumn Leaf pattern, orig box, 9 pcs	235.00
Cardboard Shipping Box, used	1.00
Christmas Ornament, pewter, Oh Come All Ye Faithful, mkd "Collector's Edition II by JT General Store," 1980s, orig box	12.00
Cookbook, *Mary Dunbar New Cook Book,* 1933, 63 pgs, used	55.00
Flour Canister, tin body, white plastic lid, Autumn Leaf dec, 5-3/4" h, 5" d	10.00
Fruitcake Tin, 1981	20.00
Malt Mixer, glass body, metal lid handle, wood handle, partial orig instructions	90.00
Mop, Dustmaster, green head, wooden handle, orig tag, unused	265.00
Rolling Pin, clear glass, black cap on one end, 14" l	15.00
Soap, Shure, 3 bars in box, unused	85.00

Plastic shopping bag, orange and clear, 8-5/8" h, 9" w, 4-1/4" d, $10.

Spice Tin, nutmeg, sq, 3-7/8", some minor dents 145.00

Toy, delivery van, brown and yellow metal body, rubber wheels 68.00

❖ Jewelry, Costume

Jewelry with faux stones became fashionable in the 1920s, thanks to Coco Chanel. It started as exact copies of real gemstone jewelry, but soon the jewelry designers were having fun creating exciting pieces. As technology developed, mass production began by the 1930s. By the 1950s, high style rhinestones, faux pearls, and colored glass jewelry was being signed by the designers and craftsmen.

References: Maryanne Dolan, *Collecting Rhinestone & Colored Jewelry*, 4th ed., Krause Publications, 1998; Christie Romero, *Warman's Jewelry*, 2nd ed., Krause Publications, 1998.

Collectors' Clubs: Leaping Frog Antique Jewelry and Collectable Club, 4841 Martin Luther Blvd, Sacramento, CA 95820; National Cuff Link Society, PO Box 346, Prospect Heights, IL 60070; Vintage Fashion & Costume Jewelry Club, PO Box 265, Glen Oaks, NY 11004.

Reproduction Alert.

Bracelet
   Bangle, sterling silver, scrolling abstract design, Lobel, sgd, 1960s 340.00
   Charm, 8 charms, goldtone links, Coro, sgd 40.00

Trifari pin, 2" l, $20.

Heart padlock, 1897, sterlin 90.00

Link, sterling silver, lily pad design, Danecraft, sgd ... 65.00

Rhinestones, panther, black enamel trim, Ciner, sgd .. 215.00

Brooch/Pin
   Bird in flight, Matisse style, high relief sterling silver, mkd "P. J. 21 Mexico 925, Nestor," 2-1/4" wing spread................... 65.00
   Cameo, faux carnelian surounded by clear rhinestones, scrolled mounting, Coro.............. 32.00
   Circle, white flower-shaped beads, silver filigree setting, Miriam Haskell................ 42.00
   Daisy, white enamel flower, yellow center, little red ladybug, green stem and leaf, Weiss...... 30.00
   Deer and squirrel, sterling silver, Georg Jensen, 1940s, #318, orig box 300.00
   Eagle's Head, black and ivory plastic, Lea Stein, sgd.... 70.00
   Fan, oriental design, gold-tone, bamboo handle, sgd "Haskell" 50.00
   Feather, sterling silver, Nye, 3-3/8" l............................. 48.00
   Flower, amber-faceted flower, clear rhinestones, 4" stem, gold-tone, Sarah Coventry 60.00
   Lamb, silver-tone, rhinestones, red rhinestone eyes, Trifari, sgd 325.00
   Lovebirds, coral and ivory plastic, Lea Stein, Paris, sgd 85.00
   Starfish, green, brown, and gold rhinestones, gold-tone, Florenza 65.00

Choker, pavé faux turquoise links, center aurora borealis rhinestones, gold-tone casting, Kramer, sgd, late 1950s 45.00

Cross, filigree, 18K yg, 3 large pearls................................ 120.00

Earrings, pr, clip
   Aurora borealis, blue rhinestones, Weiss 27.50
   Dangling, chandelier type, crystal and rhinestone, Carnegie 60.00
   Inlaid Dot (fried eggs), Bakelite, swirled amber and ivory, Kenneth Lane, orig card 85.00

Silver-tone filigree, chocolate pearl and rhinestone trim 4.00

Turquoise egg-shaped glass dangles, gold tops, mkd "Kramer" 30.00

Earrings, pr, screw-back, egg-shaped cherry red drops, white background, blue edge, copper, 1950s, mkd "Hogan-Bolas".....................45.00

Locket, 18K pink gold, seed pearls and ruby............................220.00

Necklace
   Faux pearls, double strand, knotted, aurora borealis stone clasp, Vendome, 16" l.....48.00
   "X" design with rhinestones, Crown Trifari, 14" l 65.00
   Wheat style links, small spacers, gold-tone, Francois, Coro, 15" l, 1937 ....27.50

Pendant
   Lion, gold-colored metal, carved amber tortoise shell type Bakelite, ivory Bakelite ring, c1960............................. 70.00
   Teardrop, polished faux coral, plastic, gold trimmed open center, 28" l gold-tone chain, Sarah Coventry 20.00

Perfume Pin, puffer fish, solid perfume container, textured gold-tone, aqua rhinestone eye, Fuller Brush, 1-3/4".......................30.00

Suite, pin and earrings
   Coro, 10K pink gold, pink stones, orig pink box, c1940 .....250.00
   Eisenberg, ice, rhinestones...................300.00

Tie Bar, gold plated, abstract design 2.00

Tie Tack
   Car, gold plated, Sarah Coventry 4.00
   Initial, "G", silver plated.........2.00

❖ Johnson Brothers

Johnson Brothers was started by three English brothers in 1883. As their dinnerware business flourished, they expanded. A fourth brother joined the firm in 1896 and he was charged with establishing a position in the American market. This venture was so successful that additional factories were established in England, Canada, and Australia. By 1968, Johnson Brothers became part of the Wedgwood Group.

Bread and Butter Plate, Old Britain Castles, blue dec on white 12.00

Breakfast Set, Rosedown, soft dusty rose, 12 pcs....................... 150.00

Cereal Bowl, Old Britain Castles, blue dec on white 18.00

Child's Plate, The Happy Clown, mkd "Ironstone, Made in England," 8" d.................... 22.00

Coffeepot, Provincial 78.00

Creamer and Sugar, Friendly Village.............................. 35.00

Cup and Saucer
Brooklyn Pattern, flow blue, mkd "Royal Semi Porcelain, Johnson Brothers, England," c1900 ....100.00
Countryside, 3" h cup, 7" d saucer 55.00
Harvest Time, 3" h cup, 7" d saucer 55.00
Old Britain Castles, blue dec on white..............................20.00

Dinner Plate
Brooklyn Pattern, flow blue, mkd "Royal Semi Porcelain, Johnson Brothers, England," c1900, 8-3/4" d..............100.00
Old Britain Castles, blue dec on white..............................22.00

Fruit Bowl, Old Britain Castles, blue dec on white 10.00

Indian Tree platter, 12-1/4" x 9-5/8", $25.

Gravy Boat and Underplate, Coaching Scenes.......................... 48.00

Plate, Mt. Rushmore, imported for Sunset Supply, Keystone, 10-3/4" d 15.00

Relish, Friendly Village, 3 part 38.50

Salad Plate, Old Britain Castles, blue dec on white 15.00

Saucer, Cherry Thieves, mkd "Staffordshire Old Granite Made in England by Johnson Brothers"................................ 5.00

Serving Platter, pink, blue, and white flowers, brown and gold leaves, worn gold edge trim, mkd "Royal Ironstone China," 11-1/2" x 15-3/4" 55.00

Soup Bowl, Old Britain Castles, blue dec on white 22.00

Teapot, Coaching Scenes....... 27.50

Vegetable Bowl, Blue Willow, 10" d 48.00

✦ ✪ Jordan, Michael

Can you believe it? This basketball legend retired on January 13, 1999. Bet this year's flea markets will be featuring more collectibles relating to this sports legend.

Reference: Oscar Gracia, *Collecting Michael Jordan Memorabilia*, Krause Publications, 1998.

Chicago Bulls Plaque, lists career accomplishments thru 1991, features Michael Slam Dunk card, 7" x 9" 25.00

Cup, plastic, 1995 McDonald's NBA Looney Toons All Star Showdown, Michael Jordan and Bugs Bunny, scratched 1.00

Jersey, autographed, UDA, Nike 1,250.00

Magazine, *Sports Illustrated*, March 13, 1989, cover story "Chicago's Indomitable Michael Jordan" 5.00

Photograph, wire service, 1989 .... 3.50

Program, NBA @ UNC Lakers, Oct 24, 1987 .... 50.00

Yo-yo, Space Jam, MIP 15.50

❖ Josef Originals

Even though the name of this company was originally misspelled by a printer, Tom and Muriel Joseph George had a success on their hands shortly after they started in 1946. Production eventually was moved to a Japanese factory, with Muriel still creating the designs. The company was sold to Applause, Inc. in 1985.

Periodical: *Josef Original Newsletter*, PO Box 475, Lynnwood, WA 98046.

Creamer, elephant, blue..........26.00

Doll, California January 80.00

Figure
Angel Praying 25.00
Carol 35.00
Birthday Girl, 10th birthday . 40.00
Down to Sleep 45.00
Dress Up Like Dad.............. 45.00
Elf Mending Pants.............. 25.00
France................................. 40.00
Heddy 40.00
Mistletoe Boy 20.00
Puff 40.00
Teddy 35.00
Wee Folks 25.00

Music Box 95.00

Night Light, mouse 45.00

#5 birthday angel, 4" h, $25.

For exciting collecting trends and newly expanded areas look for the following symbols:

✪ Hot Topic

✮ New Warman's Listing
(May have been in another Warman's edition.)

❖ Jugtown Pottery

While being serious about their craft of pottery making, founders Jacques and Juliana Busbee were noted for their off-beat operation. The pottery was started in 1920 and continued until 1958. One of their most talented potters was Ben Owens. Jacques did most of the designing and Juliana took care of promotion.

Candlesticks, pr, Chinese Translation, Chinese blue and red, 3" h 90.00
Creamer, cov, yellow, 4-3/4" h 65.00
Vase
Chinese blue glaze, imp mark, 4" h 295.00
Stoneware, 2 small handles, top cov with matte mustard glaze, bottom with clear glaze, imp mark, 8-3/4" h 875.00

❖ Jukeboxes

Let's spin those tunes! Jukeboxes provided many hours of musical entertainment. With proper care and maintenance, these early entertainment centers can still delight.

Periodicals: *Always Jukin'*, 221 Yesler Way, Seattle, WA 98104; *Antique Amusements, Slot Machines & Jukebox Gazette,* 909 26th St NW, Washington, DC 20037; *Coin-Op Classics,* 17844 Toiyable St., Fountain Valley, CA 92708; *Gameroom Magazine,* PO Box 41, Keyport, NJ 07735; *Jukebox Collector,* 2545 WE 60th Court, Des Moines, IA 50317.

AMI
Model A.......................... 1,250.00
Model C 600.00
Model E............................. 550.00
Mills, Empress model 1,500.00
Rock-Ola
Model 1432 .... 850.00
Model 1438 .... 975.00
Seeburg
Model HF100G 975.00
Model M100C 950.00
Wurlitzer
Model 616 .... 650.00
Model 780 .... 2,750.00

Receipts should contain:

1. Dealer's name
2. Dealer's address
3. Dealer's telephone number
4. Detailed description of item purchased
5. Purchase price
6. Date of purchase
7. Guarantee if any
8. Note of condition

Reproduction tip-offs.

☐ 1. Seeing this same kind of item from booth to booth
☐ 2. Looks new
☐ 3. Price is too good to be true
☐ 4. Glassware has a greasy feeling
☐ 5. Metal items have a bright orange type of rust

Things to remember to take to a flea market:

☐ 1. Notepad and pencil
☐ 2. Magnifying glass
☐ 3. Measuring tape
☐ 4. Backpack or canvas tote
☐ 5. Bottled water
☐ 6. Sun glasses and hat
☐ 7. Sun screen
☐ 8. Packing materials
☐ 9. Want lists
☐ 10. Comfortable shoes

K

✭ Kaleidoscopes

Changing colors or shapes as they twist or turn, kaleidoscopes date back to times when entertainment didn't involve a remote control. Look for examples with interesting designs plus colorful elements.

Steven kaleidoscope, 1980 Steven Mfg Co., paper tube, 8-3/4" h, $6.

Collectors' Club: Brewster Society, 9020 McDonald Drive, #8, Bethesda, MD 20817-1940.

Brass case, multicolored crystals, leather carrying case, English, c1910 .... 400.00
Paper case, child's, multicolored bits of paper, c1950 .... 5.00
Paper case, child's, Hallmark, decorated with Peanuts characters, rainbow colors on turning cylinder, 9" l 10.00
Paper case, Corning Glass Museum, multicolored bits of glass, c1980 .... 15.00
Tin case, tin screw caps for ends, multicolored bits, crystals . 200.00

❖ Kanawha

West Virginia was the home to this glass company. Its major production included colored glass and crackle glass. Kanawha Glass marked its wares with paper labels. When these labels are found intact, the price goes up slightly.

Ewer, amberina, long slender neck, applied amber handle, 8-1/4" h 70.00
Pitcher
    Amberina, tricorn rim, orig label, 3-1/2" h........................... 25.00
    Cased, red ext., milk white int., grape leaf design, applied handle, 6-1/2" h 50.00
    Crackle, gold-yellow, tricorn rim, applied handle, 4-3/4" h........................... 35.00

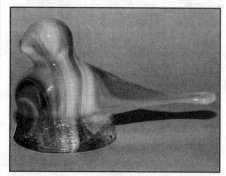

Paperweight, bird on nest, light blue with white swirl, 3" h, 5" l, $16.

Crackle, light blue, flared spout, applied blue handle, 5" h, 4" w................................. 32.00
Crackle, orange, 5-1/4" h.... 30.00
Syrup Pitcher, crackle, ruby, applied amber handle, cork stopper, stainless steel top, 6-3/4" h 65.00
Vase, crackle
    Amberina, 8" h 80.00
    Dark orange, 7-3/4" h 40.00

❖ Keeler, Brad

Brad Keeler started out making flamingo figurines which he sold to California department stores. This led to the start of another California pottery. As with some of the other success stories of the same area and locale, Brad designed the pieces himself, and, others created the molds and glazes. He included some Disney characters in his figurines and tableware designs. Keeler died in 1952, ending a promising career at an early age.

Figure
    Canary, unmarked, 4-1/2" h.......................... 35.00
    Flamingos, mkd "Brad Keeler," pr 150.00
    Playful Kittens, black, gray markings, one 7" l, other 8", mkd "BK, USA," #772 and #773, pr 140.00
Lobster Dish
    Five compartments, deep red, c1940, 15-1/4" l, 16-3/8" w 225.00
    Three compartments, gray tone, 12-1/2" l, 12-1/2" w 125.00
Planter, Pride & Joy, dog......... 50.00
Serving Dish, crab, 11"............ 80.00
Tray, figural lettuce leaf, figural tomato relish container 85.00

✭ Keen Kutter

Keen Kutter was the E. C. Simmons Hardware Co. brand. Their fine tools were welcome in the workshop and garden as well as the kitchen.

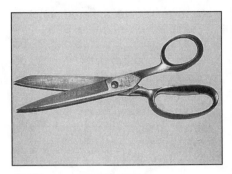

Scissors, 8" l, $12.50.

Periodical: *Winchester Keen Kutter Diamond Edge Chronicles*, Hardware Companies Kollectors' Club, 715 W 20th Ave., Hutchinson, KS 67502.

Can Opener, patent Sept 20,
  93 .... 25.00
Carpenter Pencil, slight use...... 5.00
Food Chopper, orig booklet,
  unused 15.00
Gasoline Can........................... 50.00
Hatchet 30.00
Letterhead, 1911..................... 12.00
Mallet, wood 32.00
Match Safe, cast iron, emb "E. C.
  Simmons Keen Kutter Cutlery &
  Tools"................................. 150.00
Pencil Clip, 1950s................... 17.50
Pocket Knife, pearl 28.00
Rule, 6" l, caliper, #K360 .... 60.00
Spade 125.00
Waffle Iron 90.00

✯ Kennedy, John F.

The life and times of this American President may have changed all our lives. Many were fascinated with JFK and his family during his life. After his tragic death and throughout the years, collectors have continued to keep his memory alive.

Collectors' Club: Kennedy Political Items Collectors, PO Box 922, Clark, NJ 07066-0922.

Book, *John F. Kennedy,* 1964,
  photos 35.00
Bust, by Peter C. Sedlow, limited
  edition, 8" h 325.00

Comic Book, *John F. Kennedy-Champion of Freedom,*
  1964 .... 8.00
Magazine Cover, *Newsweek,* Jackie,
  Jan 6, 1964......................... 20.00

Magazine, *Life*
  Nov 29, 1963, devoted to
    assassination 25.00
  Dec 6, 1963, devoted to
    funeral 25.00
  1968, special issue, The
    Kennedys 15.00
Newspaper, headline edition, folded,
  yellowed 25.00
Record Album, Memorial originally
  broadcast by Radio station
  WMCA, NY, Nov 22, 1963, high-
  lights of speeches, slight damage
  to cover.............................. 30.00
Salt and Pepper Shakers, pr
  Figural, JFK seated in rocking
    chair, mkd "Copyright Arrow
    1962, NYC, Japan"......... 75.00
  Porcelain, decal of JFK on one,
    Jackie on other,
    gold trim 40.00
Trivet, cork back, image of JFK and
  brothers 10.00

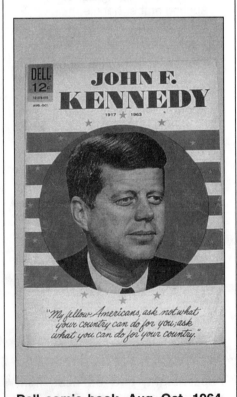

Dell comic book, Aug.-Oct. 1964, 10-1/4" x 7", $8.

✯ Kentucky Derby Glasses

The Run for the Roses is more than just the best-known horse race in the world. For collectors, the Kentucky Derby is symbolized by a commemorative drinking glass each year. It's a safe bet that examples from the 1940s through the 1960s are few and far between at most flea markets, while Derby glasses from later decades are both available and affordable. In a nutshell, here's what collectors can expect to pay for Kentucky Derby glasses from later years.

1970s 10.00-30.00
1980s 6.00-10.00
1990s 5.00-8.00

115th running, May 6, 1989, 5-1/4" h; 116th running, May 5, 1990, 5-1/4" h, each $7.50.

❖ Kewpie

Rose O'Neill created a cute character in illustrations she made for the *Ladies Home Journal* in 1909. Her Kewpies caught the attention of Joseph Kallus who created the first Kewpie dolls in 1913 through the Cameo Doll Company. Through the years, several different companies have continued O'Neill's designs, including Lefton and Enesco.

Periodical: *Traveler,* PO Box 4032, Portland, OR 92708.

Collectors' Club: International Rose O'Neill Club, PO Box 668, Branson, MO 65616.

Blanket, 5" x 6", felt fabric, 1914 Rose O'Neill copyright, fleshtone images, blue sky, tan buildings, red stitched border 8.00

Dealer Sign, "The Rose O'Neill Kewpie Collection by Enesco," sgd "O'Neill," 1991, 3-3/4" h 45.00

Doll

2-1/2" h, celluloid, some paint missing 20.00

8" h, chalk, black skin tone 65.00

9" h, vinyl, jointed at neck, shoulders, and hips, mkd "Cameo," two small discoloration marks, orig pantaloons 45.00

10" h, vinyl, head turns, mkd "Cameo" 55.00

12" h, vinyl, orig tab, mkd "Cameo" 125.00

Figure, Lefton

Bewildered 12.00

Content, 5" h 27.50

Holding foot, 3" h.................12.00

On belly, 3-3/4" l 12.00

Puzzled, 5" h 27.50

Winking, 5" h 30.00

Celluloid figure, mkd "Made in Japan/M," interlocking reverse-S import stamp, $17.50.

Night Light, figural, orig foil sticker "Lefton Trade Mark Exclusives Japan," #5718 stamped on bottom, 6-1/2" h 75.00

Pendant, small 10.00

Postcard, "Can't think of an earthly thing to say, Cept I hope you are happy Valentine's Day," Kewpie writing valentines, © Rosie O'Neill, postmarked Feb 12, 1925, published by Gibson Art Co. 20.00

☆ Key Chains

Everybody has a couple of key chains saved, whether in a desk drawer, a pocket, or perhaps a dedicated collection. It's a great starting collection for a child because they're easy to find and usually inexpensive.

Collectors' Club: License Plate Key Chain & Mini License Plate Collectors, 888 Eighth Ave, New York, NY 10019-5704.

Amoco, "As You Travel Ask Us," back with place for name and address, flicker 12.00

Ballantine Light Lager Beer, 3 ring sign, plastic, red and white, 3" h 10.00

Batman, PVC head, Funatics, MOC 2.00

Copple Motor Co., Chrysler-Plymouth, Mound City, KS, Hula dancer, flicker 12.00

Curious George, pewter, Danforth............................ 16.00

Esso Happy Motoring Key Club, 3" x 5" white card, red accent text,

Tupperware miniature bowl with lid, 3/4" h, 1-1/2" d, $2.

stapled 4" l gold accent keychain, black plastic disk with silver accent lettering, company name on front, serial number on back, c1950, unused 24.00

Ford, metal, mkd "Karriers USA" 4.00

Good Luck Penny, circular, "Bazooka Blony," reverse "Keep me and never go broke," penny dated 1957 ....12.00

Horse, 5" h, key chain in mouth.................................30.00

Johnson Feed Service, Feeding Grinding & Mixing On Your Farm, Griffin, Georgia, flicker 12.00

Kendall Oil, World's Fair, 3-1/2" x 6-1/4" black, white, and red cardboard ink blotter with 1" brass keychain tag attached, listing of auto, air, and boat 1936 records, brass disk pictures oil can and "Good Luck" inscription and text on one side, reverse with Trylon and Perisphere theme from 1939 New York World's Fair 18.00

Ship's Wheel, emb "VN Balboa," leather strap, 1" d 25.00

Silly Putty, small egg-shaped container, MOC.....................3.75

Super Bowl XXX 1996, NRFP......................................6.00

Vincent System, Exterminators—Fumigators, Tampa, Florida, flicker 12.00

Western Auto, Over 50 Years of Service, metal.....................15.00

Winnie the Pooh, brass colored 4.00

❖ Keys

Just like key chains, we've all got some keys saved. Perhaps it's a set from our first car or first house, the key to our diary, or a bicycle lock. Flea markets can be great places to find great keys to add to those collections, usually for a reasonable price.

Collectors' Clubs: Key Collectors International, 1427 Lincoln Blvd., Santa Monica, CA 90401; West Coast Lock Collectors, 1427 Lincoln Blvd., Santa Monica, CA 90401-2732.

Metal, 1-3/4" l, $3.

Cabinet
   Brass, decorative, bow........12.00
   Nickel plated, lyre design
     bow 6.50
Car
   Ford, Model T, diamond
     mark...................................3.50
   MGB, 1973, orig leather
     fob.....................................7.50
   Packard, logo key..................8.00
Door
   Bronze, Keen Kutter bow,
     4" l.....................................8.00
   Steel, standard bow and
     bit 4.50
Folding, bronze and steel,
   jack knife 17.50
Hotel
   Bit type, steel, bronze tag......4.50
   Pin tumbler, plastic tag..........2.50
Jewelers, brass, 6 point.......... 22.00
Railroad
   C & O 18.50
   IC RR 15.00
   TT RR..................................22.00
Watch, brass and steel, loop bow,
   folds.................................... 7.50

❖ Kitchen Collectibles

The kitchen is probably the one room in any house that generates more collectibles than the rest of the house. Perhaps it's all those pieces of equipment needed to prepare foods. Add to that all the dishes required to serve and store foods. Somehow, many of the old gadgets just make their way to the back of the cupboard when the latest and greatest new gadget arrives on the scene. It's those old– timers that often become the staples of kitchen collections.

References: Linda Fields, *Four & Twenty Blackbirds: A Pictorial Identification and Value Guide for Pie Birds,* published by author, (158 Bagsby Hill Lane, Dover, TN 37058); Linda Campbell Franklin, *300 Years of Housekeeping Collectibles*, Books Americana, 1992; ——, *300 Years of Kitchen Collectibles*, 4th ed., Krause Publications, 1997; *Griswold Cast Iron*, vol. 1 (1993), vol. 2 (1995), L-W Book Sales; *Griswold Manufacturing Co. 1918 Catalog Reprint*, L-W Book Sales, 1996; Barbara Mauzy, *Bakelite in the Kitchen,* Schiffer Publishing, 1998; ——, *The Complete Book of Kitchen Collecting,* Schiffer Publishing, 1997; Don Thornton, *Beat This: The Eggbeater Chronicles*, Off Beat Books (1345 Poplar Ave, Sunnyvale, CA 94087), 1994.

Periodicals: *Cast Iron Cookware News*, 28 Angela Ave, San Anselmo, CA 94960; *Cookies,* 9610 Greenview Lane, Manassas, VA 20109; *Griswold Cast Iron Collectors' News & Marketplace*, PO Box 521, North East, PA 16428; *Kettles 'n Cookware*, PO Box B, Perrysville, NY 14129; *Kitchen Antiques & Collectibles News*, 4645 Laurel Ridge Dr, Harrisburg, PA 17110; *Piebirds Unlimited,* 14 Harmony School Rd, Flemington, NJ 08822.

Collectors' Clubs: Association of Coffee Mill Enthusiasts, 5941 Wilkerson Rd, Rex, GA 30273; Cookie Cutter Collectors Club, 1167 Teal Rd, SW, Dellroy, OH 44620; Corn Items Collectors Association, Inc, 613 North Long St, Shelbyville, IL 62565; Eggcup Collectors' Corner, 67 Stevens Ave, Old Bridge, NJ 08857; Griswold & Cast Iron Cookware Association, 54 Macon Ave, Asheville, NC 28801; International Society for Apple Parer Enthusiasts, 3911 Morgan Center Rd, Utica, OH 43080; Jelly Jammers Club, 110 White Oak Dr, Butler, PA

16001; Kollectors of Old Kitchen Stuff, 501 Market St, Mifflinburg, PA 17844; National Reamer Collectors Association, 47 Midline Court, Gaithersburg, MD 20878-1996; Pie Bird Collectors Club, 158 Bagsby Hill Lane, Dover, TN 37058.

For additional listings, see *Warman's Antiques and Collectibles Price Guide* and *Warman's Americana & Collectibles.*

Angel Food Pan, 10" d 28.00
Dipper, gourd, 17" l 35.00
Egg Poacher, red enamel, gray
   enamel insert, 3-3/4" x 8"....24.00
Egg Separator, aluminum,
   9" l......................................7.00
Hot Pad Holder, black boy, chalk-
   ware, 1940s, 8" h, chips 55.00
Iced Tea Dispenser, Lord Calvert
   Hotel, Baltimore, MD, black base
   and cov, 1940s..................375.00
Mouli-Julienne, rotary cutter, 3 inter-
   changeable cutting and shredding
   discs, orig box, c1950.........30.00
Set, cookie cutter, biscuit cutter,
   donut cutter, pastry cutter, mkd
   "Calumet," Wear-Ever Aluminum,
   made in USA...................... 14.00
Strawberry Huller, Nip-It,
   1906......................................4.00
Teapot and Salt and Pepper Shak-
   ers, aluminum, four cup teapot,
   cov with red finial, orig strainer
   with red handle, orig box, mkd
   "Highly Polished Aluminum, Made
   in Japan"............................25.00
Vegetable Grater, Schroeter, tin, iron
   back, wood handle, old blue
   paint..................................40.00

Spice jars with lids, blue and black on white, Czechoslovakia, 4" h, each $25.

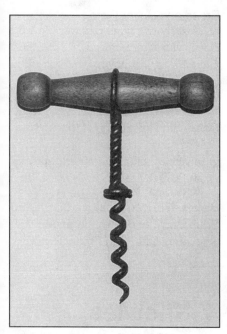

Corkscrew with turned wooden handle, 4-1/2" l, 4" handle, $5.

Wall Plaque
   Fruit, paint scuffed,
      1950s 8.00
   Parrot, chalkware, 10" x 6", chips.
      ....12.00

❖ Kitchen Glassware

One area of a kitchen collection that is brightly colored and durable is kitchen glassware. What started as a few manufacturers who were determined to create glassware that could go from the stove to the table to the refrigerator has given us products few of us could live without, like Pyrex and Corningware.

Reference: Gene Florence, *Kitchen Glassware of the Depression Years,* 5th ed., Collector Books, 1995, 1997 value update.

Collectors' Club: National Reamer Collectors Association, 47 Midline Court, Gaithersburg, MD 20878-1996.

For additional listings, see *Warman's Americana & Collectibles* and *Warman's Glass.*

Batter Bowl, black ships dec... 25.00
Bowl
   Kellogg's, green.................. 75.00
   Orange Dot, 8" d,
      custard 32.00
Butter Dish, cov
   Criss-Cross, blue,
      1/4 lb size 125.00
   Federal, amber, 1 lb 35.00
Canister, cov, 48 oz, round, Seville
   Yellow, coffee, sugar,
   or tea 135.00
Cheese Dish, cov, slicer, opaque
   white 90.00
Flour Shaker
   Deco, ivory, black lettering.. 45.00
   Roman Arch, ivory.............. 45.00
Fruit Bowl, Sunkist, pink 335.00
Grease Jar
   Red Dots, white 30.00
   Seville Yellow, black trim 35.00
Measuring Cup
   Crystal, Kellogg's.................. 8.00

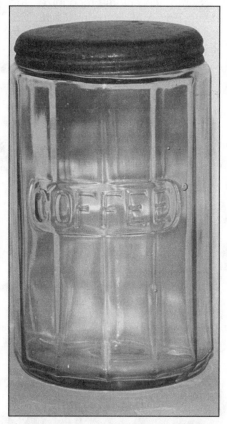

Hoosier cabinet "Coffee" jar, paneled, original tin lid, 7-1/4" h, $40.

Green, Kellogg's 22.00
Seville Yellow, 4 cup 125.00
Mixing Bowl, Criss-Cross, blue
   7-1/2" d 85.00
   8-1/2" d 100.00
Refrigerator Bowl, cov, Jennyware,
   pink, 16 oz, round 48.00
Refrigerator Dish (Leftover), cov
   4" x 4", Criss-Cross, blue.... 35.00
   4" x 8", Criss-Cross, blue.. 100.00
Salt and Pepper Shakers, pr
   Jennyware, ftd, pink............ 55.00
   Ships, red trim, red lids 55.00
Salt Box, 4-1/2" x 3-3/4",
   crystal 25.00
Spice Set, green lids, Scotty Dog
   dec, green tier holder, cinnamon,
   ginger, red pepper, paprika, mustard, cloves, allspice, set... 325.00
Sugar Bowl, Roman Arch, custard,
   red dot................................ 60.00
Tom & Jerry Set, custard, bowl and
   12 mugs 135.00

❖ Kitchen Kraft

Kitchen Kraft was kitchenware produced by Homer Laughlin in the early 1930s. It features floral decals. Most pieces are marked "Kitchen Kraft" and/or "Oven-Serve."

Casserole, cov
   Individual size, yellow 90.00
   8-1/2" d, cobalt blue.......... 110.00
Cream Soup Bowl, double handles,
   pink 7.50
Jar, cov
   Cobalt blue, small 500.00
   Green, large..................... 390.00

Mixing bowl, 10-1/2" d, $68.

Mixing Bowl, 6" d, cobalt blue, adv for Sherwood Rye 250.00
Pie Plate, 9" d, yellow 20.00
Platter, oval, yellow 50.00
Salad Fork
  Green 115.00
  Yellow 245.00
Salad Spoon, red 200.00
Salt and Pepper Shakers, pr, red
  .... 95.00

⭐ Kitchen Prayer Ladies

These pretty ladies entered the kitchen scene in the 1970s and reminded us of the power of prayer as we bustled about.

Bank, pink 275.00
Bell, pink, stress line on
  back 60.00
Bud Vase 160.00
Canister, Instant Coffee
  Blue 175.00
  Pink 130.00
Coffee Mug, blue 325.00
Cookie Jar
  Blue 350.00
  Pink 350.00
Crumb Pan 60.00

Salt and pepper shakers, Enesco, 4-1/2" h, $28.50.

⭐ Kliban

Who is that black and white cool cat? Kliban! Look for him on almost every type of object, usually with red trim and a sly smile, too.

Candlestick 50.00
Candle Tin, 2-1/2" h 28.00
Checkbook Cover, roller
  skating 15.00
Mold, hanging, Sigma, 8-1/2" w,
  11-1/2" h, 3" d 72.00
Mug, Eat Them Mousies,
  English 27.50
Pin, pewter, flying, 2" l 27.50
Placemat, woven, rect, red and
  white, unused, pr 20.00
Plate, 9" d, wearing sneakers, Kiln
  Craft 22.00
Poster, Top Cat 6.00
Potholder 5.00
Sleeping Bag, slight use 22.00
Teapot, Sigma Trend setter 47.50
Tumbler, plastic, 4-1/4" h 30.00
Wastebasket, 12" h 65.00

❖ Knowles, Edwin M. China Company

Some collectors recognize the name Edwin M. Knowles China Co. for fine dinnerware. Others associate it with limited edition collector's plates. The firm was started in 1900 in West Virginia and continued to produce good quality wares until 1963. They used several different marks, but each clearly indicates Edwin M. Knowles.

Berry Bowl, Yorktown, wheat dec
  .... 8.00

Child's plate, 1-5/8" h, 7-3/4" d, $65.

Bread and Butter Plate,
  Beverly 4.00
Bowl, Mexican motif 35.00
Cake Plate, Yorktown, white ground,
  blue daisies 7.50
Cup and Saucer, Yorktown,
  floral dec 15.00
Doll, Little Red Riding Hood,
  MIB 30.00
Gravy Boat, attached underplate,
  cream-colored ground, silver trim,
  floral decal 15.00
Platter, Mexican motif 47.50
Soup Bowl, Yorktown, floral dec 8.50
Souvenir Plate, San Francisco Bay,
  Alcatraz, Treasure Island,
  10" d 75.00

❖ Knowles, Taylor & Knowles

The other Knowles name known to collectors is Knowles, Taylor & Knowles, who were located in East Liverpool, Ohio, from 1854 to 1931. Their production included ironstone and yellow ware, as well as a translucent china known as Lotus Ware. Knowles, Taylor & Knowles also used at least nine different marks.

Butter Dish, cov, round,
  Portland 40.00
Casserole, cov, rose, green, yellow,
  purple, black, and gold florals,
  green mark, 12-1/4" x
  7-1/2" 17.50

Gravy boat with attached underplate, 7-1/4" d, $28.

Chamber Pot, white ground, gold medallions and dec 45.00

Chamber Set, tiny roses dec, 5 pcs 125.00

Dinner Plate, Grapevine, 10-1/4" d 10.00

Tier, Ebonnette, 3 snack plates, black and white 12.00

Vegetable Bowl, roosters in center, hens around edge 15.00

❖ Korean War

This sad time in the world's history is remembered by veterans and collectors. Flea markets are starting to see more items relating to the Korean War as well as later conflicts.

Blouse, USMC officer, dress blue 30.00

Book

Memoirs of General Mark Clark 15.00

Unit History Book, 25th Infantry 12.00

Weather Book for Air Crew ... 7.00

Cigarette Lighter, engraved 25.00

Combat Boots, size 9-1/2E, used 50.00

Newspaper, headline edition, war ends, 1953 .... 21.00

Pass, Safe Conduct, UN 35.00

Pin, Veteran 9.50

Screwdriver, shaped like Colt pistol 6.00

Service Ribbon 5.00

Silver Dollar, proof, 1991 Memorial commemorative 15.00

For exciting collecting trends and newly expanded areas look for the following symbols:

✪ Hot Topic

★ New Warman's Listing

(May have been in another Warman's edition.)

Favorite dealers:

Name: _____

Shop name: _____

Address: _____

_____

Phone: _____

Hours: _____

Comments: _____

Name: _____

Shop name: _____

Address: _____

_____

Phone: _____

Hours: _____

Comments: _____

Name: _____

Shop name: _____

Address: _____

_____

Phone: _____

Hours: _____

Comments: _____

Name: _____

Shop name: _____

Address: _____

_____

Phone: _____

Hours: _____

Comments: _____

Name: _____

Shop name: _____

Address: _____

_____

Phone: _____

Hours: _____

Comments: _____

Name: _____

Shop name: _____

Address: _____

_____

Phone: _____

Hours: _____

Comments: _____

L

❖ Labels

Here's a collecting category that's got lots of potential. Labels are colorful, plentiful, and usually not expensive. Brightly-colored labels were used for boxes and all kinds of products, such as oranges, lemons, pears, vegetables, tin cans, beverages, cigars, and household items, etc.

Apple, 10-1/2" x 9"
    Cliff, gorge and river scene, old
        car 4.00
    Family Choice, cartoon family
        standing behind small house,
        red background 2.00
    Orchard Boy, red-headed boy's
        face, 3 red apples, blue back-
        ground 2.00
Grape, 13" x 4"
    Arenas, spray of bright red carna-
        tions, green leaves, navy blue
        background .... .25
    Beaver, big beaver at water's
        edge, grapes, red
        background .... .75
    Rayo Sunshine, orange sunrise,
        golden rays and skies over
        lush green vineyards .... .25
Lemon, 12-1/2" x 8-3/4"
    All Year, orchard scene, moun-
        tains, cactus, desert in back-
        ground, black border 2.00
    Fallbrook, rushing mountain
        stream, pine trees, lemons,
        leaves, blossoms, black back-
        ground 1.00
    Golden State, 4 lemons, leaves,
        map of California 1.00

Fruite crate, Lily Brand, Exeter Orange Growers Assoc., white flowers, green leaves, black ground, blue border, $2.

Morning Cheer, 2 lemons, moun-
    tains, brown and shaded
    orange-gold background
    .... 2.00
Orange, 10" x 11"
    Avenue, palm and eucalyptus tree
        lined shady avenue, early auto
        .... 3.00
    Juciful, large orange and leaves,
        light blue background 2.00
    Red Bird, large red eagle, fancy
        blue and black
        background 2.00
    Strathmore, Scottish bagpiper in
        kilt, thistles, deep blue back-
        ground, red plaid border ... 2.00
    Treetop, twin Sequoia tree, yellow
        lettering, blue
        background 1.00
Pear, 10-3/4" x 7-1/4"
    Buckingham, cowboy riding buck-
        ing pig, blue background .. 3.00
    Old Gold, fancy yellow letters, red
        and blue background 1.00
    Snow Owl, fierce looking owl,
        blue background 2.00
Vegetable
    Blue Crown, jeweled crown,
        6-3/4" sq 1.00
    Elkhorn, elk's head, green peas in
        pods, brown background,
        7" x 4-1/2" .... .75
    Safe Hit, baseball player hitting a
        homer, blue background,
        5" x 7" 1.00

White Star, large white star in
    navy circle, red background,
    strip label .... .25

☆ Labino

Keep your eyes open for studio glass by Dominick Labino at flea markets. The prices seem to be really rising on these marked wares.

Creamer, 4-3/8" h, light green, mkd
    "Labino 6-1975" 220.00
Vase
    4-1/2" h, bulbous, opaque white,
        brownish red flames, cased in
        clear, mkd "Labino
        11-1974" 275.00
    4-3/4" h, sculpture type, clear,
        amber veiling pink, mkd
        "Labino 12-1982" 500.00
    4-3/4" h, sculpture type, four bub-
        ble design in pink veiling, gold
        flecks, cased in clear, mkd
        "Labino 11-1978" 470.00
    4-3/4" h, unsymmetrical, irid light
        green, mkd "Labino
        1968" 250.00
    4-7/8" h, opaque black, subtle
        ruby swags, mkd "Labino
        1969" 350.00
    5-1/4" h, sculpture type, clear,
        amber center, hourglass open-
        ing, red and black flames, mkd
        "Labino 9-1974" 485.00
    6" h, bulbous, opaque metallic irid
        green, purple highlights, mkd
        "Labino 1964" 385.00
    8-1/2" h, amethyst, second gather
        of glass in six root like prunts,
        mkd "Labino 1960" 440.00

❖ Lace

Lace has been used as trim for generations. Since the 1940s, lace collecting became a hobby for the wealthy. Those collectors were dedicated to their hobby and spent much time acquiring and studying lace examples. As these collections aged, some were sent to museums, others dispersed. Today collectors are again eagerly seeking antique lace, some to cherish as a long-ago craft, others to adorn clothing or linens.

References: Elizabeth Kurella, *Guide To Lace and Linens,* Antique Trader Books, 1998; ——, *Secrets of Real Lace*, The Lace Merchant, 1994; ——, *Pocket Guide to Valuable Old Lace and Lacy Linens*, The Lace Merchant, 1996.

Periodical: *The Lace Collector,* PO Box 222, Plainview, MI 49080.

Collectors' Club: International Old Lacers, PO Box 554, Flanders, NJ 07836.

Bridal Veil, Princess Lace, 65" x 48" oval, machine net decorated with floral and scroll design 325.00

Collar, Duchesse bobbin lace, roses, daisies, and scrollwork design, 5" at center back, 32" l, c1870 .... 125.00

Curtain, machine made lace, ecru, 36" x 72" 75.00

Doily, needle lace, rose design, round, 6" d 20.00

Yardage, machine made Valenciennes lace, all cotton, floral and scrollwork design, yard length 10.00

❖ Lady's Head Vases

Planters and vases shaped like a lady's head—we've all seen them at flea markets. But did you ever notice how many variations and styles there are? Florists in the 1940s through the early 1960s had a wide array to choose from.

Collectors' Club: Head Vase Society, PO Box 83H, Scarsdale, NY 10583.

Baby, blond hair, open eyes, pink cheeks, open mouth, pink ruffled bonnet tied under chin, pink dress, unmarked, 5-3/4" h .. 20.00

Carmen Miranda 125.00

Cowboy, brown hair, blue eyes, yellow hat and neckerchief, white shirt, yellow star-shaped badge, unmarked, 6" h 35.00

Howdy Doody 45.00

Girl, missing parasol, 4-3/4" h, $55.

Jackie Kennedy, orig foil label, mkd "#E-1852, INARCO," 6" h 650.00

Nurse, short blond hair, downcast eyes, raised right hand, white cap with Red Cross insignia, white uniform with gold accents, painted fingernails, unmarked, 5-3/4" h 70.00

Polynesian, Shawnee 60.00

❖ Lalique

Many collectors associate the name "Lalique" with French glass, but did you know Rene Lalique started as a jewelry designer? His early molded glass brooches and pendants were highlighted with semiprecious stones and are eagerly sought by Lalique collectors today. By 1905, he devoted himself to making glass tablewares, and by 1908 he began to design packaging for cosmetics and perfumes. Most of his glass was marked.

Collectors' Club: Lalique Collectors Society, 400 Veterans Blvd., Carlstadt, NJ 07072.

Reproduction Alert.

For additional listings, see *Warman's Antiques and Collectibles Price Guide* and *Warman's Glass.*

Ashtray, inscribed "Lalique France" 75.00

Bowl, Bagatelle-style, ftd, bird dec, base inscribed "Lalique France" 100.00

Cigarette Lighter, lion, butane lighter, base inscribed "Lalique France" 175.00

Dresser Jar, Epines, domical stopper bottle, molded thornbushes, strong blue patine, molded mark "R. Lalique," price for pair, one with frozen stopper, chip under edge 230.00

Perfume Bottle, Richard Hudnut Master Violet Sec, sq colorless bottle, orig contents, labels intact, some wear 145.00

Tumbler, 4" h, molded with eight recessed full-length figures, engraved "Lalique France" on base, modern 175.00

Urn, 5-1/4" h, Dampierre, Marc Lalique design 195.00

Vase

Eglantines, frosted oval, polished thorny branches and rose blossoms, center base inscribed "R. Lalique," 4-1/2" h 400.00

Elongated bulbed form, eight notched lobes, designed by Marie-Claude Lalique, engraved "Lalique France" on base, 13-1/2" h 200.00

❖ Lamps

Flea markets are great places to find all kind of lamps. Plus, they are also great places for lamp parts. Check to see all necessary parts are there and consider how much you may have to invest to have a vintage lamp rewired.

Periodical: *Light Revival,* 35 W. Elm Ave., Quincy, MA 02170.

For additional listings, see *Warman's Antiques and Collectibles Price Guide, Warman's Americana & Collectibles,* and *Warman's Glass.*

Children's

ABC Blocks, wood and plastic, linen over cardboard shade..............................25.00

TV lamp, ship, 9-1/2" h, $29.

Football Player, standing next to football standard, hollow plaster, linen over cardboard shade, mkd "WK, Japan," made for Sears, c1978....25.00

Lava, red flakes move when heated 70.00

Motion

Antique Cars, Econolite, 1957, 11" h.............................125.00

Fountain of Youth 120.00

Snow Scene, bridge, Econolite 175.00

Table, figural, 17" h, alabaster, young woman on dolphin based urn, engraved "Made in Italy, J. Papucci," some damage and repair, light fixture in urn needs to be rewired 600.00

Table, Tiffany, 21" h, 16" d new bamboo shade, new cap, old bronze patinated stick base, mkd "Tiffany Studios New York"......... 1,760.00

Television

Dragon motif, Mirmar, CA....85.00

Horse head, ceramic, 12" x 10-3/4" 30.00

Wall, folk art type, popsicle sticks, well done shade and base 100.00

☆ Lap Desk

Lap desks or folding desks were the laptop computers of the 18th and 19th centuries. They allowed a writer to have a firm writing surface, place to store papers and writing instru-

ments. Some are quite ornate and have locks and drawers, and a few even have secret compartments.

Inlaid mahogany case, mother-of-pearl motif and inlaid geometric motif, blue velvet lining in top and writing surface, orig working lock and key, 12" x 9" x 8"........ 325.00

Mahogany, cylinder roll top, drawers, heavy brass carrying handles, Victorian, 15" x 11" x 7" 335.00

Pine, painted ext, clean int, holder for ink bottle, 13" x 9" x 4-1/2" 55.00

Pine, red writing surface, 11-1/2" x 8" x 3" 60.00

Rosewood, inlaid border, orig writing surface, 14-1/4" x 9-1/2" x 5-1/4" 210.00

Wood, carved, Anglo Indian, 19th C 500.00

☆ Laundry

Here's a topic many of us would just as soon forget about, but some collectors get a lot of enjoyment from it.

Also see "Clothes Sprinklers," "Irons," and "Soap" in this edition.

Clothespin Bag, made from child's dress, bright calico, wire coat hanger top 12.00

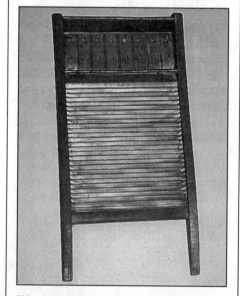

Washboard, National Washboard Co., wood and galvanized metal, 24-1/2" x 12-1/2", $55.

Clothespins

Plastic, white, red, yellow, and pink, set of 18 ....6.00

Wooden, hand made, set of 20 ....20.00

Wooden, machine made, set of 10, used............................ 7.50

Drying Rack, wooden, folding, 36" w, used 40.00

Pants Stretcher, aluminum, adjustable, pr 2.00

Sock Stretcher, wooden 30.00

Washboard

Lady's, small, glass insert... 40.00

Metal rubs 28.00

Nat'l Glass, large 30.00

Wash Tub, galvanized, round, 2 handles, some use..........45.00

❖ Law Enforcement Collectibles

Collectors are starting to actively investigate flea markets for items to add to their collections of law enforcement memorabilia. Some have a desire to salute and honor those who risk their lives to enforce the peace, while others enjoy the sense of history that's attached to these items.

Reference: Monty McCord, *Law Enforcement Memorabilia, Price and Identification Guide,* Krause Publications, 1999.

Periodical: *Police Collectors News,* RR1, Box 14, Baldwin, WI 54002.

Badge

Baltimore, MD, Junior Police............................. 15.00

Nassau NY Police Conference, miniature........................ 25.00

Button, uniform, brass-tone, 3/4" d

Birmingham Police Dept. 9.00

Charleston Police.................. 8.00

Cincinnati Police, scales of Justice 10.00

Philadelphia Police 8.00

Toledo Police 8.00

Newspaper, *National Detective and Police Review,* Vol. 13, No. 2, Indianapolis, 14-5/8" x 10-3/4", $10.

Calendar Print, 1946, humorous, Russell Sambrook illustrator, 5" x 8"

   Blue uniform hanging over No Swimming sign as policeman takes a swim 20.00

   Police officer sits waiting for turn in dentist's chair 20.00

Envelope, D. A. Farrell, Sheriff of Mills County, Glenwood, IA, return address, late 1800s, Glenwood, IA postmark 12.00

Hat, Special Officer badge, 7-1/4" d.............................. 35.00

Magazine, *Life*, Dec 6, 1968, featuring corruption of Chicago Police 12.00

Photograph, Police and Shore Patrol, black and white, crime scene, 14" x 11".................. 15.00

Tobacco Card Insert, Judge, captioned "A few points on Police Protection".......................... 25.00

Toy

   CHiPs Highway Patrol Set, c1977, H. G. Toys, window display box, MIB..............75.00

   Emergency Truck, plastic and tin, mkd "Made in Japan," 1980s, 3-1/2" l............................22.00

   Motorcycle, Triumph, orig box mkd "Made by Polistil, Italy, 1979," 3-1/2" l, MIB....................... 32.00

Police Car, Volkswagen, friction, metal, plastic wheels, Yonezama, Japan, 5" l........................... 25.00

Police Car, Porsche Acrobat Team, metal, battery operated, T.P.S., Japan, 9-1/2" l, late 1960s, MIB 80.00

❂ Lefton China

Founded by George Zoltan Lefton, this company has created china, porcelain and ceramic table wares, animals, and figurines. Lefton wares are well marked some also include a Japanese factory mark.

Reference: Loretta DeLozier, *Collector's Encyclopedia of Lefton China*, vol. 1 (1995), vol. 2 (1997), Collector Books; *1998 Lefton Price Guide.*

Collectors' Club: National Society of Lefton Collectors, 1101 Polk St, Bedford, IA 50833.

For additional listings, see *Warman's Antiques and Collectibles Price Guide.*

Bell 15.00

Egg

   Chick with rose on lid, paper label, chips 15.00

   Roosters and chick on lid, paper label, #3429.................... 25.00

Figurine, robin, 4-1/4" h, $12.

Figure

   Birthday Boys.....................30.00

   Bloomer, O531 ....30.00

   Chiropractor, 10" h.............. 15.00

   March Boy, 2300.................26.00

   January Angel, 3332...........22.00

   September Girl, 1853..........27.00

   Three Pigs 35.00

Mug

   Elf handle, green, #4284..... 15.00

   Grant.................................35.00

   Jackson.............................35.00

Salt and Pepper Shakers, pr, Miss Priss....................................20.00

Snack Set, Fleur de Lis...........50.00

Soap Dish, Christy 15.00

Teapot, Moss Rose 50.00

❖ Lenox

Walter Scott Lenox opened his porcelain factory in 1906, employing potters, decorators, etc. that he lured away from Belleek. Fine Lenox is almost translucent in appearance. The firm is still in business and offers wares at many factory outlet stores.

For additional listings, see *Warman's Antiques and Collectibles Price Guide* and *Warman's American Pottery & Porcelain.*

Bowl

   Acanthus leaf shape, ivory background, gold trim, 9" l 48.00

   Christmas, 4" sq.................... 15.00

   Coffee Pot, Cretan 0316 .... 165.00

   Cream Soup, Tuxedo pattern, green mark...................................42.00

Cup and Saucer

   Alden pattern 25.00

Shell-shaped dish, pink with white handle, 6-1/4" x 4", $15.

Figurine, Teddy's First Christmas, Teddy and Tiny Tots, 4" h, $24.50.

Golden Wheat pattern 35.00
Figure
   Snow Queen 70.00
   Stardust..............................70.00
Night Light, Leda and Swan,
   10", white bisque, sgd,
   dated 600.00
Platter, Oak Leaf, 13-1/2" l, platinum
   trim 75.00
Salt, molded seashells and coral,
   green wreath mark, 3" d 35.00
Tea Strainer, hp, small pink flowers
   .... 72.00
Vase, ivory background, gold trim,
   gold mark 65.00

✩ Letter Openers

These knife-like collectibles are handy desk accessories. They can be found in almost every material. Early advertisers found them a good way to keep their names in the hands of people who might be interested in their goods and services.

Advertising
   Borden's Elsie the Cow, flasher
      face, red plastic, 8" l........70.00
   Fuller Brush Man, clear
      plastic..................................8.00
   Kellogg Services Real Estate,
      The Busy Office, Fresno, CA,
      plastic..................................8.00

Fuller, red plastic, 7-1/4" l, $4.

NY Telephone, wood handle,
   stainless steel blade, plastic
   case, 1965, 10" l 18.00
Welsbach Lights Letter,
   10-1/2" l 95.00
Commemorative, Pennsylvania
   Independent Telephone Associa-
   tion 50th Anniversary, 1902-1952,
   plastic handle, metal blade,
   8-1/8" l 10.00
Masonic, Jordon Lodge No. 247, F &
   A. M., Robert Rogove, 1967,"
   white plastic emblem on plastic
   case 20.00
Souvenir
   Chicago World's Fair, Federal
      Building, marble handle,
      4-1/4" l blade 95.00
   Florida, alligator, celluloid ... 20.00
   San Diego, CA, Exposition build-
      ings, other side with San Diego
      Mission and US Grant
      Hotel 50.00
   Toledo, brass-colored cross,
      6-5/8" l 10.00

❖ Libbey Glass

Libbey Glass is another American success story. It began as the Libbey Glass Company in Toledo, Ohio, in 1888. Their first wares were quality cut glass. Later production included art glass and pressed wares. The Libbey Glass Company was a frequent exhibitor at World's Fairs, which allowed them to show off their wares and promote future lines. Some of their glassware is marked, but not all.

Bowl, cut glass, Somerset pattern,
   sgd, 9" d 165.00
Candy Dish, cov, cut glass, divided,
   clover shape, hobstar and prism
   dec, sgd, 7" d..................... 90.00

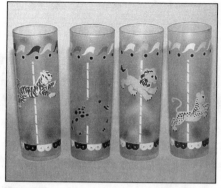

Drinking glasses, carousel motif with tiger, elephant, lion and leopard, 7" h, set of 4, $16.

Cordial, cut glass, American Pres-
   tige pattern, c1930 ....50.00
Goblet, Liberty Bell pattern, clear,
   7" h 25.00
Plate, cut glass, Gloria pattern,
   7" d 165.00
Spooner, Maize pattern, creamy
   opaque kernels of corn, blue
   husks, gold trim.................190.00
Tumble-Up, cut glass, star burst,
   hobstar, fern, and fan motifs,
   minor handle check..........725.00
Tumbler, light green, lightly swirled
   ribs, mkd, set of six 60.00
Vase, amberina, trumpet shape,
   ribbed, 12" h 450.00
Wine, Silhouette pattern, clear bowl,
   black cat silhouette in stem, sgd,
   7" h 200.00

❖ License Plates

As a driver, you won't get too far without one of these. And, few of us can throw them out when new ones are issued. So, lots of examples of license plates find their way to flea markets, to the delight of those who collect them. Since many states and organizations are now issuing specialty license plates, watch for those to rise in value too. Beginner license plate collectors should seek out a flea market devoted to automobiles. Common examples range in the $2 to $5 range. Look for examples in good condition, but expect to find some wear.

Miniature, Alaska, 1953, 4-7/8" x 12-1/4", $6.

American Legion, emb tin,
2-1/4" x 4"......................... 12.00

Betty Boop, emb tin, new,
6" x 12"................................. 6.00

Hackensack, 1966, 434, emb tin,
2" x 2-1/2"......................... 16.00

Kansas, Centennial, emb tin, never
used, orig brown envelope . 25.00

I'd Rather Be Running My Lionel
Trains, nylon...................... 18.00

Infantry, emb tin, 6" x 12".......... 5.00

US Army, emb tin, 6" x 12"....... 4.00

US Navy, emb tin, 6" x 12"....... 6.00

World's Greatest Dad, emb tin,
6" x 12"................................. 4.00

⚝ Liddle Kiddles

Introduced by Mattel in 1965, these half-pint-size dolls drew a big response from girls. But that's nothing compared to the reaction of adult collectors today, who eagerly search for these little reminders of their childhood. While the dolls themselves constitute the main attraction, accessories and go-withs, such as coloring books, are also on many "want" lists.

Collectors' Clubs: Liddle Kiddle Club—East Coast, 16 Weathervane Way, Marlboro, NJ 07746; Liddle Kiddles Klub, 3639 Fourth Ave., LaCrescenta, CA 91214.

Baby bottle, Uneeda, MOC....... 8.50

Beauty Parlor Purse Playset, 1996,
MIB...................................... 5.00

Collectors case, vinyl, holds 8 dolls,
2 slots for accessories, minor
wear, 14-1/2" x 10"............. 15.00

Colorforms, Dress-Up Kit, trays
missing, incomplete, box
damaged........................... 24.00

Coloring book, unused,
1966................................... 43.00

Doll

Anabelle Autodiddle Skediddle
Kiddle, NRFB, box with light
shelf wear.................... 107.50

Liddle Biddle Peep, no shoes,
dress lightly soiled.......... 35.00

Lolli Lemon, MIP.............. 151.50

Pretty Pride, minor play
wear............................. 100.00

Kosmic Space Ship, broken dome
hinge, 5-1/2".................... 19.00

Pop-Up Playhouse, 1967....... 45.00

Pretty Perfumes, Uneeda,
MOC................................. 17.50

Spider, goes with Liddle Middle
Muffet set.......................... 27.00

⚝ Light Bulbs

Here's a bright idea for anyone looking for something to collect—how about light bulbs? Because they were usually thrown away when no longer needed, finding vintage examples—especially those in working condition—can be a real challenge. However, that doesn't mean bulbs are always expensive. What's more, the variety of figural bulbs produced during the past century should turn on many new collectors. Displays of light bulbs can be found at the Mount Vernon Museum of Incandescent Lighting in Baltimore, Md., and the Light Bulb Museum in San Diego, Cal.

Blackout bulb, 95% finished in black
matte paint, 2" x 2" x 3-1/2" white
corrugated thin cardboard sleeve,
black and orange accent art and
lettering, "War Dept Standard"
Westinghouse bulb, tan glass,
instructions for use on sleeve,
WWII, 3-1/2" h.................. 110.00

Christmas figural miniatures

Bulldog, 75% paint, doesn't light,
2-3/4" h........................... 20.50

Cuckoo clock, 70% paint, doesn't
light, 2-1/4" h.................. 20.00

Frog, 60% paint, doesn't light,
3" h................................. 21.50

Monkey with stick, 99% paint,
doesn't light, 3" h............ 40.00

Lightbulb, 3-1/2" h, $12.

Peacock, 99% paint, doesn't light,
2-3/4" h........................... 48.00

Santa on roof, 99% paint, lights,
4" h................................. 66.00

Snowman with bag, 90% paint,
lights, 3-1/4" h................. 21.50

Snowman with pipe, 90% paint,
doesn't light, 2-3/4" h...... 31.00

Squirrel, 80% paint, doesn't light,
2-3/4" h........................... 33.00

Edison, GEM, double-hairpin,
1-piece filament, paper label,
lights............................... 130.00

Edison, Mazda flood light, paper
label, lights, 5-1/2" h ....: 28.00

Edison, replica of 1893 Thomas
Edison carbon filament lamp,
walnut base, brass tag,
5" h................................. 20.50

U.S. Incandescent Lamp Co., 1904,
St. Louis, double-loop filament,
pointed top, paper label, some
discoloring, lights,
7-1/2" h........................... 47.00

Westinghouse, Lifeguard mercury lamp, pointed top, 15" h, 7" w 26.00

❖ Lighters

Cigarette lighters have attracted collectors for years. Watch for interesting figural or advertising lighters. Look for examples in good condition, but use caution if trying to determine if a lighter is in working order.

Collectors' Clubs: International Lighter Collectors, PO Box 3536, Quitman, TX 75783; Pocket Lighter Preservation Guild & Historical Society, 380 Brooks Dr, Suite 209A, Hazelwood, MO 63042.

Bottle Shape, Phila National Expo, sterling silver, 1899 .... 43.00

Camel, brass 5.00

Colorado Insurance Group, Rolex 8.00

Dodge, 1940s 60.00

East Greenwich Dairy Co., Windmaster 15.00

Friars Club, sterling, mkd "Thailand" 140.00

Gold Filled, case mkd "Goldfilled," and "Berkly Windproof Flashlight Company of America, Jersey City, NJ, Made in USA," 2-1/4" x 1-1/2", worn 18.00

Harley Davidson, mkd "Licensed Korea" 15.00

Lays Potato Chips, chrome Zippo-style......................... 20.00

Advertising, Salem cigarettes, Zenith, 1-7/8" h, 2-1/8" w, $12.

L & M Filters, Miracle-Tip-Continental, 1957 .... 15.00

Marlboro, bottle form, wear 8.00

Ronson-Spartan, chrome, table model 20.00

Shell Gas-Techno, plastic 5.00

Siam, sterling 25.00

Tareyton Firebird 20.00

Winston Cigarettes, penguin, Japan................................. 10.00

Zippo-Camel, orange, MIB...... 30.00

❖ Lightning Rod Balls

Now if you're reading this and wondering what on earth we're talking about, take a gander at an old barn next time you're out in the country. We'll bet you'll spot an interesting colored glass ball up on top of that lightning rod. Lightning rod balls of all shapes and colors were made by several American glassmakers from 1870 to about 1920.

References: Russell Barnes, *Lightning Rod Collectibles Price Guide*, published by author; Michael Bruner and Rod Krupka, *The Complete Book of Lightning Rod Balls.*

Periodical: *The Crown Point*, 2615 Echo Lane, Ortonville, MI 48862.

Glass, light blue, chips, 5" h, $17.50.

Deep ruby red, chestnut shape, sheared mouth, no metal collars, 4" d 190.00

Electra, cone shape, embossed lettering, ruby red, sheared collared mouth, no metal collars, 4-5/8" d 230.00

Electra, round shape, embossed lettering, 4-1/2" d

　Cobalt blue, background mouth, no metal collars 160.00

　Ruby red, background mouth, no metal collars, acceptable collar chip 180.00

Embossed moon and star design, ball shape, ruby red, sheared mouths, acceptable collar chip, no metal collars, 4-3/8" d 210.00

Mercury, gold colored, ball shape, background mouth, metal collars mkd "Kretzer Brand/Trademark" 110.00

❖ Limited Edition Collectibles

It's guaranteed that you'll find some limited edition collectibles at any flea market you visit. This multi-million dollar market spills into many types of objects, with some very dedicated artists and companies offering their wares. Remember that much of the value of a limited edition object lies with the original box, packaging, etc. being with the object.

The listing below is just a sampling of what's available at flea markets.

References: Jay Brown, *The Complete Guide to Limited Edition Art Prints*, Krause Publications, 1999; *Collector's Information Bureau, Collectibles Price Guide & Directory to Secondary Market Retailers*, 9th ed., Krause Publications, 1999.

Periodicals: *Collector Editions,* 170 Fifth Ave., 12th Floor, New York, NY 10010; *Collector's Bulletin,* 22341 East Wells Rd., Canton, IL 61520; *Collectors Mart Magazine,* 700 E. State St., Iola, WI 54990; *The Treasure Trunk,* PO Box 13554, Arlington, TX 76094.

Collectors' Clubs: International Plate Collectors Guide, PO Box 487, Artesia, CA 90702, plus many company sponsored clubs and local clubs.

For additional listings, see *Warman's Antiques and Collectibles Price Guide* and *Warman's Americana & Collectibles.* Plus see specific makers, like "Bing & Grondahl" in this edition.

Christmas Ornament
    Anri, Minnie Mouse, Disney Four
        Star Collection, Disney
        Studios, 1990 ....55.00
    Danbury Mint, angel,
        4" h...................................48.00
    Gorham, snowflake, sterling
        silver, 1973.....................95.00
    Reed & Barton, Christmas Cross,
        1976, sterling silver 80.00
    Schmid, Raggedy Ann,
        1978 ....3.00
    Wallace Silversmiths, sleigh bell,
        silver plated, 1990...........50.00

Figure
    America's Heroes, policeman,
        limited to 7,500, 7" h 25.00

Moscow 1980 Olympics plate, Viletta, orig box, 8-1/2" d, $8.

Dave Grossman, Norman
    Rockwell, Back to School
    1973 .... 45.00
River Shore, lamb, 1980..... 48.00
Schmid, Stirring Up Trouble,
    1983 .... 165.00

Plate
    Annie and Grace, Edwin M.
        Knowles, MIB 40.00
    Annie and Sandy, 1982, Edwin M.
        Knowles, MIB 47.50
    Carol Burnett, 1986, Edwin M.
        Knowles, MIB 20.00
    Christmas Plate, Disneyland,
        1986, showing Walt Disney's
        1936 Christmas Greetings,
        second in series, Japan, 9" d,
        MIB.............................. 100.00
    Daddy Warbucks, 1982, Edwin M.
        Knowles, MIB 37.50
    Flowers for Mother, Schmid,
        1974 .... 85.00
    Hershey's, antique Hershey's
        label, white ironstone back-
        ground, #6 of series,
        7" d.............................. 30.00
    Hummingbird, 1986, Edwin M.
        Knowles, MIB 24.50
    Laurie & Creche, Zolan 45.00
    Little Miss Muffett, John McClel-
        land, 1981 .... 30.00
    Robin, 1986, Edwin M. Knowles,
        MIB.............................. 24.50
    Sunday Best, Reco, 1983... 50.00
    Wood Duck, Franklin Mint,
        1972 ....115.00

Sculpture
    Snow Owl, Burgess, #189 of 500
        edition, 9" h 375.00
    Youthful Cottontail, bunny in
        flowers, Burgess, #315 of 950
        edition.......................... 225.00
Stein, gorilla, 8th of Endangered
    Species series, mkd "Handcrafted
    by Ceramarte," limited edition of
    100,000, 1989, 6-1/2" h...... 32.00

❖ Lincoln, Abraham

This famous American president is a favorite among collectors. Lincoln memorabilia is also a favorite of many museums. The Henry Ford Museum recently had the chair in which Lincoln was sitting at Ford's Theater returned to their display. The curators assure collectors that no physical changes were made to this chair which still has evidence of fiber, hair, and blood from the president.

Bust, by Peter C. Sedlow, limited
    edition, 8" h, 4-1/2" w........335.00
Carte de Visite, T. R. Burhman, Bos-
    ton, photographer, untrimmed,
    c1864, 2-1/2" x 4" 50.00
Child's Tea Set, doll size, "Lincoln's
    New Salem, IL," teapot, creamer,
    sugar, two cups and saucers, mkd
    "Japan"..................................25.00
Decanter, 4 oz, 1971-72, gold eagle
    cap, orig red, white, and blue
    box 5.00
Game, Lincoln's Log Cabin Games,
    by W. H. Davidhesier, illus of
    young boy reading by fireplace on
    tin litho board, 11" sq board, parts
    of orig box 65.00
Postcard, Lincoln Memorial Reflect-
    ing Pool, Washington, photo of
    congressman on back plus his
    accomplishments 5.00
Print, President Lincoln and Mary,
    sepia, 2-1/2" x 4"................35.00

1860 campaign ribbon, white silk, facsimile signature, 6" l, $2,000.

❖ Lindbergh, Charles

Collectors are fascinated with this early aviator and his adventures. Look for items that pertain to his many flights in print, commemorative pieces, and even textiles.

Bank, G & T, 1928 .... 300.00
Book, *The Lone Eagle/Lindbergh,*
    8" x 9" stiff paper, 20 pgs, Blakely
    Printing Co., Chicago, copyright
    1929, color portrait photo ... 35.00
Children's Book, *Boy's Story of
    Charles Lindbergh,* hard
    cover 5.00
Cigarette Card, 1927 .... 26.00
First Day Cover........................ 2.25
Magazine, *Time,* June 13, 1938,
    8-1/2" x 11", color cover of Lind-
    bergh and scientist working on
    Fountain of Age, 76 black and
    white pages 15.00
Pin, Plucky Lindbergh............. 22.00
Plate, 8-1/2" d, yellow glazed china,
    color graphics of smiling Lindy,
    plane over ocean between Statue
    of Liberty and Eiffel Tower, text
    "First To Navigate The Air In
    Continuous Flight From New York
    To Paris-1927," Limoges China
    Co., Ohio, Golden Glove
    stamp 24.00
Postcard, 3-1/2" x 5-1/2"
    Red tinted, Lindbergh in cockpit of
        Spirit of St. Louis.............15.00
    Sepia-tone photo of Lindbergh
        posed next to unidentified
        gentleman on ornate balcony,
        Underwood copyright, unused
        ....25.00
Tapestry, New York to Paris...115.00

❖ Linens

No dining room or bedroom is properly dressed without linens. Collectors today treasure these textiles. Some are hand made and show exquisite craftsmanship. Others are machine made and might be just the right size to use with an antique table. Whatever the reason, enjoy them and use them with care.

Reference: Elizabeth Kurella, *Guide to Lace and Linens,* Antique Trader Books, 1998.
Periodical: *The Lace Collector,* PO Box 222, Plainview, MI 49080.
Collectors' Club: International Old Lacers, PO Box 554, Flanders, NJ 07836.

Boudoir Pillow, peach linen, embroi-
    dery, lace trim, satin bows in each
    corner, 10" x 14" 120.00
Doily
    Crocheted, pink and cream,
        7" sq 5.00
    Embroidered, oval, scalloped
        edge, scrolled design, 10" x 7"
        .... 6.50
Dresser Scarf, Damask,
    embroidered, 31-1/4" x 17" ... 25.00
Handkerchief
    7" sq, Place de la Concorne
        Paris 12.00
    7" sq, Place des Eetre
        Paris 10.00
    12" sq, purple petunias, green
        crocuses, orig labels "Pure
        Linen, Hand Rolled" 17.50
    15" sq, Oriental motif, orig silver
        tag "Hermann Irish
        Linen" 17.50
Napkin, linen, 25" sq, set of
    6 .... 20.00
Pillow Cover, linen, embroidered,
    19" x 13-1/2" 25.00
Tablecloth and Napkins
    Damask, light blue, 79-1/2" x 60",
        four 15-1/2" napkins, some
        minor stains.................... 50.00
    Irish linen, 54" sq, 4 matching
        napkins, orig box, never
        used 30.00

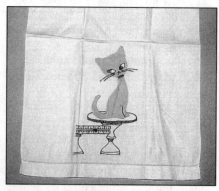

Towel, cat decoration, 19" x 12-3/4", $3.50.

Tea Towel, Irish linen, hand
embroidered
    Comical Couple, 19-1/2" x
        13-1/4" 15.00
    Dogwoods, 18-1/2" x 12", slight
        use................................. 15.00
    Purple pansies, white back-
        ground, 18" x 20", fringed
        edge 18.00

❖ Little Golden Books

Read me a story! From the time Simon & Schuster publisher the first Little Golden Book in 1942 until today, millions of stories have been read. Today's collectors have many fun titles to choose from and all are sure to find some childhood favorites.

Reference: Steve Santi, *Collecting Little Golden Books,* 3rd ed., Krause Publications, 1998.
Periodical: *The Gold Mine Review,* PO Box 209, Hershey, PA 17033.
Collectors' Club: Golden Book Club, 19626 Ricardo Ave, Hayward, CA 94541.

Annie Oakley, #221-25, 1955, name
    inside front cover, some corners
    damaged............................ 10.00
Bozo the Clown, 1st edition,
    1961 .... 20.00
Bugs Bunny's Birthday, 1st ed.,
    1950, fair condition 7.00
Captain Kangaroo, #261, 1956, pen-
    ciled name on front page 5.00
Cars and Trucks, 5th printing, 1971,
    wear to cover 12.00
Counting Rhymes, 1946, fair
    condition 8.00
Daniel Boone, #256, 1956, penciled
    name on front page.............. 6.00
Davy Crockett, #D45, 1955, penciled
    name on front page.............. 8.00
Dumbo's Book of Colors, #1015-23,
    name written on front page ... 2.00
Gordon's Jet Flight, #A48, 1961,
    activity book, insert missing
    .... 65.00
Hop, Little Kangaroo, #558 .... 5.00
Lady and the Tramp 3.00

Walt Disney's Bambi: Friends of the Forest, 1975, $5.

Little Golden Book of Dinosaurs, #355, penciled name on front page, some rubs 4.00

Little Golden Book of Dogs, #532, some cover damage............. 4.00

Little Golden Book of Horses, #459, birthday greetings written inside.................................... 4.00

Mickey's Christmas Carol, #459-09, 1983, good condition............ 2.00

My First Book, 1942, name written in front 12.00

1- 2- 3 Juggle with Me, 1st ed. 6.00

Peter Rabbit, #505, 1970, good condition................................ 2.00

Scruffy the Tugboat, #310-41, 1974, some crayon marks.............. 1.00

The Christmas Donkey, 1984 ... 3.00

The Christmas Story, 1952 .... 6.00

The Fuzzy Duckling, 1949 ...... 10.00

The Monster at the end of this Book, Starring Lovable, Furry Old Grover, Sesame St., 2nd ed. 4.00

Tootle, 1945 .... 12.00

Walt Disney's Goofy—Movie Star, 1956, red spine 27.50

Wheels, 1st ed., 1952.............. 8.00

Zorro, 1958 .... 15.00

❖ Little Orphan Annie

Poor Little Orphan Annie! Her best friend was her dog, Sandy. She's been the subject of comic strips, books, radio shows, and even a modern musical.

Ovaltine shaker, plastic, 5" h, $65.

Book, *The Little Orphan Annie Book*, James Whitcomb Riley, illus by Ethel Betts, 1908 .... 35.00

Change Purse, red vinyl, white image of Annie and Sandy, metal clasp, 1930s, 3" x 2" 45.00

Cup and Saucer, 4" d, luster ware, 1920s................................. 20.00

Doll, Knickerbocker, 10" h, 1982, orig box and extra clothes .. 20.00

Mug, Ovaltine, stoneware 50.00

Pinback Button, Los Angeles Evening Express contest, black, white, and fleshtone, 1-1/2" d 55.00

❖ Little Red Riding Hood

This popular storybook character was portrayed on all types of items. Probably the most sought after at flea markets are pottery items. These blanks were purchased by Regal China Co. in the 1940s from Hull Pottery Co., Ohio. Decorators at Regal China decorated them, allowing for the small variations in details and floral patterns found today.

Reproduction Alert.

Allspice Jar............................375.00

Bank, standing 575.00

Cereal Canister 950.00

Coffee Canister 750.00

Cookie Jar
    Gold stars, red shoes........ 300.00
    Poinsettia trim 300.00

Creamer, tab handle 275.00

Flour Canister 375.00

Match Holder, Little Red Riding Hood and Wolf, striker, Staffordshire 75.00

Milk Pitcher 400.00

Mustard, orig spoon 250.00

Salt and Pepper Shakers, pr
    3-1/4" h, incised "135889," gold trim........................ 140.00
    5-1/2" h 150.00

Sugar Bowl, cov, crawling 275.00

Sugar Canister 600.00

Tea Canister..........................750.00

Teapot, cov............................325.00

⭐ Little Tikes

When it comes to toys, many surges in collectibility begin as adults start buying back the items they remember from their childhoods. With that being the case, expect Little Likes items to continue to grow in popularity. Flea markets are excellent sources for these plastic playthings. Because the items were mass-produced, look for examples in prime condition.

Circular saw, clicks when pushed down 10.50

Dog, white with red collar.......... 7.00

Fishing set, pole, hook, 10 fish 12.50

Grandma's House, with grandma, girl, kitchen, toy box, coupe, baby carriage, table and chairs ...34.00

Kitchen set, #5528, MIB.......... 13.00

Roadway set, 68 pieces, includes train with cars, people, tunnel, station, bridge, ramp, 2 houses 26.50

Car, plastic, 6-1/4" l, $1.50.

School bus, 9 figures 8.00
Stable, with 4 fence pcs, rider, bale
    of hay, 2 horses 47.50
Toddle Tots Space Trio, astronaut,
    alien and robot 15.50
Toy box, resembles 2 stacked
    Goodyear tires 34.00
Turtle, from Pet Shop, 1984 ..... 6.50
Vacuum cleaner, goes with doll
    house 8.50

❖ Lladro Porcelains

This Spanish ceramics company was established in 1951 by brothers José, Juan, and Vincente Lladro. They made ceramic figurines and flowers. There was a lot of speculation in this segment of the collectibles market a few years ago. Whether the high prices paid will be valid when the items again return to the market place has yet to be tested.

Collectors' Club: Lladro Collectors Society, 1 Lladro Drive, Moonachie, NJ 07074.

Girl with goose and dog,
    #4866 .... 200.00
Girl with lamb, 10-3/4" h 65.00
Pepita, sombrero 175.00
Spanish Policeman 100.00
Wedding Couple 45.00

❖ Locks and Padlocks

Locks and padlocks have been around since the 1600s, so collectors potentially have many to choose from. Many collectors specialize in a particular type of lock or a particular manufacturer.

Collectors' Club: American Lock Collectors Association, 36706 Grennada, Livonia, MI 48154.

Reproduction Alert.

Commemorative
    Dan Patch, horseshoe emb on
        back, iron, 2" h 145.00
    Pan-American Exhibition, man
        riding buffalo, emb, brass,
        1901 .... 95.00
Lever
    Champion Six Lever, brass, push
        key, emb, 3-1/4" h 8.00
    Corbin, brass, emb, 3" h 10.00
    Eagle, steel, emb, 2-3/4" h ... 7.50
    King Korn, steel, emb,
        2-7/8" h 20.00
    Miller, Six Secure Levers, iron
        and brass, push key, 3-1/2" h
        .... 5.00

Yale signal lock, mkd "C&O Sig. Dept.," 3-3/8" h, $15.

SB Co., brass, emb, long
    shackle, 3" h 45.00
Railroad
    L & N, Yale, emb, pink
        tumbler 25.00
    NC & STL, switch type, Yale,
        figure eight back 30.00
    Union Pacific, switch type, brass
        lever, emb panel 45.00

❖ Loetz Glass

This pretty Austrian glass can have bright iridescent colors and sometimes is found with metal ornamentation. Most of this glass was produced at the same time Tiffany was inspiring the art glass world, and similar colors and shapes are found in Loetz glass. Some pieces are signed, but not all.

For additional listings, see *Warman's Antiques and Collectibles Price Guide* and *Warman's Glass*.

Basket, brilliant green mottled on
    clear background, highly irid blue
    and purple finish, 6-1/2" h,
    5" w 100.00
Bowl, rolled rim, applied green tad-
    poles, highly irid white back-
    ground, 7" d, 4" h 110.00
Bowl and Stand, irid deep ruby
    shading to irid pale green,
    5 crimps, 3 chased metal studs,
    reticulated 4 ftd stand,
    8" x 4" 400.00
Candlesticks, pr, slender baluster
    form, raised circular foot, gold irid,
    9-1/2" h 300.00
Dish, three applied pulled out han-
    dles, brilliant gold base, sgd in
    pontil with monogram "M" and "L,"
    8-1/2" d, 2-3/4" h 200.00
Rose Bowl, 6-1/2" d, ruffled purple,
    irid raindrop dec 265.00
Vase
    6-1/2" h, tadpole neck, white irid
        background, green
        rigaree 200.00
    6-3/4" h, 4-3/4" d, cranberry, irid
        fan and swirl optic, bulbous
        bottom, 3 dimples 190.00

8" h, 4-5/8" d, amethyst, eggshell irid, bulbous bottom.......235.00

8-1/2" h, irid green, pimpled texture, polished pontil, mkd "Loetz, Austria".............450.00

❖ Lone Ranger

Hi-Ho-Silver. The Lone Ranger and his Indian pal Tonto rode into our lives on the silver screen, over the radio waves, and later on television. As a cowboy hero, many collectors still respect the values this masked man stood for.

Periodical: *The Silver Bullet,* PO Box 553, Forks, WA 98331-0553.

Collectors' Club: Lone Ranger Fan Club, 19205 Seneca Ridge Court, Gaithersburg, MD 20879-3135.

Better Little Book, *The Lone Ranger and Dead Men's Mine,* Whitman, 1939 .... 50.00

Cereal Box, Cheerios, Frontiertown 75.00

Coloring Book, Lone Ranger Ranch, Fun Book, Whitman, Cheerios premium, 1956 .... 75.00

Gun and Holster Set, MIB..... 135.00

Hair Brush.............................. 25.00

Halloween Mask, 1960s 30.00

Lantern, 1950s..................... 150.00

Pencil, silver, bullet shape 15.00

Premium Ring, Six Shooter, metal, c1947 .... 145.00

Toothbrush Holder, plaster, painted, 1938, 4" h......................... 75.00

Watch 100.00

Jaymar jigsaw puzzle, The Lone Ranger, complete, box 7" x 10-1/8", $35.

✯ ⊘ Longaberger Baskets

These Dresden, Ohio made baskets attract a lot of buyers. Sold mostly through home shows, some baskets are now entering the secondary market. Here's a sample of some prices for some of the popular baskets. To achieve high prices, baskets must be in mint condition. Liners and protectors add slightly to value, as does a maker's signature.

Bayberry Basket, fabric liner, protector, "K. S. Lanam" wooden lid 60.00

Booking Basket
Ambrosia, 1994 .... 25.00
Chives, fabric liner and protector, 1995 .... 40.00

Baking Basket, Crisco American, napkin liner and protector, non-Longaberger wooden lid, 1993 .... 95.00

Cake Basket, swing handles, fabric liner, protector, 1993........... 50.00

Dresden Tour, fabric liner and protector, 1993 .... 45.00

Inaugural Basket, 1993, 8-1/2" h, 5-1/2" sq, $65.

Easter Basket, fabric liner, protector
1993, large 45.00
1993, orig J. W., sgd 70.00
1996............................... 35.00

Flowerpot Basket, fabric liner and protector, 1994 .... 40.00

Heartland, small purse, Longaberger signatures, 1993 .... 50.00

Hostess Basket
Appreciation, 1996.............. 35.00
Christmas Evergreen, fabric liner, protector, 1995 .... 90.00
Easter, 1991...................... 45.00
Sleigh bell, fabric liner, protector, wooden lid, 1994 .... 85.00
Wildflower, protector, 1994 .... 75.00

Key Basket
Medium, fabric liner, 1989... 25.00
Medium, green accent weaving, protector, 1994 .... 30.00
Small, green accent weaving and protector, 1994 .... 25.00
Small, red accent weaving and protector, 1995 .... 20.00
Tall, 1993 .... 20.00

Lilac Basket, fabric liner, protector, tie-on, 1994........................ 40.00

Measuring, Holiday, 13", protector, 1990................................. 80.00

Mother's Day, vanity basket, protector, 1996.................... 45.00

Pantry Basket, protector, 1989................................. 45.00

Patriot Basket, All-American, fabric liner and divided protector, 1997................................. 30.00

Petunia Basket, fabric liner and protector, 1997.................... 35.00

Purse Basket, child's, protector, 1994................................. 25.00

Season's Greetings, fabric liner, 1992................................. 55.00

Umbrella basket, "J. W.", protector, 1994................................. 100.00

❖ Lotton, Charles

Another contemporary studio glass maker, Charles Lotton started in a small studio at his home in Sauk Village, IL. His exquisite glass creations are sold through his own distributors to select retailers and at some antique shows. Several of the Lotton children are now part of the business. Expect to find pieces signed by Charles or son David.

Atomizer, selenium red 85.00
Bottle, long neck, flared lip, mandarin red 250.00
Bowl, Leaf & Vine, red background, sgd "David Lotton" 145.00
Chalice, ftd, mandarin red 160.00
Paperweight, Dana Flora, pink flower, green leaves, sgd, 1982 .... 150.00
Rose Bowl, cobalt blue background, gold zipper-style pattern ... 150.00
Vase, 5-1/4" h
   Blue, white int., #434, 1976 ....225.00
   King Tut, amethyst background, irid feather dec, pale green applied lip, 1974...........225.00

✫ ☸ Luggage

Interior decorators are known to frequent flea markets looking for interesting old suitcases, etc. What they have discovered is that these well-traveled vintage bags can make great storage containers that are also fun to display.

Child's, round, pink vinyl, black and white poodle dec, zipper closure, pink carrying loop, wear 20.00
Folding, dark plaid, zipper closure, molded plastic handle, orig hangers 15.00

"Margie" travel case, vinyl, 1962, 20th Century Fox Television Co., minor tear at base, 9" h, 14" w, 5" d, $20.

Suitcase, large, rect, camel colored leather, some wear to int. ... 45.00
Suitcase, small, rect, hard, blue, never used.......................... 25.00
Train Case, brown, light beige stripes, fitted int. with mirror, molded plastic handle, 1940s................................. 35.00
Valise, dark brown leather, padded leather handles, some wear................................ 150.00

❖ Lunch Boxes

How many moms have yelled "don't forget your lunch!" It was always easier to remember if packed in a brightly-colored lunch box, many complete with a thermos. Actually, lunch boxes or kits have been around for a long time, since the mid 1930s, certainly pre-dating those character examples usually associated with this collectible.

Periodical: *Paileontologist's Report,* PO Box 3255, Burbank, CA 91508.

Collector's Club: Step Into The Ring, 928 Jackson St., Sundusky, OH 44870.

Annie, 1981, Tribune Company Syndicate, Inc., Columbia Pictures Industries, Inc., Aladdin Industries, Inc., Nashville, TN...... 28.00
Disney Express, orig thermos, orig Aladdin tag, 1970s.............. 95.00
Disney on Parade, Mickey on balloon on lid, Donald and rest of gang on sides, orig thermos, Aladdin 50.00

Hee Haw, Thermos, tin, $85.

For exciting collecting trends and newly expanded areas look for the following symbols:

☸ Hot Topic
✫ New Warman's Listing
(May have been in another Warman's edition.)

Dukes of Hazzard, orig thermos, 1980, Aladdin......................35.00
GI Joe, 1986, plastic, no thermos, Aladdin...............................18.00
Incredible Hulk, 1978, Aladdin 42.00
Junior Miss, Aladdin................36.00
Last Chance Garage, 1994, plastic, Aladdin...............................15.00
Lawman, edge wear................85.00
Mickey Mouse Club, metal, white rim, 1976, paint scraped on rim, no thermos, Aladdin Industries 35.00
Mickey Mouse Club, metal, yellow rim, 1963, no thermos, paint scraped on edges, Aladdin Industries 40.00
Secret of NIMH, orig thermos, 1982, Aladdin................................35.00
Six Million Dollar Man, Universal City Studios, Inc., orig thermos, (thermos in poor condition), 1974, Aladdin Industries Inc., Nashville, TN 60.00
Walt Disney World, no thermos, Aladdin................................24.00
Wonderful World of Disney, Mickey with Train, Aladdin 44.00

❖ Lu-Ray Dinnerware

This pretty pattern was introduced by Taylor, Smith, Taylor in the late 1930s. Production continued until the early 1950s. The pastel shades were made in Chatham Gray, Persian Cream, Sharon Pink, Surf Green, and Windsor Blue.

Berry Bowl, Windsor Blue 15.00
Bowl, Surf Green, c1936.........60.00
Cake Plate, Persian Cream .. 115.00
Casserole, cov, Sharon Pink.155.00
Chop Plate, Persian Cream 30.00

Cream Soup, Sharon Pink,
    underplate 135.00

Demitasse Saucer, Windsor
    Blue 5.00

Dinner Plate, 9" d
    Surf Green.............................9.00
    Windsor Blue..........................9.00

Eggcup, Windsor Blue 20.00

Fruit Bowl, Persian Cream...... 10.00

Grill Plate, Surf Green 32.50

Juice Tumbler, Persian
    Cream 70.00

Pickle Dish, Sharon Pink 70.00

Platter, large, Persian
    Cream................................. 13.00

Saucer, 6" d
    Persian Cream 7.00
    Sharon Pink.......................... 7.00

Surf Green 7.00

Salt Shaker, Sharon Pink.......... 6.00

Teapot, Sharon Pink 65.00

Vegetable Bowl, Windsor
    Blue 24.00

Salt and pepper shakers, pink and blue, 3-1/2"h, $12.

Reproduction tip-offs...the sequel.

1. Nippon mark applied as a decal
2. Glassware with a hazy look
3. No sign of wear
4. Poor image
5. Incomplete marks
6. Mark is fuzzy or difficult to read
7. Obvious signs of forced wear
8. Hallmarks inconsistent with manufacturing period or method
9. Modern hardware or screws
10. Smell of fresh paint or varnish

Want List:

1. _____
2. _____
4. _____
5. _____
6. _____
7. _____
8. _____
9. _____
10. _____
11. _____
12. _____
13. _____
14. _____
15. _____
16. _____
17. _____
18. _____
19. _____
20. _____

For exciting collecting trends and newly expanded areas look for the following symbols:

✪ Hot Topic

★ New Warman's Listing

(May have been in another Warman's edition.)

★ MAD Collectibles

Collectors of *MAD Magazine* memorabilia are easy to spot at flea markets. They're the most relaxed people in sight, wearing a sly smile on their face and thinking, "Me worry?" Look for Alfred E. Neuman's smug mug on any number of items, from games to timepieces.

Buckle, Alfred E. Neuman, with belt, size 34, 1993, never worn 20.00

Bust, Alfred E. Neuman, unglazed ceramic, "Me Worry?," 4-1/2" h............................. 227.50

Card game, Parker Brothers, 1980, boxed 3.50

Desk plaque, Alfred E. Neuman, lightly soiled, 4-1/2" x 4-1/4" 6.00

MAD Magazine, #24, premiere issue, split spine, stain, one back corner missing................... 113.50

The MAD Magazine Game, Parker Brothers, $15.

Model, Alfred E. Neuman, Aurora, 1965, unassembled, orig box, complete 142.50

Pinback buttons, complete set of 24, subscription premiums, 1987, 1-1/2" d 102.50

Record, Flexi Disc, "She Got a Nose Job" by the Dellwoods, 33-1/3rpm, paper 5.00

Skateboard, Alfred E. Neuman............................ 117.50

Watch, analog, commemorates 35th anniversary, white band, Concepts Plus, 1987, orig package 45.00

❖ Maddux of California

Maddux of California started in 1938 in Los Angeles. They continued making and distributing novelties, figurines, planters, lamps, and other decorative accessories until 1974.

Compote, white, pedestal base, mkd "Maddux of California #1013," 1960s, 8" d 20.00

Console Bowl, white, oblong shell, 3" x 14-1/2", silver label 20.00

Planter, fish motif, 11-1/4" h, $18.

Figure

Bull, blue and white........... 140.00

Cockatoo, 7" h 17.50

Flamingo, mkd "Maddux of Calif. #30, Made in USA," 11" h85.00

Ruby Crowned Kinglets, pair sitting on rose bush, 8-1/4" h, small chip 48.00

Flamingo Pond, 8" h flamingo, 13" l pond, mkd "Maddux of California, #1024" 100.00

Planter, white bowl, silvered metal stand, 8" x 3-1/2", rim chip.... 9.00

Television Lamp

Mallard Duck, planter type, small chip.................................. 60.00

Rooster, mkd "Maddux of Calif, 842, Made in USA," c1950, 10" h 165.00

Stallion, white, planter type, 12-1/2" h 65.00

Vase, double flamingoes, 5" h. 65.00

❖ Magazines

Magazine collecting offers a unique perspective on American life. By reading the old magazines, you can get a clearer idea of what life was like, what products were being advertised, who was making news, etc. Some collectors buy magazines that they can take apart and see as individual advertisements or articles.

American Artist, June, 1960......7.50

American Boy, July 1927.........35.00

Atlantic Monthly, Nov, 1907.....20.00

Better Photo, 1914 ....5.00

Boy's Life, 1916, Rockwell cover 25.00

Child's Life, 1930.......................4.00

Cosmopolitan, 1907 ....7.50

Esquire, Sept, 1934 ....15.00

Farm Journal, April, 1938..........2.50

Farmer's Wife Magazine, May, 1935 ....3.00

Friends Journal, 1955 ....3.00

Golf Illustrated, Sept, 1934 .....10.00

Life

1964, July 3, Robert Kennedy, photos of family and article, Coca-Cola ad on back.... 15.00

The Literary Digest, **Oct. 22, 1921, Girl Scout cover illustrated by Norman Rockwell, $12.50.**

1965, April 9, Robert
    Kennedy...........................12.00
1968, June 14, Senator Robert F.
    Kennedy...........................15.00
McCall's, 1950, complete paper
    dolls...................................... 7.50
National Geographic, Dec, 1968 2.00
Needlecraft, 1928 .... 3.00
Newsweek, Robert Kennedy, Aug
    24, 1964 .... 15.00
New Yorker, 1948 .... 4.00
Popular Mechanics, 1952 .... 2.00
Rolling Stone, Seinfeld Final Show
    issue................................... 35.00
Saturday Evening Post
    1922, January, Leyendecker cov..
        ....24.00
    1923, Pearl Harbor..............12.00
    1936, Springtime, Norman Rock-
        well..................................12.00
Song Hits, May 1940 edition,
    Deanna Durbin on cover, 36 pgs,
    8-1/2" x 12" 20.00
Spinning Wheel, July, 1962 .... 20.00
Time, June 12, 1964, Barry Goldwa-
    ter on cover 15.00
Tobacco World, 1902................ 8.50
Travel, 1915, Santa cover....... 27.50
Woman's Home Companion,
    1916 .... 20.00

❖ Magic Collectibles

Abracadabra! Magic collectibles can too be found at flea markets. Just be careful that they don't disappear before your eyes! Actually, magic collectibles can encompass the tools of the trade or ephemera relating to great magicians.

Book
    Al Baker's Pet Secrets, Al Baker,
        illus, 1951, sgd by
        author 125.00
    *Blitz's Book of Magic, Tricks for
        Sale,* Francois Blitz, New York,
        c1880 .... 600.00
    Elusive Magical Secrets, Will
        Goldston, illus, lock and key,
        badly worn covers, London,
        c1912 .... 250.00
    Fifty TV Magic Tricks, Marshall
        Brodien, 1960s 10.00
    *The Unmasking of Robert-Hou-
        dini,* portrait frontispiece, illus,
        1908 .... 200.00
Catalog, *Magical Place of Conjuring
    Wonders, Price List of Mr. J.
    Bland's Best and Cheapest Con-
    juring Tricks*, London,
    c1895............................... 450.00
Lobby Card
    Carter Beats the Devil, Carter the
        Great, color litho, turbaned
        Carter playing cards with the
        devil, Cleveland,
        c1930 .... 400.00
    World's Super Magician, Harry
        Blackstone, RKO Orpheum

Bill Bixby The Magician Magic Set, 1974, Paramount Pictures Corp., box 14" x 20", $28.

Theatre, Davenport,
    1950s........................... 125.00
Photograph, Harry Blackstone, bust
    portrait, inscribed by Blackstone,
    1939, 8" x 10" 75.00
Poster
    El Saba, 24" x 36", three color,
        photo of acts, 1937....... 175.00
    The Great Virgil, 40" x 80", full
        color, 1940s 375.00
    Virgil, 28" x 41", three color,
        Cheating the Gallows,
        1940s........................... 250.00
Program, B. F. Keith's Theatre Pro-
    gram, Boston, Dec 19, 1921,
    including a performance by
    Houdini, 10-1/2" x 4" 95.00
Window Card, Mind Reading Abili-
    ties of Joseph Dunninger,
    1926.................................75.00

❖ Magic Lanterns

Here's one of the first types of home entertainment equipment. With a magic lantern, images could be projected and shared for all to see. These do occasionally surface at flea markets. Check to see if original slides are included with the lantern, making the treasure that much more fun to use.

Lantern
    Brass, attached alcohol
        burner...........................295.00
    Delineascope, Spencer Lens Co.,
        Buffalo, 350 slides, orig box
        ....600.00
    Germany, orig kerosene burner,
        17 glass slides, orig instruc-
        tions and box 1,890.00
    Laterna Magica, orig box and
        slides 190.00
    Optimus, converted to
        electric 90.00
Slide
    Auction scene, Civil War
        era 15.00
    Bearded Man 6.00
    Berkeley Univ, 1920.............. 4.00
    Hunt scene, horses,
        Victorian 2.00

Marching Troops 6.00
Mickey Mouse 35.00

✫ Magnifying Glasses

Did you ever play detective and scour the house with a magnifying glass in your hand? Most of us did at one time or another. And as the baby boomers age, perhaps a few of us will be looking for them to help read that fine print in the local newspaper.

Brass and rosewood, matching letter opener, 10" l 50.00
Cracker Jack prize.................. 10.00
Ivory handle, large round glass magnifying lens 125.00
Jade handle, large oval glass magnifying lens 35.00
Porcelain handle, floral dec, large round glass magnifying lens...................................... 75.00
Wood handle, large round glass magnifying lens 27.50

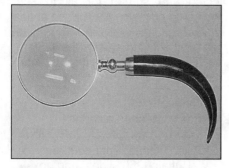

Horn handle, 9-3/4" l, 4" d, $32.

❖ Majolica

Majolica is defined as an opaque tin-glazed pottery. It has been made in many countries for centuries. Many Majolica pieces are distinctive in their use of naturalistic flowers, leaves, and other elements in bright colors. Few Majolica pieces are marked.

Periodical: *Majolica Market,* 2720 N. 45 Rd., Manton, MI 49663.

Platter, Fan and Scroll pattern, Fielding, 13-1/2" l, $450.

Collectors' Club: Majolica International Society, 1275 First Ave., Suite 103, New York, NY 10021.

Reproduction Alert.

For additional listings, see *Warman's Antiques and Collectibles Price Guide, Warman's American Pottery and Porcelain,* and *Warman's English & Continental Pottery & Porcelain.*

Butter Dish, cov, insert, Shell and Seaweed, Etruscan, minor rim nicks to lid.......................... 660.00
Butter Pat
  Butterfly, Fielding, stains... 220.00
  Grape, Clifton, rim nick..... 145.00
  Horseshoe, Wedgwood 300.00
  Calling Card Tray, fox with duck, Continental, rim chips... 100.00
Compote, pinwheel and floral, Samuel Lear, rim nick, hairline.............................. 165.00
Creamer, Blackberry, Holdcroft 150.00
Humidor, bulldog, red jacket and pipe, small nicks 440.00
Pitcher, figural, duck, shades of blue and brown.......................... 35.00
Plaque, lilies of the valley dec, large leaves with finely molded white flowers, mustard ground, reticulated, Villroy & Boch, 12" 175.00
Plate, Pond Lily, 9" d, minor glaze loss 150.00
Smoke Set, 8" h x 6" d x 6" w, monk, tobacco and cigarette holder, orig cover, match holder, and striker............................... 225.00

Teapot, 8" h, monkey handle, ostrich spout, clutched by two hands, behind spout is face of bearded man, scene of people and village on side, chipped finial 150.00
Tea Trivet, round, colorful...... 155.00
Tile, red rose center, shaded blue ground, 6" sq, mkd "Made in England, H & R Johnson, Ltd.," 45.00
Umbrella Stand, relief iris, streaked brown, green, and ochre, 18-1/2" h, 9-3/4" d............. 350.00
Vase
  11" h, 5-1/2" d, applied duck, full relief bamboo and water plants, cream glossy cylinder, gold trim........................ 270.00
  11-1/2" h, figural, black boy and girl, tulip form leaf base, pink flower and bud, boy with basket of food, girl with tray of food, pr 700.00

❖ Marbles

Playing the game of marbles may not be as popular as it once was, but collectors are still able to find great examples at flea markets. Many collectors specialize in the type of marble they search for, either agates, clambroths, hand made Benningtons, glazed and painted chinas, or unglazed and painted chinas, clay, end-of-day, Lutz, sulfide, swirl, or micas. There are some neat contemporary marbles being created by the studio glass blowers.

References: Robert Block, *Marbles Identification and Price Guide,* 2nd ed., Schiffer Publishing, 1998; Stanley A. Block, *Marble Mania,* Schiffer Publishing, 1998; Everett Grist, *Antique and Collectible Marbles,* 3rd ed., Collector Books, 1992, 1996 value update; ——, *Everett Grist's Big Book of Marbles,* Collector Books, 1993, 1997 value update; ——, *Everett Grist's Machine Made and Contemporary Marbles,* 2nd ed., Collector Books, 1995, 1997 value update.

Collectors' Clubs: Buckeye Marble Collectors Club, 437 Meadowbrook

Dr, Newark, OH 43055; Marble Collectors Unlimited, PO Box 206, Northboro, MA 01532; Marble Collectors Society of America, PO Box 222, Trumbull, CT 06611; National Marble Club of America, 440 Eaton Rd, Drexel Hill, PA 19026; Sea-Tac Marble Collectors Club, PO Box 793, Monroe, WA 98272; Southern California Marble Club, 18361-1 Strathern St, Reseda, CA 91335.

Akro Agate Co., machine made
  Blue oxblood 65.00
  Helmet patch 2.50
  Lemonade corkscrew 15.00
  Slag 1.00
Benningtons..............................1.00
Clay 1.00
Glazed painted china.............. 10.00

Lutz
  Banded, 1" d.......................250.00
  Ribbon, 1" d.......................800.00

Marble King Co., machine made
  Bumblebee 1.75
  Cub Scout 5.00
  Wasp 5.00
Mica, 1-1/2" d 200.00

Peltier Glass Co.
  Peerless Patch 5.00
  Slag 20.00
  Two-color, Rainbow,
    old type 1.50

Swirl
  Banded, 1" d 65.00
  Divided core, 3/4" d.............18.00
  Latticino core, 1-1/2" d 75.00

Clay marbles, each $1.

Ribbon core, 3/4" d.............. 75.00
Solid core, 3/4" d 25.00
Unglazed painted china 5.00

☆ Marx Toys

Louis Marx founded the Marx Toy Co. in 1921. He stressed high quality at the lowest possible price. Marx Toys tend to be very colorful, and many can be found with their original boxes, which enhances the price.

Reference: Tom Heaton, *The Encyclopedia of Marx Action Figures, A Price & Identification Guide,* Krause Publications, 1998.

Periodical: *Toy Shop,* 700 E. State St., Iola, WI 54990.

Airplane, pressed steel, silver gray,
  9-1/2" wingspan................ 150.00
Army Set, 20 flat soldiers, tin windup
  tank, tin cannon, wood
  bullets 200.00
Crazy Express Train Set, 2-5/8" x
  2-7/8" x 12-1/2" red, white, and
  blue box, silver plastic engine,
  three color tin litho cars, each
  marked "Crazy Express,"
  c1960................................. 75.00
Disneyland Jeep, Mickey, Donald,
  and gang pictured on body,
  steering wheel missing, wear,
  1950s, 9" l........................ 150.00
Electric Lightrucks, diecast, red
  body, two-tone blue plastic trailer,
  copyright 1969, orig box 15.00

Jumpin' Jeep, tin windup, $125.

Farm Set, mechanical tractor and
  mower, 1940s, orig box.....275.00
Give-A-Show Projector, 23 reels,
  MIB 40.00
Jumpin Jeep, litho tin wind-up, four
  soldier heads, machine guns and
  rifle lithographed on Jeep, 1930s,
  MIB 390.00
Old Jalopy, litho tin wind-up, Model T
  Ford, zany sayings, 1930s,
  MIB 390.00
Power House Dump Truck, steel,
  beige cargo area, blue-green cab,
  7" x 18" x 7", orig box..........85.00
Tiger on Trike, litho tin windup,
  MIB 145.00
Truck, Hi-Way Express, blue
  cap 225.00
Whiz Racer 70.00

☆ Matchbox Toys

Matchbox toys were created by Lesney in 1953. The name reflected the idea that there was a miniature toy packed in a box that resembled a matchbox. The toys were first exported to America from England in 1958 and were an instant success.

Collectors' Clubs: Matchbox Collectors Club, PO Box 977, Newfield, NJ 08344; Matchbox U.S.A., 62 Saw Mill Road, Durham, CT 06422; The Matchbox International Collectors Association, PO Box 28072, Waterloo, Ontario, Canada N2L6J8.

Bluebird Camping Trailer,
  2-1/2" l 24.00
Canteen Truck, 2-1/2" l 22.00
Dodge Daytona Turbo, 1994.....1.00
Ferrari F40, 1988 ....1.00
Ford Bronco, 1987 ....1.00
Ford Escort 1.00
Ford Transit, 1978....................2.00
International Ltd. Trailer, 1979 ..2.00
Jaguar 50.00
Jennings Cattle Truck, 4-1/2" l, no
  back gate 30.00
Korean Airlines Airbus, Sky Busters,
  1988, 4-1/4" l, 3-1/2" wingspan,
  MOC 35.00

Super King K16/18 Series Tractor, 1973, 8" l, $10.

Minnie Mouse Car, Walt Disney Productions, 1970s, MOC 50.00
Nissan 300 ZX Turbo, 1986 ...... 1.00
Pontiac Firebird SE, 1982 .... 1.00
Rig, 1993, NRFP 6.00
Scammel 6 x 6 Tractor, mkd "Pickford" on side, 2-1/2" l 40.00
Tailgator, 1994 .... 1.00
Train Car, green, 1978 .... 28.00
Wells Fargo Truck, #69, 1978 .... 24.00

❖ Matchcovers

Matchcovers have been on the scene since the early 1900s, but any before the 1930s are considered to be scarce. Collectors in this area are highly organized and have a great deal of fun trading and scouting for new matchcovers to expand their collections.

Collectors' Clubs: Rathkamp Matchcover Society, 1359 Surrey Rd., Vandalia, OH 45377; The American Matchcover Collecting Club, PO Box 18481, Asheville, NC 28814.

Baltimore Orioles, 1970s 3.75
Cam Stewart, Georgia, World War II 2.50
Capt Stearns Restaurant, Atlantic City, orig matches, pr 15.00
Champion Spark Plugs, 1930s 2.00
Fred Harvey Restaurant, 1930s 2.00
Holland Hotel, Duluth, MN, 1930s 2.00
Howard Johnson, front strike, unused 7.00

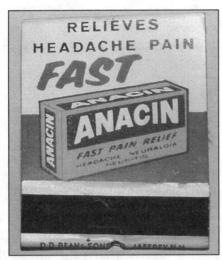

Anacin/ Dristan, $1.

Iowa Premium Pilsner Beer 8.00
Karlsbrau Beer, 1930s 2.00
Palace Clubereno 2.75
Reddy Kilowatt 4.00
Roland Falk Billiards, 1930s 4.25
Squadron Insignia, Alternate Aviation Arm, *U.S.S. Carolina,* WWII, Disney design of Fantasia's Baby Pegasus water skiing, Pepsi-Cola adv, slight wear 18.00

❖ Match Holders and Match Safes

Matches were a precious commodity many years ago. Care was taken to keep matches dry, yet handy. Match holders can be found in almost every medium and range from table or mantel top containers to wall containers. Match safes are small containers used to safely carry matches in a pocket. Many are figural and can be found in many metals. Expect to find a striking surface on some match safes.

Collectors' Club: International Match Safe Association, PO Box 791, Malaga, NJ 08328.

Match Holder

Advertising, Sharples Separator Co., tin, mother and daughter, farm scene 90.00

Bisque, rooster, beige basket, two compartments, round base 145.00
Cast Iron, high button shoe, black paint, c1890 .... 50.00
Commemorative, Reading, Pennsylvania Fire Hall, brass, celluloid insert, early 1900s 55.00
Majolica, monk, hairline in base 30.00
Porcelain, seated girl, feeding dog at table 125.00
Torquay Pottery, ship scene, mkd "A match for any Man, Shankin" 70.00

Match Safe

Advertising, Davenport Cigars, cigar shape, tin, red, white, and blue celluloid dec 65.00
Brass
 Scallop Shell, 2" l 145.00
 Walnut 200.00
Commemorative, Hudson-Fulton Celebration, 1909 .... 75.00
Nickel-plated, shoe 125.00
Pewter, pig, silvered 175.00
Silver-plated, playing card deck, King of Hearts, 2 score keeping dials, mkd "Gorham" 225.00

❖ McCoy

The J. W. McCoy Pottery was started in Roseville, OH, in 1899. Their first wares were stoneware and some art pottery. In 1911, three area potteries, Brush, J. W. McCoy and Nelson McCoy Sanitary Stoneware Co. merged, creating the Brush-McCoy Pottery Co. Fine pottery was produced for many years.

Reproduction Alert.

For additional listings, see *Warman's Antiques and Collectibles Price Guide* and *Warman's American Pottery and Porcelain.*

Bank, Centennial Bear, sgd, numbered 110.00
Clock, Jug Time, 7" h, c1924, small chip, not running 200.00
Cookie Jar, Cottage 120.00
Cornucopia, yellow 20.00

Decanter, missile 45.00
Figurine, lion 65.00
Lamp Base, 11-1/2" h, tulip motif, mkd
  "JW McCoy-Loy-Nel-Art" 150.00

Planter
  Duck and egg, yellow 30.00
  Old car................................20.00

Vase
  Brocade, green....................25.00
  Cylindrical, applied pink flower,
    6-1/2" h 38.00
  Lily, single flower, three leaves,
    7-1/2" h 42.00

Vase, Hyacinth, 8-1/4" h, $100.

Flowerpot with attached saucer, yellow, 4-5/8" h, 5-3/8" d, $22.

Wall Pocket
  Basketweave 80.00
  Butterfly, white 150.00
  Iron Trivet 40.00
  Lily 70.00
Wren House........................ 145.00

❖ McDonald's

Perhaps it's the sight of those golden arches, or the growling from your tummy that causes many of us to head to McDonald's for a quick bite and perhaps something to add to our collections.

Periodical: *Collecting Tips Newsletter,* PO Box 633, Joplin, MO 64802.

Collectors' Club: McDonald's Collectors Club, 255 New Lenox Road, Lenox, MA 01240.

Cup Holder, dark blue, orig
  package................................ 3.50
Doll, Hamburglar, played-with
  condition 15.00
Employee Cap, 12-1/2" x 11-1/2",
  flattened unused service cap,
  blue cardboard headband with
  yellow arch symbol on each side,
  white mesh open crown,
  mid-1960s.......................... 15.00
Happy Meal Prize, Genie and building 5, from Aladdin and the King
  of Thieves, MIB 4.00

Plastic plate, "Ronald McDonald Saves This Hot Summer Day...While Ol' Captain Crook Stays Safely Away!," 10" d, $3.50.

Happy Meal Box Proof Sheet, 18-
  1/4" x 23-3/4" white stiff paper
  printer's proof, full color image in
  center, four-sided box design fea-
  turing Muppet Babies characters,
  Egyptian theme, copyright 1986
  McDonald's Corp, unfolded
  .... 15.00
Map, Ronald McDonald Map of the
  Moon, 1969.......................... 7.50
Patch, cloth, red, white, blue, and
  yellow stitching, Ronald
  McDonald............................. 2.00
Puppet, hand, plastic, Ronald
  McDonald, c1977................. 2.00
Space Packet, MIP 16.00
Valentines, strip of 6 different
  valentines, 1978................... 3.00

❖ McKee Glass

Founded by the McKee Brothers in 1853, this glassware company continued production until 1961. The products it created include pattern glass, depression-era glass, kitchen and household wares.

Batter Bowl, jade-ite 45.00
Bottoms Up Tumbler, orig coaster,
  Patent #77725, light
  emerald............................. 175.00
Candlesticks, pr, custard, Laurel
  pattern................................ 35.00
Creamer, custard 24.00
Dresser Tray, milk glass.......... 35.00
Egg Cup, custard 8.50
Pitcher, Wild Rose and Bowknot,
  frosted, gilt dec 75.00

Range Shaker
  Lady, salt, pepper, flour, and
    sugar 135.00
  Roman Arch, custard, blue dots,
    salt, pepper, flour, and
    sugar 135.00

Coffee canister with lid, green, 5-1/8" h, $85.

Salt and Pepper Shakers, pr
    Amethyst, orig tops, some
        wear 24.00
    Custard, Laurel pattern 42.00
Sandwich Server, center handle,
    Rock Crystal, red.............. 165.00
Tumbler, Seville Yellow........... 17.50

❖ Medals

One way to honor a hero was to present him with a medal. Many of these were passed down through families as a treasured memento. Other types of medals are commemorative in nature.

American Legion, 1-1/4" d 8.00
Armed Forces Reserve, bar and rib-
    bon, orig card, 1-1/4" d....... 28.00
Battle of Vera Cruz, 1914, Schwaab
    & Co., Milwaukee 25.00
Camden, NJ, 12th Grand Prome-
    nade, American Legion,
    1932 .... 12.00
Conn Lodge 37, Knights of Pythias,
    name on back..................... 38.00
Drill Corps 1944, York Comy, New
    York, name on back, mkd
    "Sterling" 28.00
Efficiency, Honor, Fidelity on front,
    back "For Good Conduct,"
    1-1/4" d.............................. 16.00
For Merit, Army Air Forces, attached
    bar pin, mkd "Sterling" 35.00

United States of America Meritorious Service medal, cased, $37.

For Merit, 500 Hours, Army Air
    Forces, attached bar pin, mkd
    "Sterling" 38.00
For Merit, 1000 Hours, Army Air
    Forces, attached bar pin, mkd
    "Sterling" 38.00
Heroic or Meritorious Achievement,
    medal of honor, ribbon........ 12.00
Kodak Movie Awards, bronze, emb
    "Sponsored in Cooperation with
    UFF/UFPA and CINE," made by
    Medallic Art Co., NY, orig box,
    3" d 18.00
Official Hawaii Statehood, Medallic
    Art Co., silver, uncirculated,
    2-1/2" d.............................. 80.00
US Army, American-German War,
    2-1/2" l 65.00
United States Forces, cross with
    eagle, "1917-1918 United States
    Forces," back reads "Presented
    by the people of Williamsburg,
    Mass to (name) in grateful recog-
    nition of patriotic service in the
    World War 1917-1918," 1-1/4" x
    1-1/4" 35.00

❖ Medical Items

Ouch! Collectors of medical items don't tend to be squeamish as they search flea markets for new items to add to their collections. Some folks

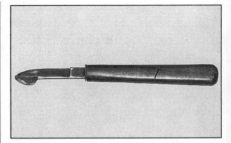

Bleeder, mkd "R. Best Sheffield England," wooden handle, 6-1/8" l, $30.

concentrate on medical apparatus and instruments, while others concentrate on other aspects of the medical profession or related ephemera.

Alcohol Burner, brass,
    sterilizer 45.00
Book, *The Physician Hand Book,
    1879,* leather bound..........500.00
Box, Dr. Greene's Nervura Nerva
    Tonic, wood, black paint, sten-
    ciled name and dec.............75.00
Capsule Filler, Sharpe and Dohme,
    chrome, orig wood box and
    instruction book, 1920s.....150.00
Counter Display, Kolynos Dental
    Cream, window type, baby reach-
    ing for tubes of product..... 115.00
Display Case, Dr. Frost's Homeo-
    pathic Remedies Build Health,
    wood, stained, litho tin door
    panel, lists 38 ailment
    remedies 475.00
Dosage Glass, Royal Pepsi Stom-
    ach Bitters, c1900, clear
    glass 40.00
Manual, *Johnson's First Aid Manual,*
    1919, 8th ed.......................24.00
Pin, 1" d, metal, "AMA, June 11-15,
    1951, Atlantic City" 12.00
Red Cross Sterilized Gauze,
    Johnson & Johnson, sealed
    box 8.00
Stethoscope, metal 125.00

❖ Meissen

Meissen is a fine porcelain that has a long and interesting history. Briefly, the original factory goes back to 1710 in Saxony, Germany. Through the years, decorating techniques were developed that led to beautiful creations that are eagerly sought by collectors today. Each period of the Meissen story has different styles, colors, and influences. Today the factory still operates, making new models as well as some true to the older styles.

There are many marks that have been used by Meissen over the years. Learning how to read these marks and understand the time period they represent will enhance a collector's knowledge of this lovely porcelain.

Reproduction Alert.

For additional listings and background information, see *Warman's English & Continental Pottery and Porcelain* and *Warman's Antiques and Collectibles Price Guide.*

Ashtray, Onion pattern, blue crossed swords mark, 5" d............... 80.00
Bread and Butter Plate, Onion pattern, 6-1/2" d.................. 75.00
Dessert Dish, painted red rose and foliage center, bouquets at corners, c1770 .... 225.00
Dessert Plate, floral dec, 20th C, 7" d, price for 4 pc set 50.00
Figure, young man and woman gathering eggs from under tree, white glaze, blue crossed swords mark, late 19th C.............. 275.00
Hot Plate, Onion pattern, handles............................ 125.00

Cup, floral design, rope-twist and stick handle, mkd "KPM," 2-3/4" h, $5.

Teabowl and Saucer, 3 purple flowers, green leaves, early 19th C, chip.................................... 325.00
Urn, white, gilt trim, two delicate snake-form handles, price for pair 500.00
Vase, 3" h, floral dec, 20th C................................ 80.00
Vegetable Dish, cov, Onion pattern, 10" w, sq 150.00

✴ Melmac

Melmac is a trade name associated with thermoset plastic dinnerware made by American Cyanamid. First introduced for commercial use, Melmac became popular with housewives in the 1950s. Collectors today are searching for interesting colors, shapes, and pieces in very good condition.

Collectors' Club: Melmac Collectors Club, 6802 Glenkirk Road, Baltimore, MD 21239.

Child's Set, bunny dec, 8-1/4" plate, 6-1/2" d cereal bowl, 4-3/4" dessert bowl, Oneida, used........ 8.00
Creamer and Sugar, blue, mkd "Made in Canada," 3" h 17.50
Magazine Advertisement, Boonton Ware, Melmac Dishes Guaranteed Against Breakage, 8-1/2" x 11" 2.00
Platter, 13-3/4" x 9-3/4", N416, pink...................................... 8.00
Set
    Avocado cups, fruit bowls, bread plates, white saucers, service for 8 .... 20.00
    Shasta Daisy pattern, dinner plates, salad plates, cereal bowls, cups and saucers, Texas Ware, service for 6 .... 60.00
    Wall Pocket, sq gray saucer as backplate, green cup as pocket, mkd "Maherware, 2, Made in USA" 10.00

❖ Metlox Pottery

The story of Metlox Pottery is one of a company formed to make one

product in the Depression that succeeded because it reorganized and became a pottery company. Up to World War II, dinnerware was produced at its Manhattan Beach plant. But during the war, the factory was again retooled to make machine parts and parts for B-52 bombers. After the war, dinnerware production began again along with some artware. Production continued until 1989.

For additional listings and history, see *Warman's Americana & Collectibles* and *Warman's American Pottery & Porcelain.*

Bowl
    Ivy, 5-1/2" d........................20.00
    Sculptured Grape, 8-1/2" d. 16.00
Bread Server, California Provincial 60.00
Casserole, cov, Sculptured Grape, 1 qt......................................50.00
Cereal Bowl, Sculptured Daisy...................................12.00
Chop Plate
    Palm.....................................10.00
    Rose-A-Day 8.00
Creamer
    Rose-A-Day 10.00
    Sculptured Grape................15.00
Cup and Saucer
    California Provincial............17.50
    Sculptured Grape................10.00
Cup, Poppytrail Homestead Provincial 4.25
Dinner Plate, Della Robbia........8.00

Platter, Homestead Provincial, 10-1/8" x 13-1/2", $36.

Dinner Service, California Ivy,
47 pc set............................ 330.00
Gravy, attached underplate,
Sculptured Grape 27.50
Miniature, White House, orig
sticker............................... 175.00
Mustard Jar, Red Rooster....... 48.00
Place Setting, Liberty Blue,
5 pc 35.00
Platter, Provincial Rose 70.00
Salad Bowl, California
Strawberry........................... 55.00
Salad Plate, Sculptured Grape,
7-1/2" d................................. 8.00
Salt and Pepper Shakers, pr,
Sammy Seal......................... 75.00
Soup Bowl, Camellia
California 17.50
Sugar, cov, Sculptured
Grape 22.00
Vegetable Bowl, divided,
Rose-A-Day......................... 10.00

❖ Mettlach

Most collectors think of steins when they hear the name "Mettlach," but this German company produced other fine pottery, including plates, plaques, bowls, teapots, etc. One of their hallmarks is underglaze printing on earthenware, using transfers from copper plates. Designs can also be relief and etched decorations and cameos. Pieces of Mettlach are well marked, showing the company name, and sometimes a shape name or that of the decorator.

Periodical: *Beer Stein Journal,* PO Box 8807, Coral Springs, FL 33075.

Collectors' Clubs: Stein Collectors International, 281 Shore Drive, Burr Ridge, IL 60521; Sun Steiners, PO Box 11782, Fort Lauderdale, FL 33339.

Coaster, #1264, girl on swing and
boy on bicycle, print under glaze,
5" d, one chipped 260.00
Plaque
#1044-542, portrait of man, blue
delft dec, 12" d 125.00
#1108, incised castle, gilt rim,
c1902, 17" d..................230.00

Stein
#1027, half liter, relief, beige, rust,
green, inlaid lid, floral and face
dec 215.00
#2057, half liter, etched, festive
dancing scene, inlaid
lid................................... 325.00
#2755, quarter liter, cameo and
etched, 3 scenes of people, Art
Nouveau design between
scenes, inlaid lid........... 560.00
#2833B, half liter 350.00
Vase, #1808, stoneware, incised foliage dec, 10" h, price for matched
pair 230.00

❖ Microscopes

Microscopes are part of the scientific collecting that is really taking off. If considering the purchase of a microscope, check to see that all the necessary parts are included and remember that the value will be enhanced by any original documentation, boxes, slides, etc.

Collectors' Club: Maryland Microscopical Society, 8261 Polk St., McLean, VA 22102.

Binocular, 18-1/2" h, mounted on
case board, 12-1/4" l binocular
tubes, single focus for both tubes,
fine focus on eyep. End, rect
mechanical stage on 4-3/8" d
rotating stage with degree scale
to 1/2º, gimballed mirror yoke,
lacquered brass, T. W. Watson, 4
Pall Mall, London, No. 287, "H. B.
Gelb," 1879....................... 750.00
Cary Type, 7" h, rack and pinion
focus of 2" d glass stage, vert.
and horiz. adjustable lens holder,
3 lenses, single mirror, dissecting
knife and tweezers, lacquered
brass, mahogany case,
c1875............................... 750.00
Compound Monocular
12" h, 8-1/4" l, 1-1/8" d tube with 1
obj. fine focus on arm, 3-1/2" d
stage with condenser and diaphragm, double mirror on calibrated rotating arm, japanned
and lacquered brass, case,
extra obj., mkd "3373,"
c1885 .... 575.00

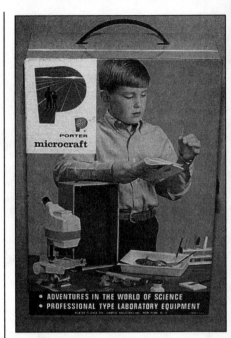

Porter Microcraft child's microscope, tin case, early 1970s, case 14" h, 9-1/2" w, 4-3/4" d, $15.

12" h, 8-1/2" l, 1-1/8" d tube with
1 obj. fine focus on arm, rect
stage, 5 hole diaphragm, double mirror on rotating arm,
extra eyepiece, orig case,
japanned and lacquered brass,
sgd "Wm. H. Armstrong Co.,
Indianapolis, Ind., #11737,"
c1893............................ 635.00
13-3/4" h, 9-5/8" l, 1-1/8" d tube
with single obj, rack and pinion
focus, rect table, 4 hole diaphragm, single mirror, 1 eyep.,
2 obj., japanned and lacquered
brass, case, Bausch & Lomb
Optical Co., Rochester, NY,
#1761, c1882............. 1,100.00
Folding Compound Monocular, 10-
1/4" h, 6-1/4" l x 1-1/2" d tube, triple nosepiece, micrometer drum
fine focus on arm, calibrated draw
tube, rect stage, condenser, double mirror, japanned and lacquered brass, heavy metal case,
Spencer, Buffalo, c1900.... 750.00

❖ Militaria

Throughout history men have been marching off to war. Those who return often bring home mementos of their travels. Years later, these treasures end up at flea markets, where eager collectors find them.

References: There are many good reference books available on all periods of military history.

Periodicals: *Men at Arms*, 222 W Exchange St, Providence, RI 02903; *Militaria Magazine*, PO Box 995, Southbury, CT 06488; *Military Collector Magazine*, PO Box 245, Lyon Station, PA 19536; *Military Collector News*, PO Box 702073, Tulsa, OK 74170; *Military Images*, RD1 Box 99A, Henryville, PA 18332; *Military Trader*, PO Box 1050, Dubuque, IA 52004; *North South Trader's Civil War*, PO Box Drawer 631, Orange, VA 22960; *Wildcat Collectors Journal*, 15158 NE 6th Ave, Miami, FL 33162; *WWII Military Journal*, PO Box 28906, San Diego, CA 92198.

Collectors' Clubs: American Society of Military Insignia Collectors, 526 Lafayette Ave, Palmerton, PA 18071; Association of American Military Uniform Collectors, PO Box 1876, Elyria, OH 44036; Company of Military Historians, North Main St, Westbrook, CT, 06498; Imperial German Military Collectors Association, 82 Atlantic St, Keyport, NJ 07735; Karabiner Collector's Network, PO Box 5773, High Point, NC 27262; Militaria Collectors Society, 137 S Almar Dr, Ft Lauderdale, FL 33334; Orders and Medals Society of America, PO Box 484, Glassboro, NJ 08028.

Reproduction Alert.

For additional listings, see *Warman's Antiques and Collectibles Price Guide* and specific topics in this edition.

Army Blanket, wool, slight use 15.00
Bayonet, Model 1873, 3-1/2" w blade, Indian War 80.00
Cabinet Card, Mathew Brady, No. 395, Shipping 1st Conn. Siege train at Yorktown, Union soldiers loading supplies on ship... 350.00
Cartridge Box, leather, white cloth strap, very worn, missing plate, War of 1812 .... 75.00

World War I corpsman's bag, cloth, 10-3/4" x 11", $10.

Bumper sticker, Go Navy, 2-7/8" x 9", $2.

Coat, Air Force, leather, brown, size 46 .... 200.00
Coffee Mug, ironstone, Marine insignia 10.00
Flag, wool, 34 stars, Civil War era, 48" x 108" 1,150.00
Pennant, Army-Navy Game, felt, c1950.................................... 5.00
Postcard, Naval Academy, c1960.................................... 2.00
Snuff Box, gutta percha, round, relief scene of battle, ships, coastline, buildings, French inscription "Prise d'Yorck 1781," Battle of Yorktown........................... 750.00
Spy Glass, pocket, brass, Naval, round holder, brown leather grip, 16" l 115.00
Tie Rack, World War I............. 12.00
Trivet, ceramic tile in metal frame, West Point 20.00

❖ Milk Bottles

Before the advent of paper and plastic containers, milk was sold in glass bottles. Today's flea markets often contain great examples of different sizes and designs. Keep your eyes open for interesting slogans.

Periodical: *The Udder Collectibles*, HC73 Box 1, Smithville Flats, NY 13841.

Collectors' Club: National Association of Milk Bottle Collectors, Inc., 4 Ox Bow Road, Westport, CT 06880.

Blue Bell Farms, Irvington, NJ, quart, round, orange pyro, Cop-the Cream 150.00
Borden's, name in script above Elsie, quart, squatty, red pyro 20.00
Cream top, generic, quart, sq, dish of ice cream, green and orange................................ 15.00
Dairylea, quart, sq, red, Miss Dairylea, fruits and vegetables illus...................................... 17.50
Empire State Dairy Co., Brooklyn, half pint, round, emb, state seal in frame................................... 12.00
Hoods, quart, round, cow in framed log, red pyro........................ 15.00

Borden's, Gail Borden Signature Quality Milk, amber, 2 qts, $12.50.

Model Farms, Milford, PA, half pint, round, emb in slug plate, Raw Milk 15.00

Palmerton Sanitary Dairy, Palmerton, PA, quart, sq, emb, cream top 12.50

Universal Store Bottle, 5¢ deposit, quart, round, emb 10.00

❖ Milk Glass

Milk glass is an opaque white bodied glass. This type of glass was made by many manufacturers and saw its heyday early in the century, when interesting patterns of tablewares and accessories were made. In the early 1960s, milk glass again became fashionable as a few companies again produced it.

References: There are several older reference books that collectors still use to determine makers and pattern names.

Collectors' Club: National Milk Glass Collectors Society, 46 Almond Drive, Hershey, PA 17033.

Animal Covered Dish
  Hen, basketweave base 175.00
  Setter Dog, sgd "Flaccus," repair to lid 150.00
Bowl, Daisy, allover leaves and flower dec, open scalloped edge, 8-1/4" d.............................. 85.00
Celery Vase, Blackberry, scalloped rim, 6-5/8" h.......................115.00

Cake stand, cherry blossom decor, 5-7/8" h, 9-1/8" d, $50.

Plate, 3 foxes reading book, hp green, brown and gold, 7-1/8" d, $28.50.

Creamer and Sugar, Trumpet Vine, fire painted dec, sgd "SV" 135.00
Easter Egg, emb chick............ 60.00
Jar, cov, owl, figural 45.00
Mug, Ivy in Snow 45.00
Spooner, Monkey, scalloped rim 140.00
Tumbler, Royal Oak, fire painted dec, green band 50.00

❖ Miniature Bottles

Flea markets are great places to find these clever bottles. Often they are samples or designed to be single servings for restaurant or commercial use.

Acme Beer, stubby, decal 6.50
Budweiser, stubby, paper label 17.50
Carstairs, lipstick shaped, 1950s.................................... 8.00
Fort Pitt Beer, stubby 3.00
Gold Bond Beer 20.00
Hamms Preferred 5.00
Maple Farms, VT, maple syrup..................................... 1.00
Old Dutch, stubby 24.00
Tavern Pale............................ 12.00

❖ Miniatures

The world of tiny objects keeps fascinating collectors. Some are attracted to the craftsmanship of these tiny treasures, while others are interested in finding examples to display. Keep scale in mind when purchasing miniatures for use in a doll house.

Periodicals: *Doll Castle News*, PO Box 247, Washington, NJ 07882; *Miniature Collector*, Scott Publications, 30595 Eight Mile Rd, Livonia, MI 48152; *Nutshell News*, 21027 Crossroads Circle, PO Box 1612, Waukesha, WI 53187.

Collectors' Clubs: International Guild Miniature Artisans, PO Box 71, Bridgeport, NY 18080; Miniature Industry Association of America Member News, 2270 Jacquelyn Dr, Madison, WI 53711; National Association of Miniature Enthusiasts, 2621 Anaheim, CA 92804-3883.

Armoire, tin litho, purple and black 35.00
Bed, four poster, mahogany stain, hand made..........................40.00
Bird Cage, brass, stand, 7" h 70.00
Blanket Chest, 6 board construction, old worn paint dec.............200.00
Christmas Tree, decorated......50.00
Desk, Chippendale style, slant front, working drawers..................65.00
Sofa, porcelain and metal 35.00
Stove, Royal, complete 120.00
Table, tin, painted brown, white top, floral design 35.00
Umbrella Stand, brass, ormolu, sq, emb palm fronds 65.00
Wash Bowl and Pitcher, cobalt blue glass, minor chips.............275.00

Tea service, Britannia metal, teapot, creamer, 4 cups and saucers, $72.

❖ Mirrors

Mirror, mirror on the wall… Mirrors are something we all depend on, and many of us use them as decorative accents in our homes and offices. Flea markets are a great source to find interesting examples in almost every decorating style.

Art Deco, wall, carved fruit and foliage at crest and on sides, 31" l, 41-1/2" h 95.00
Art Nouveau, hand held, sterling silver, monogrammed 115.00
Arts and Crafts, wall, shaped cutouts, center rect mirror, scalloped details, orig paper label "Michigan Chair Co., Grand Rapids, MI," c1915 .... 150.00
Bentwood, walnut, arched top, gilt liner, replaced mirror, 32" l 200.00
Chippendale, wall, walnut veneer, scroll, old mirror, 26" x 15-3/4" 375.00
Empire
    Pier, mahogany, rect mirror plate, carved leaf and ring and block turned frame, 21" w, 35" h..............................325.00
    Wall, flame mahogany, ogee molded frame, rect mirror plate, c1850, 27-1/2" w, 37" h .. 195.00
George III Style, wall, walnut, gilt phoenix and liner, carved and scrolling frieze, 24" x 45" 400.00
Hepplewhite, shaving, stand with round mirror frame, arm to hold shaving brush, orig mirror with some silvering damage 300.00

Hand mirror, 2-tone plastic, lace and floral pattern, beveled glass, 14-3/4" x 4-3/4", $8.

Sheraton, wall, architectural type, gilded frame, eglomise reverse glass painting, orig mirror glass discolored, replaced painting, old regilding, some flakes, 41-1/4" h, 23-3/4" w 775.00
Victorian, hand held, silver plated, emb florals and hearts 75.00

❖ Model Kits

Model kits have been on the collecting scene since the 1930s. Early kits tended to be scale models. Later model kits were created in plastics or cast resin and soon encompassed many characters as well as the airplanes and cars that most associate with model kits.

Collectors' Clubs: International Figure Kit Club, PO Box 201, Sharon Center, OH, 44274; Kit Collectors International, PO Box 38, Stanton, CA 90680.

Apollo 11, Young Model Builders Club, Aurora, MIB 45.00
Batman, Aurora, 1964, MIB 375.00
Copperhead Rear Engine Dragster, AMT, MIB 30.00
Corvette, MPC, 1985, MIB...... 15.00

The Fonz and His Bike, MPC, $25.

Dodge Touchtone Terror Pick-Up, IMC, MIB..............................60.00
Goofy Klock, Lindberg, 1960s, MIB 80.00
Huey Attack Helicopter, Revell, 1969, MIB 30.00
PT Boat 211, Young Model Builders Club, Revell, 1974, MIB......40.00
Sebring Sports Roadster, Hawk, partially built, 1962..............15.00

❖ Monroe, Marilyn

Marilyn Monroe was a model-turned-actress who captured the hearts of movie goers in the 1950s. Her tragic life has been the subject of numerous magazine articles, television shows, etc.

Collectors' Club: All About Marilyn, PO box 291176, Los Angeles, CA 90029.

Bust, 20-1/2" h, life size, flesh tones, bright red lips, front inscribed "Marilyn Monroe," c1954, some wear to paint 325.00
Calendar, 1974, orig envelope 30.00
Car, 1955 Cadillac, white, image of Marilyn on hood and both doors, 12" l....................................50.00
Commemorative Coin, Marilyn on one side, Joe DiMaggio on other, 1-1/2" d 10.00
Cookie Jar..............................50.00
Doll, emerald evening gown, Collector's Series, MIB 25.00
Magazine, article and photos
    Avant Garde, #2, March, 1968 ....70.00
    Coronet, Feb 1961..............16.00
    Eye, August 1955 ....14.50
    Look, July 5, 1960...............25.00
    Picture Scope, March 1958 ....16.00
    Tempo, July, 1953...............10.00
Movie Bill, Blue Moon Theater, Blue Mound, Kansas, *Gentlemen Prefer Blondes,* plus other current movies, Oct 1954, 9" x 11" 15.00
Salt and Pepper Shakers, pr...20.00

❖ Monsters

Perhaps it was those Saturday afternoon matinees, or those science-fiction books we read as kids that have caused many collectors to seek out monster-related memorabilia. And, these lucky folks are finding many examples of their favorite demons at flea markets.

Reference: Dana Cain, *Collecting Monsters of Film and TV,* Krause Publications, 1997.

Periodical: *Toy Shop,* 700 E. State Street, Iola, WI 54990.

Action Figure, Frankenstein,
 MOC 140.00
Book, *Dracula,* New English Library, Times Mirror, Vol. 1, No. 1.,
 9" x 11-1/2", full color, comic book format, 20 pgs, orig poster
 inside 18.00
Cigarette Lighter, Godzilla,
 MOC 125.00
Halloween Costume, Attack of the Killer Tomatoes, Collegeville,
 1991, MIB 30.00
Lighter, Godzilla, c1984,
 MOC 48.00
Model, Dracula, Aurora, 1972,
 MIB 195.00
Pop-Up Book, *Nightmare Before Christmas* 30.00
Pulp Magazine, *Amazing Stories,* May 1931, features Alien ... 48.00

GAF View-Master reel No. J23, Godzilla in "Godzilla's Rampage", 1978, $12.50.

Puzzle, Frankenstein Jr., Whitman,
 1968 .... 35.00
Snow Dome, Creature from the Black Lagoon, MIB 25.00
Soakie, Wolfman 75.00
Toy, Planet of the Apes, tree house,
 orig box 45.00
View-Master Reel, Godzilla, set of 3, orig booklet, 1978 .... 12.50

★ Moon and Stars

This popular glassware pattern has its origins in America's pattern glass industry with a pattern made by John Adams & Co., Pittsburgh, PA, about 1880. Today's collectors are treated to new colors and variations because of the work of Tom and John Weishar of Island Mould, Wheeling, WV. Joseph Weishar started reproducing pieces in the 1960s from a few original items. Since 1988, about 30 to 40 pieces have been made in this pattern. Some reproductions were also made by L. E. Smith, but those are unmarked. Weishar Enterprises now marks its new Moon & Star items.

Reference: George and Linda Breeze, *A Collector's Guide To Moon & Star.*

Ashtray, amberina 20.00
Compote, period, clear 120.00
Creamer and Sugar, amber 40.00
Cruet, blue 45.00
Dinner Plate, clear, late 15.00
Goblet, clear 20.00

Covered dish, red, 7-7/16" h, $32.

Sherbet, clear, late 15.00
Tumbler, blue, late................... 17.50
Vase, amber 20.00
Wine, period 35.00

❖ Morgantown Glass

Based in Morgantown, West Virginia, this hand made glass manufacturer created lovely tablewares and household items. The colors produced by Morgantown are bright and clear. Morgantown introduced several innovative techniques and forms.

Collectors' Club: Old Morgantown Glass Collectors' Guild, PO Box 894, Morgantown, WV 26507.

For additional listings, see *Warman's Antiques and Collectibles Price Guide* and *Warman's Glass.*

Champagne
 Jockey, crystal 50.00
 Monroe, red and crystal 35.00
Claret, Golf Ball, red............... 75.00
Cocktail
 Chanticleer, Copen blue 35.00
 Golf Ball, Stiegel Green 35.00
 Majestic, red and crystal 32.50
Cordial
 Mayfair, crystal 35.00
 Plantation, cobalt blue 145.00
Goblet
 Golf Ball, red 42.50
 Virginia, crystal 24.50
High Ball, Mexicana, ice,
 5" h 115.00
Ivy Ball, Golf Ball, red, 4" w 95.00
Night Set, Trudy Baby, blue
 opaque............................. 125.00
Parfait, Golf Ball, cobalt
 blue 125.00
Plate, Mexicana, Ice, 6" d 18.00
Tumbler, American Beauty, crystal,
 3-3/4" h 45.00
Wine
 Old English, Spanish red 35.00
 Plantation, cobalt blue 125.00

❖ Mortens Studios

Collectors identify the name Mortens Studios with fine-crafted porcelain dog figurines.

Borzoi, #749 .... 145.00
Boxer Puppy, sitting 20.00
Collie, recumbent, brown and off-
    white, 7-1/2" l, 4" h 185.00
Dachshund 65.00
Fox Terrier 185.00
Irish Setter, #856 .... 115.00
Kerry Blue Terrier 85.00
Pointer, #851 .... 120.00
Pug, #738 .... 145.00
Puppy, yellow 35.00
Spaniel, black and white, minor
    glaze chips 80.00
Terrier, sitting 45.00

❖ Morton Potteries

Morton Pottery Works was established in Morton, Illinois, in 1922. Production of dinnerware, earthenware, and table accessories were made there until 1976. They also specialized in kitchenwares and novelties for chain stores and gift shops.

Bank, hen, hand painted dec,
    4" h 38.50

Cookie Jar
    Basket of fruit 55.00
    Hen, chick finial, white, black
        wash dec 165.00
    Panda, black and white 85.00

Night Light
    Old woman in a shoe, yellow and
        red 45.00
    Teddy bear, brown glaze, hand
        painted dec 50.00

Planter
    Covered Wagon, separate oxen,
        set 70.00
    Rabbit, umbrella, blue
        egg 20.00
    Salt and Pepper Shakers, pr, chicks,
        white, black wash, pr 115.00
    Toothpick Holder, chick, white, black
        wash 60.00

Planter, red glaze, 4-1/8" d, 2-7/8" h, $12.

❖ Moss Rose Pattern

Several English and American pottery companies made this pretty pattern. It's easily identified by its pink rose bud and leaves. Some pieces also have gold trim.

Butter Pat, sq, mkd
    "Meakin" 25.00
Cake Plate, two emb
    handles 40.00
Creamer and Sugar, mkd "Haviland,
    Limoges" 150.00
Cup and Saucer, mkd "Haviland,
    Limoges" 30.00
Dinner Plate, 9-1/2" d, mkd
    "Haviland" 25.00
Gravy Boat, matching underplate,
    mkd "Green Co.,
    England" 35.00
Nappy, 4-1/2" d, mkd
    "Edwards" 18.50
Sauce Dish, 4-1/2" d, mkd
    "Haviland" 20.00
Teapot, bulbous, gooseneck spout,
    basketweave trim, mkd
    "T & V" 95.00

✴ Mother's Day Collectibles

Here's a holiday one had better not forget! The first Mother's Day celebration was held in Philadelphia, PA,

in 1907, but it wasn't until 1914 that it became a national observance. Most of us think of cards, flowers, and candy as the traditional Mother's Day gifts, but there are also ornaments, limited edition collector plates, etc. And, let's give the florists credit for creating some pretty arrangements in containers that are now dated and will become collectible too.

Limited Edition Plate
    Bing and Grondahl, H. Thelander,
        artist, 1971, Hare and Young,
        6" d 40.00
    Precious Moments, Samuel J.
        Butcher, "Mother's Day 1990,"
        4" d 7.00
    Schmid Bro., Sister Berta Hummel, "Devotion for Mother,"
        1976 .... 32.50
Magazine, MAD, #79, June, 1963,
    Special Mother's Day
    Issue 15.00
Magazine Ad, Western Union,
    "Remember Your Mother,"
    1955 .... 6.00
Ornament for Mother-to-Be, mother
    hen nests on bow-wrapped egg,
    mkd "Hallmark Handcrafted,"
    1992, orig box 20.00
Planter, white ceramic, swans,
    FTD 3.50
Table Decoration, tissue paper type,
    image of Victorian Mother,
    "Remember your mother on
    Mother's Day. Second Sunday in
    May," 11" x 14" 15.00

1980 collector's plate, Rockwell Society of America, illustrated by Norman Rockwell, 8-5/8" d, $15.

✳ Motorcycle Collectibles

Here's a collecting area where most of the collectors are also riders of this unique form of transportation, or perhaps they had a motorcycle in their past. Whatever the motivation, it's a great collectible and one sure to increase in value over the next few years.

Collectors' Clubs: American Motorcycle Association, PO Box 6114, Westerville, OH 43081; Antique Motorcycle Club of America, PO Box 300, Sweetser, IN 46987-0300; Women on Wheels, PO Box 546, Sparta, WI 54656-9546.

Catalog, Harley-Davidson Motorcycles, accessories, 8-1/2" x 11" 1954 catalog, horizontal format, blue and yellow accents, 36 pages 25.00

Flyer, Harley-Davidson Motorcycles, Christmas, 6" x 9", accessories, Baltimore, MD dealer imprint, some inked notations 10.00

Magazine Tear Sheet
   Harley-Davidson, *Farm Life,* 1919 2.00
   Honda Mini Trail, 1969, large sheet 2.50

Member Card and Patch, 2-1/4" x 4", buff paper with orange accent, American Motorcycle Association, typewritten member identification,

Big Twin, Harley-Davidson bean bag plush, 1997, $10.

1952 expiration date, 2" x 2-1/4" fabric patch, green, red, and yellow on blue background .. 35.00

Patch, 7-1/2", Harley-Davidson Motorcycles, embroidered, gold trademark in center, flanked by silver wings on black felt background, early 1950s 75.00

Stationery, 8-1/2" x 11", white sheet, 2" red, pink, and gray logo design, Indian Motorcycles Dealer, profile of Indian head at left, text "Motorcycles for Sport, Business, and Police," wheel and wing design across top, Alabama dealer imprint, three-digit phone number, c1920 .... 20.00

❖ Movie Memorabilia

Going to the movies has always been a fun event. Today collectors actively seek memorabilia from their favorite flicks or related to a particular star or studio.

Periodicals: *Big Reel,* PO Box 1050, Dubuque, IA 52004; *Collecting Hollywood Magazine,* PO Box 2512, Chattanooga, TN 37409; *Goldmine,* 700 E State Street, Iola, WI 54990; *Movie Advertising Collector,* PO Box 28587, Philadelphia, PA 19149.

Autograph
   Book, *They Got Me Covered,* Bob Hope, 5-1/4" x 7-3/4", soft cover, full color cover art of Hope, 96 pgs of text and illus of Hope's life, copyright 1941 Bob Hope California, 1st edition 24.00
   Photo, Our Gang Reunion, sgd by Tommy "Butch" Bond, 8" x 10" high-gloss black and white, 7 adults posed behind their respective character standing figure, blue handwritten title and inscription 55.00

Cookie Jar, James Dean 50.00

Doll
   Alfalfa, MIB 35.00
   Spanky, MIB 35.00

Figure, plaster
   Groucho, 16" h 90.00

16mm film, "Aids to Beauty," Excel Movies, Hal Roach 'Our Gang' Comedy, $25.

   Marx Brothers, 18" h, set .. 175.00

Herald
   James Cagney in Great Guy, 5-5/8" x 8", single fold, greentone and redtone, scenes of movie with Cagney and Mae Clark, early 1930s Grand National Picture 10.00
   The Terror of Tiny Town, 8-1/2" x 11", black and white sheet, image of laughing midgets wearing western garb, 1942, Fox Theaters 10.00

Magazine, *Charlie Chaplin,* English 60.00

Photograph, Van Johnson & June Allyson in "La Isla Encantada" M-G-M 16.00

Postcard, Judy Garland's Home, linen, unused 15.00

Salt and Pepper Shakers, pr, James Dean 20.00

Sheet Music, *As Time Goes By Casablanca,* 9" x 12", 1942 Warner Bros film, Humphrey Bogart, Ingrid Bergman, and Paul Henreid shown on cov, slight wear 65.00

Spoon, figural, facsimile autograph, set of six includes Marion Davies, Gloria Swanson, Norma Shearer, Ramon Navarro, Mae Murray, Douglas Fairbanks, each designed with heart at top, signature along handle, made by Oneida Community Par Plate, c1930 .... 35.00

❖ Movie Posters

A specialized niche of movie collecting is posters. Created by the studios to promote their movies, they are usually brightly colored and make great display pieces. One of the most popular types of poster is commonly called a "One Sheet" and is 27" x 41." The following listings are all one sheets and are in full color.

Periodicals: *Collecting Hollywood,* American Collectors Exchange, 2401 Broad St., Chattanooga, TN 37408; *Hollywood Collectibles,* 4099 McEwen Drive, Suite 350, Dallas, TX 75244; *Movie Poster Update,* American Collectors Exchange, 2401 Broad St., Chattanooga, TN 37408.

Adventures of Robin Hood, Errol Flynn, 1950s reissue 300.00

Frank Buck in *Jungle Terror,* 1940s 200.00

Great Plane Robbery, Jack Holt, Columbia, 1940 .... 85.00

Laurel and Hardy in *The Big Noise,* Fox, 1944, Tooker Litho.... 300.00

Little Rascals in *Awful Tooth,* 1950s 175.00

Paleface, Bob Hope and Jane Russell, Paramount, 1948 ...... 100.00

"*In The Bank,*" Charles Chaplin, framed full sheet trimmed to 37" x 27", $575.00.

Sweet Rosie O'Grady, Betty Grable, Robert Young, Adolphe Menjou, Fox, 1943 .... 150.00

Thunderball, Sean Connery, 1965 .... 125.00

Up the River, Preston Foster, Tony Martin, 1938 .... 100.00

❖ Moxie

Moxie is the oldest continuously produced soft drink in the country. Begun in 1884, its roots go back to Moxie Nerve Food, which was developed by Dr. Augustine Thompson of Union, Maine. It was first manufactured in Lowell, MA. Today it is produced in Georgia.

Collectors' Club: New England Moxie Congress, 445 Wyoming Ave., Millburn, NJ 07041.

Display Bottle, 36" h, three-dimensional oversized wood display, paper label, tin bottle cap, small doors in back, metal lined to hold ice, some loss to paper label 1,300.00

Mat, 23" sq, cardboard, black letters, black logo of Moxie man pointing at you, double sided 25.00

Pin, 2" h, diecut tin, Moxie girl holding emb glass of Moxie in one hand, vintage bottle in other, replaced pin 60.00

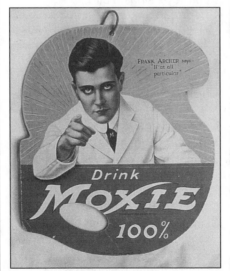

Fan, pointing Moxie Man, diecut, copyright 1922, $40.

Sign

19-1/4" h, 27-1/4" w, emb tin, Drink Moxie Distinctively Different, poor condition 70.00

21-1/2" h, 19" w, tin, Drink Moxie, poor condition 40.00

27" h, 19-1/2" w, self framed tin oval, "Yes, We Sell Moxie Very Healthful Feeds The Nerves," Kaufmann & Strauss Co. litho 450.00

28" h, 39" w, diecut cardboard, easel back, titled "Frank Archer invites you to visit Moxieland," shows factory 110.00

40" h, 19-1/2" w, diecut cardboard, easel back, trademark Moxie boy, poor condition 60.00

Smoke Stand, 28" h, 8" w, wood, figural, mkd "Drink Moxie" on base and 2 sides, woman maid shape, orig paint 500.00

Statue, 8-1/2" h, 9-1/4" w, three-dimensional chalk, man riding trademark Horsemobile 250.00

✸ Mugs

While no one is sure about the first mug to be produced, many early pottery manufacturers included mugs in their patterns. Today collectors tend to focus on advertising or character-related mugs.

Bennington, stoneware, double glazed, white and blue, double ring handle 12.00

Funny Face, set of 4, orig box 50.00

Garfield, face, striped handle 7.50

Grog, BC Comics 5.00

Hallmark, Friends Help You Hang On, mountain climber and goat 3.00

Maine Antique Digest, white, red logo 5.00

Maxwell House Coffee, blue ... 10.00

Morton Pottery Works, 1 pt size, Rockingham glaze, c1910 .. 65.00

Nestle's, globe shape, clear glass 3.50

Oh No, 4 0!, black, white letters 5.00

Red Rooster, Metlox 15.00

Stoneware, salt-glazed, tooled design, cobalt bands, 5" h, $34.

❖ Mulberry China

Mulberry China closely resembles the blurry look of flow blue patterns, but in a dark purple tone to almost black. The name comes from the resemblance of the color to crushed mulberries. It was often made by the same factories that produced Flow Blue.

Berry Dish, Bryonia, 4" d 35.00

Plate, Bokara pattern, 10-1/4" d, $45.

Creamer
  Corean 120.00
  Marble, Wedgwood 90.00
Cup Plate, Shapoo 85.00
Dinner Plate, Corea 45.00
Gravy Boat, Calcutta 110.00
Milk Pitcher, Temple, 8" h 225.00
Plate, Sage Hall, Smith
  College 55.00
Platter, Pelew, 12-1/2" l 165.00
Sugar Bowl, cov, Corean 10.00
Tea Cup and Saucer,
  Bryonia 60.00
Teapot, cov
  Calcutta 250.00
  Corean 265.00
Vegetable Bowl, cov,
  Vincennes 165.00

❖ Music Boxes, Novelty Types

Music boxes were invented by the Swiss about 1825. They can now be found in many shapes, sizes, and materials. When buying a music box at a flea market, ask the dealer if it works properly and perhaps you'll hear the pretty tune.

Collectors' Club: Musical Box Society International, 12140 Anchor Lane SW, Moore Haven, FL 33471.

Bird Cage, singing bird,
  German 250.00
Children on Merry Go Round, wood,
  figures move, plays "Around the
  World in 80 Days,"
  7-3/4" h 30.00
Christmas Tree, revolving,
  German 65.00
Dancing Dude 90.00
Easter Egg, tin, hand crank 25.00
Evening in Paris, illus of different
  cosmetics, velvet and silver
  box 125.00
Kitten with Ball, ceramic 20.00
Piano, silver plated, red velvet
  lining 45.00
Snowball, glass, Frosty the
  Snowman, red wood base,
  5" h 12.00
South of the Border 35.00

Gorham, Beautiful Dreamer, bisque blue jay, 1978, 6" h, $30.

❖ Music Related

Perhaps you're the type who likes to whistle while browsing a flea market. Bet you're likely to find some music-related collectibles.

See related categories and "Sheet Music" in this edition.

Periodical: *Goldmine,* 700 E State Street, Iola, WI 54990.

Book
  History of English Music, London,
    1895 .... 20.00
  Songs for the Family, yellow hard
    cover, c1960 .... 10.00
Calendar Print, dogs playing piano
  scene 5.00
Catalog, McKinley Music Co.,
  Chicago, IL, 1903, 50 pgs ... 20.00
Hat, marching band, blue and white,
  white plume, worn 10.00
Music Stand, chrome, folding
  type 2.00
Piano Instruction Book, beginner,
  green cover, worn 2.00
Piano Roll Cabinet, Adam style,
  mahogany veneer, painted panels
  on doors, incomplete applied
  ornament, English, 40" w, 16" d,
  38-1/4" h 330.00

Conn trumpet, brass, $45.

Sign, Mason & Hamlin Grands & Upright Pianos, Boston, New York, Chicago, emb tin, shows grand piano, framed, 19-1/2" x 27" 300.00

❖ Musical Instruments

The types of musical instruments generally found at flea markets are used, primarily by children, or as practice instruments. Expect to find wear, and perhaps they may need some repairs before they can start to make music again.

Periodicals: *Concertina & Squeezebox*, PO Box 6706, Ithaca, NY 14851; *Jerry's Musical Newsletter*, 4624 W Woodland Rd, Minneapolis, MN 55424; *Piano & Keyboard*, PO Box 767, San Anselmo, CA 94979; *Strings*, PO Box 767, San Anselmo, CA 94979; *Twentieth Century Guitar*, 135 Oser Ave, Hauppauge, NY 11788; *Vintage Guitar Classics*, PO Box 7301, Bismarck, ND 58507.

Collectors' Clubs: American Musical Instrument Society, RD 3, Box 205-B, Franklin, PA 16323; Automatic Musical Instrument Collectors Association, 919 Lantern Glow Trail, Dayton, OH 45431; Fretted Instrument Guild of America, 2344 S Oakley Ave, Chicago, IL 60608; Musical Box Society International, 887 Orange Ave. E, St. Paul, MN 55106; Reed Organ Society, Inc., PO Box 901, Deansboro, NY 13328.

Accordion, black lacquer, brass, silver, and abalone inlay, keys and decorative valve covers with carved mother-of-pearl, needs repair, some damage 95.00

Bassoon, fifteen-keyed, maple, brass mounts and keys, c1900, unstamped, 50-1/4" l 460.00

Bugle, nickel-plated, minor dents, wooden case with black paint 100.00

Clarinet, ten-keyed boxwood, key of C, c1860, brass mountings, brass keys with round covers, orig mouthpiece, 21-1/2" l 400.00

Cornet. Lyric, The Rudolph Wurlitzer Co. USA, silver-plated brass tubing engraved at the bell, three piston values with pearl buttons, stamped "P21766," fitted case, two period mouthpieces, turning crook, and mute 150.00

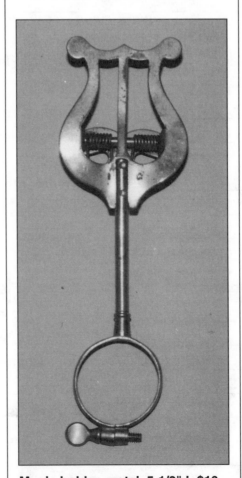

Music holder, metal, 5-1/2" l, $10.

Flute, Firth Hall and Pond, c1855, eight keys, cocuswood and nickel silver mounts, c1855, stamped "Firth, Hall & Pond, Franklin Sq, New York, 1242," inlaid lip plate, nickel-silver keys with salt spoon cup cover, adjustable stopper, 26-1/4" l, fitted mahogany case 230.00

Melodeon, rosewood veneer, lyre-shaped ends, ivory and ebony keyboard, 4-1/2 octaves, mkd "Carhart & Needham, New York," wear and veneer damage, lyre and bench mismatched, one bellows rod is missing, 32-1/2" w, 16-1/4" d, 28" h 175.00

Orguinette, "Mechanical Orguinette Co., New York," small roller organ, walnut case, silver stenciled label and dec, working condition, paper rolls, 12" w, 9-1/4" d, 10" h 500.00

Pianola, Aeolian, quartersawn oak, 36" h, 45" w, foot pedals, repairs required to bellows, 60 orig rolls 400.00

Pitch Pipe, walnut, book form, paper label on int., "WN," crack, 6" l 200.00

Ukulele, The Serenader, B & G, NY, double binding, celluloid fingerboard and head 250.00

Zither, Columbia, 47 strings, c1900 .... 275.00

☆ My Little Pony

It's said the idea for My Little Pony came about when research by Hasbro discovered that young girls see horses when they close their eyes at night. The result: ponies that even

McDonald's Happy Meal premiums, 1998, $1 each.

city kids can keep. My Little Pony memorabilia has been putting smiles on the faces of girls, young and old, since 1982.

Accessory

Alarm clock, Bubbles...........47.00

Figurine, bisque, First Born by Extra Special, 4" l............19.50

Keychains, Ivy, Light Heart, Morning Glory, Sundance, detach-able with rainbow-colored comb, each......................4.00

Satin Slipper Sweet Shop... 33.50

Sheet, fits twin bed 20.50

Sweet Dreams Crib, missing baby bottle and 2 wheels, orig box 48.00

Pony

Applejack, 1983 ....7.50

Christmas Baby, Kellogg's, NRFP.............................22.50

Firefly, pony brush and ribbon, orig card 9.00

Lucky, only available by mail-order 150.00

Merry Treat, 2nd of 3 Christmas ponies, 1984 ....13.50

Morning Glory, Birthflower Ponies line, September 1982 .....26.00

Nightglider, 1984.................35.00

Flea Market Notes

1. Market:_____

   Address/Location   _____

   Hours/Dates Open: _____

   Fees:_____

   Comments:_____

   _____

   _____

Flea Market Notes

2. Market:_____

   Address/Location   _____

   Hours/Dates Open: _____

   Fees:_____

   Comments:_____

   _____

   _____

Flea Market Notes

3. Market:_____

   Address/Location   _____

   Hours/Dates Open: _____

   Fees:_____

   Comments:_____

   _____

   _____

Flea Market Notes

4. Market:_____

   Address/Location   _____

   Hours/Dates Open: _____

   Fees:_____

   Comments:_____

   _____

   _____

Flea Market Notes

5. Market:_____

   Address/Location   _____

   Hours/Dates Open: _____

   Fees:_____

   Comments:_____

   _____

   _____

Flea Market Notes

6. Market:_____

   Address/Location   _____

   Hours/Dates Open: _____

   Fees:_____

   Comments:_____

   _____

   _____

N

❖ Napkin Rings

Figural napkin rings make a great usable collection. Many are designed to serve a specific function while still presenting a whimsical look. Victorian silver and silver plate napkin rings often are available at flea markets. For this edition, we've concentrated on the more common napkin rings.

Aluminum, engraved "World's Fair, St. Louis, 1904," and flag ... 50.00

Bakelite
  Angelfish, marbled blue,
    c1940 .... 70.00
  Elephant, navy blue,
    c1940 .... 65.00
  Popeye, decal face, caramel
    color 145.00
  Rabbit, yellow 75.00
  Rocking Horse, red 225.00
Porcelain, butterfly shape, green,
    gold colored wire antennae, pr
    .... 10.00

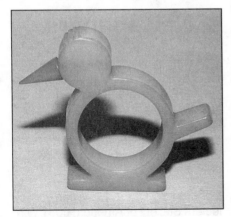

Bird form, plastic, $30.

Silver, cuff style, c1886,
    1-7/8" d 55.00
Silvered Metal, cuff style,
    cut-out "A" 6.00

❖ Nautical

Anchors Aweigh! Nautical items can encompass things with a nautical theme or items that were actually used on a ship.   .

Periodicals: *Nautical Brass,* PO Box 3966, North Ft. Myers, FL 33918; *Nautical Collector,* PO Box 949, New London, CT 06320.

Collectors' Club: Nautical Research Guild, 62 Marlboro St., Newburyport, MA 01950.

For additional listings, see *Warman's Antiques and Collectibles Price Guide.*

Bookends, pr
  Anchors, brass, mounted on faux
    stone base
    8" h 47.50
  Whale's Heads, bronze verdigris
    finish, 5-1/2" h 50.00
Diorama, ship, old paint dec,
    c1920 .... 585.00
Folk Art, carved fish, wood plaque,
c1940, life size
    Pickerel 265.00
    Rainbow Trout 295.00
    Salmon 345.00
Plaque, White Star Line, thick brass
    plate, engraved words, mounted
    on varnished mahogany board,
    18" x 7" 375.00
Print
    Clippers *Ariel & Taiping*, M. Dawson, 26" x 31" 65.00
    Ship *Triumphant,* Frank Vining
      Smith, 22" x 32" 38.50
Ship Compass, 10" d magnetic compass, teakwood box, polished
    brass gimball ring, US Navy,
    World War II era, made by John
    E. Hand & Co. 750.00
Table Lamp, brass boat cleatships
    wheel, sea navigation chart lamp
    shade, 15" h 235.00

❖ Nazi

Started as a program to revive the depressed German economy and as government revitalization, the National Socialist German Workers Party was created on Feb 24, 1920. Today the influence of this political party is referred to as "Nazi," and most understand what an impact their actions ultimately had on the world.

Banner, German, 25" w,
    41" h 200.00

Bayonet, police, dress,
    13" blade 175.00

Belt, NSDAP, police officer's, light
    tan leather belt 35.00

Car Badge, RAD, silver finish, enameled, wreath 35.00

Magazine, *Michigan State News,*
    April, 1945, several articles relating to troops and Nazi
    activities 3.50

Medal, Eastern People's, 2nd Class,
    silver metal, ribbon 25.00

Pennant, triangular, painted swastika, double sided 35.00

Poster, advertising *Mein Kampf,*
    14" x 22", pictures Hitler,
    1930s 200.00

Pinback, blue swastika on gold background, 3/4" d, $8.

❖ ⊕ Newcomb College

Started as a school to train local women in decorative arts, the Sophie Newcomb Memorial College, was an adjunct of Tulane University in New Orleans, Louisiana. Pottery was made here for almost 50 years and today is one of the hottest segments of the art pottery market.

Bowl, should dec with yellow, red, and green flowers, matte blue body, imp "NC, HF, 64, 259," 8" d 980.00

Vase

3-1/2" h, blue and red hi-glaze, incised marks, L. Nicholson 500.00

4" h, carved and painted landscape, moss-laden oaks, green and blue, pale yellow moon peeking through, imp mark "#UA-48," S. Irvine 1,700.00

5" h, carved and painted landscape of moss-laden oaks, soft pink sky, imp marks, S. Irvine, J.M. 2,400.00

6-1/2" h, carved and painted overlapping blue, green, and ivory leaves, matte glaze, imp marks, attributed to C. Chlaron, Joseph Meyer 1,500.00

Vase, floral design, sgd "S. Irvine," 4" h, $395.

6-1/2" h, 6-1/2" d, carved and painted landscape of moss-laden oaks, yellow moon, matte glaze, imp marks, S.Irvine, J. Hunt........ 3,250.00

6-1/2" h, 7-1/2" d, incised and painted pink narcissus, yellow centers, green leaves, blue matte ground, imp marks, "A. F. Simpson, J. M. #PO70, G1" 1,800.00

9-1/2" h, hi-glaze, incised and finely painted ivory, green, and blue floral design, imp marks, C. Payne 5,500.00

❖ New Martinsville Glass

Founded in 1901, the New Martinsville Glass Manufacturing Co. was located in West Virginia. Its glassware products ranged from pressed utilitarian wares to some innovative designs and colors.

Animal

Baby bear, head straight 60.00

Seal, holding ball, light lavender, candle holder.................. 75.00

Rooster, crooked tail........... 95.00

Ashtray, Moondrops, red
.... 35.00

Basket

#4427/28, Radiance, red, 8" h, metal handle................... 95.00

#4552, Janice, light blue, 11" h 300.00

Bitters Bottle, Hostmaster, cobalt blue.................................... 75.00

Bookends, pr, clipper ships..... 95.00

Bowl, Moondrops, red, 8-1/4" d, ftd 45.00

Cake Plate

Janice, 40th Anniversary silver overlay............................ 45.00

Prelude, pedestal foot 10.00

Candlesticks, pr

Janice, red........................ 200.00

Moondrops, #37/2, 4" h, brocade etching ... 130.00

Prelude, #4554, 5" h......... 130.00

Radiance, 2-lite........... 230.00

Candy Box, Radiance, 3 part, amber, etch #26 ....160.00

Champagne, Moondrops, red......................................40.00

Console Bowl, Janice, ftd, crystal 38.00

Console Set, Radiance, crystal, 12" bowl, pr 2-lite candlesticks 125.00

Cordial, Janice, red, silver trim 40.00

Creamer and Sugar, Janice, red......................................48.00

Cup and Saucer

Janice, red 30.00

Radiance, amber 30.00

Decanter, Moondrops, amber .80.00

Ivy Ball, Janice, light blue........95.00

Pitcher, Oscar, red 100.00

Punch Cup, Radiance 15.00

Punch Ladle, Radiance, red......................................125.00

Relish, Prelude, 5-part, 13" d 45.00

Swan, Janice, crystal 38.00

Tumbler

Amy, #34, ftd.......................22.50

Janice, light blue, ftd...........35.00

Janice, red, 10 oz, ftd 35.00

Moondrops, cobalt blue, 5 oz..................................24.00

Vanity Set, 3 pc, Judy, green and crystal or pink and crystal 100.00

Vase, Radiance, #4232, 10" h, crimped, etch #26 ....140.00

❖ Newspapers

Saving a newspaper about an historic event or memorable occasion seems like such an easy thing to do. Happily for newspaper collectors, folks have been doing that for centuries. Flea markets are a great place to find these interesting old newspapers.

Collectors' Club: Newspaper Collectors Society of America, 6031 Winterset, Lansing, MI 48911.

The Youth's Companion, **Vol. 80 No. 25, June 21, 1906, $3.**

Cleveland News, April 15, 1912, Titanic sinking headline 425.00

Gleason's Pictorial, March 25, 1854, front page tribute to Nathaniel Bowditch.............................. 25.00

Leslie's Illustrated Newspaper, Aug 31, 1893, Columbian Expo coverage 25.00

National Intelligencer, Washington, DC, March 11, 1841, Amistad verdict..................................... 190.00

New York Herald, Nov 9, 1864, Abraham Lincoln reelection front page story 155.00

New York Times, Oct 10, 1871, Chicago Fire front page story 185.00

New York Times, July 21, 1969, Man Walks on the Moon............. 30.00

Oakland Tribune, Extra, April 19, 1908, San Francisco Earthquake, "Citizens Are Forced To Fight Flames at Point Of Revolver" headline 145.00

❖ Niloak Pottery

Niloak Pottery was located near Benton, Arkansas. The founder of the company, Charles Dean Hyten experimented with native clays and tried to preserve their natural colors. By 1911, he had perfected a method that gave this effect, and it was named "Mission Ware." The pottery burned but was rebuilt. It reopened under the name Eagle Pottery and, by 1929, was producing novelties. Several different marks were used, helping to determine the dates of pieces. By 1946, the pottery went out of business.

Swan planter, tan glaze, 7" h, $25.

Collectors' Club: Arkansas Pottery Collectors Society, 12 Normandy Road, Little Rock, AR 72007.

For additional listings, see *Warman's Antiques and Collectibles Price Guide, Warman's Americana & Collectibles,* and *Warman's American Pottery and Porcelain.*

Bowl, Mission Ware, 7" d 110.00

Cornucopia, white, mkd "Niloak," 3-3/8" h, pair 35.00

Planter, mkd
   Elephant, standing on drum, "N" on side, maroon matte, 6" h................................... 55.00
   Frog, yellow 50.00
   Squirrel 65.00
   Swan, matte finish, pink, blue shading, 7" h 50.00
   Wishing Well....................... 25.00

Strawberry Vase, pink over gray-green over-glaze, orig paper labels, pr 150.00

Vase
   Green and tan, 6" h 20.00
   Mission Ware, flared, blue, red, and tan, 4" x 2-5/8" h 80.00
   Mission Ware, browns, reds, and blue, 6-1/4" h, 3-3/4" d . 150.00
   Ozark Dawn II, handles, 5-1/4" h..........................110.00

❖ Nippon China

The Japanese made hand painted porcelain for export from 1891 until 1921 that was marked "Nippon." When the McKinley Tariff Act was passed in 1891, the Japanese chose to use the word "Nippon." However, in 1921, the United States decided that this word would no longer be acceptable and required all imported Japanese wares to be marked "Japan."

There are over 200 documented marks or backstamps. For some makers, the color of the mark helps determine the quality of the piece; green was used for first-grade porcelain, blue for second grade, and magenta for third grade. Other types of marks were also used.

Sadly, today there are reproductions that bear marks which are very difficult to determine as genuine or fake. Carefully examine any piece, study the workmanship, and thoroughly investigate any marks.

References: There are several older reference books that provide information about marks and various makers.

Collectors' Club: Contact the International Nippon Collectors Club, 112 Oak Lane, N., Owatonna, MN 55060 to find a chapter in your local area.

Reproduction Alert.

Bowl, handpainted floral decor, 3 ball feet, 6-1/4" d, $45.

For additional listings, see *Warman's Antiques and Collectibles Price Guide.*

Ashtray, black cat on roof 125.00

Bowl

　7-1/2" d, scalloped edge, floral and gold border, green "M" in wreath mark 20.00

　9-3/4" d, eagle and shield design, blue and gold, green "M" in wreath mark 45.00

Cake Plate, 2 handles, 10" d
　... 20.00

Candy Dish, divided, scenic design, blue rising sun mark 50.00

Celery Tray, pink flowers 60.00

Child's Cup and Bowl, pulled out face, googly eyes, red bow tie
　... 175.00

Chocolate Set, hp, chocolate pot, four cups and saucers, mark 7
　... 165.0

Compote, 7-1/4" d, two handles, floral design, gold trim, blue maple leaf mark 55.00

Cup and Saucer, Orange Blossom pattern, gold trim, 3-1/4" d, 4-1/2" d saucer, blue mark..................30.00

Mayonnaise Set, 4-3/4" d bowl, underplate, spoon, floral border, magenta "M" in wreath mark
　... 50.00

Mustard Pot, 3-1/2" h, scenic design, green "M" in wreath mark
　... 40.00

Plate, 10-1/2" d, two handles, floral and gold border, red and green mark 35.00

Relish, cov, 4" h, scenic design, gold trim, matching spoon, green "M" in wreath mark.................... 50.00

Serving Tray, center handle, floral dec, magenta "M" in wreath mark 20.00

Spoon Holder, gold and white
　... 60.00

Vase

　6" h, Geisha........................525.00

　8-1/2" h, two handles, scenic design, blue pagoda mark
　...165.00

　9-3/4" h, blue floral pattern, green "M" in wreath mark
　...100.00

　10" h, portrait, Moriage......975.00

❖ Nodders and Bobbin' Heads

Here's a collecting category that folks never seem to tire of. Perhaps it's the whimsical nature of these pieces or the idea that there is constant motion. Whatever the reason, there are plenty of examples to be found at flea markets.

Collectors' Club: Bobbin' Head National Club, PO Box 9297, Daytona Beach, FL 32120.

Alligator, combination nodder/ashtray, c1940, 4" h, 5" l......... 145.00

Baseball Player

　Detroit Tigers, tiger head, white base, 1960s.................. 300.00

　Hank Aaron, 3" x 3" x 8", diecut display box, clear plastic window, 7-1/2" h painted hard plastic figure with spring-mounted head, Milwaukee Brewer Promotions, Milwaukee, WI, mid-1970s 45.00

Donkey, 6" h............................ 55.00

Football Player, Los Angeles Ram, dark blue base, gold NFL label 150.00

Foxy Grandpa, German, 1920s, 8" h 135.00

German Shepherd 48.00

Girl, hand painted 15.00

Golfer, golf club missing.......... 75.00

Kissing boy and girl, plastic, chips, 5" h, $45.

Hockey Player, bobbing head, 1960s, orig brown cardboard box, 4-1/2" h

　Boston Bruins 45.00

　Chicago Blackhawks...........40.00

　Detroit Redwings 45.00

　Montreal Canadiens............48.00

Hula Dancer, Japan, 1950s...185.00

Hula Girl 35.00

Naughty, Japan 75.00

☆ Norcrest

Here's a name for collectors to watch for. Not a lot of information has been printed about this porcelain maker, but many folks are finding their products to be charming and worth collecting.

Anniversary Plate, 45th, 10-1/2" d 10.00

Bank, wishing well, blue bird and bucket at edge, 7" h............14.50

Cup and Saucer

　Golden Wheat pattern, redmark 5.00

　Pine Cone pattern................7.50

Figure

　Boy with cart 7.00

　Dalmatian, 1960s, 6-1/4" l 15.00

　Giraffe 35.00

　Poppy, #F447, August 12.00

Salt and Pepper Shakers, pr
　Hula Girl and Ukelele Boy, paper label, 3-1/2" h 45.00

　Sad Sack, © George Baker, black ink stamp, 4-1/2" h........350.00

Wall Pocket, clock, orig label, 6" h 25.00

❖ Noritake China

Noritake China was founded by the Morimura Brothers in Nagoya, Japan, about 1904. They produced high quality dinnerware for export and also some blanks for hand painting. Although the factory was heavily damaged during World War II, production again resumed and continues today. There are over 100 different marks to help determine the pattern and date of production.

Collectors' Club: Noritake Collectors' Society, 145 Andover Place, West Hempstead, NY 11552.

Bowl, Lusterware, 4" d, 2-1/2" h 12.00

Candlesticks, pr, gold flowers and bird, blue luster ground, wreath with "M" mark, 8-1/4" h 125.00

Celery Set, celery holder, six matching salts, gold trim, green wreath marks 85.00

Creamer, Margarita pattern 15.00

Cup and Saucer
    Floroia, #83374 pattern .. 24.00
    Margarita pattern 12.00

Dinner Plate, Margarita pattern, 9-7/8" d 18.00

Dish, handle, red and gold flower border, gold trim, red wreath mark, 5-1/2" w 28.00

Easter Egg, yellow hat with blue trim, blue and pink flowers, dated 1976, satin lined box, 3" h 26.00

Gravy Boat, Margarita pattern, 9-1/2" l 35.00

Oradell creamer and sugar, $22.50.

Plate, hand-painted lake scene with swan, 6-3/8" d, $40.

Hair Receiver, Art Deco geometric designs, gold luster, wreath with "M" mark, 3-1/4" h 50.00

Jam Jar, cov, basket style, figural applied cherries on notched lid 55.00

Platter, Margarita pattern, 11-7/8" l 30.00

Salt, swan, white, orange luster 12.00

Soup Bowl, Margarita pattern . 18.00

Sugar Bowl, cov, Margarita pattern 18.00

Vegetable Bowl, cov, Margarita pattern, 11-1/2" l 45.00

❖ Noritake China, Azalea Pattern

In the 1920s, the Larkin Company of Buffalo, NY, became a prime distributor of Noritake China. Two of the most popular patterns they promoted were Azalea and Tree in the Meadow, causing them to be the most popular with collectors today. The design of Azalea pattern includes delicate pink flowers green leaves on a white background. Many pieces have gold trim, especially on handles and finials.

Basket 135.00
Bon Bon 48.00
Cake Plate 40.00
Casserole, cov 75.00
Creamer 25.00
Dinner Plate 24.00
Egg Cup 55.00

Dinner plate, 9-7/8" d, $24.

Lemon Tray 30.00
Luncheon Plate 14.00
Salad Bowl, 10" d 37.50
Teapot 100.00
Vase, fan 150.00

❖ Noritake China, Tree in the Meadow Pattern

This popular pattern was also sold by the Larkin Company. The pattern shows a scene with a meadow, sky, buildings, and, of course, trees. It's a more colorful pattern than Azalea.

Ashtray, green backstamp, 5-1/4" d 35.00
Berry Set, master bowl with pierced handles, six sauce bowls 75.00
Bowl, green backstamp, 6-3/4" l, 6" w 30.00
Cake Plate, 7-1/2" sq 38.00
Creamer and Sugar, red wreath mark 45.00
Demitasse Cup and Saucer 48.00
Plate, red-brown backstamp, 7-3/4" d 30.00
Platter, two handles 45.00
Tea Tile, green backstamp, 5" w 35.00

❖ Northwood Glass

Northwood Glass is a term used to describe the glassware made by both the Northwood Glass Company and Northwood & Co., two distinct glass companies. The histories of these companies are quite interesting and involved. Between them, fine pressed pattern glass, opalescent glass, and carnival glass were made. Today, the name Northwood has again surfaced as a glass manufacturer as Northwood family descendants are beginning to issue new pieces. The new wares will have a different mark than the familiar "N" or script signature of the older companies. Like many glass manufacturers, not every piece was marked.

Basket, white carnival, basketweave, open handles, ftd, sgd, 4" h 125.00

Bon Bon, Stippled Rays pattern, blue carnival 60.00

Bowl, Regal, 4-1/2" d, blue opalescent 20.00

Butter Dish, cov, Regal, green opalescent 110.00

Candy Dish, cov
    Ruffles and Bows, blue opalescent 45.00
    Stretch, blue iridescent, #636 .... 70.00

Creamer
    Lustre Flute, green carnival 50.00
    Pods and Posies, green pattern glass, gold trim 70.00
    Regal, blue opalescent 60.00

Cruet, Leaf Umbrella, Mauve, heat check, no stopper 500.00

Goblet
    Grape and Gothic Arches, custard, nutmeg stain 75.00
    Nearcut, colorless 40.00

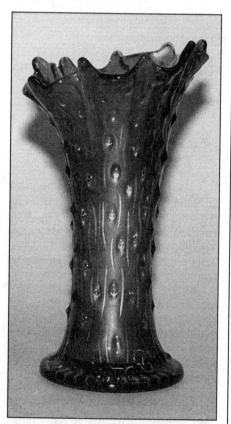

Vase, carnival glass, Tree Trunk pattern, marigold, 7-1/2" h, $265.

Jelly Compote, Poppy pattern, green 35.00

Nut Bowl, Leaf and Beads pattern, purple carnival 65.00

Pitcher, Ribbed Opal, blue . 1,450.00

Salt and Pepper Shakers, pr, orig tops
    Bow and Tassel pattern, milk glass 65.00
    Leaf Umbrella, mauve, cased 165.00

Sugar, cov
    Cherry and Plum pattern, clear, ruby and green trim 85.00
    Paneled Spring, milk glass, green and gold dec 125.00

Tumbler, Acorn Burrs, green ... 75.00

Water Set, Regent, amethyst, pitcher and six tumblers.... 800.00

❖ Nutcrackers

Clever devices to release the tasty part of a nut were invented as far back as the 19th century. Collectors today seek out interesting examples in various metals and wood.

Collectors' Club: Nutcracker Collectors' Club, 12204 Fox Run Drive, Chesterland, OH 44026.

Cat, brass 50.00
Lady's Leg, wood 35.00
Pheasant, bronze 115.00
Pliers Type
    Cast iron 15.00
    Steel, adjustable 15.00
    Sterling silver 40.00
Ram, wood, glass eyes 75.00
Rooster, cast iron 35.00
Sailor and Woman, brass 85.00

Dog, cast iron, $32.

Skull and Cross Bones, cast iron 90.00

Squirrel, cast iron 35.00

Twist and screw type, nickel-plated cast iron 15.00

❖ Nutting, Wallace

The story of Wallace Nutting is a fascinating tale of an enterprising American. He was born in 1861 attended Harvard University and several theological seminaries. In 1904, he opened a photography studio in New York, and later other branch studios. By the time he moved to Framingham, MA, in 1913, he was employing over 200 colorists, framers, and support staff. He alone took the photographs and then left explicit instructions on how they should be hand colored. Nutting died in 1941, but his wife continued the business. After her death, the business continued until 1971 when the last owner ordered the glass negatives destroyed.

Although the listing below is devoted to his pictures, remember that he also published several books, silhouettes, and sold furniture.

References: Michael Ivankovich, *Alphabetical & Numerical Index to Wallace Nutting Pictures,* Diamond Press, 1988; ——, *Collector's Guide to Wallace Nutting Pictures,* Collector Books, 1997.

Collectors' Club: Wallace Nutting Collectors Club, PO Box 2458, Doylestown, PA 18901.

A Perkiomen October, 9" x 11" 250.00
Among the Ferns, 14" x 17" 165.00
Birch Hilltop, 15" x 22" 100.00
Flume Falls, 12" x 15" 310.00
Helping Mother, 14" x 17" 400.00
On the Heights, 10" x 16" 100.00
Russet and Gold, 16" x 20" ... 315.00
The River Farm, 10" x 12" 180.00
Wilton Waters, 13" x 16" 155.00

❖ Nutting-Like Pictures

Because Wallace Nutting's pictures were so successful, copycats soon appeared on the scene. Some artists had worked for Nutting and learned the techniques. These pictures are starting to catch the eye of collectors.

Apple Tree Road, Fred Thompson 45.00

A Puritan Lady, David Davidson 75.00
At the Bend of the Road, Sawyer 35.00
Berkshire Sunset, David Davidson 80.00
Christmas Day, David Davidson 160.00
Lombardy Poplar, Fred Thompson 100.00
Mountain Road, Gibson 20.00
Mt. Washington in October, Sawyer 55.00

Silver Birches, Lake George ...50.00
Sunset on the Suwanee, Fred Thompson.......................... 45.00
The Silent Wave, David Davidson........................... 35.00
Vanity, David Davidson 70.00

For exciting collecting trends and newly expanded areas look for the following symbols:

❂ Hot Topic

★ New Warman's Listing
(May have been in another Warman's edition.)

Fellow collectors:

Name: _____
Address:_____
_____
Phone:_____
E-mail:_____

Name: _____
Address:_____
_____
Phone:_____
E-mail:_____

Name: _____
Address:_____
_____
Phone:_____
E-mail:_____

Name: _____
Address:_____
_____
Phone:_____
E-mail:_____

Name: _____
Address:_____
_____
Phone:_____
E-mail:_____

Name: _____
Address:_____
_____
Phone:_____
E-mail:_____

Name: _____
Address:_____
_____
Phone:_____
E-mail:_____

Name: _____
Address:_____
_____
Phone:_____
E-mail:_____

❖ Occupied Japan

To help repair their devasted economy, the Japanese made items to export, including porcelain, toys, and all kinds of knickknacks. Today savvy collectors know that items made during the occupation time period might be marked "Japan," "Made in Japan," or "Occupied Japan," as well as "Made in Occupied Japan."

Collectors' Club: The Occupied Japan Club, 29 Freeborn St., Newport, RI 02840.

Toby mug, 3" h, $22

Dog figurine, 2-3/4" h, 4-3/4" l, $15.

Ashtray, metal, spring loaded head of young boy smoking cigar, 4-3/4" h 55.00

Children's Play Dishes, Blue Willow, 18 pc set 375.00

Clock, bisque, dancing couple in colonial garb, floral encrusted case, 10-1/2" h 250.00

Figurine

    Couple, 7" x 4-1/2" 35.00

    Farm girl with scarf, egg basket beside her, red mark "Made in Occupied Japan," 1-1/4" x 5" 15.00

    Man, 6" h, 2" w base 25.00

    Man holding flower, 8" h, 3-1/2" w base 40.00

Flower Frog, bisque, girl with bird on shoulder, pastel highlights, gold trim 48.00

Platter, Courley pattern, heavy gold trim 30.00

Tape Measure, pig, stamped "Occupied Japan" 45.00

❖ Ocean Liner Memorabilia

The thought of a leisurely ocean cruise has enticed many to try this mode of travel. Of course, they brought back souvenirs. Today collectors are glad they did as they discover these mementos at flea markets.

Collectors' Club: Steamship Historical Society of America, Inc., 300 Ray Drive, Suite 4, Providence, RI 02906.

Ashtray, Pacific Far East Steamship, ceramic 25.00

Baggage Tag, French Line, first class, unused 7.50

Booklet, *Independence,* American Export Lines, 1966 Gala Springtime Cruise, itinerary and deck plan inserts 24.00

Brochure

    Cunard Line, Getting There is Half the Fun, 16 pgs, 1952 .... 7.50

    Italian Line, Six Cruises to the Mediterranean and Egypt, 1934 .... 15.00

Deck Plan, *RMSP Avon*, The Royal Mail Steam Packet, Dec 1909 .... 32.00

Dish, Cunard *RMS Queen Mary,* ceramic, oval, color portrait, gold edge, Staffordshire, 5" l 37.50

Menu

    SS Leonardo Da Vinci, January, 1973 .... 6.00

    SS Lurline, Matson Lines, Commodore's Dinner, March 3, 1959, 12" x 9" 20.50

Newspaper, *RMS Caronia, Ocean Times,* Aug, 1950, 4 pgs 10.00

Note paper, Cunard *White Star*, blue 5.00

Passport Cover, Red Star Line, fabric, ship illus 27.50

Playing Cards, Eastern Steamship Corp., 3/4" x 2-1/4" x 3-1/2" gold foil box, red, and black accents, full color deck, showing ship at sea, yellow and white border, revenue stamp attached to edge flap, c1950 .... 15.00

Postcard, *RMS Olympia,* unused 75.00

Souvenir Spoon, Cunard *White Star,* demitasse, silver plated 20.00

Tie Clasp, Cunard Line *RMS Queen Mary,* gold tone, red, white, and blue enameled ship 18.00

❖ Old Sleepy Eye

Old Sleepy Eye, Minnesota, was the home of the Old Sleepy Eye Flour Mill. They used a handsome Indian as their trademark. Collectors can also find his image on stoneware premiums that were issued by the mill.

Collectors' Club: Old Sleepy Eye Collectors Club, PO Box 12, Monmouth, IL 61462.

Reproduction Alert.

Bottle Opener, Old Sleepy Eye Motel 10.00

Cookbook, Sleepy Eye Milling Co., loaf of bread shape, portrait on cover 160.00

Hooked Rug, hand made........ 70.00

Letter Opener 15.00

Mug, Convention, 1980 .... 5.00

Paperweight, pot metal, bronze finish, 3" h......................... 360.00

Pitcher, stoneware
    4" h, gray ground, cobalt blue dec 325.00
    9" h, beige ground, cobalt blue dec 175.00

Postcard, postmarked 1906 .... 15.00

Sign, Old Sleepy Eye Mills, Old Sleepy Eye Cream, red band, center trademark Indian, round, 16" d................................. 200.00

Spoon, Indian head handle 125.00

Stationery, flour mill letterhead and envelope, unused, matted and framed 90.00

Sugar Bowl, stoneware, blue and white, 3" h, stains 50.00

Toothpick Holder, stoneware .. 50.00

Pitcher, No. 1., white with blue highlights, stains, $195.

❖ Olympic Collectibles

Most of us are familiar with the Olympic rings logo. Watching for that is a great way to spot Olympic collectibles. It's usually easier to find fresh examples at flea markets during years that the Olympics are held.

Periodical: *Sports Collectors Digest,* 700 E State St., Iola, WI 54990.

Collectors' Club: Olympic Pin Collector's Club, 1386 Fifth St., Schenectady, NY 12303.

Bank, Oscar Mayer Wienermobile, Official Sponsor, 1992 Olympics, 10" l 25.00

Coins, 1980, complete set 400.00

Doll, Dorothy Hamill, wearing Olympic medal 25.00

Fan, 1932 Los Angeles Olympics, folding, paper, brass sticks, chapel building illus and Olympic logo.................................... 42.00

First Day Cover, 1932 Olympiad 8.50

Handkerchief, 10" x 10-1/2" sheer white fabric, Olympic rings in five colors, other illus, Olympic stadium tower, Finnish flags, for canceled 1940 Helsinki Olympics........................... 45.00

Jacket, knit, 1976, logo on breast 18.00

Magazine Ad, 1955................... 5.00

Flag, Atlanta 1996, 12" x 18", $3.

Patch
    XVI Olympiad Melbourne 1956, 2" x 3-3/4", white silk, embroidered blue accent image, multicolored rings against red flame above Australian continent 15.00
    XIII Winter Games, Lake Placid, white, red, and blue trim, 1980, worn................................. 8.00

Photo Album, small, 1984 logo, MIB 10.00

Photograph, wire service, Cobi, mascot, Barcelona, 1989.....................................3.50

Plate, 1968, Mexico and torch illus, 7" d 70.00

Postcard, soccer, adv for Guerrillero Cigarettes, Amsterdam, 1928.....................................18.00

Poster, Olympics '64 USA Olympic Committee, 17" x 22", dark blue paper, multicolored rings, white logo at top, red logo at bottom, reverse with text explaining meaning of symbols, info about Procter & Gamble premium 12.00

Seat Cushion, 1956 Summer Games, red vinyl, yellow, white and blue Olympics logo 50.00

Stuffed Toy, mascot, Sam the Olympics Eagle, Applause, orig tags, 1980.................................25.00

Tray, tin, McDonald's, 1984, 11" x 8".................................9.00

✰ Orrefors, Kosta Boda

Here's an interesting glassware to start collecting. Made in Sweden since 1898, current pieces often reflect their historical antecedents. The crystal used is high quality, and the designers certainly develop some interesting shapes and color combinations.

Bucket, heavy walled cylinder, transparent teal blue, base inscribed "Orrefors Esp. PA 245-62 Sven Palmqvist" 200.00

Decanter, 12-1/2" h, squared crystal bottle, Romeo serenading Juliet on balcony, base engraved"Orrefors No. 880" 350.00

Jar, cov, 1000 Windows, sgd and numbered..........................450.00

Rose Bowl, round, layered, sgd "Orrefors H 748"................200.00

Sculpture, clear fish, internal teardrop bubble and eye, four piece set, each sgd "Kosta" and numbered................................260.00

Vase

6-1/8" h, cylindrical heavy walled colorless body, internal cobalt blue and amber air trap, dec of boat and gondolier with guitar, serenading woman under moonlit sky, base inscribed "Orrefors/Ariel No. 637 E.4/Edvin Ohrstrom," 1974............................5,175.00

9-1/2" h, colorless squared form, engraved portrait of partially nude woman, arms raised in full-length pose, base inscribed "Orrefors Palquist 5078," c1949...........................500.00

10" h, colorless oval, engraved with two exotic angelfish, bubbles overall, base engraved "Orrefors LA 1916," price for pair................................350.00

❖ Owl Collectibles

Whoo, whoo, who collects owl items—lots of folks! Some are enchanted with the wisdom of this regal bird, while others find owls fun and whimsical. Lucky for them, artists and designers have been incorporating the owl's image into items for years.

Advertising Trade Card, Colburn's Philadelphia Mustard, diecut................................. 10.00

Bank, tin, owl illus on each side..................................... 50.00

Blotter, "Whoo? Oswald, I told you we couldn't get away with that bone!", 2 puppies under a tree, owl sitting on branch, Harry N. Johnson, Real Estate & Insurance, Highlands, NJ 10.00

Book, *Owls in the Family,* Farley Mowat, Little, Brown & Co., 1961 .... 1.00

Book Rack, expanding............ 55.00

Calendar Plate, 1912, owl on open book 30.00

Fairy Lamp, cranberry glass, double sided, enameled lavender eyes, Clarke base 200.00

Inkwell, figural, Noritake........ 125.00
Letter Opener, brass 25.00

Napkin Ring, standing owl, silver plated................................ 150.00

Pin, blue, green, and gold enamel, amber eyes, faux pearl and rhinestone trim............................ 20.00

Salt and Pepper Shakers, pr, china, browns and white, mortarboard hats, scholarly expression, horn rim glasses 10.00

Tape Measure, brass, glass eyes, mkd "Germany" 40.00

Shawnee salt and pepper, 3-3/8" h, $35.

Want List:

1._____
2._____
3._____
4._____
5._____
6._____
7._____
8._____
9._____
10._____
11._____
12._____

P

❖ Paden City Glass

Founded in Paden City, West Virginia, in 1916, this company made lovely glassware until 1951. Paden City's wares were all handmade until 1948. Their glassware was not marked, nor was it heavily advertised like their contemporaries. Much of their success laid with blanks supplied to others to decorate. Many of their wares were sold to institutional facilities, restaurants, etc. Paden City is known for rich colors in many shades.

Bowl, Party Line, pink,
4-5/8" d................................. 9.00

Cake Plate, ftd
Black Forest, green...........125.00
Leia Bird, green, 10" d.......125.00

Candy Box, cov, flat, Crow's Foot Square, crystal, flower cut, 3 ftd, chipped edge of lid 18.00

Compote, Orchid Etch,
yellow 42.00

Cup and Saucer, Crow's Foot,
red 18.50

Goblet, Penny Line,
amethyst............................. 18.50

Iced Tea Tumbler, Penny Line,
red 22.50

Napkin Rings, Party Line,
set of 6 .... 60.00

Old-Fashioned Tumbler, Georgian,
ruby 15.00

Plate, Party Line, amber,
6" d...................................... 3.00

Covered candy dish, Orchid pattern, green, 3 compartments, 6-1/2" w, $70.

Sherbet, Penny Line,
amethyst............................. 12.50

Tumbler, Party Line, ftd, amber,
3-1/2" h................................ 9.50

Vase
Black Forest etch, black, squatty,
6-1/2" h......................... 175.00

Black Forest etch, black, Regina,
10" h............................. 250.00

Orchid etch, red, 10" h...... 395.00

Utopia etch, black, 10" h... 195.00

❖ Paden City Pottery

Located near Sisterville, West Virginia, Paden City Pottery was founded in 1914 and ceased operation in 1963. They produced semi-porcelain dinnerware with high quality decal decoration.

Bowl
Fleur De Lis pattern, 1930s,
6" d................................... 3.00

Mexicano 6.00

Bread and Butter Plate, New Virginia
.... 1.00

Casserole, cov, Bak-Serv, curled finial 20.00

Dinner Plate
Caliente, cobalt blue........... 10.00

Mexicano 7.50

Dinner Service, floral design, service for 8 plus serving pieces, wear on some pcs 250.00

Platter, yellow roses, 10-7/8" x 14", $10.

Gravy Boat, Manhattan 14.50

Plate, Pottery Ivy, mkd "Paden City Pottery Made in USA Oven Proof M54," 6" d 5.00

Platter, Sheffield..................... 10.00

Salt and Pepper Shakers, pr,
Patio................................... 10.00

Sauce Boat, Shenandoah 6.00

Serving Tray, hand wrought aluminum with Shenandoah dinner plate center, mkd "Cromwell Hand Wrought Aluminum"............ 14.50

Soup Bowl, Shenandoah 2.00

Souvenir Pitcher, Lincoln's Birthplace, green and white, brown design, 4-1/2" h.................. 10.00

Teapot, Caliente, blue 30.00

☆ Paint-by- Number Sets

For those of us who aren't artistically inclined, paint-by-number sets open a world that turns anyone into a first-class artist. Popular-culture figures are favorite subjects for paint-by-number kits. Collectors look for sets that are mint in box. However, buyers are also snapping up many finished products.

Catalog, Craft Master, 1953,
64 pgs................................29.00

Dennis the Menace Acrylic Paint by Number Set, Determined Productions, 1971, unopened, MIB 20.50

Dick Tracy Oil Paint by Number Set, Hasbro, 1967, boxed in orig shrink-wrap 65.00

Snoopy and Woodstock, 10" x 8", $6.

Dukes of Hazzard Acrylic Paint by Number Set, Craft Master, 1980, NRFB 25.00

Flamingo motif, oak frame, sgd "C.F. Massey," board 20" x 16" ... 66.00

Leonardo DaVinci's The Last Supper Paint by Number Set, Craft Master, 1964, MIB..................... 10.50

Lighthouse motif, framed, board measures 26" x 20" 46.50

Roy Rogers Paint by Number Paint Set, Post Super Sugar Crisp premium, 1954, orig box.......... 80.00

Star Wars Return of the Jedi Acrylic Paint by Number Set, Craft Master, #33009, Lando & Boush, 1983, NRFB 6.00

Western motif, man on bronco, framed, 1955, canvas 10" x 8"............................... 30.00

❖ Pairpoint

Here's a name that can confuse flea market dealers. Some associate Pairpoint with the Pairpoint Manufacturing Company or Pairpoint Corporation, a leader in silver-plated wares. Others associate it with National Pairpoint Company, a company who made glassware, plus aluminum products such as windows, and other commercial glassware. Today lead crystal glassware is still made by Pairpoint. Visit their factory in Sagamore, MA.

Basket, silver plated, 12-5/8" l, 9-1/4" w, 9-1/4" h, mkd "Pat applied for 12/1904," some wear to plating 295.00

Bowl, amethyst glass, silver label, unused............................... 75.00

Compote, silver plated, 7-5/8" w, 3-5/8" h, wear to plating...... 75.00

Cornucopia, ruby glass vase, clear glass ball connector with controlled bubbles, pr, 8-1/2" h 950.00

Fruit Tray, silver plated, birds, cherries, and leaves, 11" x 14" 195.00

Mustache Cup, silver plated, elaborate floral design, mkd "Pairpoint Mfg Co., New Bedford, Mass, Quadruple Plate, 2060," 3-1/4" h 45.00

Tea Set, silver plated 300.00

Tray, silver plated, designer Albert Steffin, 14" l, patented June 28, 1904 .... 195.00

❖ Paper Dolls

As toys, paper dolls go all the way back to the 1880s. Several early magazines, like *McCall's*, used to include paper dolls in every issue. The book form of paper dolls came into favor in the 1950s. Look for interesting characters and vintage clothing styles.

Periodicals: *Celebrity Doll Journal*, 5 Court Pl, Puyallup, WA 98372; *Cornerstones*, 2216 S. Autumn Lane, Diamond Bar, CA 91789; *Golden Paper Doll & Toy Opportunities*, PO Box 252, Golden CO, 80402-0252; *Loretta's Place Paper Doll Newsletter*, 808 Lee Ave., Tifton, GA; *Midwest Paper Dolls & Toys Quarterly*, PO Box 131, Galesburg, KS 66740; *Northern Lights Paperdoll News*, PO Box 871189, Wasilla, AK 99687; *Now & Then*, 6740 Yellowstone Blvd., Flushing, NY 11375-2614; *Paper Doll & Doll Diary*, PO Box 12146, Lake Park, FL 33403; *Paper Doll Circle*, 5 Jackson Mews, Immingham, NR, Grimsby, S Hubs DN40 2HQ, UK; *Paper Doll Gazette*, Route #2, Box 52, Princeton, IN 47670; *Paper Doll News*, PO Box 807, Vivian, LA 71082; *Paperdoll Review*, PO Box 584, Princeton, IN 47670; *PD Pal*, 5341 Gawain #883, San Antonio, TX 78218.

Collectors' Clubs: Original Paper Doll Artist Guild, PO Box 14, Kingsfield, ME 04947; Paper Doll Queens & Kings of Metro Detroit, 685 Canyon Road, Rochester, MI 48306; United Federation of Doll Clubs, 10920 N Ambassador, Kansas City, MO 64153.

America's Prettiest Girls, Magazine Cover Girls, 1944, mint..... 175.00

Annie Oakley, 1956, uncut 65.00

Barbie's Boutique, Whitman, 1973, uncut.................................. 12.00

Betsy McCall Cut-Out/Punch-Out Paper Dolls, Saalfield #1370, 8-1/4" x 11-1/2", copyright 1965, 1966 McCall Corp., USA, 16 full color pages 20.00

Carol Hess Coloring Book and Paper Dolls, Whitman, 8-3/8" x 10-3/4", copyright 1961, 128 b/w pages, two pages colored... 15.00

Dotty and Danny on Parade, Burton Playthings, #875, 1935, uncut.................................. 35.00

Joan Caulfield, Saalfield #157810, 10-3/4" x 14", copyright 1953, uncut.................................. 45.00

Lucille Ball & Desi Arnaz, Whitman, 1953, uncut......................... 80.00

Mary Poppins, 1973, partially cut....................................... 35.00

MOD Fashions Cut-Out/Punch Out Jane Fonda Paper Doll, Saalfield #1369, 8-1/4" x 11-1/2", copyright 1966, 16 full color pages..... 35.00

Our Gang, Whitman, 1931, clothes uncut.................................. 65.00

Sally Dimple, Burton Playthings, 1935, uncut......................... 35.00

Triplet Dolls, Stephens Publishing Co., c1950, uncut................ 37.50

❖ Paperback Books

Mass marketed paperback books dated back to the late 1930s. Collectors tend to focus on one type of book, or perhaps a favorite author.

Periodicals: *Books Are Everything,* 302 Martin Drive, Richmond, KY 40475; *Dime Novel Round-Up,* PO Box 226, Dundas, MN 55019; *Echoes,* 504 E. Morris Street, Seymour, TX 76380; *Golden Perils,* 5 Milliken Mills Road, Scarboro, ME 04074; *Paperback Parade,* PO Box 209, Brooklyn, NY 11228.

Baa Baa Black Sheep, Gregory Boyington, Dell 4.50
Baseball Stars of 1961, Ray Robinson, Pyramid 4.00
Battle Cry, Leon Uris, Bantam .. 5.00
Captain Rebel, Frank Yerby, Cardinal 4.50
Life and Loves of Lana Turner, W. Wright, Wisdom House......... 4.00
Nevada, Zane Grey, Bantam 7.50
Our Friend the Atom, Walt Disney, Dell 5.00
Return to Tomorrow, L. Ron Hubbard, Ace 10.00
The Wedding Journal, Walter Edmonds, Dell...................... 7.50
Woman of Kali, Gardner F. Fox, Gold Medal.......................... 6.50

Ripley's Believe It or Not, 17th Series, **Pocket Books, Sept. 1971, 50 cents.**

❖ ✪ Paper Ephemera

Collecting paper items is another one of the fastest growing collecting areas. Some folks search for bits of nostalgia to perhaps frame and decorate their homes, while others search for interesting pieces of local history or memorabilia related to a specific topic, like Coca-Cola. Ephemera takes many forms, from advertisements to books to posters, and many are covered under separate categories in this book as well as under related topics. The listings below are but a small sampling of the types of paper items commonly found at flea markets.

Periodicals: *Biblio,* 845 Willamette St., Eugene, OR 87401; *Paper & Advertising Collector,* PO Box 500, Mount Joy, PA 17552; *Paper Collectors' Marketplace,* PO Box 128, Scandinavia, WI 54977.

Collectors' Clubs: Ephemera Society, 12 Fitzroy Square, London, W1P 5HQ England; National Association of Paper & Advertising Collectors, PO Box 500, Mount Joy, PA 17552; The Ephemera Society of America, Inc., PO Box 95, Cazenovia, NY 13035; The Ephemera Society of Canada, 36 Maccauley Drive, Thornhill, Ontario L3T 5S5 Canada, plus specialized collector clubs.

For additional listings, see *Warman's Antiques and Collectibles Price Guide.*

Bill of Lading, Dayton & Michigan RR Co., Dayton, OH, 1865, letterhead, filled out for shipping purposes, red and blue printed ink...................................... 26.00

Crayola blotter, 50th anniversary, 3-3/8" x 6-1/4", $22.50.

Sinclair Dinosaur Stamp Album, 1959, 6" x 8-3/8", $4.

Blotter
    Marble Granite Works, Westport, CT, "A Happy Future," fortune-telling Mammy, HarryRoseland print, 1906, 6-1/2" x 3-1/2" 40.00
    The Soap Suds Blues, dog being bathed in tub, Harry N. Johnson, Real Estate & Insurance, Highlands, NJ 10.00
Bookmark, Palmer Violets Bloom Perfume, gold trim 15.00
Dealer's Price List, Martin Hermann, Callicon, NY, 1912, 6 pgs..... 12.00
Dance Card Booklet, Journeymen and Plasterers, 1888, attached tiny pencil........................... 60.00
Letterhead
    Bucks County Bank & Trust Co., green and white, unused .... .50
    J. W. Pepper & Son, Philadelphia, PA, building illus, typed letter 5.00
    Milford Township Ambulance Corp., red and white .... .25
Menu, Metropolitan Hotel, 4 pgs, c1974................................ 35.00
Wallpaper Book
    E. R. Hughes & Co., Dodgeville, WI, 50 pgs 12.00
    Montgomery Ward & Co., 1931, 96 pgs........................... 44.00

Wallpaper Guild, Wallpaper Room by Room, c1929, 24 pgs 16.00

Wanted Poster, Katherine Ann Power 25.00

☆ Paper Money

Here's another one of those topics where thousands and thousands of examples exist, and collectors have to be very critical of condition. There are many good reference books to help with both of these issues. And, as noted in the *Bank Note Reporter,* there was a new record set recently at auction for an 1890 $1,000 treasury note—$792,000. The note is commonly known as the Levitan Grand Watermelon. *Bank Note Reporter* goes on to explain that only three of these Grand Watermelons are known to be in private hands. Good hunting!

References, all from Krause Publications: Colin R. Bruce, II and Neil Shafer, eds., *Standard Catalog of World Paper Money, Specialized Issues,* Volume I, 8th Ed.; Chester Krause, *Wisconsin Obsolete Bank Notes and Scrip;* Eric P. Newman, *Early Paper Money of America,* 4th Ed., Dean Oates & John Schwartz, *Standard Guide to Small Size U. S. Paper Money,* 2nd Ed.; Albert Pick, *Standard Catalog of World Paper Money, General Issues,* Volume II, 8th Ed., Arlie Slabaugh, *Confederate States Paper Money,* 9th Ed.; Robert E. Wilhite, Ed., *Standard Catalog of U. S. Paper Money,* 17th Ed.

Periodical: *Bank Note Reporter,* 700 E State St., Iola, WI 54990.

Bank of State of Georgia, 1857 .... 20.00

Bank of Tennessee, 1861, 5 cents............................... 10.00

Consecutive Numbers, set of five, $1, CU FRNS, 1995 Star, District B............................ 20.00

Continental Note, Philadelphia, Feb 17, 1776, $2, decorative border, woodcuts 85.00

First Reserve Bank Note, 1929, $5 .... 150.00

$2 bill, 1963 Series, $3.

Franklin Silk Co., Ohio, $1 ...... 20.00

State of Florida, $1 .... 26.00

State of North Carolina, $2 note, 1861 .... 21.00

Tecumseh, Michigan, $1 .... 30.00

❖ Paperweights

About the same time folks invented paper, they needed something to hold it down, so along came the paperweight. They can be highly decorative or purely practical. Look for ones of interesting advertising, perhaps a unique shape, or showing an interesting location.

References: For high-end priced antique and modern glass paperweights, consult one of the many standard paperweight reference books.

Collectors' Clubs: Caithness Collectors Club, 141 Lanza Ave., Building 12, Garfield, NJ 07026; International Paperweight Society, 761 Chestnut St., Santa Cruz, CA 95060; Paperweight Collectors Association, Inc., PO Box 1263, Beltsville, MD 20704.

For additional listings of traditional glass paperweights, see *Warman's Antiques and Collectibles Price Guide* and *Warman's Glass.*

Cast Iron, 7-1/2" l, skeleton hand, realistic 125.00

Glass, rect, advertising

Coutes Clipper Mfg., Worcester, MA, illus of pair of clippers, 2-1/2" w, 4" l 75.00

Donnelly Machine Co., Brockton, MA, scalloped edge, illus of vintage factory, 3" w, 4-1/2" l 50.00

Knights of Pythias, cracked, 3-1/2" d, $25.

Heywood Shoes, shoe illus, titled "Heywood is in it," 2-1/2" w, 4" l 40.00

J. R. Leeson & Co., Boston, Linen Thread importers, spinning wheel image 80.00

Oscar R. Boehne & Co., gold scale, 2-1/2" w, 4" l 60.00

Glass, modern

Ayotte, Rick, yellow finch, perched on branch, faceted, sgd, and dated, 1979.... 750.00

Baccarat, Peace on Earth, sgd................................ 130.00

Banford, Bob, white flower, yellow flower, brown dots, green leaves, sgd 225.00

Kaziun, Charles, millefiori spider lily, green ground, pedestal........................ 365.00

Lotton, Charles, irid floral, yellow, white, and blue dec, sgd, 1975 .... 75.00

Perthshire, three-flower bouquet, 3 white lily of the valley flowers, swirl cut green and white double overlay, signature cane............................. 175.00

Souvenir, acrylic, torch inside made from materials from Statue of Liberty, 1886-1996, round, 4-1/2" d................ 20.00

☆ Parrish, Maxfield

Like many illustrators, Maxfield Parrish did commercial work. Today, some of those commercial illustrations are highly sought by collectors.

Book, *The Arabian Nights, Their Best Known Takes,* edited by Kate Douglas Wiggin and Nora A. Smith, illus by Parrish, 1929 .... 300.00

Calendar Top, Edison Mazda Reveries, 1927, framed, 6-3/4" x 10-1/4" 175.00

Child's Book, *Poems of Childhood,* 8 illus, 1955 .... 125.00

Magazine Advertisement, Goodrich Tires, black and white, 1923, unsigned, 6-3/4" x 10" 28.00

Magazine Cover
American Heritage, Dec 1970 ....25.00
Pierrot's Serenade 75.00
Schribner Magazine, 1902, bound 55.00

Matchbook, Old King Cole, St. Regis Hotel, New York City, orig wooden matches, 4-1/2" x 2" 25.00

Print
Chef Between Lobsters, 1925, 7-1/4" x 12" 150.00

Playing cards, "The Waterfall," advertise Edison Mazda Lamps, single boxed deck, $127.50.

Royal Gorge of Colorado, 1925, 16-1/2" x 20" 285.00
Wild Geese, orig frame, 15" x 12" 185.00

❖ Patriotic Collectibles

Three cheers for the red, white, and blue! And three cheers for the collectors who thrive on this type of material. There are lots of great examples just waiting to be found at America's flea markets.

Collectors' Club: Statue of Liberty Collectors' Club, 26601 Bernwood Rd., Cleveland, OH 44122.

Bank, Uncle Sam, Puriton 32.00
Bell, Statue of Liberty, hand painted, Fenton 35.00
Brooch, silver-tone, Statue of Liberty, red, white, and blue rhinestones, sgd "Wendy Gell," 4" h 65.00
Book, *The Centennial Liberty Bell,* Philadelphia, 1876, hard cover.................................... 18.00
Button, Liberty Bell, plastic shelf shank, 3/4" d......................... 2.50
Fan, diecut shield, red, white, and blue cardboard, "America First," sailor raising deck flag, warships

Flags of All Nations, reprinted from the 1953 edition of Compton's Pictured Encyclopedia, 10" x 7-1/2", $2.

in background, biplane flying overhead, back with sponsors names and song lyrics, 7" x 9" 45.00
Lapel Stud, Colonial Bicycles, red, white, and blue shield symbol 20.00
Medal, Victory Liberty Loan, US Treasury Dept 15.00
Needle Book, World's Best, Statue of Liberty, airplane, ship, world, 6 needle packets.................20.00
Note Pad Holder, kitten with red, white, and blue shield, wearing US Navy cap, 7-1/4" x 9", some wear..................................25.00

Postcard
A Daughter of the Regiment, edge wear........................ 6.00
The Glorious 4th of July, Liberty Bell, minor wear................ 6.00
Sheet Music, *Father of the Land We Love,* lyrics and music by George M. Cohan, cover artist James Montgomery Flagg, illus of George Washington on cov, 1931.................................... 12.00
Stickpin, diecut celluloid red, white, and blue American flag on front, black and white adv on back for Artistic Pianos, brass stickpin, early 1900s 30.00
Teapot, white ironstone, portrait of George Washington, excerpts from Declaration of Independence, mkd "Ellgreave Adin of Woods and Sons, England, Genuine Ironstone," 5-3/4" h 40.00
Tin, Wiles Biscuit Company, Bakers of Sunshine Biscuits, NY, signing of Constitution, Gold Rush, Statue of Liberty, bail handle, some wear 25.00
Watch Fob, silvered brass, shield shape, attached silvered brass horseshoe, raised eagle on front, red, white, and blue enameled name, American Badge Co., c1900 ....48.00

❖ Pattern Glass

Pattern glass can best be defined as tableware made in a wide range of patterns and colors. Early manufacturers developed machinery to create glassware, and as the years went by, the patterns became more intricate. Most pattern glass is usually clear, but translucent colors are also available. Remember that this was mass produced glassware, made in hundreds of different patterns in many shapes and sizes.

References: There are many older reference books which are good sources to identify a pattern name, maker, and pieces available. There are also several good resources giving solid information about the reproductions found in today's marketplace.

Collectors' Clubs: Early American Pattern Glass Society, PO Box 266, Colesburg, IA 52035; Moon and Star Collectors Club, 4207 Fox Creek, Mount Vernon, IL 62864; The National American Glass Club, Ltd., PO Box 9489, Silver Spring, MD 20907.

Reproduction Alert.

For additional listings, see *Warman's Antiques and Collectibles Price Guide, Warman's Pattern Glass,* and *Warman's Glass.*

The sampling of Pattern Glass prices listed below are clear glass unless otherwise noted.

Berry Bowl, Inverted Strawberry, 9-1/2" d, scalloped.............. 65.00
Bowl
    Delaware, green, oval 65.00

Actress sauce, clear, 2-1/2" h, 4-1/2" d, $18.

Holly, 9" l, oval, under rim flake................................. 65.00
Butter, cov
    Feather, flanked rim............ 65.00
    Finecut & Panel, vaseline..115.00
Cake Stand
    Bleeding Heart, 9" d 85.00
    Daisy & Button with Thumbprint, amber............................. 65.00
Champagne, Lily of the Valley............................... 165.00
Compote, cov, feather, ls, 5-1/2" d 75.00

Creamer
    Flowerpot............................ 32.00
    Paneled Diamond Point, applied handle 35.00
    Three Face, face below spout, frosted base 165.00
Cruet, Paneled Thistle 25.00
Eggcup, Viking........................ 40.00
Goblet
    Chain and Shield 28.00
    Curtain Tie Back 20.00
    Frazier 20.00
    Greek Key 20.00
    Halley's Comment, flint....... 40.00
    Knobby Bull's Eye............... 20.00
    Late Paneled Grape 20.00
    Late Prism with Diamond Point 20.00
    Michigan 20.00
    New Hampshire.................. 20.00
    Pennsylvania 20.00
    Shovel 20.00
    Wheat & Barley, amber....... 38.00
Honey Dish, Bleeding Heart ... 25.00

Pitcher
    Crystal Wedding, square .. 120.00
    Feathered Points 85.00
    Flowerpot............................ 65.00
    Peacock Feather 85.00
Plate, Wheat & Barley, 7" d..... 35.00
Relish, Lily of the Valley, oval.. 35.00
Salt, master, Lily of the Valley, cov repaired...................... 90.00
Salt Shaker, Three Face 75.00
Sauce, Holly, 4" d................... 25.00
Sugar, cov
    Flowerpot............................ 48.00

Hidalgo................................. 65.00
Water Set, pitcher and 6 tumblers
    Anthemion, green 345.00
    Beaumont's Floral, emerald green, gold trim 285.00
    Peerless, flint 355.00
    Red Block, ruby stained.... 330.00
Wine, Lily of the Valley.......... 175.00

❖ Peachblow Glass

This pretty art glass is colored like its name. And, as natural peaches are shaded, so is this glassware. There are marked differences in color and texture of the major glass makers who created this glass.

Reproduction Alert.

For additional listings, see *Warman's Antiques and Collectibles Price Guide* and *Warman's Glass.*

Bowl, shading from deep rose to bluish-white, white satin int., Mount Washington, 4" d.............. 150.00
Bride's Bowl, wavy ruffled rim, cased int., New Martinsville, 11" d................................. 125.00

Wheeling vase, deep red to orange to yellow, 8" h, $250.

Candlesticks, pr, Gundersen 275.00

Celery Vase, 5" sq, glossy, Wheeling 300.00

Creamer and Sugar, satin finish, ribbed, applied white handles, New England 500.00

Dish, wavy ruffled rim, New Martinsville, 5" d 100.00

Finger Bowl, cased, Webb, 4-1/2" d 195.00

Pear, hollow, free blown, crooked stem, pink shading to white, New England 300.00

Rose Bowl, Wheeling, 4" d ... 225.00

Toothpick Holder, bulbous, deep color, glossy finish, Wheeling, two cracks in outer casing 70.00

☆ Peanuts

The comic strip Peanuts has been bringing smiles to faces since 1950. Snoopy, Charlie Brown, Lucy and the rest of the gang are all creations of Charles M. Schulz. Peanuts collectibles have been licensed by Charles M. Schulz Creative Associates and United Features Syndicate.

Collectors' Club: Peanuts Collector Club, 539 Sudden Valley, Bellingham, WA 98226.

Address Book, United Features Syndicate, Inc., mkd "Made in Hong Kong," 3-3/4" x 2-1/2" 6.00

Bank, Snoopy & Friends Musicians, 5 pc set, orig boxes 175.00

Belt Buckle, Snoopy leaving home with suitcase, child's size, c1970 .... 10.00

Child's Ring, Lucy, enameled, adjustable 40.00

Hallmark Holiday Puzzle Greeting, MOC, $10.

Commemorative Coin, "The Great Pumpkin," 30th anniversary, Linus on one side, Peanuts Gang on other, black case, orig certificate of authenticity 80.00

Cookbook, Scholastic Book Services, 1st printing, Jan 1970 .... 24.00

Doll

  Lucy, rubber and plastic, mkd "United Features Syndicate, Hong Kong," 7" h 30.00

  Snoopy, dressed as graduate, plush 20.00

Flasher Button, uncut sheet, 12" x 9", 12 different 3" d buttons with Snoopy 35.00

Mug, "I'm Not Worth A Thing Before Coffee Break," Snoopy on front, mkd "Fire King" 14.50

Music Box, Schmid 65.00

PEZ, Snoopy............................ 7.00

Tumbler, plastic, 14 oz

  Charlie Brown and Lucy playing football.............................. 4.00

  Snoopy playing golf, Zak Designs 4.00

Wastebasket, tin, Snoopy 25.00

☆ Pedal Cars

The "ultimate" for many children was to own a pedal car. Pedal cars go back to about 1915, when they were made to closely resemble the automobiles of the day. After the first pedal cars became successful, other companies began to make pedal cars too. War time material supplies curbed growth for a few years, but these popular toys gained popularity again, just in time for special cars issued to tie into television programs of the 1950s and 1960s.

Periodical: *The Wheel Goods Trader,* PO Box 435, Fraser, MI 48026.

Collectors' Club: National Pedal Vehicle Association, 1720 Rupert NE, Grand Rapids, MI 49505.

Blue Streak, blue and white, BMC 450.00

Coca-Cola Truck, red and white, AMF................................. 500.00

Comet, Murray 775.00

Earth Mover, Murray 1,100.00

Fire Truck, orig ladders 325.00

Junior Trac, AMF.................. 250.00

Mustang, AMF...................... 800.00

Safari Wagon, AMF................. 50.00

Studebaker, Midwest Industries, restored........................... 950.00

Tin Lizzy, green, Garton 500.00

❖ Pencil Clips and Paper Clips

Early advertisers developed a clever way to help folks remember their names. They developed both paper clips and pencil clips. With a metal clip to do the job, they added a metal or celluloid disk to hold the advertising.

Morton pencil clip, mkd "Lou Fox, Chicago," 1-5/8" l, $20.00.

Paper Clip, celluloid button

Morton's Salt, 1-3/4" d.........28.00

Starr Egg Carrier,
1-3/4" d 125.00

Steckley's Genetics,
1-3/4" d 125.00

Pencil Clip

American Ace Flour, metal clip, metal disk with image of aviator, wearing cap and goggles, rim inscription in blue enamel, biplane image at bottom, c1930 ....40.00

Diamond Crystal Salt, celluloid button 18.00

Star Brand Shoes, silver luster metal clip, slotted grip, celluloid front label, red and white star logo and inscription "Star Brand Shoes Are Better," gold background, c1920 ....25.00

Strongheart Rations, silvered metal clip, tinted celluloid button, German Shepherd head, c1930 ....20.00

Sundial Shoes, silvered metal clip, celluloid button in brown and gold, slogan "For All The Family" 20.00

The Page Milk Company, celluloid button.............................48.00

❖ Pencil Sharpeners

Figural pencil sharpeners are starting to catch on with collectors. Many of them are brightly colored and create a wonderful grouping. Look for examples in good condition with little damage to the actual sharpener part.

Advertising

Alasco, metal, 5" w.............24.00

Eagle Pencil Co., #650, New York, 1-1/2" l.......................7.00

National Cash Register, brass replica, side crank, drawer opens 10.00

Black Boy, playing French horn, celluloid, mkd "Made in Japan," 1930s, 3-1/2" h, metal sharpener missing 175.00

Donald Duck, molded hard vinyl, yellow head, Apsco Products, Inc., orig cardboard display box, c1960................................. 35.00

Popeye, Bakelite, copyright 1929 King Features Syndicate, 1-3/4" h.............................. 95.00

Snoopy, battery operated, mkd "Snoopy, copyright 1958, 1968 United Features Syndicate, Kenner Products, Division of General Mills Fun Group Inc., Cincinnati, Ohio, made in Hong Kong," 6" l 18.00

Robot, plastic, mkd "Made in Hong Kong," 1-3/4" h 15.00

❖ Pennants

Rah Rah! Pennants used to be the flag of choice for sports events, parades, etc. Today they have become colorful collectibles.

Allegheny State Park, felt, 24" l 30.00

Cape Kennedy, 1st Man on Moon, July '69, long orig dowel 55.00

Cincinnati Redlegs, red felt, pink and white detailing, 29" l............ 60.00

Minnesota Twins, 1950s, felt, 29" l 50.00

Miss Burma Official GOP Mascot, Souvenir of Mills Bros. Circus, felt, 25" l.............................. 30.00

National Baseball Hall of Fame and Museum, Cooperstown, NY, 12" l 18.00

New York Mets, 1969, autographed by Tug McGraw, Don Clendenon, and Ron Swoboda.............. 60.00

Ohio State, university symbol, silver and red, 29" l 12.00

Panama Canal, seated lady with 2 atlases, holding sign "Succeeded and Completed, Panama 1915 Pacific," green-brown ground, San Francisco on end, 28-1/2" l 95.00

Pennsylvania Turnpike, felt, 25" l 25.00

Pete Osceola's Indian Village, Tamiami Trail, Florida, Seminole woman making dolls, 18" l 24.00

Pittsburgh Pirates, small, 1970s................................... 10.00

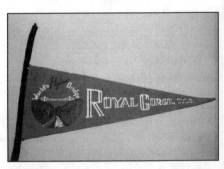

"Royal Gorge, Colo., World's Highest Bridge," orange felt, 7" x 16-1/2" plus straps, $1.

Riviera Beach, Florida, alligator, flamingo, palm tree, 18" l 22.00

Sarasota, Florida, palm trees, flamingos, sail boat, 12" l....15.00

South Carolina, Banjo Boy, white, yellow, blue, brown, and green graphics, navy blue ground, 1920s, 25-1/2" l...................70.00

Stanton, Missouri, Jesse James Hideout, Meramec Caverns, felt, 26" l....................................30.00

Tower of Jewels, San Francisco, 1915, faded dark blue, 29" l....................................125.00

Yankees, "We're #1 American League Champs," 1976 ......48.00

❖ Pennsbury Pottery

Taking it's name from the close proximity of William Penn's estate, Pennsbury, in Bucks County, Pennsylvania, this little pottery lasted from 1950 until 1970. Several of the owners had formerly worked for Stangl, which might explain some of the similarities of design and form to that New Jersey pottery.

Ashtray

Doylestown Trust 30.00

Bird

Bird on Nest...................... 300.00

Goldfinch, #102................. 200.00

Cup and Saucer, Black Rooster pattern................................20.00

Dinner Plate, Hex pattern........ 17.50

Pitcher, Eagle pattern, 6-3/8" h, $40.

Eggcup, Red Rooster
  pattern 25.00
Mug, Schiaraflia Filadelfia, owl and
  seal..................................... 30.00
Pie Plate, Apple Tree pattern . 37.50
Pitcher, Eagle pattern 40.00
Plaque
  Amish Family, 8" d..............55.00
  Pennsylvania RR 1888, Tiger
    Locomotive, 8" x 5-5/8" ...48.00
Teapot, Red Rooster pattern .. 65.00
Tea Tile, 6" d, skunk "Why Be
  Disagreeable".................... 60.00

❖ Pens and Pencils

Back in the dark ages, before computers, think pads, and other such modern day conveniences, folks actually wrote letters, etc. with pens and pencils! Today some collectors find interesting examples at flea markets.

Periodical: *Pen World Magazine,* PO Box 6007, Kingwood, TX 77325.

Collectors' Clubs: American Pencil Collectors Society, RR North, Wilmore, KS 67155; Pen Collectors of America, PO Box 821449, Houston, TX 77282.

Magazine Ad, Farber Pen,
  1946 .... 5.00

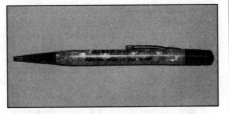

Mechanical advertising pencil, "Olson Rug Co, Chicago, From Our Looms To Your Rooms," 5-1/8" l, $3.

Pen
  Cartier, 14K, large,
    2 dents 260.00
  Conklin, Endura Model, desk set,
    2 pens, side-lever fill, black
    marble base 135.00
  Dunn, black, red barrel, gold filled
    trim, c1920 .... 45.00
  Sheaffer Lifetime Stylist, gold
    filled metal, professionally
    engraved clip, 1960s 35.00
  Wahl, maroon, gold filled trim,
    1943, slight use 25.00
  Waterman's, black, gold trim, clip,
    unused 50.00
Pencil
  Brown-McLaren MFG. Co.,
    Hamburg, Mich., Detroit Office-
    7340 Puritan Ave., Phone Uni-
    versity 3-3520, Redipoint,
    USA, celluloid................ 10.00
  Conklin, rolled gold, initials
    engraved on clip............. 85.00
  Electric Café, Detroit, Michigan,
    clip mkd "Wearever," some
    paint missing 9.00
  Mr. Peanut, engraved on both
    sides of clip, some paint miss-
    ing from top hat 12.00

❖ Pepsi-Cola

"Pepsi-Cola Hits The Spot!" That was part of a popular jingle of the 1950s. Pepsi collectibles today are hot, just as the beverage itself has remained popular since first being made in the late 1890s.

Collectors' Club: Pepsi-Cola Collectors Club, PO Box 1275, Covina, CA 91722.

Ashtray, Pepsi 40.00
Bank, vending machine
  shape 15.00
Bottle Opener
  Church key type, bit of rust ... 6.00
  Diecast flat metal, top stamped
    "Drink Pepsi-Cola," left side
    with opening for bottles, right
    side with hole to hang from
    cooler side, mkd "Vaughn
    USA," mid-1950s,
    4-1/8" l 12.00
Door Push, 31" h, 3" w, porcelain,
  Canadian 100.00
Key Chain, Beach Club, 1960s,
  unused 35.00

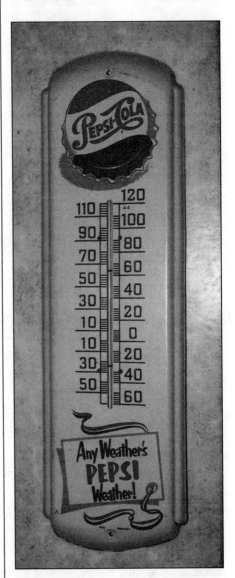

Thermometer, "Any Weather's Pepsi Weather," tin, 26-13/16" x 8-5/16", $167.50.

Bottle-shaped bottle opener, metal, "America's Biggest Value," 2-3/4" l, $12.

Machine, 52" h, Model 27, Vendorlator Mfg Co., orig light blue paint, bottle cap on front cracked 500.00

Promotional Medal................... 8.00

Sign, Have a Pepsi, bottle cap illus with man and woman, paper, 1950s, 22" x 7" 37.50

❖ Perfume Bottles

Decorative and figural perfume bottles have remained a popular area of collecting for generations. Perfume bottles can be found in many different sizes, shapes, and colors, as well as price range. Look for examples with matching stoppers and original labels.

Collectors' Clubs: International Perfume Bottle Association, PO Box 529, Vienna, VA 22180; Miniature Perfume Bottle Collectors, 28227 Paseo El Siena, Laguna Niguel, CA 92677.

Atomizer
  Cambridge, stippled gold, opaque jade, orig silk lined box, 6-1/4" h......................... 150.00
  Devilbiss, clear, threaded dec, 4" h, #127 .... 45.00

Boxed Set
  Evening In Paris 135.00
  Hudnut, Sweet Orchid, 3" h, 1920s 45.00
  Lohes, green, 3" h 40.00

Cut Glass, Button and Star pattern, rayed base, faceted stopper, 6-1/2" h.............................. 125.00

Figural, glass
  Decanter shape, opaque blue ground, enameled white leaves and grape garlands, dragonfly in center, three gold applied ball feet, clear ground stopper 125.00
  Genie slippers, glass, cork stoppers, paper labels, "Rose Oil and Cologne by H. P. & C. R. Taylor, Phila," some damage to orig labels, pr............... 125.00
  German, green glass body, colored enamel coat of arms dec, matching green stopper, 2" h................................ 65.00

Porcelain bottle with atomizer, mkd "Made in Bavaria, Western Germany," 3-1/4" h, $32.

Lay Down Type, satin glass, Diamond Quilted pattern, shading yellow to white, 6" l 415.00

Mary Gregory, cranberry ground, white enameled girl dec, colorless ball stopper 175.00

❖ PEZ

PEZ was invented in Austria as a cigarette substitute. Eduard Haas hoped his mints would catch on when he named it PEZ, an abbreviation for *Pfefferminz*. By 1952, a table top model arrived in America, but it was not until the container was redesigned for children that the candy caught on. Today many seasonal and licensed characters appear as containers. Many popular characters get periodic design updates, giving collectors variations to search for.

References: Richard Geary, *PEZ Collectibles,* Schiffer Publishing, 1994, and *More PEZ for Collectors,* 2nd ed., Schiffer Publishing, 1998.

Periodicals: *PEZ Collector's News,* PO Box 124, Sea Cliff, NY 11579; *Toy Shop,* 700 E State St., Iola, WI 54990.

Donald Duck, Garfield, each $2.

Barney Bear, 1970s 12.00
Boy with Hat, PEZ Pal, 1960 .. 12.00
Charlie Brown, frown, MIP 8.00
Donald Duck, no feet, MIP 27.50
Fozzie Bear, 1991 .... 3.00
Icee 5.50
Kermit, mkd "Made in
    Hungary" 7.50
Lamb mkd "Made in
    Yugoslavia" 6.00
Penguin, Melody Maker,
    MOC 12.00
Rabbit 7.50
Santa, mkd "Made in
    Yugloslavia" 8.00
Tom 6.00
Tuffy 7.50
Whistle, 1960s 2.50

❖ Pfaltzgraff

Here's a name most flea marketers associate with dinnerware. True, but did you know that Pfaltzgraff originally started as a stoneware company? However, by the early 1950s, they realized their future was in dinnerware production, and the company shifted its focus, quite successfully, towards that goal.

Ashtray, Gourmet 6.50
Baker, Village, rect 25.00
Bean Pot, cov, Yorktowne 35.00
Butter Dish, cov, cobalt blue ... 30.00
Chip n Dip, gray, light blue
    edge 15.00
Chowder Cup, Gourmet 4.50
Creamer, America 12.00

Folk Art pattern, 2-qt casserole, #315, $35.

Cup and Saucer
    Christmas Heirloom 7.50
    Yorktowne 5.00
Dinner Plate
    Gazebo 10.00
    Gourmet 12.00
    Windsong 12.00
    Yorktowne 10.00
Gravy Boat, attached underplate,
    Gourmet 10.00
Mug, Yorktowne 5.00
Platter, Yorktowne 10.00
Salad Plate, Village 3.50
Sugar, cov, America 15.00
Tankard, Pickled Pete, Muggsy
    series 40.00

❖ Phoenix Bird China

Phoenix Bird China is a group of pretty blue and white patterns that were made from the late 19th C through the 1940s. The dinnerware was imported to America where it was retailed by several firms, including Woolworth's, and wholesalers such as Butler Brothers.

Collectors' Club: Phoenix Bird Collectors of America, 685 S. Washington, Constantine, MI 49042.

For additional listings and a detailed history, see *Warman's Americana & Collectibles.*

Cup and Saucer 10.00
Dinner Plate, 9-3/4" d 48.00
Eggcup, double cup 15.00
Luncheon Plate, 8-1/2" d 17.50
Platter, oval, 14" l 95.00
Soup Dish, 7-1/4" d 35.00
Teapot, squatty 42.00

❖ Phoenix Glass

Phoenix Glass Company, founded in Beaver, PA, in 1880, was another one of those glass companies who started making commercial products and later got into art glass. Their molded and sculptured wares are what most dealers think of as "Phoenix" glass.

Collectors' Club: Phoenix & Consolidated Glass Collectors Club, PO Box 3847, Edmond, OK 73083.

Ashtray, Phlox, large, white,
    frosted 66.00
Basket, pink ground, relief molded
    dogwood dec, 4-1/2" h 65.00
Candlesticks, pr, blue ground,
    bubbles and swirls,
    3-1/4" h 65.00
Charger, blue ground, relief molded
    white daffodils 100.00
Ginger Jar, cov, frosted ground, bird
    finial 80.00
Planter, white ground, relief molded
    green lion, 8-1/2" l 95.00
Vase
    Bellflower, burgundy pearlized
        ground 75.00
    Flying Geese, pillow form, white
        on brown 260.00
    Philodendron, Wedgwood blue,
        white ground 160.00
    Wild Rose, amber 175.00

❖ Photographs

Photograph collecting certainly is one way to add "instant ancestors" to those picture frames you'd like to hang. Many photographs are found at flea markets. They range from the earliest type, daguerreotypes, to tintypes, to works by established photographers, to boxes and albums full of unidentified views by unidentified photographers. It's a topic that's currently hot right now. Look for photographs that have interesting composition or those which might give some perspective to the way an area looked, etc.

Reference: O. Henry Mace, *Collector's Guide to Early Photographs,* Krause Publications, 1999.

Collectors' Clubs: American Photographic Historical Society, 1150 Avenue of the Americas, New York, NY 10036; National Stereoscopic Association, PO Box 14801, Columbus, OH 43214; The Photographic Historical Society, PO Box 39563, Rochester, NY 14604.

Albumen print, common, unidentified subject or location 1.00
Ambrotype, common, unidentified subject or location 5.00
Cabinet Photo, black and white
　Garfield, J. A., signature at bottom 15.00
　Garfield, Mrs. James A., published by Ralph Frautman, New York........................15.00
CDV
　Car crash, Brooklyn street, billboards, linen mounted, c1917 ....75.00
　Girl with bisque doll 14.00
　Girl with folk art-type hobby horse 15.00
　Lady pick pocket, mug shot 45.00
　Postmortem baby 42.00
　Woolworth, lunch counter, c1940 ....55.00
Folder, Sunset Highway, 8 black and white photos, info sheet, published by J. Boyd Ellis, Arlington, WA, unused..........................5.00
Postcard, real photo of Photography Gallery, location not identified............................ 30.00
Silver Print, Chief Hairy Chin, dressed as Uncle Sam, D. F. Barry blindstamp, printed c1900, 6-1/4" x 4"..........................825.00

Real-photo postcard, Home Sweet Home, 1910 inscription, 3-1/2" x 5-1/2", $12.

Snapshot, unidentified subject or location 25
Tintype
　Common unidentified subject............................. 5.00
　Occupational, iceman 100.00
Wire Service Photograph
　Chicago White Sox, Carlton Fisk and Toronto Blue Jays Fred McGriff, 1989.................... 3.50
　The Herald Staff, names, positions, dates, taken in Atlantic City, NJ, 1908, 8" x 10" .. 16.00
　Barry Switzer and Dallas Cowboys coach Jimmy Johnson, 1989, wire service type 3.50

❖ Pickard China

This company was founded by Wilder Pickard in 1897 in Chicago. Their principal production was hand painting on European china blanks. Watch for artist-signed pieces.

Collectors' Club: Pickard Collectors Club, 300 E Grove St., Bloomington, IL 67101.

For additional listings, see *Warman's Antiques and Collectibles Price Guide* and *Warman's American Pottery & Porcelain*.

Cake Plate, open gold handles, Desert Garden pattern...... 185.00
Mug, poinsettia flowers, gold banding and trim, sgd "N. R. Clifford" 275.00
Plate
　Currants, 7-1/2" d 75.00
　Peaches, gilded and molded border, sgd "S. Heap," 9-1/8" d........................110.00
Platter, roses, gilded border, sgd "Seidel," 12" d................... 275.00
Vase, cylindrical, moonlight lake and pine forest scene, sgd "Challinor," Nippon blank, 7-3/4" h 265.00

❖ Picture Frames

Here's a topic few people admit to collecting, but most of us have many of these in our homes. And, a favorite

Wall/desk frame, wooden, grainpainted, holds 6th-plate image, 6-1/4" x 5-3/4", $35.

place for finding interesting frames is a flea market. Make sure you take measurements along if looking for a certain size frame.

Brass, table top, oval, loop hanger.................................35.00
Gold-tone, table top, easel back, small leaves in corners, 5" x 7" opening, c1955 .... 10.00
Mahogany, wide molding, large opening 95.00
Ornate gilt frame, emb with flowers, leaves, scrolls, large opening, some minor damage 100.00
Pewter, emb ribbon and floral trim, oval, small..........................80.00
Silver, table top, easel back, scrolling Art Nouveau design, small 100.00
Tortoiseshell spatter, 3 blended colors, 8-1/2" x 11" opening.....75.00
Walnut, deep, gilt liner..........125.00

☆ Pie Birds

These little birds with their beaks wide open are a bit unusual looking when found out of their natural habitat! Designed to act like a vent for a pie with a top crust, they do work well but many collectors won't think of using them for baking.

Baby Chick, English 85.00
Bird, gray and rose..................65.00

Blue Bird 75.00

Duck, Boyd Company, 4-3/4" h
  Blue 70.00
  Yellow 60.00

Duck, English, small 90.00

First Day of Spring, baby chick in
  egg 40.00

Mama Bear, blue dress,
  English 95.00

Mammy, black 245.00

Pirate, English 85.00

Rooster, English, large 90.00

❖ Pierce, Howard

Howard Pierce was another California potter who designed and created interesting figurines, dinnerware, and some accessories.

Dealer Sign 75.00

Dish, brown and white, 1950s,
  13" l 24.00

Figure
  Deer 45.00
  Fawn, sitting 27.50
  Gaggle of geese, gray 85.00
  Mouse 27.50
  Owls, pr 48.00
  Penguin, 7" h 85.00
  Quail Family, 3 figures 65.00
  Raccoon 75.00
  Roadrunner, mail 75.00
  Robin 46.00
  Sea Bird Family, 3 figures, black
    matte 65.00
  Sparrows, trio 55.00

Vase, Wedgwood jasper style, light green ground, white cameo of Oriental boy on one, girl on other, 5-3/4" h, pr 48.00

❖ Pig Collectibles

"This little piggie went to market" and so on goes the children's nursery rhyme. Actually lots of piggies are now headed to flea markets so that collectors can find them and give them a new happy home. Some of these collectors like to specialize in famous character pigs, like Babe or Porky Pig, while others prefer figurines.

Collectors' Club: The Happy Pig Collectors Club, PO Box 17, Oneida, IL 61467.

Advertising Mirror, Newton Collins Short Order Restaurant, St. Joe, MO, yellow and orange 55.00

Advertising Trade Card, Try Wright's Little Liver Pills, shows 5 pigs 12.00

Bank
  Money bag, pig standing aside, emb "My System" 115.00
  Pig-shaped, ceramic, pink and white, multicolored flowers, curly tail, 1950s 30.00

Figure
  Lobster pulling leg of red pig 115.00
  Pig riding in canoe, c1930 .... 65.00
  Playing cards, "Hearts are Trumps," 3-1/2" h 115.00
  Purse, black bisque pig sitting on top of green purse, 2-1/4" h 80.00

Pottery bank, brown glaze, mkd "Austria," 4-1/2" h, $80.

Well, gold pig, orange roof, mkd "Souvenir of Chicago, Made in Germany," 1930s 65.00

Match Holder, pair of pink bisque pigs, "Scratch My Back" and "Me Too" 120.00

Pinback Button, Swift's, multicolored cartoon of smiling pig wearing rope noose while seated in frying pan, c1901 .... 45.00

Toothpick Holder, pink pig holding camera 95.00

⭐ Pigeon Forge Pottery

Among the array of regional pottery commonly found at flea markets is Pigeon Forge Pottery, made in Pigeon Forge, Tennessee. Capitalizing on the popularity of the tourist town, many pieces were sold as souvenirs. The market is still being established for Pigeon Forge Pottery, which has started to attract more collectors in recent years. Smart flea-market buyers look for artist-signed pieces in unusual forms or glazes.

Bowl, green, ruffled lip, sgd "E. Ownby," 4-1/2" d 15.50

Bowl, red, sgd "E. Wilson," 3" h, 4" d 27.00

Butter molds, mustard, set of 4, snowflake, flower, 2 swans, impressed designs, 4" 15.50

Vase, mkd "G. Griffin," tan with brown speckles, 3-3/8" h, 3-1/2" d, $16.

Figurine, black bear
Lying on back with feet in air, sgd
"D. Ferguson,"
4" h, 6" l............................22.50
Sitting, 4" 18.25
Standing on 4 legs, 4" h 10.50
Mugs, Dogwood pattern,
set of 4 .... 12.50
Teapot, brown, squatty form,
3-1/2" h................................ 6.00
Tile, aqua with 3 yellow flowers,
signed "D. Ferguson," made to
hang, 5-3/4" sq 114.50
Vase, blue, Dogwood pattern,
3-1/2" h, 1-3/4" d 6.00
Vase, mustard, bulbous, slender
neck, sgd "E. Ownby,"
4" h...................................... 15.00
Vase, uranium orange, triple bulbous
form, sgd "E. Wilson,"
4-1/2" h.............................. 40.00

❖ Pinback Buttons

Here's a form of advertising that was an instant hit and is still popular. Look for interesting pinback buttons with advertising and political slogans of all types. Many early manufacturers included a paper insert which further exclaimed the virtues of the product being advertised. Those papers add value, as well as good condition and bright colors.

Billboard Magazine, red and white,
caricature portrait of Gee
Whiz 25.00
Bond Bread, Commander Byrd's
Plane 16.00
Boston Leading Clothiers, Continental Clothing House, black and yellow, image of Revolutionary War
soldier, c1896 .... 20.00
Cat's Paw Safety League, yellow
and black............................. 25.00
Chicago White Sox, Carlton Fisk, No.
72 of 133, 1984, 1-1/8" d........6.00
Chu Chu Gum......................... 30.00
Cinderella Stoves & Ranges,
multicolored......................... 15.00
Hostess Cake, red, white, and blue,
c1940s................................ 24.00
Own a Liberty Bond, Statue of
Liberty, 3/4" d 6.00

Junior Basic Astronaut, litho tin, 1-1/8" d, $2.

Peerless Biscuit Co., black and
white logo, bright red background,
light blue tulips, c 1912,
1-3/4" d 25.00
Red Cross Macaroni, red, white, and
blue, Long Mac cartoon, 1930s,
1-1/4" d 35.00
White House Coffee, black and
white image of White House,
paper back with slogan....... 60.00
William Tell Flour, multicolored,
Amstead & Burk Co., Springfield,
OH 45.00

❖ Pin-Up Art

Charles Dana Gibson is credited with creating the first pin-up girl with his famous Gibson Girls in the early 1900s. Other famous artists followed, creating pretty girls for calendars, magazines, advertisements, etc. It wasn't until the 1920s when the film industry got involved that their clothes seemed to be less important. Later pin-up artists, with names like Vargas, Elvgren, and Moran helped create the modern image of pin-up art.

Periodicals: *Glamour Girls: Then and Now,* PO Box 34501, Washington, DC 20043; *The Illustrator Collector's News,* PO Box 1958, Sequim, WA 98382.

Calendar
Devorss, 1944 .... 45.00

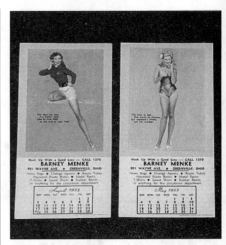

Blotters, advertise "Barney Menke, Greenville, Ohio," each $7.50.

MacPherson, 1953, Models
Sketchbook, 9-1/2" x 12-1/2",
spiral bound paper, wall type,
12 monthly pages, sgd full
color art 75.00
Petty, Esquire, 1955, desk, 5-3/4"
x 6-1/4", white cardboard eagle
frame, dark red diecut opening
around 12 monthly cardboard
sheets............................. 45.00
Petty, Fawcett, 1947 .... 70.00
Greeting Card
Bettie Page, artist Olivia 7.00
Bride, Varga 9.00
Cowboy, artist Olivia 6.00
Gal dressed up as Charlie
Chaplin, artist Olivia 7.00
Nurse, artist Olivia 6.00
Gum Card, 2-1/2" x 3", Gum Inc.,
American Beauties, Elvgren art,
full color, unsigned artwork, titled
captions, 1940s................... 15.00
Magazine, *Esquire*, Christmas,
1943, Varga fold-out, 10" x 13",
320 pgs 45.00
Pocket Knife, 3-3/4" l, silvered steel,
two blade, black and white cello
insert, one side with standing
nude, hands held discreetly over
mid-torso, wearing high heels,
similar dec on other side, c1940
.... 30.00
Print, Elgren, Two Cushion, sultry
girl in red dress playing billiards,
5" x 7", matted........................ 55.00

Rubens, Fox and Wolf Hunt, 1937, published by US Government Art Committee, headed by Eleanor Roosevelt, heavy paper, 9" x 13".............25.00

Vargas Girl, 1960s Playboy, captioned "Mr. Farnsworth…," 8-1/4" x 11".......................12.00

Stand-Up Card, 4-3/4" x 10" diecut cardboard, perforations for folding to form model figure standing on triangular display, full color Moran art, titled "Aiming To Please," pretty redhead archer, mini skirt, red high heels, c1950, unused 15.00

Stationery Kit, 7-1/2" x 9", "Thinking of You," serviceman's cardboard folder with image of lonely GI sitting on trunk trying to write letter, opens to three panel 9" x 23" with full color art of blond haired model in sarong, 50 sheets of note paper, 20 envelopes, early 1940s 55.00

✬ Pisgah Forest

This American pottery has made interesting wares. They used a layered or cameo technique, giving an interesting texture to their work. Most of their wares are clearly marked and dated.

Cream Pitcher, white cameo relief of pioneering scene, blue marbled ground, dec by Walter Stephen, raised potter's mark, mkd "1951/Stephen" 195.00

Mug, cameo dec, finely detailed clog dancers, dec by Walter Stephen, raised logo.........................115.00

Teapot, white cameo relief of pioneering scene, light blue ground, dec by Walter Stephen, raised potter's mark "1951/Stephen" 225.00

Vase, baluster, white and blue crystalline, golden ground, emb potter's mark, 5-1/2" h........... 350.00

❖ Planters

Flea markets are great places to find planters of every type. Unfortunately, many of us have "brown thumbs" and are soon left with a pretty container and little foliage. However, with careful inspection, you just might find out that your favorite planter is a real piece of Westmoreland Glass or perhaps McCoy or Roseville pottery.

We've got additional listings for planters spread all through the book, look under specific companies and also "Lady Head Vases."

Bambi, mkd "Walt Disney Productions" 65.00

Butterfly on Log, brown and white, glossy glaze, mkd "Shawnee USA 524" 12.00

Cactus and Cowboy, natural colors, Morton 17.50

Cat, coral glaze, green box, McCoy, 1950 .... 12.00

Fawns, standing pair, McCoy, 1957 .... 35.00

Flamingos, facing pair, 10" l.. 150.00

Gondola, yellow, McCoy 20.00

Mallard, head down, Royal Copley 22.00

Parrot, white, orange accents . 15.00

Pheasant, mkd "Napcoware," small chip.................................... 10.00

Straw Hat, yellow, blue ribbon 17.50

Turkey, brown, Morton 15.00

Napcoware cat-head planter, 4-1/2" h, \$35.

❖ Planter's Peanuts

The Planter's Nut and Chocolate Co. was founded in Wilkes-Barre, PA in 1906. In 1916, the company held a contest to find a mascot, and Mr. Peanut came to life. He has remained a popular advertising icon.

Collectors' Club: Peanut Pals, PO Box 4465, Huntsville, AL 35815.

Reproduction Alert.

For additional listings, see *Warman's Americana & Collectibles.*

Bank, 8-1/2" h, figural, Mr. Peanut, tan, 3-1/4" d base, coin slot in top hat, mkd "U.S.A.," c1960 ....30.00

Belt, Mr. Peanut, adjustable, Nabisco Dinah Shore Invitational Golf Tournament, "Swing into profits with Planter's," blue fabric and leather belt, brass buckle with Mr. Peanut, back of buckle stamped "1984"..................40.00

Goldwash Mr. Peanut spoon, \$10.

Coaster, tin, Mr. Peanut,
set of 4 .... 24.00
Coloring Book, unused
American Ecology 15.00
50 States 15.00
Presidents 15.00
Cookie Cutter, Mr. Peanut, plastic,
5" h 15.00
Counter Jar, metal lid,
10" h 180.00
Coupon, 6-3/4" x 8-1/2" paper sheet
by Planter's Nut & Chocolate Co.,
picturing set of single serving dish
and four individual dishes, mail
premium offer on reverse, perforated coupon at base, expiration
date of Sept 30, 1939, coupon still
attached 20.00
Olympic Coin, 1980,
Mr. Peanut.......................... 12.00

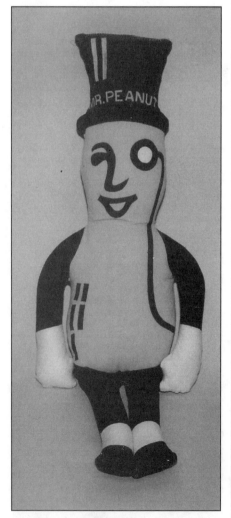

Mr. Peanut stuffed cloth doll, 18" h, $12.

Postcard, Planter's Peanuts at
Times Square, 1940s scene,
unused................................ 20.00
Serving Tray Set, 6" d tray and four
3" d individual serving trays, full
color litho image of tan peanuts
surrounding tan and black Mr.
Peanut image, gold trim accent
line, stylized gold floral pattern on
underside, unused,
c1939................................. 28.00
Waxed Papers, 7-1/4" x 8", black
and white sheet, repeated images
of Mr. Peanut, c1950, sold in lots
of 10 .... 28.00

❖ Plastic

It's hard to imagine life without
plastics. Today, collectors are starting
to become more visible as they
search out early plastics including
acrylics, Bakelite, and celluloid.

For a more detailed history and
additional listings of plastics, see
Warman's Americana & Collectibles
and "Bakelite" and "Celluloid" in this
edition.

Alarm Clock, key wind, Black Forest
works, octagonal translucent
green case.......................... 30.00
Business Card Holder, sea shells
suspended in red acrylic
base..................................... 6.50
Dress Clip, green opaque Lucite,
triangular, chevron design, rhinestone trim............................ 20.00
Mirror, hand, beveled acrylic handle
and frame, U-shaped mirror,

Ashtray, swirled multicolor, 1-3/4" h, 4-1/4" d, $1.

sterling silver floral ornament,
c1946...................................55.00
Napkin Ring, translucent Lucite, sq
shape, rounded edges, circular
center, c1960, 4-pc set 12.00
Paperweight, translucent Lucite
cube, suspended JFK half dollar,
c1965.................................. 10.00
Push Puppet, Santa, holding bell,
mkd "Made in Hong Kong for
Kohner"................................60.00
Wall Shelf, translucent neon pink,
30" l, 6" d, 1970s.................25.00

❖ Playboy Collectibles

Here's a domain that was hot in
the 1960s and 1970s. And, with the
magazine still in business, there are
always more collectibles being created with the classic Bunny image
and that distinctive logo.

Collectors' Club: Playboy Collectors
Association, PO Box 653, Phillips-
burg, MO 65722.

Ashtray, Playboy Club,
3-1/2" sq 21.00
Calendar, 1969, mint in orig
envelope 25.00
Candleholder, 6-1/4" h, 3-1/4" d
base, glass, red frosted finish,
Femin Art pictured twice, tiny
inscription "The Playboy Club"
repeated, 1960s..................25.00
Drinking Glass Set, 5-3/4" h clear
glass tumbler, weighted bottom,
black Playboy Bunny silhouette,
1960s, set of four................50.00
Lighter, black finish, Bunny logo,
engraved "Playboy," mkd "Made
in Japan"............................50.00
Mug Set, 4" d, 4-3/4" h, aluminum,
recessed profile image of Playboy
Bunny on both sides, 1960s, set
of four.................................25.00
Pen, red ink.............................5.00
Puzzle, 5" d by 6-1/2" h cardboard
canister, 500 pc jigsaw puzzle of
Sharon Clark, Playboy Playmate
of the Year, 1970
copyright 35.00
Tumbler, glass, Playboy Club,
3-1/4" h 14.00

❖ Playing Cards

Playing cards, as most of us think about them, were developed in 1885 by the U. S. Playing Card Co. of Cincinnati. However, Americans had been using cards for games and entertainment since they first arrived in the 1700s. Look for interesting designs, complete sets, and original boxes.

Collectors' Clubs: Chicago Playing Card Collectors, 1826 Mallard Lake Drive, Mariette, GA 30068; 52 Plus Joker, 204 Gorham Ave., Hamden, CT 06514; International Playing Card Society, 3570 Delaware Common, Indianapolis, IN 46220.

B & O Railroad, orig box in poor condition................................... 12.00
Camel Cigarettes, Joe Camel on each card, 75th anniversary......................... 10.00
Dallas Cowboys Cheerleaders, full deck, orig box, two jokers, info card about Cheerleaders, TransMedia, 1981 .... 12.50
Gold Medal Flour, two decks, Washburn-Crosby Foods Gold Medal logo, card backs "Eventually, Why Not Now" and company name, leather case, worn 45.00
Lombardy, linen finish, card trick included............................... 2.00
Norman Rockwell, double box.......................... 10.00
Royal Interocean Lines, Eastern Indian woman dancing on each card, flag on back of two-part box 25.00

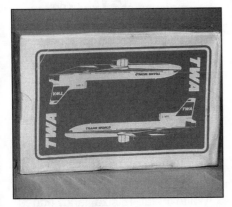

TWA, orig wrap, pictures L-1011, $2.

Union Tank Car Company, tank car on each card, joker as man juggling tank cars, double deck, orig box, 1948............................ 45.00
X-Men, worn box...................... 4.00

★ Playsets

Marx dominated the market for playsets in the 1950s and 1960s, producing a wide variety of the multipiece toys. Other makers and newer sets have followed, including some contemporary reproductions of popular vintage playsets. However, collectors remain most keenly interested in the early examples.

Periodicals: *Plastic Figure & Playset Collector*, P.O. Box 1355, LaCrosse, WI 54602-1355; *Worlds of Plastic Figures*, 815 N. 12th St., Allentown, PA 18102.

Reproduction Alert.

Marx
    Alamo, 3543, boxed 420.00
    Battleground, 4756, 1970s 255.00
    Captain Gallant of the Foreign Legion, boxed............... 725.00
    Fort Apache, 3681, 1967, MIB.............................. 175.00
    Knights and Vikings.......... 167.50
    Navarone Mountain 137.50
    Prehistoric Times, 3389.... 240.00
    Robin Hood, 4724, Series 1000 .... 280.00
    Roy Rogers Double R Bar Ranch........................... 280.00
    Super Circus.................... 256.00
    Walt Disney's Zorro 683.00
Mego
    Flash Gordon................... 150.00
    Hall of Justice, 1976 .... 105.00

Rin Tin Tin at Fort Apache, Marx, $275.

    Muhammad Ali Boxing Ring, 1976, MIB.................... 217.50
    Star Trek Enterprise, boxed, 1974 .... 207.50
    Wizard of Oz 250.00
Remco
    The Rat Patrol................... 225.00
    Wayne Foundation........... 202.50

★ Playskool

Remember Mr. Potato Head? How about wooden Lincoln Logs and Tinkertoys? Does anyone recall Weebles, which wobble but they don't fall down? Those are some of the most popular toys made by Playskool, which was founded in 1928. Playskool products are still largely designed for children 6 years old and under. Flea markets are a prime hunting ground for all manner of Playskool toys, both vintage and contemporary.

Catalog, 30 pages, 1950s 10.00
Catalog, 39 pages, 1967 price list 8.50
Coin phone, wood and metal, some wear 15.00
Doll, Dressy Bessy, cloth, 1979...................................... 28.00
Glow Worm, #866, battery-operated, face lights when squeezed, flannel fabric, 1988 .... 7.00
Lincoln Logs, #892, orig container worn, 1969......................... 52.50
Mr. Potato Head, complete, 1976, box worn 20.00
Playset
    Holiday Inn, NRFB............ 115.00

Auto puzzle, #289, 9 pieces, orig box rough, 9-3/8" x 11-1/2", $15.

McDonald's, missing one tray and playmat, orig box, 1974 ....56.00

Richard Scarry Puzzletown, Dr. Lion's Medical Center, orig box worn 45.00

Tykeworld Zoo, orig box, 1971 ....75.00

Postal Station 10.00

Puzzle, Wonder Woman on Paradise Island, 1981 .... 39.00

Sesame Street yellow rubber ducky, vinyl, 5" 10.00

Stacking toy, 10 wooden rings 31.00

Tinkertoy Starter Kit, cardboard cylinder, metal lid, 60 wooden pcs.......................... 30.00

Weebles

Mickey Mouse Clubhouse ...36.00

Weebles West, complete.....56.00

❖ Pocket Knives

Pocket knives have been made in various forms, all types of handles, and blade materials. Like other collecting categories, some collectors search out pocket knives from specific makers, while others specialize in certain handles or even advertising knives.

References: Bernard Levine, *Levine's Guide to Knives and Their Values,* Krause Publications, 1997; Jack Lewis and Roger Combs, *The Gun Digest Book of Knives,* 5th ed., Krause Publications, 1997; Jim Sargent, *Sargent's American Premium Guide to Pocket Knives & Razors,* 4th ed., Books Americana, 1995; J. Bruce Voyles, *IBCA Price Guide To Antique Knives,* 2nd ed., Krause Publications ___; ___, *IBCA Price Guide to Commemorative Knives, 1960-*

1990, Krause Publications, ___; Ken Warner, *Knives '99,* 19th ed., Krause Publications, 1998.

Periodicals: *Blade,* 700 E State St., Iola, WI 54990; *Knife World,* PO Box 3395, Knoxville, TN 37927.

Collectors' Clubs: American Blade Collectors, PO Box 22007, Chattanooga, TN 37422; Canadian Knife Collectors Club, Route 1, Milton, Ontario L9T 2X5 Canada; National Knife Collectors Association, PO Box 21070, Chattanooga, TN 37421.

Camillus

Babe Ruth, facsimile signature on side, 2-1/2" 125.00

#702, stainless 17.50

4-line stamp, black composition handle, mkd "Camillus Cutlery, Camillus, NY, USA," 3 blades, pre-1942 .... 18.00

4-line stamp, bow tie shield, black composition handle, 3 blades, pre 1942 .... 20.00

Case

XX #799, single blade 15.00

XX USA, 3 dots, #31048, single blade 18.00

Golden Gate International Exposition, creamy pearl-type handle, 2 blades, 5-1/2" l.................... 65.00

Hammer Brand, loop missing, 2-1/4" l 10.00

Hoffritz, Switzerland, stainless, 2 blades and scissors, adv "American Greetings," 2-1/4" d 25.00

Schrade Cutlery, Captain DL-2, Dura Lens diamond nail file, precision scissors, pen blade, mkd "Snap On" 12.00

Advertising, Illinois Casket Co., mkd "Utica Cultery," $21.50.

Texas Centennial, cream-colored handle with bull, bale of hay, state flag, state emblem, and "1836-1936," 2 different-sized blades 72.00

Thornton, celluloid, erotica, 1930s, 3-1/2" l, minor wear.............50.00

Zippo, 2 blades, adv "Trio Mfg Co., Inc.," 2" l............................. 18.00

❖ Pocket Watches

Pocket watches never go out of style and currently are quite fashionable. When shopping for a pocket watch at a flea market, ask a lot of questions as you carefully examine the watch—who made it, when, where, has it been repaired or cleaned recently, does it keep the proper time, etc.

Periodical: *Watch & Clock Review,* 2403 Champa St., Denver, CO 80205.

Collectors' Clubs: American Watchmakers Institute, Chapter 102, 3 Washington St., Apt 3C, Larchmont, NY 10538; Early American Watch Club Chapter 149, PO Box 5499, Beverly Hills, CA 90210; National Association of Watch & Clock Collectors, 514 Poplar St., Columbia, PA 17512.

Abe Lincoln, Illinois, silver tone, open face 290.00

American Waltham Watch Co.

14K yellow gold, model 1890 movement, 6 size, fancy hunting case, scalloped edges, engraved and dated 1897 on front cover 700.00

Gold filled case, 16 size movement, Roman numeral dial, elk on back, c1891, open face 250.00

Silver, Deuber coin silver, model 1883 movement, 18 size, open face, c1891, small chip and ding to case 295.00

Elgin National Watch Co.

Gold tone, open face 325.00

White metal, 16 size, fancy edges and back, c1906, open face, replaced crystal 250.00

Yellow gold filled, model 2 movement, 12 size, three-quarter plate, hunter case, pendant set, c1916 ....395.00

Hampden, nickel, large, open face 475.00

Howard, 14K white gold, 17 jewels, matching chain, open face 450.00

❖ Political and Campaign Items

As the cost of getting elected to political office continues to spiral upward, we can thank our forefathers for establishing the practice of creating items with their image or slogan. Intended to remind voters who they wanted to remember, these political items are now eagerly sought by collectors.

Periodicals: *The Political Bandwagon,* PO Box 348, Leola, PA 17540; *Political Collector,* PO Box 5171, York, PA 17405.

Collectors' Club: American Political Items Collectors, PO Box 340339, San Antonio, TX 78234; Third Party & Hopefuls, 503 Kings Canyon Blvd., Galesburg, IL 61401.

Reproduction Alert.

For additional listings, see *Warman's Antiques and Collectibles Price Guide* and *Warman's Americana & Collectibles,* as well as specific topics in this edition, including "John F. Kennedy," "Abraham Lincoln," and "Presidential."

Ballot Box, 12" h, 12" w, 13" d, made by Amos Pettibone, Chicago, Pat'd June 13, 1884, wood construction top and bottom, center glass cylinder, slot on top ... 70.00

Bank, Humphrey/Muskie '68, cast iron, figural donkey 32.00

Box, 8" l, 4-1/2" w, Swell Presidential Favorites Bubble Gum Cigars, "Win with Tricky Dick," red, white, and blue box, elephant and donkey motif, filled with Owl Bubble Gum Cigars 120.00

"I'm For Nixon" pinback button, 1960 campaign, 3-1/2" d, $19.75.

Bust, 13" h, Abraham Lincoln, bronzed plaster, mkd "L. W. Volk Sculptor, patent June 12, 1860" 50.00

Campaign Button
For President Herbert Hoover/For Vice-President Charles Curtis, litho jugate, bluetone photos in ovals, draped red, white, and blue flag background.... 150.00
Win with Humphrey, red, white, and blue celluloid, 1968 ... 6.50

Campaign Ticket, Wing Ticket, supporting George Briggs as Governor, woodcut of rally around flag....................................... 15.00

Clock Face, GOP/Time Setters, 9" d, celluloid, red, white, blue, gray, and black, center hole for hands, black cardboard back, 1971 .... 10.00

Coloring Book, 8-1/2" x 11", Watergate Coloring Book, color caricature cover 10.00

Doll, Ronald Reagan, Horsman, vinyl, 17" h 70.00

Mug, Republican elephant head on front, donkey inside, Rumph, 1971 .... 125.00

Novelty, 5" h gray plush elephant head, red, white, and blue striped tie, 4" l black and white fabric with "GOP" and elephant figure, fabric ears, black and white paper eyes, Gund Mfg Co., c1955-60 .... 10.00

Plate, President Garfield Memorial........................... 55.00

Poster, Goldwater Victory Rally, Madison Square Garden, red, white, and blue, 1964 .... 17.50

Sticker, diecut foil, silver, blue, and red, inscribed "Willkie/The Hope of America," 3-1/2" x 6"....... 12.00

❖ Poodles

Way back in the 1950s, poodles were supreme! From poodle skirts to television lamps, they were the favorites of many kids. Today collectors enjoy reliving some of that nostalgia at flea markets by finding those friendly pink, white, or black poodles they loved as a kid.

Ashtray, black, some wear to ear and face, 4-1/2" 5.00

Autograph Dog, white vinyl, signatures, 1950s, 4-1/2" x 7" 18.00

Beanie Baby, Gigi, MWBT and protector.............................. 18.00

Jewelry Box, wood, white, poodle dec, sgd "Kellerman Jewel Case, Japan," 1960s, 10" x 6".......25.00

Figure, Paulette....................... 30.00

Lamp, television type, poodle and puppy, mkd "Kron," 1950s, 13" h 160.00

Pin
AJC, brass color, clear rhinestone eyes, 2" x 2" 25.00
Beau, sterling, 1-1/2" x 1-3/4"............................. 35.00
Stein, Parisian Poodle, orange body, ivory pompoms, purple hair bow, mkd "Lea Stein, Paris" on clasp, 1-1/2" x 1-1/2" 95.00
Tortolani, gold-tone, faux pearls and red rhinestone eye, 1-1/2" x 2-1/4" 85.00

Pillow, poodle design, tiny rhinestone accents, tassels on each corner, 16" sq.................... 165.00

Pin Cushion, metal and fabric, nodding head and tail 35.00

Pin Cushion and Tape Measure, ceramic, brown, tongue pulls out as tape measure, mkd "Wales, Made in Japan," 6" h.......... 48.00

Planter, pink, c1940, 6-1/2" h, 8-1/2" w, 3-1/2" d.................. 45.00

Purse, wool, gold embellishment, large................................... 56.00

Wall Plaque, chalk, white head, illegible imp mark, 4-1/2" l, 4-1/4" w............................... 30.00

✯ Porcelier

Porcelain light fixtures, small appliances and a variety of tableware were some of the items produced by Porcelier Manufacturing Company, which was in business between 1926 and 1954. Collectors look for flawless items, wanting any gold trim to be unworn and items such as light fixtures to have their original pulls.

References: Susan E. Grindberg, *Collector's Guide to Porcelier China*, Collector Books, 1996.

Collectors' Clubs: Porcelier Collectors Club, 21 Tamarac Swamp Rd., Wallingford, CT 06492-5529.

Coffeepot, Mexican, 4-cup...... 30.00
Creamer, Flight........................ 10.00
Light fixture
    Ceiling-mount, 2 sockets, white with pink lilacs, needs rewired, no mounting hardware, 11" x 6-1/4"......................30.00
    Wall-mount, circular back, socket arm, white with red roses, gold accents, rewired, replaced socket............................129.00
Syrup, Barock-Colonial, 6" h .. 96.00
Teapot
    1939 New York World's Fair, 6-cup.............................305.00
    Basketweave Cameo 63.00
    Dutch Boy and Girl, 2 chips............................18.00
    Flamingo 38.00

Pitcher, floral design, 5" h, $9.50.

Nautical, 2-cup 49.00
Waffle iron, Barock-Colonial, gold dots variation 187.50

❖ Portrait Plates

Portrait plates and other types of wares with portraits of prominent people were made so that one could display such items in their homes. By such a display, you could subtly express your political affiliation or surround yourself with the popular heroes of the day. Other portrait plates were made with busts of lovely women and were intended only for decorative display.

Gibson Girl, brown hair, blue-green ground, shaded purple to pink ground, shaped gold rim, artist sgd, mkd "Austria" 50.00
Mrs. Lincoln, 6" d, Imperial China 85.00
Napoleon, Louisiana Purchase souvenir, fair buildings on rim, blue and white earthenware, high glaze, Victoria Art Company, NY, 10" d 300.00
Queen Louise, white dress, pink sash, gold rim, sgd "Mme A-K, France," 8-1/2" d............... 180.00
Thalia, black-haired woman, yellow roses in hair, red dress, Art Nouveau style border, pink ground, Hutschenreuther, c1910 ... 800.00
Woman, brown curly hair, star band on forehead, cream gown, brown border with gold overlay, mkd "C. T. Germany" and eagle mark 45.00

Empire China, unidentified woman, chipped, scratches, 10-1/8" d, $30.

Woman, brown hair, pale purple fringed lavender shawl on shoulder, gold stenciled inner rim, green border, blue "Victoria Austria" mark 125.00

❖ Postcards

Ever wonder what happened to all those postcards tourists have sent over the decades? Well, postcard collectors are searching flea markets for more examples to add to their collections. Whether they specialize in local history cards, or perhaps a specific maker or artist, lots of examples are available. Most are reasonably priced, but recently some rare postcards have been sold for record prices.

Collectors' Clubs: There are many regional Postcard Collectors Clubs. Contact one of these national organizations to find out about a chapter near you: Deltiologists of America, PO Box 8, Norwood, PA 19074; Postcard History Society, PO Box 1765, Manassas, VA 22110.

Asbury Park, looking Northeast, RR Station in foreground, unused 5.00
A Stroll on the Boardwalk showing Convention Hall, Asbury Park, New Jersey, 1934 ....3.00
A Very Happy Easter To You, Victorian child pushing egg buggy filled with forget-me-nots and baby chick, postmarked 1903, printed in Germany 8.00

Comical postcard folder, Greetings from a Nut Like Me to a Squirrel Like You, 9 double-sided cards, Asheville Postcard Co., Asheville, NC, folded 4-1/4" x 6-1/8", $2.

Beach Scene at Asbury Park, NJ, Monterey Hotel & Asbury Carlton, unused 3.00

Berkeley Carteret Hotel, Asbury Park, NJ, unused.................. 3.00

Casino & North End Hotel at Night, Asbury Park & Ocean Grove, NJ, 1950 .... 3.00

Catholic Church, Asbury Park, NJ, unused 3.00

Chalfonte Hotel & Haddon Hall, Atlantic City, NJ, 1941 .... 10.00

Deal Lake, Asbury Park, NJ, 1907 .... 2.00

Easter Greetings, angel painting words on egg car, postmarked 1909 .... 8.00

Easter Greetings, Victorian girl with chicks and hen, Raphael Tuck & Sons, printed in Germany, unused 10.00

Egg Samination, little boy examining large egg 7.50

Fishing Pier, Asbury Park, NJ, 1932 .... 3.00

General View from Boardwalk, showing Sunset Lake & Park, Asbury Park, NJ, unused 2.00

Happy Easter-Tide, boy on egg cart, wheels of forget-me-nots, pulled by two chicks, postmarked 1913, printed in Germany............... 8.00

Holy Spirit Church, Asbury Park, NJ, unused 3.00

Net Haul on Young's Million Dollar Pier, Atlantic City, NJ, 1911 .. 8.00

New Monterey Hotel & Boardwalk, Asbury Park, NJ, 1915 .... 3.50

New Park Scene, Sunset Lake, Asbury Park, NJ, 1949 .... 2.00

New York City, East River and Brooklyn Bridge.................. 10.00

R.C.A., microphone, comic appreciation, 1924 .... 10.00

Scene on the Beach, Asbury Park, NJ, 1915.............................. 3.50

Sunset in the Granite Gorge, Grand Canyon National Park, AZ, 1928 .... 3.00

The Casino & Beach, Asbury Park, NJ, unused 3.00

The Casino & Fishing Pier, Asbury Park, NJ, 1913 .... 4.00

The Guest House, North Asbury Park, NJ, unused.................. 5.00

U.S.S. Arizona, 1915 shake down cruise, leaving Brooklyn.... 100.00

View of Boardwalk & Arcade, Asbury Park, NJ, 1924..................... 4.00

Ye Olde Oyster House, 41 Union Street, Mass, linen type, unused................................. 6.00

❖ Posters

Posters have long been an effective communication tool. Their size, bright colors, and great illustrations caught the attention of many passersby. Today they are treasured and becoming more and more available at flea markets.

Periodicals: *Biblio,* 845 Willamette St, Eugene, OR 87401; *Collecting Hollywood*, American Collectors Exchange, 2401 Broad St, Chattanooga, TN 37408; *Movie Poster Update*, American Collectors Exchange, 2401 Broad St, Chattanooga, TN 37408.

For additional listings, see *Warman's Antiques and Collectibles Price Guide* and *Warman's Americana & Collectibles,* as well as "Movie Posters" in this edition.

Buddha and Heartstone, Polish magician performing tricks, English and Polish text, c1914, 14" x 26" 100.00

"National Civil Defense Week Sept. 9-15, 1956," 14" x 11-1/8", $20.

Carson & Barnes Circus, anonymous, clowns of all types, full color offset with removable date sheet, white margin wear, 1950s, 42" x 36" 75.00

Clyde Beatty-Cole Bros Combined Circus, The World's Largest Circus, "Clyde Beatty in Person," Roland Butler, lion tamer, multicolored, 19" x 26"................ 90.00

Ferry's Seeds, full color image of pretty young lass amid towering hollyhocks, light fold lines, restoration to edges, thin tears, 1925, 21" x 28" 325.00

Granite Iron Ware, paper, woman carrying milking pail, cow, "For Kitchen and Table Use," 12-1/2" x 28" 75.00

Hoxie Bros Old Time Circus Land, One Mile West of Walt Disney World, multicolored view of circus grounds and big top, 20" x 27" 65.00

Kix Cereal, Lone Ranger 6-shooter ring, General Mills premium, "Only 15 cents plus Kix box top," c1948 17" x 22"................. 225.00

Lady Esther Face Cream, printed on board, beautiful young woman in oval vignette, "A Skin Food-An Astringent," c1920, 23" x 36" 325.00

Shamrock Tobacco, canvas, seated man holding knife and tobacco, "Plug Smoking -10 cents a Cut," c1900, 17" x 23"................ 190.00

Ringling Bros Barnum & Bailey Liberty Bandwagon, color litho, ornate wagon with Merle Evans portrait, 1943, 30" x 19" 225.00

The Gondoliers, 20" x 30", full color, 1920s................................ 125.00

The Olson Shows, (carnival), 28" x 41", full color, 1950s 150.00

Waterman's Ideal Fountain Pen, paper, Uncle Sam at Treaty of Portsmouth, early 1900s, 41-1/2" x 19-1/2" 950.00

❖ Powder Jars

Pretty containers to hold powder were a staple of a lady's dressing table. And, of course, they had to be pretty or whimsical. Today collectors are just as charmed with them.

Celluloid Lid, frosted green glass jar base, wear to emb black design on top, 3-1/2" h, 4-1/4" w.... 28.00

Glass

Clear, elephant on top, raised trunk.................................28.00

Clear, lady sitting in front of beveled mirror.................55.00

Clear, lady's portrait under lid, reverse painted highlights, box shape, wear to paint, 3" x 4".................................85.00

Clear, My Pet.......................40.00

Clear, woman with child, 9" h, inside nick 145.00

Frosted, green, Art Deco lady 250.00

Frosted, green, Cameo lady 225.00

Frosted, green, Crinoline Girl 145.00

Frosted, green, hand painted flowers.............................26.00

Frosted, pink, elephant, trunk down 65.00

Frosted, pink, Scottie, small rough spot.......................25.00

Hobnail, clear, opalescent white hobnails, 4-3/8" d 25.00

Iridescent, marigold, figural poodle on top 32.00

Limoges, Remy Delinieres & Company, matte black, gilding, mkd "AG," 1895.............295.00

Musical, dresser jar, 8-1/2" h 60.00

Pink, Annette......................75.00

Clear ribbed glass base, pink plastic lid, 2-1/4" h, 4" d, $10.

✶ ✪ Precious Moments

Created by Samuel J. Butcher in 1978 and produced by Enesco, Precious Moments are now in their third decade of production. This popular line of collectibles features cute kids with inspiring messages. Accessories such as ornaments and mugs are found more frequently at flea markets than are figurines and plates, but all types of items are still fair game.

References: Rosie Wells, *Rosie's Secondary Market Price Guide for Enesco's Precious Moments Collection*, 16th Edition, Rosie Wells Enterprises, 1998; *Precious Collectibles*, 22341 E. Wells Rd., Canton, IL 61520.

Collectors' Clubs: Enesco Precious Moments Collectors' Club, P.O. Box 99, Itasca, IL 60143.

Figurine (with box unless noted)

Always In My Heart............. 80.00

Believe the Impossible 140.00

Bless Those Who Serve Their Country, 1991 .... 50.00

Boy With Dog 85.00

Porcelain mug, Jesus Loves Me Anyhow, 5" h, $15.

Dropping in for Christmas, 1982 ....52.00

Forgiving Is Forgetting, 1983 ....70.00

God is Love, Dear Valentine 36.00

God's Speed 70.00

Grandpa's Prayer, Collector's Club special edition, 1986 ....64.00

Hallelujah Country 69.00

Happiness Is The Lord........ 78.00

I Believe In Miracles, 1983.. 70.00

Indian Boy........................ 115.00

It's What's Inside That Counts, 1984 ....68.00

I Would Be Lost Without You 44.00

Jesus Is The Light, 1983..... 45.00

June, 1992.........................40.00

Let Love Reign, 1983.......... 64.00

The Lord Bless You and Keep You, 1979 ....40.00

Lord Help Us Keep Our Act Together, 1986, no box. 140.00

Love is Kind, 1983 .... 58.00

Love is Sharing, 1983......... 32.00

Love Lifted Me 92.00

Praise The Lord Anyhow, 1982 ....58.00

September 65.00

Shoot for the Stars, 1996.... 50.00

The Sweetest Club Around. 63.00

Thou Art Mine, 1983 .... 48.00

To A Very Special Mom....... 63.00

You Have Touched so Many Hearts, 1983....................56.00

We Are God's Workmanship, 1982 ....52.00

Plate

Mom's a Sweet Cookie, minor wear to gold trim, 1978..... 7.50

Mom the Egg-Spert, 3 dimples in glaze, 1978, 4".................7.50

Mother's Day 1990, 4" 7.00

✯ Premiums

Saving box tops and now bar codes has always been a way to get something from a favorite company. Many early premiums were great ways to collect items relating to your favorite radio or cowboy hero. Today these little vintage treasures are quite valuable.

Periodicals: *Box Top Bonanza,* 3403 46th Ave., Moline, IL 61265; *Premium Collectors Magazine,* 1125 Redman Ave., St. Louis, MO 63138; *The Premium Watch,* 24 San Rafael Drive, Rochester, NY 14618; *The Toy Ring Journal,* PO Box 544, Birmingham, MI 48012.

Bendee Figure, Tagamet, 4-1/2" h, flesh-colored, blue, red, and black accents, designed like smiling stomach, white gloves on arms that bend atop base, name on front in black and white letters, copyright 1988 Smith Kline & French Laboratories 35.00

Catalog, Valuable Premiums, Borden's Elsie on cover, 5" x 6-1/2" booklet, 40 pages, picturing and describing household items available as "Red Scissors Coupons," expiration date of Aug 31, 1956 .... 18.00

Sugar Bear stuffed figure, General Foods Corp., 5" h, $3.

Mask, Colonel Morton, 8-1/4" x 10-1/2" stiff paper sheet, full color punch-out mask and badge, Morton Frozen Pies, c1950, unpunched 18.00

Postcard, Tony the Tiger, 3-5/8" x 5-5/8", Tony with camper's gear, "Hi, It's Gr-r-eat Here At" as he points to sign post, black and white art on reverse, various messages to be checked off by sender, including plug for Kellogg's cereals, mid-1960s 12.00

Sign, Squirt Doll, 9-1/2" x 20-1/2", paper banner offering 18" h vinyl doll with fabric outfit through participating store or direct mail, copyright 1962 Squirt Co. ... 40.00

Squeaker Toy, Trix Rabbit, 8-1/2" h, soft vinyl, smiling figure, pink and black accent face, holding hands to chest, moveable head, Trix General Mills Inc. stamped on rear of feet, squeaks well, c1960 .... 45.00

Ticket, Max Baer vs Joe Louis, NBC Radio, 2-1/4" x 5-1/2" thin white cardboard, red and black lettering, yellow background, ticket for Sept 24, 1935 heavyweight fight, issued by Buick dealers for "Fireside Seat," event held at Yankee Stadium, attached rain check, unused 48.00

❖ Presidential

Collectors who follow the winners to the White House have additional collectibles to gather. Tried and true presidential collectors will have campaign paraphernalia and then try to gather inaugural items and other collectibles generated by an office holder. Other presidential memorabilia might deal with family members.

Periodical: *The Political Bandwagon,* PO Box 348, Leola, PA 17540; *Political Collector,* PO Box 5171, York, PA 17405.

Collectors' Club: American Political Items Collectors, PO Box 340339, San Antonio, TX 78234.

Sheet music, "Taft March," portrait of Pres. Taft, $10.

Book
> *First Ladies,* Margaret Truman, 1995, 2nd printing, dj 12.00
> *The Strange Death of President Harding,* from the diaries of Gaston B. Means as told to Mary Dixon Thacker, Guild Publishing, 1930, 324 pgs, cover worn 10.00

Cookbook, *Recipes on Parade,* 2000 world wide favorites of military officers' wives, c1964, picture of Lady Bird Johnson and her barbecued spareribs, also Mrs. John F. Kennedy's recipe on first page 24.00

First Day Cover, autographed by Gerald Ford 60.00

Inaugural Book, *The Spirit of '76,* color and black and white photos of Nixon, 1973 .... 30.00

Inaugural Medal, bronze, George Bush, orig box, 1989 .... 30.00

Inaugural Program
> Bill Clinton, glossy content, full color photos, 24 pgs 15.00
> Lyndon Johnson, gold presidential seal, Jan 20, 1965, full color and black and white photos and text 20.00

Magazine Cover, *Time*
> Johnson and Goldwater collage, Sept 25, 1964 .... 5.00

Johnson and Humphrey, Sept 4,
1964 ....8.00

President Clinton, Dec, 1998 ...50

President Johnson, Man of the
Year, Jan 1, 1965 ....8.00

Newspaper, *Daily Mirror*, April 16,
1945, tabloid size, covers funeral
of Franklin Roosevelt, slightly
browned with age 17.50

Nodder, Dwight Eisenhower, composition, brown hat, blue coat,
c1956, 6" h 100.00

Pen, gold presidential logo, facsimile
LBJ signature on black plastic,
gold metal top and clip, felt tip
frayed 15.00

Pencil, Hoover for President, 1928,
yellow, unsharpened 20.00

Pinback Button, George Washington, sepia portrait, 1920s.... 20.00

Print, The Presidents of the United
States, Washington to Polk,
Kellogg & Comstock, hand colored litho, gilt frame, 20-1/4" h,
17-1/4" w 200.00

Sheet Music, *The New Frontier,*
black and white portrait of
Kennedy on cover, facsimile signature, red, white, and blue flag,
Capitol dome on cover 27.50

❖ Presley, Elvis

"You ain't nothin' but a hound
dog…"—what lyrics of a rock n' roll
legend. Elvis was quite a hit in his
day, and even after his 1977 death,
sales of his memorabilia continue.
Fans still flock to his home and
swoon when they hear his songs.

Collectors' Club: Elvis Forever TCB
Fan Club, PO Box 1066, Pinellas
Park, FL 33281; Graceland News
Fan Club, PO Box 452, Rutherford,
NJ 07070.

Album, LP

Our Memories of Elvis, black
label, DNT 75.00

Personally Elvis, blue label, double pocket, silhouette 50.00

Spinout, black label, DOT, RCA,
white top..........................35.00

Welcome to My World, black
label, DNT 30.00

**Postmark Collection Elvis key
chain, orig card, Specialty House
of Creation International, 8-3/8" x
4-3/8", $3.50.**

Calendar, 1977, Tribute to Elvis,
Boxcar Enterprises,
12" x 13" 50.00

Cassette Tapes, three tapes, boxed
set, limited edition, poster,
book.................................... 15.00

Cookie Jar, riding in car 100.00

Game, King of Rock,
unopened 25.00

Magazine, *Saturday Evening Post,*
July/August, 1985, "Legends that
Won't Die".......................... 10.00

Poster Book 10.00

Puzzle, The King, Springbok, 1992,
1000 pieces 50.00

Sheet Music, 1954, *Love Me* .. 35.00

❖ Princess Diana

Her tragic death in 1997 stopped
the world for a brief time. Collectibles
ranging from things made during her
lifetime, such as wedding commemo-
ratives, and later memorial pieces are
readily available at flea markets.

Ale Glass, Royal Wedding 32.00

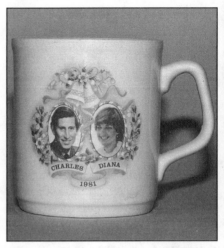

**Coffee mug, ceramic, "Charles
Diana 1981," England, 3-1/2" h,
$19.**

Beer Can, Felinfoel Brewery, Wales,
1981, official Royal Wedding
commemorative, bottom
opened................................ 15.00

Coach Replica, Matchbox, replica of
coach used in wedding, made for
Her Majesty's 40th Anniversary,
limited edition, MIB 65.00

First Day Cover, Marshall
Islands 3.00

Slippers, figural head of sleeping
Diana and Charles, c1980,
unused, orig tags 48.00

Tea Towel, Irish linen, portraits of
Diana and Charles, Prince of
Wales plumes, 28-1/2" x
18-1/2" 20.00

Thimble, HRH Prince William of
Wales, to commemorate his 1st
birthday, portrait of Prince and
Mother, June, 1983............. 27.00

❖ Prints

Prints are a great way for the common folk to have copies of fine artwork
for their homes or offices. Fortunately
publishers decades ago, like Currier &
Ives, discovered this so there are
many vintage prints to choose from.
Today limited edition prints vie for the
same collector dollars.

References: Jay Brown, *The Com-
plete Guide to Limited Edition Art
Prints,* Krause Publications, 1999;
Michael Ivankovich, *Collector's Value*

Guide to Early 20th Century American Prints, Collector Books, 1998. Plus there are many other excellent reference books available about prints, fine arts, and artists.

Periodicals: *Journal of the Print World,* 1008 Winona Road, Meredith, NH 03253; *On Paper,* 39 E. 78th St., #601, New York, NY 10021.

Reproduction Alert.

For additional listings, see *Warman's Antiques and Collectibles Price Guide.*

American Homestead Summer, hand colored litho, walnut cross corner frame, gilded liner, minor stains 220.00

Child with Doll, bear, Bessie Guttmann 150.00

Clown Acrobats, Robert Riggs, dedicated in pencil, matted 400.00

Cupid Asleep, Cupid Awake, 6-1/2" x 8-1/2", dated 1897, framed 50.00

Currier, folio, The Way To Happiness, small folio.................. 45.00

Gilbert, C. Allen, All Is Vanity, black and white, 10" x 12" 25.00

Hero, Rockwell Kent, litho on paper, sgd lower right, famed 350.00

Levi's, illus cowboy on bull, 1978, 14" x 19" 35.00

Summer on the Susquehanna, folio chromolithograph, 24" h, 30" w, framed, stains.................. 200.00

The New Brood, Currier & Ives, hand colored litho, minor stains, framed 200.00

The Rent Day, folio, hand colored engraving, minor darkening at map opening, matted and framed, 25-7/8" x 33-1/2" h............ 220.00

The Visitor, Frank W. Benson, etching on paper, numbered in pencil, 3" x 5", matted 435.00

❖ Punch Boards

Feel like taking a chance? For those lucky collectors who enjoy finding punchboards, flea markets often offer several choices of boards.

As You Like It, 1¢ punch, glamour girl....................................... 24.00

Beat the Seven 25.00

Block Buster, 5¢ punch, double jackpot 20.00

Five Tens, 10¢ punch, cash board 24.00

Home Run Derby, baseball diamond header 50.00

Lulu Bell, 5¢ punch, large 18.00

Pick A Cherry, fruit seals 24.00

Sunshine, risque, unused 45.00

Take Me Home, small 15.00

★ Puppets

Puppets come in all shapes and sizes, from hand operated to elaborate marionettes to ventriloquist dummies and little push puppets, giving collectors a real variety. The fun part about collecting puppets is that all probably have made people laugh and smile and probably still have lots of smiles left to share with their new owners.

Hand, all used condition
  Boglin, purple, yellow eyes, 1980s, 8" h 16.00
  Donkey, Kamar 10.00
  Goofy, Gabriel, 1977........... 10.00
  Snuggle Bear........................ 8.75
  Tweety Bird, 10" h.............. 13.50

Marionette, all used condition
  Clown................................. 42.00
  Mr. Bluster......................... 635.00

"Christ on the Way to Emmaus," **mkd "Painted by Furst," orig frame, print 23" x 16", $115.**

Off We Go!, 5 cents, 12-1/2" x 10", $20.

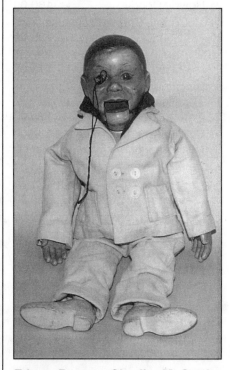

Edgar Bergen Charlie McCarthy doll, composition, Effanbee, 14-1/2" h, $595.

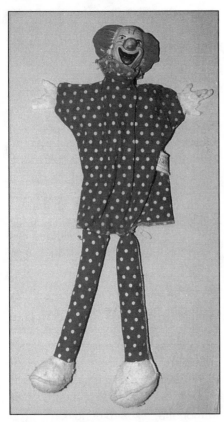

Bozo the Clown walking puppet, Renall Dolls, $45.

Howdy Doody	150.00
McCarthy, Charlie, composition, 12" h	125.00
Mickey Mouse, Bob Baker limited edition, MIB	175.00
Pinocchio, Walt Disney Enterprises, composition, 12" h	125.00
Siamese Temple Dancer	130.00

Push Puppet, all used condition

Atom Ant	30.00
Cowboy on White Horse, by Kohner, Socko label	45.00
Donald Duck	30.00
Mickey Mouse	30.00
Olive Oyl	35.00
Pluto	25.00
Popeye	35.00
Santa Mouse	35.00
Terry the Tiger	30.00

Ventriloquist Dummy, all used condition

Bart Simpson, custom made	200.00
Bozo	42.00
Jerry Mahoney	60.00
Three Stooges	100.00
Willie Talk, Horsman	42.00

❖ Purinton Pottery

Purinton Pottery is another Ohio pottery company who made dinnerware and some tablewares along with special orders. This company was founded in 1936 in Wellsville and continued until 1959.

Periodical: *Puritan Pastimes,* PO Box 9394, Arlington, VA 22219.

Bank, Uncle Sam	32.00
Bean Pot, Normandy Plaid	37.50
Canister Set, Fruit, 4-pc, blue trim	150.00
Coffee Mug, Plaid	3.00

Cookie Jar

Fruit, red trim	60.00
Howdy Doody, professionally restored	475.00
Creamer, Apple, double spouts	15.00
Cup and Saucer, Apple	18.00
Dinner Plate, Apple, sq	25.00
Grease Jar, cov, Fruit, blue trim	35.00
Marmalade, cov, Maywood	35.00
Platter, Brown Intaglio, 11" l oval	37.50
Sugar, Apple	15.00
Tea and Toast Set, Intaglio	48.00
Vegetable Dish, Normandy Plaid, divided	42.00

Apple pitcher with ice lip, 7-1/4" h, $45.

❖ Purses

Here's a topic about an item most ladies would not be without. Collectors are intrigued with the styles, colors, and different textures of bygone eras.

Alligator, brown, designer type 50.00

Evening

Brocade, Art Deco, engraved gold filled frame	75.00
Faille, black, marcasite set mounting, gold onyx monogram, c1930	70.00
Satin, pink, silver bugle beads, ivory colored seed pearls, silver frame and clasp, trimmed in white rhinestones, silver chain handle, Jolle Original, 9" x 7-1/2" x 1"	110.00
Lucite, trapezoid, cream colored, gold-tone frame, rigid handle, snap clasp, navy lining and side gussets, c1950, 8" w	185.00
Mesh, Mandalian, enameled	190.00
Straw, two handles, gold-tone ball type clasp, c1950	20.00

Pierced brass and plastic, 7-3/4" x 4" plus handle, $28.50.

❖ Puzzles

What's got lots of pieces and hours of fun? Puzzles and flea market browsers can find some great puzzles. Actually, puzzles have been around about as long as America, starting as ways to keep children occupied. By the 1890s, adults wanted to have some fun, too, and some very intricate puzzles were created. Ask the dealer if the puzzle is complete and if any pieces are damaged. Missing pieces can drastically reduce the price.

Collectors' Clubs: American Game Collectors Association., PO Box 44, Dresher, PA 19025.

For additional listings, see *Warman's Antiques and Collectibles Price Guide.*

Cottage by the Winter, Joseph K. Strauss, plywood, interlocking, orig box 20.00

Making Friends, Apple for the Horse, K. Kohler artist, Parker Brothers, Pastime, 1927, 200 pcs, 2 replaced 60.00

Advertising, Folger's Coffee, container 3-1/2" h, 2-5/8" d, $8.

Now I Lay Me, family type scene, Parker Brothers, Pastime, 1929, orig box 20.00

Pickett's Charge at Gettysburg, 1930s 25.00

Rexall Drug Store, Mountain Splendor, 1930s, diecut, orig envelope, several pcs missing 4.00

The New Toys, Christmas, 1910s, plywood, orig box 12.00

Windmill, W. J. Krola artist, 1909, solid wood, orig box 20.00

❖ Pyrex

Pyrex was developed by the researchers at Corning Glass in the early 1910s. By 1915, they launched their Pyrex line with a 12-piece set. Fry Glass Company was granted permission by Corning to produce Pyrex under their Fry Oven Glass label in 1920. Cooks today still use many Pyrex products. It's a kitchenware collectible that is just starting to become popular with collectors. Many of these collectors are eager to find advertising and paper ephemera dealing with Pyrex.

Baker, cov, delphite blue
  3-3/8" x 4-1/4" 12.00
  6-3/4" x 4-1/4" 22.00
Bean Pot, cov, clear, 2 qt 12.00
Casserole, cov, 2 qt, round, robin's egg blue base, clear cover, light use 15.00

Double Boiler, mkd "Flameware" 17.50
Freezer Server, Butterprint 12.00
Mixing Bowl, delphite blue
  7" d, rolled rim, slight discoloring 4.00
  11-1/2" d, rolled rim, sq base 20.00
Percolator, Flameware, Deluxe, 4 cup size 10.00
Pie Plate, clear, 10" 10.00
Serving Dish, Bluebelle 20.00

Mixing bowl, green with white flowers, 8-3/4" d, $6.

For exciting collecting trends and newly expanded areas look for the following symbols:

⊙ Hot Topic

★ New Warman's Listing

(May have been in another Warman's edition.)

Favorite periodicals:

1. *Maine Antique Digest*
2. *Antique Week*
3. *Warman's Today's Collector*
4. *Sports Collectors Digest*
5. *The Depression Glass Daze*
6. *Antique Trader Weekly*
7. _____
8. _____
9. _____
10. _____

11. _____
12. _____
13. _____
14. _____
15. _____
16. _____
17. _____
18. _____
19. _____
20. _____

For exciting collecting trends and newly expanded areas look for the following symbols:

⊛ Hot Topic

★ New Warman's Listing

(May have been in another Warman's edition.)

❖ Quilts

Colorful bits and pieces of material sewn together make up quilts. Wonderful examples can be found at flea markets, from vintage hand-made, one-of-a-kind quilts to newer designer quilts that might fit a specific color scheme. There is something special about the charm a vintage quilt can lend a room.

References: There are many excellent quilt identification books available to collectors. Many collectors are also quilt makers and may find the quilt books by Krause Publications of interest, including Patricia J. Morris and Jeannette T. Muir's *Worth Doing Twice, New Quilts from Old Tops.*

Periodical: *Quilters Newsletter,* PO Box 4101, Golden, CO 80401.

Collectors' Club: American Quilter's Society, PO Box 3290., Paducah, KY 42001; The National Quilting Association, Inc., PO Box 393, Ellicott City, MD 21043.

Crazy, pieced velvet, multicolored, arranged in 16 squares, colorful velvet border, late 19th C, 72" x 74" 900.00

Cross and Crown, yellow, red, and olive patches, yellow borders, red backing, 84" x 83" 450.00

Fan, multicolored pieces, red accents, trimmed in red, 74" x 85" 485.00

Floral Medallions, pastel pink, green and yellow appliques, swag border, minor stains, 82" x 90" 420.00

Four Patch, green, brown, red, and blue printed calico horizontal panels, diamond and zigzag quilting, Mennonite, PA, 19th C 230.00

Log Cabin, yellow, brown, red, green, brown, pink, and white bars, broad red and black borders, rope quilting, red, yellow, and green calico backing, 81" x 81" 250.00

Nine Patch variation, blue, gray, and tan, white background and backing, 73" x 72" 365.00

Pinwheels, multicolored patches, blue and gold ground, minor stains, 68" x 70" 250.00

Star of Bethlehem, yellow, pink, purple, green, gray, and blue, white ground, pink and green borders, c1940, 85" x 85" 25.00

Sunbonnet Sue, some wear, 1930s 125.00

❖ Quimper

Known for its colorful peasant design, Quimper is a French faience that dates back to the 17th Century. As times and styles changed, the patterns were also influenced, but still continue to have a certain charm that is special to Quimper.

Reference: Sue and Al Bagdade, *Warman's English & Continental Pottery & Porcelain,* 3rd ed., Krause Publications, 1998.

For additional listings, see *Warman's Antiques and Collectibles Price Guide.*

Bowl, 2 musicians playing bagpipe and flute beneath Crest of Brittany and crown, acanthus leaf border, green sponged handles, raised yellow and orange seashells, sgd "HR Quimper" on front and "HR Quimper 12" on back 495.00

Butter Dish, cov, 2 small chips 350.00

Cake Plate, pedestal base, black-haired male peasant playing bagpipes, surrounded by floral sprays and floral garland border, pattern repeated on underside and base, mkd "HR Quimper" on front 385.00

Cup and Saucer, armorial pattern, cup with Crest of Brittany and stylized leaf and blue flowers on red croisille and blue dot field, blue polka dots, saucer with shield of Ste. Servan and 2 lions and crown above, intersection 1st period "PB" mark............... 365.00

Plate, male peasant in blue pantaloons, green jacket, black hat, green, yellow, blue and rust florals, green and rust border with blue dots, yellow, green, and blue lined rim, "HB" mark, 9" d 300.00

Tray, Breton Broderie pattern, male and female portraits facing each other in center, wide cobalt blue border with raised orange dashes and dots, scalloped rim, "HB Quimper" mark.................. 325.00

9 Patch, red and yellow, handsewn, some wear, 78" x 64", $100.

Bell, c1920-30, 3" h, $140.

For exciting collecting trends and newly expanded areas look for the following symbols:

✪ Hot Topic

✮ New Warman's Listing

(May have been in another Warman's edition.)

✪ Racing Collectibles Auto

"Start your engines" is music to the ears of racing collectors. Auto racing has become one of the hottest spectator sports of the 1990s. NASCAR and other racing organizations are cashing in on the popularity with specially issued collectibles and race souvenirs.

Collectors' Club: National Indy 500 Collectors Club, 10505 N. Delaware St., Indianapolis, IN 46280.

Autograph, 8" x 10" photo signed
   Mario Andretti.......................30.00
   Al Unser 27.50
   Bobby Unser 25.00
   Rusty Wallace 35.00
Cigarette Lighter, Mickey Thompson Speed Equipment, metal chrome finish, 2-1/4" l...................... 30.00

Nascar, John Deere car, 1/24 scale, Racing Champion's 1998 Collector Series, $20.

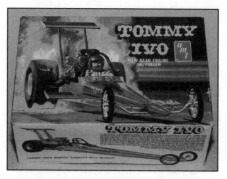

Drag Racing, AMT model kit, Tommy Ivo, $15.

Drinking Glass
   Indianapolis 500 Mile Race Motor Speedway, 5-1/8" h, frosted glass, design pictured twice in black and white art, racing flags and inscriptions, red racing car, c1960................. 30.00
   1959 Indianapolis Speedway, 4-1/2" h, weighted bottom, clear glass, black and white speedway symbol, facsimile black printed autograph of Tony Hulman, reverse lists previous 500 mile winners from 1911 to 1958, gold top edge 18.00
Driver Lapel Button, NASCAR, 1957 .... 140.00
Jello Mold, race car, plastic, Art Deco styling 50.00
Magazine, *Racing Pictorial,* 1963 .... 15.00
Necktie, Indianapolis 500, 1940s 42.00
Photograph, Daytona Beach, 1915, 10-1/2" x 3-1/2", photo of Speedway, Pepp's Pool, and Hotel, 3-pc set.............................. 45.00
Playset, Gerry Anderson's Mike Mercury Supereal Race Set, MIB 145.00
Press Pass, 1996.................... 75.00
Tablecloth, Daytona, 1950s 75.00

✤ Racing Collectibles, Other

If you're not into auto racing, there are other racing collectibles that can be found at flea markets. Keep your eyes open for air racing, dog racing, and other fast-paced collectibles.

Collectors' Club: Sport of Kings Society, 1406 Annen Lane, Madison, WI 53711.

Game, The New World to World Airship Race, Chicago Game Co., orig box 100.00
Picture Frame, commemorative, inscribed "Winner, Park Service Station, Third Annual Goodyear Dealer's Zeppelin Race, July-August 1931," 20-1/4" x 26...................................... 125.00
Pinback Button
   American Air Races, mechanic, red and cream, 1923 ...... 50.00
   Dan Patch Days, brown horse, white ground, 1967 Savage, MN commemorative celebration.................................. 25.00
   Jockey Portrait, American Pepsin Gum............................... 30.00
   Los Angeles National Air Races, red and white, 1928........ 75.00
Print, Air Racing with Roscoe Turner, Hubbell, Thompson's Products, 1940s, 12-1/2" x17" 100.00
Stickpin, brass, jockey cap over entwined initials, green and white enamel accents, 1906......... 28.00
Ticket, Kentucky Derby, race won by Swaps............................... 42.00

✤ Radio Characters and Personalities

The golden age of radio created a whole cadre of heroes and characters for the listeners. Like the stars of today, these folks had fans and fan clubs and created premiums and memorabilia to meet the demands of the earliest collectors.

Periodicals: *Friends of Old Time Radio,* PO Box 4321, Hamden, CT 06514; *Hello Again,* PO Box 4321, Hamden, CT 06514; *Nostalgia Digest and Radio Guide,* PO Box 421, Morton Grove, IL 60053; *Old Time Radio Digest,* 10280 Gunpowder Road, Florence, KY 41042.

Collectors' Clubs: National Lum & Abner Society, #81 Sharon Blvd, Dora, AL 35062; North American Radio Archives, 134 Vincewood Drive, Nicholasville, KY 40356; Radio Collectors of America, 8 Ardsley Circle, Brockton, MA 02402, plus many more specialized clubs devoted to a particular character or show.

Birthday Card, Amos n' Andy, Check and Double Check, inked birthday note, Rust Craft, ... 24.00

Blotter, The Shadow, orange, blue, and white, red silhouette, 1940s 28.00

Book, *'R' You Listening?* Tony Wons, radio scrapbook, CBS, Reilly & Lee, 1931, 1st ed., dj............ 9.00

Game, Amos n' Andy Shooting Game, Transogram Co., early 1930s, wear........................ 75.00

Magazine, *Post*
    Arthur Godfrey, 1955...........10.00
    Jack Benny article, 1963.................................15.00

Map, Jimmy Allen, full color, printed letter on back, 1934.......... 125.00

Membership Badge, Pilot Patrol, Phantom............................ 32.00

Record cleaner, "Bing Crosby, Decca Records, Roxy Music Shop, Everything Musical, LaPorte, Indiana," 3-1/2" d, $30.

Newsletter, Jimmy Allen, red, white, and green holiday design and signatures on front cover, black and white photos on back, 4 pgs................................... 65.00

Newspaper, Lum and Abner, *Pine Edge News*, Spring, 1936, orig mailing envelope 48.00

Pinback Button
    Adventurers Club, Frank Buck, 1936 .... 20.00
    Magic Club, Mandrake the Magician.......................... 60.00
    Uncle Don, Taystee Bread.............................. 55.00

Radio Guide, Amos n' Andy, photo, orig envelope..................... 32.00

Ring, Jack Armstrong, Dragon's Eye, crocodile design, green stone, 1940...................... 150.00

Valentine, Joe Penner, mechanical diecut, Joe holding duck on shoulder, inscribed "I'll Gladly Buy A Duck," c1935 .... 30.00

Whistle, Jimmie Allen, brass, c1936.............................. 30.00

Whistle Ring, Jack Armstrong, Egyptian symbols, orig mailing envelope, c1938 .... 135.00

❖ Radios

Today a radio brings us news, weather, and some tunes. But to generations past, it brought all those things plus laughter, companionship, and entertainment. The mechanical device that allowed connection to this new exciting world was developed and refined at the beginning of the 20th century. New technology caused changes in the shapes and materials of early radio receivers.

References: There are many older reference books to help identify radios.

Periodicals: *Antique Radio Classified,* PO Box 2, Carlisle, MA, 01741; *Antique Radio Topics,* PO Box 28572, Dallas, TX 75228; *Horn Speaker,* PO Box 1193, Mabank, TX 75147; *Radio Age,* 636 Cambridge Road, Augusta, GA 30909; *Transistor Network,* RR 1, Box 36, Bradford, NH 03221.

Collectors' Clubs: Antique Radio Club of America, 300 Washington Trails, Washington, PA 15301; Antique Wireless Assoc., 59 Main St., Bloomfield, NY 14469; New England Antique Radio Club, RR 1, Box 36, Bradford, NH 03221; Vintage Radio & Phonograph Society, Inc., PO Box 165345, Irving, TX 75016.

Admiral, #218, portable, leatherette, 1958...................................42.00

Arvin, #522A, ivory metal case, 1941...................................65.00

Crosley, Litfella, 1-N, cathedral 185.00

Detrola, cathedral style 150.00

Dumont, RA-346, table, scroll work, 1956...................................125.00

Emerson, #570, Memento, picture holder, 1945 .... 115.00

General Electric, #515, clock radio, 1950s.................................30.00

Grebe, MU-1, table model, with chain, 1925 ....220.00

Majestic, #92, console, 1929.................................125.00

Philco, #40-180, console, wood case 135.00

Radio Corp. of America, RCA
    Radiola, #18.................... 60.00
    Portable, #8BT-7LE, 1957.....38.00

Zenith, #500D, plastic, 1959...................................55.00

✯ Raggedy Ann

Who's always got a smile Raggedy Ann. This happy creation of Johnny Gruelle has lived on for decades. You can find her and her friend Andy, their dog and friends in children's literature and all kinds of decorative accessories.

Children's Book
    Raggedy Ann & Hoppy Toad, Perks, 1946 ....30.00
    Raggedy Ann & Laughing Book, Perks, 1946 ....30.00
    Raggedy Ann & Marcella's First Day At School, Wonder Book, #588 ....22.00
    Raggedy Ann, Beloved Belindy and the Laughing Brook, American Crayon Co., 1944 ....68.00

Sweet and Dandy Sugar Candy Scratch and Sniff Book, Golden Press, 1976, well read............. 15.00Cookie Jar

California Originals, incised mark on lid and "859 USA," 13-3/4" h 175.00

Certified International, 11" h..............................125.00

Creamer, figural, foil label, Royal Sealy, 4-1/2" h 35.00

Hasbro Softies, 13" h, $15.

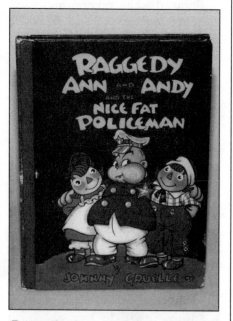

Raggedy Ann and Andy and the Nice Fat Policeman, Bobbs-Merrill, 1960, $30.

Doll

    Hasbro Commemorative Edition, 1996, 12" h...................... 40.00

    Knickerbocker, large, damage to foot 30.00

    Knickerbocker, small........... 35.00

Game, Raggedy Ann's Magic Pebble Game, Milton Bradley, copyright 1941 Johnny Gruelle Co., orig box............................... 95.00

Music Box, ceramic, Raggedy Ann and Andy, plays "This Old Man" 45.00

Print, copy of orig Johnny Gruelle drawing, 6" x 9".................... 35.00

Pop-Up Book

    Raggedy Ann and Andy, 45 rpm record, 1974, played with.................................... 5.00

    Raggedy Ann & the Daffy Taffy Pull, 1972 .... 15.00

❖ Railroad Collectibles

"All aboard!" Transportation of goods and passengers across this great country was a dream of the early railroad men. Today, we take it kind of for granted that these giants will keep moving along tracks laid so many years ago. Collectors can tell you about their favorite railroad lines or types of collectibles. Many of them probably have already enjoyed a visit to one of the several railroad museums or enjoyed a ride on a vintage steam train like the one that runs in Strasburg, PA. When you do that, you just have to close your eyes to imagine yourself back in a time when things moved a little more slowly, but perhaps, more elegantly.

Periodicals: *Key, Lock and Lantern*, 3 Berkeley Heights Park, Bloomfield, NJ 07003; *Main Line Journal*, PO Box 121, Streamwood, IL 60107; *Railfan & Railroad*, PO Box 700, Newton, NJ 07860-0700; *Trains*, PO Box 1612, Waukesha, WI 53187; *US Rail News*, PO Box 7007, Huntingdon Woods, MI 48070.

Collectors' Clubs: Canadian Railroad Historical Association, 120 Rue St. Pierre, St. Constant, Quebec J5A 2G9 Canada; Chesapeake & Ohio Historical Society Inc., PO Box 79, Clifton Forge, VA 24422; Illinois Central Railroad Historical Society 14818 Clifton Park, Midlothian, IL 60445; New York Central System Historical Society, Inc., PO Box 58994, Philadelphia, PA 19102-8994; Railroad Enthusiasts, 102 Dean Rd, Brookline, MA 02146; Railroad Club of America, Inc., PO Box 8292, Chicago, IL 60680; Railroadiana Collectors Association, 795 Aspen Drive, Buffalo Grove, IL 60089; Railway and Locomotive Historical Society PO Box 1418, Westford, MA 01886; Twentieth Century Railroad Club, 329 West 18th St, Suite 902, Chicago, IL 60616.

Book, *Oliphant's Earning Power of Railroads 1946,* James H. Oliphant & Co., 1946, 556 pgs.... 10.00

New York Central Lines lantern, clear globe, Dietz, $75.

Brochure, Florida East Coast Railway & Steamship Co., January, 1900, 39 pgs 150.00

Caboose Marker, Atlantic Coast Line RR Co., 1900, 4-way lamp 385.00

Calendar, Burlington Zephyr, 1943 .... 90.00

China, dish, Santa Fe Super Chief................................... 65.00

Coaster, Central RR, New Jersey, Statue of Liberty logo, set of 6 .... 15.00

Coloring Book, Union Pacific RR give-away, 29 pgs, 1954, 8" x 10" 20.00

Commemorative Plate, 10-1/2" d, B & O Railroad, blue transfer scene of Harper's Ferry, Lamberton China, 13-1/4" d turned wood frame 165.00

Creamer, Canadian Pacific, SP, mkd "England"............................ 25.00

Hat Rack, overhead type, coach, wood and brass, 6 brass double-sided hooks 200.00

Headrest Cover, PRR, tan ground, brown logo, 15" x 18" 15.00

Magazine, *Railway Age*............ 5.00

Menu, Amtrak, Good Morning, single card, 7" x 11" 3.50

Padlock, Rock Island, orig key....................................... 35.00

Pass

Ft Wayne, Cincinnati & Louisville and White Water, 2-1/2" x 3-3/4" white card, green accents, purple ink stamp facsimile signature of president, 1889 ....12.00

Ohio, Indiana, and Western, 2-1/4" x 3-3/4", black and white, ornately printed, signed in ink by general manager, 1889 ....12.00

Ribbon, Brotherhood of Railroad Men, Grand Union Picnic, Harrisburg, PA, June 27, 1901, 1-7/8" x 3-3/4", beige, gold accent lettering 10.00

Sign, Seaboard RR, "Explosives," 1948 .... 19.00

Step, Pullman RR Station, wood, hand cut-out on top, 21" w, 10" h................................... 25.00

Sugar Tongs, Canadian Pacific, SP, mkd "England" 20.00

Timetable

Erie Railroad, 1907............. 32.00

L&N Kansas City Southern, 1955 .... 8.50

Southern Pacific RR, 1915 .... 22.00

☆ Ramp Walkers

Here's a collectible where the prices might be a surprise to you. Remember those little plastic toys we all played with as a kid? No batteries required, just a sturdy surface that we could tilt so the little critter could walk away. Well, today's collectors are walking all over flea markets to find them.

Cow, plastic, 2-1/4" h 45.00

Cowgirl, plastic, c1945, 6-1/2" h............................. 95.00

Donald Duck, pushing wheelbarrow, Marx, plastic, 1950s 120.00

Elephant, plastic, mkd "Made in Hong Kong," 2-1/4" h.......... 65.00

Farmer, plastic, 2-5/8" h.......... 60.00

Little Girl, plastic, orig weight ball, 6-1/2" h 115.00

Mammy, wood and cloth, c1920, 5" h 245.00

Nanny pushing carriage.......... 22.00

Penguin Ramp, plastic, mkd "Made in Hong Kong," 2-5/8" h 60.00

Popeye and Wimpy, plastic, Marx, copyright 1964, orig box, never played with 80.00

Soldier, wood and cloth, c1920, 4-3/4" h 65.00

☆ Razor Blade Banks

Razor blade banks were designed as a safe place to deposit used razor blades, hence the name. But, just because they were useful, they didn't have to be ordinary. Many of the ceramic and pottery makers created whimsical figural banks which compliment the tin and advertising razor blade banks also found at flea markets. The listings below are all for ceramic or pottery banks.

Barber Head, Ceramic Arts Studio................................82.00

Barber Pole 76.00

Bum, colorful outfit 105.00

Frog 15.50

Happy Shaver, Cleminson 18.00

Mule, adv for Listerine on bottom...............................25.00

❖ Reamers

Feel like putting the squeeze on something? How about an orange, lemon, or grapefruit? Reamer collectors know just how to make their favorite juice and end up sweetly smiling when making a new purchase to add to their collection. They will tell you that reamers can be found in all types of materials, shapes, and sizes.

Collectors' Club: National Reamer Collectors Association, 47 Midline Court, Gaithersburg, MD 20878.

China

Bavaria, white, red, yellow, and green flowers dec, gold trim, 2-pc type.........................60.00

England, white, orange, and yellow flowers, 3-1/2" h...68.00

Figural, china

Elephant, nick on trunk 300.00

Pear, yellow and orange glaze, green leaves, 2-pc type 55.00

Glass

Light Jade-ite, Jeannette, 2 cup, 2-pcs..............................45.00

Glass, Criss-Cross, green, 6" d, $20.

Pink, Criss-Cross, Hazel Atlas,
orange size 295.00
Transparent green, pointed cone,
tab handle, Federal.........30.00

Metal

Dunlap's Improved, iron hinge,
9-1/2" l............................35.00
Nasco-Royal, scissors type,
6" l 10.00
Williams, iron, hinged, glass
insert, 9-3/4" l..................48.00

❖ Records

Spin me a tune! Records have evolved from early cylinders for Mr. Edison's first phonographs to the flat rounds of today. Records can be found in several sizes, and if you hunt long enough, you can probably find almost any type of music you wish. Record albums can cross over into other collecting areas when they are by a special artist, such as Elvis, or have a wonderful cover. One area of record collecting that is currently catching on in a big way is devoted to children's records where there is a picture image right on the record.

Periodical: *Goldmine,* 700 E State St., Iola, WI 54990.

Reference: Tim Neely, *Goldmine Price Guide to 45 RPM Records,* 2nd ed., Krause Publications, 1999. Plus there are many other good reference books available.

Advertising, Lucky Strike 20.00
Belafonte, Harry, LP, Streets I Have
Walked, 1963 .... 35.00
Berry, Chuck, Johnny B. Goode, 78
RPM, Chess 10.00
Best of the Crests.................. 40.00
Bye Bye Birdy, Columbia, orig cast,
1980 .... 17.50
Checker, Chubby, Limbo Party,
Parkway, LP, 1962.............. 20.00
Crosby, Bing, The Songs I Love, six
long play records, mint in orig
case................................. 75.00
Disney's Christmas Carol, picture
disc................................... 25.00
Ellington, Duke, Jubilee Stomp,
Okeh, 41013, 1938............. 15.00

Peter, Paul and Mary "In The Wind," Warner Bros., $5.

Haley, Bill, Shake, Rattle and Roll,
Decca, 5260 .... 35.00
Miller, Glenn, Glenn Miller Story,
Unbreakable, LP, Decca,
1954 .... 22.00
Oklahoma, Decca, orig cast,
1953 .... 42.00
Presley, E., Touch of Gold, Volume
2, EPA-5101, maroon
label.................................. 85.00
Shari Lewis Party Record, 6" sq
black and white thin cardboard
vinyl-coated sheet, 5-3/4" d vinyl
record with black and white photo
of Shari, 2 puppets, Allied Creative Services, Inc.,
c1950................................. 25.00
Superman, the Movie, 1978,
2 record set, LP 24.00
Welling & McGhee, Ring the Bells of
Heaven, Champion,
16660 .... 17.50

❖ Red Wing Pottery

Collectors identify items made by several potteries in the Red Wing, Minnesota area all as Red Wing. All were high quality. Some produced pottery and stoneware. A wing mark was used on many of them.

Collectors' Clubs: Red Wing Collectors Society, 624 Jones Street, Eveleth, MN 55734; The RumRill Society, PO Box 2161, Hudson, OH 44326.

For additional listings, see *Warman's Americana & Collectibles* and *Warman's American Pottery & Porcelain.*

Ashtray, horse head,
#M1472..............................80.00
Beverage Server, coffeepot
style 85.00
Butter Crock, "Hazel Creamery But-
ter," bail handle, 5 lb size,
lid 275.00
Churn, 5 gallon, 4" wing, oval, orig
lid 275.00
Console Bowl, deer flower frog, mkd
"Red Wing 526", two big
chips 130.00
Cornucopia, Swirl, #736..........32.00
Cookie Jar
Drummer Boy...................600.00

Wing ashtray, red glaze, 7-3/8" l, $44.

Bob White hors d'oeuvre server, figural quail, 8-1/2" h, $75.

Friar Tuck, blue 200.00
Round Up 400.00

Crock

1 gallon, Linden Apiary
    adv 175.00
2 gallon, 4" wing, no oval ..100.00

Mug, blue banded...................40.00
Refrigerator Jar, 5 lb, blue, diffused,
    no lid, hairlines 85.00
Teapot, Mediterranean...........65.00

Vase

Boot, #651 ....70.00
Brushed Ware, #144 crane
    motif 55.00
Dark green, M1564,
    9-1/2" h 40.00
Gray and rose, B1426 ....30.00
#1155 ....45.00

Pie plate, 4 lines in brown, yellow and green, some chips/cracks, 7-3/4" d, $200.

❖ Redware

Called redware because of its red clay body, this pottery has its roots back in colonial times when red clay was plentiful and easy to use. By adding glazes, more colors could be introduced. Modern craftsmen have kept the redware tradition alive and can be found working in several parts of the country today.

For additional listings, see *Warman's Antiques and Collectibles Price Guide* and *Warman's American Pottery & Porcelain.*

Bank, apple shape, red and yellow
    paint dec, 3-1/4" h 165.00
Bowl, white stripe dec, brown glaze,
    6-1/2" d.............................. 65.00
Creamer, yellow slip design, green
    accents, ribbed strap handle,
    4-3/8" h............................. 475.00
Cup, flared lip, applied handle, clear
    glaze with mottled amber, minor
    wear and glaze flakes 95.00
Jar, ovoid, int. glazed, imp "John
    Bell, Waynesboro," chips and
    hairlines, 7-1/2" h 150.00
Pie Plate, yellow slip, minor edge
    chips, 7-1/2" d 275.00
Turk's Head Mold, fluted swirls, clear
    glaze, brown sponging,
    8-3/4" d............................. 200.00

❖ Regal China Corporation

Here's a china ware maker which was owned by a different type of business, Jim Beam Distilleries. Their wares include those wonderful decanters you think of as Beam bottles, plus several types of advertising wares and items made for specific clients, such as Quaker Oats and Kraft Foods.

Cookie Jar, cov

Barn 300.00
Kraft Teddy Bear................. 90.00
Quaker Oats 85.00

Creamer and Sugar, Old Mac-
    Donald, rooster and hen..... 47.50

Decanter, Jim Beam, empty

Antique Trader, 1968.......... 10.00
Cat, 1967 .... 10.00
Cherubs, 1974 .... 12.00
Ford, 1978 .... 25.00
Hawaii, 50th State 15.00
Ohio 10.00
Sailfish, 1957, 14" h........... 10.00
Telephone, 1979................ 13.00

Lamp Base, 12-3/4" h, Davy
    Crockett 125.00
Salt and Pepper Shakers, pr, Van
    Telligen, huggers 24.00
Tobacco Jar, Fox, Jim Beam... 60.00

❖ Religious Collectibles

Hunting for religious collectibles at flea markets is a great idea, but not in lieu of going to church services. (Well, perhaps before or after Sunday services.) However, no matter when you shop, you're likely to find something of interest.

Collectors' Clubs: Foundation International for Restorers of Religious Medals, PO Box 2652, Worcester, MA 01608; Judaica Collectors Society, PO Box 854, Van Nuys, CA 91408.

Book, *Mother Teresa: A Life In Pictures,* Royle & Woods, Bloomsbury, 1992, 159 pgs 12.50
Buddha, bronze, early
    20th C 120.00
Chalice, 8" h, sterling, cross on
    base, gilded inside bowl.... 450.00
Charity Container, cylindrical, sheet
    copper, German, 1800s,
    5" d 265.00
Child's Book, *Old Testament*, comic
    book format, 232 pgs, published
    by M. C. Gaines, 1943, worn,
    repaired............................. 12.00
Cross, pendant, sterling silver,
    matching chain, Mexican
    hallmarks 95.00
Doorstop, cast iron, shaped like
    church door, 6" h.............. 165.00
Icon, Greek, The Mother of God of
    the Life Bearing Font, tempera on
    wood panel, 19" x 15" 1,250.00
Kadish Cup, sterling silver, applied
    flowers, trellis, and medallions,
    circular floral foot,
    5-1/2" h 150.00

Hanging glass plaque with chain frame, orig box, Cross Publishing Co., 4-1/4" x 10-1/4", $25.

Painting, The Holy Family, Continental, oil on canvas, framed,
27" x 23" 335.00

Retablo, Our Lady of Sorrows, painted on tin, Mexican, late
19th C 250.00

Santos, The Christ Child, carved and painted wood, Philippine,
14" h 110.00

❖ Riviera

This popular Homer Laughlin pattern was introduced in 1938 and sold by the Murphy Company. It was not all marked, but some pieces have been found with a gold backstamp. It was made in Laughlin's Century shape in dark blue (which is considered rare), light green, ivory, mauve blue, red, and yellow.

Periodical: *Laughlin Eagle,* 1270 63rd Terrace, South, St. Petersburg, FL 33705.

After Dinner Cup and Saucer, ivory................................. 125.00

Butter Dish, 1/2 lb, ivory 155.00

Casserole, cov
Light green 95.00
Mauve blue........................110.00

Creamer, light green or red..... 18.00

Deep Plate, ivory 45.00

Juice Pitcher, mauve blue..... 350.00

Juice Tumbler, light green....... 85.00

Nappy, yellow 50.00

Oatmeal bowl
Ivory 95.00
Light green 85.00
Mauve blue..........................85.00
Red.......................................95.00

Creamer, orange, 2-7/8" h, 6" l, $12.

Yellow 85.00

Sugar Bowl, cov
Light green 30.00
Mauve blue......................... 45.00
Red...................................... 45.00

Teapot, light green 185.00

Tumbler, handle
Light green 55.00
Mauve............................... 75.00
Red...................................... 95.00
Yellow 96.00

✰ Road Maps

Perhaps you used one of these to find a new flea market, bet there are a couple of older maps tucked away in the back of a drawer at your house, just like mine. It certainly is an area where good examples are plentiful and not too expensive.

AAA, Greenbook, Road Reference and Tourist Guide, for states east of Mississippi, Ontario, and Quebec, faded gold on green leather cover, large fold-out map, 1928, some wear and fading 30.00

Florida, Official Road Map, 1973 .... 3.00

Mendenhalls Road Map of Ohio, written directions in lieu of pictures 55.00

Oklahoma, Official Road Map, Phillips 66, 1942 .... 20.00

Pennsylvania, Official Road Map, message and facsimile signature of Governor Thornburg 4.50

Rand McNally, Indian on front cover, Coca-Cola adv on back 95.00

Turkey, 1973 .... 3.00

Wisconsin, Official Road Map, c1940.................................. 6.00

Enco North Dakota map with 1960 census, $3.50.

❖ Robots

These mechanical marvels have delighted movie goers and science fiction buffs for years. The first documented robot is Atomic Robot Man, and he first appeared about 1948. From there on, the Japanese dominated the robot market. By the 1970s, more companies had begun to create robot toys and they started to be exported from Hong Kong and other foreign places. Some of the older Japanese models are commanding big prices. Perhaps you'll find an interesting model next time you land at a flea market.

Periodical: *Robot World & Price Guide,* PO Box 184, Lenox Hill Station, New York, NY 10021; *Toy Shop,* 700 E State Street, Iola, WI 54990.

For additional listings, see Warman's Americana & Collectibles.

Action Figure, Robot Zone, five 2-1/2" h figures, 1985, mkd "Made in British Colony of Hong Kong," MOC 25.00

Bank, wind-up, plastic, dumps coin in slots when revolving, mkd "Made in Hong Kong," orig box 25.00

Figure, Rosie, Jetson's, plastic, Applause, orig sticker, 1990 .... 25.00

Top, Shogun Rocket, plastic, Mattel, 1978, MIP 15.00

Toy

Moon Stroller, wind-up, arms swing, moving radar, mkd "Made in Hong Kong," 3-1/4" h, orig box with slightwear...35.00

Mystery Action, battery operated, bump-and-go action, plastic, mkd "Made in Hong Kong," orig box, 8-1/2" h...................25.00

Magic Mike, plastic, battery-operated, orig box, 11" h, $15.

Rascal, wind-up, mkd "1978, Tomy Corp., Made in Taiwan," MIP, 2" h 20.00

Robot Sentinel, battery operated, walks, arms move, lights, 4 shooting missiles, plastic, mkd "Made in China by Kamco," 1980s, 13" h, MIB 55.00

Saturn, battery operated, walks, lights up eyes, mkd "Made in Hong Kong by Kamco," missiles missing, 13" h......... 38.00

Silver colored, wind-up, mkd "Made in Hong Kong," 4" h, orig box 35.00

Tang, General Foods, 7-1/4" h.......................... 30.00

TR2 Talking, mkd "Made in Hong Kong," orig box............... 65.00

❖ Rock n' Roll

"Rock, Rock, Rock Around the Clock!" Remember the good ol' days with American Bandstand and the great singers Dick Clark introduced us to? No matter what kind of music you associate with rock n' roll, chances are good that some neat collectibles will be rocking at your favorite flea market.

Belt, Michael Jackson, metal buckle, Lee, 1984, 29" l 30.00

Book

KISStory, autographed by band members, coffee table size............................... 175.00

Mick Jagger: Primitive Cool, Christopher Sanford, St. Martin's, 1994 .... 12.00

Woodstock 69, Scholastic Book Services, 1970 .... 25.00

Book Cover, orange and red title paper, 3 black and white book covers, one with Pat Boone, one with Sal Mineo, third generic signer, 1958 Cooga Mooga Products, Inc., NY, unused in clear plastic bag 18.00

Colorforms, KISS, MIB............ 27.50

Doll Outfit, Michael Jackson, c1984, LIN, MOC 28.00

Game, Duran Duran into the Arena, Milton Bradley, 1985 .... 18.00

Record, Billy Joel, "Turnstiles," Columbia, 1976, $2.50.

Lunch Box, The Osmonds, metal, orig thermos, unused, 1973 .... 95.00

Pinback Button, black and white photo

Bob-a-Loo, WABC, disc jockey 70.00

Dick Clark, dark green ground 15.00

Frankie Avalon-Venus, bright pink ground 25.00

Record Case, cardboard, full color photo and signature of Dick Clark, blue, white plastic handle, brass closure, holds 45 RPM records................................. 45.00

Tie Clip, Dick Clark American Bandstand, gold-tone metal 15.00

View-Master Reel, Last Wheelbarrow to Pokeyville, Monkees, orig booklet 12.00

❖ Rockwell, Norman

This famous American artist was born in 1894 and, by the time he died, in 1978, he had created over 2,000 paintings. Many of these paintings were reproduced as magazine covers, illustrations, calendars, etc. It was the allure of the every day man, woman, or child that was found in these paintings that drew you into the scene.

Besides the artwork, many of his illustrations have been translated to limited edition collectibles, giving collectors the faces and gentle ideas of his work.

Collectors' Club: Rockwell Society of America, PO Box 705, Ardsley, NY 10502.

For additional listings, see *Warman's Antiques and Collectibles Price Guide* and *Warman's Americana & Collectibles.*

Bell, Christmas, Dave Grossman,
    1975 .... 40.00

Doll, Mary Moline, made in Germany
    Anne....................................70.00
    Mimi.....................................70.00
    Tina 70.00

Figure
    Dave Grossman Designs, Inc.,
        The Graduate, 1983........35.00
    Gorham, Jolly Coachman,
        1982..................................50.00
    Lynell Studios, Cradle of Love,
        1980..................................85.00
    Rockwell Museum, Bride and
        Groom, 1979...................95.00

Ingot, Franklin Mint, Spirit of Scouting, 1972, 12-pc set.......... 295.00

Magazine Cover
    Boys' Life, June, 1947.........45.00
    Family Circle, Dec, 1967.....15.00
    Red Cross, April, 1918........25.00
    Saturday Evening Post, Jan 26,
        1918...............................95.00

Collector's plate, "The Ship Builder," The Edwin M. Knowles China Co., orig box, 8-5/8" d, $18.

Saturday Evening Post, Feb 18,
    1922 .... 90.00
Saturday Evening Post, April 19,
    1950 .... 85.00
Saturday Evening Post, Sept 7,
    1957 .... 35.00
Saturday Evening Post, Jan 13,
    1962 .... 20.00
Scouting, Dec, 1944 .... 15.00

Plate
    Dave Grossman Designs, Huckleberry Finn, 1980 .... 45.00
    Four Seasons, 1975, set of four
        .... 85.00
    Franklin Mint, The Carolers,
        1972 .... 175.00
    Gorham, Boy Scout,
        1975 .... 65.00
    Lynell Studios, Mother's Day,
        1980 .... 45.00
    River Shore, Jennie & Tina,
        1982 .... 45.00
    Rockwell Museum, First Prom,
        1979 .... 35.00
    Rockwell Society, Golden Christmas, 1976 .... 60.00
    Royal Devon, One Present Too
        Many, 1979..................... 30.00

❖ Rogers, Roy

This popular cowboy hero made a positive impression on many young minds. Today collectors are drawn to Roy Rogers memorabilia to remember and commemorate the morals and honesty he stressed.

Collectors' Club: Roy Rogers-Dale Evans Collectors Association, PO Box 1166, Portsmouth, OH 45662-1166.

Bedspread 115.00
Camera 110.00
Collectors Plate, orig box and certificate.................................... 35.00
Comic Book, April, 1954 .... 24.00
Guitar, orig box, 1950s.......... 140.00
Pocket Knife........................... 60.00
Thermos................................. 55.00
Yo-Yo, orig display box with
    12 yo-yos.......................... 250.00
Watch, Roy and Dale........... 120.00

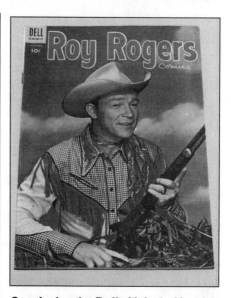

Comic book, Dell, Vol. 1, No. 84, Dec. 1954, $24.

❖ Rookwood

Founded in 1880, Rookwood Pottery underwent several metamorphoses as a business and in the types of pottery it produced, from art pottery to utilitarian wares. The distinctive mark used indicates the clay or body mark, the size, the decorator mark, a date mark, and the factory mark. Learning to accurately read these marks will enhance understanding and appreciation for Rookwood Pottery.

For additional listings, see *Warman's Antiques and Collectibles Price Guide* and *Warman's American Pottery & Porcelain.*

Bookends, pr, rook, olive green,
    c1928 .... 425.00
Bowl, yellow matte, incised Arts and
    Crafts dec, 6" d 200.00
Candlesticks, pr, matte, emb grape
    leaves, dark and light green
    glaze, 1922, restored........ 250.00
Figure, crane, #6972,
    1954................................. 175.00
Flower Frog, #2251,
    1915................................. 325.00
Paperweight, elephant, 1928,
    3-1/2" d 250.00
Pitcher, oviform, incised palm
    leaves, gold and blue highlights,
    imp "Rookwood 1893,"
    6-1/2" h 245.00

Ashtray, "Human Institution, Serving Human Needs, 1888-1938," green matte glaze, 5-3/4" d, $75.

Vase
- #913E, incised blue, white, and green fish, vellum glaze, imp mark, artist monogram for Lorinda Epply, 1908, 6" h 1,610.00
- #1124D, production, 1913, 8-1/2" h, as is 175.00
- #1343, wax matte, yellow, band of flowers, sgd "Pulman," 1931, 5" h................................450.00
- #2367, 1921, 18" h glaze crack 275.00

❖ Rose Bowls

A rose bowl is defined as a round or ovoid shaped bowl with a small opening, often found crimped, pinched, scalloped, petaled, or pleated. They were designed to hold potpourri or rose petals.

Collectors' Club: Rose Bowl Collectors, PO Box 244, Danielsville, PA 18038.

Amethyst, irid finish, etched "Thos. Webb & Son, England," minor rim flakes, 4-1/2" h 175.00
Bohemian, amber stained cut to clear, grape and vine dec, 3-1/2" h.............................. 20.00
Custard Glass, ovoid, rose and swag dec, nutmeg stain highlights, ftd, chips on one foot 20.00

Glass, cobalt blue, 4-3/4" h, $10.

Fenton
- Cranberry, orig stand 42.00
- Misty Blue, satin, incised flowers, 8" d................................. 47.95
Milk Glass, Katy pattern, Imperial.............................. 10.00
Mount Washington, opaque white, hp florals, 4-3/4" h 75.00
Satin
- Blue shaded to white, DQ, 3-3/4" h.......................... 65.00
- Raspberry pink shading to white, 4-1/2" h.......................... 25.00
- Yellow, herringbone, 6" h................................ 65.00
Venetian, gold and pink, 4-1/2" d.............................. 35.00

❖ Roselane Pottery

This California pottery was founded in 1938 in Pasadena. Production included some dinnerware and accessories. Roselane Pottery is perhaps best known for its figures, many of which have jeweled eyes and are known as "Sparklers" to collectors.

Bust, Oriental, pearl luster glaze, 9" h, pr 30.00
Console Bowl, black matte ext., turquoise glaze int., 1950s, 13-3/4" l 25.00

Figure, Sparklers
- Basset Hound 15.00
- Chihuahua 57.00
- Deer, pair 15.00
- Dog family......................... 42.00
- Elephant........................... 50.00
- Giraffe 22.00
- Quail, 6" h 45.00
Siamese Cat and Kittens, 4-1/4" h 40.00
Swimming Duck 50.00

❖ Rosemeade Pottery

Located in Whapeton, North Dakota from 1940 to 1961, this pottery created many figures and novelties. They are known for their accurate wildlife designs. Several marks were used by this company.

Ashtray
- Bear, emb "Breckenridge, Minnesota" 315.00
- Duck................................ 50.00
Bell, elephant 300.00
Flower Frog, rust colored, script mark, 3" h 25.00
Pansy Ring, white, 8-1/2" d, 2" h 35.00
Salt and Pepper Shakers, pr
- Blue Fish, orig paper label, 2-3/4" h.......................... 45.00
- Chihuahuas....................... 450.00
- Gopher, large 145.00
- Leaping Deer 145.00
- Mice 35.00
- Running Rabbits 145.00
- White Duck, orig paperl label................................. 50.00

❖ Rosenthal China

Rosenthal China has been made in Selb, Bavaria since 1880 and continues today. Major production centers around dinnerware and some accessories.

Cake Plate, grape dec, scalloped ruffled edge, ruffled handles, 12" w 75.00

Dish, floral motif, gold trim, 5" x 2-3/4", $5.

Creamer and Sugar, pate-sur-pate type blue cherries dec
.... 125.00
Cup and Saucer, San Souci pattern, white.................................... 20.00
Demitasse Cup and Saucer, Marie pattern................................ 25.00
Figure, clown, 6" h................ 225.00
Lemon Plate, handles, hp, peacock, early 1920s, sgd "Knapp" 300.00
Plate, comic lion dec, 4" d 20.00
Vase
  Modeled owls on branch, 7" h..............................165.00
  Multicolored roses, 11" h............................125.00

❖ Roseville Pottery

This popular Ohio pottery began in the early 1890s. Its wares are well known by collectors. Featuring matte colors, wares were offered in several pattern lines and are well marked. A series of high gloss glazed wares were introduced in the 1940s. Reproductions in the late 1990s have hurt the Roseville market.

References: Several older reference books are available to assist collectors in identifying patterns and marks.

Collectors' Club: Roseville of the Past, PO Box 656, Clarcona, FL 32710.

Reproduction Alert.

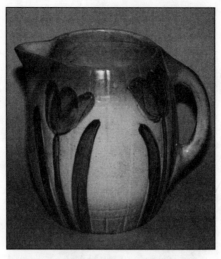

Tulip pitcher, 7-1/4" h, $150.

For additional listings, see *Warman's Antiques and Collectibles Price Guide, Warman's Americana & Collectibles,* and *Warman's American Pottery & Porcelain.*

Bookends, Gardenia, gray 300.00
Bowl
  Blueberry, blue, 412-6 ...... 130.00
  Moss Blue, high sides, #294-12 .... 275.00
  Nursery Rhyme................. 150.00
  Thorn Apple, 6" d............. 140.00
Bowl and Flower Frog, Clematis, mkd "Roseville USA 458-10," c1944.............................. 195.00
Bud Vase, Dahl Rose, double175.00
Candle holders, pr, Carnelian II 70.00

Magnolia vase, blue, 9" h, $250.

Candlesticks, pr
  Carnelian I 140.00
  Pine Cone, #451-4............ 325.00
Child's Feeding Plate, rolled edge
  Nursery Rhyme................. 150.00
  Tom Tom 90.00
Compote, Magnolian, 13" h... 110.00
Conch Shell, Peony, blue...... 185.00
Console Bowl, Bushberry, #414-10............................. 180.00
Cornucopia, White Rose, 145-8, double 175.00
Creamer, Juvenile, duck 100.00
Cup and Saucer, Zephyr Lily, blue.................................... 125.00
Ewer, Silhouette, maroon, #716-6" 175.00
Flower Frog, Clematis, #50, chipped 75.00
Mug
  Duck with boots 150.00
  Dutch 110.00
  Rabbit 140.00
Pitcher
  Blended Landscape, 7-1/2" h...................... 140.00
  Carnelian II, mottled green and cream, rough bottom 175.00
Plate, Juvenile, rabbit, rolled edge, 7" d 155.00
Tea Set, Bushberry, damage to cup and saucer 250.00
Vase
  Dahl Rose, 4" x 10".......... 190.00
  Donatello, 10" h 230.00
  Failine #648, 7" h, brown .. 700.00
  Freesia, #128-16, brown, rim defect............................ 400.00
  Iris, blue, #927-10, restored base chip................................ 285.00
  Laurel, 6" h, brown........... 185.00
  Peony, 14" h, yellow, small base repair 325.00
  Pine Cone, brown, 279-9 .... 230.00
  Poppy, 872-9, base chips 120.00
  Primrose, blue.................. 175.00
  Rozane, 8" h, honeycomb, pastel roses........................... 375.00
  Russco, 7" h 160.00
  Silhouette, blue, nude, fan, #783-7, small base repair 400.00
Wall Pocket, Carnelian.......... 185.00

❖ Royal Bayreuth

Another Bavarian firm, Royal Bayreuth has its roots back in the late 1790s and is still producing dinnerware. The name is well known to collectors for the figural lines that were quite popular in the late 1880s. One interesting type of porcelain Royal Bayreuth introduced is known as "Tapestry Ware." The texture of this ware was caused by adding a piece of fabric, then decorating and glazing and firing the piece.

Collectors' Clubs: Royal Bayreuth Collectors Club, 926 Essex Circle, Kalamazoo, MI 49008; Royal Bayreuth International Collectors' Society, PO Box 325, Orrville, OH 44667.

For additional listings, see *Warman's Antiques and Collectibles Price Guide* and *Warman's English & Continental Pottery and Porcelain.*

Bell, Nursery Rhyme, children
   dancing.............................. 295.00
Celery Tray, Tomato pattern ... 95.00
Cracker Jar, Grapes, green dec,
   no lid.................................. 95.00

Creamer, figural
   Bird of Paradise.................225.00
   Clown, red..........................275.00
   Elk..55.00
   Frog, green.........................250.00
   Robin..................................200.00
   Spikey Shell, white, 3-1/2" h,
     blue mark.....................135.00

Creamer, tapestry
   Brittany women, double handle,
     4" h................................125.00
   Mountain sheep, hunt scene,
     4" h................................110.00

Cup and Saucer
   Boy with turkey...................125.00
   Man in boat fishing............125.00
Hatpin Holder, courting couple,
   cutout base, gold dec, blue
   mark 400.00
Match Holder, tapestry, Arab
   scene.............................. 100.00

Jack and the Beanstalk pitcher, 4-1/4" h, $145.

Milk Pitcher, 3-1/2" h, pinched spout,
   mountain sheep................ 125.00
Mustard, cov
   Spikey Shell, 3-1/2" h, mkd "Germany" 135.00
   Tomato, figural leaf under
     plate 75.00
Pitcher, 7" h, turkey and cock
   fighting............................. 375.00
Plate, 7-1/2" d
   Man and dogs..................... 95.00
   Man in boat fishing 95.00
Plate, 8-1/2" d, boy and
   donkeys 95.00
Salt and Pepper Shakers, pr, Rose
   Tapestry, pink roses.......... 375.00
Vase, 4" h, Babes in the Woods
   Girl with Doll 475.00
   Girls with Witch................ 495.00

❖ Royal China

Manufactured in Sebring, Ohio, from 1924 to 1986, Royal China made a large variety of dinnerware patterns. Collectors today are particularly fond of several patterns, including Currier & Ives, Bucks County, Colonial Homestead, Fair Oaks, Memory Lane, Old Curiosity Shop, and Willow Ware.

Collectors' Club: Currier & Ives Dinnerware Collectors Club, RD 2, Box 394, Hollidaysburg, PA 16648.

For additional listings and more detailed history, see *Warman's Americana & Collectibles.*

Bread and Butter Plate
   Bucks County........................2.50
   Memory Lane........................3.25
Butter Dish, cov, Colonial
   Homestead 27.50
Casserole, cov, Bucks County 72.00
Coffee Mug
   Colonial Homestead 20.00
   Willow Ware........................22.00
Creamer, Currier and Ives.........7.50
Cup and Saucer
   Bucks County........................3.75
   Colonial Homestead 3.00
   Currier and Ives....................4.50
   Memory Lane........................5.00
Dinner Plate
   Bucks County........................8.00
   Colonial Homestead 5.00
   Currier and Ives....................6.00
   Old Curiosity Shop...............4.50
   Willow Ware........................4.00
Fruit Bowl
   Bucks County........................2.75
   Currier and Ives....................3.50

Plate, Bucks County, 10-1/16" d, $8.

Old Curiosity Shop 3.00
Gravy Boat, underplate, Old
    Curiosity Shop....................28.00
Platter, Willow Ware, oval,
    11" l....................................25.00
Salad Plate
    Bucks County........................8.25
    Willow Ware.........................10.00
Salt and Pepper Shakers, pr,
    Bucks County.....................20.00
Soup Bowl, Colonial
    Homestead...........................8.50
Sugar Bowl, Currier and Ives,
    angled handles...................17.50
Vegetable Dish, divided,
    Fair Oaks...........................28.00

❖ Royal Copenhagen

Many collectors think of Royal Copenhagen as making blue and white Christmas plates. However, this Danish firm has also made dinnerware, figurines, and other table wares.

Bowl, reticulated blue and white,
    round...............................125.00
Christmas Plate
    1981....................................35.00
    1982....................................50.00
Cup and Saucer, #1870..........75.00
Figure
    #1276, chimney sweep and
        lady.............................800.00

Christmas plate, Julen, 1914, $37.50.

#1314, girl knitting 350.00
#3165, wire haired fox
    terrier............................ 150.00
Inkwell, Blue Fluted pattern,
    matching tray.................... 165.00
Plate, #1624, 8" d 50.00
Tray, Blue Fluted pattern,
    10" l 65.00
Vase, 7" h, sage green and gray
    crackled glaze 150.00

❖ Royal Copley

Royal Copley was a trade name used by the Spaulding China Company of Sebring, Ohio. Concentrating on the tableware and novelty market, Royal Copley was sold through retail stores to consumers who wanted a knick-knack or perhaps something pretty to use on their table.

Periodical: *The Copley Courier,* 1639 N. Catalina St., Burbank, CA 91505.

Baby Mug, fish handle, as is... 60.00
Bank, rooster
    Green, gold trim.................. 70.00
    Multicolored 50.00
Dish, bluebird.......................... 15.00

Pitcher, floral pattern, high-gloss glaze, 8" h, $22.

Figure
    Bear 25.00
    Dog with yellow basket 32.95
    Fawn and deer....................21.50
    Mallard Duck, 7" h 20.00
    Pig.......................................22.00
Lamp, Flower Tree 70.00
Planter
    Blossom, large 8.00
    Cow.....................................20.00
    Doe and fawn......................20.00
    Girl leaning on planter.........10.00
    Mallard Duck.......................30.00
    Puppy and mailbox 15.00
Planter, salmon, gold trim,
    as is 80.00

❖ Royal Doulton

This English pottery firm has had a long and interesting history. They have produced all types of figurines, character jugs, toby jugs, dinnerware, Beswick, Bunnykins, and stoneware. One popular dinnerware line is known as Dicken Ware, named for the Dickens' characters included in the design. The listing below is a sampling of the kinds of Royal Doulton wares to be found at flea markets.

References: Susan and Al Bagdade, *Warman's English & Continental Pottery & Porcelain*, 3rd Edition, Krause Publications, 1998; Jean Dale, *Charlton Standard Catalogue of Royal Doulton Animals*, 2nd ed., Charlton Press, 1998; ——, *Charlton Standard Catalogue of Royal Doulton Beswick Figurines*, 6th ed., Charlton Press, 1998.

Periodicals: *Collecting Doulton,* BBR Publishing, 2 Stratford Ave, Elsecar, Nr Barnsley, S Yorkshire, S74 8AA, England; *Doulton Divvy,* PO Box 2434, Joliet, IL 60434.

Collectors' Clubs: Heartland Doulton Collectors, PO Box 2434, Joliet, IL 60434; Mid-America Doulton Collectors, PO Box 483, McHenry, IL 60050; Royal Doulton International Collectors Club, PO Box 6705, Somerset, NJ 08873; Royal Doulton International Collectors Club, 850 Progress Ave, Scarborough Ontario M1H 3C4 Canada.

Animal

Brown Bear, HN2659	175.00
Bunnykins, Aerobic	150.00
Cat with Bandaged Paw, 3-1/4" h	45.00
Dalmatian, HN1113	250.00
Elephant, Flambe, HN489A	200.00
Fox Terrier, HN1068	1,750.00
Pine Martin, HN2656	275.00
Stalking Tiger, Flambe, HN809	700.00

Christmas Carol Plate

#1, 1982	35.00
#2, 1983	35.00

Figure

Best Friends, HN3935, designed by Alan Maslankowski, 1995 ....100.00

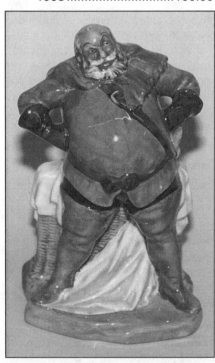

Flagstaff figurine, H.N. 2054, 7" h, $175.

Blue Beard, HN2015, designed by L. Harradine, purple, green, and brown, 1953-92, green backstamp, 11" h 600.00

Bridget, HN2070, 1951-1973, gold, brown, and lavender, designer "L. Harradine," green backstamp and registration marks, 7-3/4" h 465.00

Cherie, HN2341, designed by M. Davies, 1966-92, green backstamp.................... 135.00

Christmas Morn, HN3212 .... 145.00

Danielle, HN3001, designed by P. Gee, c1990-96, white green backstamp.................... 150.00

Family, HN2720, designed by E. J. Griffiths, 1981, 12" h.......................... 190.00

Happy Anniversary, HN3254, designed by D. V. Tootle, 1989, 12" h.......................... 175.00

Jane Eyre, HN3842, designed by Pauline Parsons, 8-1/4" h......................... 375.00

Mendicant, HN1365, designed by L. Harradine, brown, green backstamp, #39, incised, 1929-1969, 8-1/4" h............... 340.00

Rosie, HN4094, designed by Nada Pedley, 8" h......... 185.00

Royal Govenor's Cook, HN2233, designed by M. Davies, dark blue, white, and brown, 1960-83, 6" h.......................... 565.00

Sit, HN3123, designed by Alan Maslankowski, c1991, 4-1/2" h.......................... 120.00

Sweet and Twenty, HN1298, designed by L. Harradine, 1928-69, green backstamp, 5-3/4" h......................... 425.00

The Balloon Man, HN1954 .... 200.00

Plate

Alfred Jingle	145.00
Bottom from Mid-Summer's Night Dream, 9-3/4" d	185.00
Gullivers	95.00
Henry VIII	135.00
Orchids	85.00
Pansies, border of large pansies, cream ground, 9-3/4" d	95.00
Sir Andrew, 10-1/2" d	180.00

The Parson, 10-1/2" d	85.00
Toxophilite	95.00

❖ Royal Dux

Here's a lovely porcelain, made in Bohemia starting about 1860. Some of the most popular designs are their Art Nouveau inspired wares. Look for their distinctive raised triangle mark or acorn mark to help identify genuine Royal Dux.

Figure

Boy with accordion.............. 65.00

Bulldog, pink triangle mark, blue stamped circle "Czech Republic" 110.00

Elephant, pastel blue, white, and beige, triangular gold mark, stick, oval "Made in Czech Republic" sticker, 4-1/4" h.......................... 50.00

Poodle, 7-1/2" l 75.00

Sheepherder, #2261, and Peasant Girl, #2262, 9" h, price for pr 250.00

Vase, 6-1/2" h, 3-3/4" l, Art Deco, gold sticker, back stamp "Royal Dux Bohemia, Hand Painted, Made in Czech Republic," raised pink triangle, 6 incised numbers...........................60.00

Dog figurine, pink triangle mark, 11-3/4" l, $120.

✷ Royal Winton

Known best for it's pretty chintz patterns, Royal Winton also made some other dinnerware and tablewares. This firm was started by the Grimwade brothers, and some marks bear their name in additional to Royal Winton and other information.

Pin tray, rim chip, 4-5/8" l, 3-1/2" w, $12.50.

For additional listings, see *Warman's English & Continental Pottery & Porcelain* as well as "Chintz" in this edition.

Candlesticks, pr, Delphinium, hand painted, octagonal 80.00
Cup and Saucer, Spring, #2506 .... 125.00
Figure, Dickens character, Sam Weller, red jacket 155.00
Jug, 8-1/2" h, Fish, gurgles when pours 45.00
Place Setting, Ivory, mkd "Wye," black Art Deco design with multi-colored flowers 12.00
Snack Set, plate and cup, Tiger Lily pattern 85.00
Soup Plate, Rosebud pattern, 8-1/4" d.............................. 15.00
Souvenir Ware
  Plate, Nassau in the Bahamas...........................8.00
  Teapot, Old Canada, scenes and gold trim, 1953 ....21.75
Tea Cup
  Eversham pattern, 2-3/4" h....95.00
  Hibiscus, gold trim, 2-3/4" h...28.50

❖ Royal Worcester

Here's another venerable English pottery that's a favorite with collectors. Some of their porcelains are hand decorated while others take advantage of a transfer print decora-

tion technique which Royal Worcester perfected. Again, look for a mark which will help date the piece, give clues as to the decorator, etc.

For additional listings, see *Warman's Antiques and Collectibles Price Guide* and *Warman's English & Continental Pottery and Porcelain.*

Bowl, scalloped border, shell molded body, fruit and floral spray, blue and white transfer dec, first period, mid-18th C, 10" d.. 325.00
Cup and Saucer, Imari pattern, c1910................................. 48.00
Egg Coddler, silver lid with ring on top
  3" h, peach on front, leaf with berries on back............... 20.00
  3-1/4" h, two different bird scenes on each coddler, mkd "Royal Worcester Porcelain, Made in England", pr.................... 30.00
Figure
  Politician, white glaze, hat rim restored, minor staining 300.00
  Saturday's Child, boy........ 130.00
  The Thief 225.00
Mustard Pot, cylindrical, blue and white transfer, floral clusters, floral finial, first period, mid 18th C, 4" h 325.00
Plate, Tewkesbury, natural colors, gold edge, artist sgd "Nickolis," 1953 mark, 10-3/4" d 200.00
Saucer, Marble Hill Cottage, black transfer dec 75.00
Urn, cov, pierced dome top, painted floral sprays, basketweave molded base, early 20th C, 11-1/2" h 200.00
Vase, floral dec, gilt trim, reticulated, 3-1/4" h 115.00

❖ Roycroft

Roycroft is a familiar name to Arts and Crafts collectors. The Roycrofters were founded by Elbert Hubbard in East Aurora, New York. He was a talented author, lecturer, and manufacturer. Perhaps his greatest contribution was the campus he created with shops to teach and create furniture, metals, leather working, and printing.

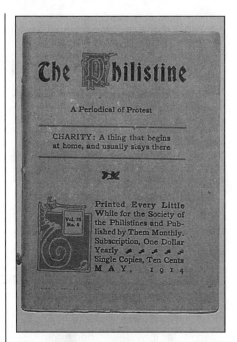

The Philistine, A Periodical of Protest, May 1914, $5.

Collectors' Clubs: Foundation for the Study of Arts & Crafts Movement, Roycroft Campus, 31 S. Grove St., East Aurora, NY 14052; Roycrofters-At-Large Association, PO Box 417, East Aurora, NY 14052.

Bookends, metal, emb quail, early orb and cross mark........... 340.00
Bowl, hammered copper, rolled rim, shouldered, 3 point feet, red patina, imp mark, traces of orig brass wash, 10-1/4" d 450.00
Candle Lamp, blue art glass, baluster form, flaring foot, stamped mark, electrified 175.00
Purse, leather, tooled dec, clutch type, 10-1/8" l.................... 175.00
Tray, hand hammered copper, orig dark patina, octagonal, handles, imp mark, 10" d................ 300.00
Vase, hammered copper, orig patina, orb and cross mark, minor wear to base, 4-1/2" d 425.00

❖ R.S. Germany

R. S. Germany wares are also known as Schlegelmilch porcelain in reference to the brothers who founded several potteries in the Thuringia and Upper Silesia region of

Teapot, creamer, sugar, orange over white lustre, teapot 6" h, $55 set.

Poland/Germany in the 1860s until the 1950s. Generally, R. S. Germany wares feature florals and detailed backgrounds. Handles and finials tend to be fancy.

Biscuit Jar, cov, roses dec, satin finish, loop handles, gold knob, 6" h 95.00

Bon Bon Dish, pink carnations, gold dec, silver-gray ground, inside looped handle, 7-3/4" l 45.00

Chocolate Pot, white rose florals, blue mark 95.00

Demitasse Cup and Saucer, pink roses, gold stenciled dec, satin finish, blue mark 95.00

Nut Bowl, cream and yellow roses, green scalloped edge, 5-1/4" d............................. 65.00

Plate, white flowers, gold leaves, green ground, gilded edge, dark green mark, gold script signature, 9-3/4" d............................. 45.00

Tray, 4" x 9", white roses 45.00

❖ R.S. Prussia

Like R. S. Germany, this porcelain was made by Reinhold Schlegelmilch in the same region. Designed to be used for export, the wares are mostly table accessories or dinnerware. Pieces of R. S. Prussia tend to be more expensive then their R. S. cousins, primarily because of better molds and decoration.

Collectors' Club: International Association of R. S. Prussia Collectors, Inc., 212 Wooded Falls Road, Louisville, KY 40243.

Creamer and sugar, unmkd 5-3/4" h, $150.

Reproduction Alert.

Cake Plate, floral with 3 medallions of cherubs.......................... 500.00

Cake Plate, turkey and evergreens 500.00

Celery Dish, green florals 175.00

Chocolate set, cov chocolate pot, 6 cups and saucers, pink and red roses, gold luster, angular handles, red mark.................. 995.00

Ferner, mold 876, florals on purple and green ground, unsigned.......................... 175.00

Hair Receiver, green lilies of the valley flowers, white ground, red mark 95.00

Plate, poppies dec, raised molded edge and gilt trim, 8-3/4" d.............................. 75.00

Toothpick Holder, pink and white roses, green shadows, jeweled, six small feet, red mark..... 250.00

❖ Ruby Stained Glass

Pattern glass with ruby stained highlights can be a great find at flea markets. Look for examples that are in good condition with little wear to the ruby staining or any gold trim. Many pieces of ruby stained glass were used as souvenirs and can be found with names, places, and dates engraved on them.

Berry Set, Tacoma pattern 7 pc................................... 310.00

Celery Tray, Tacoma pattern... 65.00

Compote, Tacoma pattern 110.00

Dish, canoe shape, Tacoma pattern................................. 75.00

Mug

Button Arches pattern, engraved "Atlantic City," 3" h, 2-3/4" d 35.00

Heart Band pattern, 2-7/8" h, 2-1/2" d 30.00

Rose Bowl, Tacoma pattern, 6-1/2" d 85.00

Spooner, Royal Crystal pattern................................. 75.00

Syrup

Late Block Pattern, orig top 300.00

Pioneer's Victoria pattern, orig top 350.00

Prize pattern, orig top 325.00

Truncated Cube pattern.... 250.00

Toothpick Holder

Double Arch pattern.......... 195.00

Harvard pattern................... 80.00

Pleating pattern................... 85.00

Prize pattern 135.00

Zipper Slash pattern 45.00

Tumbler, Riverside's Victoria pattern................................. 85.00

Water Set

Hexagon Block pattern, tankard pitcher, six tumblers, 7 pcs............................. 325.00

Loop and Block pattern, 7 pcs............................. 465.00

Miniature coal bucket, worn gold lettering, wire bail, 2-5/8" h, 4" l, $18.

Pioneer's Victoria pattern, tankard pitcher, six tumblers, 7 pcs 350.00

❖ Rugs

All kinds of rugs are available at flea markets. They range from small handmade hooked or braided examples to larger room rugs or Oriental type rugs. Look for a rug that meets your needs for size, shape, color, and price. Some collectors look at hooked rugs as folk art, and they do genuinely fall into that category when they are handmade, one-of-a-kind rugs.

Flea markets might not be the best place to buy an Oriental rug, but if you feel you know what you're looking for and the price is right, see what kind of deal you can work out with the dealer. Ask about a return policy, get the dealer's name and address, and by all means carefully examine any rug you intend to buy.

Because there are so many variables in purchasing an Oriental rug, they can't be priced in the space we have available here. Consult a good Oriental rug reference book and take the time to learn about what makes a good rug great before buying.

Braided, wool suit scraps, tightly braided, some wear, 42" l oval.................................. 200.00

Hooked
Checkerboard, floral border, red, pink, black, green, yellow, gray ground, black cloth covered stretcher, 22" h, 32" w ...335.00

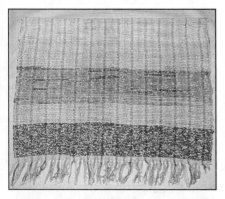

Woven throw rug, 51" x 25", $22.50.

Compass star, circular, red, gray, black, blue, and yellow, 55" d 415.00
Flowerheads, striated border, slate blue, cream, ivory, red, navy and brown, losses, fading, staining, 41" x 33".. 245.00
Saddled horse, variegated ground with grass, trees, plants, sky, New England, mounted, repairs, 30-1/2" h, 51" l 2,200.00
Rag, made on loom, multicolored, some wear, 36" w, 6" long 300.00

❖ RumRill Pottery

RumRill Pottery was made at one time by Red Wing Potteries and sold by a sales force located in Little Rock, Arkansas. Later, production was at the Florence Pottery in Ohio, and after that it was made by Shawnee Pottery, also in Ohio. Perhaps this adds to the fun for RumRill collectors in that they can further identify where the piece was made and when.

Bud Vase, #329
Green to brown................... 18.50
Ripe wheat 28.00
Ewer, H73, light green matte, 8-1/2" h 55.00
Flower Bowl, K14, blue stippled ground 32.00
Jug, ball, orange #547 .... 50.00
Planter
Log 60.00
Scalloped, pink, E12, 7" d 15.00
Urn, Rivieria glaze, ivory ext, blue int, 644, 7" h 27.50
Vase
6" h, #541-6 .... 80.00
7" h, Catalina 24.00
11" h, fan shape, blue, handles........................... 55.00

❖ Russian Items

Flea markets are great places to find Russian collectibles. From beautiful amber from the Baltic region to pieces commemorating events, there is a lot of variety. Russian craftsmen were known for the exquisite work in silver, enamels, and lacquer.

Beads, amber, graduated, screw closure, 28" l 375.00
Box, lacquer, Fedoskino, Tzar surveying wonders of Gvidon's Country 575.00
Bracelet, amber, stretch type 175.00
Compact, sterling, picture of Catherine the Great on front, puff missing.............................. 175.00
Figure, Panda, ceramic, sitting, legs up, black and white, 5-1/2" h 85.00
Medal, USSR Victory over Germany, 1941-45............................... 15.00
Painting, Russian harbor scene, pastels, Ruth Walsh, 1939, 30" x 24" 120.00
Plate, St. Petersburg Palace, sq, holes for hanging, 1991, 7-3/4" w.............................. 22.00
Samovar, 16" h, nickel-plated, sgd 140.00
Serving Spoon, sterling silver, floral pattern, c1870................... 150.00
Toy, diecast, 1:43 scale, hood and trunk open, rubber tires, 1990, 3-3/4" l, orig box.................. 15.00

Collector's plate, Tianex, Bradford Exchange, 1988, 7-3/4" d, $15.

❖ Salt and Pepper Shakers

What table would be complete without a pair of salt and pepper shakers? Flea markets are great places to spot novelty and decorative salt and pepper shakers. Most can add a smile to even a sleepy head! Generally the salt shaker has larger or more holes than the pepper.

Collectors' Club: Novelty Salt & Pepper Shakers Club, PO Box 3617, Lantana, FL 33465.

For additional listings, see *Warman's Antiques and Collectibles Price Guide* and *Warman's Antiques & Collectibles*.

Bugs Bunny and Taz with
    football................................ 15.00
Chicks emerging from egg-shaped
    cups, script mark "Japan,"
    4-1/2" h.............................. 60.00
Donald Duck and BBQ 15.00
Duck and Egg, 3-1/4" h 27.50
Fish, gray............................... 45.00
Mickey and Piano 15.00
Minnie Mouse and Vanity 15.00
Pluto and Doghouse............... 15.00
Poodles.................................. 40.00
Rabbits, yellow, snuggle type, Van
    Telligen 42.00
Refrigerators, GE, 1930 style refrig-
    erator, milk glass 30.00

Tappan, ceramic, 4-1/2" h, $37.50.

❖ Salts, Open

Before the advent of salt shakers, open salt containers were used on tables. Frequently there was a master salt to hold this precious condiment. Another way of dispensing salt was individual salts, often called salt cellars, which were placed by each place setting, along with a tiny spoon. The individual salts were usually sold as sets and can be found in silver, silver plate, and various types of glassware.

Periodical: *Salty Comments,* 401 Nottingham Road, Newark, DE 19711.

Collectors' Clubs: New England Society of Open Salt Collectors, PO Box 177, Sudbury, MA 01776; Open Salt Collectors of Atlantic Region, 56 Northview Drive, Lancaster, PA 17601.

Cut Glass, master, green cut to
    clear, silver plated holder,
    2" h 120.00
Intaglio, individual, bronze basket
    frame with "jewels," burnished
    gold scene on body,
    8-sided............................... 80.00
Noritake, individual, oval, blue and
    gold int............................... 42.00
Pattern Glass, individual
    Fine Rib, flint 35.00
    Hawaiian Lei...................... 35.00
    Three Face 42.00
Pattern Glass, master
    Barberry, pedestal 45.00
    Jacob's Ladder, pedestal
        base 40.00
    Snail, ruby stained............. 75.00
Pewter, master, cobalt blue liner,
    pedestal 70.00
Royal Bayreuth, individual, lobster
    claw 85.00

✪ ⚙ Sand Pails

Here's a topic that has caught on over the last few years. Bright litho-graphed metal sand pails were made by several of the major toy manufac-turers. They were designed with all types of characters and childhood scenes. Look for ones with bright colors. Most collectors prefer very good examples, but will tolerate some dents and signs of use.

J. Chein, some rust, 7-1/4" h plus handle, $48.

Children at Beach scene, Ohio Art,
    6" d, 6-1/4" h 90.00
Disney, Mickey, Dopey, Snow White,
    Pluto, and other characters, metal
    pail, wood handle, Chein, 1966,
    wear, slight rust, dent, 8" d,
    8" h 75.00
Easter scene, bunnies and chicks,
    6" h 85.00
Flower Garden, 6" h 60.00
Man selling flowers from cart, metal
    pail and handle, 5-1/4" d,
    6" h 32.00

❖ Sarreguemines

This porcelain is another example of tin-glazed earthware, like majolica. It was made in France and can be found in all types of design, some quite whimsical. Some have the name impressed on the back.

Covered mustard, $55.

Basket, quilted green body, heavy leopard skin crystallization, 9" h 250.00
Character Jug, lawyer 125.00
Cup and Saucer, Orange, majolica 50.00
Humidor, man with top hat 175.00
Pitcher, ugly man's head, blue int., majolica 275.00

❖ Scales

Whether it's the scales of justice or a candy scale, collectors like to find interesting examples that add weight to their collections.

Collectors' Club: International Society of Antique Scale Collectors, 176 W. Adams St., Suite 1706, Chicago, IL 60603.

Baby, white painted wicker basket 55.00
Balance, Baker's, Henry Troemner, Phila, No. 5B, cast iron, orig red paint, black and yellow trim, nickel-plated brass pans, 14" l 125.00
Candy, National Store Co., tin pan, c1910 .... 100.00
Gold, oak, all weights 225.00
Hand Held, Chatilion, wide side gauge 35.00
Postal, Sattler's, iron and brass 80.00
Store, Howe, cast iron, red base, gold highlights, brass pan, 5 weights, patent June 18, 1887 .... 85.00

Triner 89K Accuracy Scale, Triner Scale & Mfg Co., Chicago, 1 lb maximum, sheet metal base, $58.

☆ Schafer & Vater

The firm of Schafer and Vater was located in Rudolstadt, Thuringia, from about 1890 to 1962. They made porcelain dolls, figurines, and novelty wares of all types.

For additional listings, see *Warman's English & Continental Pottery & Porcelain.*

Bottle, figural, One of the Boys 150.00
Box, cov, olive green bisque, gold and bronze accents, white glazed emb cameo of lady and cupid on lid, chip on lid, 5" x 3" 225.00
Mug, figural, elk 50.00
Pin Tray, figural, lady golfer .. 235.00
Pitcher, figural
    Lady with cape, blue 130.00
    Man, hat and cane, blue and white 125.00
Pitcher, jasperware, dark green, white cameo woman's portrait, 3" h 50.00
Plaque, jasperware, dark green, white dec, mkd #2870, artist #18, 12" h 275.00
Urn, jasperware, blue and white, man and woman planting tree, 2-1/2" h 50.00
Vase
    Bisque, handles, bluish-gray, white bird on handle, tree trunk design, emb berries, nick on bird, 2" h 45.00
    Jasperware, lilac, raised Art Nouveau dec, large cobalt blue jewels, iridized and crystallized glaze, c1900-20, 6-1/4" h 225.00

❖ Schoop, Hedi

Hedi Schoop Art Creations represents another California pottery. This one was located in North Hollywood from 1942 to 1958. The company is well known for its detailed figures and other tablewares.

Bowl, 8" w, 4-1/4" h, hand crafted, mkd 75.00
Figure
    Dutch Boy and Girl, 11" h, missing one pail 95.00

Lady, seated, holding bowl, tinted bisque, high glaze turquoise, 12" h 300.00
Oriental Couple, 12" h, missing orig hat and bucket 75.00
Oriental Woman, 12" h, thumb missing 70.00
Woman holding umbrella planter, violet dress, 13" h 185.00
Planter
    Butterfly, green and gold, pr 175.00
    Rectangular, 9" w, 3" d 65.00
Vase
    8" h, feather design 110.00
    8-1/2" h, 8-1/4" d, c1940 ..... 90.00

☆ Schuco

Let's play! Schuco Toys are always well built, colorful, and ready to go. Many toy collectors are happy to find original Schuco boxes to accompany their toys.

Beach Buggy, worn orig box . 195.00
Curvo 1000 Motorcycle, red shirt, brown pants, green cycle, orig box, missing end flap 680.00
Drummer clown, litho tin wind-up 255.00
Dump truck, orig key 125.00
Electro Submarino, tin, graphics, orig instructions, 12" l, MIB 325.00
KLM Plane, Raidant 5600, battery operated 700.00
Porsche 917, battery operated, 1970, MIB 195.00

☆ ✿ Scotties

Scotties are one of the most recognizable dog breeds. Some attribute this to President Franklin Roosevelt and his dog, Fala, others identify Scotties with Jock from Lady and the Tramp. Many Scottie collectibles are found with black dogs and red and white accents. Scottie images can be found on every type of item and bring a smile with their cheerful attitude.

Reference: Candace Sten Davis and Patricia Baugh, *A Treasury of Scottie Dog Collectibles,* Collector Books, 1998.

Figural lighter, composition dog, Strikalite metal works, 3-1/4" l, $13.50.

Collectors' Clubs: Wee Scots, PO Box 1597, Winchester, VA 22604.

Ashtray, metal, figural Scottie seated next to round ash receiver, painted green 58.00
Bookends, pr, wooden, 5" h.... 32.00
Bottle, luster........................... 45.00
Bookends, pr, four dogs on each, chalkware, mkd "Melil" on side, 6-1/2" h, some chips........... 25.00
Calendar, 1959, Texaco, girl on phone with Scottie.............. 24.00
Cocktail Shaker, red checkerboard background, black Scottie .. 15.00
Doorstop, chalkware, dark brown, red collar, 11" l, some chips.................................. 28.00
Figure, chalkware, black, c1949, 8" h, 10-1/2" l..................... 65.00
Magnets, orig box 15.00
Memo Pad Holder, diecut, black plastic, red tie, hole for hanging 38.00
Salt and Pepper Shakers, pr, figural, orange Scotties playing instruments........................ 75.00
Tea Towel, pale orange linen, embroidered pair of Scotties, 12" x 18"............................. 30.00
Tumbler, 5" h, red checkerboard background, black Scottie 7.00

❖ Sebastian Miniatures

Marblehead, Massachusetts, was the home for Prescott Baston's Sebastian figurines. He started production in 1938 and created detailed historical figurines and characters from literature.

Collectors' Clubs: The Sebastian Exchange Collector Association, PO Box 10905, Lancaster, PA 17605; Sebastian Miniature Collectors Society, 321 Central St., Hudson, MA 01749.

Colonial Carriage 80.00
Gibson Girl........................... 90.00
House of Seven Gables........ 100.00
In the Candy Store, green and silver Marblehead label 135.00
Shoemaker, sgd..................... 50.00
Mark Twain 120.00
William and Hannah Penn 200.00

⭐ Sesame Street

"Sunny day, everything's A-OK!" That's the song Sesame Street collectors sing as they gleefully search through flea markets for the growing number of items related to Big Bird, Elmo and the rest of the Sesame Street gang. Wise collectors know to watch for knockoffs -- cheap, unlicensed imitations of Sesame Street products. Most of the copycats aren't worth adding to a collection.

Alarm clock, Kermit the Frog, Model 5601, Timex, 1982, 4-3/8" h 32.50
Cookie Jar, Oscar the Grouch, 1972 .... 46.00
Lamp, Big Bird under a street lamp, no shade, 13" h 15.50

45 rpm record, "Hits from Sesame Street, Vol. III," Peter Pan Records, $4.

Lunchbox and thermos, Aladdin, metal, 1979 .... 25.00
Muppet Miniatures, Hansel and Gretel set 32.50
Playset, Sesame Street Playset by Fisher-Price, 1975, orig box, missing Big Bird's nest and Gordon, foam on beds rough 200.00
Puppet, Rowlf the Dog, 15".....51.00
Radio, figural with Oscar, Ernie and Bert on stage, 7" h 17.00
Trading cards, set of 100, 1992.................................. 15.50

❖ Sevres and Sevres Type China

Sevres porcelain at a flea market? Sure, not every dealer, but some pieces of this fine French porcelain show up at flea markets. Just like today, when Sevres porcelain became so popular, imitations were made. Those are often considered "Sevres Type" and are also found at flea markets. Carefully check out the mark and the decoration on the piece. Many reproduction Sevres pieces exist, and some of the older fakes might fool buyers.

For additional listings, see *Warman's Antiques and Collectibles Price Guide* and *Warman's English & Continental Pottery & Porcelain.*

Box, cov, floral dec, 3-1/2" l...225.00
Compote, polychrome transfer printed figural landscapes, bronze mounts, 20th C, 5-1/4" h, price for matched pair 175.00
Luncheon Plate, central gilt six-pointed star, border with hunt scenes, 9-3/4" d, price for 6 pc set 325.00
Pin Box, cov, cartouche of romantic couple on cover, blue ground, oval, 6-1/2" l 275.00
Salt, 1-3/4", hp roses, paneled blue and white ground 58.00
Vase, gilt ground, enamel Art Nouveau stylized leaf and flower design, printed mark, 6" h 645.00

❖ Sewer Tile

In the late-19th and early-20th centuries, stoneware-like drain tile was often shaped into other forms and adapted to other uses, resulting in a collecting category known today as sewer tile. Produced primarily in Ohio and several Midwestern states, sewer tile was used to make everything from figural doorstops to large, stump-shaped markers used in cemeteries. Age and condition are key factors to consider when determining how much to spend on an item.

Birdhouse, round, conical roof, small
  chips, 8-1/2" h 165.00
Cat, seated, 7" h 165.00
Dog, reclining, tooled details,
  18" l 165.00
Dog, Staffordshire, seated,
  10-1/4" h 220.00
Eagle, wings at side,
  6-3/4" h 55.00
Frog, seated, 8" l 137.50
Lion, reclining on rectangular base,
  painted brown, 10" l 220.00
Pig, standing, 6-1/2" l 220.00
Planter, basket form, tooled bark
  finish, chips, 10" h 220.00
Planter, stump form, bird on crook,
  chips, 12-1/4" h 165.00
Salt and pepper shakers, tooled tree
  bark, applied handles,
  3" h, pr.............................. 275.00

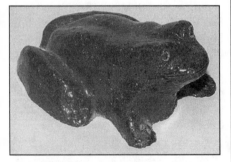

Frog, 6-1/4" l, 4-1/2" w, $65.

❖ Sewing Collectibles

"A Stitch In Time Saves Nine," or so old Ben Franklin thought. Today sewing collectors find lots of sewing memorabilia at flea markets. From tiny needle holders to interesting sewing machines, it just takes a little hunting, like finding that needle in that old haystack.

Collectors' Clubs: International Sewing Machine Collectors Society, 1000 E. Charlston Blvd., Las Vegas, NV 89104; National Button Society, 2730 Juno Place, Apt 4, Akron, OH 44313; Toy Stitchers, 623 Santa Florita Ave., Milbrae, CA 94030.

For additional listings, see *Warman's Antiques and Collectibles Price Guide* and *Warman's Americana and Collectibles.*

Darning Egg
  Ebony, sterling handle 100.00
  Porcelain, marbleized finish, one
    piece, 5-1/2" l 12.50
  Wood, 5-1/2" l, age crack ... 10.00
Display Case, 8" h, 7-1/2" w, Boye
  Needles Co., oak case, compartments for various size hooks, titled "Better than the best hook you ever used, The Boye Needle Co., Chicago, San Francisco, New York," early 20th C...... 75.00
Dress Maker Form, wire and
  cloth 50.00
Embroidery Hoop, clamp for table,
  wood 85.00
Hook Rug Machine, c1920 ..... 25.00
Instruction Manual
  Domestic Sewing Machine, model
    725 .... 10.00
  Singer Sewing Machine 400w,
    106, 107, 108, 109 and 110,
    dated 1948 .... 10.00
Loom, miniature, 9-1/2" x 12-1/2", old stringing, shuttles, some weaving intact, black stamp "N.R.A. We Do Our Part," green label "Oslind Miniature Loom" 250.00
Machine, Singer Featherweight, Model 221, black case, attachments, c1941 .... 400.00

Happy Home Rust Proof needle book, 3-1/2" x 6", $3.

Spool caddy, plastic, holds 6 spools, 4-5/8" d, $24.

Needle Book, Liberty National Life Insurance Co., Birmingham, Alabama, Statue of Liberty on front, one needle pack 8.00
Needle Case
  Egg-shaped, wood, mkd "The Columbian Egg," Germany, orig needles 155.00
  Tube shape, ivory 55.00
Pin Cushion
  Sewing drawer, thread spindle on case, orig red paint......... 90.00
  Victorian, velvet, fruits and flowers 35.00
Quilt Frame, large, fancy scroll work ends 150.00
Sewing Basket, wood, silhouette designs on side, c1930, 10" x 9" 45.00
Sewing Bird, gilt finish, pin cushion 180.00
Sign, Coats & Clark's Quality Threads, porcelain............ 900.00
Spool, woolen, mill type, 8-1/2" h, old blue paint 10.00
Thimble Holder
  Carved acorn 70.00
  Sweet grass, nickel-plated thimble........................... 95.00

❖ Shaving Mugs

"Shave and a hair cut, 2 bits!" Oh how we'd love to pay those prices again. And probably finding a barber who still uses old-fashioned shaving mugs might just be harder than finding vintage shaving mugs at a flea market. There are several different types of shaving mugs, fraternal, generic, and scuttles. By far the most popular are the occupational style mugs, those that displayed the owner's occupation. Here are some prices for those occupational type mugs.

Collectors' Club: National Shaving Mug Collectors Association, 320 S Glenwood St, Allentown, PA 18104.

For additional listings, see *Warman's Antiques and Collectibles Price Guide* and *Warman's English & Continental Pottery & Porcelain*.

Bicyclist, 3-3/4" h, 4-3/4" d, hp, name in gold, man riding bicycle, white ground, mkd "CFH/GDM" 1,250.00
Black Clouds, Limoges, name in gold 45.00
Boat Captain, hp image of fishing boat, name in gold, blue wrap on back, 3-3/4" d, 4-3/4" h.......................... 4,200.00
Drapery Cutter, drapes and scissors, name in gold.................... 195.00
Floor Safe............................. 650.00
Salesman, hand presenting calling card, name in gold........... 195.00
Steam Locomotive, tender, polychrome enamel dec, name "Philip Boyle" in gold, worn gilt trim, 3-7/8" h............................ 250.00
Skuttle, fox hunting scene, mkd "Arthur Wood England," 6-1/2" d.............................. 45.00
Tailor, tailor measuring gentleman's coat, name in gold, some wear to gold trim, 3-1/2" h............. 975.00

"Ed. Schalk," shows painter's pallet, 4"h, 3-3/4" d, $275.

❖ Shawnee Pottery

From 1937 until 1961, Shawnee Pottery operated in Zanesville, Ohio. They made kitchenwares, dinnerware and some art pottery. Two of their most recognized patterns are Corn Queen and Corn King.

References: Susan and Al Bagdade, *Warman's American Pottery and Porcelain*, Wallace-Homestead, 1994; Jim and Bev Mangus, *Shawnee Pottery*, Collector Books, 1994, 1998 value update; Mark Supnick, *Collecting Shawnee Pottery*, L-W Book Sales, 1997.

Collectors' Club: Shawnee Pottery Collectors Club, PO Box 713, New Smyrna Beach, FL 32170.

Casserole, Corn King, individual size, #73 .... 125.00
Coffeepot, Sunflower, hairline on bottom 80.00
Cookie Jar
  Drum Major...................... 345.00
  Dutch Boy, gold trim 280.00
  Dutch Boy, striped pants, inside rim chip.......................... 80.00
  Dutch Girl, gold trim.......... 315.00
  Great Northern Dutch Girl, blue trim 150.00
  Smiley Pig, red bandanna, chrysanthemum flowers, mkd "USA," 11 1/4" h 475.00

Fruit casserole, #81, 5-1/2" h, 4-7/8" d, $50.

Winnie, Shamrock............. 275.00
Figure
  Puppy................................. 40.00
  Rabbit 90.00
Fruit Bowl, Corn Queen 25.00
Mug, Corn King 35.00
Planter, Elf and Shoe, mkd "#765 Shawnee USA," 5-1/2" w, 5-1/2" l 45.00
Salt and Pepper Shakers, pr
  Chefs 20.00
  Dutch Boy and Girl............. 20.00
  Milk Cans 20.00
  Sailor Boy & Girl, gold trim.. 50.00
Teapot, cov
  Emb rose 35.00
  Floral dec.......................... 40.00
Vertical ribbed tulip................. 40.00

❖ Sheet Music

Here's a topic that might get you humming along. Sheet music is one of the hot collectibles right now. Perhaps it's nostalgia for the great tunes, or the interesting cover art. But you might want to check that old piano bench to see what kind of tunes are hiding in there.

Periodical: *The Rag Times*, 15522 Ricky Court, Grass Valley, CA 95949.

Collectors' Clubs: City of Roses Sheet Music Collectors Club, 13447 Bush St. SE, Portland, OR 97236; National Sheet Music Society, 1597 Fair Park Ave., Los Angeles, CA 90041; New York Sheet Music Society, PO Box 354, Hewlett, NY 11557; Remember That Song, 5623 N 64th St., Glendale, AZ 85301; Sonneck Society for American Music & Music in America, PO Box 476, Canton, MA 02021.

Adelaide, Guys & Dolls, photo of Brandy & Sinatra................25.00
Any Bonds Today, Irving Berlin........................16.00
A Woman In Love, Guys & Dolls, photo of Brandy & Sinatra...25.00
Coast Guard Forever 15.00
Couldn't Sleep A Wink Last Night 12.50
Down Yonder, Spade Copley...............................10.00
Father of the Land We Love, 1931.......................................8.00

Five Minutes More 12.50

Home On The Range, 1935, taped
together 10.00

If Washington Could Come To Life,
1906 .... 15.00

It's Always You 12.50

I Used To Call Her Baby, ©1919,
words by Howard Johnson,
Murray Roth and Cliff Hess 15.00

*Joan of Arc They are Calling
You* 12.00

Keep 'Em Flying 15.00

Little Red Hen, UB Iwenks, cartoon
graphics............................... 28.00

Love & Marriage 12.50

My Arms, Donna Reed and Robert
Walker 10.00

No Orchids For My Lady......... 15.00

Now Is The Hour, Bing Crosby...12.00

One Zy, Two-Zy, 1964............. 12.00

Paper Doll, Sinatra 15.00

Present Arms, name and date April
20, 1928 written on front
cover 5.00

Russian Rag............................ 8.00

The Ballad of Davy Crockett, 1954,
from Disneyland television
production 25.00

The Blond Sailor, 1945 .... 15.00

The Marines' Hymn, 1942 ...... 15.00

*When The Robin Calls It's Mate,
Then I'll Call You,* 1912 ...... 20.00

You Do, Betty Grable and Dan
Dailey 15.00

*Hi-Diddle-Diddle Novelty Fox Trot
Song,* Leo. Feist, New York, $4.

❖ Shelley China

The Shelley China company has been in business in Longton, England, since the mid 18th century and continues today. They have produced figurines and many dinnerware patterns. Many of their dinnerware patterns are known for interesting shapes. Expect to find a variety of types of decoration and marks since this firm has been around for so long.

Collectors' Club: National Shelley China Club, 5585 NW 164th Ave., Portland, OR 97229.

Child's Plate, "Little Blue Bird, How He Sings, So Happy on My Plates and Things," Mabel Lucie Attwell illus, 7" d 150.00

Cup and Saucer
Country Garden, pattern #2500, Ludlow shape 85.00
Maytime, pattern #13452, Henley shape, beige trim.......... 155.00
Morning Glory, Dainty shape 85.00
Orange pattern 170.00
Scilla, pattern #2511 .... 85.00
Shamrock pattern 85.00
Syringa pattern 85.00

Demitasse Cup and Saucer
Begonia, pattern #13427 .... 85.00
Red Rose & Daisy, pattern #12425 .... 85.00
Rosebud, pattern #13291 ... 85.00

Egg Cup, Rose 18.00

Gravy Boat and Underplate, Dainty Blue 525.00

Pin Dish, Regency, Dainty shape, sq, tab handle, gold trim 65.00

Plate, Chippendale pattern, 8" d, $55.

Place Setting, Wileman Trio, pattern #3730, 6-1/2" d plate, cup and saucer, c1898 .... 275.00

Plate
Harebell, 10-3/4" d 70.00
Rock Garden, 6" d 115.00
Teapot, Begonia................ 245.00

Vase, hand painted over transfer dec, matte finish, green mark and "799/8590," 8-1/2" h 395.00

❖ Shoe Related Collectibles

Perhaps you know the old woman who lives in a shoe or just like to buy shoes! Whatever the reason, flea markets can be a great place to find nifty additions to a shoe collection.

Advertising Display, diecut
Boston Shoes, 9" x 4-1/2" ... 35.00
Tappan Shoes.................... 15.00

Advertising Mirror, National Shoe Repairing Shop, some paint loss 10.00

Charm, lady's shoe, Swarovski crystal, enamel trim, 2-1/2" h 15.00

Charm Bracelet, gold-tone, 10 Mary Jane shoe charms, pink, light blue, sapphire, and topaz rhinestones, 7" l 95.00

Child's Book, *Tumblin Tim Joins the Circus*, story by Caryle Emery, illus by Patricia Valleau, giveaway by Acrobat Shoe Co., story book in front, coloring pages in back, neatly colored, 1945.................................. 15.00

Figure, Old Woman in a Shoe
Royal Albert, Beatrix Potter, woman knitting 36.00
Wade, 1-1/2" h.................. 24.00

Match Holder with striker, pair of high boots, Staffordshire..... 75.00

Polly Parrot Shoes blotter, 3-1/4" x 6-1/4", $13.

Shoe

Fenton, glass, cat face, orig sticker 32.00
Flow Blue, 3-1/2" l, beading 80.00
Latticino, blue and white slipper type 160.00
McCoy, Dutch shoe, white 20.00
Occupied Japan, 2-1/2" l, 1-1/2" h 4.00
Porcelain, red roses dec, 8" l 28.00
Shawnee, Button Baby, blue, 2-1/4" h 18.50
Shoe Clips, pr, yellow rhinestones, mkd "Czechoslovakia" 18.00
Tin, Two In One Wax Shoe Polish, 3-1/4" w 3.00

❖ Shot Glasses

Here's a flea market collectible that's usually always available. Watch for interesting sets of shot glasses with their original decanter or those boxed in an interesting way. Souvenir shot glasses have always been a popular memento to take home. Today they still are and, with reasonable prices, will remain a good investment.

Advertising

H. Sohns & Bros., Wine Growers, Herman, MO 65.00
J. A. Withers Mfg. Of High Grade Whiskey, Allenville, MO 65.00
Red Snapper 25.00
Cannon, "Gunshot," brown pottery, mkd "Japan," 3-1/2" h 4.50

The 1982 World's Fair, Knoxville, Tennessee, 2-1/4" h, $5.

Chicago, amethyst glass, 2-3/8" h 7.50
Here's Looking At You, natives around a palm tree, clear glass, enameled dec 12.00
Plain, glass 1.00

Promotional

Crown Royal Special Reserve, matching bag 12.00
Jim Beam, boot, 3" h 8.00
The Rat Pack movie, two sets of miniature dice in bottom, 2" h 18.00
Ruby Stained, etched "Jessie," 2-1/2" h 95.00

❖ Show Jars

Show jars are wonderful, large, crystal glass jars formerly used in drug stores, candy stores, etc. as display containers. Many double as either a candy or apothecary jar. Care should be taken to find examples where the trim on the jar matches that on the stopper.

Candy, pedestal

Hexagon bulbous globe, hexagon shaped pedestal, matching lid, ribbed neck, 15-1/2" h 850.00
Six-sided tapered jar, hexagon umbrella shaped lid, 13" h 500.00
Tapered jar, hexagon tear-shaped finial on lid, 14" h 475.00

Dakota

Globe, large flared opening at top, known as "fish bowl" type, 12-1/2" h 900.00
Globe, pedestal, 14" h 325.00
Globe, pedestal, two chips on upper rim, 10" h 100.00
Pedestal, in-making flaw on side, 8" h 225.00
Pedestal, multiple rim chips, 11-1/2" h 150.00

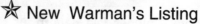

For exciting collecting trends and newly expanded areas look for the following symbols:

✿ Hot Topic

★ New Warman's Listing

(May have been in another Warman's edition.)

Clear, ground chip on pedestal base, 11-1/2" h, $135.

Egyptian

Crack in shoulder, 3-1/2" h 125.00
Minor chipping to rim of lid, 5-1/2" h 175.00
Small chip on lip, 11-1/2" h 50.00
Flor. Manzanilla, bulbous, tapered pedestal and pressed glass block and diamond pattern on neck, paneled label, some light scratching to label, 9-1/2" h 300.00

❖ Signs

Advertising signs have been staples of flea markets for many years. And with the many signs available, great examples can be found in all price ranges and made from different types of materials. Look for signs with bright colors, in good condition, and a design that appeals to you.

For additional listings, see *Warman's Antiques and Collectibles Price Guide* and *Warman's Americana and Collectibles.*

Armour's Oats, cardboard, elf and product, 18" x 14", 1920s 55.00
Ayer's Sarsaparilla, diecut cardboard, titled "The Old Folks at Home," elderly couple reading label of emb bottle, 11-1/4" h, 8" w, some creasing, overall spotting 85.00

Wooden, hp "Danger / Keep Out," white with black and red letters, 12" x 18", $60.

Butternut Bread, diecut litho, little girl eating slice of Butternut Bread, glass of milk, marmalade, and butter in foreground, multicolored, 13-1/4" h, 10-3/4" w 75.00

Candian Club, plastic and cardboard, illus of 1858 locomotive 55.00

Colgate's Cashmere Bouquet Talc Powder, diecut cardboard, two-sided, baby holding oversized tin, © 1913, 13-3/4" h, 7-1/4" w, one side in poor condition 50.00

Glendora Coffee, 14" h, 8-1/2" w, tin 125.00

Independent Lock & Key Co., 14" h, 32" l, two sided diecut tin, key shape 100.00

Knudsen Milk, diecut cardboard 140.00

Kotex Nurse, 15" h, 4-5/8" w, diecut cardboard, hanging hook . 180.00

Malt Murine, 7-3/4" h, 12-3/4" w, tin over cardboard, titled "Dr. Stork," doctor's shadow in shape of stork, Prohibition drink for babies, manufactured by Anheuser-Busch Co., © 1915 .... 50.00

Nu-Grape 70.00

Peters Shoes, trademark "Peters Shoe Co's Diamond Brand," 6" h, 24" l 35.00

Pioneer Basket, cardboard, titled "Then she bought a Pioneer Basket," shows lady in Art Deco outfit looking at broken package that she has dropped, 16" h, 12-3/4" w 25.00

Pomona Pump, tin 110.00

Purexoia Beverages Made With Distilled Water, porcelain, yellow letters, blue ground, 7" h, 28" l, badly chipped 35.00

Savings Bond, two sided, Lady Liberty with American flag 85.00

Sherwin Williams, diecut tin, enameled, 24" x 36" 450.00

Sunkist Grower, 11-1/2" x 19-1/2", heavy porcelain, red and white letters, black ground, white and green border, 1930s 300.00

Waltham Watch Co., 17-1/2" h, 33-1/2" l, factory scene, sepia tones, wood frame 65.00

❖ Silhouette Pictures

Silhouette pictures are decorative plaques with rounded or convex frames over a black image. They can have foil or colored backgrounds which enhance the presentation. They were a later generation's answer to the old hand-cut silhouettes, thus the name.

Dresser Box, wood, red metal trim, large heart shaped cut-out on top with dancing silhouettes, lined int with mirror, 8-1/2" x 6-1/2", wear.................................... 50.00

Picture, convex glass type
   Equestrian jumping fence ... 40.00
   Fairies, painted background, 1929 .... 35.00
   Hearts, shows suitor, mkd "Deltex".......................... 24.00
   Lady with Bird in Cage, pale pink background, silver stars, 8-3/4" x 10-1/2" 60.00

Kittens and ducks, 5-1/8" x 4-1/8", $12.50.

Lovebirds, boy courting girl, 2 lovebirds watching, foil accents on dress and boy's suit...30.00

Victorian Couple 40.00

❖ Silver, Plated and Sterling

Every flea market has great examples of silver in sterling and also silver plate. Look for hallmarks and maker's mark to determine the age of a piece, its silver content, and perhaps the country of origin. Also check for signs of silver polish hidden in crevices, often indicating that a piece has been polished for years. When examining a piece of plated silver, check to see that any wear is at an appropriate spot and does not detract from the overall appearance.

For additional listings, see *Warman's Antiques and Collectibles Price Guide.*

Silver Plate

Bank
   Clown with umbrella............ 35.00
   Humpty Dumpty 35.00

Champagne Bucket, cylindrical, bracket handles, applied scroll border band, monogram, Simpson, Hall, Miller & Co., 9" h 275.00

Meat Dome, Victorian, bright cut with panel of foliage swags and roses, beaded base edge, twisted branch handle, monogram, maker's mark, 18" x 10-1/2" 250.00

Punch Bowl, cylindrical, reeded circular foot, applied flowers at rim, International Silver, 12" d 200.00

Toast Rack 45.00

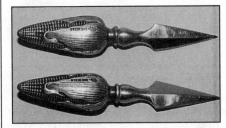

Sterling silver corn holders, figural ears of corn, 2-7/8" l, pr, $10.

Tray, rectangular, center chased with scrolls, trellis, and foliage, gadrooned and foliate handles, English, 27" l 150.00

Wine Cooler Stand, Art Deco, Reed & Barton 200.00

Silver, Sterling

Baby Spoon, ornate curled handle
   Cupid.....................................65.00
   Mother Goose 60.00

Cigarette/Compact Case, chain, all over scrolling 110.00

Curling Irons, ornate handle ... 50.00

Glove Hook, ornate handle..... 30.00

Glove Stretcher, ornate.......... 60.00

Grape Shears, grape motif dec90.00

Nail File, 6-1/2" l, head of woman as handle 30.00

Teapot, Kingston pattern, Wallace........................... 250.00

Whistle, chain, Reed and Barton, sterling, MIB 45.00

✫ Skateboards

Whooosh! Skateboarding around a flea market would be too fast to spot all the great buys. However, if you're in the market for a used skateboard, it's a great place to shop. Some of those vintage wood skateboards have neat graphics.

Black Knight, wood, graphic of Black Knight, clay wheels, 1960s, 22" l, 5-3/4" w 55.00

Butcher Block style, wood, Power Paw red plastic wheels, 23-1/2" l, 6-1/2" w 32.00

Hawaii Super Surfer, wood, graphics of Hawaiian Islands and "Hawaii" painted on top, clay wheels 50.00

Pro-Line 66-99, see-thru gold plastic, Jacksonville, FL 65.00

Roller Derby, Mustang 15, blue, gold trim, horse graphic, ball bearing wheels, 21" l, 5" w 55.00

Valterra Dragon, wood, 27" l, 8" w 20.00

✫ Sleds

You won't find the infamous "Rose Bud" sled at a flea market, but you might be able to find some other interesting examples. There are

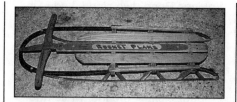

Rocket Plane, 51" l, $55.

many variations of sleds, some made for boys, girls, singles, doubles, and even some with wheels for those who lived in "snowless" climates.

Black Bird, wood, iron rod tipped runners, scrolled finials, worn black paint, polychrome striping, flowers, small landscape, and name "Black Bird" 395.00

Child's, wood, Art Deco green and red designs, c1940 .... 30.00

Flexible Flyer, No. 60J, 35 years old, 60" l 40.00

Fly 'N' Saucer, wood 75.00

Radio, 31" x 11-1/2", orig lettering............................. 125.00

❖ Slot Machines

The first slot machine was called the Liberty Bell and was developed by Charles Fey in San Francisco, CA, in 1905. Advancements were made through the years by several of the manufacturers. Some were enhancements to the playing action, others were to prevent players from cheating.

Periodicals: *Antique Amusements, Slot Machines & Jukebox,* 909 26th St NW, Washington, DC 20037; *Chicagoland Program,* 414 N Prospect Manor Ave, Mt Prospect, IL 60056; *Chicago Land Slot Machine & Jukebox Gazette,* 909 26th St, NW, Washington, DC 20037; *Coin Drop International,* 5815 W 52nd Ave, Denver, CO 80212; *Coin-Op Classics,* 17844 Toiyabe St, Fountain Valley, CA 92708; *Coin-Op Newsletter,* 909 26th St, NW, Washington, DC 20037; *Coin Slot,* 4401 Zephyr St, Wheatridge, CO 80033; *Loose Change,* 1515 South Commerce Street, Las Vegas, NV 89102.

Buckley, 25¢, red metallic enamel, chrome plated detail, oak base and sides, edge wear, working condition, 25-1/2" x 16" x 15" 1,100.00

Jennings Chief, 25-cent, wood and chrome, 28" h, 16" w, 16" d, $1,600.

Century Grand, cast iron, ornate detail, five card wheels, top banner missing, black repaint, mechanism needs repair to work properly, 11" x 10" x 50-1/2" h 825.00

Columbia, 5¢, Art Deco case, burgundy enameled finish, silver line detail, figured mahogany veneer, only minor wear, 19" x 14-5/8" x 11-1/2"............................ 1,100.00

Jennings

   5¢ and 25¢ slots, floor standing model, back lit glass panel with eagle and flags, lights and two wheels in working condition, third wheel frozen in place, 55" x 23" x 17" 500.00

   10¢ Standard Chief, chrome plated case, red trim, brass Indian head on front, wear, lock restored, 27" x 15-1/4" x 15-1/4" 1,210.00

Jennings, O. D. & Company

   Deco, 5¢, worn chrome plated detail, red enameled trim, blue repaint on top, minor crack in corner of glass, working condition, 27-3/4" x 15-1/2" x 15" 990.00

   Little Duke, 1¢, oak case, cast Art Deco detail, silver, orange, black, red, and yellow enamel dec, working condition, 22-1/2" x 12-3/4" x 9-3/16" 1,650.00

Mills

5¢, one arm bandit, laminated and carved wood, cast hand and gun, real felt hat, well done repairs, working condition, key missing, 70" h 4,100.00

25¢, orange, black, and maroon finish, some repaint, needs work, 26-3/4" x 16" x 15-1/4" 770.00

Wattling Manufacturing Co., Rol-A-Top, twin jackpot, yellow and black enameled finish, cast cornucopia, eagle, and coins, working condition, back will not open, 26-1/4" h, 15-3/4" w, 16" d...........
.... 2,420.00

☆ Smokey Bear Collectibles

Everybody knows the story of Smokey the Bear and what he stands for. He's been teaching children to beware of fire for many years.

Activity Book, *Smokey Bear's Story of the Forest*, presented by Florida Forest Service, 1959, 15 pgs, 8" x 10-1/4", unused........... 25.00

Ashtray Set, four different colors, each with emb image of Smokey, 4" d, set of four................... 20.00

Bank, Ertl

Hawkeye Motor Truck, 6-1/2" l, 1990.............................125.00

Seagrave Fire Truck, 7-1/2" l, 1991.............................125.00

Comic Book, *The True Story of Smokey Bear*, 1969, 6-1/2" x 10"......................... 25.00

Keychain................................... 5.00

Little Golden Book, 1977 .... 25.00

Plush Figure, hard plastic hat, orig Dakin hang tag and label, 1985 .... 65.00

Plastic Jr. Ranger campaign-style hat, Tonka, 12-1/2" x 11-1/4", $20.

☆ Smurf

Those cute cartoon characters come to life for flea market collectors. Watch for them on all types of items. They continue to make smiles appear.

Collectors' Club: Smurf Collectors Club International 24 Cabot Road W. Massapequa, NY 11758.

Animation Cel, matted, mkd "#240 21 65," 11" x 14" 95.00

Card Game, 1982, MIB........... 12.00

Figure

Smurf-O-Gram, Doctor's Orders, Get Well Soon 10.00

Smurf with Go-Cart, MIB 15.00

Super Smurf, with hobby horse, MIB.............................. 15.00

Keychain, figural, 2-1/4" h......... 5.00

Lunchbox, plastic, Thermos Co., 1987, no thermos 32.00

Mushroom Cottage, Peyo Schleich, orig box, description in English, French and German, 1970s, MIB 55.00

Ornament, wearing red hat, 1978 .... 1.25

Store Display, 3 pink and 5 blue baby Smurfs, 6-1/2" x 5-3/8" l 85.00

Stuffed Toy

Amour Smurf 12.00

Blue, 1979, 16" h 20.00

Papa, sitting, 10" h, soiled 6.00

Smurfette........................... 12.00

St. Patrick's Day 14.00

Sweetheart Valentine.......... 12.00

Plastic bowl, Deka Plastic, Elizabeth, NJ, 2-3/8" h, 5-1/2" d, $1.50.

☆ Snack Sets

A snack set is the combination of a plate or tray with an indent to hold a coffee cup. Perfect for a snack in front of that new invention, television, or perhaps just the item to serve refreshments on the patio. Many glass and dinnerware services included these items in the 1950s. Whole sets can be found in original boxes, perhaps attesting to the fact that although they were a great wedding present, the idea never really caught on.

Periodical: *Snack Set Searchers,* PO Box 158, Hallock, MN 56728.

Anchor Hocking

Fleurette, 8 pcs in orig box, some damage to box................ 18.00

Grape, clear, grape and leaf design, orig box 26.50

Primrose, Anchorglass, milk glass, 11" l plate, 8 pc set........................... 25.00

Bavaria, bone china, purple roses dec, 7-1/2" d plate.............. 15.00

California Pottery, bright orange, 1960s, 4 pcs, orig sticker "Cal-Style Ceramics Torrance Calif #2433"................................. 40.00

Fire King, Soreno, green, 9-3/4" d plate, 2-1/2" h cup................. 5.00

Hazel Atlas

Capri Sea Shell pattern, light blue set of 4........................... 42.50

Sea Shell, crystal, 10" x 6-1/2" tray, 3-1/2" d x 2-1/2" h cup................................. 22.50

Lefton, Golden Wheat, 8" snack plate with tab handle, low scalloped ftd cup, gold trim 12.50

Capri, azure blue, seashell pattern, boxed set of 4, $42.50.

Noritake, kidney shaped plate, white, blue luster trim, black lines, black floral dec, green mark, 8-1/2" x 7" plate, 3-1/4" h cup 35.00

Porcelain, Oriental design, purple, red, gold, light blue, yellow, and olive green, 8" d plate......... 15.00

Shelley, Flowers of Gold, pattern #141287, Dainty shape 130.00

Hand Painted, pink flowers with yellow centers, green leaves, gold edge, artist sgd "G. H. T. 1940," 8-1/2" x 7-1/4" plate, 3-1/2" d x 1-7/8" h cup 27.50

Steubenville, Woodfield pattern, 2 Tropic Green, 2 Salmon Pink, 4 Dove Gray, 9" plate, 4-1/4" w x 2-1/2" h cup, 16 pc set, one chipped plate 60.00

❖ Snow Babies

Here's a debate that's never really been settled—some folks feel that the original Snow Babies were designed to commemorate Admiral Peary's trip and his little daughter. Others believe they were just cute German figurines. Expect to find their little snow suits encrusted with bits of shiny sparkles, adding to their whimsey.

Reproduction Alert.

Bear, walking on four paws... 100.00
Elf, 1-1/2" h............................. 75.00
Snow Baby riding bear, red, white, and maroon, 2-7/8" h........ 165.00
Snow Baby on sled................. 82.75
Snow Baby playing banjo, stamped "Germany"........................ 145.00
Snow Baby waving 160.00
Snow Man, standing............... 70.00

❖ Snow Globes

Some folks call these snow globes, others prefer the name snowdomes. Whatever you call them, the fun is to shake the paperweight-type ball and see the snow fly through the water and swirl around the featured character. Many companies created snow globes over the years and they remain a popular souvenir for tourists today.

Periodical: *Roadside Attractions,* 7553 Norton Ave., Apt 4., Los Angeles, CA 90046.

Collectors' Club: Snowdome Collectors Club, PO Box 53262, Washington, DC 20009.

For additional listings, see *Warman's Americana & Collectibles.*

Berta Hummel, Tree Trimming Time..................................... 68.00
Betty Boop, musical, plays "Red Roses for a Blue Lady," 1995 .... 55.00
Chevrolet 1958 Corvette, musical, plays "Little Red Corvette," white base with Chevy logo, Westland, MIB 45.00
Cherub kneels in prayer, licensed by Kristen Haynes, Westland .. 15.00
Cherub on cloud, holding star, iridescent silvery moon, licensed by Kristen Haynes, Westland .. 15.00
Coca-Cola, Heritage Collection, polar bear scene, authorized seal, plays Coke theme, retired 1996 .... 60.00
Disney 75th Anniversary, fiber optics 75.00
Easter Bunny Train, Glama, retired, 4" l 10.00
Happy Bunny with Chick, Glama, 3" h 10.00
Little girl gazing at rose, resin pedestal base, Westland, MIB...... 20.00
Little Mermaid, Ursula............. 52.00
101 Dalmatians, McDonald's giveaway 2.25
Teletubbies............................. 36.00
Winnie the Pooh 30.00
Yogi Bear 3.00

Hallmark, Mary & Friends by Mary Hamilton, 1991, 5-1/2" h, $12.

⭐ Soakies

Remember those great figural plastic bottles we got bubble bath in when we were kids? Well, today collectors are happily reliving those days as they search flea markets for those bottles, now called "soakies."

Alvin Chipmunk, red................20.00
Atom Ant 40.00
Augie Doggie 55.00
Bozo Clown..............................35.00
Bugs Bunny, some paint loss ..25.00
Casper Ghost..........................35.00
Chewbacca 10.00
Cinderella, movable arms 25.00
Deputy Dawg, small 20.00
Dick Tracy, crack at neck 25.00
Dopey Dwarf 25.00
Dum Dum.................................65.00
Elmer Fudd 35.00
Mighty Mouse, small 25.00
Pinocchio 25.00
Pluto, with hat 25.00
Punkin Puss, repainted 65.00
Santa Claus 10.00
Squiddly Diddly 75.00
Sylvester Cat, some paint loss 35.00
Tennessee Tuxedo..................45.00

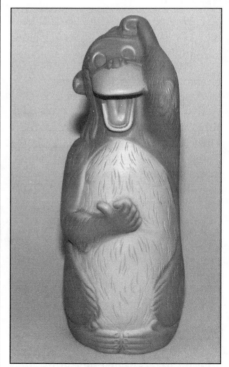

King Louie, 7-3/4" h, $35.

Smokey Bear, 8-1/2" h, $25.

Topcat
Blue vest	45.00
Red vest	55.00
Wendy Witch	45.00
Woody Woodpecker	25.00

❖ Soap Collectibles

If you're not into cleaning up with soakies, how about some soap collectibles. Again, flea markets are a great place to find all kinds of ephemera relating to soap and even some great examples of vintage soap. Look for vintage illustrations of mothers and children.

Advertising Trade Card, Lautz Brothers Master Soap, baby on pillow 10.00
Bookmark, Dingman's Soap, baby illus 9.00
Brochure, Larkin Soap, 1885 .... 17.50
Magazine Tear Sheet, Williams Shaving Soap, full color 8.00
Pocket Mirror, Dingman Soap, white letters, product, red ground, 1-7/8" d 40.00

Oatmeal Soap box, W.&H. Walker, Pittsburg USA, paper, 1-3/4" h, 6-1/2" l, 3-1/4" w, $14.

Ruler, Glory Soap Chips, folding, celluloid, blue and orange Swift & Co. trademark, 1919 calendars, 5-1/2" l 35.00
Soap
  Avon, Wildflower, flowers on paper wrapping 2.00
  Hershey's Cocoa Butter Toilet Soap, box, brown and tan, three bars of fully wrapped soap, 7" l, 3-1/2" w 40.00
Soap Box, White King, large, c1933 .... 25.00

❖ Social Cause Collectibles

Here's a topic where a collector can find memorabilia related to their favorite cause. And, feel free to interpret this area as you see fit, for isn't that what social causes are all about?

Reference: William A. Sievert, *All For the Cause: Campaign Buttons For Social Change, 1960s-1990s, Decoy Magazine,* 1997.

Badge, "Old Newsboys Day Globe-Democrat Fund For Children," attached purple ribbon, gold lettered text "Old Newsboy," c1960 .... 7.50
Flicker Card, 2-1/4" x 3-1/4", "The Tin Woodman," Heart Assn premium, colorful image pointing to his heart "Take Care Of Your Heart," Heart Assn inscription on back, c1960 .... 35.00
Pinback Button
  Eat Grapes, purple grapes, white ground, c1970 .... 8.00

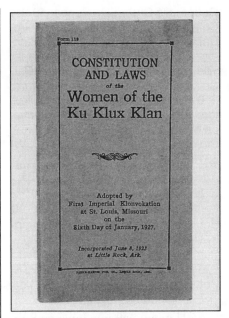

Booklet, *Constitution and Laws of the Women of the Ku Klux Klan,* **1927, 73 pgs, $25.**

Flowers for Peace, orange psychedelic lettering, yellow background, 1-3/4" d 40.00
Keep the Faith Baby, Adam Clayton Powell, c1960 .... 12.00
I Support Lesbian and Gay Rights, black and white, dark pink heart, Texas, c1960 .... 10.00
Linda Lovelace for President, 1-3/4" d cello, red, dark blue, and white lettering, early 1970s 25.00
Support the Equal Rights Amendment, dark blue and white 10.00
Take a Hippie to Lunch, black lettering, bright yellow ground, 1-1/2" d 15.00

❖ Soda

Getting thirsty? Collectors from around the country tend to call carbonated beverages by different names—it's "soda" to some, "soda pop" to others, and "pop" to other regions. Whatever your passion, flea markets are a great place to find collectibles that will "wet your whistle."

Periodical: *Club Soda,* PO Box 489, Troy, IN 83871.

Collectors Clubs: Dr. Pepper 10-2-4 Collectors Club, 3508 Mockingbird, Dallas, TX 75205; Grapette Collectors Club, 2240 Highway 27N, Nashville, AR 71852; National Pop Can Collectors, PO Box 7862, Rockford, IL 61126; Painted Soda Bottle Collectors Association, 9418 Hilmer Drive, La Mesa, CA 91942; Root Beer Float, PO Box 571, Lake Geneva, WI 53167.

Advertisement, Hires, quarter page, black and white, "Pop & I Drink", 1894 .... 25.00
Bottle Opener, Fresh Up with Seven-Up, 1-1/2" w, 3-1/2" l, diecast metal, slogan emb on both sides, 1960s 12.00
Bottle Topper, "Drink Swallow's Old Fashioned 5¢," big keg illus, 1941 .... 8.00
Chalkboard, Aircraft Gingerale 80.00
Coin, Moxie Bottle Wagon, aluminum, detailed image of horse-drawn street vending wagon, huge bottle replica holding vendor dispensing drink to 2 children, 3 adults waiting, inscribed "Moxie Nerve Food 5¢," reverse inscription "Good for One Drink of Moxie at the Moxie Bottle Wagon," early 1900s......................... 45.00
Match Book, Kist Soda 6.00
Mug, A & W Root Beer, glass, 3-1/4" h................................ 8.00
Service Pin, 7Up, 1930s 105.00
Sign
    AAA Root Beer, cardboard........................45.00
    Drink Hires, paper, cameo of young lady behind tray with flared glass and emb bottle of Hires Root Beer, some restoration, framed, 19-1/2" h, 14" w 125.00
    Drink Nehi Beverages, tin, Donaldson Sign KY, 11" x 30", colorful 250.00

For exciting collecting trends and newly expanded areas look for the following symbols:

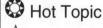 Hot Topic

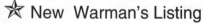 New Warman's Listing

(May have been in another Warman's edition.)

7Up Easter "Fresh Up" cardboard bottle display, 10" x 5-1/4", $18.

Drink Squirt, diecut cardboard, 5" x 6-1/2", scalloped border, full color image on both sides............................... 30.00
English Club Beverages, tin strip......................... 75.00
Hires Rootbeer, 6-3/4" h, 5" w, diecut cardboard stand-up, light creasing at edges . 190.00
Hires, 13-1/2" h, 19" l, emb tin, young flapper girl with glass of Hires Root Beer, titled "...and it's always pure, Hires, in bottles," framed 200.00
Triple AAA Root Beer 5¢, cardboard, 1940s, orange with red letters, picture of bottle, 7" x 13"..... 30.00
Thimble, 7/8" h, 5/8" d, Orange Crush, emb aluminum, unused............................... 60.00
Window Decal, Dr. Pepper, "Try A Frosty Pep...Drink Dr. Pepper & Ice Cream," plastic, NOS.... 90.00

❖ Soda Bottles

Nothing is better on a hot day than a bottle of soda pop. Watch for bottles from regional bottlers.

References: Ralph and Terry Kovel, *Kovels' Bottles Price List*, 10th Edition, Crown Publishers, 1996; Rick Sweeney, *Collecting Applied Color*

Label Soda Bottles, published by author (9418 Hilmer Dr., La Mesa, CA 91942).

Periodical: *Antique Bottle and Glass Collector*, P.O. Box 187, East Greenville, PA 18041.

Collectors' Club: Painted Soda Bottle Collectors Association, 9418 Hilmer Dr., La Mesa, CA 91942.

Alter & Wilson Mfg., light green applied top, 7" h.................20.00
Bacon's Soda Works, light green, blob top, 7" h........................9.00
Bank, 7Up, soda-can shape, white, orange and green, 1950s, 12 oz, flat top, steel 40.00
Banner, Lime Cola, canvas 40.00
Battery Operated Toy, Sprite-Lymon, talking, vinyl, MIB...............35.00
Beanie, Dr Pepper, orig charms.........................18.00
Blotter, Nehi Soda, 1930s 4.00
Booklet, 7Up
    Floats, 8 pgs, foldout type, recipes, 1961 ....4.00
    7Up Goes to a Party, 16 pgs, 1961 ....5.00
Bottle
    Dillon Beverage, 7 oz, painted label, cowboy on bucking bronco, c1950, refilled, recapped 10.00
    Donald Duck Cola, 7 oz, figural, 1950s, full, recapped 25.00
    Ma's Root Beer, clear, white pyro label.................................8.00
    Moxie, emb name, wire cap 9.00
Bottle Carrier
    Kist Soda, cardboard 5.00
    RC Cola, aluminum.............12.00
Bottle Display, 7-Up, 1949.........6.50
Bryant's Root Beer, This Bottle Makes Five Gallons, amber, applied top, 4-1/2" h.............5.00
Calendar
    Dr Pepper, 1937, Earl Moran art, framed 150.00
    Nu-Grape, 1941 ....40.00
Can, Dr Pepper, cone top 20.00
Cape Arco Soda Works, Marshfield, OR, round, light green, applied top, 7" h 10.00

Carton, Squirt, red and white card-board, front says "2 Free Bottles of Squirt and Never an afterthirst!" on 1 side, recipes on reverse, 1959 Squirt Co., 4" h, 5" w 10.00

Clock, 7Up, "You Like It, It Likes You," wood frame 75.00

Cooler, Squirt, round............... 95.00

Coupon, Royal Crown, free card, 1950s 5.00

Deadwood, SD, blob top....... 125.00

Deamer Grass Valley, aqua, blob top, 7-1/4" hg....................... 7.50

Dr Pepper, Colorado............... 18.00

Door Pull, tin, Drink Hire's 50.00

English Soda, light green, applied top, 8" h 18.00

Fan, cardboard, wood handle
　Dr Pepper...........................40.00
　Goold's Orangeade 25.00

Fizz, Southern State Siphon Bottling Co., golden amber, 11" h................................. 17.50

Hawaiian Soda Works, aqua, emb, 7-1/2" h.............................. 9.00

Hippo Size Soda Water, clear, crown top, 10" h............................. 6.50

Jackson's Napa Soda, crown cap, 7-1/4" h................................ 7.50

Label, Dr Pepper, paper 12.00

Los Angeles Soda Works, aqua, 8" h....................................... 5.00

Magazine Advertisement, *Ladies Home Journal*, 1895, back page, matted 45.00

Mechanical Pencil, Orange Crush.................................. 22.00

Mendocin Bottling Works, A.L. Reynolds, light green, 7" h 8.00

Menu Board, Orange Crush ... 55.00

Mission Dry Sparkling, black 9-3/4" h................................ 4.00

Mug
　Buckeye Root Beer, stoneware 12.50
　Dad's Root Beer.................12.00
　Graft's Root Beer...............100.00
　Hire's Root Beer, glass, 1940s 12.00
　Hunter's Root Beer...........112.00
　Jim Dandy Root Beer 125.00
　Twin Kiss Root Beer, 3" h..................................15.00

Nevada City Soda works, ETR Powell, aqua, applied top, 7" h.... 9.00

Orange Crush Co., pat July 20, 1926, light green, 9" h 4.00

Pencil Clip, 7/8" d, celluloid
　Orange Crush, black and white inscription, orange ground, c1930 .... 12.00
　7Up, black, white and red logo 10.00
　Perrier, clear, bowling-pin shape, paper label, 8-1/2" h......... 3.00

Pinback Button
　Cherry Smash, George Washington portrait, dark red shaded to olive green ground, black inscription, c1911 .... 35.00
　Dad's Root Beer, litho, bottle cap, yellow, red, blue, white and black, c1940 .... 20.00
　7Up, Fresh Up Freddie, red, white, blue and yellow litho, c1959 .... 50.00

Pitcher, Orange Crush, chrome lid......................... 115.00

Playing Cards, Nu-Grape, single deck, slide out box.............. 25.00

Push Bar, porcelain
　Nesbitt's, French................. 75.00
　Pure Spring Ginger Ale, 1950s 65.00
　7Up, bilingual, 1950s.......... 50.00
　Up-Town, lemon-lime, French, 1950s 50.00
　Rapid City Bottling Works, light green, crown cap, 8" h 5.00
　Ross's Royal Belfast Ginger Gale, green, diamond shape, paper label, 10" h 7.50
　Sandahl Beverages, clear, 8" h 5.00
　Scott & Gilbert Co., San Francisco, brown, crown top, 10" h 6.00

Sign
　B-1 Lemon Soda, 12" x 14" x 6", light-up 25.00
　Canada Dry, porcelain........ 40.00
　Dixie Springs Soda, 14" x 20", cardboard stand-up, Eskimos pulling sled 30.00
　Grapette, 12" x 24", tin, emb, 1940s 40.00
　Hires, 5" x 14", tin, emb, some flaking, 3 small holes 75.00

Nehi, 14" x 14" Drink Nehi Beverages, white and red, raised metal................................. 60.00

Mission Orange of California, 25" h, tin, 1950s.............. 90.00

Nesbitt's Orange, 48" x 16", tin, 1938 .... 175.00

Nu-Grape Soda, tin, yellow and blue, dated March 9, 1920 .... 125.00

Orange, Lemon, Lime Crush, emb tin............................350.00

RC
　11-1/2" x 29-1/2", red and white, emb letters adv crown, tin...................................... 50.00
　12" x 18", Drink Royal Crown, Better Taste Calls for RC, diamond shape, red and white, raised letters................... 50.00
　42" x 34", Drink Royal Crown Cola, Best by Taste Test, red, yellow, white, 12" privilege space, raised metal, 1954 .... 295.00
　51" x 38", Drink Royal Crown Cola, red, white and blue, 12" privilege space, raised metal................................. 165.00

Squirt, 8" h, cardboard, double sided, c1949 ....25.00

Sunrise Orange, tin, bottled by Coca-Cola...........................90.00

Solano Soda Works, aqua, 8" h 6.00

Tahoe Soda Springs Natural Mineral Water, light green, 7-1/2" h 10.00

Thermometer, tin
　Crush, 5" x 17", 1960s........ 65.00
　Nesbitt's, French, 5" x 17" ..55.00

Tip Tray, Royal Crown Cola 40.00

Tray, Hires Root Beer, 1935....90.00

Union Glass Works, dark blue, blob top......................................20.00

Watch, 7Up, promotion for Jerry Lewis Telethon, windup, pink border, Cherry 7Up, orig box and mailer 30.00

Watch Fob
　Drink Chero-Cola 5¢ 60.00
　Hires Root Beer, octagonal, raised "Drink Hires," boy, early 1900s.................................75.00
　Williams Bros., San Jose, CA...8.00

❖ Soda Fountain

The image of a soda fountain conjures up different scenes for collectors. Some remember a counter with stools with rotating tops. Others think of round tables with chairs with wire legs. Whatever it looked like, all can agree that the culinary results were the same.

Collectors' Club: National Association of Soda Jerks, PO Box 115, Omaha, NE 68101; The Ice Screamers, PO Box 465, Warrington, PA 18976.

Can, Abbott's Ice Cream, half gallon, illus of Amish girl, c1940 .... 18.50

Catalog
   Bastian-Blessing Co., Chicago, IL, soda fountain parts and carbonators, 1955 ....32.00
   Stanley Knight Corp., Chicago, IL, soda fountains, instructions, and specifications, c1944
   ....35.00

Dispenser
   Hallford's Lemon and Lime Superfine since '69, 5¢, hand blown glass, hand painted label, 8" d, 9" h................60.00

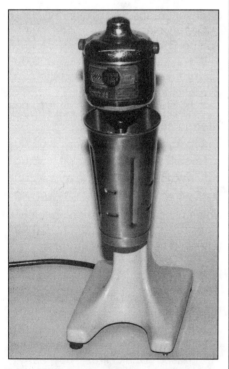

Hamilton Beach No. 18, green porcelain, rewired, $250.

Root Beer, Buckeye, tree-trunk shape, minor chips 375.00
Display Rack, Beech-Nut Chewing Gum, c1920 .... 300.00
Jar, Borden's Malted Milk, glass label 175.00
Menu Board, 7Up, tin, 1966, board reads "Freshen Up" 75.00
Milkshake Machine, Hamilton Beach, triple head, green ... 50.00
Pinback Button, Hi-Hat Ice Cream Soda, 10¢, McCory's, c1940 .... 18.00
Sign, Orange County Fountain, porcelain on steel, yellow oval center, blue and white lettering, dark blue ground, 24" x 18" 120.00
Straw Jar, glass, red metal lid, 1950s 175.00

❖ Souvenirs

We've all done it. Brought back some memento from a vacation, perhaps some shells or some piece of china, a spoon, or a tea towel. Often these spur of the moment purchases really don't quite fit in with the decor, or perhaps next year's vacation proved to be even better, and the old souvenirs are cast aside. That's great for flea market dealers who are more than glad to help recycle goodies from one household to another.

Ashtray, metal, figural
   Atlantic City, NJ, double hearts, cut-out mermaid and dolphin, scenes of lighthouse, convention hall, Miss America Pageant, mkd "Made in Japan," 3-1/2" x 5" 22.00
   Coney Island, Statue of Liberty and other NY views, c1940, 5-1/2" x 3-1/2" 75.00
Badge, paperweight type, "Oldest House, St. Augustine, FL" .. 45.00
Book
   Souvenir of Washington DC, 20 color pictures, 1912........ 10.00
   Waldorf Astoria, 1939, hard bound, tipped in illus 65.00
   Woodstock, pictorial album, 1969 .... 80.00
Bracelet, New York City, enamel dec, Statue of Liberty, Coney Island, other sites, c1930 ... 45.00

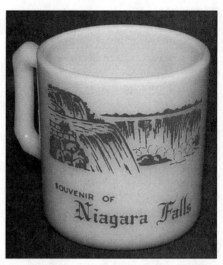

Milk glass mug, Souvenir of Niagara Falls, Hazel Atlas, 3" h, $8.

Egg Timer, wooden, "I Am Master Of This House," hand painted dec, foil label "Souvenir of Pocono Mts," 3-3/4" h 40.00
Mailer, New York-Unlock the Beauty of a Great City, 9 panels of sites, simulated lock on cover, dangling cardboard key, opens to 16" x 20" 18.00
Paperweight, Mt. Rushmore, Deer and Star 125.00
Patch
   Atlantic City Surf Fishing Tournament, 3-3/4" x 5" 12.00
   Atlantic City Tuna Tournament, 3-3/4" x 5" 12.00
Pillow Cover, Washington, DC, verse, fringe, 12" sq 8.50
Pin Cushion, Dutch shoe, place for thimble and thread, wood burned picture of Dutch windmill on one side, Galveston, TX on other, 5" l....................................... 12.00
Salt and Pepper Shakers, metal, Empire State Building and Statue of Liberty, tarnished 60.00
Tablecloth, Alaska 30.00
Tea Towel, Florida, orig tag "Kay Dee, Hand Prints, Hope Valley, Linen," 17" x 31" 18.00

❖ Souvenir Buildings

Perhaps your dream is to travel around the world. But until you can afford that luxury, try collecting minia-ture buildings. They offer fun and interesting variations and you don't have to worry about all that packing!

Collector's Club: Souvenir building Collectors Society Po Box 70, Nellys-ford, VA 22958-0070

Alamo, San Antonio, TX, 2" x 4" x 3-1/2", copper finish............... 17.00

Adler Planetarium, Chicago, IL, incense burner, 3" x 4" d, copper finish.................................. 44.00

Arc de Triomphe, Paris, 1-3/4" x 1-1/2" x 1", copper finish 6.00

Brandenberg Gate, Berlin, 4" x 3-3/4" x 2", antique bronze, wood base 38.00

Bunker Hill Monument, Boston, MA, copper finish...................... 14.00

Capitol, Washington, DC
Jewelry Box, 4-1/4" x 5" x 3-1/2", gold, mkd "JB" on bottom 55.00
Souvenir, 2-1/4" x 3-1/2" x 2" 6.00

Coit Tower, San Francisco, 6-1/2" h, 2-1/4" sq base, antique bronze finish.............................. 78.00

Cologne Cathedral, Germany, 4-1/8" x 3-3/4" x 1-1/2", antique pewter or silver finish 14.00

Coliseum, Rome, 1-1/2" x 2-1/4" x 2", copper finish.................. 15.00

Dollar Savings Bank, Pittsburgh, PA, 3-1/8" x 4" x 3", silvered lead bank 88.00

Easton National Bank, Easton, PA, 4-1/2" x 3-3/4" x 2-1/2", bank, copper finish...................... 68.00

Eiffel Tower, Paris
3" x 1" x 1", copper, antique brass or silver finish....................8.00
6" x 2-1/2" x 2-1/2", copper, antique brass or silver finish...............................13.00

Empire State Building, New York City
Prewar, no spire
3-1/2" x 1-1/2" x 1", antique brass finish...............................28.00
5-3/4" x 2-1/2" x 2", silver finish...............................63.00
Postwar, with radio antenna spire
3-1/2" x 1-1/4" x 3/4", gold plastic 3.00
5" x 1-3/4" x 1-1/4", antique brass finish...............................7.00

7-1/2" x 2-3/4" x 1-1/4", copper finish.............................. 14.00

Field Museum of Natural History, Chicago, IL, 1" x 4-1/4" x 3", silver or copper finish 33.00

Flatiron Building, New York City, 5-1/2" h, cast iron bank, silvery finish 158.00

Ft. Dearborn, Chicago, IL, 4" x 3-1/8" x 2", green or tan paint, souvenir of 1933 Chicago World's Fair 38.00

General Motors Building, Detroit, MI, 3-3/4" x 6-1/4" x 4", antique bronze finish 110.00

La Giralda, Seville, Spain, 7-1/2" h, antique brass, 2-1/4" black marble base...................... 50.00

Havoline Tower, thermometer, souvenir of 1933 Chicago World's Fair, 4-5/8" h
Cast iron, ivory paint........... 37.00
Plastic, marble base 22.00

Immaculate Conception National Shrine, Washington, DC, antique copper finish
3" x 3" x 2" 16.00
5" x 5" x 4" 38.00

Ivan's Bell Tower, Moscow, 3-1/2" x 2" x 1-1/4", solid brass, marble base........................ 91.00

Jefferson Memorial, Washington, DC, 1-1/2" x 2" x 2", copper finish 16.00

Kraft International Headquarters, Chicago, IL, 3-1/8" x 2-3/4" x 3-1/4", silvered lead paperweight, cast by A.C. Rehberger 80.00

Leaning Tower of Pisa, Italy
3-1/2", silver finish, metal ashtray 34.00
5" x 1-3/4" d, white alabaster 28.00

Lincoln Memorial, Washington, DC, 1-1/2" x 3" x 2, copper finish 8.00

Louisiana State Capitol, Baton Rouge, LA, 7" x 5-1/2" x 2-3/4", antique copper finish 88.00

Metropolitan Life Insurance Co., New York City, 5-1/4" x 3-3/4" x 2-1/4", silver or gold finish 118.00

Miami Beach Federal Savings, Miami, FL, 5-1/2" x 3-1/2" x 3-1/4", brass finish, Banthrico Bank 68.00

Mormon Temple, Salt Lake City, UT, 4" x 2-1/4" x 3-3/8", copper finish 30.00

Notre Dame, Paris, 2" x 3" x 1-1/2", bronze finish 16.00

Parthenon, Athens, Greece, 3-1/4" x 6" x 3-1/2", copper, marble base 98.00

Pilgrim Memorial Monument, Provincetown, MA, 4-3/4" h, 2-1/4" d base 22.00

Rockefeller Center (RCA Building), New York City
2-5/8" x 2" x 1", copper finish..............................27.00
4-1/4" x 3" x 1-3/8", silver finish..............................89.00

Sacre Coeur, Paris, 4-1/2" x 4-1/4" x 2-1/2", antique brass...........32.00

Singing Tower, Bok Tower, Lake Wales, FL, 5" h, 1-3/4" d base 21.00

Space Needle, Seattle, WA, 6" h, revolving turret, silver or copper finish 22.00

Statue of Liberty, New York City
2" h 3.00
4-1/2" h 5.50
6" h 8.00

St. Basil's Cathedral, Moscow, 4" x 3-1/2" x 3-1/2" h, solid brass, marble base 300.00

St. Mary's Cathedral, Florence, Italy, 2-1/2" x 3-1/2" x 2-1/2", silver finish.............................27.00

St. Peter's Cathedral, Rome, 3-1/2" x 3-1/2" x 2-1/2", silver finish 28.00

Syracuse Savings Bank, Syracuse, NY, 5-1/2" x 4" x 3", copper finish 68.00

Taj Mahal, Agra, India, 8" x 7" x 7", white marble, night-light......64.00

United Nations Building, New York City, 3" x 4" x 2-1/2", antique brass...................................22.00

U.S. Fidelity & Guaranty Co., 5-3/4" x 7-1/4" x 6", building as combina-tion cigar humidor, inkwell and clock, cast by Art Metal Works, NJ, antique bronze finish ..190.00

Washington Monument, Washington, DC
3-1/4" h, silver, salt and pepper set...................................27.00
6" h, copper, thermometer 9.00

Woolworth Building, New York City,
4" x 1-3/4" x 1-1/4",
gold finish 26.00
Zembo Museum, Harrisburg, PA,
2-1/2" x 4-1/2" x 1-3/4", antique
copper finish 63.00

❖ Souvenir China

Guess it's human nature to want to save something of a memorable trip or vacation. Happily for souvenir china collectors, lots of folks have felt this through the years. Souvenir china can be found in lots of forms, from ashtrays to plates to pitchers to vases. Sit back and take an armchair tour with souvenir china.

Periodical: *Antique Souvenir Collectors News,* PO Box 562, Great Barrington, MA 01230.

For additional listings, see *Warman's Americana & Collectibles* and *Warman's Antiques and Collectibles Price Guide.*

Basket, Myer, Texas, white ground,
hand painted blue bonnets,
3" h 30.00

Cup and Saucer
Hess Brothers, Allentown, PA,
colorful repeated script name,
white ground 20.00
St. Charles Hotel, New Orleans,
white 17.50
Niagara Falls, mkd "Carlsbad,
Austria" 18.00

Cup, china, white
St. Charles Hotel, New
Orleans 15.00

Cup and saucer, "Washington Palm Walk, Miami, Fla.," saucer decorated with oranges, $40.

Souvenir of the Midget's Palace,
Montreal, well-dressed male
and female midgets illus, late
1800s 65.00
Demitasse Cup and Saucer, Hotel
Roosevelt, New Orleans..... 37.50
Hatpin Holder, Capitol Building,
Washington, DC, gold trim, green
wreath mark, 4-1/2" d 125.00
Plate
Alabama, state capitol in center,
blue, Vernon Kilns 22.00
Albany, MN 40.00
Along 101 The Redwood
Highway, maroon, Vernon
Kilns 25.00
Baltimore & Ohio Railroad,
Harpers Ferry, blue and white,
10-1/2" d 95.00
Birmingham, AL, The Industrial
City, maroon, Vernon
Kilns 22.00
Boston, MA, Filene's, brown, Vernon Kilns 22.00
Carlsbad Caverns, White's City,
New Mexico 25.00
Chicago, clock in center,
maroon 22.00
Chiang Kai-Shek Memorial Hall,
Republic of China, orig box,
7-1/4" d 12.00
Cypress Gardens, Florida,
Human Kite, Human Pyramid,
Esther Williams Swimming
Pool, Beautiful Aquamaids,
8" d 25.00
Daytona Beach, FL, World's Most
Famous Beach, maroon,
Vernon Kilns 22.00
Delaware Tercentenary Celebration, 1938, black and white,
Spode 35.00
Denver, CO, state capitol in center, blue, Vernon Kilns 22.00
Greenville, SC, blue, Vernon
Kilns 22.00
Hawaii, blue Tiki, emb border,
8-1/4" 30.00
Hollywood, CA, NBC Studios,
Hollywood Bowl, Ciro's, Graumann's, Earl Carroll's, Brown
Derby, blue, Vernon
Kilns 35.00
Jacksonville, FL, Gateway to
Florida, maroon 22.00
Laguna Beach, CA, Festival of
Arts 25.00

Maine, state capitol in center,
multicolored, Vernon
Kilns 30.00
Mississippi, blue, Vernon
Kilns 22.00
My Old Kentucky Home,
10" d, cobalt blue,
Adams 75.00
Nevada, The Silver State, Hoover
Dam in center, brown, Vernon
Kilns 22.00
New Mexico, picture map ... 22.00
New York, City of Wonders,
Statue of Liberty, Coney Island,
International Airport, 1950s,
9" d 24.00
Northwestern University, multicolored, Vernon Kilns 35.00
Our West, Vast Empire, maroon,
Vernon Kilns 35.00
Peggy's Cove, Nova Scotia,
green, 10" d 15.00
Portsmouth Virginia Bicentennial,
1752-1952, light brown,
Vernon Kilns 22.00
Saint Augustine, FL, brown,
Vernon Kilns 22.00
Salem Witch, 8" d 140.00
San Diego County Fair, Delmar,
CA, Don Diego Welcomes You,
blue 35.00
SE Missouri State College, Diamond Jubilee, brown, Vernon
Kilns 25.00
Sonoma, CA, Cradle of California,
maroon, Vernon Kilns 35.00
South Dakota, state capitol in
center, maroon, Vernon Kilns
.... 22.00
Spokane, WA, The Inland Empire,
blue, Vernon Kilns 25.00
SS *Grand View Hotel*, A Steamboat in the Allegheny Mountains, 10" d, cobalt blue,
Adams 95.00
Statue of Liberty, mkd "Made
expressly for James Hill, Bedloe's Island, NY, The New
Colossus by Emma Lazarus"
on back, blue, Vernon
Kilns 35.00
Vermont, Green Mountain State,
brown, Vernon Kilns 22.00
Washington, state capital in
center, brown, Vernon
Kilns 22.00

West Virginia, state capital in center, brown 22.00

Salt and Pepper Shakers, pr, Hot Springs, SD, orig label, Rosemeade........................ 65.00

Tip Tray, Hotel Coronado........ 18.50

Vase, Western Normal College, Shenandoah, Iowa, decal of college, mkd "Made in Austria for F. L. Bauer," 7-1/2" h 90.00

❖ Souvenir Spoons

Collecting souvenir spoons has become a little more popular in the past few years. Collectors are starting to admire the tiny treasures often for their colorful decoration as well as for the place they honor. Perhaps it is their diminutive size that keeps collectors yearning for more as they display well.

Collectors' Club: American Spoon Collectors, 7408 Englewood Lane, Kansas City, MO 64133; Northeastern Spoon Collectors Guild, 52 Hillcrest Ave., Morristown, NJ 07960.

For additional listings, see *Warman's Americana & Collectibles.*

Battle Monument, Trenton, NJ........................ 35.00

Ben Franklin, Philadelphia...... 55.00

Bethesda Springs, Waukesha, WI........................ 55.00

Bismarck, ND, post office bowl........................ 45.00

Boulder, CO, name in bowl, Indian head handle 42.00

Brooklyn, NY, 13th Regiment.. 35.00

Calumet, MI, mining, Helco Shaft #2 .... 35.00

Chicago, IL, U.S. Government Building, Fort Dearborn 40.00

Columbus, bust, plated.......... 20.00

For exciting collecting trends and newly expanded areas look for the following symbols:

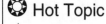 Hot Topic

★ New Warman's Listing

(May have been in another Warman's edition.)

Golden Gate, San Francisco, rose design on handle, sterling, 5-1/4" l, $15.

Columbus, OH, Lancaster pattern handle.............................. 35.00

Cornell University, Art Nouveau woman.............................. 75.00

Cuba, Morro castle 50.00

Detroit Skyline....................... 70.00

Decatur, IL, SS....................... 42.00

Elgin Watch Factory................ 85.00

Eureka, CA, courthouse.......... 30.00

Fredericton, New Brunswick, spiral handle, gold-wash bowl 60.00

Girard College................. 48.00

Girard College, Irian pattern handle.............................. 45.00

Golden Gate, San Francisco .. 45.00

Grant Monument, Chicago...... 45.00

Hope, ID............................... 30.00

Hot Springs, AK, Indian head, corn 45.00

Inclined Plane, Cincinnati, OH 35.00

Kansas City, MO, Convention Hall 45.00

Lake Worth, Palm Beach, FL.. 65.00

Madison, WI........................... 35.00

McDermott Falls, Glacier National Park bowl......................... 45.00

Michigan City, IN, ornate Art Nouveau handle 50.00

Miles Standish, fruit bowl........ 75.00

Mt. Vernon 20.00

New Orleans, SS 30.00

Old Hickory, Jackson monument 75.00

Paul Revere, Midnight Ride.... 95.00

Portland, OR, SS 40.00

Prairie du Chien, WI................ 28.00

Quebec, open-work handle..... 35.00

Reading, PA, Mt. Penn Tower, demitasse 40.00

Richlandtown, PA, demitasse 30.00

Richmond, MO, SS 32.50

Salt Lake City, UT, Mormon Temple handle, demitasse 45.00

Salem, MA, witch handle 48.00

San Francisco, Mission Dolores 1776, bear on dec handle, gold bowl 45.00

Sioux City, IA, Corn Palace, 1891.................................... 80.00

Springfield, IL, Abraham Lincoln 60.00

Statue of Liberty, Tiffany.......... 75.00

Texas, enameled star, demitasse 25.00

Union Station, Dayton, OH, picture bowl........................ 35.00

Vassar, MI, high school engraved bowl 35.00

Waseca, MN, grape pattern 55.00

Washington's Tomb................ 32.00

Wilmington, NC, floral handle, gold-wash bowl, demitasse 35.00

Yellowstone Park, etched falls bowl, bear, stag's head and buffalo's head on handle.................. 45.00

❖ Space Adventurers, Fictional

Space adventurers have always fascinated folks, from Buck Rogers in 1929 to the early awaited sequels to Star Trek. We've been spellbound by their adventures, taken to new places and returned safely back again.

References: Dana Cain, *UFO & Alien Collectibles Price Guide,* Krause Publications, 1999; Rex Miller, *The Investor's Guide to Vintage Character Collectibles,* Krause Publications, 1999; Stuart W. Wells, III, *Science Fiction Collectibles Identification & Price Guide,* Krause Publications, 1998.

Collectors' Club: Galaxy patrol, 22 Colton St., Worcester, MA 01610.

For additional listings, see *Warman's Americana & Collectibles.*

Action Figure, Space Fighter, soft vinyl robot shape, movable arms, Imperial Toy Corp., Hong Kong, 1977, 4-3/4" h, MOC........... 15.00

Activity Book, *Battlestar Galactica,* Wonder Books, Universal City Studios, Inc., unused.................... 10.00

Buck Rogers in the City Below the Sea, Whitman, 1934 ....60.00

Buck Rogers, 25th Century A.D., Whitman, 1938, Cocomalt premium..........................48.00

Badge, Buck Rogers Solar Scout 95.00

Bank, Flash Gordon, metal, rocket 35.00

Bed Sheet, Star Trek, 38" x 785", cotton and polyester, red, blue, yellow, b&w illus, light blue background, c1970............ 35.00

Belt and Buckle, Space Patrol, 4" brass buckle, rocket, decoder mounted on back, glow-in-the-dark belt, Ralston premium, early 1950s 175.00

Better Little Book, *Flash Gordon and the Perils of Mongo,*

Better Little Book, *Buck Rogers and the Doom Comet,* Whitman #1178, 1935, 432 pgs, hardcover 65.00

Book, *Bucks Rogers Collected Words of Comics,* hardcover 35.00

Book, *Star-Trek, Mission to Horatius,* Whitman TV Adventure Book, #1549, 1968, 210 pgs, 5" x 8"................................. 20.00

Book, *Tom Corbett Space Cadet/Sabotage In Space,* Grosset & Dunlap, hardcover, 212 pgs, dj......................... 15.00

Card Set, Star Wars 12 perforated 3-1/2" x 7-1/2" thin cardboard sheets, 3 color cards on each, Burger King premium, Lucasfilm Ltd., complete set of 36 cards, unpunched 15.00

Clock, Star Wars alarm, talking................................. 30.00

Coin Album, Space Patrol, 3" x 7-3/4", thin cardboard black, white and blue folder, spaceship landing and men rushing toward it,

Battlestar Galactica game, Parker Bros., box 9-3/8" x 18-3/8", $18.

diecut slots for plastic Ralston premium or Schwinn Bicycle dealer coins, c1953 .... 175.00

Colorforms Set, Buck Rogers diecut vinyl figures, box, 1979 .... 25.00

Coloring Book, Star Wars *The Empire Strikes Back,* 8" x 11", Kenner, 1982 Lucasfilm Ltd., color photo of Darth Vader and 2 Storm Troopers on front and back, 64 pgs, unused 9.00

Comic Album, Lost in Space, 7-3/4" x 10-1/4", Space Family Robinson/Lost in Space, stiff cover comic album, English reprints of Western Publishing Co. full-color comic book stories, 1965 by World Distributors Ltd., 64 pgs................................. 18.00

Comic Book, *Space Family Robinson/Lost In Space,* World Distributors Ltd., 1965 .... 20.00

Crayon Box, Buck Rogers Crayon Ship, cardboard, 6 colored pencils, c1930 .... 175.00

Decoder, 1-1/2" d, Capt Video Mysto-Coder, brass, plastic wheels, lightning-bolt design............................. 165.00

Decoder, 2-1/2" x 4", Tom Corbett Space Cadet Code, black, white and red cardboard, membership card printed on back........... 45.00

Flashlight, 7" l, Space Cadet Signal Siren Flashlight, full-color illus, orig box, c1952 .... 65.00

Flashlight, Space Patrol,12" l, silvered metal body, pointed rubber red top nose, decal inscription on fin Official Space Patrol Rocket Lite and Commander Buzz Corry, Ray-O-Vac Co., orig box, early 1950s............................... 250.00

Game, Star Wars, Destroy Death Star, Kenner, 16" sq board, 1977 .... 35.00

Gun, Captain Video Secret Ray Gun, red plastic flashlight, secret message instructions, Power Halloween Costume, Star Trek, Tng-Frengi, Ben Cooper, 1987, orig box............................... 50.00

House Candy premium........... 90.00

Handbook, Space Patrol 175.00

Lobby Card, Buck Rogers "The Enemy Stronghold," Buster Crabbe, 1938.................... 190.00

Lunch Box with thermos, Star Wars, King Seeley, 1978.............. 55.00

Lunch Box, 7" x 8" x 4", Buck Rogers, litho metal, 6-1/2" h plastic thermos............................. 45.00

Lunch Box, Tom Corbett Space Cadet, 7" x 8" x 4", litho metal, full-color space scene, dark blue galaxy background, 1954 Rockhill Radio 95.00

Magazine, *TV Star Parade,* Captain Video, 2-pg photo article, Ideal Publishing Co., 1953...........20.00

Manual, 5" x 7-1/2", Buck Rogers Solar Scouts, 16 pgs, Cream of Wheat premium, 1936 ...... 165.00

Mask that attaches to poster, smaller X-Wing and Tie Fighter attachments, MIP.........................24.00

Membership Card, 3" x 4-1/4", Flash Gordon Movie Club, green, black scene and lettering, unuse 600.00

Match Cover, Buck Rogers, Popsicle adv 17.50

Spaceship, Thunderbird 3, friction powered, 7" h, c1960..........75.00

Membership Kit Fan Photo, Tom Corbett Space Cadet, 3-1/2" x 5-1/4", glossy b&w photo, Tom with Space Rangers, facsimile blue ink signature, c1952 ....28.00

Microscope, Space Patrol, orig slides...............................195.00

Model, Return of the Jedi, B-Wing Fighter, 7" x 9-3/4" x 2", box with image of fighter flying past planet, Lucasfilm 1983 MPC, unopened 25.00

Model, Star Trek, USS Enterprise, 8-1/2" x 10" x 2-3/4" box, image of spaceship between planets, gray unassembled plastic pieces, folded b&w instruction sheet, AMT #6676, 1983 ....20.00

Mug, Return of the Jedi, 4" h, plastic, white, 1983 ....40.00

Mug, Star Trek, 3-3/4" h, white plastic, color illus, red inscription, 1975.....................................15.00

Paint Book, Buck Rogers 11" x 14", 96 pgs, Whitman, 1935.......85.00

Paint Set, Star Trek, 12" x 16" canvas portrait, Hasbro, 1974, partially used.......................60.00

Paper Cup, Space Patrol, pkg of 6, rocket ships, stars and planets motif, orig cellophane and company label 70.00

Patch, 2" x 4", cloth, Space Cadet, red, yellow and blue, Kellogg's premium 35.00

Pencil Case, Buck Rogers 5" x 8-1/2" x 1/2", cardboard, yellow illus top and bottom, green background, brass snap fastener, American Lead Pencil Co., 1936 .... 225.00

Photo, 3-1/2" x 5-1/2", b&w glossy, blue signature "Spaceman's Luck/Tom Corbett/Space Cadet," early 1950s 45.00

Pinback Button, 1-1/8" d, black, white and red, Flash Gordon Club, Chicago, Herald and Examiner 75.00

Pistol, Battlestar Galactica, Lasermatic, Mattel, MIB 50.00

Place Mat, 8-1/2" x 11", Star Wars, The Empire Strikes Back, paper, full color, Burger King, 1980 .... 7.50

Poster, Star Trek, Mr. Spock holding model of Enterprise, Personality Posters 24.00

Premium Card, Space Patrol, 2-1/2" x 3-1/2", full-color scene on front and back, text, adv for Wheat and Rice Chex Cereal, Rockets, Jets and Weapons Series, 7 cards from 40-card set, early 1950s 135.00

Press Book, Captain Video, 12" x 18", black, white and blue cover, newspaper headline style... 90.00

Press Kit, Star Wars, first movie......................... 70.00

Puppet, 8" h, Star Wars, Yoda, molded soft rubber, silver hair wisps, 1979 .... 25.00

Record, Flash Gordon, 6-1/2" d, City of Sea Caves, plastic on cardboard, 78 RPM, 1948 .... 45.00

Rocket Ship, Buck Rogers 4-1/2" l, Venus Duo-Destroyer, die-cast metal, yellow, red, trim, inscription on each side, orig box, 1937 .... 150.00

Record Storybook, Star Wars 15.00

Rocket Ship, Captain Video, 4-1/2" l, plastic, metallic lavender, removable cannons, inscription on tail fin, Lido Toy Co., orig box, early 1950s 65.00

School Bag, Tom Corbett Space Cadet, 11" x 14-1/2", plastic, Tom on center flap, rocket designs on side, red plastic handle....... 45.00

Space Helmet, Space Patrol, diecut cardboard, 6 sided, yellow, green, red design, black top with printed red lightning flashes 1230.00

Tablecloth, 54" x 88", blue, red, yellow, black and white design, white background, unopened plastic pkg, 1976........................... 25.00

Telephone, Star Wars, Darth Vader, figural, speakerphone....... 125.00

Telescope, 9" l, Flash Gordon Planet Gazer, plastic, decal portrait, orig display card, unopened plastic bubble, 1970s................... 125.00

Trekkie Outfit, Star Trek, worn during filming of TV series, "Star Trek: The Next Generation"....... 820.00

Utility Belt, Star Trek, phaser, tricorder and communicator, Remco, 1975 .... 45.00

View-Master Reel, Tom Corbett Space Cadet, set of 3, orig story folder and envelope............ 45.00

Wallet, Battlestar Galactica, vinyl, c1971, Larami, MOC 18.00

Watch, Space Patrol, silvered chrome, stainless steel back, black leather straps, "Space Patrol" inscription on dial, black numerals, U.S. Time, early 1950s............................... 165.00

Water Pistol, Flash Gordon, 7-1/2" l, blue plastic, whistle mouthpiece, inscribed "Flash Gordon Water Pistol," Marx, orig box, c1950............................... 95.00

Whitman, Coloring Book, Flash Gordon, 8-1/2" x 11", 1952
.... 35.00

Wristwatch, Tom Corbett Space Cadet, orig band.............. 150.00

❖ Space Exploration

The recent return of John Glenn to space has served to remind us how long the NASA program has been around. Collecting memorabilia relating to space flights can show how far we've come from the early Sputnik days.

Periodical: *Space Autograph News,* 862 Thomas Ave., San Diego, CA 92109.

For additional listings, see *Warman's Americana & Collectibles.*

Ashtray, 5-1/2" sq, china, Apollo 11, mission insignia, mkd "Johnson Space Center/Houston, Texas" 30.00

Autograph, envelope, inked Jack Swigert signature on back, Man on Moon stamp, canceled Kennedy Space Center, April 11, 1970.................................... 50.00

Badge, First Men on Moon, 1-3/4" white button, blue and red text listing astronauts names, date July 21, 1969, red, white, and blue ribbon with brass accent keychain holding 2" h vinyl figure of astronaut with sextant........ 20.00

Bank, 4-1/2" h, Freedom 7, plastic, silver, flight details listed on bottom, inscription on base, "Freedom 7 Capsule/Project Mercury/Redstone Rocket" 45.00

Book

First American Into Space, Robert Silverberg, Monarch Books, 142 pgs, 1961................. 20.00

NASA Astronauts Biography Book, NASA, 1968, 8" x 10-1/4", soft-cover 40.00

Clock, 4" x 4-1/2" x 2", Apollo 11, animated windup, ivory case, red, white and blue diecut, metallic blue dial, Apollo craft illus, gold-colored numerals, brass hands, mkd "Lux Clock Mfg Co." ..145.00

Coloring Book, Apollo Man On The Moon, Saalfield #4566, copyright 1969, 8-1/2" x 11", color cover of astronauts near lunar rover on moon, unused 15.00

Dish, 8" d, Apollo II Commemorative, irid glass, raised design, inscription "One Small Step," 1970s 18.00

Drinking Glass, Astronaut Neil Armstrong, 5-1/2" h, clear glass, brown and white graphics of Armstrong wearing suit, gold lettering "Wapakoneta Astronaut Neil Armstrong," list of 1961-1966 manned space flights........................ 35.00

Magazine

Life, Sept 14, 1959, 10-1/2" x 14", color cover photo of astronauts, article with profiles of each astronaut 15.00

Newsweek, First Man On Moon, Aug 11, 1969, 8-1/4" x 11", color cover, illus article......7.50

Time, First Man on Moon, July 25, 1969, 8-1/4" x 11", color cover, illus article 9.00

Medal, Apollo 11, Lunar Landing, 2" d, silver luster, lunar exploration scene, reverse with Apollo 11-First Men On The Moon, full names of astronauts, July 28, 1969 date 35.00

Mug, 3" h, china, black St. *Louis Globe-Democrat* newspaper design of July 20, 1969, Moon landing.....35.00Pennant, 5" x 10-1/2", First Men On The Moon, white cord hanger, lunar exploration scenes in blue, white, gray, and black, red, white, and blue flag, text "One Small Step...," c1969 .... 25.00

Pinback Button, 1-3/4" d, white cello, black and white photo of astronauts, red accent title "Man's First Flight Around The Moon, Dec 21-27, 1968," attached to dark blue ribbon with gold accents "Welcome Back To Earth," image of earth and moon 25.00

Apollo 13 glasses, 4-1/8" h, each, $2.

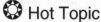

For exciting collecting trends and newly expanded areas look for the following symbols:

✿ Hot Topic

★ New Warman's Listing

(May have been in another Warman's edition.)

Place Mat, 9-1/2" x 14", Kennedy Space Center/NASA Tours, paper, scalloped border, red, white, and blue shuttle, red and blue text, c1976 .... 20.00

Plate

7" d, white plastic, astronaut in green outfit hanging upside down from spaceship as astronaut in foreground pulls tether against starry background, early 1970s..................... 15.00

7-1/4" d, "John H. Glenn Jr. First American To Orbit The World," white china, gold accent, inscriptions for Feb 20, 1962, flight................................ 35.00

Press Pass, 3" x 4-1/4", laminated, ABC News, June 18-24, 1983, Challenger Mission, b&w photos, blue, white and orange design.................................. 60.00

Print, framed, 16" x 20-1/2", tapered wood frame, black and white artist's rendering of huge elevated dome structure, cut-away view, identified as "AN/FPS-35 Radome/Sperry Gyroscope Company"........................... 25.00

Puzzle Apollo 11, 1969, MIB... 25.00

Ruler, 4-1/2" x 7", Space Shuttle 3-D Picture Ruler, red, white and blue illus card, diecut opening with 6" ruler, five images of space shuttle in flight, Vari-Vue, Mt. Vernon, NY, orig display bag, unopened 20.00

Salt and Pepper Shakers, pr, 3" h, china, blue symbol and Columbia shuttle design, inscription "Johnson Space Center, Houston, TX," early 1980s 20.00

Tie Clip, 1-1/2", Apollo 11, brass, black accents, raised Moon-landing design, landing date and astronaut names on rim, orig plastic display case 40.00

❖ Space Toys

Now that we've done some imagining about space adventurers and real space heroes, how about some toys to round out our experience? Flea markets are sure to yield some out-of-this-world treasures.

Periodical: *Toy Shop,* 700 E. State St., Iola, WI 54990.

Johillco robots, dimestore figures, each, $30.

For additional listings, see *Warman's Americana & Collectibles* and "Robots" in this edition.

Apollo Spacecraft, battery operated, Japan, MIB.......................275.00

Astronaut, litho tin, wearing space suit, carrying gun in right hand, arms swing with walking action, mkd "AN," 7-1/2" h 1,650.00

Eagle Lunar Module, battery operated, Daishin, Japan, 1969, MIB 320.00

Flying Saucer, litho tin, space pilot, revolving antenna, orange, swivel lighted engine 395.00

Helmet, Space patrol, cardboard, 1950s............................... 225.00

Moon Globe Orbitor, Japan, MIB 235.00

Playset, Apollo Exploration 85.00

Ray Gun, laser, plastic, Tim-Me, 10" l, MOC 60.00

Rocket, battery operated, MIB

Automatic docking and separating actions, Daiya, 17" l...... 275.00

Moon Rocket, litho tin, bump and go auction, revolving astronaut, flashing colored lights, mkd "MT, Japan"........... 150.00

Space Gun, friction powered, MIB 45.00

Spaceship, Burger Blaster, Heinz Catsup, MIB 145.00

Universe Car, litho tin, China, MIB 125.00

❖ Spark Plugs

Spark plug collectors are quite at home at flea markets devoted to

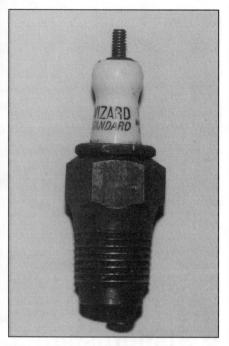

Wizard Standard, 3" l, $3.

automobiles. They look for interesting spark plugs, boxes, and other ephemera.

Champion

    J-9 14 MM, 13/16" hex,
        MIB.................................10.00

    Maytag, 14 MM, red lettering,
        used 30.00

    V-3, airplane........................15.50

    W-18, oversized 6.00

Red Head, 1-1/2" pipe thread,
    unused 40.00

Western Auto

    Endurance Red Seal, box only,
        1950s 2.00

    Wizard, orig box, MIB............3.00

❖ Spatter Glass

This colorful glassware is so named because of the spatters found in the clear glass body. The misnomer "end of day glass" has been associated with spatter glass for years. These colorful combinations weren't unplanned but many are terrific examples of a glass blower showing off his craft.

Basket, multicolored spatter, white int., cased, applied crystal thorn handle, polished pontil, Stourbridge, England, c1880

Pear, Gibson, 1992, multicolor, 5-1/4" h, $19.

    7" h, 6" w triangular
        body 285.00

    8" h, 6-1/4" w, sides pinched to
        form ruffled top 295.00

Creamer, 4" h, multicolored spatter, white int., cased, applied crystal handle, English................. 125.00

Vase

    4-1/4" h, multicolored spatter,
        cased, Stourbridge,
        c1880 .... 75.00

    5" h, silver and multicolored spatter, mica flecks, white int., cased, attributed to Stevens & Williams........................ 195.00

    7-1/4" h, white, yellow, and pink spatter, cased, applied crystal handles, English,
        c1880 .... 325.00

Water Set, Leaf Mold, cased cranberry spatter, 6 pc set....... 850.00

❖ Spongeware

Ever see pottery that looked like someone had taken paint and just sponged all over the piece - well that's spongeware. Most spongeware is available in blue on a white ground, but other interesting color variations do exist. Care should be taken when examining a piece of spongeware as modern craftsmen are making some examples that rival their antique ancestors.

Blue and white pottery pitcher, 1 gal., 9" h, $300.

Reproduction Alert.

For additional listings, see *Warman's Antiques and Collectibles Price Guide.*

Batter Bowl, large, blue and white, pouring spout 225.00

Bowl, large, heart panel, variegated sponging 325.00

Butter Crock, cov, blue and gray, grapevine design, Robinson Clay Products...........................225.00

Creamer, green and blue sponging on cream ground, 3" h 110.00

Milk Pitcher, black sponging, white ground, 7-1/2" h 195.00

Pitcher, barrel shape, green, gold, and brown sponging, 10" h 120.00

Sugar Bowl, cov, floral reserve, brown sponging, English, 19th C, 4" h 115.00

⚙ Sporting Collectibles

Whatever sport is your passion, you're bound to find some interesting examples of ephemera and other collectibles while browsing a flea market.

Reference: Sports Collectors Digest Editors, *1999 Sports Collectors Almanac*, Krause Publications, 1998.

For additional listings, see *Warman's Antiques and Collectibles Price Guide, Warman's Americana & Collectibles,* and specific categories in this edition.

Action Figure, Muhammad Ali, The Champ, Mego, 3" x 9" x 13-1/2" platform base blister card, Ali in white boots, fabric boxing shorts, second blister card holding accessories, copyright 1976 Herbert Muhammad Enterprises, Inc. 130.00

Badge

Jersey City Ali Welcome, 3-1/2" d, black and white cello, for June 29, 1979, exhibition charity bout, shows NJ Gov. Byrne, Jersey City Mayor Tommie Smith, Muhammad Ali and his body guard 55.00

National Weightlifting and Mr. America Championship, 4-3/4", brass accent, "Official Badge," at top, blue and white ribbon, gold accent lettering, "Senior National A.A.U. Weightlifting and Mr. America Championships May 12-13, 1950, Academy of Music, Phila, Pa" text, orig manila envelope.............................. 15.00

Book, *Giant Book of Sports,* covers baseball, football, boxing, tennis, bowling, and basketball, dedicated to the Memory of Babe Ruth, 185 pgs, 8-1/2" x 11-3/4" 20.00

First Day Covers, 9th Annual National Sports Collectors Convention, Atlantic City, NJ, July 8, 1988, silk emb, set of three 18.00

Game, Bowling, Parker Brothers, orig box, 1896 .... 65.00

Magazine, *Life,* Nov, 1971, tennis article and cover................... 8.50

Medal, World Weightlifting Championships, 1947, 5" bronze, detailed image of Independence Hall at top, name "Patron" under clear celluloid, attached bright yellow ribbon holding 1-1/2" d detailed medal showing muscular man lifting weights, inscribed "World's Weightlifting Championships Sept 26-27, 1947 Philadelphia, Penna, U.S.A.," orig 3" x 5-1/4" white card 12.00

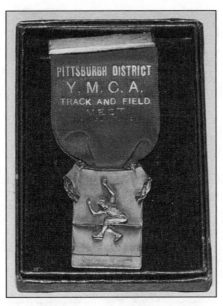

Medal, high jump, "Pittsburgh District Y.M.C.A. Track and Field Meet, Sat. July 7, 1934," red cloth ribbon, pinback, orig box, 3-3/4" h, $15.

Pinback Button

American Bowling Congress, 1932, 32nd Annual Tournament, Detroit................... 82.00

Devil's Lake Regatta, blue and white, 1934..................... 15.00

US Open Tennis Championship, 1975 .... 18.50

❂ Sporting Goods

So you'd rather participate in sports than watch? Need some kitschy decor items for your family room? Well, head for the flea market and look for some of these neat collectibles.

See specific listings for fishing rods, skateboards, etc.

Baseball Glove, used for Little League 35.00

Camping, coffeepot, aluminum, four aluminum cups fit inside 15.00

Goalie Mitt, hockey, used........ 20.00

Goalie Pads, indoor soccer, used................................... 20.00

Hockey stick, used

Bauer Supreme, used by Eric Lindros 300.00

Wilson Professional Softball, Wilson Sporting Goods Co., orig box, $6.

Easton, used by Sergei Zubov 95.00

Lacrosse stick, wood, used.............................. 40.00

Snow Shoes, pr, used 125.00

❖ Staffordshire Items

The Staffordshire district of England is well known for the quality porcelain they have produced through the centuries. This region was home to many potteries who supplied dinnerware, table items, and novelties such as mantel figures and toby jugs, etc.

For additional listings, see *Warman's Antiques and Collectibles Price Guide* and *Warman's English & Continental Pottery & Porcelain.*

Bank, cottage shape, 5-1/4" h, repairs................................195.00

Box, cov, oval, raised panels, finial, green, black, and gold traces....................................60.00

Chamber Pot, cov, 9" h, Columbia, mkd "W. Adams," short hairline in bottom................................80.00

Cup and Saucer, handleless, dark blue transfer of vase with flowers, imp "Clews," small chips, wear....................................95.00

Figure

Gentleman, seated, book and spectacles, polychrome enamel, damaged, old repairs 275.00

Rabbit, black and white, green and brown base, 3-1/4" h, wear and enamel flaking 315.00

Dogs, textured finish, 3-1/2" h, pr, $275.

Squirrel, sitting upright, holding nut, naturalistic stump base, ear repaired...................125.00

Mantel Ornament, cottage, Potash Farm, hairlines, 9" h 175.00

Plate, blue feathered edge, emb rim design, 10" d 55.00

Waste Bowl, Forget-Me-Not, red transfer, edge roughness, 5-5/8" d.............................. 60.00

❖ Stamps

Stamp collecting has long been one of the most popular hobbies. Like many other hobbies, it is crucial that participants spend time reading and researching stamps and their values. And, as they learn more, they will learn to enjoy the fine art of collecting.

References: George Cuhaj, ed., *Krause-Minkus Standard Catalog of Canadian & United Nations Stamps,* Krause Publications, 1998; Arlene Dunn, ed., *Brookman Price Guide for Disney Stamps,* 2nd edition, Krause Publications, 1998; Robert Furman, *The 1999 Comprehensive Catalogue of United States Stamp Booklets, Postage and Airmail,* Krause Publications, 1998, plus many others.

Periodical: *Stamp Collector,* 700 E. State St., Iola, WI 54990, plus others.

Collectors' Clubs: American Philatelic Society, PO Box 8000, State College, PA 16803; International Stamp Collectors Society, PO Box 854, Van Nuys, CA 91408. Contact either one of these to inquire about local chapters.

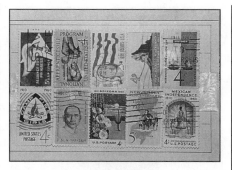

U.S. anniversary issues, early 1960s, each 15 cents.

❖ Stangl

Stangl Pottery was an active pottery in the Flemington, New Jersey, area. They produced colorful dinnerware, table wares and are well known for their interesting bird figurines.

Collectors' Club: Stangl/Fulper Collectors Club, PO Box 538, Flemington, NJ 08822.

For additional listings, see *Warman's Antiques and Collectibles Price Guide* (Stangl Birds) and *Warman's Americana & Collectibles* (dinnerware).

Basket, #3414........................ 20.00

Butter Dish, cov, Country Garden 42.00

Child's Dish and Cup, ABC's, chip on rear of plate 85.00

Chop Plate, Harvest................ 42.00

Cigarette Box, cov, goldfinch .. 55.00

Coffeepot, Blue Rooster 90.00

Creamer

Blue Rooster...................... 27.50

Cup and Saucer

Country Garden.................. 20.00

Harvest 22.00

Terra Rose......................... 24.00

Town and Country, brown ... 20.00

Decorative Plate, quail, small chip on back 25.00

Dinner Plate

Country Garden.................. 40.00

Terra Rose 15.00

Thistle................................ 19.50

Egg Cup, Country Garden 15.00

Gravy Boat, Thistle 24.00

Mug, Town and Country, blue..................................... 22.00

Stangl Pottery bowl, fruit motif, 2-1/2" h, 8-3/4" d, $36.

Teapot, Harvest....................... 80.00

Vase, 7" h, orange, #3102....... 75.00

Wig Stand, lady's head, brown 500.00

✶ Stanhope

Remember those Easter Eggs that you peaked in one end to see an Easter scene at the other end? Well, that's a large form of a Stanhope. Stanhopes are little scenes tucked in miniature holders. Sometimes the cases are shaped like cameras and the viewer sees different images when holding the camera up to the light. Other Stanhopes are shaped like miniature binoculars.

Disney 40th Anniversary, a scene from "Aladdin's Oasis" at Disneyland 4.00

Easter Egg, composition and plastic, blue egg, multicolored scene, c1950 .... 5.00

Eiffel Tower, binoculars shape, bone, brass ring, c1900, 1-1/2" l 55.00

Garfield, General James A., scenes and incidents from his life, 1831-1881........................ 100.00

Lord's Prayer, cross shape, silvertone, baguettes dec, 1950s, 1-1/2" l, 1" w....................... 35.00

Napoleon, figure, 2" h, bronzed.............................. 80.00

Rock City, plastic camera with 15 views, mkd "Brownie Mfg Co., West Germany," 2-1/4" x 1-1/4" 10.00

Rome, Coliseum, St. Peters, binoculars shape, 1-1/8" l 35.00
Rosary 21.50
The Apparition of Knock County, Mayo, Ireland, bone, 1-5/8" l................................ 22.00

✳ Stanley Tools

Some of the finest tools were created by the Stanley Tool Co. Today they are becoming more and more collectible. Look for examples free of rust and damage, but expect to find some wear from usage.

Periodical: *Stanley Tool Collectors News,* 208 Front St., PO Box 227, Marietta, OH 45750.

Beader, No. 66, full set of replacement blades, fences, 70% orig plating.............................. 100.00
Butt Gauge, No. 95G, yellow box, reinforced corners 22.50
Clapboard Maker, No. 88, adjustable, orig box, early label ... 40.00
Marking Gauge, Williams' Patent, 1857 patent date, 7" l 445.00
Plane, No. 50, combination, 15 cutters, B casting, 70% orig plating..............................110.00
Router, #71-1/2", patent date 1901 .... 48.00
Rule, folding........................... 20.00
Saw Set, No. 42, orig box....... 15.00

Level, wooden with brass viewer, Stanley Rule & Level Co., 1890 patent date, 12" l, $20.

❖ Star Trek

"Beam Me Up Scottie" certainly is a phrase many collectors associate with Star Trek. The adventures of this space team started on television in September of 1966 and lasted until June 1969. By 1978 syndicated broadcasts were reaching 51 countries, and the number of Star Trek fan clubs kept growing. *Star Trek, The Motion Picture* was released in 1979 and has been followed by additional movies.

Comic book, *Star Trek: A Triangle of Peril*, No. 40, Sept. 1976, Western Publishing Co., 10-1/8" x 6-1/8", $22.50.

Collectors' Clubs: International Federation of Trekkers, PO Box 84, Groveport, OH, 43125; Starfleet, 200 Hiawatha Blvd., Oakland, NJ 07436; Star Trek: The Official Fan Club, PO Box 111000, Aurora, CO 80042.

Activity Book, Whitman, 1979 .... 18.00
Book and Record, *Passage to Moauv,* 1975 Paramount Pictures, 20 pg comic book format 18.00
Bowl and Mug, plastic, "The Motion Picture," 1979 .... 24.00
Game, board, Hasbro, 1974 ... 55.00
Halloween Costume, TNG-Ferengi, Ben Cooper, 1987, orig box............................. 55.00
Lunch Box.............................. 50.00
Mobile, Enterprise, paper, orig envelope...................... 37.50
Poster, Mr. Spock holding model of Enterprise, Personality Posters 25.00
Utility Belt, Remco, phaser, tricorder, and communicator, 1975 .... 48.00

❖ ⬟ Star Wars

"May the force be with you" is one of phrases associated with this series of movies. George Lucas brought such special effects to the screen that fans of all ages were mesmerized. Twentieth Century Fox was clever

enough to give Kenner a broad license to produce movie-related toys and items, creating a wealth of Star Wars materials for collectors.

Reference: Stuart W. Wells, III, *Science Fiction Collectibles Identification & Price Guide,* Krause Publications, 1998.

Periodical: *The* Star Wars *Collector,* 20982 Homecrest Court, Ashburn, VA 22011.

Collectors' Club: Official Star Wars Fan Club, PO Box 111000, Aurora, CO 80042.

Action Figure, Kenner, MOC
Chewbacca, *Empire Strikes Back* 60.00
Darth Vader, *Return of the Jedi*................................48.00
Imperial Gunner, *Power of the Force* 110.00
Lando Calrissian, *Empire Strikes Back* 48.00
Alarm Clock, talking, MIB........85.00
Book, pop-up..........................20.00
Card game, Escape from Death Star, Kenner, 1977..............45.00
Cake Decoration, Wilton
Boba Fett 15.00
C-3PO................................5.00
Charm Bracelet, Stormtrooper and Chewbacca 15.00
Coloring Book, 1979, 11-3/4" x 8-1/4" 22.00
Game, Escape from Death Star, Kenner, copyright 1977.......25.00
Helmet, Darth Vader, Don Post, orig box, 1977 .... 115.00
Model Kit 35.00

Golden Trivia Game, Star Trek Edition, Western Publishing Co., box 12-1/2" sq, $18.

Micro Machines, Endor, $25.

Mug, Luke Skywalker,
   Sigma 24.00
Notebook, spiral bound,
   Mead 6.50
Paint Set, Darth Vader............ 12.00
Postcard, Greetings Earthlings,
   Droids.................................... .25
Stamp Kit, H. E. Harris & Co.,
   orig box, unused................. 12.00
Vehicle, Land Speeder,
   MIP...................................... 48.00
Watch, wind-up, Bradley......... 85.00

✳ St. Clair Glass

Here's a glass manufacturer that started making glassware using molds obtained from out-of-business companies. St. Clair specialized in making new colors in these pieces, but also some pieces in colors similar to the originals. The glass is usually marked and is eagerly sought by collectors in some areas.

Bell, Rosette pattern, chocolate
   glass, 6-1/4" h 55.00
Bicentennial Plate, blue carnival,
   5-1/2" d.............................. 40.00
Figure, buffalo, caramel slag .. 40.00
Paperweight
   Apple, red...........................82.00
   Bell shape, turquoise, sgd...55.00
   Bird, yellow, sgd 50.00
   Blue flowers........................40.00
   Owl, sulfide, yellow base, sgd
      "Maude and Bob" 180.00
   Pear, green........................100.00
   Turtle, clear and brown, sgd
      "Maude and Bob,"
      1982..............................155.00
Salt, open, wheelbarrow, caramel
   slag..................................... 15.00
Tumbler, Cactus, cobalt blue......28.00

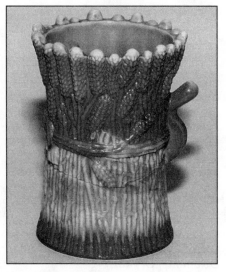

Toothpick holder, wheat sheaf, chocolate glass, emb "Bob and Maude 1974," 3-1/8" h, $35.

✳ Steiff

Steiff bears and toys are recognized by that familiar button ear tag. Steiff's first teddy bear appeared in 1903 and was an instant hit. The company still operates today, and collectors know the name means quality and a well made toy.

Collectors' Clubs: Steiff Club USA, 225 Fifth Ave., Suite 1033, New York, NY 10010; Steiff Collectors Club, PO Box 798, Holland, OH 43528.

Bunny, Manni, button 85.00
Circus Seal, with ball, on
   stand................................... 85.00
Hen, gold and black spotted feath-
   ers, yellow plush head, felt tail,
   black button eyes, c1949.... 85.00
Kangaroo, plush, glass eyes,
   2 plastic Joeys in pouch 70.00
Leopard.................................... 90.00
Llama, standing, white, brown
   spots................................. 110.00
Owl, 10" h 75.00
Parrot, Lora, glass eyes.......... 75.00
Rabbit, jointed, mohair,
   6-1/2" h 110.00
Squirrel, Perri, plush 45.00
Teddy Bear
   Light brown plush, glass eyes,
      jointed, c1950.............. 350.00
   Tan mohair, ear button, chest tag,
      jointed, c1980................. 75.00

Jointed teddy bear, white, orig tag, 9-1/2" h, $200.

✳ Steins

Finding steins at flea markets is great fun. Look for advertising or novelty steins, and don't overlook the limited ones made to commemorate a special event, like a fire truck housing.

Periodical: *Regimental Quarterly,* PO Box 793, Frederick, MD 21705.

Collectors' Club: Stein Collectors International, PO box 5005, Laurel, MD 20726; Sun Steiners, PO Box 11782, Fort Lauderdale, FL 33339.

For additional listings, see *Warman's Antiques and Collectibles Price Guide.*

Budweiser, 1991, basketball, orig
   box.................................... 15.00
Figural
   Ape, dressed in hobo tuxedo
      jacket, top hat, drinking from
      stein, smoking pipe, pewter
      thumbrest, 9-1/2" h 100.00
   Jolly Man, sitting on stump, play-
      ing accordion, pewter thum-
      brest and lid rim,
      9-1/2" h 150.00
Mekelbach, half liter, Hassfurt Town-
   ship, pewter lid and thumbrest,
   raised lettering and seal on lid,
   German inscription on front, blue

and whtie border and green wreath, 5-1/2" h 100.00

Mettlach

#171, half liter, figures representing monthly activities, blue background, inlaid top, pewter rim and thumbrest, 9-1/2" h, minor rubbing 90.00

2-1/4 liter, PUG, pewter lid and thumbrest, print of musical cherubs, man and woman performing ceremony, 17" h 250.00

Oktoberfest, German beer garden scene, Ceramarte, 1996, 5-3/4" h 20.00

Olympics, deep relief, full color, official logo, Atlanta, 1996, mkd "Made in Brazil, Ceramarte," 5-3/4" h 25.00

Regimental, German, half liter, pewter lid with image of solider with gun and lion, thumbrest with majestic lion, 12-1/2" h, wear on handle 250.00

Stoneware, German, half liter, gray, pewter lid and thumbrest, porcelain lid reads "Mohl Bekomms," five panels with raised figures 60.00

Avon, tall ships in a harbor, mkd "Handcrafted in Brazil exclusively for Avon Products Inc., 1977," pottery, metal lid, 9" h, $28.

❖ Stereoptican and Cards

Here's another way to bring antiques into your family entertainment area. Think of a stereoptican as the pre-cursor of the modern View-Master. Stereopticans were made as table-top models or hand-held and could take the viewer on a world tour just by changing the cards. Stereoviews covered many topics, from comedy to disasters, everyday scenes and tourist sites.

Collectors' Club: National Stereoscopic Association, PO Box 14801, Columbus, OH 43214.

Stereoview

Bristol, steamship scene 18.50

Civil War, Libby Prison, Anthony #3365, yellow mount 45.00

Crystal Palace, yellow mount 27.50

Cuba, street scene 18.00

Deer hunting, Keystone #26396 .... 8.50

Edison, Thomas, Keystone view of Edison in lab 90.00

Fishing in the Pool, copyright 1903, T. W. Ingersoll, No. 499 .... 6.00

Fireman, steam pumper, 1870 .... 50.00

Funeral of Abraham Lincoln, Anthony #2948 .... 75.00

Gypsies, in front of text 24.00

Harding, W., president addressing Boy Scouts 25.00

Portland Fire, 1866, Soule #469 .... 12.00

Savannah, Bonaventura Cemetery 10.00

Viewer

Hand-held, aluminum hood, wooden folding handle 125.00

Hand-held, walnut, screw on handle, velvet hood 115.00

For exciting collecting trends and newly expanded areas look for the following symbols:

⚙ Hot Topic

★ New Warman's Listing

Card, Keystone View Co. #17391, "Love Bids Him Stay but Duty Calls to the Man in Khaki," 3-1/2" x 7", $1.50.

Pedestal, Keystone, school and library type, black crinkle metal finish 95.00

Stand, Bates-Holmes, paper or wood hood 195.00

❖ Steuben Glass

The Steuben Glass Works was established in Corning, NY, in 1904. They produced many types of glass, from crystal to art glass. A trip to the Corning Museum today is always a treat, and you can actually see Steuben glass being made while there. Look for the traditional fleur-de-lis mark on Steuben Glass. It won't be found on every piece, and beware of faked signatures.

For additional listings, see *Warman's Antiques and Collectibles Price Guide* and *Warman's Glass.*

Bowl, blown into mold, amber, catalog #7696 ....300.00

Champagne, ruby, crystal stem, catalog #6521, set of 8 ....500.00

Cologne, 5" h, catalog #6887
  Flemish Blue 225.00
  Wisteria 300.00

Compote, Cerise, ruby and crystal, twisted stem, catalog #6043 ....325.00

Perfume, Verre de Soie, green jade stopper, catalog #1455 .....300.00

Puff Box, Green Jade, catalog #2910 ....325.00

Sherbet Set, catalog #2960, gold Aurene stemmed bowl, calcite stem, matching undertray, sgd "F. Carder Aurene" on base ...300.00

Vase

    Celeste Blue, catalog #6298, fan shape, optic ribbed version, triple wafer stem, pedestal base stamped with fleur-de-lis mark..............................320.00

    Rosaline, catalog #345......300.00

❖ Stocks and Bonds

Just as today's Wall Street stocks and bonds fluctuate, so do the prices of vintage stocks and bonds, just not as quickly. Many collectors enjoy researching the companies who issued stock; some enjoy the intricate vignettes.

Periodical: *Bank Note Reporter*, 700 E State Street, Iola, WI 54990.

Collectors' Clubs: Bond and Share Society, 26 Broadway at Bowling Green, Room 200, New York, NY 10004; Old Certificates Collector's Club, 4761 W. Waterbuck Drive, Tucson, AZ 85742.

Atchison, Topeka & Santa Fe Railroad, $1000 bond, two vignettes of railroad station interior, issued.................................. 20.00

Ben-Hur Motor Car, globe vignette, issued by not canceled, 1917 .... 85.00

Ford International Capital Corporation, $1000 bond, 1968 ...... 15.00

Fruit of the Loom, script certificate for fractional share of common stock, 1938........................... 7.50

King Productions, Inc., unissued stock certificate book, 9-3/4" x 16" black textured hardbound book, 26 green bank note design stock certificates, vignette of two workers in factory, wheels and turbines against city skyline, bound serially numbered, c1940 .... 75.00

Penn National Bank & Trust Co. of Reading, Pennsylvania, vignette of colonial man, issued but not canceled, 1930................... 20.00

Pepsi-Cola United Bottlers, vignette of goddess holding world globe and Pepsi bottle, issued..... 15.00

State of New York, Canal Department, Draper, Toppan & Co., NY, engravers, 1842 .... 18.50

United Airlines, $1000 share, 1970s.................................... 7.50

❖ Stoneware

Stoneware was meant to be both utilitarian and decorative. Early potters boasted of its durability and added cobalt blue flourishes to advertise their location, or perhaps a flower or bird as decoration. Today collectors seek out interesting examples. Some specialize in certain potters, while others collect by form, such as canning jars or crocks.

Butter Crock, brushed cobalt blue foliage, imp label "R. C. R. Phila.," applied handles, chips, filled in base chip, 12" d 600.00

Canning Jar, cobalt blue stenciled and freehand design, "Excelsior Works, Issac Hewitt, Jr., Rices Landing, PA" 335.00

Crock, three-gallon

    C. W. Braun, Buffalo, NJ, cobalt blue dotted bird perched on branch, minor damage . 750.00

    Macumber & Tannahill, Ithaca, NY, cobalt blue double flower on flowering tree, c1875 .... 495.00

Churn, Union Stoneware Co., Red Wing, Minn., 5 gal, birch leaf mark, $250.

Jug, N. Clark, Jr., Athens, NY, mkd "3," bluish-brown floral dec, gray salt glaze, golden highlights, strap handle, imp label, some bubbling to dec 350.00

Preserve Jar, red clay, cobalt blue stenciled and brushed dec, chips, 8" h 215.00

Water Cooler, unmarked, double ear handles, cobalt blue quill work, "8" with flourish, gray salt glaze, green pebbled highlights, hairline in lip, wooden spigot and turned plug, 20" h......................... 175.00

✦ Stork Club

Standing on one leg and wearing a top hat, the logo for the Stork Club served as a perfect symbol for the popular New York dinner club, which was located at 3 East 53rd St. Almost anything related to the Stork Club is highly prized by collectors today, with unpretentious items such as cologne bottles fetching surprisingly high prices.

Ashtray, ceramic, round, outer edge emb "Stork Club," 4-3/4" d 71.00

Cologne, men's, paper label mkd "Stork Club Men's Cologne" with stork logo, glass bottle, orig box, 4-1/2" h 175.00

Lipstick, enameled case, used, 2-1/2" h 102.50

Menu, paper, dated Oct. 26, 1950.....................................61.00

Necktie, silk, burgundy background, design of top hats and canes, stork logo at bottom, mkd "Phelps-Terkel California" .355.00

Playing cards, Congress, orig box.............................202.50

Ashtray, pottery, mkd "For Fatima Ashes Only," $162.50.

Records, Columbia, "A Night at the Stork Club," Stork Club Orchestra led by Sherman Billingsley, 4-record set 40.00

Sheet music, *Doctor, Lawyer, Indian Chief*, from Paramount Picture's "The Stork Club," 1945, edge wear, corner folds............... 10.50

Souvenir, "Lucky Stork Club Penny," encased 1937 wheat cent .. 15.00

Swizzle stick, white milk glass, gray/black printing, *"Stork Club 3 East 53rd Street, N. Y. C. Sherman Billingsley, Mgr"* stork logo 115.00

Tip tray, plastic, black, white stork logo, 6-1/2" x 5" 305.00

✶ Strawberry Shortcake

Who's that freckle-faced kid in the puffy bonnet? It's Strawberry Shortcake, of course. Strawberry Shortcake memorabilia is both available and affordable, meaning it's perfect flea market material as well as a great collectible for children and adults.

Collectors' Clubs: Strawberry Shortcake Collectors' Club, 1409 72nd St., North Bergen, NJ 07047-3827; Strawberry Shortcake Doll Club, 405 E. Main Cross, Greenville, KY 42345.

Carrying case, strawberry shape 15.00

Charms and jewelry
  Charm, Jelly Bear................50.00
  Charm, Pupcake 50.00
  Charm, Raspberry Tart........50.00
  Charm, Strawberry Shortcake........................50.00
  Charm set, Apricot, Lemon, Custard, some wear 100.00
  Necklace, Strawberry Shortcake, hand over mouth.............25.00
  Ring, Strawberry Shortcake........................20.00

Comforter, Strawberry Shortcake 25.00

Curtain set, Strawberry Shortcake 25.00

Doll
  Angel Cake with Souffle, MIB.................................45.00

Milk glass mug, 1980, 4" h, $5.

Apple Dumplin with Tea Time Turtle, 1st ed, MIB.......... 60.00

Apricot with Hopsalot, MIB................................ 65.00

Butter Cookie with JellyBear, MIB................................ 40.00

Dancin' Strawberry Shortcake, MIB................................ 95.00

Lem & Ada with Sugar Woofer, MIB................................ 90.00

Lime Chiffon with Parfait Parrot, MIB................................ 40.00

Mint Tulip with Marsh Mallard, MIB................................ 80.00

Orange Blossom, MIB 45.00

Sour Grapes with Dregs, MIB................................ 70.00

Strawberry Shortcake, 1st ed, MIB................................ 75.00

Lunch Box, Aladdin, 1980 .. 32.00

Lunch Box, Cheinco, two handles, tin 10.00

Playset
  Lime Chiffon, Dance n' Berry-cise, 1991, MIP 35.00
  Raspberry Tart, Rock n' Berry Roll, 1991, MIP.............. 45.00
  Strawberry Shortcake, Berry Beach Park, 1991, MIP............................. 45.00
  Strawberry Shortcake, Berry Beauty Shop, 1991, MIP............................. 45.00
  Strawberry Shortcake, Berry Sweet Sleepover, 1991, MIP................................. 45.00

✪ String Holders

Here's a useful collectible that's really taken off in the past few years. Probably some of this renewed popularity can be the decorator look which often includes some of these colorful figures. Look for examples that are bright and colorful, free of chips or damage, and include the original hanger.

Apple, chalkware, 7-3/4" h 95.00

Black Man and Woman, chalkware, matched pair 275.00

Boy, top hat and pipe, chalkware, 9" h 125.00

Cast Iron, ball shape, designed to be hung from ceiling 75.00

Cat, ball of twine, white cat, red/orange ball, chalkware, 7" h 75.00

Cat, ball of twine and bow, black cat, white face, green bow, chalkware, 6-1/2" h 100.00

Chef, black, chalkware, 8" h 165.00

Chef, white, chalkware, 7-1/4" h 145.00

Dutch Girl, chalkware, 7" h 100.00

Mammy, holding flowers, chalkware, 6-1/2" h 185.00

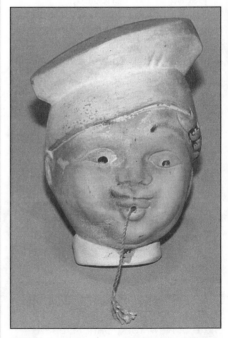

Chef, chalkware, 7-1/8" x 5-1/8", $42.

Pear, chalkware, 7-3/4" h 85.00
Pineapple, face, chalkware,
   7" h 165.00
Senor, chalkware, bright colors,
   8-1/4" h 90.00
Strawberry, chalkware,
   6-1/2" h 115.00

✵ Structo

Want to play cars and trucks? Structo made some great metal toys that have delighted children for years.

Army Cub Jeep, #200, pressed
   steel, orig box 75.00
Cargo truck, steel, #702 .... 75.00
Dump Truck, diecast, painted white,
   red sheet metal body, extension
   frame, dual rubber tires, side
   decals, 12" l, MIB 225.00
Fix It Tow Truck, #910, pressed
   steel, MIB 200.00
Overland freight truck, #704 ... 90.00

❖ Stuffed Toys

Steiff was the originator of stuffed toys. By the middle of the 20th century, stuffed toys of every type, color, and animal were made. Some were sold in stores, others used for carnival prizes. Today many of these animals find their way to flea markets, hoping someone will give them a new home.

Periodical: *Soft Dolls & Animals,* 30595 Eight Mile, Livonia, MI 48152.

Bambi, Gund, c1953 .... 65.00
Beagle, plush, glass eyes,
   9" h 28.00
Cat, sleeping, mohair, 5" l 100.00
Donkey, gray plush body, brown
   glass eyes, brown yarn mane,
   gray tail, wheeled base,
   c1950 .... 110.00
Duck, calico, embroidered wing and
   eye, hand made, c1950 ...... 12.00
Frog, green velvet back, white satin
   underside, c1960 .... 15.00
Monkey, Curious George, plush, yellow knitted sweater, red cap,
   c1975, 36" h 48.00
Pig, pink plush, pink felt corkscrew
   tail, black and white felt
   eyes 22.00
Raccoon, Gund 20.00
Walrus, pink, Gund 25.00

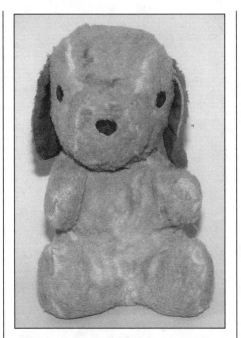

Dog, Gund, early 1960s, 8" h, $15.

✵ Sugar Packets

Here's a sweet topic. Collectors used to find many of their most interesting examples while traveling and enjoying diners and restaurants. Many sugar packets had interesting scenes or even advertising. Today some sugar packets are finding their way to flea markets, especially those that were made in sets. Because the collecting interest is relatively small, expect to find sugar packets ranging from $.25 and upward.

❖ Sugar Shakers

Two sweet categories in a row! Sugar shakers are also called muffineers and were designed to sprinkle powdered sugar, so the holes in their tops tend to be large. When looking for sugar shakers, check to see that the top and bottom started life together. Like salt shakers, tops do wear out, and replacement tops only detract slightly from the value.

Coin Spot, cranberry,
   new lid 150.00
Mt. Washington, opaque white
   ground, flowers dec,
   orig top 350.00

Clear glass with plastic top, Measuring Device Corp., 7", $8.50.

Nippon China, white, gold
   beading 65.00
R. S. Prussia, pearl finish, shaded
   roses and green leaves, scal-
   loped base, red mark 250.00
Spanish Lace
   Blue opalescent, light blue
      color 275.00
   Vaseline opalescent 300.00
Tomato Shape, Mt. Washington
   .... 410.00

❖ Sun Bonnet Babies

These cute little gals did everything in their sun bonnets with the big brims. They washed and ironed and played on all types of material, from Royal Bayreuth china wares to postcards.

Cake Plate, babies washing, Royal
   Bayreuth, 10-1/4" d 400.00
Cup and Saucer, babies fishing,
   Royal Bayreuth 250.00
Plate, babies ironing, Royal
   Bayreuth 110.00
Postcard, Weekly series,
   set of 7 .... 75.00

Postcard, Wash Day, illustrated by B.L. Corbett, J.I. Austin Co., Chicago, $20.

❖ Super Heroes

Shazam! Super heroes have been influencing the minds and checkbooks of collectors for decades. Batman, Green Hornet, Captain Midnight, Superman, etc., and all kinds of villains have come to life from comic books, radio, television and movie tales.

Reference: Rex Miller, *The Investor's Guide to Vintage Character Collectibles,* Krause Publications, 1999.

Periodical: *The Adventures Continue,* 935 Fruitsville Pike, #105, Lancaster, PA 17601.

Collectors' Club: Air Heroes Fan Club, 19205 Seneca Ridge Club, Gaithersburg, MD 20879; Batman TV Series Fan Club, PO Box 107, Venice, CA 90291; Rocketeer Fan Club, 10 Halick Court, East Brunswick, NJ 08816.

For additional listings, see *Warman's Americana & Collectibles* and related topics in this edition.

Balloon Whistle, Captain Marvel, red and yellow, 1941 .... 42.00
Bendy, Green Hornet.............. 50.00
Candy Container, Wonder Woman, 1960s 95.00
Coloring Book, *Six Million Dollar Man,* Saalfield, unused....... 20.00
Comic Book, *The Amazing World of Superman,* 1973, map of Krypton............................... 8.50
Costume, Aquaman, Ben Cooper, 1967 .... 210.00
Cape, Superman, home made, c1975 .... 20.00
Doll, Wonder Woman, MIB 90.00
Hair Brush, Superman, wood, c1942 .... 95.00

Superman model kit, Aurora, 1964, assembled, $50.

Puzzle, Aquaman, action scene, Whitman, 1967 .... 45.00
Rubber Stamp Kit, Buck Rogers, MIB 45.00
Spoon, Green Hornet figure on handle, 1955........................ 20.00
Stamp Album, Captain Midnight, Air Heroes, Skelly Gas............. 80.00
Toy, Spider-Man Helicopter, NRFB............................... 115.00
View-Master Set, Battle of the Mon, Buck Rogers, 1978, MIP 27.50
Wallet, Superman, leather and plastic, made in Hong Kong, 1976 .... 27.50

✪ Surveyor's Equipment

Keep your eyes open while out surveying at your favorite flea market. Perhaps you'll spot an interesting piece of used surveying equipment. With today's electronics and computers, many old rods and transits are being sold. Instruments with original cases are worth more. Time will tell whether collectors like their instruments brightly polished or with the original patina left intact.

For additional listings, see *Warman's Antiques and Collectibles Price Guide.*

Alidade, Keuffel & Esser Co., Model No 5093A, high post plane table, 10" telescope, one beveled edge, strider level, orig case, c1940................................ 360.00

Compass, W. Davenport, Phila., detachable brass sight vanes, worn fitted dovetailed mahogany case with brass fittings......920.00
Level, Worth, 12", plumb, brass top 35.00
Military Level, Berger & Sons, Boston, 9-1/4" l telescope with high precision vial, c1950 ....375.00
Transit, Bostrom, orig box 50.00

❖ Swankyswigs

Collectors never seem to tire of finding these little glasses. Kraft Cheese Spreads were originally packed in these colorful juice glasses as early as the 1930s. Over the years many variations and new patterns have been introduced.

Collectors' Club: Swankyswig's Unlimited, 201 Alvena, Wichita, KS 67203.

Antique, brown coal bucket and clock.....................................4.00
Bands, red and black 3.00
Bustlin' Betsy 2.50
Checkerboard, green, red, and dark blue, 3-1/2" h 25.00
Dots and Circles, black, blue, green, or red 4.50
KiddieCup, pig and bear, blue...2.00
Modern Flowers, dark and light blue, red or yellow
    Cornflower 3.25
    Forget-me-not.......................3.25
    Jonquil 3.00

Clear with blue and red stripes, 3-3/8" h, $5.

Sailboat, red, green, or dark blue, racing or sailing 25.00

❖ Swarovski Crystal

The Swarovski family can trace its glass making tradition back to Austria and 1895. Today they are still identified with high quality crystal. Look for a swan logo on most pieces. The original box and packaging will add to the price.,

Periodicals: *Swan Seekers News,* 9740 Campo Road, Suite 134, Spring Valley, CA 91977; *The Crystal Report,* 1322 N. Barron St., Eaton, OH 45320.

Collectors' Clubs: Swan Seekers, 9740 Campo Road, Suite 134, Spring Valley, CA 91977; Swarovski Collectors Society, 2 Slater Road, Cranston, RI 02920.

Charm, musical clef note, enamel and crystal, 1-3/4" h 15.00

Christmas Ornament, snowflake, 1990 .... 35.00

Figure
  Bear, miniature, 1-1/8" h....200.00
  Butterfly, miniature, 1" h 125.00
  Dachshund, large, 3" l.......125.00
  Elephant, large,
    frosted tail 115.00
  Rabbit, large.....................250.00
  Swan, 1" h 125.00

Fur Clip, gold-tone, crystal stones, sterling silver setting, sgd "Eisenberg Original, Sterling," 2-1/2" h, pr...................... 695.00

Pendant, red and black enameled child's sled, crystal on top, 2" h 35.00

❖ Swizzle Sticks

Here's another example of something people tend to save as a souvenir. Who hasn't tucked one into their pocket? And after awhile, you've got a "collection started" so why not search for some more examples during your next trip to a flea market.

Commemorative, plastic
  Aircal, 5" l 1.00
  Beefeater, clear, red lettering, 7" l...................................... .25

Cunard Lines, 6" l 1.00
Howard Johnson's, 5-1/2" l... 1.00
Lawrence Welk Welkome Inn,
  6" l 1.00
Mirage, Las Vegas, 6" l......... 1.00
Savarin Restaurant, 6" l........ 1.00
Ski Southwest, 4" l................ 1.00
SS Independence, 5-1/2" l.... 1.00
The Royal Lahaina Hotel 1.00
The Sands, Las Vegas 1.00
TWA, 6" l.............................. 1.00

Glass
  Amber, 6" l 3.00
  Figural black caricature on top, set of 6 .... 130.00

Plastic
  Hawaiian girl 1.00
  Mr. Peanut, Everybody Loves A Nut 5.00
  Native mask.......................... 1.00
  Sword .... .25

❖ Syracuse China

Founded in Syracuse, New York, in the mid 1800s, this china company is still in operation. Along with the many dinnerware patterns they've produced over the years, they have also made several patterns for commercial accounts, such as the C & O Railroad. Currently, their restaurant wares are popular with collectors.

Ashtray, Chessie, C & O Railroad, 4" d 95.00
Creamer, Chessie, C & O Railroad 20.00
Cup and Saucer, Adobe Ware, Rodeo Cowboy, stenciled "Adobe Ware, Syracuse China, 5-EE USA," c1950 .... 38.00

Cup/saucer, Wayside, Carefree True China, $1.

Place Setting, Chicken in the Rough, golfing rooster, 4 pc set.......95.00
Plate
  AAA, 50th Anniversary, Oct 4, 1950, mkd "Iroquois China, Syracuse, NY" 55.00
  Boone's Portland Maine Restaurant, 9-1/2" d................... 35.00
  Chessie, C & O Railroad..... 30.00
  Toddle House Restaurant, 12 bakers around border, mkd "Good as the Best," 7-1/4" d 32.00
Serving Platter, Sabella, fish chef logo, green mark, 12" x 9-1/2"
  .... 35.00
Soup Bowl, Anderdsen Restaurant, Pea Soup Characters, Hap-Pea and Pea-Wee, 9" d............. 45.00

❖ Syrup Pitchers

Here's another specialized type of glassware for your table or sideboard. It was designed to hold syrup. Look for metal tops to be in good condition, but some use-related wear is acceptable.

Coin Spot & Swirl, blue opalescent 185.00
Coreopis, red satin................ 350.00
Daisy & Fern, cranberry opalescent 210.00
Hazel Atlas, clear body, plastic top........................... 90.00
Inverted Thumbprint, blue 200.00
Lattice, blue opalescent 335.00

Aunt Jemima, plastic, F.&F. Mold & Die Works, 5-1/2" h, $75.

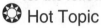

For exciting collecting trends
and newly expanded areas look
for the following symbols:

⊕ Hot Topic

☆ New Warman's Listing

(May have been in another Warman's edition.)

☆ Taxidermy

Many a hunter has returned home with his trophy and had it mounted. What happens to these when the hunter (or his family) no longer wants this prized possession? Many times it's off to the flea market. Look for animals in good condition and well mounted. Any damage would lower the prices listed below.

Bear, black, full bodied 650.00
Crocodile, full bodied 425.00
Eland, mounted head 250.00
Lion, mounted head 400.00
Moose, mounted head 500.00
Tusks, elephant, 4-1/2' long,
    pr 5,000.00
Warthog, mounted head 200.00
Water Buck, mounted head .. 100.00

❖ Taylor, Smith & Taylor

Taylor, Smith & Taylor was started by W. L. Smith, John N. Taylor, W. L. Taylor, Homer J. Taylor, and Joseph G. Lee in Chester, West Virginia in 1899. By 1903, the firm reorganized and the Taylors bought out Lee. By 1906, Smith bought out the Taylors. They continued making dinnerware and tablewares until 1981 when the plant closed. The Smith family sold its interest to Anchor Hocking in 1973.

For additional listings, see *Warman's Americana & Collectibles* and "LuRay" pattern in this edition.

Covered butter, 2-1/2" h, 7-3/4" l, 3-3/4" w, $22.50.

Bowl, Vistosa, cobalt blue,
    8" d 65.00
Butter Dish, cov, Empire 20.00
Cake Plate, Laurel, 10-1/4" d.. 12.00
Casserole, Fairway 20.00
Chop Plate
    Plymouth 20.00
    Vistosa, light green, 11" d... 85.00
    Creamer and Sugar, Vistosa, light
        green 45.00
Cup and Saucer
    Delphian 7.50
    Marvel................................. 6.00
    Vogue 6.50
Dinner Plate
    Empire, 10" d..................... 12.00
    Fairway, 9-1/2" d................. 8.50
    Pebbleford, 10" d............... 10.00
Gravy Boat, Paramount 12.50
Platter, Beverly....................... 12.00
Salad Bowl, Marvel 17.50
Salt and Pepper Shakers, pr,
    Versatile.............................. 6.00
Soup Bowl, Vistosa, deep
    yellow 24.00
Teapot, Vistosa, deep yellow .. 85.00

❖ Teapots

To devoted tea drinkers, the only way to properly brew a cup of tea is in a teapot. Thankfully there are many wonderful examples of teapots available to collectors. From decorative porcelain teapots to whimsical figural teapots, the array is endless.

Periodicals: *Tea Talk,* PO Box 860, Sausalito, CA 94966; *Tea Time*

Gazette, PO Box 40276, St. Paul, MN 55104.

For additional listings, see specific companies, such as "Hall China," in this edition.

English
    Abrams, cosy pot, pitcher shape,
        patents...........................50.00
    Ellgreave, Wood & Sons,
        floral...............................32.00
    Portmeirion, Meridian, speckled
        glaze...............................28.00
    Sadler, floral, raised mark ...30.00
    Wedgwood, jasperware, 6 cup,
        20th C..........................175.00
Figural
    Betty Boop 35.00
    Dickens character, Beswick,
        English...........................85.00
        Doc 35.00
        Lucy................................50.00
        McCormick, black 35.00
    Minnie Mouse 35.00
Japan
    Brown, raised dots (coralene
        type), flowers 14.00
    Brown lustre, sq, 2 cup 12.00
    Buff sharkskin, bisque, orange-
        peel glaze, unmkd 30.00
    Cube shape, hp, c1930.......22.00
    Violets, china, c1950...........18.00
Porcelain
    English, Abrams, cosy pot,
        pitcher shape, patents 50.00

Hall, green, 7" h, $25.

English, Wade, majolica style,
    basket and fruit 40.00
German, Royal Hanover, hand
    painted 75.00

Pottery
Brown, 2 cup, mkd
    "U.S.A." 18.00
Brown Betty, colored rings,
    various sizes $28.00
Frankoma, autumn yellow, warm-
    ing stand 45.00
Granny Ann, Shawnee, mkd
    "U.S.A." 80.00
Granny Woods, English.......40.00
Green glaze, crude,
    unmkd 15.00
Torquay, motto ware, small, Wat-
    combe, English 38.00

❖ Teddy Bears

Everybody has loved one of these
at one time, and many collectors start
by buying one or two that remind
them of a childhood companion.
Whatever the motivation, teddy bears
are still one of the hottest collectibles.
Look for teddy bears that are in good
condition, perhaps showing a sign or
two of a little loving. Some collectors
are more discriminating about condition and know they may pay an extra
premium.

Periodicals: *National Doll & Teddy
Bear Collector*, PO Box 4032, Portland, OR 97208; *Teddy Bear &
Friends*, PO Box 420235, II Commerce Blvd., Palm Coast, FL 32142;
Teddy Bear Review, 170 Fifth Ave.,
12th Floor, New York, NY 10010.

Collectors' Clubs: Good Bears of
the World, PO Box 13097, Toledo,
OH 43613; My Favorite Bear: Collectors Club for Classic Winnie the
Pooh, 468 W Alpine #10, Upland, CA
91786; Teddy Bear Boosters Club,
19750 SW Peavine Mountain Road,
McMinnville, OR 97128.

For additional listings, see *Warman's
Antiques and Collectibles Price
Guide,* as well as Steiff and other cat-
egories in this edition.

Bear Cub, 6-1/2" h, shell base,
    Trench Art.......................... 85.00

Carnival-type, 28" h, $15.

Koala Me, store display,
    10" h 75.00
Musical, Swiss, 16" h,
    mohair 350.00
Petsey, Steiff, blond, button 95.00
Teddy Ruxpin, orig box, 2 tapes,
    orig books 100.00
This Bear, Possum Trot, brown
    plush, orig tags 75.00
Yes-No Bear, Schuco, mohair,
    20" h, 1950s 1,200.00
Westinghouse, adv, 1983........ 15.00

✴ Telephone Cards

Here's a new collecting area that is
just starting to catch on in American
flea markets. It's been all the rage in
Europe for years. Telephone cards
are PVC cards about the size and
shape of traditional credit cards. They
are made with an interesting design,
sometimes in series and often in a
limited number.

American Innovations Ltd.,
    1997 .... 5.00

**Sweet Sue premium phone card,
3-31-97 expiration date, 2-1/8" x
3-3/8", $1.**

Atlanta Olympic Games, 1996,
    instructions in Russian........ 10.00
Bell Cab Taxi Co., Los Angeles,
    1996.................................... 15.00
Kurier, Russian newspaper, instruc-
    tions in Russian, 1997 .... 10.00
Lou Gehrig, 1994 .... 15.00
Union Bail Bond Co., Los Angeles,
    1997.................................... 10.00
Wizard of Oz
    Ruby Slippers 7.50
    Scarecrow.......................... 12.50
    Tin Man.............................. 10.00
Whitney Houston..................... 9.00

❖ Telephones & Related

Talk, talk, talk. That's what we've
been doing since this wonderful
invention caught on with our ancestors. As technology changes, some
folks are starting to notice that perhaps telephones are something to
collect. Add to that some interesting
ephemera and you've got a great collecting area.

Collectors' Clubs: Antique Tele-
phone Collectors Association, PO
Box 94, Abilene, KS 67410; Mini-
Phone Exchange, 5412 Tilden Road,
Bladensburg, MD 20710; Telephone
Collectors International, 19 N. Cherry
Drive, Oswego, IL 60543.

Bank, Ertl, Ford Model T Runabout,
    American Telephone & Telegraph
    Co. adv 35.00

Western Electric, rotary dial, 1970s, $24.

Calendar, Illinois Bell Telephone, 1947, wallet size, adv on back 10.00

Candy Container, glass, black plastic receiver, red woven cord, mkd "J. H. Millstein Co., Jeannette, Pa.," orig bottom cardboard with advertising, c1945, minor chip 45.00

Mouthpiece, Whispering Glass Mouthpiece, dated 1916 ... 175.00

Postcard, Bell Telephone Co. Building, Kansas City, MO, 1924 .... 5.00

Poster, evolution since 1876, 30 illus, 20" x 24", rolled 90.00

Salt and Pepper Shakers, pink wall telephone, orig box mkd "Party Line," c1950 .... 25.00

Sign

New York Telephone Co., 8" d, porcelain, trademark bell 150.00

United Utilities System, Public Telephone, porcelain, 2-sided, L-shape, flange wall mount 200.00

Telephone

Candlestick, brass, Western Electric 75.00

Candlestick, dial, brass, separate ringer 300.00

Co-pay, gray, box with key 95.00

Desk, black, brass dial, reconditioned 95.00

Figural, '57 Chevy, red, push-button, modular plugs, unused 37.50

Figural, Mickey Mouse, 1978, Western Electric 150.00

Figural, Pizza Inn, cartoon figure of mustache-wearing pizza tosser, wearing red and black outfit, white base, company name on front in red, touch-tone phone, Taiwan, late 1970s, 10" h 25.00

Figural, Snoopy, push button dial 75.00

Ship, US Navy, World War II vintage, brass bells on top, mounted on mahogany slab with anchor brass plate attached above phone, restored, 20" x 11" 1,175.00

Wall, single box, Kellogg, refinished 200.00

Wall single box, Kellogg, oak case, mouth base mkd "Kellogg," 25-1/2" l 200.00

Wall, single box, Western Electric 190.00

Telephone Almanac

1940, Bell System Telephone Subscribers, American Telephone & Telegraph 5.00

1959, Michigan Bell Telephone Co., slight discoloration 2.50

Telephone Book

Beloit, WI, 1954 .... 5.00

Villisca, Iowa, 1962 .... 17.50

Washington, D.C. March, 1948, Yellow Pages Directory, slight use 55.00

❖ Television Characters and Personalities

"Now on with the show" was Ed Sullivan's promise to the audience as folks waited to be entertained. Today's flea markets are a great place to find vintage items relating to early television and the many characters who became stars.

Reference: Rex Miller, *The Investor's Guide to Vintage Character Collectibles,* Krause Publications, 1999, plus many others on specific stars and character memorabilia.

Periodicals: *Big Reel,* PO Box 1050, Dubuque, IA 52004; *Television Chronicles,* 10061 Riverside Drive, #171, North Hollywood, CA 91602; *The TV Collector,* PO Box 1088, Easton, MA 02334.

For additional listings, see *Warman's Americana & Collectibles,* plus other categories in this edition.

Activity Book, Soupy Sales, 8-1/4" x 11", photo of Soupy on cover, 64 b&w pages, some color on text, games and art, Treasure Books, 1965 Soupy Sales 12.00

Activity Box Kit, Captain Kangaroo, 1956, shoe-box type 60.00

Activity Set, Captain Kangaroo, shoe box size, c1956, unused 75.00

Advertisement, Red Skelton Pledge of Allegiance, 1969 .... 20.00

Autograph

Check, Elizabeth Montgomery, Sept. 1974, personal check to Pacific Telephone 150.00

Photograph sgd by cast

Gilligan's Island 275.00

Lost in Space 370.00

Bank, Romper Room, Do-Bee, Hasbro 55.00

Big Little Book, *Lassie Adventure in Alaska,* Whitman, 1967 .... 15.00

Book

I Spy, Message From Moscow, Whitman, Robert Culp and Bill Cosby on cover, hardcover, 1966 .... 20.00

TV's Top Ten Shows and Their Stars, Peggy Herz, Scholastic Book Service, 1976, paperback 8.00

Starsky & Hutch Detective Game, Milton Bradley, $15.

You're Never Too Young,
Lawrence Welk,
autographed...................15.00

Card Game, Beverly Hillbillies,
Milton Bradley, complete 24.00

Card Set
Dukes of Hazzard, 1983......24.00
Gomer Pyle, b&w photos,
1960................................90.00

Chalk, 2-3/4" x 3-1/2" x 1",
features 3 Chipmunks on front,
used pieces of chalk, Creston
Crayon & Toy Co., c1980
....12.00

Cigar Band, Hawaii Five-O, full color
....2.50

Colorforms, Daniel Boone, Fess
Parker, 1964, unused 85.00

Coloring Book, unused
Beverly Hillbillies, Whitman,
1963................................24.00
Gilligan's Island, Whitman,
1965...............................135.00
Ozzie's Girls, Saalfield Publish-
ing, copyright 1973 Filmways
Television Corp 40.00

Game
Cookbook, *Buffy's Cookbook,* Jody
Cameron, Family Affair, Buffy roll-
ing out dough illus on glossy color
cover, Berkeley Medallion .. 14.00
Comic Book, *I Love Lucy,* Dell, #3,
1954 .... 135.00
Dog Training Kit, Lassie Trick
Trainer, Mousley, 1956, orig train-
ing devices, picture album, photo
cards of Lassie and trainer Rudd
Weatherwax, orig box....... 275.00

Doll
Capt. Kangaroo, 21", Baby Barry
Toys, c1965, orig box 385.00
Cher, 12" h, posable, plastic and
vinyl, Mego, orig box,
1970s 50.00
Farrah Fawcett, 1977,
MIB................................25.00
Honey West, 12" h, posable
plastic, Gilbert, 1965,
orig box 370.00
I Dream of Jeannie, Libby Major-
ette Doll Co., Barbara Eden,
c1966, 18" h,
orig box 2,437.00

Man from U.N.C.L.E., Gilbert,
1965, orig box Ilya
Kuryakin 385.00
Napoleon Solo 385.00
M.C. Hammer, boom box,
MIB................................. 20.00
Oscar Goldman, MIB.......... 25.00
Shaun Cassidy, from Hardy Boys,
MIB................................. 20.00
Six Million Dollar Man, 1973,
MIB................................. 35.00
Toni Tennille, 1977, MIB 25.00
Fan Club Pack, Richard Diamond,
Private Detective, David Janssen,
c1959.............................. 130.00

Game
Adventures of Lassie, Lisbeth
Whiting Co., 1955........... 50.00
Down You Go, Selchow & Righter
Co., copyright 1954........ 18.00
Flying Nun, Milton Bradley,
1968, sealed................. 200.00
F Troop, Ideal, 1965 .... 165.00
Have Gun Will Travel, Parker
Bros., 1959..................... 75.00
Howdy Doody 75.00
Ironside Game, Ideal,
1967 .... 185.00
Lost in Space.................... 180.00
Mister Ed, Parker Brothers, copy-
right 1962, missing dice and
markers 45.00
Mod Squad, Remco,
1968 .... 200.00
Name That Tune................. 25.00
NBC Peacock, Selchow &
Righter, 1966, sealed ... 200.00
Rin-Tin-Tin, Transogram,
1955 .... 40.00
Road Runner, Milton Bradley,
Warner Bros., 1968 .... 65.00
Route 66, Transogram, travel
type, 1962 .... 225.00
Twelve O'Clock High, Milton Bradley, 1965, deck of 40 oversized playing cards....... 100.00
Glass, Dick Van Dyke Show,
7-1/2" h, white design, studio
spotlight shows title on center
of light, derby on top, cane
resting on spotlight's pole,
1960s 135.00

Gum Card, complete 55 card set
Land of the Giants, 1968 ..220.00
Man from U.N.C.L.E., Topps,
1965, orig box...............550.00
Gum Card Box, McHale's Navy,
Fleer, 1965, illus pop-open
diecut lid 115.00

Gum Card Wrapper
Beverly Hillbillies, Topps,
1963 ....85.00
Hogan's Heroes, Fleer,
1965 .... 100.00

Halloween Costume
Flipper, cloth, black velvet trim,
crack in mask 40.00
Fred Flintstone, cloth, Ben Cooper, orig box...................40.00
Howard the Duck, Collegeville,
1986, orig box................45.00
Lambchop, Shari Lewis, Halco,
1961, orig box................35.00
The Fonz, Happy Days, Ben Coo-
per, 1976, orig box..........30.00
Jewelry, Captain Video, secret seal
ring, c1950 .... 150.00
Kerchief, Howdy Doody, 18" sq, red,
blue, green and orange, Howdy at
the rodeo, 1950s................65.00
Kit, M*A*S*H Make Your Own Dog
Tag, 2 steel chains, Tristar, 1981,
unused 18.00
Lamp, figural, sitting Howdy
Doody 175.00

Lunch Box
Charlie's Angels, Aladdin, metal,
6-1/2" h thermos 72.00
Gunsmoke, Aladdin, 1959, metal
box............................... 150.00
Munsters, 1965, lunch box and
thermos, various scenes and
portraits 400.00
S.W.A.T., plastic, Thermos, King
Seeley, 1975, blue, multicolored images, thermos
missing 95.00

Magazine,
Confidential, Aug. 1966, Sammy
Davis cover......................8.00
Life
Oct. 30, 1970, Dick Cavett 7.00
March 26, 1971, Walter Cronk-
ite cover........................8.00

May 7, 1971, Germaine Greer
cover, Howdy Doody
article 8.00

Dec. 10, 1971, Cybil Shephard
cover, Today Show
article 6.00

Look

Nov. 11, 1958, Ozzie & Harriet
cover..........................12.00

March 23, 1971, Marcus Welby
cover..........................10.00

Post, Dec. 4, 1965, Bonzana
cover..........................15.00

TV Guide

April 3, 1953, Lucille Ball's
newborn baby 400.00

Feb. 3, 1973, Bill Cosby....7.50

July 5, 1975, Tony Orlando &
Dawn 6.50

Aug. 6, 1981, Archie Bunker,
O'Conner 6.00

Jan. 9, 1982, Michael
Landon..........................7.00

TV Junior, March 1959 ....20.00

TV Mirror, 1963, March, Vince
Edwards..........................4.00

TV Star Parade, 1973, July,
Lawrence Welk cover, Rock
Hudson article 4.00

Medic Set, M*A*S*H, Ja-Ru, copy-
right 1981, 20th Century Fox Film
Corp, 6" x 10" blister card,
MOC 18.00

Mirror, Miss Piggy, Sigma, glazed
ceramic, easel back and hook for
hanging, early 1980s 80.00

Mug, 3-1/2" h, Dennis the Menace,
molded plastic, painted, early
1950s 15.00

Night-Light, Flintstones, Fred and
Barney..............................25.00

Nodder, Dr. Kildare, Lego,
7" h, ceramic, Richard
Chamberlain....................125.00

Paint Set

Flipper Stardust, Hasbro1966,
missing 1 picture and vial of
paint 50.00

Flying Nun, Hasbro, 1967,
sealed 140.00

Winky Dink, licensed by CBS,
16" x 12", c1950, MIB ...100.00

Photograph, Robert Redford in "
Jeremiah Johnson," ABC Sunday

Night Movie, Dec 19,
1976 .... 10.00

Pinback Button, Bullwinkle for President, red, white, and blue flag,
1972 copyright, 2-1/4" d 40.00

Planter, 2-3/4" x 6-1/4" x 4-1/2" h,
glazed ceramic, Lawrence Welk,
lime green, flared accordion
design, name in relief on 1 side,
musical notes and bubbles on
reverse, 1950s................... 48.00

Play Suit, Rifleman, Play-Master,
1959, mint condition, orig photo
box.................................. 250.00

Poster Put-Ons, Charlie's Angels,
self-adhesive picture posters, Bi-
Rite Enterprises, Chicago, IL,
1977, MIP 24.00

Premium

Lassie, Giant Picture Premium,
Best-in-Children's Books,
1961 ....110.00

Sgt. Preston, framed color portrait, Quaker Oats,
1950 .... 200.00

Prototype Toy, Man from U.N.C.L.E.

Projector Gun, Marx, 1965, battery-operated film projector in
shape of gun 1,560.00

Shooting Arcade, Marx, 1966,
hand-lettered box 650.00

Puppet, hand

Captain Kangaroo 3.00

Cookie Monster, Sesame
Street............................ 4.00

Push Puppet

Huckleberry Hound............. 45.00

Pebbles 50.00

Puzzle

Ben Casey, 13-1/2" x 24", Milton
Bradley, 1962 .... 25.00

Family Affair, Whitman, 10 pcs,
Uncle Bill sitting in chair with
cast and sling, Buffy and Jody
attending, 1970 .... 25.00

Happy Days, Fonz.............. 15.00

Howdy Doody 25.00

Voyage to the Bottom of the Sea,
Milton Bradley, 1964, 4 tray
puzzles, orig box 450.00

Record

Addams Family, 12-1/4" sq orig
cardboard slip case, 33-1/3

RPM record with 6 TV music
themes, RCA Victor label,
1965 ....25.00

Get Smart, United Artists, Don
Adams on cover, LP, orig
jacket, 1960s 25.00

Howdy Doody and the Air-O-Doodle, RCA, Little Nipper, 2 yellow 78 RPM records, foldout
paper jacket, 6-pg story book
about Air-O-Doodle,
1950s...........................45.00

Theme from Dr. Kildare, MGM
Studios, 45 RPM,
1960s...........................10.00

Robot, Lost in Space, 12" h, plastic,
Remco, 1966, metallic blue body,
red arms, near mint condition,
orig box 850.00

Shampoo Bottle, Farrah Fawcett,
Faberge, 1977, 7" h,
plastic..............................170.00

Slide Show, Mr. Ed Give-A-Show,
Kenner, 1962 ....15.00

Thermos, Beverly Hillbillies,
6-1/2" h, litho metal, red plastic
cap, full-color scene, Aladdin,
c1962 ....75.00

Towel, Queen for a Day, contestant
dressing-room type, NBC,
c1956 ....140.00

Toy

Flying Nun, Ray Plastic Inc.,
copyright 1970 Screen Gems,
Inc., color photo of Sally Fields,
plastic figure, launching unit,
some wear to orig box 50.00

Starsky & Hutch, diecast car, 3" l,
metal and plastic,
1970s.............................35.00

T-shirt, Josie & the Pussycats,
cotton 17.00

TV Kit, Winky Dink & You, Super
Magic TV Kit, Standard Toycraft,
1968................................235.00

View Master Reel, orig envelope,
16-pg illus story booklet
Lost in Space, Sawyers,
1967 ....165.00

Star Trek, GAF, 1969 .... 110.00

Wallet, CHiPS, orig display card,
MGM, MOC........................18.00

Waste Can, Laugh-In, 13" h, oval,
litho metal, color photos on 1
side, "Sock It to Me" slogan on
reverse, 1968....................42.00

Whistle, Dragnet 15.00

Wristwatch

Howdy Doody, 1971,
orig band 95.00
Tammy, half face is blue, other is
white, blue band,
1960s 125.00

Yo-Yo, 2-1/4" d, Official Pee Wee
Herman Brand, white plastic, colorful image of Pee Wee, name in
different colors, image repeated
on both sides, late 1980s ... 12.00

❖ Television Sets

Used television sets are something that occasionally show up at
flea markets. Often their size and
bulk finds them still sitting on the
truck or in the back of a booth. Before
plugging in a vintage television set,
have someone knowledgeable check
over the circuits and old tubes.

Collectors' Clubs: Antique Wireless
Association, 59 Main St., Holcomb,
NY 14469-9336; Mid-Atlantic Radio
Club, PO Box 67, Upperco, MD
21155.

GE, portable, cream colored plastic
case, black and white, working
condition, one knob
chipped............................ 25.00
Hallicrafters, T-54, c1950...... 250.00
Philco, reconditioned, floor
model 325.00
Pilot, TV-37, magnifier
model 120.00
RCA, CT-100, first RCA
color set........................... 550.00
Zenith, portable, black plastic case,
black and white, working
condition........................... 35.00

❖ Temple, Shirley

Her smile and curly hair were her
trademarks as she stole the hearts of
movie goers in the 1940s. Her
mother carefully licensed items with
her image, from dolls to glassware,
jewelry and even soap. More
recently, several of the limited edition
companies have revived interest in
Shirley Temple by creating new collectibles with vintage images.

Book, *Story of Shirley Temple,*
1934 .... 28.00
Doll, Ideal
1982
Captain January 60.00
Heidi Stowaway 60.00
1984
36" h, vinyl, MIB................ 650.00
Doll Dress, 1930s, for 18" or 20" doll,
orig tags.............................. 90.00
Figure, limited edition, Nostalgia
Collectibles, made in Japan
Curly Top 60.00
Standup and Cheer 60.00
Movie Book, *The Little Colonel,*
Saalfield, 4-3/4" x 5-1/4", hard
cover, black and white movie
scenes, full color front cover
.... 40.00

**Doll, Ideal, 1954, sleep eyes, 18" h,
$280.**

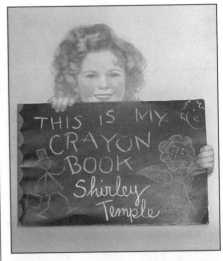

This Is My Crayon Book, **Authorized Edition, The Saalfield Publishing Co., 1935, 13" x 13", $25.**

Plate, limited edition, Nostalgia
Collectibles, made in Japan
Baby Take A Bow................ 65.00
Standup and Cheer............. 65.00
Pocket Mirror, 1937 Fox Film
Corp. 35.00
Scrapbook, Saalfield #1722, copy-
right 1936, full color front and
back covers, Shirley wearing pink
dress, white bonnet, spiral
binding, used 40.00
Sheet Music, *Goodnight My Love,*
name written in pencil on
front..................................... 21.00

❖ Tennis
Collectibles

Tennis anyone? Here's another
sport where the collectibles are starting
to command more and more notice.
Look for ephemera and equipment with
endorsements by famous players.

Dexterity Puzzle, Tennis-O-Rama,
plastic and paper 4.00
Figure
Minnie Mouse playing tennis,
copyright "Walt Disney Productions," orig Disneyland paper
price sticker, 1970s......... 40.00
Snoopy, porcelain,
orig box............................ 20.00

J.C. Higgins tennis balls, Sears, Roebuck and Co., $12.50.

Magazine, *Sports Illustrated,*
    July 15, 1974, Connors and
    Evert 10.00
Needle Folder, Broadway French
    Cleaners & Dyers, Detroit, illus of
    young girl holding tennis
    racket 10.00
Program, United States Lawn Tennis
    Championships, West Side Ten-
    nis Club, Forest Hills, NY, Sept,
    1947 .... 42.00
Tennis Balls
    Dunlop, Mr. Peanut 9.00
    Dunlop, Vinnie Richards......25.00
    MacGregor, red and white plaid
        can 25.00
    Spaulding, Pancho Gonzales,
        blue label.........................20.00
    Wilson, Jack Kramer illus, red and
        white...............................55.00

Tennis Racket
    Knickerbocker, wood 45.00
    Spaulding, needs
        restringing 10.00
Wilson Sporting Goods, Maureen
    Connolly, full color portrait on
    handle, 1950s..................... 25.00

❖ Thermometers

We've got Galileo to thank for the first practical thermometer. There have certainly been a few advances since that 1593 start. One of the most collectible types of thermometers are those used as advertising. Look for examples that are free of rust or damage and have working mercury or other temperature-telling liquids.

Collectors' Club: Thermometer Collectors Club of America, 6130 Rampart Drive, Carmichael, CA 96508.

Reproduction Alert.

For additional information, see *Warman's Americana & Collectibles.*

American Alcohol, 26-1/2" h, 19-1/2"
    w, tin, inside of arrow points at
    words "American Denatured
    Alcohol," some soiling, some
    chipping 80.00
Auto King, bottle of Auto King Motor
    Oil attached to wooden thermom-
    eter, 21" h, slight alligator finish to
    back 250.00
Dayton Coal Coke Fuel Oil Co.,
    wooden, 15" x 6".............. 120.00
Gulf Gas, 13" l, 1950s............. 40.00
Johnson Service Co., Milwaukee, WI,
    12-1/2" h, some wear.......... 145.00
Lumber Co., 13" l, 1950s 35.00
Penn Fishing Tackle Mfg Co.,
    15" x 6", 1950s 100.00
Quickie, 1950........................ 145.00

**For exciting collecting trends
and newly expanded areas look
for the following symbols:**

❂ Hot Topic

★ New Warman's Listing

(May have been in another Warman's edition.)

Winston cigarettes, tin, 13-1/2" x 6", $55.

Standard Oil, Floyd Zeigler, Agent,
    Sarasota, Florida, metal frame,
    metal easel back.................32.00
Taylor Permacolor, wooden,
    15" x 6" 120.00
Tru-Ade, 1950 ....155.00
Vojta Motors, SD, girl in red dress on
    telephone, 1941 ....75.00

❖ Thimbles

Thimble, thimble, who's got the thimble? Collectors do! And, they enjoy their tiny treasures. Finding thimbles at flea markets is probably easier than it sounds since there are so many different kinds of thimbles—advertising, commemorative, political, porcelain, and all types of metal thimbles.

Periodical: *Thimbletter,* 93 Walnut Hill Road, Newton Highlands, MA 02161.

Collectors' Clubs: The Thimble Guild, PO Box 381807, Duncanville, TX 75138; Thimble Collectors International, 8289 Northgate Drive, Rome, NY 13440.

Aluminum, plain	4.00

Commemorative
California, gold-tone, white background with bear, 3/4" l	10.00
Mackinaw Bridge, copper-tone, showing bridge	10.00
New York, pink shield with Statue of Liberty, New York, The Empire State	10.00
North Carolina, porcelain, Cardinal and "N. C."	5.00
Virginia Beach, silver-tone, seagull	10.00

Figural, ceramic, 2-1/4" h
Donald Duck	15.00
Goofy	15.00
Minnie Mouse	17.50
Miniature, Arcadia, gold thimble, gold thread	30.00

Porcelain
Anniversary, violet flower, gold band, mkd "Fine Bone China, Ashleydale, England"	8.00

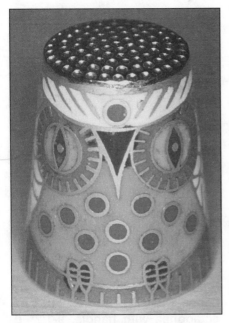

Owl, brass and enamel, $14.

Bird	5.50
Blue and red flowers, mkd "Avon"	6.00
Orange flowers	5.00
Pink and blue flowers	6.00
Silver, plain, 5/8" l	5.00

★ Ticket Stubs

Here's another collectible that most of us have tucked in a drawer and probably have almost forgotten. However, there are dedicated collectors of tickets for all kinds of events, from charities to sporting events to theatrical shows, expositions, fairs, etc. Most tickets are small in size and easy to display in an album, making them a compact type of collectible.

Children's Day, March 31, 1894, *San Francisco Chronicle,* coupons attached, unused	135.00

Railroad
PA RR	.50
Pitt & Lake Erie, passenger, 1918	2.00
Rose Bowl, 1952	55.00
Ship, *Italia Societa Di Navigazione Marco Polo,* from Valparaiso to La Guaira	6.00

World's Fair
Panama-Pacific International Exposition, tan and brown, Nov 2, 1915, used	45.00
Souvenir of the California Midwinter International Exposition, Souvenir San Francisco Day, July 4, 1894, four fair buildings on back, 4-3/4" x 3-1/2"	85.00

❖ Tiffany Studios

Louis Comfort Tiffany was an interesting man. While he was a patron of arts and crafts, he was also a skilled craftsman. His work in many mediums, but primarily glass, earned him acclaim for the beautiful things he created or designed.

Reproduction Alert.

For additional listings, see *Warman's Antiques and Collectibles Price Guide* and *Warman's Glass.*

Beaker, sterling silver, reeded foot, flared rim, 3-3/4" h	100.00
Bowl, squared dimpled form, transparent aquamarine, foot inscribed "L. C. Tiffany Favrile," 4-1/4" d, 2-1/2" h, price for pair	490.00
Calling Card Receiver, bronze, mkd "Tiffany Studios"	75.00
Candlestick, heavy walled amber glass stick, 10 prominent swirled ribs, fine gold luster, inscribed "L. C. T.," labeled, 6-3/4" h	400.00

Desk Accessories, Zodiac pattern, bronze
Calendar Holder	95.00
Pen Brush	175.00
Rocker Blotter	120.00
Paper Rack, bronze, Chinese pattern, dark patina, some green wash in pattern recesses, three-tier, imp "Tiffany Studios New York 1756," some metal corrosion	260.00
Serving Fork, sterling silver, Wave Edge pattern	150.00
Tile, pressed molded irid blue glass, stylized blossom motif, imp "Patent Applied For," small chip, 4" sq	375.00

Vase
Elongated bulbous body, 10 prominent ribs below flattened rim, gold irid, inscribed "L. C. Tiffany Favrile," and number, 7-1/4" h	525.00
Flared conical irid gold glass insert, ribbed bronze pedestal foot, imp "Louis C. Tiffany Furnaces, Inc., 160," 15" h	865.00
Oval body, teal blue, lined in opal white glass, smooth matte lustrous surface, inscribed "L. C. Tiffany Favrile 1753E," 5-3/4" h	750.00

❖ Tiffin Glass

Glass was made in Tiffin, Ohio, by A. J. Beatty & Sons, starting about 1888. The factory became part of the United States Glass conglomerate and continued to provide high quality glassware. The company closed in 1980, ending a long tradition that included many types of glassware as well as many brilliant colors.

Collectors' Club: Tiffin Glass Collectors' Club, PO Box 554, Tiffin, OH 44883.

Bud Vase
  Cherokee Rose, 6" h 38.00
  Fuschia, 10" h 45.00
Champagne
  Charlton...............................22.00
  Mystic..................................26.00
  Rosalind 20.00
Cocktail, Cherokee Rose........ 16.00
Cordial
  June Night 40.00
  Rambling Rose....................28.00
Goblet
  Cordelia, crystal 22.00
  Mystic..................................28.00
  Thistle..................................22.00
Parfait, Mystic......................... 27.00

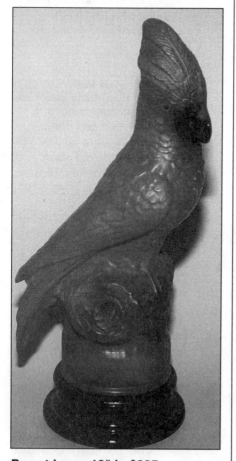

Parrot lamp, 13" h, $325.

Sherbet, Cordelia, crystal,
  high type 15.00
Tumbler
  Rambling Rose, flat 13.00
  Rosalind, ftd 20.00
Vase, black satin, red poppies dec,
  #16255 .... 125.00
Wine
  Rosalind 25.00
  Thistle................................. 17.00

❖ Tiles

Tiles have been used as a functional design element for decades. Collectors have also recognized the beauty of tiles and search them out.

American Encaustic Tiling Co.,
  white, black design of horseman
  riding through brush,
  4-1/4" sq 48.00
Batchelder, imp bird design, blue
  ground, imp mark, 6" sq, price for
  pair 175.00
California Art, landscape, tan and
  green, 5-3/4" sq 65.00
Marblehead, blue and white ships,
  4-5/8" sq, price for pair 125.00
Minton Hollins & Co., urn and floral
  relief, green ground, 6" sq .. 48.00
Mosaic Tile Co., Delft windmill, blue
  and white, framed, 8" sq..... 55.00
U. S. Encaustic Tile Works, flowered
  wreath, light green, 6" sq.... 20.00

Delft, running dog, 5-1/8" sq, $10.50.

❖ Tins

One of the most decorative aspects of collecting vintage advertising is to collect tins. They were designed to catch the consumer's eye with interesting graphics and/or colors. Today collectors seek them out for many of the same reasons.

For additional listings, see *Warman's Antiques and Collectibles Price Guide* and *Warman's Americana & Collectibles.*

Airflost Talcum, pictures baby and
  claw foot tub........................95.00
Bagdade Coffee, Maximum Products Co, Vancouver, Canada, 5 lb,
  slip cover, same image both
  sides, wrong lid, 8-3/4" h 70.00
Buster Popcorn, 10 lb, 9-1/2" h,
  6-1/2" w..............................75.00
Canco Candy, 5 lb tin, Piggies
  dec 235.00
Campfire Marshmallows, Campfire
  Kitchens, 7-1/4" d, 2" h 70.00
Colman's, no graphics...............7.00
Comfort Powder Talcum, pictures
  nurse and baby, c1910 .....600.00
Dr. Chevallier's Red Spruce Gum
  Paste, Canadian, English and
  French texts, Indian Chief in
  center, some scattered edge
  wear..................................50.00

Hiawatha's Wedding Journey, Loose-Wiles Biscuit Co., 2 lb 8 oz, octagonal, with handle, 9-1/2" d, $125.

El-Be, no graphics 7.00

Evening In Paris, 5" h, round .. 10.00

French's, graphics 9.00

Glover's Liver Pill Dog Medicine, 2" w, 3-1/8" l, 1/2" h, tin litho, hinged lid, illus dog and text on cov 90.00

Italina Antacid, 1930s, colorful 30.00

Johnson & Johnson Baby Talc 60.00

Libbey's Miniature Asparagus 95.00

Log Cabin Syrup 60.00

Mammy Salted Peanuts, pictures Mammy, some wear 2,500.00

Monarch Cocoa, 3" h 50.00

Mount Cross Coffee, J. S. Brown Mercantile Co., 3 lb, 7-1/2" h 70.00

National Biscuit 15.00

Old Master Coffee, 9-1/4" h, 5-1/2" d, 3 lb, snap lid, few dents 75.00

Omar Cigarettes 15.00

O-So-Easy Mop, 1920s 50.00

Plee-zing, no graphics 7.00

Rose Kist Popcorn 48.00

Runkle's Cocoa, 2" h 15.00

Shur-Fine, no graphics 7.00

Sudan Spice, graphics 9.00

B&L Brand Oysters, Bivalve Oyster Packing Co., Bivalve, Md., 7-1/2" h, 6-5/8" d, $30.

Towle's Log Cabin Syrup, 7" h, 4" w, 6" d, one side with illus of young girl in doorway holding tin ... 70.00

Twas the Night Before Christmas, candy, art deco style 245.00

Widlar's Spice, no graphics 7.00

❖ Tinware

As a metal, tinware was inexpensive, durable, and easy to work with for early craftsmen. Today we regard some of those early wares with high esteem. Decorated tinware is also known as Tole or Toleware.

Candle Box, cylindrical, hanging, some battering, 14-1/2" h 225.00

Candle Mold
   Four tubes, half mold, light rust, 5-1/4" h 325.00
   Eight tubes, curved feet, ear handle, 11-1/4" h 345.00

Canister, red, green, and yellow floral dec, white band, orig alligatored dark brown japanning 420.00

Candle mold, round, 12 tubes, some battering, old split in base, 12" h plus ring, $495.

Cheese Sieve, heart shape, resoldered hanging ring, 6" h 360.00

Egg Cooker, 10-1/2" h 55.00

Foot Warmer, punched diamonds and circles, mortised hardwood case, turned corner posts, 8-1/2" l 150.00

Lantern, mkd "Dietz Scout," 7-5/8" h 90.00

Sugar Canister, dark brown japanning, silver leaf and scroll stencil design around "Sugar," snap closure, 9-3/4" x 8-3/4" 175.00

Wall Pocket, punched heart design, old decoration, 7-3/4" h 250.00

❖ Tip Trays

Tip trays are small colorful trays left on a table so that a patron could leave a tip for the wait staff. Their colorful lithographed decorations make them an interesting collectible. Because these little beauties saw a lot of use, carried coins, etc., expect to find signs of wear, perhaps some denting.

Reproduction Alert.

Boston Herald, vintage news boy running with paper exclaiming "The Boston Herald New England's Greatest Newspaper," orange perimeter ring, H. D. Beach Co. Litho, 3-1/2" d 140.00

"Dowagiac Grain Drills, The Standard of Excellence, Dowagiac Drills and Seeders are the Leaders," wear, 4-1/4" d, $28.

Columbus Brewing Co., image of Christopher Columbus, Chas. W. Shonk Co. litho, some scratching, 4-1/4" d 70.00

Evinrude, titled "On a Crest of the Wave," woman in boat, vintage outboard motor, 4" d 155.00

Gypsy Hosier, center with trademark sultry gypsy girl dancing, camp scene in background, 6" d 120.00

Helvetia, 4" d 25.00

Indianapolis Brewing Co., titled "The World's Standard of Perfection," shows unopened bottle of Gold Medal Beer, minor scratching and soiling, 5-1/4" d................... 50.00

Monticello Whiskey, colonial scene in front of Monticello, Chas. W. Shonk Co., litho, light overall crazing and soiling, 4-1/2" h, 6-1/4" l 50.00

National Cigar Stand, sensuous woman pulling petals off daisy, 6" d 120.00

Stollwerck, trademark for Stollwerck Gold Brand chocolate and cocoa, Kaufmann & Strass & Co. litho, some staining, 5" d 45.00

Wrigley's Soap, black cat sitting on pile of soap, Chas W. Shonk Co., litho, small dent, 3-1/2" d............................. 145.00

Yuengling's Beer, young lady with big hat, rim wear, 4-1/4" d............................. 130.00

✫ Titanic Collectibles

There are two types of Titanic Collectibles. The oldest are those that were generated when the great ship was built and first launched. The public then was eager for news about this disaster just as we would be today. There were newspaper reports, books written, and other memorabilia. The second classification of Titanic memorabilia relates to the recent movie and its popularity.

Collectors' Clubs: Titanic Historical Society, 208 Main Street, Indian Orchard, MA 01151; Titanic International, Inc., PO Box 7007, Freehold, NJ 07728-7007.

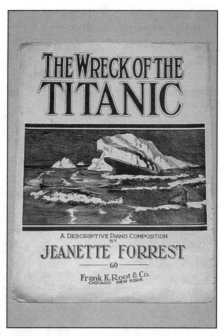

Sheet music, *The Wreck of the Titanic,* **worn, 13-5/8" x 10-1/8", $55.**

Book, *Wreck & Sinking of the Titanic,* Marshall Everett, 1912, worn condition 150.00

Key Chain, Titanic, White Star Line, MOC 3.95

Magazine, *National Geographic,* December, 1985 .... 2.25

Model Kit, Minicraft 350 scale, Japan, 30" l, MIB 55.00

Movie Prop, certificate of authenticity

  Oar Lock, brass 450.00

  Passageway Lamp, brass 250.00

Photograph, movie set, set of 27 4" x 6" photos, showing film crews, actors, 1977 .... 35.00

Poster, Pepsi, L. DiCaprio....... 10.00

Print, 6" d round sealed bubble frame, shells and seaweed dec on frame 250.00

Puzzle, *NY Times,* April 25, 1912, headline, MIB 5.00

❖ Toasters

You need a good breakfast to help you get through a hard day at the flea market. Better include some toast in that feast. That breakfast staple has

Tin, 5" h, 6-5/8" sq, $7.

been around for generations, and the toaster has been evolving too. Watch for interesting designs and shapes in toasters. However, like other electrical appliances, be careful if you try to use any vintage toaster.

Periodical: *A Toast To You,* 26245 Calle Cresta, Temecula, CA 92590.

Collectors' Clubs: Electric Breakfast Club, PO Box 306, White Mills, PA 18473-0306; Upper Crust, PO Box 529, Temecula, CA 92593.

Challenge, #10552, Art Deco design, 2 slice, chrome plated 20.00

General Mills, 2 slice pop-up, chrome body, wheat dec, black Bakelite base, early 1940s 38.00

Knapp Monach Reverso, lightweight nickel-plated body, rounded corners, black painted base, flip-flop doors with tab handles........ 35.00

Ohio Art, child's play toaster, mkd "Pfaltzgraff," 8" l, 5-1/2" h.... 18.00

Sunbeam, Model B, flat, chrome body, round reeded legs, hexagonal Bakelite feet, double wire cages flip over horizontally, small drop bail handles for carrying, 1920s, 5" x 9".................... 145.00

Toast-A-Lator, conveyor belt toaster.............................. 125.00

❖ Tobaccoania

Tobaccoania is a term coined to reflect the joys of smoking, and includes cigar, cigarette, and pipe smoking. As a collectible, tobaccoania seems to be as strong today as it was several years ago.

Collectors' Club: Society of Tobacco Jar Collectors, 3011 Falstaff Road, #307, Baltimore, MD 21209-2960.

Advertisement, 21" h, 14" w, cardboard, Mail Pouch, The Real Man's Choice, litho image of someone playing bellows organ, some soiling and scuffs 20.00

Pocket Tin, vertical, 4-1/2" h, 3" w

Central Union 100.00

Forest and Stream, Fisherman image 100.00

Peachy 100.00

Puritan Mixture, Continental Tobacco Co. 50.00

Times Square 200.00

Pouch, orig contents

Arrow 15.00

Biggerhair Tobacco Chew or Smoke, black native with curly hair, big earrings, nose ring, 5" h 30.00

Harp 15.00

Star, empty 10.00

Sure Shot, colored scene of Indian shooting arrow into air, 5" h 20.00

Uncle Daniel Fine Cut Tobacco, colorful image of Uncle Dan, white whiskers and hat, red background, yellow field, 3-1/2" h 15.00

Sign

9-1/2" h, 9-1/2" w, paper, Winner Plug, race horses jumping through oversized stirrup, framed 60.00

12-3/4" h, 7" w, paper, Crusader Tobacco, trademark logo of armor-clad crusader, framed 45.00

14-1/2" h, 10-1/4" l, Kinney Tobacco Co, paper, man flirting with woman while sitting on wall plastered with all types of Kinney Brothers advertising, framed 100.00

17-1/2" h, 14-1/2" l, Piper Heidsieck Chewing Tobacco, tin over cardboard, shows plug of tobacco bursting with champagne flavor, tin shown at top 65.00

19-1/2" h, 24-3/4" l, Redford's Tobaccos, paper, shows tobacco plantation scene, scene framed in tobacco leaves, naming various products, framed 175.00

Tobacco Jar

Fisherman 275.00

Old Man 350.00

Scotsman 275.00

❖ Tobacco Tags

The colorful tags used to identify bundles of tobacco that were sold at country tobacco auctions have become collectible. Watch for interesting shapes and names or places to help identify the original locale of the tag.

Collectors' Club: Tobacco Tin Tag Collectors Club, Route 2, Box 55, Pittsburg, TX 75686-9516.

Bachman's Fiddle 18.50

Brown & Williamson, Sun Cured 10.00

Close Figures 28.00

Flat Iron 13.50

Golden Slipper 6.00

Gravely's Second 10.00

Legal Tender 9.50

Little Henry 11.50

Little Mattie 9.50

New Coon 28.00

New Moon 10.00

Old Bob 28.00

Old Lorillard Climax Plug, 5/8" d 3.00

For exciting collecting trends and newly expanded areas look for the following symbols:

✪ Hot Topic

★ New Warman's Listing

(May have been in another Warman's edition.)

Old Navy, Zahm 5.00

Scotten's Brown Slag 10.00

Spur 22.50

Uncle Sam 14.00

❖ Tobacco Tins

Everybody remembers the old joke about letting Prince Albert out of the can. Today's collectors of tobacco tins search for Prince Albert and many other colorful characters who grace the front of tobacco tins.

Battle Royal, United States Tobacco Co, Hakser & Marcuse, flat, pocket, 4-1/2" h, 2-3/4" w, 1" d 100.00

California Nugget Chalk Cut, shaped like cake of soap, gold background, green, gold, and red lettering, 3" l, 2-1/2" w 110.00

Catcher Tobacco, canister 95.00

Hiawatha, Spaulding & Merrick, 8-1/2" d 150.00

Mayo's Cut Plug, lunch box 40.00

Old Colony, pocket 125.00

Peachy, vertical, pocket, 4" h, 2-1/2" w 100.00

Red Belt, pocket 95.00

Kentucky Club Mixture tin, 14 oz, 6-1/2" h, 4-3/4" w, 3-3/4" d, $8.

The American Tobacco Co. USA, green ground, black transfer of Indian brave with war bonnet, 2-3/4" d, 1-1/2" h25.00

Times Square, vertical, pocket, 4-1/2" h, 3" w 200.00

Uncle Daniel, Scotten-Dillon Co, 8-1/2" d 50.00

❖ Tokens

Tokens are small medallions or coin type objects. Some tokens are used in lieu of currency for transportation, such as a railroad token. Other tokens were forms of advertising or perhaps were used for admission to an event. Look for tokens where you tend to find coins and medals.

References: Many coin reference books also contain information about tokens.

Collectors' Clubs: Active Token Collectors Organization, PO Box 1573, Sioux Falls, SD 57101-1573; American Numismatic Association, 818 N. Cascade Ave, Colorado Springs, CO 80903-3279; American Vecturist Association, PO Box 1204, Boston, MA 02104-1204; Indiana, Kentucky & Ohio Token & Medal Society, 1725 N 650 West, Columbia City, IN 46725; Love Token Society, 130 Cornel Road, Audubon, NJ 01806-2857; Michigan Token & Medal Society, PO Box 572, Comstock Park, MI 49321; National Token Collector's Association, PO Box 5596, Elko, NV 98902; New Jersey Exonumia Society, 112 Carlton Ave., Collingswood, NJ 08108-3501; Token & Medal Society, PO Box 366, Brayntown, MD 20617-0366.

Advertising, aluminum, White Sewing Machine, one side reads "White is King" with picture of sewing machine, other side "The White is Sold Everywhere, White Sewing Machine Co., Cleveland, O, USA" 12.00

Lassie Gold Award for Meritorious Action, brass, 1" d 45.00

National Horse Show Association of America, 1995, silver-tone, 3" d 5.00

Lucky Buddha / Virgo the Virgin, copper, 1-1/8" d, $2.

Sambo's Restaurant, "Good for a 10 Cent Cup of Coffee at Sambo's Restaurants Anywhere," issued in Salem, Oregon, wood 12.00

Token Holder, 2 tokens, back mkd "The Goerke Co., Broad St, Newark, NJ" 28.00

Tower of Jewels, other side with California bear, bay with ship and sun rays, gold-tone 1-1/2" d 32.00

US Marine Corp, Third Battalion, brass 5.00

World's Fair

　Montana Exposition Fund, angel on bow of ship, fair name and date 1915 .... 35.00

　New York, 1964, Peace Through Understanding, 1-1/2" d 15.00

　Panama Canal Completion Exposition, San Francisco, Eureka, flag and bear, steamship and 1915 on back, tarnished 35.00

❖ Tools

Considering this great country was built from the ground up, tools have been with us for a long time. And treated properly, good tools last for years. Many eventually make their way to flea markets. Tool collectors tend to find flea markets to be like gold mines when they are searching for something new to add to their collections.

Collectors' Clubs: Collectors of Rare & Familiar Tools Society of New Jersey, 38 Colony Court, New Providence, NJ 07974-2332; Early American Industries Association, 167 Bakersville Road, South Dartsmouth, MA 02748; New England Tool Collectors Association, 11-1/2 Concord Ave., Saint Johnsbury, VT 05819; Tool Group of Canada, 7 Tottenham Road, Ontario MC3 2J3 Canada, plus many regional and specialized groups.

Anvil, 4" l, "Compliments of John Fink Metal Works, San Francisco and Seattle Wash" 30.00

Axe head, single bit, Black Raven 20.00

Bailey, Stanley #3, with lateral 30.00

Beading Tool, Stanley #166, guide, 8 blades 175.00

Block Plane, low angle, Stanley, adjusted throat, black japanned 35.00

Box Scraper, Stanley, #70, needs cleaning 20.00

Broad Axe, W. Hunt, 6" h, orig handle 50.00

Carving Chisels, S. J. Addis Cast Steel, Masonic hallmark, set of 12 .... 125.00

Ford wrench, 4-3/8" l, $5.

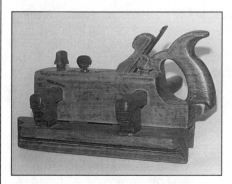

Plane, mkd "H.N. Holway," 11" l, $90.

Compass Plane, Stanley #20, all orig, nickel finish.............. 175.00

Draw Knife, D. R. Barton 1882, 22" l, orig finish.......................... 85.00

Foot Measure, Korrecto, directions on back.............................. 32.00

Plane

    Stanley #8, some surface rust.................................45.00

    Stanley #196 ....950.00

Router, unmarked, wrought iron, 1/2", wood handles, needs cleaning............................ 25.00

Router Plane, Stanley #71, Pat. 1884 .... 50.00

Saddle Maker's Knife, H. G. Comph & Co., Albany, NY, crescent shape, rosewood handle, orig tooled leather scabbard...... 45.00

Socket Chisel

    9/16" gouge, mkd "Lakeside" 15.00

    1-1/4" gouge, mkd "Butcher Cast Steel," handle split 15.00

    2", heavy, needs handle 17.00

Scraper Plane, Stanley #112, #32 tooth blade 175.00

Woodworking Plane, "The Cincinnati Tool Co. Hargrove" on blade, spoke shave, 10-1/2" l........ 45.00

❖ Toothbrush Holder

Getting kids to brush their teeth has been a challenge for decades. One way to help this activity was a character to hold toothbrushes. They certainly make a neat collectible. But because many are made of plaster or bisque, expect to find some damage and loss to the paint.

Collectors' Club: Toothbrush Holder Collectors Club, PO Box 371, Barnesville, MD 20838-0371.

Drum Major, tube tray 90.00

Girl with Dog, tube tray 80.00

Lone Ranger, plaster, painted, 4" h.................................... 75.00

Mickey and Minnie Mouse, bisque.............................. 350.00

Bennington, 4" h, 3-3/8" w, 2-1/2 d, $95.

Mickey Mouse, bisque, one arm moveable, other connected to body, string tail missing, paint worn, late 1930s 225.00

Soldier.................................... 85.00

Three Pigs 155.00

❖ Toothpick Holders

Here's another tabletop accessory that was always present on the table or sideboard in Victorian times and later. Typically they are high enough for a toothpick to stand on end and large enough to hold many toothpicks. Over the years, toothpick holders have been made in all different types of materials.

Collectors' Club: National Toothpick Holders Collectors Society, PO Box 417, Safety Harbor, Fl 34695-0417.

Bisque, Kate Greenaway-style little girl standing beside basket................................. 75.00

China

    Meissen, clown.................. 70.00

    Royal Bayreuth, elk 120.00

    R. S. Prussia, pink and green luster ground, floral trim 45.00

Figural head, ceramic, Germany, 2" h, $22.50.

Glass

    Cut Glass, pedestal, chain of hobstars dec....................... 150.00

    Milk Glass, parrot and top hat, c1895.............................. 45.00

Pattern Glass

    Daisy and Button, blue........ 75.00

    Kansas................................ 45.00

    Texas, gold trim.................. 50.00

Silver Plate, chick standing next to egg, engraved "Just Picked Out," Victorian, plate very worn ...25.00

☆ Torquay Pottery

This English pottery is often called Motto Ware because it usually contains a motto written into the clay. Some of the sayings are quite humorous. The pieces were hand decorated and usually well marked.

Collectors' Clubs: North American Torquay Society, 12 Stanton, Madison, CT 06443; Torquay Pottery Collectors Society, 23 Holland Ave, Cheam, Sutton, Surrey SM2 6HW UK.

Bowl, Allervale, "Du'ee mak yerzel at 'ome," 3-3/4" d.................... 18.00

Candle Holder, "Last in bed put the light out," 5-3/4" d............. 120.00

Creamer, house dec, "Don't make a fool of pleasure" 26.00

Finger Bowl, "Time Ripens All Things," 4-1/4" d................. 27.00

Shaving Mug, scuttle, "The nearer the razor, the closer the shave," Dad on back, 6-1/2" l........ 215.00

Teapot, small, house dec, 4" h................................... 120.00

Tulip Vase, hand painted, cobalt blue ground, hummingbird and floral design, black mark and #32, 7-1/2" h.............................. 98.00

❖ Tortoise Shell Items

The mottled brown design known as tortoise shell was so popular with Victorians that many items were made of actual tortoise shell as well as being imitated in glassware and pottery. With the invention of celluloid and plastics, imitation celluloid saw a revival. Today, real tortoise shell falls under the protection of the Endangered Species Act. But, remember when many vintage tortoise shell items were made, the entire tortoise was being used for food and other purposes, so the shell was also used.

Box, cov, circular, painted figure by riverscape, French, late 19th C, minor losses, 3" d............. 495.00

Calling Card Case, mother-of-pearl and ivory inlaid dec, c1825, 4" x 3"............................... 225.00

Glove Box, domed lid, ornate ivory strapping, sandalwood int, 3-1/2" h............................. 375.00

Patch Box, silver corner dec, ivory trim, 2" l............................ 200.00

Snuff Box, oval, silver dec, 1-1/2" x 3"........................ 325.00

Travel Set, case, comb, nail file, hand mirror, shoe horn, hair brush, soap box, toothpaste box, toothbrush box, powder box, nail buff, monogrammed "B.M.A," case worn........................... 40.00

❖ Toys

Every toy at a flea market is collectible. Some are worth more than others. Factors that influence price include: age, condition, orig box, desirability, or maker. Probably the most deciding factor in the purchase of an antique toy is the one that makes the heart of the collector skip a beat, something that says that toy is important. The sampling below is just a mere peek into the giant toy box that many flea markets represent to collectors.

References: Dana Cain, *UFO & Alien Collectibles Price Guide,* Krause Publications, 1999; Sharon and Bob Huxford, *Schroeder's Collectible Toys,* 4th ed., Collector Books, 1998; Dana Johnson, *Collector's Guide to Diecast Toys & Scale Models,* 2nd ed., Collector Books, 1998; Mike and Sue Richardson, *Diecast Toy Aircraft,* New Cavendish, 1998; Vincent Santelmo, *GI Joe Identification & Price Guide, 1964-1998,* Krause Publications, 1999; Elizabeth Stephan, ed., *O'Brien's Collecting Toys, 9th edition,* Krause Publications, 1999; *Toy Shop* Magazine Editors, *1999 Toy Shop Annual,* Krause Publications, 1998; Gerhard G. Walter, *Tin Dream Machines: German Tin Toy Cars and Motorcycles of the 1950s and 1960s,* New Cavendish, 1998; Stuart W. Wells, III, *Science Fiction Collectibles Identification & Price Guide,* Krause Publications, 1998, plus many, many more.

Periodicals: *Antique Toy World,* PO Box 34509, Chicago, IL 60634; *Model and Toy Collector Magazine,* PO Box 347240, Cleveland, OH 44134; *The Games Annual,* 5575 Arapahoe Rd, Suite D, Boulder, CO 80303; *Toy Farmer,* 7496 106th Ave., SE, Lamoure, ND 58458; *Toy Shop,* 700 E. State St, Iola, WI 54990; *Toy Trader,* PO Box 1050, Dubuque, IA 52004.

Collectors' Clubs: American Game Collectors Association, PO Box 44, Dresher, PA, 19025; Antique Toy Collectors of America, Two Wall Street, 13th Floor, New York, NY, 10005; Canadian Toy Collectors Society, 67 Alpine Ave., Hamilton, Ontario L9A 1A7 Canada; Gamers Alliance, PO Box 197, East Meadow, NY 11554; plus many regional and specialized clubs.

For additional listings, see *Warman's Antiques and Collectibles Price Guide* and *Warman's Americana & Collectibles,* as well as specific company listings in this edition.

Army Radio Jeep, Line Mar 7-1/4", white body, orig drawer, worn box 195.00

Astin Martin Competition Model, Corgi, MIB........................100.00

Banjo Cowboy, litho tin windup, Line Mar, 5-1/2" h 175.00

Barney Rubble's Car, Corgi, MOC 25.00

Betty Crocker Junior Baking Kit, Ideal, 1952, MIB..................90.00

Boxing Gloves, child size, Benlee, 2 pairs in box 125.00

Bunny, three-wheeler bike, litho tin wind-up, mkd "MTU, China" 65.00

Camper Truck, all tin, litho, friction, 8" l, MIB 175.00

Car Carrier, Tonka, c1960 ....45.00

Car, Mattel, 8-1/4" l, hard-plastic friction, experimental, yellow and silver, SS wheel 75.00

Car, Sun Rubber,4-door limousine type, white rubber wheels, 4" l, 1-1/2" h
    Blue.....................................15.00
    Red 15.00

Casper Flipover Tank, Line Mar, litho tin windup..........................300.00

Charlie's Angels Chevy Van, Corgi, MIB 60.00

Buddy L Traveling Zoo truck, $195.

Manoil dimestore figures, man with scythe, scarecrow, lead, each $10.

Chevrolet Caprice, Corgi, MIB 60.00

Chevy Police Car, battery-operated tin, Line Mar, 9" l 100.00

Chrysler Imperial, Corgi, MIB 85.00

Coney Island Roller Coaster, 22" w, 15" deep, two large bus type cars, bright graphics, Techonix, Germany, MIB 395.00

Corvette, Tonka, tin 50.00

Crackers, The Talking Parrot, Mattel MIB 165.00

Crazy Clown in Crazy Car, litho tin wind-up, Japan, MIB 175.00

Double Decker London Bus, adv for Mobil and Shell, all tin, rubber wheels, friction, 7" l, MIB 175.00

Digger the Dog, Hasbro, plastic, vinyl tail and ears, orig yellow hat and leash string, 13-3/4" l... 15.00

Donald Duck and Pluto, Sun Rubber, red car 85.00

Duck, blue shirt, red bandanna, big orange star badge, rubber, sgd "The Walt Disney Company Tootsie Toy Made in China," 5-1/4" h 35.00

Dump Truck, red and green, Tonka, 1955 .... 100.00

Ferris Wheel, colorful seats and graphics, Ohio Art 295.00

Dump Truck, Tonka, #180, green bed, professionally restored 175.00

Electric Food Center, 1950s, Ideal, MIB 35.00

Farm Truck, Tonka 85.00

Farmer in the Dell, Mattel, litho tin, musical, c1953, 9-1/2" x 9-1/2" x 7" 90.00

Fire Chief Car, pull toy, metal, clanging bell, T. Cohen, 1940s, MIB 275.00

Fire Pumper, Tonka, 1964 .... 95.00

Ford Consul Classic 315, Corgi, MIB 80.00

Ford Dragster, Glow Worm, white, #163, MIB 85.00

Ford Escort 13GL, Corgi, MIB 30.00

Ford Sedan, Tootsietoy 40.00

Fred Flintstone's Car, Corgi, MOC 25.00

Give-A-Show Projector, Kenner, boxed 35.00

Guitar, Mattel, cowboy, orig box 40.00

Hillman Husky, Corgi, MIB 160.00

Hot Dog Wagon, Ideal, MIB .. 315.00

Hot Roadster, #28, Corgi, yellow 25.00

Indian Joe, Alps, NMIB 65.00

James Bond Moonraker Shuttle, Corgi, MIB 90.00

Jerry's Banger, Corgi, ... 15.00

Katerina, Shako figure, litho tin, Lindstrom, 1930s 175.00

Kojak's Buick, Corgi, MIB 100.00

Merry-Go-Round, three bears sitting in tea cups on saucers, litho tin, Japan, 1950s, MIB 275.00

Machine Gun, Mattel, air cooled, MIB 200.00

Marlin, #263, red and black, 1/43 scale, Corgi, MIB 100.00

Mercedes-Benz 240D, Corgi, MIB 45.00

Mickey Mouse Talking Telephone, Hasbro, battery operated, 1964, MIB 175.00

Moon Base Space 1999, Mattel, Star Flash Computer Kit 50.00

Mr. Dan, coffee drinking man, raises coffee pot, pours the drinks, Japan, MIB 95.00

Mr. Potato Head, Hasbro, 7-1/2" x 10" x 2" box, 2-1/4" d Styrofoam ball head, plastic accessories, orig color illus instruction sheet, Hasbro, #2000, c1950, orig box 40.00

Policeman on Motorcycle, tin, friction, MIB 75.00

Porky Pig, Sun Rubber, multicolored molded rubber, c1950, orig box 95.00

Power Shovel, Line Mar, tin friction, 8" l 100.00

Race Car, Auburn Rubber 65.00

Race Car, Sun Rubber, silver body, white rubber wheels, 2" x 4" x 1" 45.00

Reading Bear, turns page of tin book, Japan, MIB 145.00

Road Grader, Tonka 75.00

Sand Loader, Line Mar, yellow, MIB 35.00

Santa Claus, all tin, holding Merry Xmas sign, rings bell, Japan, MIB 175.00

Satellite Launcher, 3 satellites, orig instructions, 1950s Ideal catalog, box fair 125.00

Scooter the Tooter, Hasbro, plastic, clown, flexible vinyl arms, bluebird on hat 10.00

Service Truck, Tonka, #01, medium blue, professionally restored 125.00

Sky Ranger, tin zeppelin and prop plane revolving around naval tower lighthouse, Unique Art, 1930s 390.00

Hasbro Romper Room clown, plastic, 1980, 11-1/2" h, $8.

Slot Car, TCR, Ideal, Dirt Modified Mustang, blue and yellow, MIB...................................... 25.00

Snow Plow, Line Mar, tin friction, 7" l...................................... 50.00

Super Stock Car, silver and yellow, Corgi, Castrol trim.............. 25.00

Telephone Bear, picks up phone, places it back on stand, and phone rings, tin and cloth, Japan, MIB.................................. 145.00

Tank.. 25.00

The Big Press, Ideal, printing press 45.00

Top, Whizzer, Mattel, 1969, MIB.. 35.00

Trombone, 10" l, tin, brass-color, works................................... 60.00

Truck, Sun Rubber, streamlined design, green paint, white rubber tires, c1930, 2" x 4-1/2" x 1-1/2" 45.00

UPS Package Car, brown hard plastic truck, orig brown and white box, copyright UPS 1977, friction, 2" x 5-1/2" x 2-1/2" box....... 45.00

UPS Truck, hard plastic, clicker on front tires, copyright UPS, Made in China, 1977, 5-1/2" l....... 45.00

Violin Player, Line Mar, litho tin windup, red, white and blue tuxedo, 5-1/2" h................ 200.00

Weebles Haunted House, Hasbro, plastic furniture, glow-in-the-dark Ghost Weeble, Witch Weeble, Boy Weeble and Girl Weeble 20.00

Girard handcar, tin windup, 5-3/4" h, 6" l, $250.

Whistling Train Station, Mattel, litho tin, MIB 65.00

Winnebago............................. 70.00

Wrecker, Tonka, c1960 .... 85.00

❖ Toy Dimestore Figures

Children have been fascinated with three-dimensional lead, iron, rubber, and plastic toy soldiers for many years. About the time of World War II, dimestores started to carry soldiers which were very popular with their young customers. They could be purchased one at a time, making each set unique, unlike the English lead soldiers which were sold in sets.

Periodicals: *Old Toy Soldier,* 209 N. Lombard, Oak Park, IL 60302; *Plastic Figure & Playset Collector,* PO Box 1355, LaCrosse, WI 54602; *Plastic Warrior,* 905 Harrison St., Allentown, PA 18103; *Toy Shop,* 700 E. State St., Iola, WI 54490; *Toy Soldier Review,* 127 74th St., North Bergen, NJ 07047.

Aircraft Spotter, Manoil 27.50

Bandit, hands up, Grey Iron.... 42.00

Baseball Player, Auburn Rubber............................... 35.00

Bugler, pre-war, tin helmet, Barclay 20.00

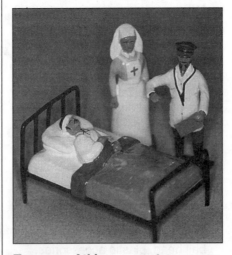

Tommy Atkins, contemporary, doctor and nurse, $16 each, wounded soldier, $32.

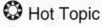
Colonial Soldier, Grey Iron 17.50

Cowboy, mounted, firing pistol, Barclay................................ 24.00

Farmer, sowing grain, Manoil 20.00

Flag Bearer, post-war, Manoil 24.00

Football Player, Auburn Rubber 35.00

Indian, with tomahawk and shield, Barclay................................ 10.00

Machine Gunner, kneeling, Auburn Rubber 15.00

Marine Officer, pre-war, marching, sword, blue uniform, tin hat 27.50

Nurse, white uniform, Barclay................................ 24.00

Officer, post-war, pot helmet, Barclay, orig sword 175.00

Pirate, Barclay........................ 15.00

Policeman, raised arm, Barclay................................ 12.00

Soldier

Charging, Barclay 7.50

Gas mask and flare gun, Manoil............................ 20.00

Searchlight, Auburn Rubber............................ 30.00

Wounded soldier, Manoil 17.50

Two as rocket team, Barclay 25.00

❖ Toy Train Accessories

Toy train accessories, like Plasticville houses, tunnels, miniature figures and fences, are often found at flea markets. Look for these tiny treasures to add to your train set-up.

Airport Hangar, Lionel 36.00

Bachman Hotel, Plasticville, HO 6.00

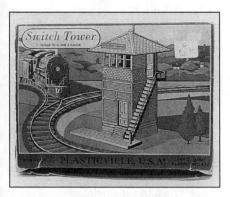

Switch tower, #1402/79, Plasticville, orig box, $15.

Barnyard Animal Set,
    Plasticville 20.00
Billboard, Plasticville............... 10.00
Diner, Plasticville, orig box, some
    wear 25.00
Fence and Gate, Plasticville 3.25
Foot Bridge, Plasticville, #1051 7.00
Gas Station, Plasticville, MIB.. 66.50
Green House, Plasticville, MIB 65.00

House, Plasticville
    Cape Cod 10.00
    Ranch...................................5.00
Moving and Storage Van,
    Plasticville, NRFB.............. 35.00
Outhouse, Plasticville, O or S
    gauge 10.00
Spruce Trees, pr, Plasticville 9.00

Trestle Set
    American Flyer, #780 ....42.00
    Lionel, #111 ....24.00
Union Station, Plasticville 18.00
Waiting Room, American Flyer,
    metal 30.00

Water Tower
    American Flyer, red and white
        checkerboard sides, bubbling
        type 100.00
    Lionel.....................................82.00
    Plasticville 6.00
Windmill, Plasticville,
    O gauge 12.00

❖ Toy Trains

Toy trains are one of the most popular types of toys that collectors invest in today. Early toy trains were cast iron and quickly progressed to well-crafted trains of different types of metals and materials. Names like American Flyer, Ives, and Lionel are well known. The prices listed below are for sets of trains.

References: Excellent references exist for every kind of toy train.

Periodicals: *Classic Toy Trains,* PO Box 1612, Waukesha, WI 53187; *LGB Telegram,* 1573 Landvater, Hummelstown, PA 17036; *Lionel Collector Series Marketmaker, Trainmaster,* 3224 NW 47th Terrace, Gainesville, FL 32606; *O Scale Railroading,* PO Box 239, Nazareth, PA 18064; *S. Gaugian,* 7236 Madison Ave., Forest Park, IL 60130.

Collectors' Clubs: American Flyer Collectors Club, PO Box 13269, Pittsburgh, PA 15234; LGB Model Railroad Club, 1854 Erin Drive, Altoona, PA 16602; Lionel Collectors Club of America, PO Box 479, LaSalle, IL 61301; Lionel Operating Train Society, 18 Eland Ct, Fairfield, OH 45014; Marklin Club-North America, PO Box 51559, New Berlin, WI 53151; Marklin Digital Special Interest Group, PO Box 51319, New Berlin, WI 53151; The National Model Railroad Association, 4121 Cromwell Road, Chattanooga, TN 37421; The Toy Train Operating Society, Inc., Suite 308, 25 West Walnut St., Pasadena, CA 91103; Train Collector's Association, PO Box 248, Strasburg, PA 17579.

American Flyer
    American Legion Ltd., locomotive, box car, American pullman, observation car, maroon litho and roofs, S gauge 675.00

Lionel 3100 Great Northern 4-8-4, engine (shown) and tender, orig box, $400.

Burlington Zephyr Streamliner,
    passenger, O gauge 725.00
Minnie Ha-Ha, locomotive,
    3 coaches, orange and gray,
    minor wear.................... 295.00
Passenger, #253 locomotive, two
    #610 cars, #612 dark green,
    maroon inserts, 1924,
    O gauge........................ 295.00
Ives, passenger set, locomotive, tender, 3 cars, S gauge.......... 150.00

Lionel
    Freight, #33, #35, #36, olive
        green, S gauge, 1920... 350.00
    Passenger, #352E, #103 locomotive, #332 baggage car, #339, coach, #341 observation car, 1926, S gauge, orig box, minor wear to locomotive 550.00
Marx, Seaboard Air Line RR Co.,
    citrus colors, boxed set..... 450.00

❖ Trading Cards, Non-Sport

As the name implies, these colorful cards were made to be traded. Often they were packed with food products. Many times they appeared in series form, and you needed to eat a lot of cereal or whatever product to get the complete series. To today's collector, that's where the value lies, in complete series, with individual cards ranging from about a quarter and up at most flea markets.

Collectors' Clubs: Cartophilic Society, 116 Hillview Road, Ensbury Park, Bournemouth BH10 5BJ UK; United States Cartophilic Society, PO Box 4020, Saint Augustine, FL 32085-4020.

Alfa-Romeo Auto Racing, Player
    Cigarettes, 1936 ....5.50
Casper, Fleer, 1960, set of 66
    cards 165.00
Senior Service Cigarettes, set of 48
    photo cards of airplanes,
    1938.................................90.00
Star Trek, The Motion Picture, 1979,
    set of 88 cards 32.00
Walt Disney, Brooke Bond Foods,
    Ltd., London, late 1980s, set of 25
    cards 65.00

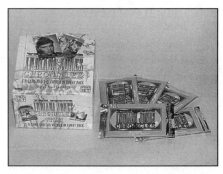

The Young Indiana Jones Chronicles, Pro Set, 36 packs, $10.

❖ ⊛ Tramp Art

Here's a hot part of the flea market scene! Now considered to be folk art by some, these pieces were crafted by someone with limited materials, tools, and sometimes skill. By adding bits and pieces together, layers became objects such as picture frames, boxes of all kinds, etc.

Reference: Clifford A. Wallach and Michael Cornish, *Tramp Art, One Notch At A time,* Wallach-Irons Publishing, 1998.

Bank, secret access to coins, 6" h, 4" w, 4" d 335.00
Clock, mantel, rd stain, drawers in base, 22" h, 14" w 495.00
Crucifix, wooden pedestal base, wooden carved figure, 16" h, 7" w, 4-1/2" d 195.00
Document Box, diamond designs, sgd and dated, 14" h, 9-1/2" w 375.00
Frame, horseshoe design, light and dark wood, 13" h, 12" w ... 495.00

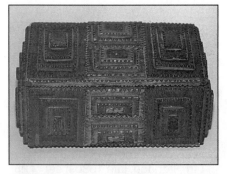

Wooden box, 5" h, 9" l, 6" w, $190.

Jewelry Box, covered with hearts, painted silver over gold, velvet lining, 6" h, 11" w, 6" d 600.00
Pedestal, lift off lid, velvet lining, 6-1/2" h, 10" w, 7" d 225.00
Pocket Watch Holder, ftd, 9" h, 5-1/2" w 375.00
Sewing Box, covered, velvet pin cushion on top, 8-1/2" h, 11-1/2" w, 8-1/2" d 275.00
Wall Pocket, shelf, diamonds motif, 8-1/2" h, 16" w, 4-3/4" d 150.00

❖ Transistor Radios

Remember how kewl it was to walk around as a teenager, holding your radio up so only you could hear it! Those transistor radios spelled freedom from electrical cords and sometimes were even in kewl shapes and colors. Most of us didn't care that they only got AM stations, it was the "old folks" that listened to FM anyway. Today collectors like to find them with original cases, instructions, and little wear.

Bulova, transistor, orig case.... 45.00
Champion Spark Plug, figural, AM only 56.00

Panasonic R-70, green, orig box, $32.

Elvis Presley, AM 40.00
Emerson, #888, Vanguard, transistor, portable, 1958 .... 65.00
GE, P-910C, aqua 12.50
Guild Radio, telephone shape, crank changes stations, 18" h 95.00
Lionel, MIB 35.00
Panasonic, 1950s, blue 55.00
Realtone 6 .... 48.00
Silvertone, #9205, transistor, plastic, 1959 .... 42.00
Sony, TFM-151, transistor, 1960 .... 60.00
Toy telephone and cigarette lighter, plastic, 1950s, 5-1/2" h 20.00
Tropicana 15.00
Zenith
    RG 47J, Hong Kong 4.00
    Royal 500 Deluxe 45.00
    Royal 710 .... 30.00

❖ Transportation

Memorabilia relating to the transportation of goods and people has long been a favorite with collectors. Perhaps it's the romance of the open road or the fun of finding out about far-away places. Whatever the mode of transportation, you'll find some ephemera relating to it.

Reference: Barbara J. Conroy, *Restaurant China: Identification & Value Guide For Restaurant, Airline, Ship & Railroad Dinnerware,* Collector Books, 1998.

Token, "Good For One Fare, New York City Transit Authority," brass, 11/16" d, $1.

Periodical: *Airliners*, PO Box 52-1238, Miami, FL 33152.

Collectors' Clubs: Aeronautic & Air Label Collectors Club, PO Box 1239, Elgin, IL 60121; Gay Airline Club, PO Box 69A04, West Hollywood, CA 90069; Bus History Association, 965 McEwan, Windsor Ontario N9B 2G1 Canada; Central Electric Railfans' Association, PO Box 503, Chicago, IL 60690; International Bus Collectors Club, 1518 "C" Trailee Drive, Charleston, SC 29407; National Association of Timetable Collectors, 125 American Inn Rd, Villa Ridge, MO 63089; Steamship Historical Society of America, Inc, Ste #4, 300 Ray Drive, Providence, RI 02906; Titanic Historical Society, PO Box 51053, Indian Orchard, MA 01151; Titanic International, PO Box 7007, Freehold, NJ 07728; Transport Ticket Society, 4 Gladridge Close, Earley, Reading Berks RG6 2DL England; World Airline Historical Society, 13739 Picarsa Dr., Jacksonville, FL 32225.

Blotter, Firestone Bicycle Tires, black, white, orange, and blue, 1920s, unused 20.00
Booklet, St. Lawrence route to Europe, Canadian Pacific, 1930, 16 pgs, 8" x 11" 25.00
Bus Calendar, Greyhound, 1940 .... 80.00
Fan, Air India, adv 4.00
Game, Pirates & Travelers, 1911, trifold board, boxed pcs 120.00
Luggage Tag, Canadian Pacific, stringed cardstock, red, white, and blue ship signs, c1930, 5" x 3" 15.00
Stickpin, brass, bug pedaling bicycle, mkd "Compliments of United States Tire Co.," 1920s 27.50
Traffic Light, rewired 85.00

✴ Traps

Snap! Gotcha! Hunters have been trapping since the old days when fur traders trapped and traded goods. Today many traps are considered to be collectible. Again, be careful if you test one of these out!

Collectors' Clubs: National Trappers Association, PO Box 3667, Bloomington, IL 61701; North American Trap Collectors Association, PO Box 94, Galloway, OH 43119-0094.

Beaver, Jump #13 .... 46.00
S. Newhouse #1, Oneida Community, c1904 .... 10.00
Sargent & Co. #1, muskrat 22.50
Stop Thief #3, Oneida Community 15.00
Wolf #4, Oneida Community ... 72.00

❖ Trays

Trays are another type of advertising collectible. Like tip trays, expect to find interesting lithographed scenes and advertising for all types of products. Also expect to find some signs of usage.

Reproduction Alert.

Anheuser-Busch Brewing, 12" d, trademark eagle and letter "A," Chas. W. Shonk Co. litho, inpainting, coated to enhance image 60.00
Bartlett Spring Mineral Water, 13" d, doe and fawn drinking from pure mountain spring, oversized bottle of mineral water in background, Kaufmann & Strauss Co. litho 150.00
Buffalo Brewing Co., 13" d, woman with flowing hair, Kaufmann & Strauss Co. litho, varnished, some overall scratching and soiling 100.00
Centennial Brewing, 13-1/2" l, 16-1/2" w, factory scene, some inpainting, tray in poor condition 50.00
Dick & Bros' Quincy Beer, factory scene, early wagons and automobilia, some chipping to rim, fading, scratching 200.00
Enterprise Brewing Co. Old Tap Abe, toothless happy old man, minor wear to rim, some staining to background 175.00
Golden West Brewing Co., factory scene, early trolleys and horse drawn carts, American Art Works, some chipping and soiling 300.00

Kaiser Willhelm Bitters Co., oversized bottle with trademark label, "For Appetite and Digestion" 70.00
Maier Brewing, woman in orange outfit, Maier trademark on side, © 1909, Kaufmann & Strauss Co. litho, some overall scratching 100.00
Moerlein Beer, trademark "Crowned Wherever Exhibited" in fancy filigree, rim shows different expositions, Chas. W. Shonk Co., minor inpainting 50.00
National Brewery Co. White Seal Beer, factory scene, horse drawn wagon, early blob top bottle, Griesedieck Bros, proprietors, chipping and scratching 185.00
Old Pepper Whisky, 11-3/4" l, 16-1/2" w, colonial soldiers enjoying libation around oversized bottle of Old Pepper Whisky, Meek & Beach Co. litho, rim chips 200.00
Olympia Brewing Co., 12" d, trademark Turnwater "It's the Water," Savage Manufacturing Co., overall scratching, soiling, and light surface rust 90.00
Pacific Brewing & Malting Co., Mt. Tacoma illus, orig 1912 work order from Chas. W. Shonk Co. on back 50.00
Park Brewing Co., factory scene, early railroad, horse drawn carts, and automobilia, Chas. W. Shonk Co. litho, some inpainting, 12" d 60.00

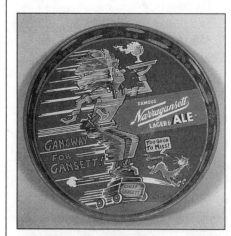

Narragansett, litho tin, illustration of Chief Gansett by Dr. Seuss, $125.

Rising Sun Brewing Co., 12" d, pre-prohibition, titled "Bohemian Girl," young lady enjoying glass of Bohemia Beer, © 1911, Kaufmann & Strauss Co. litho, some inpainting, light surface rust, coated 100.00

Robinson's Pilsner Beer, 12" d, factory scene, refrigerating room, grain dryer, bottling building, stables, wagon sheds, early railroad and multiple horse drawn wagons, Haeusermann litho 90.00

Stegmaier Brewing Co. factory scene, early railroad and automobilia, minor scratching and rubbing 70.00

Terre Haute Brewing Co., room full of colonials raise their empty glasses to flying cherubs who are bringing "That Ever-Welcome Beer" 125.00

❖ Trivets

Trivets are handy to have to hold hot irons and pots. Over the years, some have become quite decorative.

Brass, cast
  Cathedral, #4 ....45.00
  Heart, scrolls, 8" w 65.00
  Masonic, 8" 48.00
Shield shape, leafy foliage, English registry mark, 6-3/4" h 20.00

Iron trivet, Wm Howell Co., Geneva, Ill., 6-7/8" x 4-1/4", $32.50.

Cast Iron
  Bless Our House 20.00
  Cat's head, 8-3/4" d 150.00
  Horseshoe, clasped hands, Good Luck, gold paint 25.00
  Spade shape, shield, cannon, and crossed swords dec 72.00
Sterling Silver, round, cork 40.00
Wrought Iron
  Cross with crown 25.00
  Heart 65.00

✶ Trolls

These funny looking characters marched onto the scene in the 1960s. With their bright colors and busy hair, they have been bringing collectors good luck.

Periodicals: *Troll Monthly,* 216 Washington St., Canton, MA 02021; *Trollin,* PO Box 601292, Sacramento, CA 95860.

Bank, ceramic 15.00
Bear, orig box 58.00
Couple, elderly, large 95.00
Doll, girl, 6" h, hard vinyl, movable head, blond hair, red felt playsuit, Thomas Dam, c1970 .... 35.00
Fox 35.00
Gorilla 35.00
Mug, traveling type, plastic, gray ground, blue image and lid ..... .50
Norfin, female, c1970, 12" h ... 28.00
Scandia House, 12" h 85.00

✶ Trophies

How many of us have received a trophy for some event and it now resides in the back of a closet? Some trophies find their way to flea markets and then attract new buyers. Look for interesting names or dates on a trophy.

Fred Astaire Dance Studios Qualification Trophy, 7" h, brass colored metal, Astaire figure dancing with woman, dark wood base, attached nameplate, c1950 .... 120.00

Poultry trophy, "To Miss Betty Braun, First Local Bantam Display, Poultry Exhibition, 1922" 7-1/4" h, $14.

Golf, sterling silver, Rochester Country Club, 1954, mkd "Royal Danish USA International Sterling," 3" h 45.00

Lewis & Clark Exposition, 1905, Mt. Hood, Oregon, silver plate, mkd "Quadruple & Co." 2" h 40.00

Little League, Regional Champs, 1970 .... 10.00

Police Pistol Tournament, "*New York Mirror,* 19th Annual International Police Pistol Tournament, Teaneck Pistol Range, NJ," 4-3/4" h brass policeman figure, some dents 60.00

Swimming, female, figural, silver plate, 1950s, 12-1/4" h 125.00

❖ Turtle Collectibles

Turtle collectors will not find a flea market slow going. There will probably be several interesting examples to add to their growing collections.

Animation Art Cel, Teenage Mutant Ninja Turtles, certificate of authenticity, copyright dates, 1985 to 1991, matted, 11" x 14" 85.00

Beanie Baby, Speedy the Turtle, retired, protector on orig tag 65.00

Glass turtle, blue, Gibson, 1996, 3-1/4" l, $17.

Earrings, sterling silver, 1" l 8.50

Pin

    Ciner, yellow enameled shell, green rhinestones, red rhinestone eye, 1-1/2" x 1-1/4" 50.00

    Unmarked, silver-tone, enameled, rhinestone trim 10.00

Paperweight

    Cast iron 35.00

    Porcelain, Royal Crown Derby, 4-1/2" l, MIB 125.00

Pill Box, sterling silver, 1-1/2" l, 1-1/8" w 35.00

Planter, McCoy 40.00

Tape Measure, brushed gold metal, red rhinestone eyes, 3" x 2-1/2" 130.00

☆ TV Guides

These little television-oriented magazines have been steadily growing in value. There is usually an article about the star featured on the cover, plus other interesting tidbits for television memorabilia collectors.

1953, Queen Elizabeth 12.00
1967, Ed Sullivan 7.50
1976, George Kennedy 5.00
1976, Redd Foxx 5.00
1977, Frank Sinatra 5.00
1977, Milton Berle and Esther Williams 9.00
1984, Pierce Brosnan 12.50
1986, Farrah Fawcett 5.00
1986, Nicollette Sheridan 5.00
1986, Lucille Ball 15.00

Winter Olympics '84, Feb. 4-10, 1984, $1.

☆ Twin Winton

Twin Winton had production facilities in both Pasedena and San Juan Capistrano, California in the early 1950s. Their wares are well known to cookie jar collectors, but don't overlook some of their other tablewares and accessories.

Bank, Fox Pirate

Cookie Jar

    Cat 60.00
    Grandma 75.00
    Raggedy Ann, Mopsy 71.00
    Ranger Rabbit 66.00
    Dealer's Sign 300.00
    Figure, black football player, 6" h, 1972 .... 75.00

Napkin Holder

    Dutch Girl 20.00
    Ranger Bear 45.00
    Pitcher, Hillbilly, glaze flake on spout 33.00

Salt and Pepper Shakers, pr

    Kitten 46.00
    Lion 40.00
    Squirrel 20.00
    Teddy Bear 48.00

❖ Typewriters & Accessories

Tap, tap, ding! Remember that bell that used to ring when the carriage returned on an old typewriter? Well, to some typewriter collectors that sound is still heard. You can find them searching flea markets for vintage typewriters, accessories and related ephemera. Vintage typewriters are another example of a collectible where you should thoroughly inspect the keys, motor, and wiring, before trying to use it.

Periodicals: *Ribbon Tin News,* 28 The Green, Watertown, CT 06795-2118; *The Typewriter Exchange,* 2125 Mount Vernon Street, Philadelphia, PA 19130.

Collectors' Club: Early Typewriter Collectors Association, 2591 Military Ave., Los Angeles, CA 90064.

Advertisement

    Royal, 1962 .... 13.00
    Royal Portable, 1970s 3.00
Postcard, Remington Plant 15.00

Ribbon Tin

    Columbia Twins 15.00
    Eberhard 10.00
    Remington 7.50
    Vogue Royale 5.00

Typewriter

    Adler 7, oak case 335.00
    L. C. Smith #8, 12" carriage 20.00
    Remington, portable, #5 ..... 40.00
    Simplex 50.00
    Tom Thumb, orig case 15.00
    Underwood #5 .... 155.00

American-Flyer typewriter, American Flyer Mfg. Co., tin, orig box, $65.

✭ Umbrellas

While you might not want to open one in your house, it's great fun to find vintage umbrellas and parasols at flea markets. Look for interesting handles, fabrics in good condition and working order.

Beach, beige cloth, long wooden spiked pole, c1940, some wear and fading 40.00
Black, large size, "J" shaped Bakelite handle.................... 45.00
Brown, light beige stripes, clear lucite handle, some wear ... 10.00
Golf, bright red and white, wood handle 35.00
Holly Hobbie, child size, plastic 7.50
Parasol, beige, boa trim, shepherd's crook handle, c1900 .... 100.00
Parasol, white linen, crochet work trim, c1890 .... 120.00

✭ Unicorns

This mystical beast has charmed many hearts. Today collectors search them out and enjoy finding the various ways they are interpreted in glass, ceramic, and even on paper.

Collectors' Club: Unicorns Unanimous, 248 N. Larchmont Blvd, Los Angeles, CA 90004.

Beanie Baby, Mystic the Unicorn, protector on orig tag 18.00
Bell, bronzed pot metal, figural unicorn handle, 6-1/2" h 20.00
Candleholder, Vandor, MIB..... 12.00
Clip Board, brass 24.00

Figure, ceramic
Lefton, gold horns and hooves, pastel pink ribbons, floral accents, #10912, retired, pair 30.00
White, ivory, blue, and black, fired-on gold horn, applied silk flowers............................ 75.00
Garden Ornament, Unicorn Gargoyle, gypsum, Windstone, 13-3/4" h, orig box 85.00
Mirror, hand, Vandor, MIB 10.00
Pin, vermeil, black enameled horn, red, green, blue, and pink cabochons, rhinestone accents, mkd "Reinad," 3-1/2" x 3" 450.00
Print, black and white, sgd "Lisa Johnson, 1979," matted and framed, 11" x 14" 25.00
Sculpture, glass, hand blown, Scott Hartshorn, 4" h 30.00
Stuffed Toy
White plush, satin ribbons, shimmering gold horn, iridescent mane 22.00
White plush, silver horn and hooves, Gund, 10" h 10.00

❖ Universal Pottery

This popular pottery company was organized in 1934 by the Oxford Pottery Company, in Cambridge, Ohio. The plant merged and bought several other small potteries over the years. Universal Pottery made dinnerware and kitchenware until 1960, when all their plants closed. Because of the mergers, several different brand names were used, including Oxford Ware, Harmony House, etc.

For additional listings, see *Warman's Americana & Collectibles* and *Warman's American Pottery & Porcelain.*

Bittersweet
Drip Jar, cov 20.00
Platter 32.00
Salad Bowl 20.00
Calico Fruit
Custard Cup, 5 oz 5.00
Milk Jug, 3 qt 25.00
Salt and Pepper Shakers, pr 17.50
Cattails
Bread Box, double compartment 30.00

Kitchen Bouquet mixing bowl, 8-3/4" d, $12.

Casserole, cov, 8-1/4" d 17.50
Pie server............................ 20.00
Platter, oval 20.00
Refrigerator Pitcher............. 40.00
Rambler Rose
Dinner Plate 10.00
Gravy Boat.......................... 10.00
Soup Bowl, flat...................... 5.00
Woodvine
Cup and Saucer.................... 9.00
Vegetable Bowl, oval 9.50

❖ U.S. Glass

Known to collectors and dealers as U.S. Glass, the United States Glass Company started as a conglomerate of several glass houses in 1891. Because of the mergers created by the formation of this company, many smaller glass houses probably existed a little longer. The first wares under this new company were pressed pattern glass pieces. Another of their innovations was the States series. Some of these patterns were existing patterns renamed, others were new designs. As the years went on, they developed some of the newer, sleeker, more elegant depression-era patterns. The last of U.S. Glass factories to close was Tiffin Glass.

Prices listed below are for clear pieces, unless otherwise indicated.

Banana Stand, Colorado, blue.....................................65.00
Bowl, Bull's Eye and Daisy, ruby stained 30.00
Bride's Basket, Delaware, silver plated frame.........................75.00
Butter Dish, cov, Almond Thumbprint, non-flint.....................40.00

Cake Stand, Connecticut,
non-flint 40.00
Celery Tray, Vermont,
gold trim 30.00
Compote, cov, New Hampshire, high
standard, 5" d 5.00

Carnival glass compote, strawberry design, Marigold bowl on a clear stem, 3-1/2" h, 6" d, $45.

Creamer
California, emerald green ... 50.00
Texas, gold trim 45.00
Vermont, gold trim 32.00
Finger Bowl, Nevada 25.00
Goblet
California, emerald green ... 55.00
Galloway, non-flint 75.00
Manhattan 25.00
Juice Tumbler, Pennsylvania .. 10.00
Olive, Iowa 15.00
Pickle Castor, Galloway, silver
plated holder and lid 85.00
Punch Bowl, Almond Thumbprint,
non-flint.............................. 75.00
Punch Cup, Iowa 15.00
Relish, Maryland 15.00
Rose Bowl, Galloway.............. 25.00
Salt and Pepper Shakers, pr
California 45.00
Kentucky............................ 24.00

Sauce Dish, Nevada 10.00
Spooner, Bull's Eye and Daisy 25.00
Sugar, cov
Colorado 75.00
Vermont, gold trim............... 35.00
Toothpick, Delaware, rose,
gold trim 45.00
Tumbler, Almond Thumbprint,
non-flint.............................. 20.00
Whiskey, Pennsylvania,
gold trim 24.00
Wine, Connecticut, non-flint 35.00

For exciting collecting trends and newly expanded areas look for the following symbols:

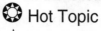 Hot Topic

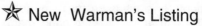 New Warman's Listing

(May have been in another Warman's edition.)

Books I'd like to find

1._____
2._____
3._____
4._____
5._____
6._____
7._____
8._____
9._____
10._____
11._____
12._____
13._____
14._____
15._____
16._____
17._____
18._____
19._____
20._____

❖ Valentines

Collecting Valentine's Day sentiments is a pleasure for many folks. The earliest cards were hand–made. After the greeting card business became more fully developed, valentines were included, and many nice examples exist. Many collectors prefer the diecut cards that are sometimes found with layers or pull-down decorations. Others prefer mechanical or animated cards that have some moving part.

Collectors' Club: National Valentine Collectors Association, PO Box 1404, Santa Ana, CA 92702.

For additional listings, see *Warman's Antiques and Collectibles Price Guide* and *Warman's Americana & Collectibles*.

Comic, McLoughlin, c1900,
4" x 6" 7.50
Diecut, heart shapes, small 5.00
Hand Made, hand painted card, attached clothespin doll, orig matching box, 1926 .... 40.00
Hand Painted, watercolor folk art, cherubs with heart 35.00
Honeycomb Tissue, wide-eyed children playing house, German, 1920s, 5" x 8" 25.00
Mechanical, Charles Twelvetrees design of children and snowman, 1920s, 8" x 7" 32.50
Paper Lace, simple lace folder, c1870, 5" x 7" 20.00
Silk Fringed
Prang, double-sided, 1880s, 3" x 5" 18.00

Mechanical valentine, fox motif, leaf moves to cover face, 6-3/8" x 5-1/2", $4.

Tuck, artist sgd, c1890,
5" x 7" 25.00
Stand-Up, easel back
Automobile, windows open, small 12.00
Children, figural 6.00
Flower basket, pasteboard, 1918 .... 9.00

❖ Van Briggle Pottery

The Van Briggle Pottery was founded in 1869 by an Ohio artist, Artus Van Briggle. For health reasons, he moved his pottery to Colorado Springs in 1901. After his death in 1904, his wife, Anna, continued the pottery for a few years. Reading the marks can give valuable clues as to the date and maker. The really pricey pieces of Van Briggle are early works, and prime examples can command hundreds of dollars. However, there are plenty of more ordinary pieces which are great for a beginning collector.

Ashtray, Hopi Indian maiden kneeling, grinding corn, turquoise Ming glaze, 6-1/2" w 75.00
Bust, child reading book,
6-1/2" h 65.00
Dish, turquoise blue, removable flower frog 125.00
Figure, Indian maiden, white... 95.00
Flower Bowl with Frog, green and brown, 9" x 12" 47.50

Paperweight, rabbit, maroon, c1930, 3" d 70.00
Vase
Shape #165, stylized spiderwort, light green matte, blue green leaves, slight brown peppering, pinched handles, incised logo, dated 1903, 6" h 1,375.00
Shape #830, carved poppy buds, sinewy stems, matte purple glaze, green ground, incised "AA/Van Briggle/Colo., Springs/830," c1901-20, 7-1/4" h 1,600.00
Shape #861, blue, tan, and green, short line to lip, c1912, 8-1/4" h 275.00

✭ Vandor

Vandor is a relative newcomer to the flea market scene. Their specialized wares bring vintage characters back to life and are well received. Because the wares are mainly from the 1990s, make sure to get the original box, packaging, etc.

Bank, Howdy Doody 25.00
Cookie Jar
Betty Boop, holiday..............35.00
Mona Lisa 85.00
Egg Cup, Sweet Pea..............45.00
Mug, Brutus...........................15.00
Music Box, Popeye and Olive Oyl 75.00
Salt and Pepper Shakers, pr
Betty Boop, shopper 15.00
Man in top hat.....................15.00
Popeye................................95.00
Teapot, cov
Betty Boop, car 12.50
Cherry Woods.......................5.00

✭ Van Telligen

Designer Ruth Van Telligen created some fun characters for the Royal China and Novelty Company of Chicago. The items were produced by Regal China and were limited to a few cookie jar designs and salt and pepper shakers. The cookie jars were made in limited numbers and tend to be quite hard to find.

Salt and Pepper Shakers, pr
Black Boy and Dog 45.00

Bunnies, hugging	25.00
Duck	35.00
Huggie Bear	18.00
Mary and Lamb	45.00
Peek-A-Boos, red and white	120.00

Salt Shaker, single

Dutch Girl	60.00
Mary	22.50
Mermaid	95.00

✫ Vaseline Glass

Vaseline glass gets its name from its unusual yellow-green color. The color is created by adding uranium salts to the glassware batch. Today collectors test their vaseline glass with a black light or even a Geiger counter as it is somewhat radioactive. Production was restricted to pattern glass and some opalescent wares. The white swirls of the opalescent highlights create a pretty contrast to the unusual base color.

Reproduction Alert.

Bread Plate, Daisy and Button with Crossbars, pattern glass	35.00
Butter Dish, cov, Spanish Lace, opalescent, Northwood	445.00
Celery Vase, Daisy and Button with Crossbars, pattern glass	50.00
Console Set, 10" d compote, matching 9" h candlesticks	500.00
Creamer, Wreath and Shell, opalescent, dec	135.00
Cruet, Everglades, opalescent	275.00
Jelly Compote, Iris with Meander, opalescent	95.00

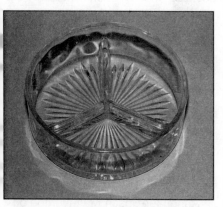

Divided dish, depression-era, 1-3/4" h, 5-1/4" d, $20.

Pitcher, Fluted Scrolls, opalescent	300.00
Spooner, Palm Beach, opalescent	95.00
Sugar, cov, Diamond Spearhead, opalescent	235.00
Toothpick Holder, Daisy and Button	35.00
Tumbler, Fluted Scrolls	50.00

❖ Vending Machines

Got a penny for a gumball? Vending machines with gumballs, peanuts, and other goodies captured many pennies and loose change. Actually, these simple vending machines go back to about 1910 and have been with us in some form ever since.

References: Several good older reference books exist on this topic and are recommended for those who want to learn more about vending machines.

Periodicals: *Antique Amusements, Slot Machines & Jukebox Gazette,* 909 26th St NW, Washington, DC 20037; *Around the Vending Wheel,* 54217 Costana Ave, Lakewood, CA 90712; *Coin Drop International,* 5815 W 52nd Ave, Denver, CO 80212; *Coin Machine Trader,* 569 Kansas SE, PO Box 602, Huron, SD 57350; *Coin-Op Newsletter,* 909 26th St, NW, Washington, DC, 20037; *Coin Slot,* 4401 Zephyr St, Wheat Ridge, CO 80033; *Gameroom,* 1014 Mt Tabor Rd, New Albany, IN 47150; *Loose Change,* 1515 S Commerce St, Las Vegas, NV 89102; *Pin Game Journal,* 31937 Olde Franklin Dr, Farmington, MI, 48334; *Scopitone Newsletter,* 810 Courtland Dr, Ballwin, MO 63021.

Aspirin, Winthrop Metal Products, 10¢, c1940	45.00
Cigar, Malkin Phillies, steel meal, 10¢, c1930	95.00
Combs, Advance Machine, Model #4, 10¢, c1950	45.00

Gum

Adams, stick gum, Tutti-Frutti, wood upright case, 1¢, c1890	750.00

5-cent gum/candy dispenser, 11-1/2" h, 8" x 10" tray, $135.

Advance, stick gum, metal upright case, c1925	90.00
Columbus, ball gum, cast iron and round glove, Model A, c1915	200.00
Kayum, stick or pack gum, metal case, Adams or Beechnut decal, c1947	225.00
Victor, gum ball, plastic top, Topper, c1950	50.00
Hot Nuts, Cebco Products, cast aluminum, c1930	190.00
Matches, Kelley Mfg., boxes, 1¢, c1920	225.00
Postcard, Exhibit Supply, 1¢, c1930	125.00
Stamps, Postage and Stamp Machine Co., metal, 5¢ and 10¢, c1948	45.00

✫ Ventriloquist Dummies

Charlie McCarthy and Jerry Mahoney easily come to mind when thinking about vintage ventriloquist dummies. How fascinated we used to be with this form of entertainment. And, because there were many amateur ventriloquists, their dummies do occasionally find their way to flea markets. Look for well made hand-made examples or those made by well known doll companies.

Ventriloquist Dummy, all used condition

Bart Simpson, custom made.............................200.00

Boy, hand made, wearing child's blue suit, white shirt 90.00

Bozo 42.00

Jerry Mahoney 60.00

Madame look-a-like, hand made, but well done...................95.00

Monkey, hand made, plush fur, one arm quite long 35.00

Old Lady, wire frame glasses, purple hat, plastic hand bag, hand made.......................75.00

Three Stooges...................100.00

Willie Talk, Horsman............42.00

❖ Vernon Kilns

Founded in Vernon, California, the firm was formerly called Poxon China. After it was sold to Faye Bennison in 1931, it was renamed Vernon Kilns. The company then flourished and made high quality dinnerware and other items. One of their most successful lines were souvenir plates. The company survived until 1958, when it sold its trade name, molds, and remaining stock.

Periodical: *Vernon Views,* PO Box 945, Scottsdale, AZ 85252.

Cake Plate, Organdie, 12" d... 20.00

Chop Plate, Hawaiian Flowers, blue, 14" d 42.00

Creamer and Sugar, Brown-Eyed Susan 12.00

Cup and Saucer
    Chatelaine, topaz 40.00
    Moby Dick, brown................22.00

Dinner Plate, Hawaiian Flowers, blue, 9" d 32.00

Egg Cup, Organdie................. 27.50

Mug, Brown-Eyed Susan........ 25.00

Pitcher, Raffia, 2 qt 40.00

Platter, Winchester 73, oval, 12-1/2" l 145.00

Salad Plate, Chatelaine, topaz 25.00

Salt and Pepper Shakers, pr, Gingham............................. 15.00

Souvenir Plate
    Georgia, 10" d 15.00

Plate, Fruitdale, 10-1/2" d, $13.

Honolulu, Hawaii, pineapple border, several scenes, mkd "Made Exclusively for the Liberty House by Vernon Kilns, USA," 10-1/2" d 50.00

Nebraska University 30.00

Oklahoma State Agricultural and Mechanical College, backstamp "Vernon Kilns, designed especially for Creech's, Stillwater, Oklahoma"................ 30.00

Texas Southwest Methodist University, Dallas, backstamp "Made exclusively for Titche-Goettinger Co.".............. 35.00

Teapot, Mayflower................... 48.00

Tid-Bit Tray, Tam O'Shanter, 3 tiers, wood handle 45.00

☆ Victorian

This is one of those topics clearly open to individual interpretation. It takes its name from the reign of Queen Victoria, but clearly lasted for years after her reign ceased. Today decorators and dealers use it to describe things from that era that generally are ornate, richly colored and often richly textured. As a "look", it's fussy and somewhat heavy, but it also feels right at home in some older homes. Look for ornate furniture, period prints, and even ephemera to use as accents.

Boudoir Chair, lady's, wicker, ornate curliques, bead garlands ..335.00

Bud Vase, sterling silver, unidentified hallmarks, 8" h.................... 90.00

Fan, ostrich feathers, ribbon, white, some losses 120.00

Trade card, "Mikado Cologne, Fleming Bros., Pittsburgh," 5-1/8" x 3-1/2", $5.

Frame, 12" x 13", double heart shape openings, wood, brass corners............................... 60.00

Mirror, 12" x 12", beveled, ornate................................. 155.00

Print, Gibson Girl type portrait, some hand colored accents, framed............................... 125.00

Rose Bowl, glass, rich cranberry color 65.00

Sheet, 90" sq, matching pillow case, cutwork and embroidered cherubs, bows, and flowers 110.00

Valance and Mantle Cloth, 60" x 29", silk, large pink roses, moss green background, fringe............ 225.00

☆ Vienna Art

The Vienna Art Company was responsible for many interesting lithographed items. Look for intricate scenes which often include the advertised product. The colors tend to be rich. However, because the tin items were designed to be used, expect to find some scratching or signs of use when purchasing Vienna Art at flea markets.

Calendar, adv Harvard Brewing Co. Pure Malt Beverages, Lowell, Mass USA, lady with large pink ribbons in her hair, white gown, ornamental gilt border....... 150.00

Plate, 10" d, adv
    Anheuser-Busch Malt-Nurtine on back, front with lady in low cut diaphanous top.............. 95.00

Compliments of the American Sheet and Tinplate Co., Pittsburgh, maid with flowing brunette brown hair, plunging neckline, gilt border.........90.00

Dr. Pepper, beautiful lady holding stem of lilies, silhouetted against floral background, some rim chips, overall soiling and staining...................650.00

Dr. Pepper, Gypsy lady, some rim chips, staining on back............. 650.00

Joslin Dry Goods Co. adv on back, Gypsy lady.............90.00

Tray

9-1/2" d, adv Joseph Glennons New Brewery, art plate #207, Lenore, blond lady, rose colored gown, burgundy and gilt lined border.....................80.00

9-1/2" d, adv Stegmaier Brewing Co. Wilkes Barre, PA, lady with flowing hair dec with flowers, cobalt blue border, sapphire blue and gilt dec..............80.00

10" d, adv Anheuser-Busch Malt Nutrine, St. Louis, lady with flowing brown hair, low gown, green, gold, white, and pink on mantel border, dated 1905.................................65.00

10" d, adv Heim Breweries Select, East St. Louis, Ills, art plate #104, Poesie, lady with flowing brown hair, springs of leaves in her hair, pink low-cut gown, gold, cream, brown, and green border 75.00

10" d, adv Hotel Majestic, color litho of maiden in rose colored gown, holding vase of flowers, gilt border......................150.00

10" d, adv Independent Special Brew Beer, sultry young maid, plunging neckline, long brown flowing hair, red hat with pearls throughout hair, holds pink rose, Victorian burgundy border, red and white flowers, dated 1905.....................100.00

10" d, beautiful maid with white gown, long brown flowing hair, red hat, Art Nouveau green, gilt, and brown border, back mkd "Royal Saxony Art Plate #105, Irene, Chs. W. Shonk Co.,"................................60.00

10" d, bust of beautiful maiden, pink gown, sprigs of leaves, multicolored border, reverse mkd "Royal Saxony Art Plate #104, Poesie, Chs. W. Shonk Co." 90.00

☆ Vietnam War

With the passing of time since the Vietnam War, there is growing interest in military and civilian items related to the conflict. Items from "The Nam" and those from back in "The World" are seen with increasing frequency at flea markets, where good pieces can still be found at reasonable prices.

Service-related

Canteen, 2-qt, collapsible, no cover, 1968..................... 20.00

C-Rations, unopened 35.00

Flight jacket, G-1, US Navy, leather, size 40............. 260.00

Insect net for helmet, instruction tag attached 22.00

Jungle boots, unissued, early Vibram sole style, with instruction tag, 1967 .... 55.00

Magazine pouch, M16, rubberized canvas, early issue . 25.00

Shoulder tab, RVN Ranger, white silk, light-red border, "23 Vietnamese Ranger Bn" 73.00

Tour jacket, mkd "Camranh 1969-70," cloth, embroidered designs, zipper damage 81.50

Vietnam Veterans Memorial Fund pin, orig card, 1", $1.50.

Vietnam Veterans Memorial
Collector's Plate, Villroy & Boch, depicts statue of 3 servicemen 20.00

Stamps, Scott 2109, plate block of 4 .... 2.00

❖ View-Master

Gimme, gimme, I want to see, too! From the time view-masters and their reels were first created in 1939 until today, they have been educating and entertaining us. During World War II, shortages caused a cut-back in production, until the Army and Navy recognized that this would be a good way to train troops. After the war, demand soared and was met by several different companies.

Collectors' Club: National Stereoscopic Association, PO Box 14801, Columbus, OH 43214.

Aladdin & the Wonderful Lamp, Part One, 1951, Sawyers, Inc., orig jacket, FT-50A......................8.00

Aladdin & the Wonderful Lamp, Part Two, 1951, Sawyers, Inc., orig jacket and booklet, FT-50B.................................9.00

Fantasyland I, Sawyers, Inc. 854-A, Disneyland No. 4, orig jacket.................................8.00

Fantasyland II, Sawyers, Inc., 854-B, Disneyland No. 4, orig jacket 8.00

Fantasyland III, Sawyers, Inc. 854-C, Disneyland No. 4, orig jacket 8.00

Flintstones, View-Master International, 1980, MOC..............17.50

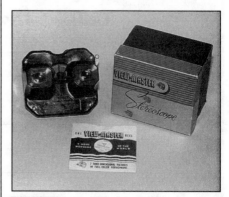

Sawyer's View-Master, orig box and reels, $16.

France, Sawyers, sealed pack.................... 17.50

Frontierland I, Sawyers, Inc. 852-A, Disneyland No. 2, orig jacket 8.00

Frontierland II, Sawyers, Inc., 852-B, Disneyland No. 2, orig jacket 8.00

Frontierland III, Sawyers, Inc., 852-C, Disneyland No. 2, orig jacket 8.00

GI Joe Adventures, GAF 24.00

Laugh-In, 3 reels, orig envelope, 1968 .... 45.00

Mount Rushmore, GAF, 1966 .... 17.50

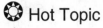
Snow White and the Seven Dwarfs, The Magic Mirror, FT-4A, Sawyers, 1955, orig sleeve 10.00

Space Mouse, Sawyer, 1964 .. 25.00

The Magic Carpet, FT-51, Sawyers, 1951, orig sleeve 9.00

Welcome Back Kotter, 3 reels, story booklet, color photo cover, 1977 .... 25.00

Wild Animals of the World, GAF, 1958 .... 14.50

❖ Viking Glass

Located in New Martinsville, West Virginia, this glass company has recently ceased production under the last of the original family owners, Dalzell-Viking. They produced various brightly colored glassware items through the years and also made some crackle glass. Look for a silver and pink foil label on some items.

Ashtray
   Amber, crackle glass, 7" l ... 15.00

Teal blue, triangular, orig foil label, 3-3/4" w 17.50

Bust, Madonna....................... 30.00

Candy Dish, teal blue 40.00

Compote, cov, orange 22.00

Fairy Lamp, red satin 55.00

Figure
   Duck, dark blue................... 40.00
   Elephant, frosted................. 20.00
   Penguin, dark blue.............. 65.00

Goblet, orange and gold, 4-5/8" h 12.00

Juice Set, cobalt blue, 5 pcs ... 30.00

Bird-shaped bowl, smoky brown, 4-1/2" h, 10-1/4" l, 8-5/8" w, $14.

Flea Market Notes

1. Market:_____

   Address/Location   _____

   Hours/Dates Open: _____

   Fees:_____

   Comments:_____

   _____

   _____

Flea Market Notes

2. Market:_____

   Address/Location   _____

   Hours/Dates Open: _____

   Fees:_____

   Comments:_____

   _____

   _____

Flea Market Notes

3. Market:_____

   Address/Location   _____

   Hours/Dates Open: _____

   Fees:_____

   Comments:_____

   _____

   _____

Flea Market Notes

4. Market:_____

   Address/Location   _____

   Hours/Dates Open: _____

   Fees:_____

   Comments:_____

   _____

   _____

W

✩ ✪ Wade Ceramics

The British firm known as The Wade Group started making industrial ceramics. By the late 1920s, they started to make figurines which were well received. They also added a dinnerware and accessories line to their production. Many dealers know the name Wade from the Red Rose Tea premiums.

References: Pat Murray, *The Charlton Standard Catalogue of Wade,* Vol One, 2nd ed., 1966; Vol. Two, 2nd ed., 1966; Vol. Three, 1998; *The Charlton Standard Catalogue of Wade Whimsical Collectibles,* 4th ed., 1998, Charlton Press.

Collectors' Clubs: The Official International Wade Collectors Club, Royal Works, Westport, Road, Burslem, Stoke-On-Trent, ST6 4AP England; Wade Watch, 8199 Pierson Court, Arvada, CO 80005.

Candlestick, baby seal, gray and black 37.50
Circus Figures, set of 15 entertainers and animals 30.00
Dish, ballerina 12.00
Figure
    Kissing bunnies 115.00
    Lucky Leprechaun, cobbler, 1950s 32.00
Mary Had A Little Lamb 7.50
Storybook Chimp, wearing skirt 5.00
Ginger Jar, red and black flowers, white ground 32.50

Humpty Dumpty, Fox, each $8.50.

Red Rose Tea Figure
    Buffalo 3.50
    Camel 3.00
    Cockatoo 8.00
    Elephant 2.50
    Hippo 3.00
    Kangaroo 2.50
    Raccoon 2.50
    Tiger 2.50
Stein, beer barrel shape, sgd "T. J.," 7-1/2" h 35.00
Turtle, with lid 35.00
Wall Plaque, yacht, green, blue, and beige 45.00

❖ Waffle Irons

One of the best things to find at many flea markets is the ice cream waffle stand. There they have commercial waffle irons working hard to keep up with the demand for that wonderful creation. However, if your favorite flea market doesn't include such a gourmet treat, perhaps you'd prefer to collect waffle irons. If that's the case, look for examples with interesting waffle patterns and, if used, no damage or missing parts.

Armstrong, Model W, heat indicator and thermometer light on top, round nickel body, black wood handles, orig cord 50.00
Coleman, Art Deco style, chrome, low profile, small black and white porcelain top impala insert, black Bakelite handles 85.00
Electrahot, two 6" sets of plates mounted on oval base, heat indicators 35.00
Hotpoint, round chrome body, top dec, ivory Bakelite handle, scalloped base 45.00
Stover Junior #8 .... 160.00
Wagner Ware, stove top type, 3" d 85.00

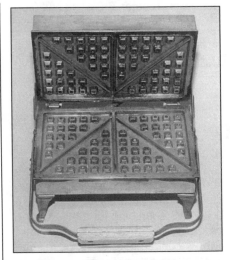

Westinghouse Model WA-4, 1921 patent date, wooden handle, works, 9" h, 5-1/4" w $37.50.

✩ Wagner Ware

Wagner Manufacturing made cast iron hollow ware, brass castings and, later, made aluminum cookware and other household wares. The company prospered from 1891 to the late 1950s under the care of the Wagner family. The firm was bought in 1959 by Textron, who held it until 1969.

Periodical: *Kettles n' Cookware,* Drawer B, Perrysville, NY 14129.

Ashtray, frying pan shape, mkd "1050" 10.00
Coffeepot, 1902 .... 55.00
Corn Stick Pan 15.00
Lid, glass, emb "Wagner Ware, C-10," 11-7/8" d 24.00
Orange Squeezer, #453B 30.00
Popover Pan 20.00

Cast-iron Dutch oven, #1268/A, 10-1/4" d, $55.

Sandwich Toaster, 6-3/4" sq ... 320.00

Skillet

#6 .... 10.00
#12 .... 55.00

✯ Walgreen's Collectibles

Walgreen's is an American institution. Being one of the oldest drug stores in the country contributes to collectors searching for early tins and products with the Walgreen's name. Others concentrate on things relating to other aspects of the store.

Ashtray, glass, Walgreen's
    Restaurant 25.00
Book, *Pharmacist to the Nation,*
    1989 .... 12.00
Cup and Saucer, Syracuse
    China 8.50
Grill Plate, Syracuse China,
    9-1/2" d 26.00
Matchcover, mkd "Walgreens Drugs
    Bismadine," 1930 .... 11.00
Menu, Coke cooler, small size .. 6.00
Mug, commemorative, 1997 ..... 6.50
Spoon, silver plate, mkd "Property of
    Walgreen's" 7.50

Tin

Amelita Dusting Powder,
    orig puff 10.00
Epsom Salts 15.00

✯ Wallace China

Wallace China was founded in 1931 in Vernon, California. It made commercial and residential dinnerware until 1959. Their western designs are favorites with collectors. The Westward Ho pattern is a good example of chinaware they created for a hotel. Their Willow design is also popular with Blue Willow collectors. Wallace China is well marked.

Cereal Bowl, Magnolia 20.00

Chili Bowl

Western brands motif 70.00
Westward Ho 55.00
Cup and Saucer, western brands
    motif 70.00

Dinner Plate
Rodeo 115.00
Westward Ho 85.00
Grill, El Rancho 12.00

Serving Plate
Old Hawaii, oval 30.00
Shadow Leaf 20.00
Teapot, individual size,
    Hibiscus 55.00

✯ ✪ Wall Pockets

Wall pockets are clever pottery holders designed to be hung on walls. Potteries such as Roseville and Weller made wall pockets in the same lines as their vases, bowls, etc. Collectors search for these potteries plus interesting examples from other lesser known makers. Wall pockets were very hot collectibles a few years ago, driven by the decorator market. Today they are becoming easier to find at flea markets, but the prices haven't declined.

Reference: Betty and Bill Newbound, *Collector's Encyclopedia of Wall Pockets, Identification and Values,* Collector Books, 1996, 1998 value update.

Collectors' Club: Wall Pocket Collectors Club, 1356 Tahiti, St. Louis, MO 63128.

Acorn, light brown, mkd "Frankoma
    190" 25.00
Cowboy Boot, blue and white,
    speckled, mkd "Frankoma
    133" 30.00
Cup and Saucer, blue,
    B-24 .... 265.00
Fish, yellow stripes, mkd "Gilner
    Calif C" 25.00
Harlequin heads, boy and girl,
    Japan 65.00
Horseshoe, horse head
    center 30.00
Lily, yellow, McCoy 25.00
Panel, 9" l, brown,
    Roseville 325.00
Peacock, blue, mkd "USA" 35.00
Pitcher, pink and blue, B-26 .. 265.00
Straw Hat, mkd "Stewart G. McCullock Calif" 20.00
Teapot, pink apple dec,
    Shawnee 32.00

Abingdon, #435, white, 8-1/2" x 8-3/8", $120.

Umbrella, black, white handle, mkd
    "McCoy USA" 40.00
Whisk Broom, blue, B-27 ...... 265.00
Woodland, pre-1950 .... 175.00
Zephyr Lily, brown,
    Roseville 245.00

❖ Watch Fobs

A watch fob is a useful and/or decorative item that is attached to a man's pocket watch by a strap. Its main function is to assist the user in removing the watch from a pocket. The heyday of watch fobs was late in the 19th century when many manufacturers created them to advertise products, commemorate special events, or as decorative and useful objects. Most watch fobs are made of metal and struck from a steel die. Some are trimmed with enamel or may even have a celluloid plaque. When found with their original watch strap or original packaging, the value is enhanced.

Collectors' Clubs: Canadian Association of Watch Fob Collectors, PO Box 787, Caledonia, Ontario, NDA IAO Canada; International Watch Fob Association, Inc., RR5, PO Box 210, Burlington, IA 52601; Midwest Watch Fob Collectors, Inc.,6401 W. Girard Ave., Milwaukee, WI 53210.

Reproduction Alert.

National Sportsman, brass, 1-1/2" d, $52.

For additional listings, see *Warman's Americana & Collectibles.*

Advertising

Brown Gin & Liquors, brass, raised moose head, reverse mkd "Sold by H. Obermauer & Co., Pittsburgh, PA," 1-1/2" d 60.00

Caterpillar Construction Equipment, silvered metal, tread tractor earth mover, reverse inscribed with dealer's name, orig strap 40.00

Evening Gazette, baseball shape, scorecard back, 1912......95.00

Joliet Corn Shellers 150.00

Kelly Springfield Tires, white metal, raised illus of female motorist, "Kelly Springfield Hand Made Tires" on back, 2" d................................80.00

Pontiac, with key chain, 3/4" d..............................45.00

Red Goose Shoes, enameled red goose 100.00

Commemorative

American Legion, Cleveland State Convention, 1946, diecut brass 35.00

Princeton University, brass, 1908................................48.00

World Championship Rodeo Contest, Chicago 45.00

❖ Waterford Crystal

The name Waterford Crystal is easily identified with high quality crys-

tal. The firm was started in 1729, in Waterford, Ireland. Look for a very finely etched mark or a foil type label. Waterford continues to make exquisite glassware today.

For additional listings, see *Warman's Antiques and Collectibles* and *Warman's Glass.*

Christmas Ornament, c1995... 17.50
Clock, ABC block 60.00

Figure

Dolphin 110.00
Eagle 140.00
Lion...................................150.00
Rocking Horse................... 80.00
Shark 125.00

Frame, ABC block, 4" x 6" 55.00
Goblet, Colleen 65.00
Paperweight, Capital.............. 90.00

Vase

Glendora, 9" h 195.00
#227-974-6200, 9" h......... 175.00

✦ ❂ Watering Cans

Here's a topic that was really hot at last summer's flea markets. It seemed like everywhere you looked there was a watering can. Again, it's the decorator influence that encouraged those with a country-style interior to add a few watering cans. And, while all this flower watering has been going on, more vintage lithographed tin children's watering cans also appeared on the scene. They too have become an eagerly sought after item.

Ceramic, Czechoslovakian, white ground, blue-green shading and trim, 2 swans swimming, 5-1/4" h .60.00Sterling Silver, narrow spout, small size 45.00

Child's, litho on tin

Ohio Art, turquoise and orange flowers, pink hearts, yellow ground, 8-1/4" h 35.00

Pretty garden, bright colors, c1920, very slight use, 6-1/4" h 150.00

Super Smurf in Shower 10.00

Victorian children in garden, handle loose, scratches, wear, 8" h 60.00

Plastic elephant, Ohio Art, 8-1/2" h, $7.

Copper, round, long narrow spout, round closed sprinkler head 66.00

Tin, brass spray head..............35.00

❖ Watt Pottery

Although the name Watt Pottery wasn't used until about 1920, founder W. J. Watt was involved in the pottery business as early as 1886. He worked at several pottery companies before purchasing the Crooksville, OH, Globe Stoneware Company. With the help of his sons Harry and Thomas, son-in-law C. L. Dawson, daughter Marion Watt, and numerous other relatives, he began production of this uniquely American pottery. Most Watt dinnerware features underglaze decoration on a sturdy off-white or tan body. Much of Watt dinnerware found its way to America's housewives by outlets such as Safeway and Woolworth and grocery chains. A fire destroyed the factory in October of 1965 and it was never rebuilt.

Collectors' Club: Watt Pottery Collectors USA, Box 26067, Fairview Park, OH 44126.

Reproduction Alert.

For additional listings, see *Warman's Americana & Collectibles.*

Apple #96 casserole, two-tone leaves, 8-3/4" d, $115.

Baker, Cherry, cov, #53 .... 100.00
Bean Pot, Apple, cov 200.00
Canister, cov, Apple, #72 ...... 265.00
Cereal Bowl Apple 24.00
Creamer, Apple, #62 .... 175.00
Ice Tea Dispenser, NESTEA, green,
    restaurant size 385.00
Mug, Brownstone, blue, #12168.00
Pie Plate, Apple 150.00
Salad Bowl, Apple, #73 .... 65.00

❖ Weather Vanes

Weather vanes were originally designed to help determine which way the wind was blowing, showing farmers which direction a potential weather system was coming from. Back in the old days, farmers used their own resources to figure out what the weather was going to be like, not the six o'clock news. However, just because it was going to be on top of the barn didn't mean it had to be ordinary. Look for large weather vanes made of copper, sheet metal, cast or wrought iron, wood, or zinc. Expect to find some signs of weathered wear on vintage weather vanes.

Reproduction Alert.

For additional listings, see *Warman's Antiques and Collectibles Price Guide.*

Arrow, gilt iron and copper,
    repainted, very minor losses,
    29-1/2" l 815.00
Beaver, painted over giltwood, early
    20th C, 48" l 460.00
Cow, molded zinc, late 19th C,
    dents, repainted, very minor
    holes, 29" l 230.00

Running horse, sheet metal, repainted black, 12-1/4" x 19", $26.

Horse
    Prancing, gilt copper, attributed to
        W. A. Snow, Boston, minor
        dents, splits, repairs, surface
        imperfections, 25-1/2" h,
        34" l 2,415.00
    Running, gilt molded copper,
        imperfections,
        17-3/4" l 1,850.00
Rooster, gilt over copper, iron stand,
    bullet holes, 28-1/2" h,
    24" l 770.00

❖ Wedgwood

Another name that usually denotes quality, this time in English ceramics. Josiah Wedgwood built a factory at Etruria, England, between 1766 and 1769, after having been in the ceramics business for a few years. Wedgwood's early products included caneware, unglazed earthenware, black basalt, creamware, and jasperware. Bone china was introduced between 1812 and 1822. Over the years these and other wares have been made, marked, and well used. Today, Wedgwood still continues its tradition of fine quality.

Periodical: *ARS Ceramics,* 5 Dogwood Court, Glen Head, NY 11545.

Collectors' Clubs: Wedgwood International Seminar, 22 DeSavry Crescent, Toronto, Ontario M4S 2T2 Canada; The Wedgwood Society, The Roman Villa, Rockbourne, Fordingbridge, Hants, SP6 3PG, England; The Wedgwood Society of Boston, 28 Birchwood Drive, Hampstead, NH 03841; The Wedgwood Society of

New York, 5 Dogwood Court, Glen Head, NY 11545; Wedgwood Society of Southern California, Inc., PO Box 4385, North Hollywood, CA 91617.

For additional listings, see *Warman's Antiques and Collectibles Price Guide* and *Warman's English & Continental Pottery & Porcelain.*

Basket, Queen's Ware, oval, under-
    tray, basketweave molded bodies,
    pierced galleries, green and black
    enamel oak leaves and trim, imp
    mark, early 19th C, 9" l 290.00
Bowl, jasper, solid light blue, white
    foliate relief, polished int., imp
    mark, c1800, 5" d 550.00
Bust, Locke, black basalt, raised
    base, imp title and mark, c1865,
    7-3/4" h 525.00
Celery Dish, bone china, gilt dia-
    mond border, printed mark, foot
    rim, light gilt wear, c1820 .. 175.00
Dinner Plate, lavender on cream,
    shell edge 35.00
Egg Shaped Box, cov, 1978, incised
    "Wedgwood, England, V," 2" h,
    3" l 65.00
Fruit Plate, majolica, turquoise bas-
    ketweave, 6-1/2" d 250.00
Game Pie, caneware, oval, molded,
    rabbit finial, imp mark, 1865, 7"l,
    orig liner cracked 445.00
Match Box, jasper, dark blue ... 90.00
Medallion, jasper, light green dip,
    oval, portrait of Admiral Richard
    Howe, imp title and mark, 3-1/2" x
    4-1/4" 260.00

Collector's plate, Children's Story 1971, "The Sandman" by Hans Christian Andersen, orig box, 6" d, $46.

Pitcher, black basalt, club, enameled floral dec, imp mark, c1860, 6-1/2" h.............................. 345.00

Plaque, jasper, solid black, applied white classical relief of muses, imp mark, 19th C, wood frame, rect 490.00

Teapot, blue transfer printed earthenware, Oaklands, imp and printed marks, 1909, spout chips, cover stained.................... 200.00

Vase

Creamware, molded grape vines and foliage, painted band of strawberries, mid 19th C, minor damage, 6" h...................90.00

Diceware, tricolor, pale blue dip, yellow quatrefoils, white ground, pierced flower frog cover with white applied quatrefoils, #82 of limited edition of 200, mkd "Wedgwood, Made in England, H82HB, 74," c1974, 5-1/4" h, 4-5/8" d 1,275.00

Jasper, solid pale blue, white relief of children playing Blind Man's Bluff, mounted to white marble base, se with oval Wedgwood pale blue jasper medallion with white relief of children playing, imp mark, late 18th C, minor damage, modern cover 1,850.00

Wine Cooler, redware, fruiting vines on molded body, raised mask handles, imp mark, early 19th C, 10" h 550.00

❖ Weller Pottery

Samuel Weller started a small pottery factory near Zanesville, Ohio, in 1872. He started producing utilitarian stoneware. By 1882, he moved to larger quarters and expanded his lines. As the years continued, more designers arrived, and the lines were expanded to include commercial wares. As art pottery became popular, Weller developed lines to answer that need also. Today, some of the art pottery lines are highly sought after. The company managed to stay in business during World War II, but by 1948 it had ceased operations.

For additional listings, see *Warman's Antiques and Collectibles Price*

Louwelsa mug, hp cherries, 6" h, $225.

Guide, Warman's Americana & Collectibles, and *Warman's American Pottery & Porcelain.*

Ashtray, Coppertone, frog seated at end 115.00

Basket
    Melrose, 10" 155.00
    Silvertone, 8" 350.00

Bowl
    Cameo, 6" d........................ 95.00
    Fleron, green 80.00

Ewer, Greenbrier, 11-1/2"...... 200.00

Flower Frog
    Kingfisher, 6" 475.00
    Muskota swan, chip repair 145.00

Hanging Basket, Ivory Ware, marked with half kiln ink stamp...... 110.00

Jardiniere
    Claywood, cherries and trees 95.00
    Roma, cat chasing canary 175.00

Milk Pitcher, 4" h, Zona........... 75.00

Mug, Claywood 75.00

Tub, Flemish, 4-1/2" d............. 75.00

For exciting collecting trends and newly expanded areas look for the following symbols:

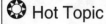 Hot Topic

★ New Warman's Listing

(May have been in another Warman's edition.)

Claywood vase, 3 1/2" h, $58.

Vase

Eocean, 8" h 400.00

Eocean, 10-1/2" h 250.00

Etna, 8-3/4" h, sgd front and bottom, thistle dec, celadon leaves, dusty rose flowers, champagne pink and smoky slate ground.................. 800.00

Hudson, 9" h, florals, sgd "McLaughlin"................. 900.00

Louella, gray, hp, nasturtiums.................. 220.00

❖ Western Collectibles

The American West has always held a fascination. Whether you're a collector interested in history or a decorator striving to achieve a western motif using authentic items, flea markets yield many items to catch your eye.

Periodicals: *American Cowboy,* PO Box 6630, Sheridan, WY 82801; *Boots,* Lone Pine Road, PO Box 766, Challis, ID 83226; *Cowboy Collector Newsletter,* PO Box 7486, Long Beach, CA 90807; *Cowboy Guide,* PO Box 6459, Sante Fe, NM 87502; *Rope Burns,* PO Box 35, Gene Autry, OK 73436; *The Westerner,* PO Box 5253, Vienna, WV 26105.

Collectors' Clubs: American Cowboy Culture Association, 4124 62nd Drive, Lubbock, TX 79413; National Bit, Spur & Saddle Collectors Association, PO Box 3098, Colorado Springs, CO 80934; Western Americana Collectors Society, PO Box 620417, Woodside, CA 94062.

Annual, Annie Oakley, 1964....40.00

Spurs, worn, 6-1/2" l, $110.

Award, aluminum cowboy hat, mkd "Nelson's 8th Round-Up, Qualified Cow Puncher," 1934, 5" x 4-3/8" x 2" 40.00

Belt Buckle, bucking bronc, MIB 40.00

Book

My Sixty Years on the Plains: Trapping, Trading, and Indian Fighting, W. T. Hamilton, 1905, portrait frontispiece, plates by Charles Russell, first edition 150.00

Old Frontiers: The Story of the Cherokee Indians, John P. Brown, 1938....................70.00

The Cowboys Own Brand Book, Duncan Emrich, hard bound, 1954, ex-library 7.50

Coasters, cowboy, set of four in holder 15.00

Cowboy Hat, Stetson, pencil roll, orig box 150.00

Figure, cowboy, Stetson 35.00

Holster, leather, double, studs, jewels, 1950s 65.00

Lamp, 8" h, figural cowboy boot, mkd "Made in Occupied Japan" 85.00

Magic Lantern Slides, set of 60, Colorado by a Tenderfoot, railroad, mining towns, Pikes Peak, waterfalls, Denver, c1907.......... 225.00

Saddle Stand, wood 100.00

Spurs, pr, N & J, brass, horse head 225.00

Wall Lamp, cast iron silhouette of bronco buster 30.00

❖ Westmoreland Glass

Founded in 1899 in Grapeville, PA, the Westmoreland Company originally made hand crafted high quality glassware. During the 1920s, they started to make reproductions and decorated wares. Production continued until 1982. Over the years they made crystal, black, various colored milk glass pieces, and many other colors. Today, it's probably the milk glass pieces that are the most interesting to collectors.

Collectors' Clubs: National Westmoreland Glass Collectors Club, PO Box 625, Irwin, PA 15692; Westmoreland Glass Collectors Club, 2712 Glenwood, Independence, MO 64052; Westmoreland Glass Society, PO Box 2883, Iowa City, IA 52244.

Bowl

Old Quilt, milk glass, 6" d, ftd 18.00

Paneled Grape, milk glass, 10" d 50.00

Bud Vase, Roses & Bows, milk glass, 10" h, paneled grape dec...................................... 45.00

Candelabra, 3–light, Paneled Grape, milk glass......................... 285.00

Candlesticks, pr

Old Quilt, milk glass, 3" h 20.00

Paneled Grape, milk glass, 2–light............................ 37.50

Candy Dish, cov, Old Quilt, milk glass, sq

High foot 30.00

Low foot............................. 25.00

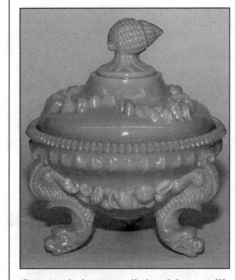

Covered butter, light blue milk glass, 3 feet, $42.

Cheese Dish, cov, Old Quilt, milk glass 45.00

Cologne Bottle, Paneled Grape, milk glass 45.00

Compote, cov, 7", Paneled Grape, milk glass............................. 45.00

Creamer and Sugar, Della Robia, milk glass 18.00

Cruet, Old Quilt, milk glass 25.00

Cup, Della Robia..................... 45.00

Cup and Saucer

Paneled Grape, milk glass 22.50

Plain, beaded edge, milk glass 12.00

Dresser Set, Paneled Grape, milk glass, 4 pcs..................... 250.00

Dresser Tray

Daisy, milk glass 20.00

Paneled Grape, milk glass, decorated 125.00

Sunflower, milk glass 30.00

Goblet

Della Robia, milk glass 18.00

Paneled Grape, milk glass.. 18.00

Thousand Eye, crystal 12.00

Honey Dish, cov, Beaded Grape, milk glass, sq 20.00

Iced Tea Tumbler

Old Quilt, milk glass, 5-1/4" h, ftd 18.00

Paneled Grape, milk glass, 12 oz 22.00

Pin Dish, square, milk glass...... 7.00

Pitcher, pint, Paneled Grape, milk glass 47.50

Planter, Paneled Grape, milk glass, 5" x 9" 40.00

Plate

Milk Glass, beaded edge, apple dec................................. 12.00

Old Quilt, milk glass, 8" d....32.00

Punch Set, Della Robia, crystal bell shaped punch bowl, 6 cups 45.00

Salad Plate, Della Robia, crystal, dark stained fruit 24.00

Relish, 3–part, Paneled Grape, milk glass 40.00

Tidbit, Beaded Grape, milk glass, 2 tiers 45.00

Tray

Grape, milk glass 25.00

Heavy Scroll, all–over gold dec................................... 25.00

Maple Leaf, 9" d 12.00

Tumbler, milk glass, ftd
Apple 20.00
Old Quilt, 4-1/4" h 10.00
Peach 20.00
Wedding Bowl, Roses & Bows, milk glass, 10" h......................... 65.00

❖ Wheaton Glass

Wheaton Glass is located in central New Jersey and today operates a wonderful museum and working glass site in Millville. Flea markets are seeing few of their limited edition bottles and objects. Perhaps this will change as collectors begin to search for Wheaton objects again.

Ashtray, ruby 3.00

Bottle
George Washington 5.00
Great American Series, Mark Twain, W72, blue carnival...........................30.00
Jenny Lind, set of three, red, green, and cobalt blue 12.00
President Series, 12 bottles 30.00
Bud Vase, ruby 10.00

Flask, "Dwight David Eisenhower, Peace With Justice," purple, 8" h, $7.50.

Decanter, Robert F. Kennedy, green 5.00
Paperweight, figural green pepper 20.00

❖ Whirligigs

Like weather vanes, many early whirligigs were used to help determine weather patterns. Others were made for ornamentation. Most are made of wood and can be found painted. The more action a whirligig exhibits, the higher the price will probably be.

Duck, yellow, wings move 25.00
Locomotive, painted and carved wood and metal, mechanized engine and signal man, old weathered surface, minor imperfections, America, early 20th C 750.00
Man sawing log, wood, painted red, white, and green 60.00
Roadrunner, moving legs 25.00
Soldier, holding small American flag, painted uniform.................... 20.00
Windmill, moving blades, pressure treated wood....................... 50.00
Woman, arm raises pump handle................................. 50.00
Red Goose Shoes, yellow litho tin, yellow and red symbol, made by Kirchof Co., 1930s 35.00

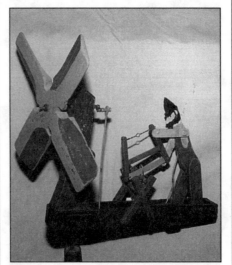

Man sawing wood, painted wood figure and blades, 15" h, 17" l, $60.

⭐ White Knob Windups

Just give a twist or two to the little white knob, and these plastic playthings teeter across any hard, flat surface. Because of their small size they are most commonly found in showcases. Only recently have they received much attention, which has started to send prices scurrying. Of course, ask permission to test any white knob windup before buying it. Few nonfunctioning examples are worth owning.

Collectors' Clubs: White Knob Wind-Up Collectors Club, 61 Garrow St., Auburn, NY 13021-4605.

Alien, H.R. Geiger, MIP, 3" 10.00
Bobotto, robot, SCL, 1983, MOC 10.50
Dairy Queen, ice cream sundae 6.00
Marvin, comic strip character, Straco, 1983, shop-worn card.................................... 13.50
Mickey Mouse, Tomy, 3-1/4" 11.00
Pac Man, Tomy, MOC, 2-1/2" 10.50
Penguin, pushes smaller penguin, magnetic, plays song 60.00

Owl, Tomy, 2-1/8" h, $5.

Snoopy, football motif, red jersey,
Aviva.................................... 10.00
Snoopy, Christmas motif, soiling to
Santa hat, Aviva 12.50
Starrior robot, Tomy, MOC...... 13.00
Star Wars, Chewbacca, 3"...... 13.00
Star Wars, R2-D2, 3" 8.00
Star Wars, Yoda, 3" 15.00
Sumo wrestler, Sekiguchi, multiple
actions 155.00

❖ Wicker

Wicker furniture evokes a summer time feeling, even in the cold of winter. Wicker can be found in natural rattan or painted. The Victorians loved it. Today the look is still popular. Look for pieces with original upholstery in very good condition and without too many layers of paint. Many pieces of wicker cannot be stripped without damaging the materials.

Chair
Arm, wide flat arm rests continue
to back, broad seat,
repainted 200.00
Corner, elaborate scrolling, bird
cage arms and supports,
natural finish..................650.00
Photographer's, elaborate
scrolled back and arms,
painted white.................450.00
Ferner, white, metal liner,
rectangular, repainted several
times................................. 185.00
Foot Stool, upholstered seat,
painted 195.00
Music Stand, Wakefield Rattan Co.,
three shelves, orig paper label,
c1883 .... 285.00
Rocker, Wakefield Rattan Co.,
serpentine edges, braided trim,
wooden rockers, painted
white................................. 265.00
Suite, sofa, two matching arm
chairs, ottoman, some damage to
wicker, worn old upholstery, as
found condition 300.00

For exciting collecting trends and newly expanded areas look for the following symbols:

⊕ Hot Topic

✫ New Warman's Listing

(May have been in another Warman's edition.)

✫ Winchester

This favorite American firearms manufacturer has a quite a following with collectors. Those with sharp vision can find all kinds of ephemera and advertising.

Collectors' Club: Winchester Club of America, 3070 S. Wyandot, Englewood, Co 80110.

Ammunition, 50-110-300 for Model
1886 rifles, orig box in good condition, orig labels, 20
cartridges.......................... 200.00
Banner, Headquarters for Winchester Rifles & Shotguns, fringed
hem, wood rod,
19-1/2" x 29"..................... 150.00
Book, *The Book of Winchester
Engraving,* first edition, dust
jacket 500.00
Calendar, 1915, eagle attacking
mountain goats, Forbes Litho
Mfg. Co., artist sgd "Lynn Bogue
Hunt," paper, framed, 29-1/2" h,
14-1/2" w, calendar pad
missing 1,500.00
Catalog
Winchester Rifles, John Wayne
cover, 1982..................... 10.00
Winchester-Western, New Haven,
CT, 1976, 5-3/4" x 7-1/2" 40.00
Counter Felt, Shoot Where
You Aim 175.00

12-gauge shotgun shells, box only, 4-1/8" x 4-1/8" x 2-1/2", $4.

Print, signed, framed, hunter standing tall with his Winchester as
ferocious wolves attack, © 1906,
29" h, 15-1/4" w 3,300.00
Stickpin, Ask for Winchester
Nublack, brass, shotgun shell
shape, green enamel shell casing
with inscription,
early 1900s 125.00

✫ Winnie the Pooh

A.A. Milne's "tubby little cubby all stuffed with fluff" has become a best friend to countless children. It's no wonder Pooh, Piglet, Eeyore and the rest of the gang are eagerly sought by collectors. Mass marketing of Pooh in recent years has brought a flood of newer collectibles onto the market. However, buyers can still find a fair share of vintage Pooh items at flea markets.

Animation cel, "Winnie the Pooh and
Tigger Too!," from limited ed of
2,500, certificate of
authenticity........................ 125.00
Book, *Winnie the Pooh and Tigger
Too!,* Disney's Wonderful World of
Reading, Grolier Enterprises,
hardcover, mint in orig mailer,
9-1/2" x 7" 19.00
Bracelet, Ampaco Ltd., 1960s,
MOC 35.00
Collector's plate, 1997 Pooh &
Friends Chrsitmas Collectors'
Plate, 8-1/4" d 29.00

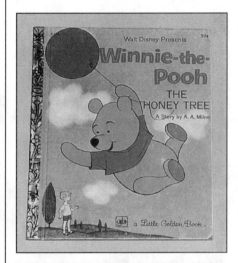

Little Golden Book, *Walt Disney Presents Winnie-the-Pooh: The Honey Tree,* **1977, 19th printing, $1.**

Cookie jar, Winnie the Pooh, cold paint, mkd "#900 Walt Disney Productions U.S.A., Made by California Originals".......... 275.00

Cookie jar, Winnie the Pooh Holiday Treehouse, Disney Store exclusive, MIB.................. 325.00

Doll, stuffed Eeyore, Gund, 1964, 9" h, 13-1/2" l.................... 100.00

Drinking glass, Winnie the Pooh for President, mkd "Sears" 26.00

Light fixture, ceiling light, Pooh and friends, glass, Sears exclusive, 13" sq 43.00

Movie Poster, "Winnie the Pooh and Tigger Too!," 1-sheet, folds, 27" x 41".. 74.00

Ornament, Winnie the Pooh Magic Ornament, talks, 1993........ 28.00

Perfume bottle, Tigger, glass, sold at Walt Disney World, 5" h...... 31.00

Pinback button, Disneyland, shows Pooh in center, green background 15.00

Record, "Winnie the Pooh and Christopher Robin Songs," 78rpm 39.00

Wall hangings, different Pooh characters, heavy cardboard..... 49.00

✯ Wizard of Oz

MGM gave birth to an institution when it released "The Wizard of Oz" in 1939, although L. Frank Baum's stories of Oz date to the early part of the 20th century. While vintage Oz items are competitively sought and can be pricey, a variety of contemporary collectibles fit into any collector's budget. Among the newer items are numerous pieces commemorating the film's 50th anniversary in 1989.

Periodical: Beyond the Rainbow Collector's Exchange, Elaine Willingham, P.O. Box 31672, St. Louis, MO 63131-0672.

Collectors' Clubs: Emerald City Club, 153 E. Main St., New Albany, IN 47150; The International Wizard of Oz Club, P.O. Box 10117, Berkeley, CA 94709-5117.

Book, *The Patchwork Girl of Oz* by L. Frank Baum, Reilly & Lee, 1913, no dustjacket 96.00

***Dorothy and the Wizard of Oz*, The Reilly & Lee Co., 1908, $75.**

Book, *The Road to Oz* by L. Frank Baum, Reilly & Lee, 1909, loose spine, no dustjacket............ 71.00

Collector's plate, Knowles China, 7th in series, man in hot air balloon, art by James Auckland, MIB 42.00

Cookbook, *The Wonderful Wizard of Oz Cookbook* by Monica Bayley, hardcover, 1st ed, 1981 ...... 52.00

Cookie jar, Dorothy & Toto, Star Jars, limited production of 1,939, 1994 .... 350.00

Doll, Barbie as Dorothy, Hollywood Legend Series, 1994, MIB 227.50

Doll, Dorothy of Emerald City, Madame Alexander, #94-D, 1994, MIB, 7-1/2"........................ 130.00

Game, Wizard of Oz Collector's Edition Monopoly Game, Parker Brothers, MIB 85.00

Lunchbox and thermos, Aladdin, 50th anniversary, 1989 .... 73.00

Playset, Wizard of Oz, Mego, complete 250.00

Sheet music, *Over the Rainbow*, 1939, pages separated....... 43.50

✯ Wolverine Toys

The Wolverine Supply & Manufacturing Company was founded in 1903. The first type of toys they produced were lithographed sand toys. Next came girls' housekeeping toys, soon followed by action games as well as cars and trucks.

Automatic Coal Loader, litho tin 80.00

Diving Submarine, litho tin windup, 13" l...................................195.00

Do The Twist, dancer on pedestal, MIB 75.00

Drum Major, #27, round base, c1930, 13-1/4" h 225.00

Gee Whiz Racehorse Game, 1930s, 15" l...................................145.00

Icebox, tin...............................55.00

Jet Roller Coaster, all tin, 22" l extended, 1930s 275.00

Kitchen Cabinet, #280, 1949, complete with toy groceries, orig box...........................195.00

Sand Toy, Cap't Sandy Andy, orig box......................................200.00

Shooting Gallery, orig box.....175.00

Sunny Suzy, electric iron, orig box..............................25.00

❖ Wood Collectibles

Wooden objects of all types are found at flea markets. Look for objects that are interesting, well made, and fit into your decorating scheme. Today's decorators often prefer a weathered look, while others prefer natural finished wood or an aged patina.

Collectors' Club: International Wood Collectors Society, 5900 Chestnut Ridge Road, Riner, VA 24149.

Apple Box, pine, old red paint, conical feet, 10" l.....................310.00

Artist's Model, articulated, minor losses and breaks, late 19th C 1,100.00

Checkerboard, 14-3/4" sq, inlaid, mahogany and maple, 20th C, minor veneer damage.......110.00

Duck toy, wooden, orig paint, 6" h, 6" l, $37.50.

Churn, stave construction, metal bands, turned lid, dasher, old refinishing, 21-1/2" h 150.00

Cutting Board, round top, shaped base, metal blade, 18" l...... 35.00

Drying Rack, mortised construction, chamfered, shoe feet, old blue repaint over yellow, 24-1/2" w 220.00

Egg Timer, candlestick telephone shape, wood, stamped "Cornwall Wood Products, So. Paris, Maine," 5" h 45.00

Niddy Noddy, hardwood, old yellow paint, one end with age crack................................... 110.00

Press, orig hardware, patina, dove-tailed construction, carved spout, 17" 150.00

Salad Bowl, varnished int, bright hand painted flowers, matching serving fork and spoon....... 25.00

Towel Bar, walnut, three horizontal bars on tapering squared posts, scrolled trestle feet, New England, early 19th C, 37-1/2" w 175.00

❖ World War I

Fueled by the assassination of Austrian Archduke Franz Ferdinand by a Serbian national in June of 1914, World War I was set off with Germany invading Belgium and France. Shortly after that, Russia, England, and Turkey joined the war. By 1917, the United States and Italy had become involved, too. By the time peace had been reached in 1919, many people had lost their lives, and the damage was wide spread. Memorabilia relating to World War I was carefully laid aside, hoping it would be the last war. Alas, it was not.

Periodicals: *Men at Arms*, 222 W Exchange St, Providence, RI 02903; *Military Collector Magazine*, PO Box 245, Lyon Station, PA, 19536; *Military Collectors' News*, PO Box 702073, Tulsa, OK 74170; *Military Trader*, PO Box 1050, Dubuque, IA 52004; *Wildcat Collectors Journal*, 15158 NE 6 Ave, Miami FL 33162.

Collectors' Clubs: American Society of Military Insignia Collectors, 526 Lafayette Ave, Palmerton, PA 18701; Association of American Military Uniform Collectors, PO Box 1876, Elyria, OH 44036; Company of Military Historians, North Main St, Westbrook, CT 06498; Orders and Medals Society of America, PO Box 484, Glassboro, NJ 08028.

Badge, American Red Cross-Military Welfare, cap, enamel.......... 24.00

Bayonet, orig case 24.00

Helmet, 28th Div. Medical Corps, orig ptd emblem, no liner or chin-strap, $55.

Candleholder, German, sword handle fits into candleholder, silver inlay reads "To Mom & Dad from Gordon," just above handle, no blade 95.00

Gas Mask, carrying can, shoulder strap, canister attached to bottom, German 50.00

Handkerchief, Remember Me, soldier and girl in center, red, white, and blue edge 24.00

Helmet, US, 3rd Army insignia .. 72.00

Painting, pastel on paper, German soldier, fine Victorian frame, 30" x 38" 500.00

Photograph, Officer Training Camp, Chickamuga Park, GA, 1917, 7" x 31" 85.00

Sheet Music, *American Patrol March*, 1914........................ 15.00

Watch Fob, flag on pole, USA, beaded, blue 48.00

❖ World War II

Several world events came together in 1939 to create World War II. The German Third Reich was engaged in an arms race; the Depression compounded the situation. After Germany invaded Poland, Allied and Axis alliances were formed and the war was underway. From 1942 to 1945, the whole world was involved, and almost every industry was war-related. Peace was not achieved until August of 1945. Again, after those horrible years, memorabilia was laid aside. Today collectors are discovering artifacts, equipment, and remembrances of this war at flea markets.

Periodicals: *Men at Arms*, 222 W Exchange St, Providence, RI 02903; *Military Collector Magazine*, PO Box 245, Lyon Station, PA, 19536; *Military Collectors' News*, PO Box 702073, Tulsa, OK 74170; *Military Trader*, PO Box 1050, Dubuque, IA 52004; *Wildcat Collectors Journal*, 15158 NE 6 Ave, Miami FL 33162; *World War II*, 7741 Miller Drive, SE, Suite D2, Harrisburg, PA 20175; *WWII Military Journal*, PO Box 28906, San Diego, CA 92198.

Collectors' Clubs: American Society of Military Insignia Collectors, 526 Lafayette Ave, Palmerton, PA 18701; Association of American Military Uniform Collectors, PO Box 1876, Elyria, OH 44036; Company of Military Historians, North Main St, Westbrook, CT 06498; Imperial German Military Collectors Association, 82 Atlantic St., Keyport, NJ 07735; Orders and Medals Society of America, PO Box 484, Glassboro, NJ 08028.

Book, *The American Heritage Picture History of World War II,* 1966, 640 pgs, color and black and white photos 15.00

Dexterity Puzzle, 3-1/4" x 4-1/4" x 7/8", Atom Bomb, dark blue tin litho frame, glass cover over paper playing surface, black and yellow, silhouette of Japan, A. C. Gilbert Co., 1946 .... 150.00

Drinking Glass, Remember Pearl Harbor, 4-3/4" h, clear, red letters pale to white and then blue, artwork of Pearl Harbor and Hawaiian Islands, warships, and aircraft 65.00

Parade Ticket, 1946, New York City Victory Parade, 3-1/2" x 5" stiff paper, black and pink text, issued by Mayor's Committee for 82nd Airborne Division Victory Parade on Jan 12, for reviewing stand, facsimile signatures of Mayor Wil-

War Bonds poster, "Heed their Call...," $75.

V Mail stationery, box with 35 sheets/envelopes, $10.

liam O'Dwyer and Committee Chairman Grover Whalen ... 30.00

Postcard, 3-1/4" x 5-1/2", "Three Dirty Dogs Remember Pearl Harbor," black and white, Axis leaders portraits, unused 30.00

Punch-Out Kit, Model Battleship, 7" x 10", full color envelope with scene of battleship on open sea, colorful thin cardboard sheet, Reed & Associates, early 1940s, unused 45.00

Salt and Pepper Shakers, pr, figural, Gen MacArthur, glazed ceramic, 2" x 2-1/2", tan hat, long yellow pipe 85.00

Sheet Music, *What Do You Do In The Infantry* 15.00

Sign, 12" x 18" full color, Kool Cigarettes, Kool penguin as Army sentry on duty, carrying rifle and smoking cigarette, Kool packs in cartridge belt and munitions factory in background, top text "Keep Alert-Smoke Kools," slight damage, colors bright 135.00

Wings
    Glider 30.00
    Liason 30.00

❖ World's Fairs and Expositions

The first really great world's exposition was the Great Exhibition of 1851 in London. Since that time, there have been many world's fairs, expositions, and celebrations. Today collectors tend to specialize in a particular fair or type of memorabilia.

Periodical: *World's Fair,* PO Box 339, Corte Madera, CA 94976.

Collectors' Club: World's Fair Collectors' Society, PO Box 20806, Sarasota, FL 34276.

Ashtray
    1939, Thinking of you at the World's Fair, NY, 1939, blue and black enamel, do-it-yourself type 130.00
    1964, New York, silver-tone metal, building panorama, back incised "Copyright 1961, Unisphere, Presented by United States Steel, Made in Japan," 5-3/4" d 48.00

Booklet, "My Diary of the New York World's Fair," 1939, 6-1/2" x 8-3/4", compliments of Hotel Chesterfield at Radio City, Times Square, 16 pgs, 21 black and white photos of fair exhibit buildings and New York City attractions 25.00

Stein, Louisiana World Exposition May 12-Nov. 11, 1984, pottery, 7" h, $13.50.

Coaster Set, 1964-65 New York, tin litho, Unisphere color image, text on back with details, set of four 12.00

Foil Stickers, New York World's Fair, 1939-40, 4-3/4" x 5-1/2" clear cellophane pack, double-sided sheet with gold, blue, and orange foil stickers on one side, silver, blue, and orange on other side, 12 images on both sides 25.00

Guide Book

"Second Edition Official Guide Book, 1939, New York," 5" x 8", soft cover, Art Deco style cover of Trylon/Perisphere at night, 256 black and white pgs 25.00

"World's Fair 1934 Official Guide Book," 5-1/2" x 8-1/2", full color Art Deco cover, 192 pages 25.00

Hot Pad, A Century of Progress, 1933, 6" x 8" cardboard, detailed silver accented relief image of exposition in center, surrounded by transportation theme, dark tan suede covering 15.00

Key Chain, Golden Gate bridge in center, "International Exposition" on bottom, 1-1/4" h 40.00

Magazine, New York World's Fair 1939, *Life* 35.00

Mug, 2-3/4" d, 5" h, brown glass, designed like mason jar, brass accent metal straps, notched wooden handle, New York Unisphere painted in white on front, Siesta Ware, 1964 .... 15.00

Pennant, 1939 Golden Gate International Exposition, San Francisco Bay, pastel Portals of the Pacific Building, red ground, 14-3/4" l 45.00

Photo Wheel, Chicago, 1939.. 60.00

Plate, St. Louis, 1904 Fair, 7" d, glass, molded flower vine design, reverse painted gold and white design, image of Festival Hall & Cascade Gardens in center, gold accent paint worn off flower rim 15.00

Program, "Official Daily Program of the Pan American Exposition," features for Elmira College Day, Sat, Oct 26, 1901 .... 25.00

Playing Cards, 1933 Century of Progress, World's Fair, single deck, boxed, $38.

Salt and Pepper Shakers, pr, 2" x 3-3/4" h, Eneloid plastic, blue Trylon and Perisphere, orange base, inscribed "New York World's Fair" 35.00

Shot Glass, ruby stained, "World's Fair 1933, Leona Hess," 2-1/4" h 55.00

Vinegar Bottle, 1939, milk glass 20.00

❖ Wrestling Memorabilia

The last sport of this edition is one that involves fewer players than team sports, but is physically demanding. It has also created a unique kind of memorabilia for its collectors and devotees.

Periodicals: *Sports Cards Magazine & Price Guide,* 700 E State St, Iola, WI 54990; *Sports Collectors Digest*, 700 E State St, Iola, WI 54990.

Autographed Photo, 8" x 10"
Goldberg, Bill 22.00
Lugar, Lex........................... 18.00
Nash, Kevin 20.00

Figure, L. L. Rittgers, 1941, 3 pc set, referee looking mad at standing wrestler looking down at opponent tied up in ball 295.00

Plaque, autographed
Goldberg............................ 45.00
Hollywood Hogan 45.00
Sting 45.00

Sports Card, WMF Superstars, foil 30.00

Cloth doll, Hulk Hogan, 24" h, $12.

❖ Wright, L. G.

L. G. Wright is a curious company. It started manufacturing glassware using old molds of other companies. Some of these are done in colors or textures not originally manufactured in a particular pattern. Some pattern glass collectors embraced this as a way to add color or another form to their collections. However, L. G. Wright also made some reproductions in original colors, causing great confusion for unsuspecting collectors. Today, as their reproductions broaden in scope and color, some folks are now collecting L. G. Wright wares as examples of that glass company and are not encumbered by the reproduction aspect.

Cocktail, Paneled Grape, #55, blue opalescent 25.00

Creamer and Sugar, Beaded Curtain, cranberry 160.00

Epergne, aqua blue crest...... 775.00

Goblet, Paneled Grape, #55, blue opalescent 30.00

Plate, Paneled Grape, #55, blue opalescent
6" d 15.00
9-3/4" d 30.00

Vase, Corn, blue opalescent ...90.00

Wine, Paneled Grape, #55, blue opalescent 30.00

❖ Wright, Russel

Russel Wright was an American industrial designer who took an active passion for life and the streamlined look to new heights. He influenced several companies and their designs, such as Chase Brass and Chrome, and General Electric.

One area where his influence was greatly felt was in dinnerware design. The Steubenville Pottery responded with a pattern called American Modern. This pattern was made from 1939 to 1959. The original issue colors were Bean Brown, Chartreuse Curry, Coral, Granite Grey, Seafoam Blue, and White. Later color additions include: Black Chutney, Cedar Green, Cantaloupe, Glacier Blue, and Steubenville Blue. Wright also created other dinnerware patterns, but American Modern remains the one that is most sought after by collectors.

American Modern pattern

Bread and Butter Plate, 6" d
Bean Brown..........................10.00
Granite Grey...........................5.00

Casserole, cov
Granite Grey........................65.00
Seafoam Blue......................45.00

Celery Dish
Bean Brown.........................28.00
Granite Grey 25.00

Chop Plate
Chartreuse Curry.................35.00
Granite Grey........................30.00

Cup and Saucer
Coral....................................12.00
Granite Grey........................14.00

Dinner Plate
Cedar Green 10.00
Granite Grey........................13.00

Fruit Bowl, lug
Coral....................................17.50
Granite Grey........................15.00

Platter
Coral....................................35.00
Granite Grey........................28.00

Salad Bowl
Granite Grey........................85.00
Seafoam Blue......................90.00

Bread plate, tan, 6" d, $5.

Salad Plate
Coral....................................17.50
Granite Grey........................15.00

Salt Shaker
Chartreuse Curry................14.00
Granite Grey........................10.00

Soup, lug
Bean Brown.........................27.50
Granite Grey........................15.00

Vegetable Bowl, open
Coral....................................35.00
Granite Grey........................25.00

Water Pitcher
Granite Grey......................100.00
Seafoam Blue...................125.00

❖ Wristwatches

Got the time? The first "real" wristwatch dates back to about 1850, but it wasn't until about 1880 that wristwatches became the stylish element we consider them to be. By the 1930s, the idea caught on well enough that sales of wristwatches finally surpassed sales of pocket watches.

References: To help identify your wristwatch, there are many excellent reference books, but most have older copyrights. Check a local bookseller or library for assistance.

Periodical: *International Wrist Watch*, 242 West Ave, Darien, CT 06820.

Collectors' Clubs: International Wrist Watch Collectors Chapter 146, 5901C Westheimer, Houston, TX 77057; National Association of Watch & Clock Collectors, 514 Poplar Street, Columbia, PA 17512; The Swatch Collectors Club, PO Box 7400, Melville, NY 11747.

Gruen
Man's, 10K wg, precision autowind, Tonneau case, black lizard band 65.00
Man's, 14K yg, orig strap .. 300.00

Hamilton, lady's, Art Deco, bezel and shoulders set with round baguette diamonds, platinum mount, black cord strap, white gold filled clasp, minor discoloration to dial 460.00

Lorus, Mickey Mouse, c1980, band simulates animation film of Mickey walking, MIB 25.00

Movado, man's, 14K yg, tank, stepped lugs, slightly bowed sides, gold-tone dial, Roman numerals and abstract indicators, subsidiary seconds dial, worn leather strap, crystal loose......................230.00

Omega, 18K yg, Seamaster, man's 250.00

Rolex, man's, perpetual, stainless steel, Air King, silver-tone dial, applied abstract indicators, sweep second hand, oyster bracelet with clasp, discoloration to dial, scratches to crystal 575.00

Tiffany & Co.
Lady's, 18K yg, back wind, texture gold dial with black Roman numerals and abstract indictors, diamond frame, textured gold bracelet, orig box..........................920.00
Man's, 18K yg, lapis lazuli color dial, stepped bezel, black crocodile strap 635.00

Uti, Paris, lady's, 18K yg, silver-tone dial, applied gold-tone indicators, leather strap with keyhole form closure, hallmarks, wear to strap....................................575.0

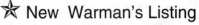

For exciting collecting trends and newly expanded areas look for the following symbols:

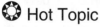 Hot Topic

★ New Warman's Listing

(May have been in another Warman's edition.)

❖ Yard Long Photos and Prints

To most collectors, a long narrow print is considered a "yard long" print. The format can be either horizontal or vertical. Yard long prints first appeared about 1900 and some were used as premiums as well as advertising. Many calendars were created in this format. The prices listed below are for yard long prints which have been nicely framed.

Many photographs were also made in this format, too. These were especially popular with school groups so that the entire student body could be included in a photo. Military units also favored this size.

Calendar

1911, Pabst Extra, American Girl, C. W. Henning, full length, cardboard roll at bottom 350.00

1927, Pompeian, The Bride, sgd "Rolf Armstrong" 350.00

Photograph

1919, USS *Siboney* Arriving at US Naval Base, August 8, 1919 .... 175.00

1936, Quakertown High School, Class of '36, in front of Capitol 75.00

Print

Battle of the Chicks, Ben Austrian, © 1920 by The Art Interchange Co. of New York 250.00

Easter Greetings, Paul DeLong- pre, © 1894 by Knapp Co. Litho 400.00

Hula Girl, sgd "Gene Pressler" 350.00

La France Roses, Paul DeLong- pre, © 1903, advertising Spie- hler's Perfume 300.00

❖ Yellow Ware

Named for its yellow body, it's a pottery made from common yellow clays. Some variations exist from pumpkin to light shades, because of the natural clay. Yellow ware was frequently made as useful household wares, such as bowls, cups, rolling pins. Most yellow ware was not marked and decorations are simple, if present at all.

Canning Jar, barrel shape, 6-3/4" h 110.00

Creamer, brown stripes, white band, blue seaweed dec, shallow flake on base, 4-3/4" h 440.00

Food Mold, turk's head, 7-1/2" d 145.00

Mug, flared sides, white slip dec 150.00

Pie Funnel, 2-1/2" h 125.00

Pie Plate, 10" d 90.00

Rolling Pin, wooden handles, adv 125.00

Mixing bowl, blue and pink stripes, 4-5/8" h, 8-1/4" d, $40.

★ Yo-Yos

Q: What keeps coming back when you toss it away? A: A yo-yo. Few people can truly throw away a yo-yo, which means there are many examples available on today's market. In addition to vintage items, look for contemporary yo-yo's featuring popular culture figures, advertising yo-yos

and commemorative examples. Yo-yo collections can be seen free of charge at The Yozeum in Tucson, Ariz., and the National Yo-Yo Museum in Chico, Cal.

Collectors' Clubs: American Yo-Yo Association, 627 163rd St. South, Spanaway, WA 98387.

Big D Trickster, Dell, 1961, MIP 125.00

Bowling ball, Duncan, Sports Line Model, #1070, MOC 55.00

Butterfly, Duncan, red, plastic ... 7.50

Campbell's Kids, Duncan 26.00

Cat's Eye, Duncan, green and gold jeweled eyes 305.00

Coca-Cola, 1992 Summer Olympics 25.00

Freddy Krueger Nightmare on Elm Street, Spectra Star, 1989, worn orig card 8.00

Grateful Dead, Searching for the Sound Summer Tour '92, wood, pictures Phil Lesh, Hummingbird Toy Co. 32.00

Hot Wheels, Mattel, tire motif, red chrome hubcaps, 1990, MOC 13.00

Jurassic Park, 1992, MIP 21.50

Mark Martin, Goodyear tire motif, pictures #6 Valvoline car, 1993, MIP 7.00

McDonald's, Pro-yo Whiz-z, arm and hand moves up and down ... 20.50

Nightmare Before Christmas, Spectra Star, #1584 .... 45.00

Oreo Cookie 10.50

Pee Wee Herman, Spectra Star, 1988, MOC 8.50

Planter's Mr. Peanut 20.50

Spider-Man, Duncan, 1978 ..... 25.50

Duncan butterfly, plastic, worn decal, 2-1/4" d, $5.

Z

❖ Zanesville Pottery

The area around Zanesville, Ohio, was home to several potteries. The Zanesville Art Pottery started production about 1900. Their first wares were utilitarian, and they soon ventured into art pottery production. The firm was bought by S. A. Weller in 1920 and became part of Weller Pottery at that time.

Bowl, fluted edge, mottled blue glaze, 6-1/2" d 45.00

Jardiniere, ruffed rim, cream to light amber peony blossoms, shaded brown ground 75.00

Vase, portrait of light gray horse, light olive green to blue-green ground, matte ext., glossy brown int., sgd "R. G. Turner," 10-1/4" h 825.00

For exciting collecting trends and newly expanded areas look for the following symbols:

❂ Hot Topic

★ New Warman's Listing
(May have been in another Warman's edition.)

Favorite dealers:

Name: _____

Shop name:_____

Address:_____

_____

Phone:_____

Hours:_____

Comments:_____

Name: _____

Shop name:_____

Address:_____

_____

Phone:_____

Hours:_____

Comments:_____

Name: _____

Shop name:_____

Address:_____

_____

Phone:_____

Hours:_____

Comments:_____

Name: _____

Shop name:_____

Address:_____

_____

Phone:_____

Hours:_____

Comments:_____

Name: _____

Shop name:_____

Address:_____

_____

Phone:_____

Hours:_____

Comments:_____

Name: _____

Shop name:_____

Address:_____

_____

Phone:_____

Hours:_____

Comments:_____

Appendix A:
Antiques and Collectibles Periodicals

The antiques and collectibles marketplace is fortunate to have some great publications in the form of weekly or monthly newspapers and magazines. Although many of these are regional publications, others are larger in scope. The periodicals listed below contain general information. For specialized material, please check the specific categories listed in *Warman's Flea Market Price Guide.*   Many of these publications can be found at your local news stand or book store. Frequently, complimentary copies can be obtained at flea markets. Look for them!

American Collector
225 Main Street, Suite 300
Northport, NY 11768-1737
516-261-8337
http://www.tias.com/mags/IC/AntiqueDollWorld/

American History Illustrated
741 Miller Drive
Harrisburg, PA 20175
703-771-9400
http://www.thehistorynet.com

Americana Magazine
29 W 38th Street
New York, NY 10018
212-398-1550

Antique Almanac, The
PO Box 1613
Bowie, TX 76230-1613
817-872-6186

Antique & Collectables
PO Box 13560
El Cajon, CA 92022
619-593-2925

Antique & Collectible News
PO Box 529
Anna, IL 62906-0529
618-833-2158

Antique Collecting Magazine
Antique Collectors' Club Ltd.
5 Church Street
Woodbridge
Suffolk 1P12 1DS, UK
http://www.antiquecc.com/mag/magtoc.htm

Antique Collector & Auction Guide, The
PO Box 38
Salem, OH 44480
216-337-3419

Antique Dealer & Collectors Guide, The
200 Meacham Avenue
Elmont, NY 11003

Antique Gazette
6949 Charlotte Pike, Suite 106
Nashville, TN 37209-4200
615-352-0941

Antique Press, The
12403 N. Florida Avenue
Tampa, FL 33612
813-935-7577

Antique Review
PO Box 538
Columbus, OH 43085-0538
614-885-9757

Antique Shoppe, The
PO Box 2175
Keystone Heights, FL 32656
352-475-5326

Antique Showcase
103 Lakeshore Road
St. Catharines
Ontario L2N 2T6 Canada
905-646-7744

Antiquer's Guide to the Susquehanna Region
PO Box 388
Sidney, NY 13838
607-563-8339

Antique & Auction News
PO Box 500
Mount Joy, PA 17552-0500
717-633-4300

Antiques & Collectibles
150 Linden Avenue
PO Box 33
Westbury, NY 11590
516-334-9650

Antiques & Collecting Magazine
1006 S Michigan Avenue
Chicago, IL 60605-9840
312-939-4767

Antiques & Fine Art
25200 La Paz Road
Laguna Hills, CA 92653-5135

Antiques & The Arts Weekly (The Newtown Bee)
5 Church Hill Road
PO Box 5503
Newtown, CT 06470-5503
203-426-3141

Antiques Today
977 Lehigh Circle
Carson City, NV 89705-7160
702-267-4600

Antiques West
3450 Sacramento Street, Suite 618
San Francisco, CA 94118
415-221-4645

Antiques!
27 Queen Street East, Suite 707
Box 1860
Toronto M5C 2M6 Canada
416-944-3880

Antiques-Collectibles
PO Box 268
Greenvale, NY 11548
516-767-0312

Antique Trader Weekly, The
PO Box 1050
Dubuque, IA 52004-1050
800-334-7165
http://www.csmonline.com

Antique Traveler, The
PO Box 656
Mineola, TX 75773
800-446-3588

AntiqueWeek
Central or Eastern Edition
PO Box 90
Knightstown, IN 46148-0090
765-345-5133
http://www.antiqueweek.com

Arizona Antique News & South-
west Antiques Journal
PO Box 26536
Phoenix, AZ 85068-6536
602-943-9137

Art & Antiques
3 E 54th Street
New York, NY 10022-3108
212-752-5557

Auction Action News
131 E James Street
Columbus, WI 53925
414-623-3767

Auction Price Check Newsletter
8728 U. S. Highway 19
Port Richey, FL 34608
813-869-9114

Brimfield Antique Guide, The
RFD 1 Box 20
Brimfield, MA 01010-9802
413-245-9329

Buckeye Marketeer, The
PO Box 954
Westerville, OH 43086-0954
614-895-1663

Cape Cod Antiques & Arts
PO Box 400
Yarmouth Port, MA 02675-0400
508-362-2111

Carolina Antique News
PO Box 24114
Charlotte, NC 28224-4114

Collectible Canada
103 Lakeshore Road
St. Catharines
Ontario L2N 2T6 Canada
905-647-0995

Collectibles/Flea Market Finds
1700 Broadway
New York, NY 10019-5905
212-541-7100

Collector Magazine
436 W Fourth Street #222 at
Park Avenue
Pomona, CA 91766-1620
909-620-9014

Collector Magazine & Price Guide
PO Box 1050
Dubuque, IA 52004-1050
800-334-7165
http://www.csmonline.com

Collector's Digest
PO Box 23
Banning CA 92220-0023
909-849-1064

Collectors Journal
PO Box 601
Vinton, IA 52349-0601
319-472-4763

Collector's Mart
700 E State Street
Iola, WI 54990-0001
715-455-2214

Collectors News
PO Box 156
Grundy Center, IA 50638-0156
319-824-6981
http://collectors-news.com

Collectors' Classified
PO Box 347
Hollbrook, MA 02343-0347
617-961-1463

Collector's Marketplace, The
PO Box 25
Stewartsville, NJ 08886-0025
http://www.4-collectors.com

Collector, The
PO Box 148
Heyworth, IL 61745-0158
309-473-2466

Comic Buyer's Guide
700 E State Street
Iola, WI 54990-0001
715-455-2214

Cotton & Quail Antique Trail
PO Box 326
Monticello, FL 32344-0326
800-757-7755

Depression Glass Daze, The
PO Box 57
Otisville, MI 48463-0057
810-631-4593

Elvin's Small Fortune
PO Box 229
Rexford, NY 12148-0229
518-384-1182

Georgian Antiques Digest
PO Box 429
Tornbury
Ontario NGH 2P0 Canada
519-599-5017

Goldmine
700 E State Street
Iola, WI 54990-0001
715-455-2214

Great Lakes Trader
132 S Putnam
Williamstown, MI 48895
517-655-5621

Hawaii Antiques
PO Box 853
Honolulu, HI 96808-0853
808-591-0049

Historic Traveler
741 Miller Drive
Harrisburg, PA 20174
703-771-9400
http://www.thehistorynet.com

Hudson Valley Antiquer, The
PO Box 561
Rhinebeck, NY 12572-0561
914-876-8766

Inside Antiques
11912 Mississippi Avenue #E
Los Angeles, CA 90025
310-826-8583

Journal America
PO Box 459
Hewitt, NJ 07421-0459
201-728-8355

Magazine Antiques, The
575 Broadway
New York, NY 10012
212-941-2800

Maine Antique Digest
PO Box 1429
Waldoboro, ME 04572-1429
207-832-7534
http://mainantiquedigest.com

MassBay Antiques
PO Box 192
Ipswich, MA 01938-0192
508-777-7070

Master Collector
12513 Birchfalls Drive
Raleigh, NC 27614-9675
800-772-6673
http://www.mastercollector.com

Memories
1515 Broadway
New York, NY 10036
212-719-4000

MidAtlantic Antiques Magazine
PO Box 908
Henderson, NC 27536-0908
919-492-4001

Mountain States Collector
PO Box 2525
Evergreen, CO 80439-2525
303-987-3994

New England Antiques Journal,
The
PO Box 120
Ware, MA 01082-0120
413-967-3505

New Hampshire Antiques
Monthly
PO Box 546
Farmington, NH 03835-0546
603-755-4568

News Antique Shopper, The
37600 Hills Tech Drive
Farmington, MI 48331-5727

New York Antique Almanac
PO Box 2400
New York, NY 10021-0057

New York-Pennsylvania Collector, The
PO Box Drawer C
Fishers, NY 14453
716-924-8230

Northeast Journal of Antiques &
Art
PO Box 635
Hudson, NY 12534
518-828-1616

Numismatic News
700 E State Street
Iola, WI 54990-0001
715-455-2214

Ohio Collectors' Magazine
PO Box 1522
Piqua, OH 45356

Old Cars Price Guide
700 E State Street
Iola, WI 54990-0001
715-455-2214

Old Cars Weekly News &
Marketplace
700 E State Street
Iola, WI 54990-0001
715-455-2214

Old News is Good News Antiques
Gazette, The
PO Box 305
Hammond, LA 70403-1069
504-429-0575

Old Stuff
PO Box 1084
Meminnville, OR 97128-1084

Old Times, The
PO Box 340
Maple lake, MN 55350-0340
800-539-1810

Renninger's Antique Guide
PO Box 495
Lafayette Hill, PA 19444-0495
610-828-4614

Southern Antiques
PO Box 1107
Decatur, GA 30031-1107
404-289-0954

Sports Cards
700 E State Street
Iola, WI 54990-0001
715-455-2214

Sports Collectors Digest
700 E State Street
Iola, WI 54990-0001
715-455-2214

Stamp Collector
700 E State Street
Iola, WI 54990-0001
715-455-2214

Swap Meet Shopper, The
PO Box 35123
Panama City, FL 32412
http://members.aol.com/smshopper/index.html

Toy Shop
700 E State Street
Iola, WI 54990-0001
715-455-2214

Treasure Chest
PO Box 245
North Scituate, RI 02847-0245
212-496-2234

Unravel the Gavel
9 Hurricane Road #1
Belmont, NH 03220-5603
http://www.the-forum.com/gavel

Upper Canadian, The
PO Box 653
Smiths Falls
Ontario K7A 5B8 Canada
613-283-1168

Vintage Collector, The
PO Box 764
Hotchkiss, CO 81419-0764
970-872-2226

Vintage Times, The
5692 Zebulon Road, #368
Macon, GA 31202
912-757-4755

Warman's Today's Collector
700 E State Street
Iola, WI 54990-0001
715-455-2214

Wayback Times, The
RR #1, Rednersville Road
Belleville
Ontario K8N 4Z1 Canada
613-966-8749

West Coast Peddler
PO Box 5134
Whittier, CA 90607
310-698-1718

Western CT/Western MA Antiquer, The
PO Box 561
Rhinebeck, NY 12572-0561
914-876-8766

Wonderful Things
PO Box 2288
Winter Park, Fl 32790-2288
406-332-0954

Yankee Magazine
PO Box 37017
Bonne, IA 50037-0017
http://www.new-england.com/store/store.YKsub.html

Yesteryear
PO Box 2
Princeton, WI 54968-0002
920-787-4808

Index

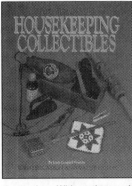